# Macaulay's
# History of England

FROM THE ACCESSION OF JAMES II

IN FOUR VOLUMES · VOLUME FOUR

INTRODUCTION BY
DOUGLAS JERROLD

DENT: LONDON
EVERYMAN'S LIBRARY
DUTTON: NEW YORK

NO. *37*

SBN: 460 00037 3

# CONTENTS

## VOLUME FOUR

v

# CHAPTER XX

IT is now time to relate the events which, since the battle of La Hogue, had taken place at Saint Germains.

James, after seeing the fleet which was to have convoyed him back to his kingdom burned down to the water edge, had returned in no good humour to his abode near Paris. Misfortune generally made him devout after his own fashion; and he now starved himself and flogged himself till his spiritual guides were forced to interfere.*

It is difficult to conceive a duller place than Saint Germains was when he held his Court there; and yet there was scarcely in all Europe a residence more enviably situated than that which the generous Lewis had assigned to his suppliants. The woods were magnificent, the air clear and salubrious, the prospects extensive and cheerful. No charm of rural life was wanting; and the towers of the most superb city of the Continent were visible in the distance. The royal apartments were richly adorned with tapestry and marquetry, vases of silver and mirrors in gilded frames. A pension of more than forty thousand pounds sterling was annually paid to James from the French Treasury. He had a guard of honour composed of some of the finest soldiers in Europe. If he wished to amuse himself with field sports, he had at his command an establishment far more sumptuous than that which had belonged to him when he was at the head of a great kingdom, an army of huntsmen and fowlers, a vast arsenal of guns, spears, buglehorns and tents, miles of network, staghounds, foxhounds, harriers, packs for the boar and packs for the wolf, gerfalcons for the heron and haggards for the wild duck. His presence chamber and his antechamber were in outward show as splendid as when he was at Whitehall. He was still surrounded by blue ribands and white staves. But over the mansion and the domain brooded a constant gloom, the effect, partly of bitter regrets and of deferred hopes, but chiefly of the abject superstition which had taken complete possession of his own mind, and which was affected by almost all those who aspired to his favour. His palace wore the aspect of a monastery. There were three places of worship within the spacious pile. Thirty or forty ecclesiastics were lodged in the building; and their apartments were eyed with envy by noblemen and gentlemen

* Life of James, ii. 479.

who had followed the fortunes of their Sovereign, and who thought it hard that, when there was so much room under his roof, they should be forced to sleep in the garrets of the neighbouring town. Among the murmurers was the brilliant Anthony Hamilton. He has left us a sketch of the life of Saint Germains, a slight sketch indeed, but not unworthy of the artist to whom we owe the most highly finished and vividly coloured picture of the English Court in the days when the English Court was gayest. He complains that existence was one round of religious exercises; that, in order to live in peace, it was necessary to pass half the day in devotion or in the outward show of devotion; that, if he tried to dissipate his melancholy by breathing the fresh air of that noble terrace which looks down on the valley of the Seine, he was driven away by the clamour of a Jesuit who had got hold of some unfortunate Protestant loyalists from England, and was proving to them that no heretic could go to heaven. In general, Hamilton said, men suffering under a common calamity have a strong fellow feeling and are disposed to render good offices to each other. But it was not so at Saint Germains. There all was discord, jealousy, bitterness of spirit. Malignity was concealed under the show of friendship and of piety. All the saints of the royal household were praying for each other and backbiting each other from morning to night. Here and there in the throng of hypocrites might be remarked a man too high-spirited to dissemble. But such a man, however advantageously he might have made himself known elsewhere, was certain to be treated with disdain by the inmates of that sullen abode.*

Such was the Court of James, as described by a Roman Catholic. Yet, however disagreeable that Court may have been to a Roman Catholic, it was infinitely more disagreeable to a Protestant. For the Protestant had to endure, in addition to all the dulness of which the Roman Catholic complained, a crowd of vexations from which the Roman Catholic was free. In every competition between a Protestant and a Roman Catholic the Roman Catholic was preferred. In every quarrel between a Protestant and a Roman Catholic the Roman Catholic was supposed to be in the right. While the ambitious Protestant looked in vain for promotion, while the dissipated Protestant looked in vain for amusement, the serious Protestant looked in vain for spiritual instruction and consolation. James might, no doubt, easily have obtained permission for those members of the Church of England who had sacrificed every thing in his

* Hamilton's Zeneyde.

cause to meet privately in some modest oratory, and to receive
the eucharistic bread and wine from the hands of one of their
own clergy : but he did not wish his residence to be defiled by
such impious rites. Doctor Dennis Granville, who had quitted
the richest deanery, the richest archdeaconry and one of the
richest livings in England, rather than take the oaths, gave
mortal offence by asking leave to read prayers to the exiles of
his own communion. His request was refused ; and he was so
grossly insulted by his master's chaplains and their retainers
that he was forced to quit Saint Germains. Lest some other
Anglican doctor should be equally importunate, James wrote to
inform his agents in England that he wished no Protestant
divine to come out to him.* Indeed the nonjuring clergy were
at least as much sneered at and as much railed at in his palace
as in his nephew's. If any man had a claim to be mentioned
with respect at Saint Germains, it was surely Sancroft. Yet it
was reported that the bigots who were assembled there never
spoke of him but with aversion and disgust. The sacrifice of
the first place in the Church, of the first place in the peerage,
of the mansion at Lambeth and the mansion at Croydon, of
immense patronage and of a revenue of more than five thousand
a year was thought but a poor atonement for the great crime
of having modestly remonstrated against the unconstitutional
Declaration of Indulgence. Sancroft was pronounced to be
just such a traitor and just such a penitent as Judas Iscariot.
The old hypocrite had, it was said, while affecting reverence
and love for his master, given the fatal signal to his master's
enemies. When the mischief had been done and could not be
repaired, the conscience of the sinner had begun to torture him.
He had, like his prototype, blamed himself and bemoaned himself.
He had, like his prototype, flung down his wealth at the feet of
those whose instrument he had been. The best thing that he
could now do was to make the parallel complete by hanging
himself.†

James seems to have thought that the strongest proof of
kindness which he could give to heretics who had resigned
wealth, country, family, for his sake, was to suffer them to be

* A View of the Court of St. Germains from the Year 1690 to 1695,
1696 ; Ratio Ultima, 1697. In the Nairne Papers is a letter in which the
nonjuring bishops are ordered to send a Protestant divine to Saint Germains. This letter was speedily followed by another letter revoking the
order. Both letters will be found in Macpherson's collection. They both
bear date Oct. 16. 1693. I suppose that the first letter was dated according
to the New Style and the letter of revocation according to the Old Style.

† Ratio Ultima, 1697 ; History of the late Parliament, 1699.

beset, on their dying beds, by his priests. If some sick man,
helpless in body and in mind, and deafened by the din of bad
logic and bad rhetoric, suffered a wafer to be thrust into his
mouth, a great work of grace was triumphantly announced to
the Court; and the neophyte was buried with all the pomp of
religion. But if a royalist, of the highest rank and most stain-
less character, died professing firm attachment to the Church
of England, a hole was dug in the fields; and, at dead of night,
he was flung into it and covered up like a mass of carrion.
Such were the obsequies of the Earl of Dunfermline, who had
served the House of Stuart with the hazard of his life and to
the utter ruin of his fortunes, who had fought at Killiecrankie,
and who had, after the victory, lifted from the earth the still
breathing remains of Dundee. While living he had been
treated with contumely. The Scottish officers who had long
served under him had in vain entreated that, when they were
formed into a company, he might still be their commander.
His religion had been thought a fatal disqualification. A
worthless adventurer, whose only recommendation was that he
was a Papist, was preferred. Dunfermline continued, during
a short time, to make his appearance in the circle which
surrounded the Prince whom he had served too well; but it
was to no purpose. The bigots who ruled the Court refused
to the ruined and expatriated Protestant Lord the means of
subsistence: he died of a broken heart; and they refused him
even a grave.*

The insults daily offered at Saint Germains to the Protestant
religion produced a great effect in England. The Whigs
triumphantly asked whether it were not clear that the old
tyrant was utterly incorrigible; and many even of the nonjurors
observed his proceedings with shame, disgust and alarm.†
The Jacobite party had, from the first, been divided into two
sections, which, three or four years after the Revolution, began
to be known as the Compounders and the Noncompounders.

* View of the Court of Saint Germains from 1690 to 1695. That
Dunfermline was grossly ill used is plain even from the Memoirs of
Dundee, 1714.
† So early as the year 1690, that conclave of the leading Jacobites which
gave Preston his instructions made a strong representation to James on this
subject. "He must overrule the bigotry of Saint Germains, and dispose
their minds to think of those methods that are more likely to gain the
nation. For there is one silly thing or another daily done there, that comes
to our notice here, which prolongs what they so passionately desire." See
also A Short and True Relation of Intrigues transacted both at Home and
Abroad to restore the late King James, 1694.

The Compounders were those who wished for a restoration, but for a restoration accompanied by a general amnesty, and by guarantees for the security of the civil and ecclesiastical constitution of the realm. The Noncompounders thought it downright Whiggery, downright rebellion, to take advantage of His Majesty's unfortunate situation for the purpose of imposing on him any condition. The plain duty of his subjects was to bring him back. What traitors he would punish and what traitors he would spare, what laws he would observe and with what laws he would dispense, were questions to be decided by himself alone. If he decided them wrongly, he must answer for his fault to heaven and not to his people.

The great body of the English Jacobites were more or less Compounders. The pure Noncompounders were chiefly to be found among the Roman Catholics, who, very naturally, were not solicitous to obtain any security for a religion which they thought heretical, or for a polity from the benefits of which they were excluded. There were also some Protestant nonjurors, such as Kettlewell and Hickes, who resolutely followed the theory of Filmer to all the extreme consequences to which it led. But, though Kettlewell tried to convince his countrymen that monarchical government had been ordained by God, not as a means of making them happy here, but as a cross which it was their duty to take up and bear in the hope of being recompensed for their sufferings hereafter, and though Hickes assured them that there was not a single Compounder in the whole Theban legion, very few churchmen were inclined to run the risk of the gallows merely for the purpose of reestablishing the High Commission and the Dispensing Power.

The Compounders formed the main strength of the Jacobite party in England : but the Noncompounders had hitherto had undivided sway at Saint Germains. No Protestant, no moderate Roman Catholic, no man who dared to hint that any law could bind the royal prerogative, could hope for the smallest mark of favour from the banished King. The priests and the apostate Melfort, the avowed enemy of the Protestant religion and of civil liberty, of Parliaments, of trial by jury and of the Habeas Corpus Act, were in exclusive possession of the royal ear. Herbert was called Chancellor, walked before the other officers of state, wore a black robe embroidered with gold, and carried a seal : but he was a member of the Church of England ; and therefore he was not suffered to sit at the Council Board.*

* View of the Court of Saint Germains. The account given in this View is confirmed by a remarkable paper, which is among the Nairne MSS.

The truth is that the faults of James's head and heart were incurable. In his view there could be between him and his subjects no reciprocity of obligation. Their duty was to risk property, liberty, life, in order to replace him on the throne, and then to bear patiently whatever he chose to inflict upon them. They could no more pretend to merit before him than before God. When they had done all, they were still unprofitable servants. The highest praise due to the royalist who shed his blood on the field of battle or on the scaffold for hereditary monarchy was simply that he was not a traitor. After all the severe discipline which the deposed King had undergone, he was still as much bent on plundering and abasing the Church of England as on the day when he told the kneeling fellows of Magdalene to get out of his sight, or on the day when he sent the Bishops to the Tower. He was in the habit of declaring that he would rather die without seeing England again than stoop to capitulate with those whom he ought to command.* In the Declaration of April 1692 the whole man appears without disguise, full of his own imaginary rights, unable to understand how any body but himself can have any rights, dull, obstinate and cruel. Another paper which he drew up about the same time shows, if possible, still more clearly, how little he had profited by a sharp experience. In that paper he set forth the plan according to which he intended to govern when he should be restored. He laid it down as a rule that one Commissioner of the Treasury, one of the two Secretaries of State, the Secretary at War, the majority of the Great Officers of the Household, the majority of the Lords of the Bedchamber, the majority of the officers of the army, should always be Roman Catholics.†

It was to no purpose that the most eminent Compounders sent from London letter after letter filled with judicious counsel and earnest supplication. It was to no purpose that they demonstrated in the plainest manner the impossibility of establishing Popish ascendency in a country where at least forty-nine fiftieths of the population and much more than forty-

---

Some of the heads of the Jacobite party in England made a representation to James, one article of which is as follows : " They beg that Your Majesty would be pleased to admit of the Chancellor of England into your Council : your enemies take advantage of his not being in it." James's answer is evasive. " The King will be, on all occasions, ready to express the just value and esteem he has for his Lord Chancellor."

* A short and true Relation of Intrigues, 1694.

† See the paper headed " For my Son the Prince of Wales, 1692." It is printed at the end of the Life of James.

nine fiftieths of the wealth and the intelligence were Protestant.
It was to no purpose that they informed their master that the
Declaration of April 1692 had been read with exultation by his
enemies and with deep affliction by his friends, that it had been
printed and circulated by the usurpers, that it had done more
than all the libels of the Whigs to inflame the nation against
him, and that it had furnished those naval officers who had
promised him support with a plausible pretext for breaking
faith with him, and for destroying the fleet which was to have
convoyed him back to his kingdom. He continued to be deaf
to the remonstrances of his best friends in England till those
remonstrances began to be echoed at Versailles. All the
information which Lewis and his ministers were able to obtain
touching the state of our island satisfied them that James
would never be restored unless he could bring himself to make
large concessions to his subjects. It was therefore intimated
to him, kindly and courteously, but seriously, that he would do
well to change his counsels and his counsellors. France could
not continue the war for the purpose of forcing a Sovereign on
an unwilling nation. She was crushed by public burdens.
Her trade and industry languished. Her harvest and her
vintage had failed. The peasantry were starving. The faint
murmurs of the provincial Estates began to be heard. There
was a limit to the amount of the sacrifices which the most
absolute prince could demand from those whom he ruled.
However desirous the Most Christian King might be to uphold
the cause of hereditary monarchy and of pure religion all over
the world, his first duty was to his own kingdom ; and, unless
a counterrevolution speedily took place in England, his duty to
his own kingdom might impose on him the painful necessity of
treating with the Prince of Orange. It would therefore be wise
in James to do without delay whatever he could honourably
and conscientiously do to win back the hearts of his people.

Thus pressed, James unwillingly yielded. He consented to
give a share in the management of his affairs to one of the most
distinguished of the Compounders, Charles Earl of Middleton.

Middleton's family and his peerage were Scotch. But he
was closely connected with some of the noblest houses of
England : he had resided long in England : he had been
appointed by Charles the Second one of the English Secretaries
of State, and had been entrusted by James with the lead of the
English House of Commons. His abilities and acquirements
were considerable : his temper was easy and generous : his
manners were popular ; and his conduct had generally been

consistent and honourable. He had, when Popery was in the ascendant, resolutely refused to purchase the royal favour by apostasy. Roman Catholic ecclesiastics had been sent to convert him; and the town had been much amused by the dexterity with which the layman baffled the divines. A priest undertook to demonstrate the doctrine of transubstantiation, and made the approaches in the usual form. "Your Lordship believes in the Trinity." "Who told you so?" said Middleton. "Not believe in the Trinity!" cried the priest in amazement. "Nay," said Middleton; "prove your religion to be true if you can: but do not catechize me about mine." As it was plain that the Secretary was not a disputant whom it was easy to take at an advantage, the controversy ended almost as soon as it began.* When fortune changed, Middleton adhered to the cause of hereditary monarchy with a stedfastness which was the more respectable because he would have had no difficulty in making his peace with the new government. His sentiments were so well known that, when the kingdom was agitated by apprehensions of an invasion and an insurrection, he was arrested and sent to the Tower: but no evidence on which he could be convicted of treason was discovered; and, when the dangerous crisis was past, he was set at liberty. It should seem indeed that, during the three years which followed the Revolution, he was by no means an active plotter. He saw that a Restoration could be effected only with the general assent of the nation, and that the nation would never assent to a Restoration without securities against Popery and arbitrary power. He therefore conceived that, while his banished master obstinately refused to give such securities, it would be worse than idle to conspire against the existing government.

Such was the man whom James, in consequence of strong representations from Versailles, now invited to join him in France. The great body of Compounders learned with delight that they were at length to be represented in the Council at Saint Germains by one of their favourite leaders. Some noblemen and gentlemen, who, though they had not approved of the deposition of James, had been so much disgusted by his perverse and absurd conduct that they had long avoided all connection with him, now began to hope that he had seen his error. They had refused to have any thing to do with Melfort; but they communicated freely with Middleton. The new minister conferred also with the four traitors whose infamy has been made preeminently conspicuous by their station, their

* Burnet, i. 683.

abilities, and their great public services; with Godolphin, the great object of whose life was to be in favour with both the rival Kings at once, and to keep, through all revolutions and counterrevolutions, his head, his estate and a place at the Board of Treasury; with Shrewsbury, who, having once in a fatal moment entangled himself in criminal and dishonourable engagements, had not had the resolution to break through them; with Marlborough, who continued to profess the deepest repentance for the past and the best intentions for the future; and with Russell, who declared that he was still what he had been before the day of La Hogue, and renewed his promise to do what Monk had done, on condition that a general pardon should be granted to all political offenders, and that the royal power should be placed under strong constitutional restraints.

Before Middleton left England he had collected the sense of all the leading Compounders. They were of opinion that there was one expedient which would reconcile contending factions at home, and lead to the speedy pacification of Europe. This expedient was that James should resign the Crown in favour of the Prince of Wales, and that the Prince of Wales should be bred a Protestant. If, as was but too probable, His Majesty should refuse to listen to this suggestion, he must at least consent to put forth a Declaration which might do away the unfavourable impression made by his Declaration of the preceding spring. A paper such as it was thought expedient that he should publish was carefully drawn up, and, after much discussion, approved.

Early in the year 1693, Middleton, having been put in full possession of the views of the principal English Jacobites, stole across the Channel, and made his appearance at the Court of James. There was at that Court no want of slanderers and sneerers whose malignity was only the more dangerous because it wore a meek and sanctimonious air. Middleton found, on his arrival, that numerous lies, fabricated by the priests who feared and hated him, were already in circulation. Some Non-compounders too had written from London that he was at heart a Presbyterian and a republican. He was however very graciously received, and was appointed Secretary of State conjointly with Melfort.*

* As to this change of ministry at Saint Germains see the very curious but very confused narrative in the Life of James, ii. 498—515.; Burnet, ii. 219.; Mémoires de Saint Simon; A French Conquest neither desirable nor practicable, 1693; and the Letters from the Nairne MSS. printed by Macpherson.

It very soon appeared that James was fully resolved never to resign the Crown, or to suffer the Prince of Wales to be bred a heretic; and it long seemed doubtful whether any arguments or entreaties would induce him to sign the Declaration which his friends in England had prepared. It was indeed a document very different from any that had yet appeared under his Great Seal. He was made to promise that he would grant a free pardon to all his subjects who should not oppose him after he should land in the island; that, as soon as he was restored, he would call a Parliament; that he would confirm all such laws, passed during the usurpation, as the Houses should tender to him for confirmation; that he would waive his right to the chimney money; that he would protect and defend the Established Church in the enjoyment of all her possessions and privileges; that he would not again violate the Test Act; that he would leave it to the legislature to define the extent of his dispensing power; and that he would maintain the Act of Settlement in Ireland.

He struggled long and hard. He pleaded his conscience. Could a son of the Holy Roman Catholic and Apostolic Church bind himself to protect and defend heresy, and to enforce a law which excluded true believers from office? Some of the ecclesiastics who swarmed in his household told him that he could not without sin give any such pledge as his undutiful subjects demanded. On this point the opinion of Middleton, who was a Protestant, could be of no weight. But Middleton found an ally in one whom he regarded as a rival and an enemy. Melfort, scared by the universal hatred of which he knew himself to be the object, and afraid that he should be held accountable, both in England and in France, for his master's wrongheadedness, submitted the case to several eminent Doctors of the Sorbonne. These learned casuists pronounced the Declaration unobjectionable in a religious point of view. The great Bossuet, Bishop of Meaux, who was regarded by the Gallican Church as a father scarcely inferior in authority to Cyprian or Augustin, showed, by powerful arguments, both theological and political, that the scruple which tormented James was precisely of that sort against which a much wiser King had given a caution in the words, "Be not righteous overmuch." * The authority of the French divines

---

* Life of James, ii. 509. Bossuet's opinion will be found in the Appendix to M. Mazure's history. The Bishop sums up his arguments thus: " Je dirai donc volontiers aux Catholiques, s'il y en a qui n'approuvent point la déclaration dont il s'agit ; Noli esse justus multum ; neque plus sapias quam necesse est, ne obstupescas." In the Life of James it is

was supported by the authority of the French government. The language held at Versailles was so strong that James began to be alarmed. What if Lewis should take serious offence, should think his hospitality ungratefully requited, should conclude a peace with the usurpers, and should request his unfortunate guests to seek another asylum? It was necessary to submit. On the seventeenth of April 1693 the Declaration was signed and sealed. The concluding sentence was a prayer. "We come to vindicate our own right and to establish the liberties of our people; and may God give us success in the prosecution of the one as we sincerely intend the confirmation of the other!" * The prayer was heard. The success of James was strictly proportioned to his sincerity. What his sincerity was we know on the best evidence. Scarcely had he called on heaven to witness the truth of his professions, when he directed Melfort to send a copy of the Declaration to Rome with such explanations as might satisfy the Pope. Melfort's letter ends thus: "After all, the object of this Declaration is only to get us back to England. We shall fight the battle of the Catholics with much greater advantage at Whitehall than at Saint Germains." †

Meanwhile the document from which so much was expected had been despatched to London. There it was printed at a secret press in the house of a Quaker: for there was among the Quakers a party, small in number, but zealous and active, which had imbibed the politics of William Penn.‡ To circulate such a work was a service of some danger: but agents were found. Several persons were taken up while distributing copies in the streets of the city. A hundred packets were stopped in one day at the Post Office on their way to the fleet. But, after a short time, the government wisely gave up the endeavour to suppress what could not be suppressed, and published the Declaration at full length, accompanied by a severe commentary.§

---

asserted that the French Doctors changed their opinion, and that Bossuet, though he held out longer than the rest, saw at last that he had been in error, but did not choose formally to retract. I think much too highly of Bossuet's understanding to believe this.

* Life of James, ii. 505.

† "En fin celle cy—j'entends la déclaration—n'est que pour rentrer, et l'on peut beaucoup mieux disputer des affaires des Catholiques à Whytehall qu'à Saint Germain."—Mazure, Appendix.

‡ Baden to the States General, June 1/12. 1693. Four thousand copies, wet from the press, were found in this house.

§ Baden's Letters to the States General of May and June 1693; An

The commentary, however, was hardly needed. The Declaration altogether failed to produce the effect which Middleton had anticipated. The truth is that his advice had not been asked till it mattered not what advice he gave. If James had put forth such a manifesto in January 1689, the throne would probably not have been declared vacant. If he had put forth such a manifesto when he was on the coast of Normandy at the head of an army, he would have conciliated a large part of the nation, and he might possibly have been joined by a large part of the fleet. But both in 1689 and in 1692 he had held the language of an implacable tyrant; and it was now too late to affect tenderness of heart and reverence for the constitution of the realm. The contrast between the new Declaration and the preceding Declaration excited, not without reason, general suspicion and contempt. What confidence could be placed in the word of a Prince so unstable, of a Prince who veered from extreme to extreme? In 1692 nothing would satisfy him but the heads and quarters of hundreds of poor ploughmen and boatmen who had, several years before, taken some rustic liberties with him at which his grandfather Henry the Fourth would have had a hearty laugh. In 1693 the foulest and most ungrateful treasons were to be covered with oblivion. Caermarthen expressed the general sentiment. "I do not," he said, "understand all this. Last April I was to be hanged. This April I am to have a free pardon. I cannot imagine what I have done during the past year to deserve such goodness." The general opinion was that a snare was hidden under this unwonted clemency, this unwonted respect for law. The Declaration, it was said, was excellent; and so was the Coronation oath. Every body knew how King James had observed his Coronation oath; and every body might guess how he would observe his Declaration. While grave men reasoned thus, the Whig jesters were not sparing of their pasquinades. Some of the Noncompounders, meantime, uttered indignant murmurs. The King was in bad hands, in the hands of men who hated monarchy. His mercy was cruelty of the worst sort. The general pardon which he had granted to his enemies was in truth a general proscription of his friends. Hitherto the Judges appointed by the usurper had been under a restraint, imperfect indeed, yet not absolutely nugatory. They had known that a day of reckoning might

---

Answer to the Late King James's Declaration published at Saint Germains, 1693.

come, and had therefore in general dealt tenderly with the persecuted adherents of the rightful King. That restraint His Majesty had now taken away. He had told Holt and Treby that, till he should land in England, they might hang royalists without the smallest fear of being called to account.[*]

But by no class of people was the Declaration read with so much disgust and indignation as by the native aristocracy of Ireland. This then was the reward of their loyalty. This was the faith of kings. When England had cast James out, when Scotland had rejected him, the Irish had still been true to him ; and he had, in return, solemnly given his sanction to a law which restored to them an immense domain of which they had been despoiled. Nothing that had happened since that time had diminished their claim to his favour. They had defended his cause to the last : they had fought for him long after he had deserted them : many of them, when unable to contend longer against superior force, had followed him into banishment ; and now it appeared that he was desirous to make peace with his deadliest enemies at the expense of his most faithful friends. There was much discontent in the Irish regiments which were dispersed through the Netherlands and along the frontiers of Germany and Italy. Even the Whigs allowed that, for once, the O's and Macs were in the right, and asked triumphantly whether a prince who had broken his word to his devoted servants could be expected to keep it to his foes ? [†]

[*] James, ii. 514. I am unwilling to believe that Ken was among those who blamed the Declaration of 1693 as too merciful.

[†] Among the Nairne Papers is a letter sent on this occasion by Middleton to Macarthy, who was then serving in Germany. Middleton tries to soothe Macarthy and to induce Macarthy to soothe others. Nothing more disingenuous was ever written by a Minister of State. "The King," says the Secretary, "promises in the foresaid Declaration to restore the Settlement, but, at the same time, declares that he will recompense all those who may suffer by it by giving them equivalents." Now James did not declare that he would recompense any body, but merely that he would advise with his Parliament on the subject. He did not declare that he would even advise with his Parliament about recompensing all who might suffer, but merely about recompensing such as had followed him to the last. Finally he said nothing about equivalents. Indeed the notion of giving an equivalent to every body who suffered by the Act of Settlement, in other words, of giving an equivalent for the fee simple of half the soil of Ireland, was obviously absurd. Middleton's letter will be found in Macpherson's collection. I will give a sample of the language held by the Whigs on this occasion. "The Roman Catholics of Ireland," says one writer, "although in point of interest and profession different from us, yet, to do them right, have deserved well from the late King, though ill from us ; and for the late King to leave them and exclude them in such an instance of uncommon

While the Declaration was the subject of general conversation in England, military operations recommenced on the Continent. The preparations of France had been such as amazed even those who estimated most highly her resources and the abilities of her rulers. Both her agriculture and her commerce were suffering. The vineyards of Burgundy, the interminable cornfields of the Beauce, had failed to yield their increase : the looms of Lyons were silent ; and the merchant ships were rotting in the harbour of Marseilles. Yet the monarchy presented to its numerous enemies a front more haughty and more menacing than ever. Lewis had determined not to make any advance towards a reconciliation with the new government of England till the whole strength of his realm had been put forth in one more effort. A mighty effort in truth it was, but too exhausting to be repeated. He made an immense display of force at once on the Pyrenees and on the Alps, on the Rhine and on the Meuse, in the Atlantic and in the Mediterranean. That nothing might be wanting which could excite the martial ardour of a nation eminently high-spirited, he instituted, a few days before he left his palace for the camp, a new military order of knighthood, and placed it under the protection of his own sainted ancestor and patron. The new cross of Saint Lewis shone on the breasts of the gentlemen who had been conspicuous in the trenches before Mons and Namur, and on the fields of Fleurus and Steinkirk ; and the sight raised a generous emulation among those who had still to win an honourable fame in arms.*

In the week in which this celebrated order began to exist Middleton visited Versailles. A letter in which he gave his friends in England an account of his visit has come down to us.† He was presented to Lewis, was most kindly received, and was overpowered by gratitude and admiration. Of all the wonders of the Court,—so Middleton wrote,—its master was the greatest. The splendour of the great King's personal merit threw even the splendour of his fortunes into the shade. The language which His Most Christian Majesty held about English politics was, on the whole, highly satisfactory. Yet in

---

ingratitude that Protestants have no reason to stand by a Prince that deserts his own party, and a people that have been faithful to him and his interest to the very last."—A short and true Relation of the Intrigues, &c., 1694.

* The edict of creation was registered by the Parliament of Paris on the 10th of April 1693.

† The letter is dated the 19th of April 1693. It is among the Nairne MSS., and was printed by Macpherson.

one thing this accomplished prince and his able and experienced ministers were strangely mistaken. They were all possessed with the absurd notion that the Prince of Orange was a great man. No pains had been spared to undeceive them; but they were under an incurable delusion. They saw through a magnifying glass of such power that the leech appeared to them a leviathan. It ought to have occurred to Middleton that possibly the delusion might be in his own vision and not in theirs. Lewis and the counsellors who surrounded him were far indeed from loving William. But they did not hate him with that mad hatred which raged in the breasts of his English enemies. Middleton was one of the wisest and most moderate of the Jacobites. Yet even Middleton's judgment was so much darkened by malice that, on this subject, he talked nonsense unworthy of his capacity. He, like the rest of his party, could see in the usurper nothing but what was odious and contemptible, the heart of a fiend, the understanding and manners of a stupid, brutal, Dutch boor, who generally observed a sulky silence, and, when forced to speak, gave short testy answers in bad English. The French statesmen, on the other hand, judged of William's faculties from an intimate knowledge of the way in which he had, during twenty years, conducted affairs of the greatest moment and of the greatest difficulty. He had, ever since 1673, been playing against themselves a most complicated game of mixed chance and skill for an immense stake: they were proud, and with reason, of their own dexterity at that game; yet they were conscious that in him they had found more than their match. At the commencement of the long contest every advantage had been on their side. They had at their absolute command all the resources of the greatest kingdom in Europe; and he was merely the servant of a commonwealth, of which the whole territory was inferior in extent to Normandy or Guienne. A succession of generals and diplomatists of eminent ability had been opposed to him. A powerful faction in his native country had pertinaciously crossed his designs. He had undergone defeats in the field and defeats in the senate: but his wisdom and firmness had turned defeats into victories. Notwithstanding all that could be done to keep him down, his influence and fame had been almost constantly rising and spreading. The most important and arduous enterprise in the history of modern Europe had been planned and conducted to a prosperous termination by him alone. The most extensive coalition that the world had seen for ages had been formed by him, and would be instantly dissolved if his superintending care were withdrawn. He had gained two kingdoms by statecraft, and a third by conquest; and he was still maintaining himself in the possession of all three in spite of both foreign and domestic foes. That these things had been effected by a poor creature, a man of the most ordinary capacity, was an assertion which might easily find credence among the nonjuring parsons who congregated at Sam's Coffee-house, but which moved the laughter of the veteran politicians of Versailles.

While Middleton was in vain trying to convince the French that William was a greatly overrated man, William, who did full justice to Middleton's merit, felt much uneasiness at learning that the Court of Saint Germains had called in the help of so able a counsellor.* But this was only one of a thousand causes of anxiety which during that spring pressed on the King's mind. He was preparing for the opening of the campaign, imploring his allies to be early in the field, rousing the sluggish, haggling with the greedy, making up quarrels, adjusting points of precedence. He had to prevail on the Cabinet of Vienna to send timely succours into Piedmont. He had to keep a vigilant eye on those Northern potentates who were trying to form a third party in Europe. He had to act as tutor to the Elector of Bavaria in the Netherlands. He had to provide for the defence of Liege, a matter which the authorities of Liege coolly declared to be not at all their business, but the business of England and Holland. He had to prevent the House of Brunswick Wolfenbuttel from going to blows with the House of Brunswick Lunenburg: he had to accommodate a dispute between the Prince of Baden and the Elector of Saxony, each of whom wished to be at the head of an army on the Rhine; and he had to manage the Landgrave of Hesse, who omitted to furnish his own contingent, and yet wanted to command the contingents furnished by other princes.†

And now the time for action had arrived. On the eighteenth of May Lewis left Versailles: early in June he was under the walls of Namur. The Princesses, who had accompanied him,

* "Il ne me plait nullement que M. Middleton est allé en France. Ce n'est pas un homme qui voudroit faire un tel pas sans quelque chose d'importance, et de bien concerté, sur quoy j'ay fait beaucoup de reflections que je reserve à vous dire à vostre heureuse arrivée."—William to Portland from Loo. April 18/28. 1693.

† The best account of William's labours and anxieties at this time is contained in his letters to Heinsius—particularly the letters of May 1. 9. and 30. 1693.

held their court within the fortress. He took under his immediate command the army of Boufflers, which was encamped at Gembloux. Little more than a mile off lay the army of Luxemburg. The force collected in that neighbourhood under the French lilies did not amount to less than a hundred and twenty thousand men. Lewis had flattered himself that he should be able to repeat in 1693 the stratagem by which Mons had been taken in 1691 and Namur in 1692 ; and he had determined that either Liege or Brussels should be his prey. But William had this year been able to assemble in good time a force, inferior indeed to that which was opposed to him, but still formidable. With this force he took his post near Louvain, on the road between the two threatened cities, and watched every movement of the enemy.

Lewis was disappointed. He found that it would not be possible for him to gratify his vanity so safely and so easily as in the two preceding years, to sit down before a great town, to enter the gates in triumph, and to receive the keys, without exposing himself to any risk greater than that of a staghunt at Fontainebleau. Before he could lay siege either to Liege or to Brussels he must fight and win a battle. The chances were indeed greatly in his favour : for his army was more numerous, better officered and better disciplined than that of the allies. Luxemburg strongly advised him to march against William. The aristocracy of France anticipated with intrepid gaiety a bloody but a glorious day, followed by a large distribution of the crosses of the new order. William himself was perfectly aware of his danger, and prepared to meet it with calm but mournful fortitude.* Just at this conjuncture Lewis announced his intention to return instantly to Versailles, and to send the Dauphin and Boufflers, with part of the army which was assembled near Namur, to join Marshal Lorges who commanded in the Palatinate. Luxemburg was thunderstruck. He expostulated boldly and earnestly. Never, he said, was such an opportunity thrown away. If His Majesty would march against the Prince of Orange, victory was almost certain. Could any advantage which it was possible to obtain on the Rhine be set against the advantage of a victory gained in the heart of Brabant over the principal army and the principal captain of the coalition ? The Marshal reasoned : he implored : he went

---

* He speaks very despondingly in his letter to Heinsius of the 30th of May. Saint Simon says : " On a su depuis que le Prince d'Orange écrivit plusieurs fois au prince de Vaudmont, son ami intime, qu'il était perdu et qu'il n'y avait que par un miracle qu'il pût échapper."

on his knees; but in vain; and he quitted the royal presence in the deepest dejection. Lewis left the camp a week after he had joined it, and never afterwards made war in person.

The astonishment was great throughout his army. All the awe which he inspired could not prevent his old generals from grumbling and looking sullen, his young nobles from venting their spleen, sometimes in curses and sometimes in sarcasms, and even his common soldiers from holding irreverent language round their watchfires. His enemies rejoiced with vindictive and insulting joy. Was it not strange, they asked, that this great prince should have gone in state to the theatre of war, and then in a week have gone in the same state back again? Was it necessary that all that vast retinue, princesses, dames of honour and tirewomen, equerries and gentlemen of the bed-chamber, cooks, confectioners and musicians, long trains of waggons, droves of led horses and sumpter mules, piles of plate, bales of tapestry, should travel four hundred miles merely in order that the Most Christian King might look at his soldiers and then return? The ignominious truth was too evident to be concealed. He had gone to the Netherlands in the hope that he might again be able to snatch some military glory without any hazard to his person, and had hastened back rather than expose himself to the chances of a pitched field.* This was not the first time that His Most Christian Majesty had shown the same kind of prudence. Seventeen years before he had been opposed under the walls of Bouchain to the same antagonist. William, with the ardour of a very young commander, had most imprudently offered battle. The opinion of the ablest generals was that, if Lewis had seized the opportunity, the war might have been ended in a day. The French army had eagerly asked to be led to the onset. The King had called his lieutenants round him and had collected their opinions. Some courtly officers to whom a hint of his wishes had been dexterously conveyed had, blushing and stammering with shame, voted against fighting. It was to no purpose that bold and honest men, who prized his honour more than his life, had proved to him that, on all principles of the military art, he ought to accept the challenge rashly given by the enemy. His Majesty had gravely expressed his sorrow that he could not, consistently with his public duty, obey the impetuous movement of his blood, had turned his rein, and had galloped back to his quarters.† Was it not frightful to think what rivers

* Saint Simon; Monthly Mercury, June 1693; Burnet, ii. 111.
† Mémoires de Saint Simon; Burnet, i. 404.

of the best blood of France, of Spain, of Germany and of England, had flowed, and were destined still to flow, for the gratification of a man who wanted the vulgar courage which was found in the meanest of the hundreds of thousands whom he had sacrificed to his vainglorious ambition?

Though the French army in the Netherlands had been weakened by the departure of the forces commanded by the Dauphin and Boufflers, and though the allied army was daily strengthened by the arrival of fresh troops, Luxemburg still had a superiority of force ; and that superiority he increased by an adroit stratagem. He marched towards Liege, and made as if he were about to form the siege of that city. William was uneasy, and the more uneasy because he knew that there was a French party among the inhabitants. He quitted his position near Louvain, advanced to Nether Hespen, and en-camped there with the river Gette in his rear. On his march he learned that Huy had opened its gates to the French. The news increased his anxiety about Liege, and determined him to send thither a force sufficient to overawe malecontents within the city, and to repel any attack from without.* This was exactly what Luxemburg had expected and desired. His feint had served its purpose. He turned his back on the fortress which had hitherto seemed to be his object, and hastened towards the Gette. William, who had detached more than twenty thousand men, and who had but fifty thousand left in his camp, was alarmed by learning from his scouts, on the eighteenth of July, that the French General, with near eighty thousand, was close at hand.

It was still in the King's power, by a hasty retreat, to put the narrow, but deep, waters of the Gette, which had lately been swollen by rains, between his army and the enemy. But the site which he occupied was strong ; and it could easily be made still stronger. He set all his troops to work. Ditches were dug, mounds thrown up, palisades fixed in the earth. In a few hours the ground wore a new aspect ; and the King trusted that he should be able to repel the attack even of a force greatly outnumbering his own. Nor was it without much appearance of reason that he felt this confidence. When the morning of the nineteenth of July broke, the bravest men of Lewis's army looked gravely and anxiously on the fortress which had suddenly sprung up to arrest their progress. The allies were protected by a breastwork. Here and there along the entrenchments were formed little redoubts and half moons.

* William to Heinsius, July $\frac{7}{17}$. 1693.

A hundred pieces of cannon were disposed along the ramparts. On the left flank, the village of Romsdorff rose close to the little stream of Landen, from which the English have named the disastrous day. On the right was the village of Neerwinden. Both villages were, after the fashion of the Low Countries, surrounded by moats and fences ; and, within these enclosures, the little plots of ground occupied by different families were separated by mud walls five feet in height and a foot in thickness. All these barricades William had repaired and strengthened. Saint Simon, who, after the battle, surveyed the ground, could hardly, he tells us, believe that defences so extensive and so formidable could have been created with such rapidity.

Luxemburg, however, was determined to try whether even this position could be maintained against the superior numbers and the impetuous valour of his soldiers. Soon after sunrise the roar of cannon began to be heard. William's batteries did much execution before the French artillery could be so placed as to return the fire. It was eight o'clock before the close fighting began. The village of Neerwinden was regarded by both commanders as the point on which every thing depended. There an attack was made by the French left wing commanded by Montchevreuil, a veteran officer of high reputation, and by Berwick, who, though young, was fast rising to a high place among the captains of his time. Berwick led the onset, and forced his way into the village, but was soon driven out again with a terrible carnage. His followers fled or perished : he, while trying to rally them, and cursing them for not doing their duty better, was surrounded by foes. He concealed his white cockade, and hoped to be able, by the help of his native tongue, to pass himself off as an officer of the English army. But his face was recognised by one of his mother's brothers, George Churchill, who held on that day the command of a brigade. A hurried embrace was exchanged between the kinsmen ; and the uncle conducted the nephew to William, who, as long as every thing seemed to be going well, remained in the rear. The meeting of the King and the captive, united by such close domestic ties, and divided by such inexpiable injuries, was a strange sight. Both behaved as became them. William uncovered, and addressed to his prisoner a few words of courteous greeting. Berwick's only reply was a solemn bow. The King put on his hat : the Duke put on his hat ; and the cousins parted for ever.

By this time the French, who had been driven in confusion

out of Neerwinden, had been reinforced by a division under the command of the Duke of Bourbon, and came gallantly back to the attack. William, well aware of the importance of this post, gave orders that troops should move thither from other parts of his line. This second conflict was long and bloody. The assailants again forced an entrance into the village. They were again driven out with immense slaughter, and showed little inclination to return to the charge.

Meanwhile the battle had been raging all along the entrenchments of the allied army. Again and again Luxemburg brought up his troops within pistolshot of the breastwork : but he could bring them no nearer. Again and again they recoiled from the heavy fire which was poured on their front and on their flanks. It seemed that all was over. Luxemburg retired to a spot which was out of gunshot, and summoned a few of his chief officers to a consultation. They talked together during some time ; and their animated gestures were observed with deep interest by all who were within sight.

At length Luxemburg formed his decision. A last attempt must be made to carry Neerwinden ; and the invincible household troops, the conquerors of Steinkirk, must lead the way.

The household troops came on in a manner worthy of their long and terrible renown. A third time Neerwinden was taken. A third time William tried to retake it. At the head of some English regiments he charged the guards of Lewis with such fury that, for the first time in the memory of the oldest warrior, that far famed band gave way.* It was only by the strenuous exertions of Luxemburg, of the Duke of Chartres, and of the Duke of Bourbon, that the broken ranks were rallied. But by this time the centre and left of the allied army had been so much thinned for the purpose of supporting the conflict at Neerwinden that the entrenchments could no longer be defended on other points. A little after four in the afternoon the whole line gave way. All was havoc and confusion. Solmes had received a mortal wound, and fell, still alive, into the hands of the enemy. The English soldiers, to whom his name was hateful, accused him of having in his sufferings shown pusillanimity unworthy of a soldier. The Duke of Ormond was struck down in the press ; and in another moment he would have been a corpse, had not a rich diamond

* Saint Simon's words are remarkable. "Leur cavalerie," he says, "ey fit d'abord plier des troupes d'élite jusqu'alors invincibles." He adds, "Les gardes du Prince d'Orange, ceux de M. de Vaudemont, et deux régimens Anglais en eurent l'honneur."

on his finger caught the eye of one of the French guards, who justly thought that the owner of such a jewel would be a valuable prisoner. The Duke's life was saved; and he was speedily exchanged for Berwick. Ruvigny, animated by the true refugee hatred of the country which had cast him out, was taken fighting in the thickest of the battle. Those into whose hands he had fallen knew him well, and knew that, if they carried him to their camp, his head would pay for that treason to which persecution had driven him. With admirable generosity they pretended not to recognise him, and suffered him to make his escape in the tumult.

It was only on such occasions as this that the whole greatness of William's character appeared. Amidst the rout and uproar, while arms and standards were flung away, while multitudes of fugitives were choking up the bridges and fords of the Gette or perishing in its waters, the King, having directed Talmash to superintend the retreat, put himself at the head of a few brave regiments, and by desperate efforts arrested the progress of the enemy. His risk was greater than that which others ran. For he could not be persuaded either to encumber his feeble frame with a cuirass, or to hide the ensigns of the garter. He thought his star a good rallying point for his own troops, and only smiled when he was told that it was a good mark for the enemy. Many fell on his right hand and on his left. Two led horses, which in the field always closely followed his person, were struck dead by cannon shots. One musket ball passed through the curls of his wig, another through his coat : a third bruised his side and tore his blue riband to tatters. Many years later grey-haired old pensioners who crept about the arcades and alleys of Chelsea Hospital used to relate how he charged at the head of Galway's horse, how he dismounted four times to put heart into the infantry, how he rallied one corps which seemed to be shrinking: " That is not the way to fight, gentlemen. You must stand close up to them. Thus, gentlemen, thus." " You might have seen him," an eyewitness wrote, only four days after the battle, " with his sword in his hand, throwing himself upon the enemy. It is certain that, one time, among the rest, he was seen at the head of two English regiments, and that he fought seven with these two in sight of the whole army, driving them before him above a quarter of an hour. Thanks be to God that preserved him." The enemy pressed on him so close that it was with difficulty that he at length made his way over the Gette. A small body of brave men, who shared his peril to the last, could hardly keep off the pursuers as he crossed the bridge.*

Never, perhaps, was the change which the progress of civilisation has produced in the art of war more strikingly illustrated than on that day. Ajax beating down the Trojan leader with a rock which two ordinary men could scarcely lift, Horatius defending the bridge against an army, Richard the Lionhearted spurring along the whole Saracen line without finding an enemy to stand his assault, Robert Bruce crushing with one blow the helmet and head of Sir Henry Bohun in sight of the whole array of England and Scotland, such are the heroes of a dark age. In such an age bodily vigour is the most indispensable qualification of a warrior. At Landen two poor sickly beings, who, in a rude state of society, would have been regarded as too puny to bear any part in combats, were the souls of two great armies. In some heathen countries they would have been exposed while infants. In Christendom they would, six hundred years earlier, have been sent to some quiet cloister. But their lot had fallen on a time when men had discovered that the strength of the muscles is far inferior in value to the strength of the mind. It is probable that, among the hundred and twenty thousand soldiers who were marshalled round Neerwinden under all the standards of Western Europe, the two feeblest in body were the hunchbacked dwarf who urged forward the fiery onset of France, and the asthmatic skeleton who covered the slow retreat of England.

The French were victorious : but they had bought their victory dear. More than ten thousand of the best troops of Lewis had fallen. Neerwinden was a spectacle at which the oldest soldiers stood aghast. The streets were piled breast high with corpses. Among the slain were some great lords and some

* Berwick ; Saint Simon ; Burnet, i. 112, 113. ; Feuquières ; London Gazette, July 27. 31., Aug. 3. 1693 ; French Official Relation ; Relation sent by the King of Great Britain to their High Mightinesses, Aug. 2. 1693 ; Extract of a Letter from the Adjutant of the King of England's Dragoon Guards, Aug. 1. ; Dykvelt's Letter to the States General, dated July 30. at noon. The last four papers will be found in the Monthly Mercuries of July and August 1693. See also the History of the Last Campaign in the Spanish Netherlands by Edward D'Auvergne, dedicated to the Duke of Ormond, 1693. The French did justice to William. " Le Prince d'Orange," Racine wrote to Boileau, " pensa être pris, après avoir fait des merveilles." See also the glowing description of Sterne, who, no doubt, had many times heard the battle fought over by old soldiers. It was on this occasion that Corporal Trim was left wounded on the field, and was nursed by the Beguine.

renowned warriors.   Montchevreuil was there, and the mutilated
trunk of the Duke of Uzes, first in order of precedence among
the whole aristocracy of France.   Thence too Sarsfield was
borne desperately wounded to a pallet from which he never
rose again.   The Court of Saint Germains had conferred on
him the empty title of Earl of Lucan : but history knows him
by the name which is still dear to the most unfortunate of
nations.   The region, renowned in history as the battle field,
during many ages, of the most warlike nations of Europe, has
seen only two more terrible days, the day of Malplaquet and
the day of Waterloo.   During many months the ground was
strewn with skulls and bones of men and horses, and with fragments of hats and shoes, saddles and holsters.   The next summer the soil, fertilised by twenty thousand corpses, broke forth
into millions of poppies.   The traveller who, on the road from
Saint Tron to Tirlemont, saw that vast sheet of rich scarlet
spreading from Landen to Neerwinden, could hardly help fancy-
ing that the figurative prediction of the Hebrew prophet was
literally accomplished, that the earth was disclosing her blood,
and refusing to cover the slain.*

There was no pursuit, though the sun was still high in the
heaven when William crossed the Gette.   The conquerors were
so much exhausted by marching and fighting that they could
scarcely move ; and the horses were in even worse condition
than the men.   Their general thought it necessary to allow
some time for rest and refreshment.   The French nobles
unloaded their sumpter horses, supped gaily, and pledged one
another in champagne amidst the heaps of dead ; and, when
night fell, whole brigades gladly lay down to sleep in their
ranks on the field of battle.   The inactivity of Luxemburg did
not escape censure.   None could deny that he had in the action
shown great skill and energy.   But some complained that he
wanted patience and perseverance.   Others whispered that he
had no wish to bring to an end a war which made him necessary
to a Court where he had never, in time of peace, found favour
or even justice.†   Lewis, who on this occasion was perhaps
not altogether free from some emotions of jealousy, contrived,
it was reported, to mingle with the praise which he bestowed on
his lieutenant blame which, though delicately expressed, was

* Letter from Lord Perth to his sister, June 17. 1694.
† Saint Simon mentions the reflections thrown on the Marshal.   Feuquières, a very good judge, tells us that Luxemburg was unjustly blamed,
and that the French army was really too much crippled by its losses to
improve the victory.

perfectly intelligible. " In the battle," he said, "the Duke of Luxemburg behaved like Condé; and since the battle the Prince of Orange has behaved like Turenne."

In truth the ability and vigour with which William repaired his terrible defeat might well excite admiration. "In one respect," said the Admiral Coligni, "I may claim superiority over Alexander, over Scipio, over Cæsar. They won great battles, it is true. I have lost four great battles; and yet I show to the enemy a more formidable front than ever." The blood of Coligni ran in the veins of William; and with the blood had descended the unconquerable spirit which could derive from failure as much glory as happier commanders owed to success. The defeat of Landen was indeed a heavy blow. The King had a few days of cruel anxiety. If Luxemburg pushed on, all was lost. Louvain must fall, and Mechlin, Nieuport, and Ostend. The Batavian frontier would be in danger. The cry for peace throughout Holland might be such as neither States General nor Stadtholder would be able to resist.* But there was delay; and a very short delay was enough for William. From the field of battle he made his way through the multitude of fugitives to the neighbourhood of Louvain, and there began to collect his scattered forces. His character is not lowered by the anxiety which, at that moment, the most disastrous of his life, he felt for the two persons who were dearest to him. As soon as he was safe, he wrote to assure his wife of his safety.† In the confusion of the flight he had lost sight of Portland, who was then in very feeble health, and had therefore run more than the ordinary risks of war. A short note which the King sent to his friend a few hours later is still extant.‡ "Though I hope to see you this evening, I cannot help writing to tell you how rejoiced I am that you got off so well. God grant that your health may soon be quite restored. These are great trials, which he has been pleased to send me in quick succession. I must try to submit to his pleasure without murmuring, and to deserve his anger less."

His forces rallied fast. Large bodies of troops which he had, perhaps imprudently, detached from his army while he supposed

---

* This account of what would have taken place, if Luxemburg had been able and willing to improve his victory, I have taken from what seems to have been a very manly and sensible speech made by Talmash in the House of Commons on the 11th of December following. See Grey's Debates.

† William to Heinsius, July $\frac{29}{30}$. 1693.

‡ William to Portland, July $\frac{20}{31}$. 1693.

that Liege was the object of the enemy, rejoined him by forced marches.  Three weeks after his defeat he held a review a few miles from Brussels.  The number of men under arms was greater than on the morning of the bloody day of Landen : their appearance was soldierlike ; and their spirit seemed unbroken.  William now wrote to Heinsius that the worst was over.  " The crisis," he said, "has been a terrible one.  Thank God that it has ended thus."  He did not, however, think it prudent to try at that time the event of another pitched field. He therefore suffered the French to besiege and take Charleroy ; and this was the only advantage which they derived from the most sanguinary battle fought in Europe during the seventeenth century.

The melancholy tidings of the defeat of Landen found England agitated by tidings not less melancholy from a different quarter.   During many months the trade with the Mediterranean Sea had been almost entirely interrupted by the war. There was no chance that a merchantman from London or from Amsterdam would, if unprotected, reach the Pillars of Hercules without being boarded by a French privateer ; and the protection of armed vessels was not easily to be obtained. During the year 1692, great fleets, richly laden for Spanish, Italian and Turkish markets, had been gathering in the Thames and the Texel.   In February 1693, near four hundred ships were ready to start.   The value of the cargoes was estimated at several millions sterling.   Those galleons which had long been the wonder and envy of the world had never conveyed so precious a freight from the West Indies to Seville.   The English government undertook, in concert with the Dutch government, to escort the vessels which were laden with this great mass of wealth.   The French government was bent on intercepting them.

The plan of the allies was that seventy ships of the line and about thirty frigates and brigantines should assemble in the Channel under the command of Killegrew and Delaval, the two new Lords of the English Admiralty, and should convoy the Smyrna fleet, as it was popularly called, beyond the limits within which any danger could be apprehended from the Brest squadron.   The greater part of the armament might then return to guard the Channel, while Rooke, with twenty sail, might accompany the trading vessels and might protect them against the squadron which lay at Toulon.   The plan of the French government was that the Brest squadron under Tourville and the Toulon squadron under Estrees should meet in the neighbourhood of the Straits of Gibraltar, and should there lie in wait for the booty.

Which plan was the better conceived may be doubted. Which was the better executed is a question which admits of no doubt. The whole French navy, whether in the Atlantic or in the Mediterranean, was moved by one will. The navy of England and the navy of the United Provinces were subject to different authorities; and, both in England and in the United Provinces, the power was divided and subdivided to such an extent that no single person was pressed by a heavy responsibility. The spring came. The merchants loudly complained that they had already lost more by delay than they could hope to gain by the most successful voyage; and still the ships of war were not half manned or half provisioned. The Amsterdam squadron did not arrive on our coast till late in April; the Zealand squadron not till the middle of May.\* It was June before the immense fleet, near five hundred sail, lost sight of the cliffs of England.

Tourville was already on the sea, and was steering southward. But Killegrew and Delaval were so negligent or so unfortunate that they had no intelligence of his movements. They at first took it for granted that he was still lying in the port of Brest. Then they heard a rumour that some shipping had been seen to the northward; and they supposed that he was taking advantage of their absence to threaten the coast of Devonshire. It never seems to have occurred to them as possible that he might have effected a junction with the Toulon squadron, and might be impatiently waiting for his prey in the neighbourhood of Gibraltar. They therefore, on the sixth of June, having convoyed the Smyrna fleet about two hundred miles beyond Ushant, announced their intention to part company with Rooke. Rooke expostulated, but to no purpose. It was necessary for him to submit, and to proceed with his twenty men of war to the Mediterranean, while his superiors, with the rest of the armament, returned to the Channel.

It was by this time known in England that Tourville had stolen out of Brest, and was hastening to join Estrees. The return of Killegrew and Delaval therefore excited great alarm. A swift sailing vessel was instantly despatched to warn Rooke of his danger: but the warning never reached him. He ran before a fair wind to Cape Saint Vincent; and there he learned that some French ships were lying in the neighbouring Bay of Lagos. The first information which he received led him to

\* London Gazette, April 24., May 15. 1693.

believe that they were few in number; and so dexterously did they conceal their strength that, till they were within half an hour's sail, he had no suspicion that he was opposed to the whole maritime strength of a great kingdom. To contend against fourfold odds would have been madness. It was much that he was able to save his squadron from utter destruction. He exerted all his skill. Two or three Dutch men of war, which were in the rear, courageously sacrificed themselves to save the fleet. With the rest of the armament, and with about sixty merchant ships, Rooke got safe to Madeira and thence to Cork. But more than three hundred of the vessels which he had convoyed were scattered over the ocean. Some escaped to Ireland; some to Corunna; some to Lisbon; some to Cadiz: some were captured, and more destroyed. A few, which had taken shelter under the rock of Gibraltar, and were pursued thither by the enemy, were sunk when it was found that they could not be defended. Others perished in the same manner under the batteries of Malaga. The gain to the French seems not to have been great: but the loss to England and Holland was immense.*

Never within the memory of man had there been in the City a day of more gloom and agitation than that on which the news of the encounter in the Bay of Lagos arrived. Many merchants, an eyewitness said, went away from the Royal Exchange, as pale as if they had received sentence of death. A deputation from the merchants who had been sufferers by this great disaster went up to the Queen with an address representing their grievances. They were admitted to the Council Chamber, where she was seated at the head of the Board. She directed Somers to reply to them in her name; and he addressed to them a speech well calculated to soothe their irritation. Her Majesty, he said, felt for them from her heart; and she had already appointed a Committee of the Privy Council to inquire into the cause of the late misfortune, and to consider of the best means of preventing similar misfortunes in time to come.† This answer gave so much satisfaction that the Lord Mayor

---

* Burchett's Memoirs of Transactions at Sea; Burnet, ii. 114, 115, 116.; the London Gazette, July 17. 1693; Monthly Mercury of July; Letter from Cadiz, dated July 4.

† Narcissus Luttrell's Diary; Baden to the States General, July $\frac{14}{24}$. $\frac{July\ 25}{Aug.\ 4}$. Among the Tanner MSS. in the Bodleian Library are letters describing the agitation in the City. "I wish," says one of Sancroft's Jacobite correspondents, "it may open our eyes and change our minds. But by the accounts I have seen, the Turkey Company went from the Queen and Council full of satisfaction and good humour."

soon came to the palace to thank the Queen for her goodness, to assure her that, through all vicissitudes, London would be true to her and her consort, and to inform her that, severely as the late calamity had been felt by many great commercial houses, the Common Council had unanimously resolved to advance whatever might be necessary for the support of the government.*

The ill humour which the public calamities naturally produced was inflamed by every factious artifice. Never had the Jacobite pamphleteers been so savagely scurrilous as during this unfortunate summer. The police was consequently more active than ever in seeking for the dens from which so much treason proceeded. With great difficulty and after long search the most important of all the unlicensed presses was discovered. This press belonged to a Jacobite named William Anderton, whose intrepidity and fanaticism marked him out as fit to be employed on services from which prudent men and scrupulous men shrink. During two years he had been watched by the agents of the government : but where he exercised his craft was an impenetrable mystery. At length he was tracked to a house near Saint James's Street, where he was known by a feigned name, and where he passed for a working jeweller. A messenger of the press went thither with several assistants, and found Anderton's wife and mother posted as sentinels at the door. The women knew the messenger, rushed on him, tore

---

* London Gazette, August 21. 1693 ; L'Hermitage to the States General, $\frac{\text{July } 28.}{\text{Aug. } 7.}$ As I shall, in this and the following chapters, make large use of the despatches of L'Hermitage, it may be proper to say something about him. He was a French refugee, and resided in London as agent for the Waldenses. One of his employments had been to send newsletters to Heinsius. Some interesting extracts from those newsletters will be found in the work of the Baron Sirtema de Grovestins. It was probably in consequence of the Pensionary's recommendation that the States General, by a resolution dated $\frac{\text{July } 24.}{\text{Aug. } 3.}$ 1693, desired L'Hermitage to collect and transmit to them intelligence of what was passing in England. His letters abound with curious and valuable information which is nowhere else to be found. His accounts of parliamentary proceedings are of peculiar value, and seem to have been so considered by his employers.

Copies of the despatches of L'Hermitage, and, indeed, of the despatches of all the ministers and agents employed by the States General in England from the time of Elizabeth downward, now are, or will soon be, in the library of the British Museum. For this valuable addition to the great national storehouse of knowledge, the country is chiefly indebted to Lord Palmerston. But it would be unjust not to add that his instructions were most zealously carried into effect by the late Sir Edward Disbrowe, with the cordial cooperation of the enlightened men who have charge of the noble collection of Archives at the Hague.

his hair, and cried out "Thieves" and "Murder." The alarm was thus given to Anderton. He concealed the instruments of his calling, came forth with an assured air, and bade defiance to the messenger, the Censor, the Secretary, and Little Hooknose himself. After a struggle he was secured. His room was searched; and at first sight no evidence of his guilt appeared. But behind the bed was soon found a door which opened into a dark closet. The closet contained a press, types and heaps of newly printed papers. One of these papers, entitled Remarks on the Present Confederacy and the Late Revolution, is perhaps the most frantic of all the Jacobite libels. In this tract the Prince of Orange is gravely accused of having ordered fifty of his wounded English soldiers to be burned alive. The governing principle of his whole conduct, it is said, is not vainglory, or ambition, or avarice, but a deadly hatred of Englishmen and a desire to make them miserable. The nation is vehemently adjured, on peril of incurring the severest judgments, to rise up and free itself from this plague, this curse, this tyrant, whose depravity makes it difficult to believe that he can have been procreated by a human pair. Many copies were also found of another paper, somewhat less ferocious but perhaps more dangerous, entitled A French Conquest neither desirable nor practicable. In this tract also the people are exhorted to rise in insurrection. They are assured that a great part of the army is with them. The forces of the Prince of Orange will melt away: he will be glad to make his escape; and a charitable hope is sneeringly expressed that it may not be necessary to do him any harm beyond sending him back to Loo, where he may live surrounded by luxuries for which the English have paid dear.

The government, provoked and alarmed by the virulence of the Jacobite pamphleteers, determined to make Anderton an example. He was indicted for high treason, and brought to the bar of the Old Bailey. Treby, now Chief Justice of the Common Pleas, and Powell, who had honourably distinguished himself on the day of the trial of the bishops, were on the Bench. It is unfortunate that no detailed report of the evidence has come down to us, and that we are forced to content ourselves with such fragments of information as can be collected from the contradictory narratives of writers evidently partial, intemperate and dishonest. The indictment, however, is extant; and the overt acts which it imputes to the prisoner undoubtedly amount to high treason.* To exhort the subjects

* It is strange that the indictment should not have been printed in

of the realm to rise up and depose the King by force, and to add to that exhortation the expression, evidently ironical, of a hope that it may not be necessary to inflict on him any evil worse than banishment, is surely an offence which the least courtly lawyer will admit to be within the scope of the statute of Edward the Third. On this point indeed there seems to have been no dispute, either at the trial or subsequently.

The prisoner denied that he had printed the libels. On this point it seems reasonable that, since the evidence has not come down to us, we should give credit to the judges and the jury who heard what the witnesses had to say.

One argument with which Anderton had been furnished by his advisers, and which, in the Jacobite pasquinades of that time, is represented as unanswerable, was that, as the art of printing had been unknown in the reign of Edward the Third, printing could not be an overt act of treason under a statute of that reign. The Judges treated this argument very lightly ; and they were surely justified in so treating it. For it is an argument which would lead to the conclusion that it could not be an overt act of treason to behead a King with a guillotine or to shoot him with a Minie rifle.

It was also urged in Anderton's favour,—and this was undoubtedly an argument well entitled to consideration,—that a distinction ought to be made between the author of a treasonable paper and the man who merely printed it. The former could not pretend that he had not understood the meaning of the words which he had himself selected. But to the latter those words might convey no idea whatever. The metaphors, the allusions, the sarcasms, might be far beyond his comprehension ; and, while his hands were busy among the types, his thoughts might be wandering to things altogether unconnected with the manuscript which was before him. It is undoubtedly true that it may be no crime to print what it would be a great crime to write. But this is evidently a matter concerning which no general rule can be laid down. Whether Anderton had, as a mere mechanic, contributed to spread a work the tendency of which he did not suspect, or had knowingly lent his help to raise a rebellion, was a question for the jury ; and the jury might reasonably infer from his change of his name, from the secret manner in which he worked, from the strict watch kept by his wife and mother, and from the fury with

---

Howell's State Trials. The copy which is before me was made for Sir James Mackintosh.

which, even in the grasp of the messengers, he railed at the government, that he was not the unconscious tool, but the intelligent and zealous accomplice of traitors. The twelve, after passing a considerable time in deliberation, informed the Court that one of them entertained doubts. Those doubts were removed by the arguments of Treby and Powell ; and a verdict of Guilty was found.

The fate of the prisoner remained during some time in suspense. The Ministers hoped that he might be induced to save his own neck at the expense of the necks of the pamphleteers who had employed him. But his natural courage was kept up by spiritual stimulants which the nonjuring divines well understood how to administer. He suffered death with fortitude, and continued to revile the government to the last. The Jacobites clamoured loudly against the cruelty of the Judges who had tried him and of the Queen who had left him for execution, and, not very consistently, represented him at once as a poor ignorant artisan who was not aware of the nature and tendency of the act for which he suffered, and as a martyr who had heroically laid down his life for the banished King and the persecuted Church.*

The Ministers were much mistaken if they flattered themselves that the fate of Anderton would deter others from imitating his example. His execution produced several pamphlets scarcely less virulent than those for which he had suffered. Collier, in what he called Remarks on the London Gazette, exulted with cruel joy over the carnage of Landen, and the vast destruction of English property on the coast of Spain.† Other writers did their best to raise riots among the labouring people. For the doctrine of the Jacobites was that disorder, in whatever place or in whatever way it might begin, was likely to end in a Restoration. A phrase which, without a commentary, may seem to be mere nonsense, but which was really full of meaning, was often in their mouths at this time, and was indeed a password by which the members of the party recognised each other : " Box it about : it will come to my father." The hidden sense of this gibberish was, " Throw the country into confusion : it will be necessary at last to have recourse to King James." ‡ Trade was not prosperous ; and many industrious men were out of work. Accordingly songs addressed

---

* Most of the information which has come down to us about Anderton's case will be found in Howell's State Trials.

† The Remarks are extant, and deserve to be read.

‡ Narcissus Luttrell's Diary.

to the distressed classes were composed by the malecontent
street poets. Numerous copies of a ballad exhorting the
weavers to rise against the government were discovered in the
house of that Quaker who had printed James's Declaration.*
Every art was used for the purpose of exciting discontent
in a much more formidable body of men, the sailors; and
unhappily the vices of the naval administration furnished the
enemies of the State with but too good a choice of inflammatory
topics. Some seamen deserted: some mutinied: then came
executions; and then came more ballads and broadsides
representing those executions as barbarous murders. Reports
that the government had determined to defraud its defenders
of their hard earned pay were circulated with so much effect
that a great crowd of women from Wapping and Rotherhithe
besieged Whitehall, clamouring for what was due to their
husbands. Mary had the good sense and good nature to
order four of those importunate petitioners to be admitted into
the room where she was holding a Council. She heard their
complaints, and herself assured them that the rumour which
had alarmed them was unfounded.† By this time Saint
Bartholomew's day drew near; and the great annual fair, the
delight of idle apprentices and the horror of Puritanical Aldermen, was opened in Smithfield with the usual display of dwarfs,
giants, and dancing dogs, the man that ate fire, and the
elephant that loaded and fired a musket. But of all the shows
none proved so attractive as a dramatic performance which, in
conception, though doubtless not in execution, seems to have
borne much resemblance to those immortal masterpieces of
humour in which Aristophanes held up Cleon and Lamachus
to derision. Two strollers personated Killegrew and Delaval.
The Admirals were represented as flying with their whole fleet
before a few French privateers, and taking shelter under the
guns of the Tower. The office of Chorus was performed by a
Jackpudding who expressed very freely his opinion of the naval
administration. Immense crowds flocked to see this strange
farce. The applauses were loud: the receipts were great; and

* Narcissus Luttrell's Diary.

† There are still extant a handbill addressed to All Gentlemen Seamen
that are weary of their Lives; and a ballad accusing the King and Queen
of cruelty to the sailors.

> "To robbers, thieves, and felons, they
> Freely grant pardons every day.
> Only poor seamen, who alone
> Do keep them in their father's throne,
> Must have at all no mercy shown."

Narcissus Luttrell gives an account of the scene at Whitehall.

the mountebanks, who had at first ventured to attack only the unlucky and unpopular Board of Admiralty, now, emboldened by impunity and success, and probably prompted and rewarded by persons of much higher station than their own, began to cast reflections on other departments of the government.    This attempt to revive the license of the Attic Stage was soon brought to a close by the appearance of a strong body of constables who carried off the actors to prison.*    Meanwhile the streets of London were every night strewn with seditious handbills.    At all the taverns the zealots of hereditary right were limping about with glasses of wine and punch at their lips. This fashion had just come in ; and the uninitiated wondered much that so great a number of jolly gentlemen should have suddenly become lame.    But those who were in the secret knew that the word Limp was a consecrated word, that every one of the four letters which composed it was the initial of an august name, and that the loyal subject who limped while he drank was taking off his bumper to Lewis, James, Mary, and the Prince.†

It was not only in the capital that the Jacobites, at this time, made a great display of their wit.    They mustered strong at Bath, where the Lord President Caermarthen was trying to recruit his feeble health.    Every evening they met, as they phrased it, to serenade the Marquess.    In other words they assembled under the sick man's window, and there sang doggrel lampoons on him.‡

It is remarkable that the Lord President, at the very time at which he was insulted as a Williamite at Bath, was considered as a stanch Jacobite at Saint Germains.    How he came to be so considered is a most perplexing question.    Some writers are of opinion that he, like Shrewsbury, Russell, Godolphin and Marlborough, entered into engagements with one king while eating the bread of the other.    But this opinion does not rest on sufficient proofs.    About the treasons of Shrewsbury, of Russell, of Godolphin and of Marlborough, we have a great mass of evidence, derived from various sources, and extending

* L'Hermitage, Sept. $\frac{5}{15}$. 1693 ; Narcissus Luttrell's Diary.

† Narcissus Luttrell's Diary.

‡ Narcissus Luttrell's Diary.    In a pamphlet published at this time, and entitled A Dialogue between Whig and Tory, the Whig alludes to "the public insolences at the Bath upon the late defeat in Flanders."    The Tory answers, "I know not what some hotheaded drunken men may have said and done at the Bath or elsewhere."    In the folio Collection of State Tracts, this Dialogue is erroneously said to have been printed about November 1692.

over several years. But all the information which we possess about Caermarthen's dealings with James is contained in a single short paper written by Melfort on the sixteenth of October 1693. From that paper it is quite clear that some intelligence had reached the banished King and his Ministers which led them to regard Caermarthen as a friend. But there is no proof that they ever so regarded him, either before that day or after that day.* On the whole, the most probable explanation of this mystery seems to be that Caermarthen had been sounded by some Jacobite emissary much less artful than himself, and had, for the purpose of getting at the bottom of the new scheme of policy devised by Middleton, pretended to be well disposed to the cause of the banished King, that an exaggerated account of what had passed had been sent to Saint Germains, and that there had been much rejoicing there at a conversion which soon proved to have been feigned. It seems strange that such a conversion should even for a moment have been thought sincere. It was plainly Caermarthen's interest to stand by the sovereigns in possession. He was their chief minister. He could not hope to be the chief minister of James. It can indeed hardly be supposed that the political conduct of a cunning old man, insatiably ambitious and covetous, was much influenced by personal partiality. But, if there were any person to whom Caermarthen was partial, that person was undoubtedly Mary. That he had seriously engaged in a plot to depose her, at the risk of his head if he failed, and with the certainty of losing immense power and wealth if he succeeded, was a story too absurd for any credulity but the credulity of exiles.

* The Paper to which I refer is among the Nairne MSS., and will be found in Macpherson's collection. That excellent writer Mr. Hallam has, on this subject, fallen into an error of a kind very rare with him. He says that the name of Caermarthen is perpetually mentioned among those whom James reckoned as his friends. I believe that the evidence against Caermarthen will be found to begin and to end with the letter of Melfort which I have mentioned. There is indeed, among the Nairne MSS., which Macpherson printed, an undated and anonymous letter in which Caermarthen is reckoned among the friends of James. But this letter is altogether undeserving of consideration. The writer was evidently a silly hotheaded Jacobite, who knew nothing about the situation or character of any of the public men whom he mentioned. He blunders grossly about Marlborough, Godolphin, Russell, Shrewsbury and the Beaufort family. Indeed the whole composition is a tissue of absurdities.

It ought to be remarked that, in the Life of James compiled from his own Papers, the assurances of support which he received from Marlborough, Russell, Godolphin, Shrewsbury, and other men of note are mentioned with very copious details. But there is not a word indicating that any such assurances were ever received from Caermarthen.

Caermarthen had indeed at that moment peculiarly strong reasons for being satisfied with the place which he held in the counsels of William and Mary. There is but too strong reason to believe that he was then accumulating unlawful gain with a rapidity unexampled even in his experience.

The contest between the two East India Companies was, during the autumn of 1693, fiercer than ever. The House of Commons, finding the Old Company obstinately averse to all compromise, had, a little before the close of the late session, requested the King to give the three years' warning prescribed by the Charter. Child and his fellows now began to be seriously alarmed. They expected every day to receive the dreaded notice. Nay, they were not sure that their exclusive privilege might not be taken away without any notice at all: for they found that they had, by inadvertently omitting to pay the tax lately imposed on their stock at the precise time fixed by law, forfeited their Charter; and, though it would, in ordinary circumstances, have been thought cruel in the government to take advantage of such a slip, the public was not inclined to allow the Old Company any thing more than the strict letter of the bond. Every thing was lost if the Charter were not renewed before the meeting of Parliament. There can be little doubt that the proceedings of the corporation were still really directed by Child. But he had, it should seem, perceived that his unpopularity had injuriously affected the interests which were under his care, and therefore did not obtrude himself on the public notice. His place was ostensibly filled by his near kinsman Sir Thomas Cook, one of the greatest merchants of London, and Member of Parliament for the borough of Colchester. The Directors placed at Cook's absolute disposal all the immense wealth which lay in their treasury; and in a short time near a hundred thousand pounds were expended in corruption on a gigantic scale. In what proportions this enormous sum was distributed among the great men at Whitehall, and how much of it was embezzled by intermediate agents, is still a mystery. We know with certainty however that thousands went to Seymour and thousands to Caermarthen.

The effect of these bribes was that the Attorney General received orders to draw up a charter regranting the old privileges to the Old Company. No minister, however, could, after what had passed in Parliament, venture to advise the Crown to renew the monopoly without conditions. The Directors were sensible that they had no choice, and reluctantly consented to accept the new Charter on terms substantially the same with those which the House of Commons had sanctioned.

It is probable that, two years earlier, such a compromise would have quieted the feud which distracted the City. But a long conflict, in which satire and calumny had not been spared, had heated the minds of men. The cry of Dowgate against Leadenhall Street was louder than ever. Caveats were entered: petitions were signed; and in those petitions a doctrine which had hitherto been studiously kept in the background was boldly affirmed. While it was doubtful on which side the royal prerogative would be used, that prerogative had not been questioned. But as soon as it appeared that the Old Company was likely to obtain a regrant of the monopoly under the Great Seal, the New Company began to assert with vehemence that no monopoly could be created except by Act of Parliament. The Privy Council, over which Caermarthen presided, after hearing the matter fully argued by counsel on both sides, decided in favour of the Old Company, and ordered the Charter to be sealed.*

The autumn was by this time far advanced, and the armies in the Netherlands had gone into quarters for the winter. On the last day of October William landed in England. The Parliament was about to meet; and he had every reason to expect a session even more stormy than the last. The people were discontented, and not without cause. The year had been every where disastrous to the allies, not only on the sea and in the Low Countries, but also in Servia, in Spain, in Italy, and in Germany. The Turks had compelled the generals of the Empire to raise the siege of Belgrade. A newly created Marshal of France, the Duke of Noailles, had invaded Catalonia and taken the fortress of Rosas. Another newly created Marshal, the skilful and valiant Catinat, had descended from the Alps on Piedmont, and had, at Marsiglia, gained a complete victory over the forces of the Duke of Savoy. This battle is memorable as the first of a long series of battles in which the Irish troops retrieved the honour lost by misfortunes and misconduct in domestic war. Some of the exiles of Limerick showed, on that day, under the standard of France, a valour which distinguished them among many thousands of brave men. It is remarkable that on the same day a battalion of the persecuted and expatriated Huguenots

* A Journal of several Remarkable Passages relating to the East India Trade, 1693.

stood firm amidst the general disorder round the standard of Savoy, and fell fighting desperately to the last.

The Duke of Lorges had marched into the Palatinate, already twice devastated, and had found that Turenne and Duras had left him something to destroy. Heidelberg, just beginning to rise again from its ruins, was again sacked, the peaceable citizens butchered, their wives and daughters foully outraged. The very choirs of the churches were stained with blood : the pyxes and crucifixes were torn from the altars : the tombs of the ancient Electors were broken open : the corpses, stripped of their cerecloths and ornaments, were dragged about the streets. The skull of the father of the Duchess of Orleans was beaten to fragments by the soldiers of a prince among the ladies of whose splendid Court she held the foremost place.

And yet a discerning eye might have perceived that, unfortunate as the confederates seemed to have been, the advantage had really been on their side. The contest was quite as much a financial as a military contest. The French King had, some months before, said that the last piece of gold would carry the day ; and he now began painfully to feel the truth of the saying. England was undoubtedly hard pressed by public burdens : but still she stood up erect. France meanwhile was fast sinking. Her recent efforts had been too much for her strength, and had left her spent and unnerved. Never had her rulers shown more ingenuity in devising taxes or more severity in exacting them : but by no ingenuity, by no severity, was it possible to raise the sums necessary for another such campaign as that of 1693. In England the harvest had been abundant. In France the corn and the wine had again failed. The people, as usual, railed at the government. The government, with shameful ignorance or more shameful dishonesty, tried to direct the public indignation against the dealers in grain. Decrees appeared which seemed to have been elaborately framed for the purpose of turning dearth into famine. The nation was assured that there was no reason for uneasiness, that there was more than a sufficient supply of food, and that the scarcity had been produced by the villanous arts of misers, who locked up their stores in the hope of making enormous gains. Commissioners were appointed to inspect the granaries, and were empowered to send to market all the corn that was not necessary for the consumption of the proprietors. Such interference of course increased the suffering which it was meant to relieve. But in the midst of the general distress there was an artificial plenty in one favoured spot. The most arbitrary prince must always stand in some awe of an immense mass of human beings collected in the neighbourhood of his own palace. Apprehensions similar to those which had induced the Cæsars to extort from Africa and Egypt the means of pampering the rabble of Rome induced Lewis to aggravate the misery of twenty provinces for the purpose of keeping one huge city in good humour. He ordered bread to be distributed in all the parishes of the capital at less than half the market price. The English Jacobites were stupid enough to extol the wisdom and humanity of this arrangement. The harvest, they said, had been good in England and bad in France ; and yet the loaf was cheaper at Paris than in London ; and the explanation was simple. The French had a sovereign whose heart was French, and who watched over his people with the solicitude of a father, while the English were cursed with a Dutch tyrant, who sent their corn to Holland. The truth was that a week of such fatherly government as that of Lewis would have raised all England in arms from Northumberland to Cornwall. That there might be abundance at Paris, the people of Normandy and Anjou were stuffing themselves with nettles. That there might be tranquillity at Paris, the peasantry were fighting with the bargemen and the troops all along the Loire and the Seine. Multitudes fled from those rural districts where bread cost five sous a pound to the happy place where bread was to be had for two sous a pound. It was necessary to drive the famished crowds back by force from the barriers, and to denounce the most terrible punishments against all who should not go home and starve quietly.*

Lewis was sensible that the strength of France had been overstrained by the exertions of the last campaign. Even if her harvest and her vintage had been abundant, she would not have been able to do in 1694 what she had done in 1693 ; and it was utterly impossible that, in a season of extreme distress, she should again send into the field armies superior in number on every point to the armies of the coalition. New conquests were not to be expected. It would be much if the harassed and exhausted land, beset on all sides by enemies, should be able to sustain a defensive war without any disaster.

* See the Monthly Mercuries and London Gazettes of September, October, November and December 1693 ; Dangeau, Sept. 5. 27., Oct. 21., Nov. 21. ; the Price of the Abdication, 1693.

So able a politician as the French King could not but feel that it would be for his advantage to treat with the allies while they were still awed by the remembrance of the gigantic efforts which his kingdom had just made, and before the collapse which had followed those efforts should become visible.

He had long been communicating through various channels with some members of the confederacy, and trying to induce them to separate themselves from the rest. But he had as yet made no overture tending to a general pacification. For he knew that there could be no general pacification unless he was prepared to abandon the cause of James, and to acknowledge the Prince and Princess of Orange as King and Queen of England. This was in truth the point on which every thing turned. What should be done with those great fortresses which Lewis had unjustly seized and annexed to his empire in time of peace, Luxemburg which overawed the Moselle, and Strasburg which domineered over the Upper Rhine ; what should be done with the places which he had recently won in open war, Philipsburg, Mons and Namur, Huy and Charleroy ; what barrier should be given to the States General ; on what terms Lorraine should be restored to its hereditary Dukes ; these were assuredly not unimportant questions. But the all important question was whether England was to be, as she had been under James, a dependency of France, or, as she was under William and Mary, a power of the first rank. If Lewis really wished for peace, he must bring himself to recognise the Sovereigns whom he had so often designated as usurpers. Could he bring himself to recognise them ? His superstition, his pride, his regard for the unhappy exiles who were pining at Saint Germains, his personal dislike of the indefatigable and unconquerable adversary who had been constantly crossing his path during twenty years, were on one side ; his interests and those of his people were on the other. He must have been sensible that it was not in his power to subjugate the English, that he must at last leave them to choose their government for themselves, and that what he must do at last it would be best to do soon. Yet he could not at once make up his mind to what was so disagreeable to him. He however opened a negotiation with the States General through the intervention of Sweden and Denmark, and sent a confidential emissary to confer in secret at Brussels with Dykvelt, who possessed the entire confidence of William. There was much discussion about matters of secondary importance : but the great question remained unsettled. The French agent

used, in private conversation, expressions plainly implying that
the government which he represented was prepared to recognise
William and Mary : but no formal assurance could be obtained
from him. Just at the same time the King of Denmark informed
the allies that he was endeavouring to prevail on France not to
insist on the restoration of James as an indispensable condition
of peace, but did not say that his endeavours had as yet been
successful. Meanwhile Avaux, who was now Ambassador at
Stockholm, informed the King of Sweden, that, as the dignity
of all crowned heads had been outraged in the person of James,
the Most Christian King felt assured that not only neutral
powers, but even the Emperor, would try to find some expedient
which might remove so grave a cause of quarrel. The expedient at which Avaux hinted doubtless was that James should
waive his rights, and that the Prince of Wales should be sent
to England, bred a Protestant, adopted by William and Mary,
and declared their heir. To such an arrangement William
would probably have had no personal objection. But we may
be assured that he never would have consented to make it a
condition of peace with France. Who should reign in England
was a question to be decided by England alone.*

It might well be suspected that a negotiation conducted in
this manner was merely meant to divide the confederates.
William understood the whole importance of the conjuncture.
He had not, it may be, the eye of a great captain for all the
turns of a battle. But he had, in the highest perfection, the
eye of a great statesman for all the turns of a war. That
France had at length made overtures to him was a sufficient
proof that she felt herself spent and sinking. That those
overtures were made with extreme reluctance and hesitation
proved that she had not yet come to a temper in which it was
possible to have peace with her on fair terms. He saw that
the enemy was beginning to give ground, and that this was the
time to assume the offensive, to push forward, to bring up every
reserve. But whether the opportunity should be seized or lost
it did not belong to him to decide. The King of France might
levy troops and exact taxes without any limit save that which
the laws of nature impose on despotism. But the King of
England could do nothing without the support of the House
of Commons ; and the House of Commons, though it had

* Correspondence of William and Heinsius ; Danish Note, dated Dec.
$\frac{21}{31}$. 1693. The note delivered by Avaux to the Swedish government at
this time will be found in Lamberty's Collection and in the Mémoires et
Négotiations de la Paix de Ryswick.

hitherto supported him zealously and liberally, was not a body on which he could rely. It had indeed got into a state which perplexed and alarmed all the most sagacious politicians of that age. There was something appalling in the union of such boundless power and such boundless caprice. The fate of the whole civilised world depended on the votes of the representatives of the English people; and there was no public man who could venture to say with confidence what those representatives might not be induced to vote within twenty-four hours.* William painfully felt that it was scarcely possible for a prince dependent on an assembly so violent at one time, so languid at another, to effect any thing great. Indeed, though no sovereign did so much to secure and to extend the power of the House of Commons, no sovereign loved the House of Commons less. Nor is this strange: for he saw that House at the very worst. He saw it when it had just acquired the power and had not yet acquired the gravity of a senate. In his letters to Heinsius he perpetually complains of the endless talking, the factious squabbling, the inconstancy, the dilatoriness, of the body which his situation made it necessary for him to treat with deference. His complaints were by no means unfounded; but he had not discovered either the cause or the cure of the evil.

The truth was that the change which the Revolution had made in the situation of the House of Commons had made another change necessary; and that other change had not yet taken place. There was parliamentary government: but there was no Ministry; and, without a Ministry, the working of a parliamentary government, such as ours, must always be unsteady and unsafe.

It is essential to our liberties that the House of Commons should exercise a control over all the departments of the executive administration. And yet it is evident that a crowd of five or six hundred people, even if they were intellectually much above the average of the members of the best Parliament, even if every one of them were a Burleigh, or a Sully, would be unfit for executive functions. It has been truly said that every large collection of human beings, however well educated, has a strong tendency to become a mob; and a country of which the Supreme Executive Council is a mob is surely in a perilous situation.

* " Sir John Lowther says, nobody can know one day what a House of Commons would do the next; in which all agreed with him." These remarkable words were written by Caermarthen on the margin of a paper drawn up by Rochester in August 1692. Dalrymple, Appendix to part ii. chap. 7.

Happily a way has been found out in which the House of Commons can exercise a paramount influence over the executive government, without assuming functions such as can never be well discharged by a body so numerous and so variously composed. An institution which did not exist in the times of the Plantagenets, of the Tudors or of the Stuarts, an institution not known to the law, an institution not mentioned in any statute, an institution of which such writers as De Lolme and Blackstone take no notice, began to exist a few years after the Revolution, grew rapidly into importance, became firmly established, and is now almost as essential a part of our polity as the Parliament itself. This institution is the Ministry.

The Ministry is, in fact, a committee of leading members of the two Houses. It is nominated by the Crown: but it consists exclusively of statesmen whose opinions on the pressing questions of the time agree, in the main, with the opinions of the majority of the House of Commons. Among the members of this committee are distributed the great departments of the administration. Each Minister conducts the ordinary business of his own office without reference to his colleagues. But the most important business of every office, and especially such business as is likely to be the subject of discussion in Parliament, is brought under the consideration of the whole Ministry. In Parliament the Ministers are bound to act as one man on all questions relating to the executive government. If one of them dissents from the rest on a question too important to admit of compromise, it is his duty to retire. While the Ministers retain the confidence of the parliamentary majority, that majority supports them against opposition, and rejects every motion which reflects on them or is likely to embarrass them. If they forfeit that confidence, if the parliamentary majority is dissatisfied with the way in which patronage is distributed, with the way in which the prerogative of mercy is used, with the conduct of foreign affairs, with the conduct of a war, the remedy is simple. It is not necessary that the Commons should take on themselves the business of administration, that they should request the Crown to make this man a bishop and that man a judge, to pardon one criminal and to execute another, to negotiate a treaty on a particular basis or to send an expedition to a particular place. They have merely to declare that they have ceased to trust the Ministry, and to ask for a Ministry which they can trust.

It is by means of Ministries thus constituted, and thus changed, that the English government has long been conducted in general conformity with the deliberate sense of the House of Commons, and yet has been wonderfully free from the vices which are characteristic of governments administered by large, tumultuous and divided assemblies. A few distinguished persons, agreeing in their general opinions, are the confidential advisers at once of the Sovereign and of the Estates of the Realm. In the closet they speak with the authority of men who stand high in the estimation of the representatives of the people. In Parliament they speak with the authority of men versed in great affairs and acquainted with all the secrets of the State. Thus the Cabinet has something of the popular character of a representative body; and the representative body has something of the gravity of a cabinet.

Sometimes the state of parties is such that no set of men who can be brought together possesses the full confidence and steady support of a majority of the House of Commons. When this is the case, there must be a weak Ministry; and there will probably be a rapid succession of weak Ministries. At such times the House of Commons never fails to get into a state which no person friendly to representative government can contemplate without uneasiness, into a state which may enable us to form some faint notion of the state of that House during the earlier years of the reign of William. The notion is indeed but faint; for the weakest Ministry has great power as a regulator of parliamentary proceedings; and in the earlier years of the reign of William there was no Ministry at all.

No writer has yet attempted to trace the progress of this institution, an institution indispensable to the harmonious working of our other institutions. The first Ministry was the work, partly of mere chance, and partly of wisdom, not however of that highest wisdom which is conversant with great principles of political philosophy, but of that lower wisdom which meets daily exigencies by daily expedients. Neither William nor the most enlightened of his advisers fully understood the nature and importance of that noiseless revolution,—for it was no less,—which began about the close of 1693, and was completed about the close of 1696. But every body could perceive that, at the close of 1693, the chief offices in the government were distributed not unequally between the two great parties, that the men who held those offices were perpetually caballing against each other, haranguing against each other, moving votes of censure on each other, exhibiting articles of impeachment against each other, and that the temper of the House of Commons was wild, ungovernable and uncertain. Every body could perceive that at the close of 1696, all the principal servants of the Crown were Whigs, closely bound together by public and private ties, and prompt to defend one another against every attack, and that the majority of the House of Commons was arrayed in good order under those leaders, and had learned to move, like one man, at the word of command. The history of the period of transition and of the steps by which the change was effected is in a high degree curious and interesting.

The statesman who had the chief share in forming the first English Ministry had once been but too well known, but had long hidden himself from the public gaze, and had but recently emerged from the obscurity in which it had been expected that he would pass the remains of an ignominious and disastrous life. During that period of general terror and confusion which followed the flight of James, Sunderland had disappeared. It was high time: for of all the agents of the fallen government he was, with the single exception of Jeffreys, the most odious to the nation. Few knew that Sunderland's voice had in secret been given against the spoliation of Magdalene College and the prosecution of the Bishops: but all knew that he had signed numerous instruments dispensing with statutes, that he had sate in the High Commission, that he had turned or pretended to turn Papist, that he had, a few days after his apostasy, appeared in Westminster Hall as a witness against the oppressed fathers of the Church. He had indeed atoned for many crimes by one crime baser than all the rest. As soon as he had reason to believe that the day of deliverance and retribution was at hand, he had, by a most dexterous and seasonable treason, earned his pardon. During the three months which preceded the arrival of the Dutch armament in Torbay, he had rendered to the cause of liberty and of the Protestant religion services of which it is difficult to overrate either the wickedness or the utility. To him chiefly it was owing that, at the most critical moment in our history, a French army was not menacing the Batavian frontier and a French fleet hovering about the English coast. William could not, without staining his own honour, refuse to protect one whom he had not scrupled to employ. Yet it was no easy task even for William to save that guilty head from the first outbreak of public fury. For even those extreme politicians of both sides who agreed in nothing else agreed in calling for vengeance on the renegade. The Whigs hated him as the vilest of the slaves by whom the late government had been served, and the Jacobites as the vilest of the traitors by whom it had been overthrown. Had he remained in England, he would probably have died by the hand of the executioner, if indeed the executioner had not been anticipated by the populace. But in Holland a political refugee, favoured by the Stadtholder, might hope to live unmolested. To Holland Sunderland fled, disguised, it is said, as a woman ; and his wife accompanied him. At Rotterdam, a town devoted to the House of Orange, he thought himself secure. But the magistrates were not in all the secrets of the Prince, and were assured by some busy Englishmen that His Highness would be delighted to hear of the arrest of the Popish dog, the Judas, whose appearance on Tower Hill was impatiently expected by all London. Sunderland was thrown into prison, and remained there till an order for his release arrived from Whitehall. He then proceeded to Amsterdam, and there changed his religion again. His second apostasy edified his wife as much as his first apostasy had edified his master. The Countess wrote to assure her pious friends in England that her poor dear lord's heart had at last been really touched by divine grace, and that, in spite of all her afflictions, she was comforted by seeing him so true a convert. We may, however, without any violation of Christian charity, suspect that he was still the same false, callous, Sunderland who, a few months before, had made Bonrepaux shudder by denying the existence of a God, and had, at the same time, won the heart of James by pretending to believe in transubstantiation. In a short time the banished man put forth an apology for his conduct. This apology, when examined, will be found to amount merely to a confession that he had committed one series of crimes in order to gain James's favour, and another series in order to avoid being involved in James's ruin. The writer concluded by announcing his intention to pass all the rest of his life in penitence and prayer. He soon retired from Amsterdam to Utrecht, and at Utrecht made himself conspicuous by his regular and devout attendance on the ministrations of Huguenot preachers. If his letters and those of his wife were to be trusted, he had done for ever with ambition. He longed indeed to be permitted to return from exile, not that he might again enjoy and dispense the favours of the Crown, not that his antechambers might again be filled by the daily swarm of suitors, but that he might see again the turf, the trees and the family pictures of his country seat. His only wish was to be suffered to end his troubled life at Althorpe ; and he would be content to forfeit his head if ever he went beyond the palings of his park.*

While the House of Commons, which had been elected during the vacancy of the throne, was busily engaged in the work of proscription, he could not venture to show himself in England. But when that assembly had ceased to exist, he thought himself safe. He returned a few days after the Act of Grace had been laid on the table of the Lords. From the benefit of that Act he was by name excluded: but he well knew that he had now nothing to fear. He went privately to Kensington, was admitted into the closet, had an audience which lasted two hours, and then retired to his country house.†

During many months he led a secluded life, and had no residence in London. Once in the spring of 1691, to the great astonishment of the public, he showed his face in the circle at Court, and was graciously received.‡ He seems to have been afraid that he might, on his reappearance in Parliament, receive some marked affront. He therefore, very prudently, stole down to Westminster, in the dead time of the year, on a day to which the Houses stood adjourned by the royal command, and on which they met merely for the purpose of adjourning again. Sunderland had just time to present himself, to take the oaths, to sign the declaration against transubstantiation, and to resume his seat. None of the few peers who were present had an opportunity of making any remark.§ It was not till the year 1692 that he began to attend regularly. He was silent: but silent he had always been in large assemblies, even when he was at the zenith of power. His talents were not those of a public speaker. The art in which he surpassed all men was the art of whispering. His tact, his quick eye for the foibles of individuals, his caressing manners, his power of insinuation, and, above all, his apparent frankness, made him irresistible in private conversation. By means of these qualities he had governed James, and now aspired to govern William.

To govern William, indeed, was not easy. But Sunderland succeeded in obtaining such a measure of favour and influence

* See Sunderland's celebrated Narrative which has often been printed, and his wife's letters, which are among the Sidney papers, published by the late Serjeant Blencowe.

† Van Citters, May $\frac{8}{18}$. 1690.                              ‡ Evelyn, April 24. 1691.
§ Lords' Journals, April 28. 1693.

as excited much surprise and some indignation. In truth, scarcely any mind was strong enough to resist the witchery of his talk and of his manners. Every man is prone to believe in the gratitude and attachment even of the most worthless persons on whom he has conferred great benefits. It can therefore hardly be thought strange that the most skilful of all flatterers should have been heard with favour, when he, with every outward sign of strong emotion, implored permission to dedicate all his faculties to the service of the generous protector to whom he owed property, liberty, life. It is not necessary, however, to suppose that the King was deceived. He may have thought, with good reason, that, though little confidence could be placed in Sunderland's professions, much confidence might be placed in Sunderland's situation ; and the truth is that Sunderland proved, on the whole, a more faithful servant than a much less depraved man might have been. He did indeed make, in profound secresy, some timid overtures towards a reconciliation with James. But it may be confidently affirmed that, even had those overtures been graciously received,—and they appear to have been received very ungraciously,—the twice turned renegade would never have rendered any real service to the Jacobite cause. He well knew that he had done that which at Saint Germains must be regarded as inexpiable. It was not merely that he had been treacherous and ungrateful. Marlborough had been as treacherous and ungrateful; and Marlborough had been pardoned. But Marlborough had not been guilty of the impious hypocrisy of counterfeiting the signs of conversion. Marlborough had not pretended to be convinced by the arguments of the Jesuits, to be touched by divine grace, to pine for union with the only true Church. Marlborough had not, when Popery was in the ascendant, crossed himself, shrived himself, done penance, taken the communion in one kind, and, as soon as a turn of fortune came, apostatized back again, and proclaimed to all the world that, when he knelt at the confessional and received the host, he was merely laughing at the King and the priests. The crime of Sunderland was one which could never be forgiven by James ; and a crime which could never be forgiven by James was, in some sense, a recommendation to William. The Court, nay, the Council, was full of men who might hope to prosper if the banished King were restored. But Sunderland had left himself no retreat. He had broken down all the bridges behind him. He had been so false to one side that he must of necessity be true to the other. That he was in the main true to the government which now protected him there is no reason to doubt ; and, being true, he could not but be useful. He was, in some respects, eminently qualified to be at that time an adviser of the Crown. He had exactly the talents and the knowledge which William wanted. The two together would have made up a consummate statesman. The master was capable of forming and executing large designs, but was negligent of those small arts in which the servant excelled. The master saw farther off than other men ; but what was near no man saw so clearly as the servant. The master, though profoundly versed in the politics of the great community of nations, never thoroughly understood the politics of his own kingdom. The servant was perfectly well informed as to the temper and the organization of the English factions, and as to the strong and weak parts of the character of every Englishman of note.

Early in 1693, it was rumoured that Sunderland was consulted on all important questions relating to the internal administration of the realm : and the rumour became stronger when it was known that he had come up to London in the autumn before the meeting of Parliament and that he had taken a large mansion near Whitehall. The coffeehouse politicians were confident that he was about to hold some high office. As yet, however, he had the wisdom to be content with the reality of power, and to leave the show to others.*

His opinion was that, as long as the King tried to balance the two great parties against each other, and to divide his favour equally between them, both would think themselves ill used, and neither would lend to the government that hearty and steady support which was now greatly needed. His Majesty must make up his mind to give a marked preference to one or the other ; and there were three weighty reasons for giving the preference to the Whigs.

In the first place, the Whigs were on principle attached to the reigning dynasty. In their view the Revolution had been, not merely necessary, not merely justifiable, but happy and glorious. It had been the triumph of their political theory. When they swore allegiance to William, they swore without scruple or reservation ; and they were so far from having any doubt about his title that they thought it the best of all titles. The Tories, on the other hand, very generally disapproved of that vote of the Convention which had placed him on the

* L'Hermitage, Sept. $\frac{1}{2}\frac{3}{3}$., Oct. $\frac{2}{1}\frac{}{3}$. 1693.

throne. Some of them were at heart Jacobites, and had taken the oath of allegiance to him only that they might be able to injure him. Others, though they thought it their duty to obey him as King in fact, denied that he was King by right, and, if they were loyal to him, were loyal without enthusiasm. There could, therefore, be little doubt on which of the two parties it would be safer for him to rely.

In the second place, as to the particular matter on which his heart was at present set, the Whigs were, as a body, prepared to support him strenuously, and the Tories were, as a body, inclined to thwart him. The minds of men were at this time much occupied by the question, in what way the war ought to be carried on. To that question the two parties returned very different answers. An opinion had during many months been growing among the Tories that the policy of England ought to be strictly insular; that she ought to leave the defence of Flanders and the Rhine to the States General, the House of Austria and the Princes of the Empire; that she ought to carry on hostilities with vigour by sea, but to keep up only such an army as might, with the help of the militia, be sufficient to repel an invasion. It was plain that, if this system were adopted, there might be an immediate reduction of the taxes which pressed most heavily on the nation. But the Whigs maintained that this relief would be dearly purchased. Many thousands of brave English soldiers were now in Flanders. Yet the allies had not been able to prevent the French from taking Mons in 1691, Namur in 1692, Charleroy in 1693. If the English troops were withdrawn, it was certain that Ostend, Ghent, Liege, Brussels would fall. The German Princes would hasten to make peace, each for himself. The Spanish Netherlands would probably be annexed to the French monarchy. The United Provinces would be again in as great peril as in 1672, and would accept whatever terms Lewis might be pleased to dictate. In a few months, he would be at liberty to put forth his whole strength against our island. Then would come a struggle for life and death. It might well be hoped that we should be able to defend our soil even against such a general and such an army as had won the battle of Landen. But the fight must be long and hard. How many fertile counties would be turned into deserts, how many flourishing towns would be laid in ashes, before the invaders were destroyed or driven out! One triumphant campaign in Kent and Middlesex would do more to impoverish the nation than ten disastrous campaigns in Brabant. It is remarkable that this dispute between the two great factions was, during seventy years, regularly revived as often as our country was at war with France. That England ought never to attempt great military operations on the Continent continued to be a fundamental article of the creed of the Tories till the French Revolution produced a complete change in their feelings.* As the chief object of William was to open the campaign of 1694 in Flanders with an immense display of force, it was sufficiently clear to whom he must look for assistance.

In the third place, the Whigs were the stronger party in Parliament. The general election of 1690, indeed, had not been favourable to them. They had been, for a time, a minority: but they had ever since been constantly gaining ground: they were now in number a full half of the Lower House; and their effective strength was more than proportioned to their number: for in energy, alertness and discipline, they were decidedly superior to their opponents. Their organization was not indeed so perfect as it afterwards became: but they had already begun to look for guidance to a small knot of distinguished men, which was long afterwards widely known by the name of the Junto. There is, perhaps, no parallel in history, ancient or modern, to the authority exercised by this council, during twenty troubled years, over the Whig body. The men who acquired that authority in the days of William and Mary continued to possess it, without interruption, in office and out of office, till George the First was on the throne.

One of these men was Russell. Of his shameful dealings with the Court of Saint Germains we possess proofs which leave no room for doubt. But no such proofs were laid before the world till he had been many years dead. If rumours of his guilt got abroad, they were vague and improbable: they rested on no evidence: they could be traced to no trustworthy author; and they might well be regarded by his contemporaries as Jacobite calumnies. What was quite certain was that he sprang from an illustrious house, which had done and suffered great things for liberty and for the

* It is amusing to see how Johnson's Toryism breaks out where we should hardly expect to find it. Hastings says, in the Third Part of Henry the Sixth,

> " Let us be back'd with God and with the seas
> Which He hath given for fence impregnable,
> And with their helps alone defend ourselves."

"This," says Johnson in a note, " has been the advice of every man who, in any age, understood and favoured the interest of England."

Protestant religion, that he had signed the invitation of the thirtieth of June, that he had landed with the Deliverer at Torbay, that he had in Parliament, on all occasions, spoken and voted as a zealous Whig, that he had won a great victory, that he had saved his country from an invasion, and that, since he had left the Admiralty, every thing had gone wrong. We cannot therefore wonder that his influence over his party should have been considerable.

But the greatest man among the members of the Junto, and, in some respects, the greatest man of that age, was the Lord Keeper Somers. He was equally eminent as a jurist and as a politician, as an orator and as a writer. His speeches have perished : but his State papers remain, and are models of terse, luminous, and dignified eloquence. He had left a great reputation in the House of Commons, where he had, during four years, been always heard with delight ; and the Whig members still looked up to him as their leader, and still held their meetings under his roof. In the great place to which he had recently been promoted, he had so borne himself that, after a very few months, even faction and envy had ceased to murmur at his elevation. In truth, he united all the qualities of a great judge, an intellect comprehensive, quick and acute, diligence, integrity, patience, suavity. In council, the calm wisdom which he possessed in a measure rarely found among men of parts so quick and of opinions so decided as his, acquired for him the authority of an oracle. The superiority of his powers appeared not less clearly in private circles. The charm of his conversation was heightened by the frankness with which he poured out his thoughts.* His good temper and his good breeding never failed. His gesture, his look, his

---

* Swift, in his Inquiry into the Behaviour of the Queen's last Ministry, mentions Somers as a person of great abilities, who used to talk in so frank a manner that he seemed to discover the bottom of his heart. In the Memoirs relating to the Change in the Queen's Ministry, Swift says that Somers had one and only one unconversable fault, formality. It is not very easy to understand how the same man can be the most unreserved of companions, and yet err on the side of formality. Yet there may be truth in both the descriptions. It is well known that Swift loved to take rude liberties with men of high rank, and fancied that, by doing so, he asserted his own independence. He has been justly blamed for this fault by his two illustrious biographers, both of them men of spirit at least as independent as his, Samuel Johnson and Walter Scott. I suspect that he showed a disposition to behave with offensive familiarity to Somers, and that Somers, not choosing to submit to impertinence, and not wishing to be forced to resent it, resorted, in selfdefence, to a ceremonious politeness which he never would have practised towards Locke or Addison.

tones were expressive of benevolence. His humanity was the more remarkable, because he had received from nature a body such as is generally found united with a peevish and irritable mind. His life was one long malady : his nerves were weak : his complexion was livid : his face was prematurely wrinkled. Yet his enemies could not pretend that he had ever once, during a long and troubled public life, been goaded, even by sudden provocation, into vehemence inconsistent with the mild dignity of his character. All that was left to them was to assert that his disposition was very far from being so gentle as the world believed, that he was really prone to the angry passions, and that sometimes, while his voice was soft, and his words kind and courteous, his delicate frame was almost convulsed by suppressed emotion. It will perhaps be thought that this reproach is the highest of all eulogies.

The most accomplished men of those times have told us that there was scarcely any subject on which Somers was not competent to instruct and to delight. He had never travelled ; and, in that age, an Englishman who had not travelled was generally thought incompetent to give an opinion on works of art. But connoisseurs familiar with the masterpieces of the Vatican and of the Florentine gallery allowed that the taste of Somers in painting and sculpture was exquisite. Philology was one of his favourite pursuits. He had traversed the whole vast range of polite literature, ancient and modern. He was at once a munificent and severely judicious patron of genius and learning. Locke owed opulence to Somers. By Somers Addison was drawn forth from a cell in a college. In distant countries the name of Somers was mentioned with respect and gratitude by great scholars and poets who had never seen his face. He was the benefactor of Leclerc. He was the friend of Filicaja. Neither political nor religious differences prevented him from extending his powerful protection to merit. Hickes, the fiercest and most intolerant of all the nonjurors, obtained, by the influence of Somers, permission to study Teutonic antiquities in freedom and safety. Vertue, a strict Roman Catholic, was raised by the discriminating and liberal patronage of Somers from poverty and obscurity to the first rank among the engravers of the age.

The generosity with which Somers treated his opponents was the more honourable to him because he was no waverer in politics. From the beginning to the end of his public life he was a steady Whig. His voice was indeed always raised, when his party was dominant in the State, against violent and vindictive counsels; but he never forsook his friends, even when their perverse neglect of his advice had brought them to the verge of ruin.

His powers of mind and his acquirements were not denied, even by his detractors. The most acrimonious Tories were forced to admit, with an ungracious snarl, which increased the value of their praise, that he had all the intellectual qualities of a great man, and that in him alone, among his contemporaries, brilliant eloquence and wit were to be found associated with the quiet and steady prudence which ensures success in life. It is a remarkable fact, that, in the foulest of all the many libels that were published against him, he was slandered under the name of Cicero. As his abilities could not be questioned, he was charged with irreligion and immorality. That he was heterodox all the country vicars and foxhunting squires firmly believed: but as to the nature and extent of his heterodoxy there were many different opinions. He seems to have been a Low Churchman of the school of Tillotson, whom he always loved and honoured; and he was, like Tillotson, called by bigots a Presbyterian, an Arian, a Socinian, a Deist, and an Atheist.

The private life of this great statesman and magistrate was malignantly scrutinised; and tales were told about his libertinism which went on growing till they became too absurd for the credulity even of party spirit. At last, long after he had been condemned to flannel and chicken broth, a wretched courtesan, who had probably never seen him except in the stage box at the theatre, when she was following her vocation below in a mask, published a lampoon in which she described him as the master of a harem more costly than the Great Turk's. There is, however, reason to believe that there was a small nucleus of truth round which this great mass of fiction gathered, and that the wisdom and selfcommand which Somers never wanted in the senate, on the judgment seat, at the council board, or in the society of wits, scholars and philosophers, were not always proof against female attractions.*

* The eulogies on Somers and the invectives against him are innumerable. Perhaps the best way to come to a just judgment would be to collect all that has been said about him by Swift and by Addison. They were the two keenest observers of their time; and they both knew him well. But it ought to be remarked that, till Swift turned Tory, he always extolled Somers, not only as the most accomplished, but as the most virtuous of men. In the dedication of the Tale of a Tub are these words, "There is no virtue, either of a public or private life, which some circumstances of your own have not often produced upon the stage of the world;" and

Another director of the Whig party was Charles Montague. He was often, when he had risen to power, honours and riches, called an upstart by those who envied his success. That they should have called him so may seem strange; for few of the statesmen of his time could show such a pedigree as his. He sprang from a family as old as the Conquest: he was in the succession to an earldom, and was, by the paternal side, cousin of three earls. But he was the younger son of a younger brother; and that phrase had, ever since the time of Shakspeare and Raleigh, and perhaps before their time, been proverbially used to designate a person so poor as to be broken to the most abject servitude or ready for the most desperate adventure.

Charles Montague was early destined for the Church, was entered on the foundation of Westminster, and, after distinguishing himself there by skill in Latin versification, was sent up to Trinity College, Cambridge. At Cambridge the philosophy of Des Cartes was still dominant in the schools. But a few select spirits had separated from the crowd, and formed a fit audience round a far greater teacher.* Conspicuous among the youths of high promise who were proud to sit at the feet of Newton was the quick and versatile Montague. Under such guidance the young student made considerable proficiency in the severe sciences: but poetry was his favourite pursuit; and when the University invited her sons to celebrate royal marriages and funerals, he was generally allowed to have surpassed his competitors. His fame travelled to London: he was thought a clever lad by the wits who met at Will's, and the lively parody which he wrote, in concert with his friend and fellow student Prior, on Dryden's Hind and Panther, was received with great applause.

At this time all Montague's wishes pointed towards the Church. At a later period, when he was a peer with twelve thousand a year, when his villa on the Thames was regarded as the most delightful of all suburban retreats, when he was said to revel in Tokay from the Imperial cellar, and in soups made out of birds' nests brought from the Indian Ocean, and costing three guineas a piece, his enemies were fond of

---

again, "I should be very loth the bright example of your Lordship's virtues should be lost to other eyes, both for their sake and your own." In the Discourse of the Contests and Dissensions at Athens and Rome, Somers is the just Aristides. After Swift had ratted he described Somers as a man who "possessed all excellent qualifications except virtue."
* See Whiston's Autobiography.

reminding him that there had been a time when he had eked out by his wits an income of barely fifty pounds, when he had been happy with a trencher of mutton chops and a flagon of ale from the College buttery, and when a tithe pig was the rarest luxury for which he had dared to hope. The Revolution came, and changed his whole scheme of life. He obtained, by the influence of Dorset, who took a peculiar pleasure in befriending young men of promise, a seat in the House of Commons. Still, during a few months, the needy scholar hesitated between politics and divinity. But it soon became clear that, in the new order of things, parliamentary ability must fetch a higher price than any other kind of ability; and he felt that in parliamentary ability he had no superior. He was in the very situation for which he was peculiarly fitted by nature; and during some years his life was a series of triumphs.

Of him, as of several of his contemporaries, especially of Mulgrave and of Sprat, it may be said that his fame has suffered from the folly of those editors who, down to our own time, have persisted in reprinting his rhymes among the works of the British poets. There is not a year in which hundreds of verses as good as any that he ever wrote are not sent in for the Newdigate prize at Oxford and for the Chancellor's medal at Cambridge. His mind had indeed great quickness and vigour, but not that kind of quickness and vigour which produces great dramas or odes: and it is most unjust to him that his Man of Honour and his Epistle on the Battle of the Boyne should be placed side by side with Comus and Alexander's Feast. Other eminent statesmen and orators, Walpole, Pulteney, Chatham, Fox, wrote poetry not better than his. But fortunately for them, their metrical compositions were never thought worthy to be admitted into any collection of our national classics.

It has long been usual to represent the imagination under the figure of a wing, and to call the successful exertions of the imagination flights. One poet is the eagle: another is the swan: a third modestly compares himself to the bee. But none of these types would have suited Montague. His genius may be compared to that pinion which, though it is too weak to lift the ostrich into the air, enables her, while she remains on the earth, to outrun hound, horse and dromedary. If the man who possesses this kind of genius attempts to ascend the heaven of invention, his awkward and unsuccessful efforts expose him to derision. But if he will be content to stay in the terrestrial region of business, he will find that the faculties which would not enable him to soar into a higher sphere will enable him to distance all his competitors in the lower. As a poet Montague could never have risen above the crowd. But in the House of Commons, now fast becoming supreme in the State, and extending its control over one executive department after another, the young adventurer soon obtained a place very different from the place which he occupies among men of letters. At thirty, he would gladly have given all his chances in life for a comfortable vicarage and a chaplain's scarf. At thirty-seven, he was First Lord of the Treasury, Chancellor of the Exchequer and a Regent of the kingdom; and this elevation he owed not at all to favour, but solely to the unquestionable superiority of his talents for administration and debate.

The extraordinary ability with which, at the beginning of the year 1692, he managed the conference on the Bill for regulating Trials in cases of Treason, placed him at once in the first rank of parliamentary orators. On that occasion he was opposed to a crowd of veteran senators renowned for their eloquence, Halifax, Rochester, Nottingham, Mulgrave, and proved himself a match for them all. He was speedily seated at the Board of Treasury; and there the clearheaded and experienced Godolphin soon found that his young colleague was his master. When Somers had quitted the House of Commons, Montague had no rival there. Sir Thomas Littleton, once distinguished as the ablest debater and man of business among the Whig members, was content to serve under his junior. To this day we may discern in many parts of our financial and commercial system the marks of the vigorous intellect and daring spirit of Montague. His bitterest enemies were unable to deny that some of the expedients which he had proposed had proved highly beneficial to the nation. But it was said that these expedients were not devised by himself. He was represented, in a hundred pamphlets, as the daw in borrowed plumes. He had taken, it was affirmed, the hint of every one of his great plans from the writings or the conversation of some ingenious speculator. This reproach was, in truth, no reproach. We can scarcely expect to find in the same human being the talents which are necessary for the making of new discoveries in political science, and the talents which obtain the assent of divided and tumultuous assemblies to great practical reforms. To be at once an Adam Smith and a Pitt is scarcely possible. It is surely praise enough for a busy politician that he knows how to use the theories of others, that he discerns, among the schemes of innumerable projectors, the precise scheme which is wanted and which is practicable, that he shapes it to suit pressing circumstances and popular humours, that he proposes it just when it is most likely to be favourably received, that he triumphantly defends it against all objectors, and that he carries it into execution with prudence and energy; and to this praise no English statesman has a fairer claim than Montague.

It is a remarkable proof of his selfknowledge that, from the moment at which he began to distinguish himself in public life, he ceased to be a versifier. It does not appear that, after he became a Lord of the Treasury, he ever wrote a couplet, with the exception of a few well turned lines inscribed on a set of toasting glasses which were sacred to the most renowned Whig beauties of his time. He wisely determined to derive from the poetry of others a glory which he never would have derived from his own. As a patron of genius and learning he ranks with his two illustrious friends, Dorset and Somers. His munificence fully equalled theirs; and, though he was inferior to them in delicacy of taste, he succeeded in associating his name inseparably with some names which will last as long as our language.

Yet it must be acknowledged that Montague, with admirable parts and with many claims on the gratitude of his country, had great faults, and unhappily faults not of the noblest kind. His head was not strong enough to bear without giddiness the speed of his ascent and the height of his position. He became offensively arrogant and vain. He was too often cold to his old friends, and ostentatious in displaying his new riches. Above all, he was insatiably greedy of praise, and liked it best when it was of the coarsest and rankest quality. But, in 1693, these faults were less offensive than they became a few years later.

With Russell, Somers and Montague, was closely connected, during a quarter of a century a fourth Whig, who in character bore little resemblance to any of them. This was Thomas Wharton, eldest son of Philip Lord Wharton. Thomas Wharton has been repeatedly mentioned in the course of this narrative. But it is now time to describe him more fully. He was in his forty-seventh year, but was still a young man in constitution, in appearance and in manners. Those who hated him most heartily,—and no man was hated more heartily,—admitted that his natural parts were excellent, and that he was equally qualified for debate and for action. The history of his mind deserves notice : for it was the history of many thousands of minds. His rank and abilities made him so conspicuous that in him we are able to trace distinctly the origin and progress of a moral taint which was epidemic among his contemporaries.

He was born in the days of the Covenant, and was the heir of a covenanted house. His father was renowned as a distributor of Calvinistic tracts, and a patron of Calvinistic divines. The boy's first years were past amidst Geneva bands, heads of lank hair, upturned eyes, nasal psalmody, and sermons three hours long. Plays and poems, hunting and dancing, were proscribed by the austere discipline of his saintly family. The fruits of this education became visible, when, from the sullen mansion of Puritan parents, the hotblooded, quickwitted young patrician emerged into the gay and voluptuous London of the Restoration. The most dissolute cavaliers stood aghast at the dissoluteness of the emancipated precisian. He early acquired and retained to the last the reputation of being the greatest rake in England. Of wine indeed he never became the slave ; and he used it chiefly for the purpose of making himself the master of his associates. But to the end of his long life the wives and daughters of his nearest friends were not safe from his licentious plots. The ribaldry of his conversation moved astonishment even in that age. To the religion of his country he offered, in the mere wantonness of impiety, insults too foul to be described. His mendacity and his effrontery passed into proverbs. Of all the liars of his time he was the most deliberate, the most inventive and the most circumstantial. What shame meant he did not seem to understand. No reproaches, even when pointed and barbed with the sharpest wit, appeared to give him pain. Great satirists, animated by a deadly personal aversion, exhausted all their strength in attacks upon him. They assailed him with keen invective : they assailed him with still keener irony ; but they found that neither invective nor irony could move him to any thing but an unforced smile and a goodhumoured curse ; and they at length threw down the lash, acknowledging that it was impossible to make him feel. That, with such vices, he should have played a great part in life, should have carried numerous elections against the most formidable opposition by his personal popularity, should have had a large following in Parliament, should have risen to the highest offices of the State, seems extraordinary. But he lived in times when faction was almost a madness ; and he possessed in an eminent degree the qualities of the leader of a faction. There was a single tie which he respected. The falsest of mankind in all relations but one, he was the truest of Whigs. The religious tenets of his family he had early renounced with contempt: but to the politics of his family he stedfastly adhered through all the temptations and dangers of half a century. In small things and in great his devotion to his party constantly appeared. He had the finest stud in England; and his delight was to win plates from Tories. Sometimes when, in a distant county, it was fully expected that the horse of a High Church squire would be first on the course, down came, on the very eve of the race, Wharton's Careless, who had ceased to run at Newmarket merely for want of competitors, or Wharton's Gelding, for whom Lewis the Fourteenth had in vain offered a thousand pistoles. A man whose mere sport was of this description was not likely to be easily beaten in any serious contest. Such a master of the whole art of electioneering England had never seen. Buckinghamshire was his own especial province; and there he ruled without a rival. But he extended his care over the Whig interest in Yorkshire, Cumberland, Westmoreland, Wiltshire. Sometimes twenty, sometimes thirty, members of Parliament were named by him. As a canvasser he was irresistible. He never forgot a face that he had once seen. Nay, in the towns in which he wished to establish an interest, he remembered, not only the voters, but their families. His opponents were confounded by the strength of his memory and the affability of his deportment, and owned that it was impossible to contend against a great man who called the shoemaker by his Christian name, who was sure that the butcher's daughter must be growing a fine girl, and who was anxious to know whether the blacksmith's youngest boy was breeched. By such arts as these he made himself so popular that his journeys to the Buckinghamshire Quarter Sessions resembled royal progresses. The bells of every parish through which he passed were rung, and flowers were strewed along the road. It was commonly believed that, in the course of his life, he expended on his parliamentary interest not less than eighty thousand pounds, a sum which, when compared with the value of estates, must be considered as equivalent to more than three hundred thousand pounds in our time.

But the chief service which Wharton rendered to the Whig party was that of bringing in recruits from the young aristocracy. He was quite as dexterous a canvasser among the embroidered coats at the Saint James's Coffeehouse as among the leathern aprons at Wycombe and Aylesbury. He had his eye on every boy of quality who came of age ; and it was not easy for such a boy to resist the arts of a noble, eloquent and wealthy flatterer, who united juvenile vivacity to profound art and long experience of the gay world. It mattered not what the novice preferred, gallantry or field sports, the dicebox or the bottle. Wharton soon found out the master passion, offered sympathy, advice and assistance, and, while seeming to be only the minister of his disciple's pleasures, made sure of his disciple's vote.

The party to whose interests Wharton, with such spirit and constancy, devoted his time, his fortune, his talents, his very vices, judged him, as was natural, far too leniently. He was widely known by the very undeserved appellation of Honest Tom. Some pious men, Burnet, for example, and Addison, averted their eyes from the scandal which he gave, and spoke of him, not indeed with esteem, yet with goodwill. A most ingenious and accomplished Whig, the third Earl of Shaftesbury, author of the Characteristics, described Wharton as the most mysterious of human beings, as a strange compound of best and worst, of private depravity and public virtue, and owned himself unable to understand how a man utterly without principle in every thing but politics should in politics be as true as steel. But that which, in the judgment of one faction, more than half redeemed all Wharton's faults, seemed to the other faction to aggravate them all. The opinion which the Tories entertained of him is expressed in a single line written after his death by the ablest man of that party ; " He was the most universal villain that ever I knew." * Wharton's political adversaries thirsted for his blood, and repeatedly tried to shed it. Had he not been a man of imperturbable temper, dauntless courage and consummate skill in fence, his life would have been a short one. But neither anger nor danger ever deprived him of his presence of mind : he was an incomparable swordsman ; and he had a peculiar way of disarming opponents which moved the envy of all the duellists of his time. His friends said that he had never given a challenge, that he had never refused one, that he had never taken a life, and yet that he had never fought without having his antagonist's life at his mercy.†

* Swift's note on Mackay's Character of Wharton.
† This account of Montague and Wharton I have collected from innumerable sources. I ought, however, to mention particularly the very curious Life of Wharton published immediately after his death.

The four men who have been described resembled each other so little that it may be thought strange that they should ever have been able to act in concert. They did, however, act in the closest concert during many years. They more than once rose and more than once fell together. But their union lasted till it was dissolved by death. Little as some of them may have deserved esteem, none of them can be accused of having been false to his brethren of the Junto.

While the great body of the Whigs was, under these able chiefs, arraying itself in order resembling that of a regular army, the Tories were in a state of an ill drilled and ill officered militia. They were numerous; and they were zealous: but they can hardly be said to have had, at this time, any chief in the House of Commons. The name of Seymour had once been great among them, and had not quite lost its influence. But, since he had been at the Board of Treasury, he had disgusted them by vehemently defending all that he had himself, when out of place, vehemently attacked. They had once looked up to the Speaker, Trevor: but his greediness, impudence and venality were now so notorious that all respectable gentlemen, of all shades of opinion, were ashamed to see him in the chair. Of the old Tory members Sir Christopher Musgrave alone had much weight. Indeed the real leaders of the party were two or three men bred in principles diametrically opposed to Toryism, men who had carried Whiggism to the verge of republicanism, and who had been considered not merely as Low Churchmen, but as more than half Presbyterians. Of these men the most eminent were two great Herefordshire squires, Robert Harley and Paul Foley.

The space which Robert Harley fills in the history of three reigns, his elevation, his fall, the influence which, at a great crisis, he exercised on the politics of all Europe, the close intimacy in which he lived with some of the greatest wits and poets of his time, and the frequent recurrence of his name in the works of Swift, Pope, Arbuthnot, and Prior, must always make him an object of interest. Yet the man himself was of all men the least interesting. There is indeed a whimsical contrast between the very ordinary qualities of his mind and the very extraordinary vicissitudes of his fortune.

He was the heir of a Puritan family. His father, Sir Edward Harley, had been conspicuous among the patriots of the Long Parliament, had commanded a regiment under Essex, had, after the Restoration, been an active opponent of the Court, had supported the Exclusion Bill, had harboured dissenting preachers, had frequented meetinghouses, and had made himself so obnoxious to the ruling powers that, at the time of the Western Insurrection, he had been placed under arrest, and his house had been searched for arms. When the Dutch army was marching from Torbay towards London, he and his eldest son Robert declared for the Prince of Orange and a free Parliament, raised a large body of horse, took possession of Worcester, and evinced their zeal against Popery by publicly breaking to pieces, in the High Street of that city, a piece of sculpture which to rigid precisians seemed idolatrous. Soon after the Convention became a Parliament, Robert Harley was sent up to Westminster as member for a Cornish borough. His conduct was such as might have been expected from his birth and education. He was a Whig, and indeed an intolerant and vindictive Whig. Nothing would satisfy him but a general proscription of the Tories. His name appears in the list of those members who voted for the Sacheverell clause ; and, at the general election which took place in the spring of 1690, the party which he had persecuted made great exertions to keep him out of the House of Commons. A cry was raised that the Harleys were mortal enemies of the Church ; and this cry produced so much effect that it was with difficulty that any of them could obtain a seat. Such was the commencement of the public life of a man whose name, a quarter of a century later, was inseparably coupled with the High Church in the acclamations of Jacobite mobs.*

Soon, however, it began to be observed that in every division Harley was in the company of those gentlemen who held his political opinions in abhorrence : nor was this strange : for he affected the character of a Whig of the old pattern ; and before the Revolution it had always been supposed that a Whig was a person who watched with jealousy every exertion of the prerogative, who was slow to loose the strings of the public purse, and who was extreme to mark the faults of the ministers of the Crown. Such a Whig Harley still professed to be. He did not admit that the recent change of dynasty had made any change in the duties of a representative of the people. The new government ought to be observed as suspiciously, checked as severely, and supplied as sparingly as the old one. Acting on these principles he necessarily found himself acting with men whose principles were diametrically opposed to his. He

* Much of my information about the Harleys I have derived from unpublished memoirs written by Edward Harley, younger brother of Robert. A copy of these memoirs is among the Mackintosh MSS.

liked to thwart the King : they liked to thwart the usurper : the consequence was that, whenever there was an opportunity of thwarting William, the Roundhead stayed in the House or went into the lobby in company with the whole crowd of Cavaliers.

Soon Harley acquired the authority of a leader among those with whom, notwithstanding wide differences of opinion, he ordinarily voted. His influence in Parliament was indeed altogether out of proportion to his abilities. His intellect was both small and slow. He was unable to take a large view of any subject. He never acquired the art of expressing himself in public with fluency and perspicuity. To the end of his life he remained a tedious, hesitating and confused speaker.* He had none of the external graces of an orator. His countenance was heavy; his figure mean and somewhat deformed, and his gestures uncouth. Yet he was heard with respect. For, such as his mind was, it had been assiduously cultivated. His youth had been studious ; and to the last he continued to love books and the society of men of genius and learning. Indeed he aspired to the character of a wit and a poet, and occasionally employed hours which should have been very differently spent in composing verses more execrable than the bellman's.† His time however was not always so absurdly wasted. He had that sort of industry and that sort of exactness which would have made him a respectable antiquary or King at Arms. His taste led him to plod among old records ; and in that age it was only by plodding among old records that any man could obtain an accurate and extensive knowledge of the law of Parliament. Having few rivals in this laborious and unattractive pursuit, he soon began to be regarded as an oracle

* The only writer who has praised Harley's oratory, as far as I remember, is Mackay, who calls him eloquent. Swift scribbled in the margin, " A great lie." And certainly Swift was inclined to do more than justice to Harley. "That lord," said Pope, "talked of business in so confused a manner that you did not know what he was about ; and every thing he went to tell you was in the epic way ; for he always began in the middle."— Spence's Anecdotes.

† "He used," said Pope, "to send trifling verses from Court to the Scriblerus Club almost every day, and would come and talk idly with them almost every night even when his all was at stake." Some specimens of Harley's poetry are in print. The best, I think, is a stanza which he made on his own fall in 1714 ; and bad is the best.

> " To serve with love,
> And shed your blood,
> Approved is above ;
> But here below
> The examples show
> 'Tis fatal to be good."

on questions of form and privilege. His moral character added not a little to his influence. He had indeed great vices; but they were not of a scandalous kind. He was not to be corrupted by money. His private life was regular. No illicit amour was imputed to him even by satirists. Gambling he held in aversion; and it was said that he never passed White's, then the favourite haunt of noble sharpers and dupes, without an exclamation of anger. His practice of flustering himself daily with claret was hardly considered as a fault by his contemporaries. His knowledge, his gravity and his independent position gained for him the ear of the House; and even his bad speaking was, in some sense, an advantage to him. For people are very loth to admit that the same man can unite very different kinds of excellence. It is soothing to envy to believe that what is splendid cannot be solid, that what is clear cannot be profound. Very slowly was the public brought to acknowledge that Mansfield was a great jurist, and that Burke was a great master of political science. Montague was a brilliant rhetorician, and, therefore, though he had ten times Harley's capacity for the driest parts of business, was represented by detractors as a superficial, prating pretender. But from the absence of show in Harley's discourses many people inferred that there must be much substance; and he was pronounced to be a deep read, deep thinking gentleman, not a fine talker, but fitter to direct affairs of state than all the fine talkers in the world. This character he long supported with that cunning which is frequently found in company with ambitious and unquiet mediocrity. He constantly had, even with his best friends, an air of mystery and reserve which seemed to indicate that he knew some momentous secret, and that his mind was labouring with some vast design. In this way he got and long kept a high reputation for wisdom. It was not till that reputation had made him an Earl, a Knight of the Garter, Lord High Treasurer of England, and master of the fate of Europe, that his admirers began to find out that he was really a dull puzzleheaded man.*

Soon after the general election of 1690, Harley, generally voting with the Tories, began to turn Tory. The change was so gradual as to be almost imperceptible, but was not the less

* The character of Harley is to be collected from innumerable panegyrics and lampoons: from the works and the private correspondence of Swift, Pope, Arbuthnot, Prior and Bolingbroke, and from multitudes of such works as Ox and Bull, the High German Doctor, and The History of Robert Powell the Puppet Showman.

real.   He early began to hold the Tory doctrine that England ought to confine herself to a maritime war.   He early felt the true Tory antipathy to Dutchmen and to moneyed men.   The antipathy to Dissenters, which was necessary to the completeness of the character, came much later.   At length the transformation was complete ; and the old haunter of conventicles became an intolerant High Churchman.   Yet to the last the traces of his early breeding would now and then show themselves ; and, while he acted after the fashion of Laud, he sometimes wrote in the style of Praise God Barebones.*

Of Paul Foley we know comparatively little.   His history, up to a certain point, greatly resembles that of Harley : but he appears to have been superior to Harley both in parts and in elevation of character.   He was the son of Thomas Foley, a new man, but a man of great merit, who, having begun life with nothing, had created a noble estate by ironworks, and who was renowned for his spotless integrity and his munificent charity.   The Foleys were, like their neighbours the Harleys, Whigs and Puritans.   Thomas Foley lived on terms of close intimacy with Baxter, in whose writings he is mentioned with warm eulogy.   The opinions and the attachments of Paul Foley were at first those of his family.   But he, like Harley, became, merely from the vehemence of his Whiggism, an ally of the Tories, and might, perhaps, like Harley, have been completely metamorphosed into a Tory, if the process of transmutation had not been interrupted by death.   Foley's abilities were highly respectable, and had been improved by education.   He was so wealthy that it was unnecessary for him to follow the law as a profession ; but he had studied it carefully as a science.   His morals were without stain ; and the greatest fault which could be imputed to him was that he paraded his independence and disinterestedness too ostentatiously, and was so much afraid of being thought to fawn that he was always growling.

Another convert ought to be mentioned.   Howe, lately the most virulent of the Whigs, had been, by the loss of his place, turned into one of the most virulent of the Tories.   The deserter brought to the party which he had joined no weight

---

* In a letter dated Sept. 12. 1709. a short time before he was brought into power on the shoulders of the High Church mob, he says : " My soul has been among lyons, even the sons of men, whose teeth are spears and arrows, and their tongues sharp swords.   But I learn how good it is to wait on the Lord, and to possess one's soul in peace."   The letter was to Carstairs.   I doubt whether Harley would have canted thus if he had been writing to Atterbury.

of character, no capacity or semblance of capacity for great affairs, but much parliamentary ability of a low kind, much spite and much impudence. No speaker of that time seems to have had, in such large measure, both the power and the inclination to give pain.

The assistance of these men was most welcome to the Tory party; but it was impossible that they could, as yet, exercise over that party the entire authority of leaders. For they still called themselves Whigs, and generally vindicated their Tory votes by arguments grounded on Whig principles.*

From this view of the state of parties in the House of Commons, it seems clear that Sunderland had good reason for recommending that the administration should be entrusted to the Whigs. The King, however, hesitated long before he could bring himself to quit that neutral position which he had long occupied between the contending parties. If one of those parties was disposed to question his title, the other was on principle hostile to his prerogative. He still remembered with bitterness the unreasonable and vindictive conduct of the Convention Parliament at the close of 1689 and the beginning of 1690; and he shrank from the thought of being entirely in the hands of the men who had obstructed the Bill of Indemnity, who had voted for the Sacheverell clause, who had tried to prevent him from taking the command of his army in Ireland, and who had called him an ungrateful tyrant merely because he would not be their slave and their hangman. He had once, by a bold and unexpected effort, freed himself from their yoke; and he was not inclined to put it on his neck again. He personally disliked Wharton and Russell. He thought highly of the capacity of Caermarthen, of the integrity of Nottingham, of the diligence and financial skill of Godolphin. It was only by slow degrees that the arguments of Sunderland, backed by the force of circumstances, overcame all objections.

On the seventh of November 1693 the Parliament met; and the conflict of parties instantly began. William from the throne pressed on the Houses the necessity of making a great exertion to arrest the progress of France on the Continent.

* The anomalous position which Harley and Foley at this time occupied is noticed in the Dialogue between a Whig and a Tory, 1693. "Your great P. Fo—y," says the Tory, "turns cadet, and carries arms under the General of the West Saxons. The two Har—ys, father and son, are engineers under the late Lieutenant of the Ordnance, and bomb any bill which he hath once resolv'd to reduce to ashes." Seymour is the General of the West Saxons. Musgrave had been Lieutenant of the Ordnance in the reign of Charles the Second.

During the last campaign, he said, she had, on every point, had a superiority of force; and it had therefore been found impossible to cope with her. His allies had promised to increase their armies; and he trusted that the Commons would enable him to do the same.*

The Commons at their next sitting took the King's speech into consideration. The miscarriage of the Smyrna fleet was the chief subject of discussion. The cry for inquiry was universal: but it was evident that the two parties raised that cry for very different reasons. Montague spoke the sense of the Whigs. He declared that the disasters of the summer could not, in his opinion, be explained by the ignorance and imbecility of those who had charge of the naval administration. There must have been treason. It was impossible to believe that Lewis, when he sent his Brest squadron to the Straits of Gibraltar, and left the whole coast of his kingdom from Dunkirk to Bayonne unprotected, had trusted merely to chance. He must have been well assured that his fleet would meet with a vast booty under a feeble convoy. As there had been treachery in some quarters, there had been incapacity in others. The State was ill served. And then the orator pronounced a warm panegyric on his friend Somers. "Would that all men in power would follow the example of my Lord Keeper! If all patronage were bestowed as judiciously and disinterestedly as his, we should not see the public offices filled with men who draw salaries and perform no duties." It was moved and carried unanimously, that the Commons would support their Majesties, and would forthwith proceed to investigate the cause of the disaster in the Bay of Lagos.† The Lords of the Admiralty were directed to produce a great mass of documentary evidence. The King sent down copies of the examinations taken before the Committee of Council which Mary had appointed to inquire into the grievances of the Turkey merchants. The Turkey merchants themselves were called in and interrogated. Rooke, though too ill to stand or speak, was brought in a chair to the bar, and there delivered in a narrative of his proceedings. The Whigs soon thought that sufficient ground had been laid for a vote condemning the naval administration, and moved a resolution attributing the miscarriage of the Smyrna fleet to notorious and treacherous mismanagement. That there had been mismanagement could not be disputed; but that there had been foul play

* Lords' and Commons' Journals, Nov. 7. 1693.
† Commons' Journals, Nov. 13. 1693; Grey's Debates.

had certainly not been proved. The Tories proposed that the word " treacherous " should be omitted. A division took place ; and the Whigs carried their point by a hundred and forty votes to a hundred and three. Wharton was a teller for the majority.*

It was now decided that there had been treason, but not who was the traitor. Several keen debates followed. The Whigs tried to throw the blame on Killegrew and Delaval, who were Tories : the Tories did their best to make out that the fault lay with the Victualling Department, which was under the direction of Whigs. But the House of Commons has always been much more ready to pass votes of censure drawn in general terms than to brand individuals by name. A resolution clearing the Victualling Office was proposed by Montague, and carried, after a debate of two days, by a hundred and eighty-eight votes to a hundred and fifty-two.† But when the victorious party brought forward a motion inculpating the admirals, the Tories came up in great numbers from the country, and, after a debate which lasted from nine in the morning till near eleven at night, succeeded in saving their friends. The Noes were a hundred and seventy, and the Ayes only a hundred and sixty-one. Another attack was made a few days later with no better success. The Noes were a hundred and eighty-five, the Ayes only a hundred and seventy-five. The indefatigable and implacable Wharton was on both occasions tellers for the minority.‡

In spite of this check the advantage was decidedly with the Whigs. The Tories who were at the head of the naval administration had indeed escaped impeachment : but the escape had been so narrow that it was impossible for the King to employ them any longer. The advice of Sunderland prevailed. A new Commission of Admiralty was prepared ; and Russell was named First Lord. He had already been appointed to the command of the Channel fleet.

His elevation made it necessary that Nottingham should retire. For, though it was not then unusual to see men who were personally and politically hostile to each other holding high offices at the same time, the relation between the First Lord of the Admiralty and the Secrerary of State, who had charge of what would now be called the War Department, was

* Commons' Journals, Nov. 17. 1693.
† Ibid. Nov. 22. 27. 1693 ; Grey's Debates.
‡ Commons' Journals, Nov. 29. Dec. 6. 1693 ; L'Hermitage, Dec. $\frac{1}{11}$.
1693.

of so peculiar a nature that the public service could not be well conducted without cordial cooperation between them; and between Nottingham and Russell such cooperation was not to be expected. "I thank you," William said to Nottingham, "for your services. I have nothing to complain of in your conduct. It is only from necessity that I part with you." Nottingham retired with dignity. Though a very honest man, he went out of office much richer than he had come in five years before. What were then considered as the legitimate emoluments of his place were great: he had sold Kensington House to the Crown for a large sum; and he had probably, after the fashion of that time, obtained for himself some lucrative grants. He laid out all his gains in purchasing land. He heard, he said, that his enemies meant to accuse him of having acquired wealth by illicit means. He was perfectly ready to abide the issue of an inquiry. He would not, as some ministers had done, place his fortune beyond the reach of the justice of his country. He would have no secret hoard. He would invest nothing in foreign funds. His property should all be such as could be readily discovered and seized.*

During some weeks the seals which Nottingham had delivered up remained in the royal closet. To dispose of them proved no easy matter. They were offered to Shrewsbury, who of all the Whig leaders stood highest in the King's favour: but Shrewsbury excused himself, and, in order to avoid further importunity, retired into the country. There he soon received a pressing letter from Elizabeth Villiers. This lady had, when a girl, inspired William with a passion which had caused much scandal and much unhappiness in the little Court of the Hague. Her influence over him she owed not to her personal charms, —for it tasked all the art of Kneller to make her look tolerably on canvass,—not to those talents which peculiarly belong to her sex,—for she did not excel in playful talk, and her letters are remarkably deficient in feminine ease and grace,—but to powers of mind which qualified her to partake the cares and guide the counsels of statesmen. To the end of her life great politicians sought her advice. Even Swift, the shrewdest and most cynical of her contemporaries, pronounced her the wisest of women, and more than once sate, fascinated by her conversation, from two in the afternoon till near midnight.† By

* L'Hermitage, Sept. $\frac{1}{11}$., Nov. $\frac{7}{17}$. 1693.
† See the Journal to Stella, lii. liii. lix. lxi.; and Lady Orkney's Letters to Swift.

degrees the virtues and charms of Mary conquered the first place in her husband's affection. But he still, in difficult conjunctures, frequently applied to Elizabeth Villiers for advice and assistance. She now implored Shrewsbury to reconsider his determination, and not to throw away the opportunity of uniting the Whig party for ever. Wharton and Russell wrote to the same effect. In reply came flimsy and unmeaning excuses : " I am not qualified for a court life : I am unequal to a place which requires much exertion : I do not quite agree with any party in the State : in short, I am unfit for the world : I want to travel : I want to see Spain." These were mere pretences. Had Shrewsbury spoken the whole truth, he would have said that he had, in an evil hour, been false to the cause of that Revolution in which he had borne so great a part, that he had entered into engagements of which he repented, but from which he knew not how to extricate himself, and that, while he remained under those engagements, he was unwilling to enter into the service of the existing government. Marlborough, Godolphin and Russell, indeed, had no scruple about corresponding with one King while holding office under the other. But Shrewsbury had, what was wanting to Marlborough, Godolphin and Russell, a conscience, a conscience which indeed too often failed to restrain him from doing wrong, but which never failed to punish him.*

In consequence of his refusal to accept the Seals, the ministerial arrangements which the King had planned were not carried into entire effect till the end of the session. Meanwhile the proceedings of the two Houses had been highly interesting and important.

Soon after the Parliament met, the attention of the Commons was again called to the state of the trade with India ; and the charter which had just been granted to the Old Company was laid before them. They would probably have been disposed to sanction the new arrangement, which, in truth, differed little from that which they had themselves suggested not many months before, if the Directors had acted with prudence. But the Directors, from the day on which they had obtained their charter, had persecuted the interlopers without mercy, and had quite forgotten that it was one thing to persecute interlopers in the Eastern Seas, and another to persecute them in the port of London. Hitherto the war of the monopolists against the private trade had been generally carried on at the distance

---

* See the letters written at this time by Elizabeth Villiers, Wharton, Russell and Shrewsbury, in the Shrewsbury Correspondence.

of fifteen thousand miles from England.  If harsh things were done, the English did not see them done, and did not hear of them till long after they had been done ; nor was it by any means easy to ascertain at Westminster who had been right and who had been wrong in a dispute which had arisen three or four years before at Moorshedabad or Canton.  With incredible rashness the Directors determined, at the very moment when the fate of their company was in the balance, to give the people of this country a near view of the most odious features of the monopoly.  Some wealthy merchants of London had equipped a fine ship named the Redbridge.  Her crew was numerous, her cargo of immense value.  Her papers had been made out for Alicant : but there was some reason to suspect that she was really bound for the countries lying beyond the Cape of Good Hope.  She was stopped by the Admiralty, in obedience to an order which the Company obtained from the Privy Council, doubtless by the help of the Lord President.  Every day that she lay in the Thames caused a heavy expense to the owners.  The indignation in the City was great and general.  The Company maintained that from the legality of the monopoly the legality of the detention necessarily followed.  The public turned the argument round, and, being firmly convinced that the detention was illegal, drew the inference that the monopoly must be illegal too.  The dispute was at the height when the Parliament met. Petitions on both sides were speedily laid on the table of the Commons ; and it was resolved that these petitions should be taken into consideration by a Committee of the whole House. The first question on which the conflicting parties tried their strength was the choice of a chairman.  The enemies of the Old Company proposed Papillon, once the closest ally and subsequently the keenest opponent of Child, and carried their point by a hundred and thirty-eight votes to a hundred and six.  The Committee proceeded to inquire by what authority the Redbridge had been stopped.  One of her owners, Gilbert Heathcote, a rich merchant and a stanch Whig, appeared at the bar as a witness.  He was asked whether he would venture to deny that the ship had really been fitted out for the Indian trade.  "It is no sin that I know of," he answered, "to trade with India ; and I shall trade with India till I am restrained by Act of Parliament."  Papillon reported that in the opinion of the Committee, the detention of the Redbridge was illegal.  The question was then put, that the House would agree with the Committee. The friends of the Old Company ventured on a second division, and were defeated by a hundred and seventy-one votes to a hundred and twenty-five.*

The blow was quickly followed up. A few days later it was moved that all subjects of England had equal right to trade to the East Indies unless prohibited by Act of Parliament; and the supporters of the Old Company, sensible that they were in a minority, suffered the motion to pass without a division.†

This memorable vote settled the most important of the constitutional questions which had been left unsettled by the Bill of Rights. It has ever since been held to be the sound doctrine that no power but that of the whole legislature can give to any person or to any society an exclusive privilege of trading to any part of the world.

The opinion of the great majority of the House of Commons was that the Indian trade could be advantageously carried on only by means of a joint stock and a monopoly. It might therefore have been expected that the resolution which destroyed the monopoly of the Old Company would have been immediately followed by a law granting a monopoly to the New Company. No such law, however, was passed. The Old Company, though not strong enough to defend its own privileges, was able, with the help of its Tory friends, to prevent the rival association from obtaining similar privileges. The consequence was that, during some years, there was nominally a free trade with India. In fact, the trade still lay under severe restrictions. The private adventurer found indeed no difficulty in sailing from England: but his situation was as perilous as ever when he had turned the Cape of Good Hope. Whatever respect might be paid to a vote of the House of Commons by public functionaries in London, such a vote was, at Bombay or Calcutta, much less regarded than a private letter from Child; and Child still continued to fight the battle with unbroken spirit. He sent out to the factories of the Company orders that no indulgence should be shown to the intruders. For the House of Commons and for its resolutions he expressed the bitterest contempt. "Be guided by my instructions," he wrote, "and not by the nonsense of a few ignorant country gentlemen who have hardly wit enough to manage their own private affairs, and who know nothing at all about questions of trade." It appears that his directions were obeyed. Every where in the East, during this period of anarchy, the

* Commons' Journals, Jan. 6. 8. 169¾.
† Ibid. Jan. 19. 169¾.

servant of the Company and the independent merchant waged war on each other, accused each other of piracy, and tried by every artifice to exasperate the Mogul government against each other.*

The three great constitutional questions of the preceding year were, in this year, again brought under the consideration of Parliament. In the first week of the session, a Bill for the Regulation of Trials in cases of High Treason, a Triennial Bill, and a Place Bill were laid on the table of the House of Commons.

None of these bills became a law. The first passed the Commons, but was unfavourably received by the Peers. William took so much interest in the question that he came down to the House of Lords, not in his crown and robes, but in the ordinary dress of a gentleman, and sate through the whole debate on the second reading. Caermarthen spoke of the dangers to which the State was at that time exposed, and entreated his brethren not to give, at such a moment, impunity to traitors. He was powerfully supported by two eminent orators, who had, during some years, been on the uncourtly side of every question, but who, in this session, showed a disposition to strengthen the hands of the government, Halifax and Mulgrave. Marlborough, Rochester and Nottingham spoke for the bill: but the general feeling was so clearly against them that they did not venture to divide. It is probable, however, that the reasons urged by Caermarthen were not the reasons which chiefly swayed his hearers. The Peers were fully determined that the bill should not pass without a clause altering the constitution of the Court of the Lord High Steward: they knew that the Lower House was as fully determined not to pass such a clause; and they thought it better that what must happen at last should happen speedily, and without a quarrel.†

The fate of the Triennial Bill confounded all the calculations of the best informed politicians of that time, and may therefore well seem extraordinary to us. During the recess, that bill had been described in numerous pamphlets, written for the most

* Hamilton's New Account.

† The bill I found in the Archives of the Lords. Its history I learned from the Journals of the two Houses, from a passage in the Diary of Narcissus Luttrell, and from two letters to the States General, both dated on $\frac{\text{Feb. 27.}}{\text{March 9.}}$ 1694, the day after the debate in the Lords. One of these letters is from Van Citters; the other, which contains fuller information, is from L'Hermitage.

part by persons zealous for the Revolution and for popular principles of government, as the one thing needful, as the universal cure for the distempers of the State. On the first, second and third readings in the House of Commons no division took place. The Whigs were enthusiastic. The Tories seemed to be acquiescent. It was understood that the King, though he had used his Veto for the purpose of giving the Houses an opportunity of reconsidering the subject, had no intention of offering a pertinacious opposition to their wishes. But Seymour, with a cunning which long experience had matured, after deferring the conflict to the last moment, snatched the victory from his adversaries, when they were most secure. When the Speaker held up the bill in his hands, and put the question whether it should pass, the Noes were a hundred and forty-six, the Ayes only a hundred and thirty-six.*

Some eager Whigs flattered themselves that their defeat was the effect of a surprise, and might be retrieved. Within three days, therefore, Monmouth, the most ardent and restless man in the whole party, brought into the Upper House a bill substantially the same with that which had so strangely miscarried in the Lower. The Peers passed this bill very expeditiously, and sent it down to the Commons. But in the Commons it found no favour. Many members, who professed to wish that the duration of parliaments should be limited, resented the interference of the hereditary branch of the legislature in a matter which peculiarly concerned the elective branch. The subject, they said, is one which especially belongs to us : we have considered it : we have come to a decision ; and it is scarcely parliamentary, it is certainly most indelicate, in their Lordships, to call upon us to reverse that decision. The question now is, not whether the duration of parliaments ought to be limited, but whether we ought to submit our judgment to the authority of the Peers, and to rescind, at their bidding, what we did only a fortnight ago. The animosity with which the patrician order

---

* Commons' Journals, Nov. 28. 1693 ; Grey's Debates. L'Hermitage expected that the bill would pass, and that the royal assent would not be withheld. On November $\frac{1}{7}$. he wrote to the States General, "Il paroist dans toute la chambre beaucoup de passion à faire passer ce bil." On $\frac{Nov. 28.}{Dec. 8.}$ he says that the division on the passing "n'a pas causé une pétite surprise. Il est difficile d'avoir un point fixe sur les idées qu'on peut se former des émotions du parlement, car il paroist quelquefois de grandes chaleurs qui semblent devoir tout enflammer, et qui, peu de tems après, s'évaporent." That Seymour was the chief manager of the opposition to the bill is asserted in the once celebrated Hush Money pamphlet of that year.

was regarded was inflamed by the arts and the eloquence of Seymour. The bill contained a definition of the words, "to hold a Parliament." This definition was scrutinised with extreme jealousy, and was thought by many, with very little reason, to have been framed for the purpose of extending the privileges, already invidiously great, of the nobility. It appears, from the scanty and obscure fragments of the debates which have come down to us, that bitter reflections were thrown on the general conduct, both political and judicial, of the Peers. Old Titus, though zealous for triennial parliaments, owned that he was not surprised at the ill humour which many gentlemen showed. "It is true," he said, "that we ought to be dissolved: but it is rather hard, I must own, that the Lords are to prescribe the time of our dissolution. The Apostle Paul wished to be dissolved: but, I doubt, if his friends had set him a day, he would not have taken it kindly of them." The bill was rejected by a hundred and ninety-seven votes to a hundred and twenty-seven.*

The Place Bill, differing very little from the Place Bill which had been brought in twelve months before, passed easily through the Commons. Most of the Tories supported it warmly; and the Whigs did not venture to oppose it. It went up to the Lords, and soon came back completely changed. As it had been originally drawn, it provided that no member of the House of Commons, elected after the first of January, 1694, should accept any place of profit under the Crown, on pain of forfeiting his seat, and of being incapable of sitting again in the same Parliament. The Lords had added the words, "unless he be afterwards again chosen to serve in the same Parliament." These words, few as they were, sufficed to deprive the bill of nine tenths of its efficacy, both for good and for evil. It was most desirable that the crowd of subordinate public functionaries should be kept out of the House of Commons. It was most undesirable that the heads of the great executive departments should be kept out of that House. The bill, as altered, left that House open both to those who ought and to those who ought not to have been admitted. It very properly let in the Secretaries of State and the Chancellor of the Exchequer; but

* Commons' Journals; Grey's Debates. The engrossed copy of this Bill went down to the House of Commons and is lost. The original draught on paper is among the Archives of the Lords. That Monmouth brought in the bill I learned from a letter of L'Hermitage to the States General, Dec. $\frac{1}{11}$. 1693. As to the numbers on the division, I have followed the Journals. But in Grey's Debates, and in the letters of Van Citters and L'Hermitage, the minority is said to have been 172.

it let in with them Commissioners of Wine Licenses and Commissioners of the Navy, Receivers, Surveyors, Storekeepers, Clerks of the Acts and Clerks of the Cheque, Clerks of the Green Cloth and Clerks of the Great Wardrobe. So little did the Commons understand what they were about that, after framing a law, in one view most mischievous, and in another view most beneficial, they were perfectly willing that it should be transformed into a law quite harmless and almost useless. They agreed to the amendment; and nothing was now wanting but the royal sanction.

That sanction certainly ought not to have been withheld, and probably would not have been withheld, if William had known how unimportant the bill now was. But he understood the question as little as the Commons themselves. He knew that they imagined that they had devised a most stringent limitation of the royal power; and he was determined not to submit, without a struggle, to any such limitation. He was encouraged by the success with which he had hitherto resisted the attempts of the two Houses to encroach on his prerogative. He had refused to pass the bill which quartered the Judges on his hereditary revenue; and the Parliament had silently acquiesced in the justice of the refusal. He had refused to pass the Triennial Bill; and the Commons had since, by rejecting two Triennial Bills, acknowledged that he had done well. He ought, however, to have considered that, on both these occasions, the announcement of his refusal was immediately followed by the announcement that the Parliament was prorogued. On both these occasions, therefore, the members had half a year to think and to grow cool before the next sitting. The case was now very different. The principal business of the session was hardly begun: estimates were still under consideration: bills of supply were still depending; and, if the Houses should take a fit of ill humour, the consequences might be serious indeed.

He resolved, however, to run the risk. Whether he had any adviser is not known. His determination seems to have taken both the leading Whigs and the leading Tories by surprise. When the Clerk had proclaimed that the King and Queen would consider of the bill touching free and impartial proceedings in Parliament, the Commons retired from the bar of the Lords in a resentful and ungovernable mood. As soon as the Speaker was again in his chair there was a long and tempestuous debate. All other business was postponed. All committees were adjourned. It was resolved that the House would, early the next morning, take into consideration the state of the nation. When the morning came, the excitement did not appear to have abated. The mace was sent into Westminster Hall and into the Court of Requests. All members who could be found were brought into the House. That none might be able to steal away unnoticed, the back door was locked, and the key laid on the table. All strangers were ordered to retire. With these solemn preparations began a sitting which reminded a few old men of some of the first sittings of the Long Parliament. High words were uttered by the enemies of the government. Its friends, afraid of being accused of abandoning the cause of the Commons of England for the sake of royal favour, hardly ventured to raise their voices. Montague alone seems to have defended the King. Lowther, though high in office and a member of the cabinet, owned that there were evil influences at work, and expressed a wish to see the Sovereign surrounded by counsellors in whom the representatives of the people could confide. Harley, Foley and Howe carried every thing before them. A resolution, affirming that those who had advised the Crown on this occasion were public enemies, was carried with only two or three Noes. Harley, after reminding his hearers that they had their negative voice as the King had his, and that, if His Majesty refused them redress, they could refuse him money, moved that they should go up to the Throne, not, as usual, with a Humble Address, but with a Representation. Some members proposed to substitute the more respectful word Address : but they were overruled ; and a committee was appointed to draw up the Representation.

Another night passed ; and, when the House met again, it appeared that the storm had greatly subsided. The malignant joy and the wild hopes which the Jacobites had, during the last forty-eight hours, expressed with their usual imprudence, had incensed and alarmed the Whigs and the moderate Tories. Many members too were frightened by hearing that William was fully determined not to yield without an appeal to the nation. Such an appeal might have been successful : for a dissolution, on any ground whatever, would, at that moment, have been a highly popular exercise of the prerogative. The constituent bodies, it was well known, were generally zealous for the Triennial Bill, and cared comparatively little about the Place Bill. Many Tory members, therefore, who had recently voted against the Triennial Bill, were by no means desirous to run the risks of a general election. When the Representation which Harley and his friends had prepared was read, it was thought offensively strong. After being recommitted, shortened and softened, it was presented by the whole House. William's answer was kind and gentle ; but he conceded nothing. He assured the Commons that he remembered with gratitude the support which he had on many occasions received from them, that he should always consider their advice as most valuable, and that he should look on counsellors who might attempt to raise dissension between him and his Parliament as his enemies : but he uttered not a word which could be construed into an acknowledgment that he had used his Veto ill, or into a promise that he would not use it again.

The Commons on the morrow took his speech into consideration. Harley and his allies complained that the King's answer was no answer at all, threatened to tack the Place Bill to a money bill, and proposed to make a second representation pressing His Majesty to explain himself more distinctly. But by this time there was a strong reflux of feeling in the assembly. The Whigs had not only recovered from their dismay, but were in high spirits and eager for conflict. Wharton, Russell and Littleton maintained that the House ought to be satisfied with what the King had said. "Do you wish," said Littleton, "to make sport for your enemies ? There is no want of them. They besiege our very doors. We read, as we come through the lobby, in the face and gestures of every nonjuror whom we pass, delight at the momentary coolness which has arisen between us and the King. That should be enough for us. We may be sure that we are voting rightly when we give a vote which tends to confound the hopes of traitors." The House divided. Harley was a teller on one side, Wharton on the other. Only eighty-eight voted with Harley, two hundred and twenty-nine with Wharton. The Whigs were so much elated by their victory that some of them wished to move a vote of thanks to William for his gracious answer : but they were restrained by wiser men. "We have lost time enough already in these unhappy debates," said a leader of the party. "Let us get to Ways and Means as fast as we can. The best form which our thanks can take is that of a money bill."

Thus ended, more happily than William had a right to expect, one of the most dangerous contests in which he ever engaged with his Parliament. At the Dutch Embassy the rising and going down of this tempest had been watched with intense interest ; and the opinion there seems to have been that the King had on the whole lost neither power nor popularity by his conduct.*

* The bill is in the Archives of the Lords. Its history I have collected

Another question, which excited scarcely less angry feeling in Parliament and in the country, was, about the same time, under consideration. On the sixth of December, a Whig member of the House of Commons obtained leave to bring in a bill for the Naturalisation of Foreign Protestants. Plausible arguments in favour of such a bill were not wanting. Great numbers of people, eminently industrious and intelligent, firmly attached to our faith, and deadly enemies of our deadly enemies, were at that time without a country. Among the Huguenots who had fled from the tyranny of the French King were many persons of great fame in war, in letters, in arts and in sciences ; and even the humblest refugees were intellectually and morally above the average of the common people of any kingdom in Europe. With French Protestants who had been driven into exile by the edicts of Lewis were now mingled German Protestants who had been driven into exile by his arms. Vienna, Berlin, Basle, Hamburg, Amsterdam, London, swarmed with honest laborious men who had once been thriving burghers of Heidelberg or Manheim, or who had cultivated vineyards along the banks of the Neckar and the Rhine. A statesman might well think that it would be at once generous and politic to invite to the English shores and to incorporate with the English people emigrants so unfortunate and so respectable. Their ingenuity and their diligence could not fail to enrich any land which should afford them an asylum ; nor could it be doubted that they would manfully defend the country of their adoption against him whose cruelty had driven them from the country of their birth.

The first two readings passed without a division. But, on the motion that the bill should be committed, there was a debate in which the right of free speech was most liberally used by the opponents of the government. It was idle, they said, to talk about the poor Huguenots or the poor Palatines. The bill was evidently meant for the benefit, not of French Protestants or German Protestants, but of Dutchmen, who would be Protestants, Papists or Pagans for a guilder a head, and who would, no doubt, be as ready to sign the Declaration against Transubstantiation in England as to trample on the Cross in Japan. They would come over in multitudes. They would swarm in every public office. They would collect the customs,

from the Journals, from Grey's Debates, and from the highly interesting letters of Van Citters and L'Hermitage. I think it clear from Grey's Debates that a speech which L'Hermitage attributes to a nameless "quelq'un" was made by Sir Thomas Littleton.

and gauge the beer barrels. Our Navigation Laws would be virtually repealed. Every merchant ship that cleared out from the Thames or the Severn would be manned by Zealanders and Hollanders and Frieslanders. To our own sailors would be left the hard and perilous service of the royal navy. For Hans, after filling the pockets of his huge trunk hose with our money by assuming the character of a native, would, as soon as a pressgang appeared, lay claim to the privileges of an alien. The intruders would soon rule every corporation. They would elbow our own Aldermen off the Royal Exchange. They would buy the hereditary woods and halls of our country gentlemen. Already one of the most noisome of the plagues of Egypt was among us. Frogs had made their appearance even in the royal chambers. Nobody could go to Saint James's without being disgusted by hearing the reptiles of the Batavian marshes croaking all round him: and if this bill should pass, the whole country would be as much infested by the loathsome brood as the palace already was.

The orator who indulged himself most freely in this sort of rhetoric was Sir John Knight, member for Bristol, a coarse-minded and spiteful Jacobite, who, if he had been an honest man, would have been a nonjuror. Two years before, when Mayor of Bristol, he had acquired a discreditable notoriety by treating with gross disrespect a commission sealed with the great seal of the Sovereigns to whom he had repeatedly sworn allegiance, and by setting on the rabble of his city to hoot and pelt the Judges.* He now concluded a savage invective by desiring that the Serjeant at Arms would open the doors, in order that the odious roll of parchment, which was nothing less than a surrender of the birthright of the English people, might be treated with proper contumely. "Let us first," he said, "kick the bill out of the House; and then let us kick the foreigners out of the kingdom."

On a division the motion for committing the bill was carried by a hundred and sixty-three votes to a hundred and twenty-eight.† But the minority was zealous and pertinacious; and the majority speedily began to waver. Knight's speech, re-touched and made more offensive, soon appeared in print without a license. Tens of thousands of copies were circulated by the post, or dropped in the streets; and such was the strength of national prejudice that too many persons read this ribaldry with assent and admiration. But, when a copy was

* Narcissus Luttrell's Diary, September 1691.
† Commons' Journals, Jan. 4. 169⅔.

produced in the House, there was such an outbreak of indignation and disgust, as cowed even the impudent and savage nature of the orator. Finding himself in imminent danger of being expelled and sent to prison, he apologized, and disclaimed all knowledge of the paper which purported to be a report of what he had said. He escaped with impunity: but his speech was voted false, scandalous and seditious, and was burned by the hangman in Palace Yard. The bill which had caused all this ferment was prudently suffered to drop.*

Meanwhile the Commons were busied with financial questions of grave importance. The estimates for the year 1694 were enormous. The King proposed to add to the regular army, already the greatest regular army that England had ever supported, four regiments of dragoons, eight of horse, and twenty-five of infantry. The whole number of men, officers included, would thus be increased to about ninety-four thousand.† Cromwell, while holding down three reluctant kingdoms, and making vigorous war on Spain in Europe and America, had never had two thirds of the military force which William now thought necessary. The great body of the Tories, headed by three Whig chiefs, Harley, Foley and Howe, opposed any augmentation. The great body of the Whigs, headed by Montague and Wharton, would have granted all that was asked. After many long discussions, and probably many close divisions, in the Committee of Supply, the King obtained the greater part of what he demanded. The House allowed him four new regiments of dragoons, six of horse, and fifteen of infantry. The whole number of troops voted for the year amounted to eighty-three thousand, the charge to more than two millions and a half, including about two hundred thousand pounds for the ordnance.‡

* Of the Naturalisation Bill no copy, I believe, exists. The history of that bill will be found in the Journals. From Van Citters and L'Hermitage we learn less than might have been expected on a subject which must have been interesting to Dutch statesmen. Knight's speech will be found among the Somers Papers. He is described by his brother Jacobite, Roger North, as "a gentleman of as eminent integrity and loyalty as ever the city of Bristol was honoured with."

† Commons' Journals, Dec. 5. 169¾.

‡ Commons' Journals, Dec. 20. and 22. 169¾. The Journals did not then contain any notice of the divisions which took place when the House was in committee. There was only one division on the army estimates of this year, when the mace was on the table. That division was on the question whether 60,000l. or 147,000l. should be granted for hospitals and contingencies. The Whigs carried the larger sum by 184 votes to 120. Wharton was a teller for the majority, Foley for the minority.

The naval estimates passed much more rapidly ; for Whigs and Tories agreed in thinking that the maritime ascendency of England ought to be maintained at any cost. Five hundred thousand pounds were voted for paying the arrears due to seamen, and two millions for the expenses of the year 1694.*

The Commons then proceeded to consider the Ways and Means. The land tax was renewed at four shillings in the pound ; and by this simple but powerful machinery about two millions were raised with certainty and despatch.† A poll tax was imposed.‡ Stamp duties had long been among the fiscal resources of Holland and France, and had existed here during part of the reign of Charles the Second, but had been suffered to expire. They were now revived ; and they have ever since formed an important part of the revenue of the State.§ The hackney coaches of the capital were taxed, and were placed under the government of commissioners, in spite of the resistance of the wives of the coachmen, who assembled round Westminster Hall and mobbed the members.‖ But, notwithstanding all these expedients, there was still a large deficiency ; and it was again necessary to borrow. A new duty on salt and some other imposts of less importance were set apart to form a fund for a loan. On the security of this fund a million was to be raised by a lottery, but a lottery which had scarcely any thing but the name in common with the lotteries of a later period. The sum to be contributed was divided into a hundred thousand shares of ten pounds each. The interest on each share was to be twenty shillings annually, or, in other words, ten per cent., during sixteen years. But ten per cent. for sixteen years was not a bait which was likely to attract lenders. An additional lure was therefore held out to capitalists. On one fortieth of the shares much higher interest was to be paid than on the other thirty-nine fortieths. Which of the shares should be prizes was to be determined by lot. The arrangements for the drawing of the tickets were made by an adventurer of the name of Neale, who, after squandering away two fortunes, had been glad to become groom porter at the palace. His duties were to call the odds when the Court played at hazard, to provide cards and dice, and to decide any dispute which might arise on the bowling green or at the gaming table. He was eminently

* Commons' Journals, Nov. 25. 169¾.
† Stat. 5 W. & M. c. 1.                    ‡ Stat. 5 & 6 W. & M. c. 14.
§ Stat. 5 & 6 W. & M. c. 21. ; Narcissus Luttrell's Diary.
‖ Stat. 5 & 6 W. & M. c. 22. ; Narcissus Luttrell's Diary.

skilled in the business of this not very exalted post, and had made such sums by raffles that he was able to engage in very costly speculations, and was then covering the ground round the Seven Dials with buildings. He was probably the best adviser that could have been consulted about the details of a lottery. Yet there were not wanting persons who thought it hardly decent in the Treasury to call in the aid of a gambler by profession.*

By the lottery loan, as it was called, one million was obtained. But another million was wanted to bring the estimated revenue for the year 1694 up to a level with the estimated expenditure. The ingenious and enterprising Montague had a plan ready, a plan to which, except under the pressure of extreme pecuniary difficulties, he might not easily have induced the Commons to assent, but which, to his large and vigorous mind, appeared to have advantages, both commercial and political, more important than the immediate relief to the finances. He succeeded, not only in supplying the wants of the State for twelve months, but in creating a great institution, which, after the lapse of more than a century and a half, continues to flourish, and which he lived to see the stronghold, through all vicissitudes, of the Whig party, and the bulwark, in dangerous times, of the Protestant succession.

In the reign of William old men were still living who could remember the days when there was not a single banking house in the city of London. So late as the time of the Restoration every trader had his own strong box in his own house, and, when an acceptance was presented to him, told down the crowns and Caroluses on his own counter. But the increase of wealth had produced its natural effect, the subdivision of labour. Before the end of the reign of Charles the Second, a new mode of paying and receiving money had come into fashion among the merchants of the capital. A class of agents arose, whose office was to keep the cash of the commercial houses. This new branch of business naturally fell into the hands of the goldsmiths, who were accustomed to traffic largely in the precious metals, and who had vaults in which great masses of bullion could lie secure from fire and from robbers. It was at the shops of the goldsmiths of Lombard Street that all the

* Stat. 5 W. & M. c. 7.; Evelyn's Diary, Oct. 5. Nov. 22. 1694; A Poem on Squire Neale's Projects ; Malcolm's History of London. Neale's functions are described in several editions of Chamberlayne's State of England. His name frequently appears in the London Gazette, as, for example, on July 28. 1684.

payments in coin were made.    Other traders gave and received nothing but paper.

This great change did not take place without much opposition and clamour.    Oldfashioned merchants complained bitterly that a class of men who, thirty years before, had confined themselves to their proper functions, and had made a fair profit by embossing silver bowls and chargers, by setting jewels for fine ladies, and by selling pistoles and dollars to gentlemen setting out for the Continent, had become the treasurers, and were fast becoming the masters, of the whole City.    These usurers, it was said, played at hazard with what had been earned by the industry and hoarded by the thrift of other men. If the dice turned up well, the knave who kept the cash became an alderman : if they turned up ill, the dupe who furnished the cash became a bankrupt.    On the other side the conveniences of the modern practice were set forth in animated language. The new system, it was said, saved both labour and money. Two clerks, seated in one counting house, did what, under the old system, must have been done by twenty clerks in twenty different establishments.    A goldsmith's note might be transferred ten times in a morning ; and thus a hundred guineas, locked in his safe close to the Exchange, did what would formerly have required a thousand guineas, dispersed through many tills, some on Ludgate Hill, some in Austin Friars, and some in Tower Street.*

Gradually even those who had been loudest in murmuring against the innovation gave way and conformed to the prevailing usage.    The last person who held out, strange to say, was Sir Dudley North.    When, in 1680, after residing many years abroad, he returned to London, nothing astonished or displeased him more than the practice of making payments by drawing bills on bankers.    He found that he could not go on Change without being followed round the piazza by goldsmiths, who, with low bows, begged to have the honour of serving him. He lost his temper when his friends asked where he kept his cash.    " Where should I keep it," he asked, " but in my own house ? "    With difficulty he was induced to put his money into the hands of one of the Lombard Street men, as they were called. Unhappily, the Lombard Street man broke, and some of his customers suffered severely.    Dudley North lost only fifty

* See, for example, the Mystery of the Newfashioned Goldsmiths or Brokers, 1676 ; Is not the Hand of Joab in all this ? 1676 ; and an answer published in the same year.   See also England's Glory in the great Improvement by Banking and Trade, 1694.

pounds: but this loss confirmed him in his dislike of the whole mystery of banking. It was in vain, however, that he exhorted his fellow citizens to return to the good old practice, and not to expose themselves to utter ruin in order to spare themselves a little trouble. He stood alone against the whole community. The advantages of the modern system were felt every hour of every day in every part of London; and people were no more disposed to relinquish those advantages for fear of calamities which occurred at long intervals than to refrain from building houses for fear of fires, or from building ships for fear of hurricanes. It is a curious circumstance that a man who, as a theorist, was distinguished from all the merchants of his time by the largeness of his views and by his superiority to vulgar prejudices, should, in practice, have been distinguished from all the merchants of his time by the obstinacy with which he adhered to an ancient mode of doing business, long after the dullest and most ignorant plodders had abandoned that mode for one better suited to a great commercial society.*

No sooner had banking become a separate and important trade, than men began to discuss with earnestness the question whether it would be expedient to erect a national bank. The general opinion seems to have been decidedly in favour of a national bank: nor can we wonder at this: for few were then aware that trade is in general carried on to much more advantage by individuals than by great societies; and banking really is one of those few trades which can be carried on to as much advantage by a great society as by an individual. Two public banks had long been renowned throughout Europe, the Bank of Saint George at Genoa, and the Bank of Amsterdam. The immense wealth which was in the keeping of those establishments, the confidence which they inspired, the prosperity which they had created, their stability, tried by panics, by wars, by revolutions, and found proof against all, were favourite topics. The bank of Saint George had nearly completed its third century. It had begun to receive deposits and to make loans before Columbus had crossed the Atlantic, before Gama had turned the Cape, when a Christian Emperor was reigning at Constantinople, when a Mahomedan Sultan was reigning at Granada, when Florence was a Republic, when Holland obeyed a hereditary Prince. All these things had been changed. New continents and new oceans had been discovered. The Turk was at Constantinople: the Castilian was at Granada: Florence had its hereditary Prince: Holland was a Republic: but the

* See the Life of Dudley North, by his brother Roger.

Bank of Saint George was still receiving deposits and making loans. The Bank of Amsterdam was little more than eighty years old : but its solvency had stood severe tests. Even in the terrible crisis of 1672, when the whole Delta of the Rhine was overrun by the French armies, when the white flags were seen from the top of the Stadthouse, there was one place where, amidst the general consternation and confusion, tranquillity and order were still to be found ; and that place was the Bank. Why should not the Bank of London be as great and as durable as the Banks of Genoa and of Amsterdam ? Before the end of the reign of Charles the Second several plans were proposed, examined, attacked and defended. Some pamphleteers maintained that a national bank ought to be under the direction of the King. Others thought that the management ought to be entrusted to the Lord Mayor, Aldermen and Common Council of the capital.* After the Revolution the subject was discussed with an animation before unknown. For, under the influence of liberty, the breed of political projectors multiplied exceedingly. A crowd of plans, some of which resemble the fancies of a child or the dreams of a man in a fever, were pressed on the government. Preeminently conspicuous among the political mountebanks, whose busy faces were seen every day in the lobby of the House of Commons, were John Briscoe and Hugh Chamberlayne, two projectors worthy to have been members of that Academy which Gulliver found at Lagado. These men affirmed that the one cure for every distemper of the State was a Land Bank. A Land Bank would work for England miracles such as had never been wrought for Israel, miracles exceeding the heaps of quails and the daily shower of manna. There would be no taxes ; and yet the Exchequer would be full to overflowing. There would be no poor rates : for there would be no poor. The income of every landowner would be doubled. The profits of every merchant would be increased. In short, the island would, to use Briscoe's words, be the paradise of the world. The only losers would be the moneyed men, those worst enemies of the nation, who had done more injury to the gentry and yeomanry than an invading army from France would have had the heart to do.†

* See a pamphlet entitled Corporation Credit ; or a Bank of Credit, made Current by Common Consent in London, more Useful and Safe than Money.

† A proposal by Dr. Hugh Chamberlayne, in Essex Street, for a Bank of Secure Current Credit to be founded upon Land, in order to the General Good of Landed Men, to the great Increase in the Value of Land, and the

These blessed effects the Land Bank was to produce simply by issuing enormous quantities of notes on landed security. The doctrine of the projectors was that every person who had real property ought to have, besides that property, paper money to the full value of that property. Thus, if his estate was worth two thousand pounds, he ought to have his estate and two thousand pounds in paper money.* Both Briscoe and Chamberlayne treated with the greatest contempt the notion that there could be an overissue of paper as long as there was, for every ten pound note, a piece of land in the country worth ten pounds. Nobody, they said, would accuse a goldsmith of overissuing as long as his vaults contained guineas and crowns to the full value of all the notes which bore his signature. Indeed no goldsmith had in his vaults guineas and crowns to the full value of all his paper. And was not a square mile of rich land in Taunton Dean at least as well entitled to be called wealth as a bag of gold or silver? The projectors could not deny that many people had a prejudice in favour of the precious metals, and that therefore, if the Land Bank were bound to cash its notes, it would very soon stop payment. This difficulty they got over by proposing that the notes should be inconvertible, and that every body should be forced to take them.

The speculations of Chamberlayne on the subject of the currency may possibly find admirers even in our own time. But

---

no less Benefit of Trade and Commerce, 1695 ; Proposals for the supplying their Majesties with Money on Easy Terms, exempting the Nobility, Gentry, &c., from Taxes, enlarging their Yearly Estates, and enriching all the Subjects of the Kingdom by a National Land Bank ; by John Briscoe. "O fortunatos nimium bona si sua norint Anglicanos." Third Edition, 1696. Briscoe seems to have been as much versed in Latin literature as in political economy.

* In confirmation of what is said in the text, I extract a single paragraph from Briscoe's proposals. "Admit a gentleman hath barely 100*l.* per annum estate to live on, and hath a wife and four children to provide for: this person, supposing no taxes were upon his estates, must be a great husband to be able to keep his charge, but cannot think of laying up anything to place out his children in the world : but according to this proposed method he may give his children 500*l.* a piece and have 90*l.* per annum left for himself and his wife to live upon, the which he may also leave to such of his children as he pleases after his and his wife's decease. For first having settled his estate of 100*l.* per annum, as in proposals 1. 3., he may have bills of credit for 2000*l.* for his own proper use, for 10*s.* per cent. per annum, as in proposal 22., which is but 10*l.* per annum for the 2000*l.*, which being deducted out of his estate of 100*l.* per annum, there remains 90*l.* per annum clear to himself." It ought to be observed that this nonsense reached a third edition.

to his other errors he added an error which began and ended with him. He was fool enough to take it for granted, in all his reasonings, that the value of an estate varied directly as the duration. He maintained that if the annual income derived from a manor were a thousand pounds, a grant of that manor for twenty years must be worth twenty thousand pounds, and a grant for a hundred years worth a hundred thousand pounds. If, therefore, the lord of such a manor would pledge it for a hundred years to the Land Bank, the Land Bank might, on that security, instantly issue notes for a hundred thousand pounds. On this subject Chamberlayne was proof to ridicule, to argument, even to arithmetical demonstration. He was reminded that the fee simple of land would not sell for more than twenty years' purchase. To say, therefore, that a term of a hundred years was worth five times as much as a term of twenty years, was to say that a term of a hundred years was worth five times the fee simple; in other words, that a hundred was five times infinity. Those who reasoned thus were refuted by being told that they were usurers; and it should seem that a large number of country gentlemen thought the refutation complete.*

In December 1693 Chamberlayne laid his plan, in all its naked absurdity, before the Commons, and petitioned to be heard. He confidently undertook to raise eight thousand pounds on every freehold estate of a hundred and fifty pounds a year which should be brought, as he expressed it, into his Land Bank, and this without dispossessing the freeholder.†

* See Chamberlayne's Proposal, his Positions supported by the Reasons explaining the Office of Land Credit, and his Bank Dialogue. See also an excellent little tract on the other side entitled "A Bank Dialogue between Dr. H. C. and a Country Gentleman, 1696," and "Some Remarks upon a nameless and scurrilous Libel entitled a Bank Dialogue between Dr. H. C. and a Country Gentleman, in a Letter to a Person of Quality."

† Commons' Journals, Dec. 7. 1693. I am afraid that I may be suspected of exaggerating the absurdity of this scheme. I therefore transcribe the most important part of the petition. "In consideration of the freeholders bringing their lands into this bank, for a fund of current credit, to be established by Act of Parliament, it is now proposed that, for every 150*l.* per annum, secured for 150 years, for but one hundred yearly payments of 100*l.* per annum, free from all manner of taxes and deductions whatsoever, every such freeholder shall receive 4000*l.* in the said current credit, and shall have 2000*l.* more put into the fishery stock for his proper benefit; and there may be further 2000*l.* reserved at the Parliament's disposal towards the carrying on this present war. . . . . The freeholder is never to quit the possession of his said estate unless the yearly rent happens to be in arrear."

All the squires in the House must have known that the fee simple of such an estate would hardly fetch three thousand pounds in the market. That less than the fee simple of such an estate could, by any device, be made to produce eight thousand pounds, would, it might have been thought, have seemed incredible to the most illiterate foxhunter that could be found on the benches. Distress, however, and animosity had made the landed gentlemen credulous. They insisted on referring Chamberlayne's plan to a committee; and the committee reported that the plan was practicable, and would tend to the benefit of the nation.* But by this time the united force of demonstration and derision had begun to produce an effect even on the most ignorant rustics in the House. The report lay unnoticed on the table; and the country was saved from a calamity compared with which the defeat of Landen and the loss of the Smyrna fleet would have been blessings.

All the projectors of this busy time, however, were not so absurd as Chamberlayne. One among them, William Paterson. was an ingenious, though not always a judicious, speculator. Of his early life little is known except that he was a native of Scotland, and that he had been in the West Indies. In what character he had visited the West Indies was a matter about which his contemporaries differed. His friends said that he had been a missionary; his enemies that he had been a buccaneer. He seems to have been gifted by nature with fertile invention, an ardent temperament and great powers of persuasion, and to have acquired somewhere in the course of his vagrant life a perfect knowledge of accounts.

This man submitted to the government, in 1691, a plan of a national bank; and his plan was favourably received both by statesmen and by merchants. But years passed away; and nothing was done, till, in the spring of 1694, it became absolutely necessary to find some new mode of defraying the charges of the war. Then at length the scheme devised by the poor and obscure Scottish adventurer was taken up in earnest by Montague. With Montague was closely allied Michael Godfrey, the brother of that Sir Edmondsbury Godfrey whose sad and mysterious death had, fifteen years before, produced a terrible outbreak of popular feeling. Michael was one of the ablest, most upright and most opulent of the merchant princes of London. He was, as might have been expected from his near connection with the martyr of the

* Commons' Journals, Feb. 5. 169¾.

Protestant faith, a zealous Whig. Some of his writings are still extant, and prove him to have had a strong and clear mind.

By these two distinguished men Paterson's scheme was fathered. Montague undertook to manage the House of Commons, Godfrey to manage the City. An approving vote was obtained from the Committee of Ways and Means; and a bill, the title of which gave occasion to many sarcasms, was laid on the table. It was indeed not easy to guess that a bill, which purported only to impose a new duty on tonnage for the benefit of such persons as should advance money towards carrying on the war, was really a bill creating the greatest commercial institution that the world had ever seen.

The plan was that twelve hundred thousand pounds should be borrowed by the government on what was then considered as the moderate interest of eight per cent. In order to induce capitalists to advance the money promptly on terms so favourable to the public, the subscribers were to be incorporated by the name of the Governor and Company of the Bank of England. The corporation was to have no exclusive privilege, and was to be restricted from trading in any thing but bills of exchange, bullion and forfeited pledges.

As soon as the plan became generally known, a paper war broke out as furious as that between the swearers and the non-swearers, or as that between the Old East India Company and the New East India Company. The projectors who had failed to gain the ear of the government fell like madmen on their more fortunate brother. All the goldsmiths and pawnbrokers set up a howl of rage. Some discontented Tories predicted ruin to the monarchy. It was remarkable, they said, that Banks and Kings had never existed together. Banks were republican institutions. There were flourishing banks at Venice, at Genoa, at Amsterdam and at Hamburg. But who had ever heard of a Bank of France or a Bank of Spain?* Some discontented Whigs, on the other hand, predicted ruin to our liberties. Here, they said, is an instrument of tyranny more formidable than the High Commission, than the Star Chamber, than even the fifty thousand soldiers of Oliver. The whole wealth of the nation will be in the hands of the Tonnage Bank,—such was the nickname then in use;—and the Tonnage Bank will be in the hands of the Sovereign. The power of the purse, the one great security for all the rights of Englishmen, will be transferred from the House of Commons to the

* Account of the Intended Bank of England, 1694.

Governor and Directors of the new Company. This last consideration was really of some weight, and was allowed to be so by the authors of the bill. A clause was therefore most properly inserted which inhibited the Bank from advancing money to the Crown without authority from Parliament. Every infraction of this salutary rule was to be punished by forfeiture of three times the sum advanced; and it was provided that the King should not have power to remit any part of the penalty.

The plan, thus amended, received the sanction of the Commons more easily than might have been expected from the violence of the adverse clamour. In truth, the Parliament was under duress. Money must be had, and could in no other way be had so easily. What took place when the House had resolved itself into a committee cannot be discovered: but, while the Speaker was in the chair, no division took place.

The bill, however, was not safe when it had reached the Upper House. Some Lords suspected that the plan of a national bank had been devised for the purpose of exalting the moneyed interest at the expense of the landed interest. Others thought that this plan, whether good or bad, ought not to have been submitted to them in such a form. Whether it would be safe to call into existence a body which might one day rule the whole commercial world, and how such a body should be constituted, were questions which ought not to be decided by one branch of the Legislature The Peers ought to be at perfect liberty to examine all the details of the proposed scheme, to suggest amendments, to ask for conferences. It was therefore most unfair that the law establishing the Bank should be sent up as part of a law granting supplies to the Crown. The Jacobites entertained some hope that the session would end with a quarrel between the Houses, that the Tonnage Bill would be lost, and that William would enter on the campaign without money. It was already May, according to the New Style. The London season was over; and many noble families had left Covent Garden and Soho Square for their woods and hayfields. But summonses were sent out. There was a violent rush back to town. The benches which had lately been deserted were crowded. The sittings began at an hour unusually early, and were prolonged to an hour unusually late. On the day on which the bill was committed the contest lasted without intermission from nine in the morning till six in the evening. Godolphin was in the chair. Nottingham and Rochester proposed to strike out all the clauses which related to the Bank. Something was said about the danger of setting up a gigantic corporation which might soon give law to the King and the three Estates of the Realm. But the Peers seemed to be most moved by the appeal which was made to them as landlords. The whole scheme, it was asserted, was intended to enrich usurers at the expense of the nobility and gentry. Persons who had laid by money would rather put it into the Bank than lend it on mortgage at moderate interest. Caermarthen said little or nothing in defence of what was, in truth, the work of his rivals and enemies. He owned that there were grave objections to the mode in which the Commons had provided for the public service of the year. But would their Lordships amend a money bill? Would they engage in a contest of which the end must be that they must either yield, or incur the grave responsibility of leaving the Channel without a fleet during the summer? This argument prevailed; and, on a division, the amendment was rejected by forty-three votes to thirty-one. A few hours later the bill received the royal assent, and the Parliament was prorogued.*

In the City the success of Montague's plan was complete. It was then at least as difficult to raise a million at eight per cent. as it would now be to raise thirty millions at four per cent. It had been supposed that contributions would drop in very slowly; and a considerable time had therefore been allowed by the Act. This indulgence was not needed. So popular was the new investment that on the day on which the books were opened three hundred thousand pounds were subscribed: three hundred thousand more were subscribed during the next forty-eight hours; and, in ten days, to the delight of all the friends of the government, it was announced that the list was full. The whole sum which the Corporation was bound to lend to the State was paid into the Exchequer before the first instalment was due.† Somers gladly put the Great Seal to a charter framed in conformity with the terms prescribed by Parliament; and the Bank of England commenced its operations in the house of the Company of Grocers. There, during many years, directors, secretaries and clerks might be seen labouring in different parts of one spacious hall. The persons employed by the Bank were originally only fifty-four. They are now nine hundred. The sum paid yearly in salaries amounted at first to only four thousand three hundred and

* See the Lords' Journals of April 23, 24, 25. 1694, and the letter of L'Hermitage to the States General dated $\frac{\text{April 24.}}{\text{May 4.}}$

† Narcissus Luttrell's Diary, June 1694.

fifty pounds. It now exceeds two hundred and ten thousand pounds. We may therefore fairly infer that the incomes of commercial clerks are, on an average, about three times as large in the reign of Victoria as they were in the reign of William the Third.*

It soon appeared that Montague had, by skilfully availing himself of the financial difficulties of the country, rendered an inestimable service to his party. During several generations the Bank of England was emphatically a Whig body. It was Whig, not accidentally, but necessarily. It must have instantly stopped payment if it had ceased to receive the interest on the sum which it had advanced to the government; and of that interest James would not have paid one farthing. Seventeen years after the passing of the Tonnage Bill, Addison, in one of his most ingenious and graceful little allegories, described the situation of the great Company through which the immense wealth of London was constantly circulating. He saw Public Credit on her throne in Grocers' Hall, the Great Charter over her head, the Act of Settlement full in her view. Her touch turned every thing to gold. Behind her seat, bags filled with coin were piled up to the ceiling. On her right and on her left the floor was hidden by pyramids of guineas. On a sudden the door flies open. The Pretender rushes in, a sponge in one hand, in the other a sword which he shakes at the Act of Settlement. The beautiful Queen sinks down fainting. The spell by which she has turned all things around her into treasure is broken. The money bags shrink like pricked bladders. The piles of gold pieces are turned into bundles of rags or faggots of wooden tallies.† The truth which this parable was meant to convey was constantly present to the minds of the rulers of the Bank. So closely was their interest bound up with the interest of the government that the greater the public danger the more ready were they to come to the rescue. In old times, when the Treasury was empty, when the taxes came in slowly, and when the pay of the soldiers and sailors was in arrear, it had been necessary for the Chancellor of the Exchequer to go, hat in hand, up and down Cheapside and Cornhill, attended by the Lord Mayor and by the Aldermen, and to make up a sum by borrowing a hundred pounds from this hosier, and two hundred pounds from that ironmonger.‡

* Heath's Account of the Worshipful Company of Grocers; Francis's History of the Bank of England.
† Spectator, No. 3.
‡ Proceedings of the Wednesday Club in Friday Street.

Those times were over. The government, instead of laboriously scooping up supplies from numerous petty sources, could now draw whatever it required from an immense reservoir, which all those petty sources kept constantly replenished. It is hardly too much to say that, during many years, the weight of the Bank, which was constantly in the scale of the Whigs, almost counterbalanced the weight of the Church, which was as constantly in the scale of the Tories.

A few minutes after the bill which established the Bank of England had received the royal assent, the Parliament was prorogued by the King with a speech in which he warmly thanked the Commons for their liberality. Montague was immediately rewarded for his services with the place of Chancellor of the Exchequer.*

Shrewsbury had a few weeks before consented to accept the seals. He had held out resolutely from November to March. While he was trying to find excuses which might satisfy his political friends, Sir James Montgomery visited him. Montgomery was now the most miserable of human beings. Having borne a great part in a great Revolution, having been charged with the august office of presenting the Crown of Scotland to the Sovereigns whom the Estates had chosen, having domineered without a rival, during several months, in the Parliament at Edinburgh, having seen before him in near prospect the seals of Secretary, the coronet of an Earl, ample wealth, supreme power, he had on a sudden sunk into obscurity and abject penury. His fine parts still remained ; and he was therefore used by the Jacobites : but, though used, he was despised, distrusted and starved. He passed his life in wandering from England to France and from France back to England, without finding a resting place in either country. Sometimes he waited in the antechamber at Saint Germains, where the priests scowled at him as a Calvinist, and where even the Protestant Jacobites cautioned one another in whispers against the old Republican. Sometimes he lay hid in the garrets of London, imagining that every footstep which he heard on the stairs was that of a bailiff with a writ, or that of a King's messenger with a warrant. He now obtained access to Shrewsbury, and ventured to talk as a Jacobite to a brother Jacobite. Shrewsbury, who was not at all inclined to put his estate and his neck in the power of a man whom he knew to be both rash and perfidious, returned very guarded answers. Through some channel which is not known to us, William obtained full intelligence of what had passed on this

* Lords' Journals, April 25. 1694 ; London Gazette, May 7. 1694.

occasion.  He sent for Shrewsbury, and again spoke earnestly about the secretaryship.  Shrewsbury again excused himself. His health, he said, was bad.  "That," said William, "is not your only reason."  "No, Sir," said Shrewsbury, "it is not." And he began to speak of public grievances, and alluded to the fate of the Triennial Bill, which he had himself introduced. But William cut him short.  "There is another reason behind. When did you see Montgomery last?"  Shrewsbury was thunderstruck.  The King proceeded to repeat some things which Montgomery had said.  By this time Shrewsbury had recovered from his dismay, and had recollected that, in the conversation which had been so accurately reported to the government, he had fortunately uttered no treason, though he had heard much. "Sir," said he, "since Your Majesty has been so correctly informed, you must be aware that I gave no encouragement to that man's attempts to seduce me from my allegiance." William did not deny this, but intimated that such secret dealings with noted Jacobites raised suspicions which Shrewsbury could remove only by accepting the seals.  "That," he said, "will put me quite at ease.  I know that you are a man of honour, and that, if you undertake to serve me, you will serve me faithfully."  So pressed, Shrewsbury complied, to the great joy of his whole party ; and was immediately rewarded for his compliance with a dukedom and a garter.*

Thus a Whig ministry was gradually forming.  There were now two Whig Secretaries of State, a Whig Keeper of the Great Seal, a Whig First Lord of the Admiralty, a Whig Chancellor of the Exchequer.  The Lord Privy Seal, Pembroke, might also be called a Whig : for his mind was one which readily took the impress of any stronger mind with which it was brought into contact.  Seymour, having been long enough a Commissioner of the Treasury to lose much of his influence with the Tory country gentlemen who had once listened to him as to an oracle, was dismissed ; and his place was filled by John Smith, a zealous and able Whig, who had taken an active part in the debates of the late session.†  The only Tories who still held great offices in the executive government were the Lord President, Caermarthen, who, though he began to feel that power was slipping from his grasp, still clutched it desperately, and the first Lord of the Treasury, Godolphin, who meddled

* Life of James, ii. 520. ; Floyd's (Lloyd's) Account in the Nairne Papers, under the date of May 1. 1694 ; London Gazette, April 26. 30. 1694.

† London Gazette, May 3. 1694.

little out of his own department, and performed the duties of that department with skill and assiduity.

William, however, still tried to divide his favours between the two parties. Though the Whigs were fast drawing to themselves the substance of power, the Tories obtained their share of honorary distinctions. Mulgrave, who had, during the late session, exerted his great parliamentary talents in favour of the King's policy, was created Marquess of Normanby, and named a Cabinet Councillor, but was never consulted. He obtained at the same time a pension of three thousand pounds a year. Caermarthen, whom the late changes had deeply mortified, was in some degree consoled by a signal mark of royal approbation. He became Duke of Leeds. It had taken him little more than twenty years to climb from the station of a Yorkshire country gentleman to the highest rank in the peerage. Two great Whig Earls were at the same time created Dukes, Bedford and Devonshire. It ought to be mentioned that Bedford had repeatedly refused the dignity which he now somewhat reluctantly accepted. He declared that he preferred his Earldom to a Dukedom, and gave a very sensible reason for the preference. An Earl who had a numerous family might send one son to the Temple and another to a counting house in the city. But the sons of a Duke were all lords; and a lord could not make his bread either at the bar or on Change. The old man's objections, however, were overcome; and the two great houses of Russell and Cavendish, which had long been closely connected by friendship and by marriage, by common opinions, common sufferings and common triumphs, received on the same day the greatest honour which it is in the power of the Crown to confer.*

The Gazette which announced these creations announced also that the King had set out for the Continent. He had, before his departure, consulted with his ministers about the means of counteracting a plan of naval operations which had been formed by the French government. Hitherto the maritime war had been carried on chiefly in the Channel and the Atlantic. But Lewis had now determined to concentrate his maritime forces in the Mediterranean. He hoped that, with their help, the army of Marshal Noailles would be able to take Barcelona, to subdue the whole of Catalonia, and to compel Spain to sue for peace. Accordingly, Tourville's squadron, consisting of fifty-

* London Gazette, April 30. May 7. 1694; Shrewsbury to William, May $\frac{1}{2}$1; William to Shrewsbury, $\frac{May\ 22}{June\ 1}$; L'Hermitage, $\frac{April\ 27.}{May\ 7.}$

three men of war, set sail from Brest on the twenty-fifth of April and passed the Straits of Gibraltar on the fourth of May.

William, in order to cross the designs of the enemy, determined to send Russell to the Mediterranean with the greater part of the combined fleet of England and Holland. A squadron was to remain in the British seas under the command of the Earl of Berkeley. Talmash was to embark on board of this squadron with a large body of troops, and was to attack Brest, which would, it was supposed, in the absence of Tourville and his fifty-three vessels, be an easy conquest.

That preparations were making at Portsmouth for an expedition, in which the land forces were to bear a part, could not be kept a secret. There was much speculation at the Rose and at Garraway's touching the destination of the armament. Some talked of Rhe, some of Oleron, some of Rochelle, some of Rochefort. Many, till the fleet actually began to move westward, believed that it was bound for Dunkirk. Many guessed that Brest would be the point of attack; but they only guessed this: for the secret was much better kept than most of the secrets of that age.* Russell, till he was ready to weigh anchor, persisted in assuring his Jacobite friends that he knew nothing. His discretion was proof even against all the arts of Marlborough. Marlborough, however, had other sources of intelligence. To those sources he applied himself; and he at length succeeded in discovering the whole plan of the government. He instantly wrote to James. He had, he said, but that moment ascertained that twelve regiments of infantry and two regiments of marines were about to embark, under the command of Talmash, for the purpose of destroying the harbour of Brest and the shipping which lay there. "This," he added, "would be a great advantage to England. But no consideration can, or ever shall, hinder me from letting you know what I think may be for your service." He then proceeded to caution James against Russell. "I endeavoured to learn this some time ago from him: but he always denied it to me, though I am very sure that he knew the design for more than six weeks. This gives me a bad sign of this man's intentions."

The intelligence sent by Marlborough to James was com-

---

* L'Hermitage, May $\frac{18}{28}$. After mentioning the various reports, he says, "De tous ces divers projets qu'on s'imagine aucun n'est venu à la cognoissance du public." This is important: for it has often been said, in excuse for Marlborough, that he communicated to the Court of Saint Germains only what was the talk of all the coffeehouses, and must have been known without his instrumentality.

municated by James to the French government. That government took its measures with characteristic promptitude. Promptitude was indeed necessary; for, when Marlborough's letter was written, the preparations at Portsmouth were all but complete : and, if the wind had been favourable to the English, the objects of the expedition might have been attained without a struggle. But adverse gales detained our fleet in the Channel during another month. Meanwhile a large body of troops was collected at Brest. Vauban was charged with the duty of putting the defences in order; and, under his skilful direction, batteries were planted which commanded every spot where it seemed likely that an invader would attempt to land. Eight large rafts, each carrying many mortars, were moored in the harbour, and, some days before the English arrived, all was ready for their reception.

On the sixth of June the whole allied fleet was on the Atlantic about fifteen leagues west of Cape Finisterre. There Russell and Berkeley parted company. Russell proceeded towards the Mediterranean. Berkeley's squadron, with the troops on board, steered for the coast of Brittany, and anchored just without Camaret Bay, close to the mouth of the harbour of Brest. Talmash proposed to land in Camaret Bay. It was therefore desirable to ascertain with accuracy the state of the coast. The eldest son of the Duke of Leeds, now called Marquess of Caermarthen, undertook to enter the basin and to obtain the necessary information. The passion of this brave and eccentric young man for maritime adventure was unconquerable. He had solicited and obtained the rank of Rear Admiral, and had accompanied the expedition in his own yacht, the Peregrine, renowned as the masterpiece of shipbuilding, and more than once already mentioned in this history. Cutts, who had distinguished himself by his intrepidity in the Irish war, and had been rewarded with an Irish peerage, offered to accompany Caermarthen. Lord Mohun, who, desirous, it may be hoped, to efface by honourable exploits the stain which a shameful and disastrous brawl had left on his name, was serving with the troops as a volunteer, insisted on being of the party. The Peregrine went into the bay with its gallant crew, and came out safe, but not without having run great risks. Caermarthen reported that the defences, of which however he had seen only a small part, were formidable. But Berkeley and Talmash suspected that he overrated the danger. They were not aware that their design had long been known at Versailles, that an army had been collected to oppose them, and that the greatest engineer in the world had been employed to fortify the coast against them.    They therefore did not doubt that their troops might easily be put on shore under the protection of a fire from the ships.    On the following morning Caermarthen was ordered to enter the bay with eight vessels and to batter the French works.    Talmash was to follow with about a hundred boats full of soldiers.    It soon appeared that the enterprise was even more perilous than it had on the preceding day appeared to be.    Batteries which had then escaped notice opened on the ships a fire so murderous that several decks were soon cleared.    Great bodies of foot and horse were discernible; and, by their uniforms, they appeared to be regular troops. The young Rear Admiral sent an officer in all haste to warn Talmash.    But Talmash was so completely possessed by the notion that the French were not prepared to repel an attack that he disregarded all cautions and would not even trust his own eyes.    He felt sure that the force which he saw assembled on the shore was a mere rabble of peasants, who had been brought together in haste from the surrounding country. Confident that these mock soldiers would run like sheep before real soldiers, he ordered his men to pull for the beach. He was soon undeceived.    A terrible fire mowed down his troops faster than they could get on shore.    He had himself scarcely sprung on dry ground when he received a wound in the thigh from a cannon ball, and was carried back to his skiff.    His men reembarked in confusion.    Ships and boats made haste to get out of the bay, but did not succeed till four hundred seamen and seven hundred soldiers had fallen. During many days the waves continued to throw up pierced and shattered corpses on the beach of Brittany.    The battery from which Talmash received his wound is called, to this day, the Englishman's Death.

The unhappy general was laid on his couch; and a council of war was held in his cabin.    He was for going straight into the harbour of Brest and bombarding the town.    But this suggestion, which indicated but too clearly that his judgment had been affected by the irritation of a wounded body and a wounded mind, was wisely rejected by the naval officers.    The armament returned to Portsmouth.    There Talmash died, exclaiming with his last breath that he had been lured into a snare by treachery.    The public grief and indignation were loudly expressed.    The nation remembered the services of the unfortunate general, forgave his rashness, pitied his sufferings, and execrated the unknown traitors whose machinations had been fatal to him. There were many conjectures and many rumours. Some sturdy Englishmen, misled by national prejudice, swore that none of our plans would ever be kept a secret from the enemy while French refugees were in high military command. Some zealous Whigs, misled by party spirit, muttered that the Court of Saint Germains would never want good intelligence while a single Tory remained in the Cabinet Council. The real criminal was not named; nor, till the archives of the House of Stuart were explored, was it known to the world that Talmash had perished by the basest of all the hundred villanies of Marlborough.*

Yet never had Marlborough been less a Jacobite than at the moment when he rendered this wicked and shameful service to the Jacobite cause. It may be confidently affirmed that to serve the banished family was not his object, and that to ingratiate himself with the banished family was only his secondary object. His primary object was to force himself into the service of the existing government, and to regain possession of those important and lucrative places from which he had been dismissed more than two years before. He knew that the country and the Parliament would not patiently bear to see the English army commanded by foreign generals. Two Englishmen only had shown themselves fit for high military posts, himself and Talmash. If Talmash were defeated and disgraced, William would scarcely have a choice. In fact, as soon as it was known that the expedition had failed, and that Talmash was no more, the general cry was that the King ought to receive into his favour the accomplished Captain who had done such good service at Walcourt, at Cork and at Kinsale. Nor can we blame the multitude for raising this cry. For every body knew that Marlborough was an eminently brave, skilful and successful officer: but very few persons knew that he had, while commanding William's troops, while sitting in William's council, while waiting in William's bedchamber, formed a most artful and dangerous plot for the subversion of William's throne; and still fewer suspected the real author of the recent calamity, of the slaughter in the Bay of Camaret, of the melancholy fate of Talmash. The effect therefore of the foulest of all treasons was to raise the traitor in public estimation. Nor was he

* London Gazette, June 14. 18. 1694; Paris Gazette, $\frac{June\ 16.}{July\ 3.}$; Burchett; Journal of Lord Caermarthen; Baden, June $\frac{1\ 5}{2\ 6}$.; L'Hermitage, June s. $\frac{1\ 9}{2\ 9}$.

wanting to himself at this conjuncture. While the Royal Exchange was in consternation at this disaster of which he was the cause, while many families were clothing themselves in mourning for the brave men of whom he was the murderer, he repaired to Whitehall ; and there, doubtless with all that grace, that nobleness, that suavity, under which lay, hidden from all common observers, a seared conscience and a remorseless heart, he professed himself the most devoted, the most loyal, of all the subjects of William and Mary, and expressed a hope that he might, in this emergency, be permitted to offer his sword to their Majesties. Shrewsbury was very desirous that the offer should be accepted : but a short and dry answer from William, who was then in the Netherlands, put an end for the present to all negotiation. About Talmash the King expressed himself with generous tenderness. " The poor fellow's fate," he wrote, " has affected me much. I do not indeed think that he managed well : but it was his ardent desire to distinguish himself that impelled him to attempt impossibilities." *

The armament which had returned to Portsmouth soon sailed again for the coast of France, but achieved only exploits worse than inglorious. An attempt was made to blow up the pier at Dunkirk. Some towns inhabited by quiet tradesmen and fishermen were bombarded. In Dieppe scarcely a house was left standing : a third part of Havre was laid in ashes ; and shells were thrown into Calais which destroyed thirty private dwellings. The French and the Jacobites loudly exclaimed against the cowardice and barbarity of making war on an unwarlike population. The English government vindicated itself by reminding the world of the sufferings of the thrice wasted Palatinate ; and, as against Lewis and the flatterers of Lewis, the vindication was complete. But whether it were consistent with humanity and with sound policy to visit the crimes which an absolute Prince and a ferocious soldiery had committed in the Palatinate on shopkeepers and labourers, on women and children, who did not know that the Palatinate existed, may perhaps be doubted.

Meanwhile Russell's fleet was rendering good service to the common cause. Adverse winds had impeded his progress through the Straits so long that he did not reach Carthagena till the middle of July. By that time the progress of the French arms had spread terror even to the Escurial. Noailles

* Shrewsbury to William, June $\frac{15}{25}$. 1694. William to Shrewsbur July 1. ; Shrewsbury to William, $\frac{\text{June 22.}}{\text{July 2.}}$

had, on the banks of the Tar, routed an army commanded by the Viceroy of Catalonia ; and, on the day on which this victory was won, the Brest squadron had joined the Toulon squadron in the Bay of Rosas. Palamos, attacked at once by land and sea, was taken by storm. Gerona capitulated after a faint show of resistance. Ostalric surrendered at the first summons. Barcelona would in all probability have fallen, had not the French Admirals learned that the conquerors of La Hogue was approaching. They instantly quitted the coast of Catalonia, and never thought themselves safe till they had taken shelter under the batteries of Toulon.

The Spanish government expressed warm gratitude for this seasonable assistance, and presented to the English Admiral a jewel which was popularly said to be worth near twenty thousand pounds sterling. There was no difficulty in finding such a jewel among the hoards of gorgeous trinkets which had been left by Charles the Fifth and Philip the Second to a degenerate race. But, in all that constitutes the true wealth of states, Spain was poor indeed. Her treasury was empty : her arsenals were unfurnished : her ships were so rotten that they seemed likely to fly asunder at the discharge of their own guns. Her ragged and starving soldiers often mingled with the crowd of beggars at the doors of convents, and battled there for a mess of pottage and a crust of bread. Russell underwent those trials which no English commander whose hard fate it has been to cooperate with Spaniards has escaped. The Viceroy of Catalonia promised much, did nothing, and expected every thing. He declared that three hundred and fifty thousand rations were ready to be served out to the fleet at Carthagena. It turned out that there were not in all the stores of that port provisions sufficient to victual a single frigate for a single week. Yet His Excellency thought himself entitled to complain because England had not sent an army as well as a fleet, and because the heretic Admiral did not choose to expose the fleet to utter destruction by attacking the French under the guns of Toulon. Russell implored the Spanish authorities to look well to their dockyards, and to try to have, by the next spring, a small squadron which might at least be able to float ; but he could not prevail on them to careen a single ship. He could with difficulty obtain, on hard conditions, permission to send a few of his sick men to marine hospitals on shore. Yet, in spite of all the trouble given him by the imbecility and ingratitude of a government which has generally caused more annoyance to its allies than to its enemies, he acquitted himself well. It is but just to him to say that, from the time at which he became First Lord of the Admiralty, there was a decided improvement in the naval administration. Though he lay with his fleet many months near an inhospitable shore, and at a great distance from England, there were no complaints about the quality or the quantity of provisions. The crews had better food and drink than they had ever had before : comforts which Spain did not afford were supplied from home ; and yet the charge was not greater than when, in Torrington's time, the sailor was poisoned with mouldy biscuit and nauseous beer.

As almost the whole maritime force of France was in the Mediterranean, and as it seemed likely that an attempt would be made on Barcelona in the following year, Russell received orders to winter at Cadiz. In October he sailed to that port ; and there he employed himself in refitting his ships with an activity unintelligible to the Spanish functionaries, who calmly suffered the miserable remains of what had once been the greatest navy in the world to rot under their eyes.*

Along the eastern frontier of France the war during this year seemed to languish. In Piedmont and on the Rhine the most important events of the campaign were petty skirmishes and predatory incursions. Lewis remained at Versailles, and sent his son, the Dauphin, to represent him in the Netherlands : but the Dauphin was placed under the tutelage of Luxemburg, and proved a most submissive pupil. During several months the hostile armies observed each other. The allies made one bold push with the intention of carrying the war into the French territory : but Luxemburg, by a forced march, which excited the admiration of persons versed in the military art, frustrated the design. William on the other hand succeeded in taking Huy, then a fortress of the third rank. No battle was fought : no important town was besieged : but the confederates were satisfied with their campaign. Of the four previous years every one had been marked by some great disaster. In 1690 Waldeck had been defeated at Fleurus. In 1691 Mons had fallen. In 1692 Namur had been taken in sight of the allied army ; and this calamity had been speedily followed by the defeat of Steinkirk. In 1693 the battle of Landen had been lost ; and Charleroy had submitted to the conqueror. At length in 1694 the tide had begun to turn. The French arms had made no progress. What had

---

* This account of Russell's expedition to the Mediterranean I have taken chiefly from Burchett.

been gained by the allies was indeed not much: but the smallest gain was welcome to those whom a long run of evil fortune had discouraged.

In England, the general opinion was that, notwithstanding the disaster in Camaret Bay, the war was on the whole proceeding satisfactorily both by land and by sea. But some parts of the internal administration excited, during this autumn, much discontent.

Since Trenchard had been appointed Secretary of State, the Jacobite agitators had found their situation much more unpleasant than before. Sidney had been too indulgent and too fond of pleasure to give them much trouble. Nottingham was a diligent and honest minister: but he was as high a Tory as a faithful subject of William and Mary could be: he loved and esteemed many of the nonjurors; and, though he might force himself to be severe when nothing but severity could save the State, he was not extreme to mark the transgressions of his old friends; nor did he encourage talebearers to come to Whitehall with reports of conspiracies. But Trenchard was both an active public servant and an earnest Whig. Even if he had himself been inclined to lenity, he would have been urged to severity by those who surrounded him. He had constantly at his side Hugh Speke and Aaron Smith, men to whom a hunt after a Jacobite was the most exciting of all sports. The cry of the malecontents was that Nottingham had kept his bloodhounds in the leash, but that Trenchard had let them slip. Every honest gentleman who loved the Church and hated the Dutch went in danger of his life. There was a constant bustle at the Secretary's Office, a constant stream of informers coming in, and of messengers with warrants going out. It was said too, that the warrants were often irregularly drawn, that they did not specify the person, that they did not specify the crime, and yet that, under the authority of such instruments as these, houses were entered, desks and cabinets searched, valuable papers carried away, and men of good birth and breeding flung into gaol among felons.* The minister and his agents answered that Westminster Hall was open; that, if any man had been illegally imprisoned, he had only to bring his action; that juries were quite sufficiently disposed to listen to any person who pretended to have been oppressed by cruel and griping men in power, and that, as none of the prisoners whose wrongs were so pathetically described had ventured to resort to this obvious

* Letter to Trenchard, 1694.

and easy mode of obtaining redress, it might fairly be inferred that nothing had been done which could not be justified. The clamour of the malecontents however made a considerable impression on the public mind; and at length, a transaction in which Trenchard was more unlucky than culpable, brought on him and on the government with which he was connected much temporary obloquy.

Among the informers who haunted his office was an Irish vagabond who had borne more than one name and had professed more than one religion. He now called himself Taaffe. He had been a priest of the Roman Catholic Church, and secretary to Adda the Papal Nuncio, but had since the Revolution turned Protestant, had taken a wife, and had distinguished himself by his activity in discovering the concealed property of those Jesuits and Benedictines who, during the late reign, had been quartered in London. The ministers despised him: but they trusted him. They thought that he had, by his apostasy, and by the part which he had borne in the spoliation of the religious orders, cut himself off from all retreat, and that, having nothing but a halter to expect from King James, he must be true to King William.*

This man fell in with a Jacobite agent named Lunt, who had, since the Revolution, been repeatedly employed among the discontented gentry of Cheshire and Lancashire, and who had been privy to those plans of insurrection which had been disconcerted by the battle of the Boyne in 1690, and by the battle of La Hogue in 1692. Lunt had once been arrested on suspicion of treason, but had been discharged for want of legal proof of his guilt. He was a mere hireling, and was, without much difficulty, induced by Taaffe to turn approver. The pair went to Trenchard. Lunt told his story, mentioned the names of some Cheshire and Lancashire squires to whom he had, as he affirmed, carried commissions from Saint Germains, and of others, who had, to his knowledge, formed secret hoards of arms and ammunition. His simple oath would not have been sufficient to support a charge of high treason: but he produced another witness whose evidence seemed to make the case complete. The narrative was plausible and coherent; and indeed, though it may have been embellished by fictions, there can be little doubt that it was in substance true.† Messengers and search warrants were sent

* Burnet, ii. 141, 142.; and Onslow's note; Kingston's True History, 1697.
† See the Life of James, ii. 524.

down to Lancashire. Aaron Smith himself went thither; and
Taaffe went with him. The alarm had been given by some of
the numerous traitors who ate the bread of William. Some of
the accused persons had fled; and others had buried their
sabres and muskets and burned their papers. Nevertheless,
discoveries were made which confirmed Lunt's depositions.
Behind the wainscot of the old mansion of one Roman
Catholic family was discovered a commission signed by James.
Another house, of which the master had absconded, was
strictly searched, in spite of the solemn asseverations of his
wife and his servants that no arms were concealed there.
While the lady, with her hand on her heart, was protesting
on her honour that her husband was falsely accused, the
messengers observed that the back of the chimney did not
seem to be firmly fixed. It was removed, and a heap of
blades such as were used by horse soldiers tumbled out. In
one of the garrets were found, carefully bricked up, thirty
saddles for troopers, as many breastplates, and sixty cavalry
swords. Trenchard and Aaron Smith thought the case
complete; and it was determined that those culprits who
had been apprehended should be tried by a special commission.*

Taaffe now confidently expected to be recompensed for his
services: but he found a cold reception at the Treasury. He
had gone down to Lancashire chiefly in order that he might,
under the protection of a search warrant, pilfer trinkets and
broad pieces from secret drawers. His sleight of hand however had not altogether escaped the observation of his companions. They discovered that he had made free with the
communion plate of the Popish families, whose private hoards
he had assisted in ransacking. When therefore he applied for
reward, he was dismissed, not merely with a refusal, but with
a stern reprimand. He went away mad with greediness and
spite. There was yet one way in which he might obtain both
money and revenge; and that way he took. He made overtures to the friends of the prisoners. He and he alone could
undo what he had done, could save the accused from the
gallows, could cover the accusers with infamy, could drive
from office the Secretary and the Solicitor who were the dread
of all the friends of King James. Loathsome as Taaffe was to
the Jacobites, his offer was not to be slighted. He received
a sum in hand: he was assured that a comfortable annuity
for life should be settled on him when the business was done;

* Kingston; Burnet, ii. 142.

and he was sent down into the country, and kept in strict
seclusion against the day of trial.*

Meanwhile unlicensed pamphlets, in which the Lancashire
plot was classed with Oates's plot, with Dangerfield's plot,
with Fuller's plot, with Young's plot, with Whitney's plot, were
circulated all over the kingdom, and especially in the county
which was to furnish the jury.   Of these pamphlets the longest,
the ablest, and the bitterest, entitled a Letter to Secretary
Trenchard, was commonly ascribed to Ferguson.   It is not
improbable that Ferguson may have furnished some of the
materials, and may have conveyed the manuscript to the press.
But many passages are written with an art and a vigour which
assuredly did not belong to him.   Those who judge by internal
evidence may perhaps think that, in some parts of this remarkable tract, they can discern the last gleam of the malignant
genius of Montgomery.   A few weeks after the appearance of
the Letter he sank, unhonoured and unlamented, into the
grave.†

There were then no printed newspapers except the London
Gazette.   But since the Revolution the newsletter had become
a more important political engine than it had previously been.
The newsletters of one writer named Dyer were widely circulated
in manuscript.   He affected to be a Tory and a High Churchman, and was consequently regarded by the foxhunting lords
of manors, all over the kingdom, as an oracle.   He had already
been twice in prison : but his gains had more than compensated
for his sufferings, and he still persisted in seasoning his intelligence to suit the taste of the country gentlemen.   He now
turned the Lancashire plot into ridicule, declared that the guns
which had been found were old fowling pieces, that the saddles
were meant only for hunting, and that the swords were rusty
reliques of Edge Hill and Marston Moor.‡   The effect produced by all this invective and sarcasm on the public mind
seems to have been great.   Even at the Dutch Embassy, where
assuredly there was no leaning towards Jacobitism, there was
a strong impression that it would be unwise to bring the
prisoners to trial.   In Lancashire and Cheshire the prevailing
sentiments were pity for the accused and hatred of the prosecutors.   The government however persevered.   In October four

* Kingston.   For the fact that a bribe was given to Taaffe, Kingston
cites the evidence taken on oath by the Lords.

† Narcissus Luttrell's Diary, Oct. 6. 1694.

‡ As to Dyer's newsletter, see Narcissus Luttrell's Diary for June and
August 1693, and September 1694.

Judges went down to Manchester. At present the population of that town is made up of persons born in every part of the British Isles, and consequently has no especial sympathy with the landowners, the farmers and the agricultural labourers of the neighbouring districts. But in the seventeenth century the Manchester man was a Lancashire man. His politics were those of his county. For the old Cavalier families of his county he felt a great respect; and he was furious when he thought that some of the best blood of his county was about to be shed by a knot of Roundhead pettifoggers from London. Multitudes of people from the neighbouring villages filled the streets of the town, and saw with grief and indignation the array of drawn swords and loaded carbines which surrounded the culprits. Aaron Smith's arrangements do not seem to have been skilful. The chief counsel for the Crown was Sir William Williams, who, though now well stricken in years and possessed of a great estate, still continued to practise. One fault had thrown a dark shade over the latter part of his life. The recollection of that day on which he had stood up in Westminster Hall, amidst laughter and hooting, to defend the dispensing power and to attack the right of petition, had, ever since the Revolution, kept him back from honour. He was an angry and disappointed man, and was by no means disposed to incur unpopularity in the cause of a government to which he owed nothing, and from which he hoped nothing.

Of the trial no detailed report has come down to us; but we have both a Whig narrative and a Jacobite narrative.* It seems that the prisoners who were first arraigned did not sever in their challenges, and were consequently tried together. Williams examined or rather crossexamined his own witnesses with a severity which confused them. The crowd which filled the court laughed and clamoured. Lunt in particular became completely bewildered, mistook one person for another, and did not recover himself till the Judges took him out of the hands of the counsel for the Crown. For some of the prisoners an alibi was set up. Evidence was also produced to show, what was undoubtedly quite true, that Lunt was a man of abandoned character. The result however seemed doubtful till, to the dismay of the prosecutors, Taaffe entered the box. He swore with unblushing forehead that the whole

* The Whig narrative is Kingston's; the Jacobite narrative, by an anonymous author, has lately been printed by the Chetham Society. See also a Letter out of Lancashire to a Friend in London, giving some Account of the late Trials, 1694.

story of the plot was a circumstantial lie devised by himself and
Lunt.   Williams threw down his brief ; and, in truth, a more
honest advocate might well have done the same.   The prisoners
who were at the bar were instantly acquitted : those who had
not yet been tried were set at liberty : the witnesses for the
prosecution were pelted out of Manchester : the Clerk of the
Crown narrowly escaped with life ; and the Judges took their
departure amidst hisses and execrations.

A few days after the close of the trials at Manchester William
returned to England.   On the twelfth of November, only forty-
eight hours after his arrival at Kensington, the Houses met.
He congratulated them on the improved aspect of affairs.
Both by land and by sea the events of the year which was
about to close had been, on the whole, favourable to the allies:
the French armies had made no progress : the French fleets
had not ventured to show themselves : nevertheless, a safe and
honourable peace could be obtained only by a vigorous prosecution of the war ; and the war could not be vigorously
prosecuted without large supplies.   William then reminded the
Commons that the Act by which they had settled the tonnage
and poundage on the Crown for four years was about to expire,
and expressed his hope that it would be renewed.

After the King had spoken, the Commons, for some reason
which no writer has explained, adjourned for a week.   Before
they met again, an event took place which caused great sorrow
at the palace, and through all the ranks of the Low Church
party.   Tillotson was taken suddenly ill while attending public
worship in the chapel of Whitehall.   Prompt remedies might
perhaps have saved him : but he would not interrupt the
prayers ; and, before the service was over, his malady was
beyond the reach of medicine.   He was almost speechless :
but his friends long remembered with pleasure a few broken
ejaculations which showed that he enjoyed peace of mind to
the last.   He was buried in the church of Saint Lawrence
Jewry, near Guildhall.   It was there that he had won his
immense oratorical reputation.   He had preached there during
the thirty years which preceded his elevation to the throne of
Canterbury.   His eloquence had attracted to the heart of the
City crowds of the learned and polite, from the Inns of Court
and from the lordly mansions of Saint James's and Soho.
A considerable part of his congregation had generally consisted
of young clergymen, who came to learn the art of preaching at
the feet of him who was universally considered as the first of
preachers.   To this church his remains were now carried

through a mourning population. The hearse was followed by an endless train of splendid equipages from Lambeth through Southwark and over London Bridge. Burnet preached the funeral sermon. His kind and honest heart was overcome by so many tender recollections that, in the midst of his discourse, he paused and burst into tears, while a loud moan of sorrow rose from the whole auditory. The Queen could not speak of her favourite instructor without weeping. Even William was visibly moved. "I have lost," he said, "the best friend that I ever had, and the best man that I ever knew." The only Englishman who is mentioned with tenderness in any part of the great mass of letters which the King wrote to Heinsius is Tillotson. The Archbishop had left a widow. To her William granted a pension of four hundred a year, which he afterwards increased to six hundred. His anxiety that she should receive her income regularly and without stoppages was honourable to him. Every quarterday he ordered the money, without any deduction, to be brought to himself, and immediately sent it to her. Tillotson had bequeathed to her no property, except a great number of manuscript sermons. Such was his fame among his contemporaries that those sermons were purchased by the booksellers for the almost incredible sum of two thousand five hundred guineas, equivalent, in the wretched state in which the silver coin then was, to at least three thousand six hundred pounds. Such a price had never before been given in England for any copyright. About the same time Dryden, whose reputation was then in the zenith, received thirteen hundred pounds for his translation of all the works of Virgil, and was thought to have been splendidly remunerated.*

It was not easy to fill satisfactorily the high place which Tillotson had left vacant. Mary gave her voice for Stillingfleet, and pressed his claims as earnestly as she ever ventured to press any thing. In abilities and attainments he had few superiors among the clergy. But, though he would probably have been considered as a Low Churchman by Jane and South, he was too high a Churchman for William ; and Tenison was appointed. The new primate was not eminently distinguished by eloquence or learning : but he was honest, prudent, laborious and benevolent : he had been a good rector of a large parish and a good bishop of a large diocese : detraction had not yet been busy with his name ; and it might well be thought that a man of plain sense, moderation and integrity, was more

* Birch's Life of Tillotson ; the Funeral Sermon preached by Burnet ; William to Heinsius, $\frac{\text{Nov. 23}}{\text{Dec. 3.}}$ 1694.

likely than a man of brilliant genius and lofty spirit to succeed in the arduous task of quieting a discontented and distracted Church.

Meanwhile the Commons had entered upon business. They cheerfully voted about two million four hundred thousand pounds for the army, and as much for the navy. The land tax for the year was again fixed at four shillings in the pound: the Tonnage Act was renewed for a term of five years; and a fund was established on which the government was authorised to borrow two millions and a half.

Some time was spent by both Houses in discussing the Manchester trials. If the malecontents had been wise, they would have been satisfied with the advantage which they had already gained. Their friends had been set free. The prosecutors had with difficulty escaped from the hands of an enraged multitude. The character of the government had been seriously damaged. The ministers were accused, in prose and in verse, sometimes in earnest and sometimes in jest, of having hired a gang of ruffians to swear away the lives of honest gentlemen. Even moderate politicians, who gave no credit to these foul imputations, owned that Trenchard ought to have remembered the villanies of Fuller and Young, and to have been on his guard against such wretches as Taaffe and Lunt. The unfortunate Secretary's health and spirits had given way. It was said that he was dying; and it was certain that he would not long continue to hold the seals. The Tories had won a great victory; but, in their eagerness to improve it, they turned it into a defeat.

Early in the session Howe complained, with his usual vehemence and asperity, of the indignities to which innocent and honourable men, highly descended and highly esteemed, had been subjected by Aaron Smith and the wretches who were in his pay. The leading Whigs, with great judgment, demanded an inquiry. Then the Tories began to flinch. They well knew that an inquiry could not strengthen their case, and might weaken it. The issue, they said, had been tried: a jury had pronounced: the verdict was definitive; and it would be monstrous to give the false witnesses who had been stoned out of Manchester an opportunity of repeating their lesson. To this argument the answer was obvious. The verdict was definitive as respected the defendants, but not as respected the prosecutors. The prosecutors were now in their turn defendants, and were entitled to all the privileges of defendants. It did not follow, because the Lancashire gentlemen had been found, and very properly found, not guilty of treason, that the Secretary of State or the Solicitor of the Treasury had been guilty of unfairness or even of rashness. The House, by one hundred and nineteen votes to one hundred and two resolved that Aaron Smith and the witnesses on both sides should be ordered to attend. Several days were passed in examination and crossexamination; and sometimes the sittings extended far into the night. It soon became clear that the prosecution had not been lightly instituted, and that some of the persons who had been acquitted had been concerned in treasonable schemes. The Tories would now have been content with a drawn battle: but the Whigs were not disposed to forego their advantage. It was moved that there had been a sufficient ground for the proceedings before the Special Commission; and this motion was carried without a division. The opposition proposed to add some words implying that the witnesses for the Crown had forsworn themselves: but these words were rejected by one hundred and thirty-six votes to one hundred and nine; and it was resolved by one hundred and thirty-three votes to ninety-seven that there had been a dangerous conspiracy. The Lords had meanwhile been deliberating on the same subject, and had come to the same conclusion. They sent Taaffe to prison for prevarication; and they passed resolutions acquitting both the government and the judges of all blame. The public however continued to think that the gentlemen who had been tried at Manchester had been unjustifiably persecuted, till a Jacobite plot of singular atrocity, brought home to the plotters by decisive evidence, produced a violent revulsion of feeling.*

Meanwhile three bills, which had been repeatedly discussed in preceding years, and two of which had been carried in vain to the foot of the throne, had been again brought in; the Place Bill, the Bill for the Regulation of Trials in cases of Treason, and the Triennial Bill.

The Place Bill did not reach the Lords. It was thrice read in the Lower House, but was not passed. At the very last moment it was rejected by a hundred and seventy-five votes to a hundred and forty-two. Howe and Harley were the tellers for the minority.†

---

* See the Journals of the two Houses. The only account that we have of the debates is in the letters of L'Hermitage.

† Commons' Journals, Feb. 20. 169⅘. As this bill never reached the Lords, it is not to be found among their archives. I have therefore no means of discovering whether it differed in any respect from the bill of the preceding year.

The Bill for the Regulation of Trials in cases of Treason went up again to the Peers. Their Lordships again added to it the clause which had formerly been fatal to it. The Commons again refused to grant any new privilege to the hereditary aristocracy. Conferences were again held: reasons were again exchanged: both Houses were again obstinate; and the bill was again lost.*

The Triennial Bill was more fortunate. It was brought in on the first day of the session, and went easily and rapidly through both Houses. The only question about which there was any serious contention was, how long the existing Parliament should be suffered to continue. After several sharp debates November in the year 1696 was fixed as the extreme term. The Tonnage Bill and the Triennial Bill proceeded almost side by side. Both were, on the twenty-second of December, ready for the royal assent. William came in state on that day to Westminster. The attendance of members of both Houses was large. When the Clerk of the Crown read the words, "A Bill for the frequent Calling and Meeting of Parliaments," the anxiety was great. When the Clerk of the Parliament made answer, "Le roy et la royne le veulent," a loud and long hum of delight and exultation rose from the benches and the bar.† William had resolved many months before not to refuse his assent a second time to so popular a law.‡ There was some however who thought that he would not have made so great a concession if he had on that day been quite himself. It was plain indeed that he was strangely agitated and unnerved. It had been announced that he would dine in public at Whitehall. But he disappointed the curiosity of the multitude which on such occasions flocked to the Court, and hurried back to Kensington.§

He had but too good reason to be uneasy. His wife had, during two or three days, been poorly; and on the preceding evening grave symptoms had appeared. Sir Thomas Millington, who was physician in ordinary to the King, thought that she had the measles. But Radcliffe, who, with coarse manners and little book learning, had raised himself to the first practice

---

* The history of this bill may be read in the Journals of the Houses. The contest, not a very vehement one, lasted till the 20th of April.

† "The Commons," says Narcissus Luttrell, "gave a great hum." "Le murmure qui est la marque d'applaudissement fut si grand qu'on peut dire qu'il estoit universel."—L'Hermitage, $\frac{\text{Dec. 25.}}{\text{Jan 4.}}$

‡ L'Hermitage says this in his despatch of Nov. $\frac{20}{30}$.

§ Burnet, ii. 137. ; Van Citters, $\frac{\text{Dec. 25.}}{\text{Jan 4.}}$

in London chiefly by his rare skill in diagnostics, uttered the more alarming words, small pox. That disease, over which science has since achieved a succession of glorious and beneficient victories, was then the most terrible of all the ministers of death. The havoc of the plague had been far more rapid : but the plague had visited our shores only once or twice within living memory ; and the small pox was always present, filling the churchyards with corpses, tormenting with constant fears all whom it had not yet stricken, leaving on those whose lives it spared the hideous traces of its power, turning the babe into a changeling at which the mother shuddered, and making the eyes and cheeks of the betrothed maiden objects of horror to the lover. Towards the end of the year 1694, this pestilence was more than usually severe. At length the infection spread to the palace, and reached the young and blooming Queen. She received the intimation of her danger with true greatness of soul. She gave orders that every lady of her bedchamber, every maid of honour, nay, every menial servant, who had not had the small pox, should instantly leave Kensington House. She locked herself up during a short time in her closet, burned some papers, arranged others, and then calmly awaited her fate.

During two or three days there were many alternations of hope and fear. The physicians contradicted each other and themselves in a way which sufficiently indicates the state of medical science in that age. The disease was measles : it was scarlet fever : it was spotted fever : it was erysipelas. At one moment some symptoms, which in truth showed that the case was almost hopeless, were hailed as indications of returning health. At length all doubt was over. Radcliffe's opinion proved to be right. It was plain that the Queen was sinking under small pox of the most malignant type.

All this time William remained night and day near her bedside. The little couch on which he slept when he was in camp was spread for him in the antechamber : but he scarcely lay down on it. The sight of his misery, the Dutch Envoy wrote, was enough to melt the hardest heart. Nothing seemed to be left of the man whose serene fortitude had been the wonder of old soldiers on the disastrous day of Landen, and of old sailors on that fearful night among the sheets of ice and banks of sand on the coast of Goree. The very domestics saw the tears running unchecked down that face, of which the stern composure had seldom been disturbed by any triumph or by any defeat. Several of the prelates were in attendance. The

King drew Burnet aside, and gave way to an agony of grief. "There is no hope," he cried. "I was the happiest man on earth; and I am the most miserable. She had no fault; none: you knew her well: but you could not know, nobody but myself could know, her goodness." Tenison undertook to tell her that she was dying. He was afraid that such a communication, abruptly made, might agitate her violently, and began with much management. But she soon caught his meaning, and, with that gentle womanly courage which so often puts our bravery to shame, submitted herself to the will of God. She called for a small cabinet in which her most important papers were locked up, gave orders that, as soon as she was no more, it should be delivered to the King, and then dismissed worldly cares from her mind. She received the Eucharist, and repeated her part of the office with unimpaired memory and intelligence, though in a feeble voice. She observed that Tenison had been long standing at her bedside, and, with that sweet courtesy which was habitual to her, faltered out her commands that he would sit down, and repeated them till he obeyed. After she had received the sacrament she sank rapidly, and uttered only a few broken words. Twice she tried to take a last farewell of him whom she had loved so truly and entirely: but she was unable to speak. He had a succession of fits so alarming that his Privy Councillors, who were assembled in a neighbouring room, were apprehensive for his reason and his life. The Duke of Leeds, at the request of his colleagues, ventured to assume the friendly guardianship of which minds deranged by sorrow stand in need. A few minutes before the Queen expired, William was removed, almost insensible, from the sick room.

Mary died in peace with Anne. Before the physicians had pronounced the case hopeless, the Princess, who was then in very delicate health, had sent a kind message; and Mary had returned a kind answer. The Princess had then proposed to come herself: but William had, in very gracious terms, declined the offer. The excitement of an interview, he said, would be too much for both sisters. If a favourable turn took place, Her Royal Highness should be most welcome to Kensington. A few hours later all was over.*

The public sorrow was great and general. For Mary's blameless life, her large charities and her winning manners had

* Burnet, ii. 136. 138. ; Narcissus Luttrell's Dairy ; Van Citters, $\frac{\text{Dec. 28.}}{\text{Jan. 7.}}$ 169$\frac{4}{5}$ ; L'Hermitage, $\frac{\text{Dec. 25.}}{\text{Jan.}}$ $\frac{\text{Dec. 28.}}{\text{Jan. 7.}}$ Jan. $\frac{1}{11}$. ; Vernon to Lord Lexington, Dec. 21. 25. 28., Jan. 1. ; Tenison's Funeral Sermon.

conquered the hearts of her people. When the Commons next met they sate for a time in profound silence. At length it was moved and resolved that an Address of Condolence should be presented to the King ; and then the House broke up without proceeding to other business. The Dutch envoy informed the States General that many of the members had handkerchiefs at their eyes. The number of sad faces in the street struck every observer. The mourning was more general than even the mourning for Charles the Second had been. On the Sunday which followed the Queen's death her virtues were celebrated in almost every parish church of the Capital, and in almost every great meeting of nonconformists.*

The most estimable Jacobites respected the sorrow of William and the memory of Mary. But to the fiercer zealots of the party neither the house of mourning nor the grave was sacred. At Bristol the adherents of Sir John Knight rang the bells as if for a victory.† It has often been repeated, and is not at all improbable, that a nonjuring divine, in the midst of the general lamentation, preached on the text, "Go : see now this cursed woman and bury her : for she is a King's daughter." It is certain that some of the ejected priests pursued her to the grave with invectives. Her death, they said, was evidently a judgment for her crime. God had, from the top of Sinai, in thunder and lightning, promised length of days to children who should honour their parents ; and in this promise was plainly implied a menace. What father had ever been worse treated by his daughters than James by Mary and Anne? Mary was gone, cut off in the prime of life, in the glow of beauty, in the height of prosperity ; and Anne would do well to profit by the warning. Wagstaffe went further, and dwelt much on certain wonderful coincidences of time. James had been driven from his palace and country in Christmas week. Mary had died in Christmas week. There could be no doubt that, if the secrets of Providence were disclosed to us, we should find that the turns of the daughter's complaint in December 1694 bore an exact analogy to the turns of the father's fortune in December 1688. It was at midnight that the father ran away from Rochester : it was at midnight that

* Evelyn's Dairy ; Narcissus Luttrell's Diary ; Commons' Journals, Dec. 28. 1694 ; Shrewsbury to Lexington, of the same date ; Van Citters of the same date ; L'Hermitage, Jan. $\frac{1}{11}$. 1695. Among the sermons on Mary's death, that of Sherlock, preached in the Temple Church, and those of Howe and Bates, preached to great Presbyterian congregations, deserve notice.

† Narcissus Luttrell's Diary.

the daughter expired. Such was the profundity and such the ingenuity of a writer whom the Jacobite schismatics justly regarded as one of their ablest chiefs.*

The Whigs soon had an opportunity of retaliating. They triumphantly related that a scrivener in the Borough, a stanch friend of hereditary right, while exulting in the judgment which had overtaken the Queen, had himself fallen down dead in a fit.†

The funeral was long remembered as the saddest and most august that Westminster had ever seen. While the Queen's remains lay in state at Whitehall, the neighbouring streets were filled every day, from sunrise to sunset, by crowds which made all traffic impossible. The two Houses with their maces followed the hearse, the Lords robed in scarlet and ermine, the Commons in long black mantles. No preceding Sovereign had ever been attended to the grave by a Parliament : for, till then, the Parliament had always expired with the Sovereign. A paper had indeed been circulated, in which the logic of a small sharp pettifogger was employed to prove that writs, issued in the joint names of William and Mary, ceased to be of force as soon as William reigned alone. But this paltry cavil had completely failed. It had not even been mentioned in the Lower House, and had been mentioned in the Upper only to be contemptuously overruled. The whole Magistracy of the City swelled the procession. The banners of England and France, Scotland and Ireland, were carried by great nobles before the corpse. The pall was borne by the chiefs of the illustrious houses of Howard, Seymour, Grey, and Stanley. On the gorgeous coffin of purple and gold were laid the crown and sceptre of the realm. The day was well suited to such a ceremony. The sky was dark and troubled ; and a few ghastly flakes of snow fell on the black plumes of the funeral car. Within the Abbey, nave, choir and transept were in a blaze with innumerable waxlights. The body was deposited under a magnificent canopy in the centre of the church while the Primate preached. The earlier part of his discourse was deformed by pedantic divisions and subdivisions : but towards the close he told what he had himself seen and heard with a simplicity and earnestness more affecting than the most skilful rhetoric. Through the whole ceremony the distant booming of cannon was heard every minute from the batteries of the

* Remarks on some late Sermons, 1695 ; A Defence of the Archbishop's Sermon, 1695.
† Narcissus Luttrell's Diary.

Tower. The gentle Queen sleeps among her illustrious kindred in the southern aisle of the Chapel of Henry the Seventh.*

The affection with which her husband cherished her memory was soon attested by a monument the most superb that was ever erected to any sovereign. No scheme had been so much her own, none had been so near her heart, as that of converting the palace at Greenwich into a retreat for seamen. It had occurred to her when she had found it difficult to provide good shelter and good attendance for the thousands of brave men who had come back to England wounded after the battle of La Hogue. While she lived scarcely any step was taken towards the accomplishing of her favourite design. But it should seem that, as soon as her husband had lost her, he began to reproach himself for having neglected her wishes. No time was lost. A plan was furnished by Wren ; and soon an edifice, surpassing that asylum which the magnificent Lewis had provided for his soldiers, rose on the margin of the Thames. Whoever reads the inscription which runs round the frieze of the hall will observe that William claims no part of the merit of the design, and that the praise is ascribed to Mary alone. Had the King's life been prolonged till the works were completed, a statue of her who was the real foundress of the institution would have had a conspicuous place in that court which presents two lofty domes and two graceful colonnades to the multitudes who are perpetually passing up and down the imperial river. But that part of the plan was never carried into effect ; and few of those who now gaze on the noblest of European hospitals are aware that it is a memorial of the virtues of the good Queen Mary, of the love and sorrow of William, and of the great victory of La Hogue.

## CHAPTER XXI

On the Continent the news of Mary's death excited various emotions. The Huguenots, in every part of Europe to which they had wandered, bewailed the Elect Lady, who had retrenched from her own royal state in order to furnish bread and shelter to the persecuted people of God.† In the United

* L'Hermitage, March $\frac{1}{11}$. $\frac{4}{15}$. 1695 ; London Gazette, March 7.; Tenison's Funeral Sermon ; Evelyn's Diary.
† See Claude's Sermon on Mary's death.

Provinces, where she was well known and had always been popular, she was tenderly lamented.  Matthew Prior, whose parts and accomplishments had obtained for him the patronage of the magnificent Dorset, and who was now attached to the Embassy at the Hague, wrote that the coldest and most passionless of nations was touched.  The very marble, he said, wept.*  The lamentations of Cambridge and Oxford were echoed by Leyden and Utrecht.  The States General put on mourning.  The bells of all the steeples of Holland tolled dolefully day after day.†  James, meanwhile, strictly prohibited all mourning at Saint Germains, and prevailed on Lewis to issue a similar prohibition at Versailles.  Some of the most illustrious nobles of France, and among them the Dukes of Bouillon and of Duras, were related to the House of Nassau, and had always, when death visited that House, punctiliously observed the decent ceremonial of sorrow.  They were now forbidden to wear black ; and they submitted : but it was beyond the power of the great King to prevent his highbred and sharpwitted courtiers from whispering to each other that there was something pitiful in this revenge taken by the living on the dead, by a parent on a child.‡

The hopes of James and of his companions in exile were now higher than they had been since the day of La Hogue.  Indeed the general opinion of politicians, both here and on the Continent, was that William would find it impossible to sustain himself much longer on the throne.  He would not, it was said, have sustained himself so long but for the help of his wife.  Her affability had conciliated many who had been repelled by his freezing looks and short answers.  Her English tones, sentiments and tastes had charmed many who were disgusted by his Dutch accent and Dutch habits.  Though she did not belong to the High Church party, she loved that ritual to which she had been accustomed from infancy, and complied willingly and reverently with some ceremonies which he con-

---

* Prior to Lord and Lady Lexington, Jan. $\frac{14}{24}$. 1695.  The letter is among the Lexington papers, a valuable collection, and well edited.

† Monthly Mercury for January 1695.  An orator who pronounced an eulogium on the Queen at Utrecht was so absurd as to say that she spent her last breath in prayers for the prosperity of the United Provinces :— "Valeant et Batavi ;"—these are her last words—" sint incolumes ; sint florentes ; sint beati : stet in æternum, stet immota præclarissima illorum civitas, hospitium aliquando mihi gratissimum, optime de me meritum." See also the orations of Peter Francius of Amsterdam, and of John Ortwinius of Delft.

‡ Journal de Dangeau ; Mémoires de Saint Simon.

sidered, not indeed as sinful, but as childish, and in which he could hardly bring himself to take part. While the war lasted, it would be necessary that he should pass nearly half the year out of England. Hitherto she had, when he was absent, supplied his place, and had supplied it well. Who was to supply it now? In what vicegerent could he place equal confidence? To what vicegerent would the nation look up with equal respect? All the statesmen of Europe therefore agreed in thinking that his position, difficult and dangerous at best, had been made far more difficult and more dangerous by the death of the Queen. But all the statesmen of Europe were deceived; and, strange to say, his reign was decidedly more prosperous and more tranquil after the decease of Mary than during her life.

A few hours after he had lost the most tender and beloved of all his friends, he was delivered from the most formidable of all his enemies. Death had been busy at Paris as well as in London. While Tenison was praying by the bed of Mary, Bourdaloue was administering the last unction to Luxemburg. The great French general had never been a favourite at the French Court: but when it was known that his feeble frame, exhausted by war and pleasure, was sinking under a dangerous disease, the value of his services was, for the first time, fully appreciated: the royal physicians were sent to prescribe for him: the sisters of Saint Cyr were ordered to pray for him: but prayers and prescriptions were vain. "How glad the Prince of Orange will be," said Lewis, "when the news of our loss reaches him." He was mistaken. That news found William unable to think of any loss but his own.*

During the month which followed the death of Mary the King was incapable of exertion. Even to the addresses of the two Houses of Parliament he replied only by a few inarticulate sounds. The answers which appear in the Journals were not uttered by him, but were delivered in writing. Such business as could not be deferred was transacted by the intervention of Portland, who was himself oppressed with sorrow. During some weeks the important and confidential correspondence between the King and Heinsius was suspended. At length William forced himself to resume that correspondence: but his first letter was the letter of a heartbroken man. Even his martial ardour had been tamed by misery. "I tell you in confidence," he wrote, "that I feel myself to be no longer fit for military command. Yet I will try to do my duty; and I

* Saint Simon ; Dangeau ; Monthly Mercury for January 1695.

hope that God will strengthen me." So despondingly did he look forward to the most brilliant and successful of his many campaigns.[*]

There was no interruption of parliamentary business. While the Abbey was hanging with black for the funeral of the Queen, the Commons came to a vote, which at the time attracted little attention, which produced no excitement, which has been left unnoticed by voluminous annalists, and of which the history can be but imperfectly traced in the archives of Parliament, but which has done more for liberty and for civilisation than the Great Charter or the Bill of Rights. Early in the session a select committee had been appointed to ascertain what temporary statutes were about to expire, and to consider which of those statutes it might be expedient to continue The report was made; and all the recommendations contained in that report were adopted, with one exception. Among the laws which the committee advised the House to renew was the law which subjected the press to a censorship. The question was put, "that the House do agree with the committee in the resolution that the Act entitled an Act for preventing Abuses in printing seditious, treasonable and unlicensed Pamphlets, and for regulating of Printing and Printing Presses, be continued." The Speaker pronounced that the Noes had it; and the Ayes did not think fit to divide.

A bill for continuing all the other temporary Acts, which, in the opinion of the Committee, could not properly be suffered to expire, was brought in, passed and sent to the Lords. In a short time this bill came back with an important amendment. The Lords had inserted in the list of Acts to be continued the Act which placed the press under the control of licensers. The Commons resolved not to agree to the amendment, demanded a conference, and appointed a committee of managers. The leading manager was Edward Clarke, a stanch Whig, who represented Taunton, the stronghold, during fifty troubled years, of civil and religious freedom.

Clarke delivered to the Lords in the Painted Chamber a paper containing the reasons which had determined the Lower House not to renew the Licensing Act. This paper completely vindicates the resolution to which the Commons had come. But it proves at the same time that they knew not what they were doing, what a revolution they were making, what a power they were calling into existence. They pointed out concisely,

---

[*] L'Hermitage, Jan. $\frac{1}{11}$. 1695; Vernon to Lord Lexington, Jan. 1. 4. Portland to Lord Lexington, Jan. $\frac{1}{22}$.; William to Heinsius, $\frac{Jan. 22}{Feb. 1}$.

clearly, forcibly, and sometimes with a grave irony which is not unbecoming, the absurdities and iniquities of the statute which was about to expire. But all their objections will be found to relate to matters of detail. On the great question of principle, on the question whether the liberty of unlicensed printing be, on the whole, a blessing or a curse to society, not a word is said. The Licensing Act is condemned, not as a thing essentially evil, but on account of the petty grievances, the exactions, the jobs, the commercial restrictions, the domiciliary visits which were incidental to it. It is pronounced mischievous because it enables the Company of Stationers to extort money from publishers, because it empowers the agents of the government to search houses under the authority of general warrants, because it confines the foreign book trade to the port of London; because it detains valuable packages of books at the Custom House till the pages are mildewed. The Commons complain that the amount of the fee which the licenser may demand is not fixed. They complain that it is made penal in an officer of the Customs to open a box of books from abroad, except in the presence of one of the censors of the press. How, it is very sensibly asked, is the officer to know that there are books in the box till he has opened it? Such were the arguments which did what Milton's Areopagitica had failed to do.

The Lords yielded without a contest. They probably expected that some less objectionable bill for the regulation of the press would soon be sent up to them; and in fact such a bill was brought into the House of Commons, read twice, and referred to a select committee. But the session closed before the committee had reported; and English literature was emancipated, and emancipated for ever, from the control of the government.* This great event passed almost unnoticed. Evelyn and Luttrell did not think it worth mentioning in their diaries. The Dutch minister did not think it worth mentioning in his despatches. No allusion to it is to be found in the Monthly Mercuries. The public attention was occupied by other and far more exciting subjects.

One of those subjects was the death of the most accomplished, the most enlightened, and, in spite of great faults, the

---

* See the Commons' Journals of Feb. 11., April 12. and April 17., and the Lords' Journals of April 8. and April 18. 1695. Unfortunately there a hiatus in the Commons' Journal of the 12th of April, so that it is now possible to discover whether there was a division on the question to ee with the amendment made by the Lords.

most estimable of the statesmen who were formed in the corrupt and licentious Whitehall of the Restoration. About a month after the splendid obsequies of Mary, a funeral procession of almost ostentatious simplicity passed round the shrine of Edward the Confessor to the Chapel of Henry the Seventh. There, at the distance of a few feet from her coffin, lies the coffin of George Savile, Marquess of Halifax.

Halifax and Nottingham had long been friends: and Lord Eland, now Halifax's only son, had been affianced to the Lady Mary Finch, Nottingham's daughter. The day of the nuptials was fixed: a joyous company assembled at Burley on the Hill, the mansion of the bride's father, which, from one of the noblest terraces in the island, looks down on magnificent woods of beech and oak, on the rich valley of Catmos, and on the spire of Oakham. The father of the bridegroom was detained in London by indisposition, which was not supposed to be dangerous. On a sudden his malady took an alarming form. He was told that he had but a few hours to live. He received the intimation with tranquil fortitude. It was proposed to send off an express to summon his son to town. But Halifax, good natured to the last, would not disturb the felicity of the wedding day. He gave strict orders that his interment should be private, prepared himself for the great change by devotions which astonished those who had called him an atheist, and died with the serenity of a philosopher and of a Christian, while his friends and kindred, not suspecting his danger, were tasting the sack posset and drawing the curtain.* His legitimate male posterity and his titles soon became extinct. No small portion, however, of his wit and eloquence descended to his daughter's son, Philip Stanhope, fourth Earl of Chesterfield. But it is perhaps not generally known that some adventurers, who, without advantages of fortune or position, made themselves conspicuous by the mere force of ability, inherited the blood of Halifax. He left a natural son, Henry Carey, whose dramas once drew crowded audiences to the theatres, and some of whose gay and spirited verses still live in the memory of hundreds of thousands. From Henry Carey descended that Edmund Kean, who, in our time, transformed himself so marvellously into Shylock, Iago and Othello.

More than one historian has been charged with partiality to Halifax. The truth is that the memory of Halifax is entitled in an especial manner to the protection of history. For wha

* L'Hermitage, April $\frac{18}{28}$. 1695 ; Burnet, ii. 149.

distinguishes him from all other English statesmen is this, that, through a long public life, and through frequent and violent revolutions of public feeling, he almost invariably took that view of the great questions of his time which history has finally adopted. He was called inconstant, because the relative position in which he stood to the contending factions was perpetually varying. As well might the pole star be called inconstant because it is sometimes to the east and sometimes to the west of the pointers. To have defended the ancient and legal constitution of the realm against a seditious populace at one conjuncture and against a tyrannical government at another; to have been the foremost defender of order in the turbulent Parliament of 1680 and the foremost defender of liberty in the servile Parliament of 1685; to have been just and merciful to Roman Catholics in the days of the Popish plot and to Exclusionists in the days of the Rye House Plot; to have done all in his power to save both the head of Stafford and the head of Russell; this was a course which contemporaries, heated by passion and deluded by names and badges, might not unnaturally call fickle, but which deserves a very different name from the late justice of posterity.

There is one and only one deep stain on the memory of this eminent man. It is melancholy to think that he, who had acted so great a part in the Convention, could have afterwards stooped to hold communication with Saint Germains. The fact cannot be disputed: yet for him there are excuses which cannot be pleaded for others who were guilty of the same crime. He did not, like Marlborough, Russell, Godolphin and Shrewsbury, betray a master by whom he was trusted, and with whose benefits he was loaded. It was by the ingratitude and malice of the Whigs that he was driven to take shelter for a moment among the Jacobites. It may be added that he soon repented of the error into which he had been hurried by passion, that, though never reconciled to the Court, he distinguished himself by his zeal for the vigorous prosecution of the war, and that his last work was a tract in which he exhorted his countrymen to remember that the public burdens, heavy as they might seem, were light when compared with the yoke of France and of Rome.*

About a fortnight after the death of Halifax, a fate far more cruel than death befell his old rival and enemy, the Lord President. That able, ambitious and daring statesman was

---

* An Essay upon Taxes, calculated for the present Juncture of Affairs. 593.

again hurled down from power. In his first fall, terrible as it was, there had been something of dignity; and he had, by availing himself with rare skill of an extraordinary crisis in public affairs, risen once more to the most elevated position among English subjects. The second ruin was indeed less violent than the first: but it was ignominious and irretrievable.

The peculation and venality by which the official men of that age were in the habit of enriching themselves had excited in the public mind a feeling such as could not but vent itself, sooner or later, in some formidable explosion. But the gains were immediate: the day of retribution was uncertain; and the plunderers of the public were as greedy and as audacious as ever, when the vengeance, long threatened and long delayed, suddenly overtook the proudest and most powerful among them.

The first mutterings of the coming storm did not at all indicate the direction which it would take, or the fury with which it would burst. An infantry regiment, which was quartered at Royston, had levied contributions on the people of that town and of the neighbourhood. The sum exacted was not large. In France or Brabant the moderation of the demand would have been thought wonderful. But to English shopkeepers and farmers military extortion was happily quite new and quite insupportable. A petition was sent up to the Commons. The Commons summoned the accusers and the accused to the bar. It soon appeared that a grave offence had been committed, but that the offenders were not altogether without excuse. The public money which had been issued from the Exchequer for their pay and subsistence had been fraudulently detained by their colonel and by his agent. It was not strange that men who had arms and who had not necessaries should trouble themselves little about the Petition of Right and the Declaration of Right. But it was monstrous that, while the citizen was heavily taxed for the purpose of paying to the soldier the largest military stipend known in Europe, the soldier should be driven by absolute want to plunder the citizen. This was strongly set forth in a representation which the Commons laid before William. William, who had been long struggling against abuses which grievously impaired the efficiency of his army, was glad to have his hands thus strengthened. He promised ample redress, cashiered the offending colonel, gave strict orders that the troops should receive their due regularly, and established a military board fo the purpose of detecting and punishing such malpractices as had taken place at Royston.*

But the whole administration was in such a state that it was hardly possible to track one offender without discovering ten others. In the course of the inquiry into the conduct of the troops at Royston, it was discovered that a bribe of two hundred guineas had been received by Henry Guy, member of Parliament for Heydon and Secretary of the Treasury. Guy was instantly sent to the Tower, not without much exultation on the part of the Whigs: for he was one of those tools who had passed, together with the buildings and furniture of the public offices, from James to William: he affected the character of a High Churchman; and he was known to be closely connected with some of the heads of the Tory party, and especially with Trevor.†

Another name, which was afterwards but too widely celebrated, first became known to the public at this time. James Craggs had begun life as a barber. He had then been a footman of the Duchess of Cleveland. His abilities, eminently vigorous though not improved by education, had raised him in the world; and he was now entering on a career which was destined to end, after a quarter of a century of prosperity, in unutterable misery and despair. He had become an army clothier. He was examined as to his dealings with the colonels of regiments; and, as he obstinately refused to produce his books, he was sent to keep Guy company in the Tower.‡

A few hours after Craggs had been thrown into prison, a committee, which had been appointed to inquire into the truth of a petition signed by some of the hackney coachmen of London, laid on the table of the House a report which excited universal disgust and indignation. It appeared that these poor hardworking men had been cruelly wronged by the board under the authority of which an Act of the preceding session had placed them. They had been pillaged and insulted, not

* Commons' Journals, Jan. 12., Feb. 26., Mar. 6. ; A Collection of the Debates and Proceedings in Parliament in 1694 and 1695 upon the Inquiry into the late Briberies and Corrupt Practices, 1695 ; L'Hermitage to the States General, March $\frac{8}{18}$. ; Van Citters, Mar. $\frac{15}{26}$. ; L'Hermitage says: " Siepar cette recherche la chambre pouvoit remédier au désordre qui règne, lle rendroit un service très utile et très agréable au Roy."

† Commons' Journals, Feb. 16. 1695 ; Collection of the Debates and Proceedings in Parliament in 1694 and 1695 ; Life of Wharton ; Burnet, ii. 144.

‡ Speaker Onslow's note on Burnet, ii. 583. ; Commons' Journals, Mar. 6, 7. 1695. The history of the terrible end of this man will be found in the pamphlets of the South Sea year.

only by the commissioners, but by one commissioner's lacquey and by another commissioner's harlot. The Commons addressed the King; and the King turned the delinquents out of their places.*

But by this time delinquents far higher in power and rank were beginning to be uneasy. At every new detection, the excitement, both within and without the walls of Parliament, became more intense. The frightful prevalence of bribery, corruption and extortion was every where the subject of conversation. A contemporary pamphleteer compares the state of the political world at this conjuncture to the state of a city in which the plague has just been discovered, and in which the terrible words, "Lord have mercy on us," are already seen on some doors.† Whispers, which at another time would have speedily died away and been forgotten, now swelled, first into murmurs, and then into clamours. A rumour rose and spread that the funds of the two wealthiest corporations in the kingdom, the City of London and the East India Company, had been largely employed for the purpose of corrupting great men; and the names of Trevor, Seymour and Leeds were mentioned.

The mention of these names produced a stir in the Whig ranks. Trevor, Seymour and Leeds were all three Tories, and had, in different ways, greater influence than perhaps any other three Tories in the kingdom. If they could all be driven at once from public life with blasted characters, the Whigs would be completely predominant both in the Parliament and in the Cabinet.

Wharton was not the man to let such an opportunity escape him. At White's, no doubt, among those lads of quality who were his pupils in politics and in debauchery, he would have laughed heartily at the fury with which the nation had on a sudden begun to persecute men for doing what every body had always done and was always trying to do. But if people would be fools, it was the business of a politician to make use of their folly. The cant of political purity was not so familiar to the lips of Wharton as blasphemy and ribaldry: but his abilities were so versatile, and his impudence so consummate, that he ventured to appear before the world as an austere patriot mourning over the venality and perfidy of a degenerate age. While he, animated by that fierce party spirit which in

---

* Commons' Journals, March 8. 1695; Exact Collection of Debates and Proceedings in Parliament in 1694 and 1695; L'Hermitage, March $\frac{8}{18}$.
† Exact Collection of Debates.

honest men would be thought a vice, but which in him was almost a virtue, was eagerly stirring up his friends to demand an inquiry into the truth of the evil reports which were in circulation, the subject was suddenly and strangely forced forward. It chanced that, while a bill of little interest was under discussion in the Commons, the postman arrived with numerous letters directed to members ; and the distribution took place at the bar with a buzz of conversation which drowned the voices of the orators. Seymour, whose imperious temper always prompted him to dictate and to chide, lectured the talkers on the scandalous irregularity of their conduct, and called on the Speaker to reprimand them. An angry discussion followed ; and one of the offenders was provoked into making an allusion to the stories which were current about both Seymour and the Speaker. "It is undoubtedly improper to talk while a bill is under discussion : but it is much worse to take money for getting a bill passed. If we are extreme to mark a slight breach of form, how severely ought we to deal with that corruption which is eating away the very substance of our institutions !" That was enough : the spark had fallen : the train was ready : the explosion was immediate and terrible. After a tumultuous debate in which the cry of "the Tower" was repeatedly heard, Wharton managed to carry his point. Before the House rose a committee was appointed to examine the books of the City of London and of the East India Company.*

Foley was placed in the chair of the committee. Within a week he reported that the Speaker, Sir John Trevor, had in the preceding session received from the City a thousand guineas for expediting a local bill. This discovery gave great satisfaction to the Whigs, who had always hated Trevor, and was not unpleasing to many of the Tories. During six busy sessions his sordid rapacity had made him an object of general aversion. The legitimate emoluments of his post amounted to about four thousand a year : but it was believed that he had made at least ten thousand a year.† His profligacy and insolence united had been too much even for the angelic temper of Tillotson. It was said that the gentle Archbishop had been heard to mutter something about a

* L'Hermitage, March $\frac{8}{18}$. 1695. L'Hermitage's narrative is confirmed by the Journals, March 7. 169$\frac{4}{5}$. It appears that, just before the committee was appointed, the House resolved that letters should not be delivered out to members during a sitting.

† L'Hermitage, March $\frac{18}{28}$. 1695.

*E 37

knave as the Speaker passed by him.* Yet, great as were the
offences of this bad man, his punishment was fully proportioned
to them. As soon as the report of the committee had been
read, it was moved that he had been guilty of a high crime
and misdemeanour. He had to stand up and to put the
question. There was a loud cry of Aye. He called on the
Noes; and scarcely a voice was heard. He was forced to
declare that the Ayes had it. A man of spirit would have
given up the ghost with remorse and shame; and the unutterable ignominy of that moment left its mark even on the
callous heart and brazen forehead of Trevor. Had he returned
to the House on the following day, he would have had to put
the question on a motion for his own expulsion. He therefore
pleaded illness, and shut himself up in his bedroom. Wharton
soon brought down a royal message authorising the Commons
to elect another Speaker.

The Whig chiefs wished to place Littleton in the chair: but
they were unable to accomplish their object. Foley was
chosen, presented and approved. Though he had of late
generally voted with the Tories, he still called himself a Whig,
and was not unacceptable to many of the Whigs. He had
both the abilities and the knowledge which were necessary to
enable him to preside over the debates with dignity: but what,
in the peculiar circumstances in which the House then found
itself placed, was not unnaturally considered as his principal
recommendation, was that implacable hatred of jobbery and
corruption which he somewhat ostentatiously professed, and
doubtless sincerely felt. On the day after he entered on his
functions, his predecessor was expelled.†

The indiscretion of Trevor had been equal to his baseness;
and his guilt had been apparent on the first inspection of the
accounts of the City. The accounts of the East India
Company were more obscure. The committee reported that
they had sate in Leadenhall Street, had examined documents,
had interrogated directors and clerks, but had been unable to
arrive at the bottom of the mystery of iniquity. Some most
suspicious entries had been discovered, under the head of
special service. The expenditure on this account had, in the
year 1693, exceeded eighty thousand pounds. It was proved
that, as to the outlay of this money, the directors had placed
implicit confidence in the governor, Sir Thomas Cook. He

---

* Birch's Life of Tillotson.

† Commons' Journals, March 12, 13, 14, 15, 16, 169⅘; Vernon to
Lexington, March 15.; L'Hermitage, March ⅘.

had merely told them in general terms that he had been at a charge of twenty-three thousand, of twenty five thousand, of thirty thousand pounds, in the matter of the Charter; and the Court had, without calling on him for any detailed explanation, thanked him for his care, and ordered warrants for these great sums to be instantly made out. It appeared that a few mutinous directors had murmured at this immense outlay, and had called for a detailed statement. But the only answer which they had been able to extract from Cook was that there were some great persons whom it was necessary to gratify.

The committee also reported that they had lighted on an agreement by which the Company had covenanted to furnish a person named Colston with two hundred tons of saltpetre. At the first glance, this transaction seemed merchantlike and fair. But it was soon discovered that Colston was merely an agent for Seymour. Suspicion was excited. The complicated terms of the bargain were severely examined, and were found to be framed in such a manner that, in every possible event, Seymour must be a gainer and the Company a loser to the extent of ten or twelve thousand pounds. The opinion of all who understood the matter was that the compact was merely a disguise intended to cover a bribe. But the disguise was so skilfully managed that the country gentlemen were perplexed, and that the lawyers doubted whether there were such evidence of corruption as would be held sufficient by a court of justice. Seymour escaped without even a vote of censure, and still continued to take a leading part in the debates of the Commons.* But the authority which he had long exercised in the House and in the western counties of England, though not destroyed, was visibly diminished; and, to the end of his life, his traffic in saltpetre was a favourite theme of Whig pamphleteers and poets.†

The escape of Seymour only inflamed the ardour of Wharton and of Wharton's confederates. They were determined to

---

* On vit qu'il étoit impossible de le poursuivre en justice, chacun toutefois démeurant convaincu que c'étoit un marché fait à la main pour lui faire présent de la somme de 10,000*l.*, et qu'il avoit été plus habile que les autres novices que n'avoient pas su faire si finement leure affaires.— L'Hermitage, March 29. April 8. Commons' Journals, March 12.; Vernon to Lexington, April 26.; Burnet, ii. 145.

† In a poem called the Prophecy (1703), is the line
          " When Seymour scorns saltpetre pence."
In another satire is the line
          "Bribed Seymour bribes accuses."

discover what had been done with the eighty or ninety thousand pounds of secret service money which had been entrusted to Cook by the East India Company. Cook, who was member for Colchester, was questioned in his place : he refused to answer : he was sent to the Tower ; and a bill was brought in providing that if, before a certain day, he should not acknowledge the whole truth, he should be incapable of ever holding any office, should refund to the Company the whole of the immense sum which had been confided to him, and should pay a fine of twenty thousand pounds to the Crown. Rich as he was, these penalties would have reduced him to penury. The Commons were in such a temper that they passed the bill without a single division.* Seymour, indeed, though his saltpetre contract was the talk of the whole town, came forward with unabashed forehead to plead for his accomplice : but his effrontery only injured the cause which he defended.† In the Upper House the bill was condemned in the strongest terms by the Duke of Leeds. Pressing his hand on his heart, he declared, on his faith, on his honour, that he had no personal interest in the question, and that he was actuated by no motive but a pure love of justice. His eloquence was powerfully seconded by the tears and lamentations of Cook, who, from the bar, implored the Peers not to subject him to a species of torture unknown to the mild laws of England. "Instead of this cruel bill," he said, "pass a bill of indemnity ; and I will tell you all." The Lords thought his request not altogether unreasonable. After some communication with the Commons, it was determined that a joint committee of the two Houses should be appointed to inquire into the manner in which the secret service money of the East India Company had been expended ; and an Act was rapidly passed providing that, if Cook would make to this committee a true and full discovery, he should be indemnified for the crimes which he might confess ; and that, till he made such a discovery, he should remain in the Tower. To this arrangement Leeds gave in public all the opposition that he could with decency give. In private those who were conscious of guilt employed numerous artifices for the purpose of averting inquiry. It was whispered that things might come out which every good Englishman would wish to hide, and that the greater part of the enormous sums which had passed through Cook's hands had been paid to Portland for His Majesty's use.

* Commons' Journals from March 26. to April 8. 1695.
† L'Hermitage, April $\frac{18}{28}$. 1695.

But the Parliament and the nation were determined to know the truth, whoever might suffer by the disclosure.*

As soon as the Bill of Indemnity had received the royal assent, the joint committee, consisting of twelve lords and twenty-four members of the House of Commons, met in the Exchequer Chamber. Wharton was placed in the chair; and in a few hours great discoveries were made.

The King and Portland came out of the inquiry with unblemished honour. Not only had not the King taken any part of the secret service money dispensed by Cook; but he had not, during some years, received even the ordinary present which the Company had, in former reigns, laid annually at the foot of the throne. It appeared that not less than fifty thousand pounds had been offered to Portland, and rejected. The money lay during a whole year ready to be paid to him if he should change his mind. He at length told those who pressed this immense bribe on him, that if they persisted in insulting him by such an offer, they would make him an enemy of their Company. Many people wondered at the probity which he showed on this occasion, for he was generally thought interested and grasping. The truth seems to be that he loved money, but that he was a man of strict integrity and honour. He took, without scruple, whatever he thought that he could honestly take, but was incapable of stooping to an act of baseness. Indeed, he resented as affronts the compliments which were paid him on this occasion.† The integrity of Nottingham could excite no surprise. Ten thousand pounds had been offered to him, and had been refused. The number of cases in which bribery was fully made out was small. A large part of the sum which Cook had drawn from the Company's treasury had probably been embezzled by the brokers whom he had employed in the work of corruption; and what had become of the rest it was not easy to learn from the reluctant witnesses who were brought before the committee. One glimpse of light however was caught: it was followed; and it led to a discovery of the highest moment. A large sum was traced from Cook to an agent named Firebrace, and from Firebrace to another agent named Bates, who was well known to be closely connected with the High Church party and especially with Leeds. Bates was summoned, but absconded: messengers were sent in pursuit of him: he was caught, brought into the Exchequer

---

* Exact Collection of Debates and Proceedings.

† L'Hermitage, $\frac{\text{April 30.}}{\text{May 10.}}$ 1695; Portland to Lexington, $\frac{\text{April 23}}{\text{May 3.}}$.

Chamber and sworn. The story which he told showed that he was distracted between the fear of losing his ears and the fear of injuring his patron. He owned that he had undertaken to bribe Leeds, had been for that purpose furnished with five thousand five hundred guineas, had offered those guineas to His Grace, and had, by His Grace's permission, left them at His Grace's house in the care of a Swiss named Robart, who was His Grace's confidential man of business. It should seem that these facts admitted of only one interpretation. Bates however swore that the Duke had refused to accept a farthing. "Why then," it was asked, "was the gold left, by his consent, at his house and in the hands of his servant?" "Because," answered Bates, "I am bad at telling coin. I therefore begged His Grace to let me leave the pieces, in order that Robart might count them for me; and His Grace was so good as to give leave." It was evident that, if this strange story had been true, the guineas would, in a few hours, have been taken away. But Bates was forced to confess that they had remained half a year where he had left them. The money had indeed at last,—and this was one of the most suspicious circumstances in the case,—been paid back by Robart on the very morning on which the committee first met in the Exchequer Chamber. Who could believe that, if the transaction had been free from all taint of corruption, the guineas would have been detained as long as Cook was able to remain silent, and would have been refunded on the very first day on which he was under the necessity of speaking out?*

A few hours after the examination of Bates, Wharton reported to the Commons what had passed in the Exchequer Chamber. The indignation was general and vehement. "You now understand," said Wharton, "why obstructions have been thrown in our way at every step, why we have had to wring out truth drop by drop, why His Majesty's name has been artfully used to prevent us from going into an inquiry which has brought nothing to light but what is to His Majesty's honour. Can we think it strange that our difficulties should have been great, when we consider the power, the dexterity, the experience of him who was secretly thwarting us? It is time for us to prove signally to the world that it is impossible for any criminal to double so cunningly that we cannot track him, or to climb so high that we cannot reach

* L'Hermitage ($\frac{\text{April 30.}}{\text{May 10.}}$ 1695) justly remarks, that the way in which the money was sent back strengthened the case against Leeds.

him. Never was there a more flagitious instance of corruption. Never was there an offender who had less claim to indulgence. The obligations which the Duke of Leeds has to his country are of no common kind. One great debt we generously cancelled; but the manner in which our generosity has been requited forces us to remember that he was long ago impeached for receiving money from France. How can we be safe while a man proved to be venal has access to the royal ear? Our best laid enterprises have been defeated. Our inmost counsels have been betrayed. And what wonder is it? Can we doubt that, together with this home trade in charters, a profitable foreign trade in secrets is carried on? Can we doubt that he who sells us to one another will, for a good price, sell us all to the common enemy?" Wharton concluded by moving that Leeds should be impeached of high crimes and misdemeanours.*

Leeds had many friends and dependents in the House of Commons: but they could say little. Wharton's motion was carried without a division; and he was ordered to go to the bar of the Lords, and there, in the name of the Commons of England, to impeach the Duke. But, before this order could be obeyed, it was announced that His Grace was at the door and requested an audience.

While Wharton had been making his report to the Commons, Leeds had been haranguing the Lords. He denied with the most solemn asseverations that he had taken any money for himself. But he acknowledged, and indeed almost boasted, that he had abetted Bates in getting money from the Company, and seemed to think that this was a service which any man in power might be reasonably expected to render to a friend. Too many persons, indeed, in that age made a most absurd and pernicious distinction between a minister who used his influence to obtain presents for himself and a minister who used his influence to obtain presents for his dependents. The former was corrupt: the latter was merely goodnatured. Leeds proceeded to tell with great complacency a story about himself, which would, in our days, drive a public man, not only out of office, but out of the society of gentlemen. "When I was Treasurer, in King Charles's time, my Lords, the excise was to be farmed. There were several bidders. Harry Savile, for whom I had a great value, informed me that they had asked for his interest with me, and begged me to tell them that

* There can, I think, be no doubt, that the member who is called D in the Exact Collection was Wharton.

he had done his best for them. 'What!' said I: 'tell them all so, when only one can have the farm?' 'No matter;' said Harry: 'tell them all so; and the one who gets the farm will think that he owes it to me.' The gentlemen came. I said to every one of them separately, 'Sir, you are much obliged to Mr. Savile:' 'Sir, Mr. Savile has been much your friend.' In the end Harry got a handsome present; and I wished him good luck with it. I was his shadow then. I am Mr. Bates's shadow now."

The Duke had hardly related this anecdote, so strikingly illustrative of the state of political morality in that generation, when it was whispered to him that a motion to impeach him had been made in the House of Commons. He hastened thither: but, before he arrived, the question had been put and carried. Nevertheless he pressed for admittance; and he was admitted. A chair, according to ancient usage, was placed for him within the bar; and he was informed that the House was ready to hear him.

He spoke, but with less tact and judgment than usual. He magnified his own public services. But for him, he said, there would have been no House of Commons to impeach him; a boast so extravagant that it naturally made his hearers unwilling to allow him the praise which his conduct at the time of the Revolution really deserved. As to the charge against him he said little more than that he was innocent, that there had long been a malicious design to ruin him, that he would not go into particulars, that the facts which had been proved would bear two constructions, and that of the two constructions the most favourable ought in candour to be adopted. He withdrew, after praying the House to reconsider the vote which had just been passed, or, if that could not be, to let him have speedy justice.

His friends felt that his speech was no defence, and did not attempt to rescind the resolution which had been carried just before he was heard. Wharton, with a large following, went up to the Lords, and informed them that the Commons had resolved to impeach the Duke. A committee of managers was appointed to draw up the articles and to prepare the evidence.*

The articles were speedily drawn: but to the chain of evidence one link appeared to be wanting. That link Robart, if he had been severely examined and confronted with other witnesses, would in all probability have been forced to supply. He was summoned to the bar of the Commons. A messenger

* As to the proceedings of this eventful day, April 27. 1695, see the Journals of the two Houses, and the Exact Collection.

went with the summons to the house of the Duke of Leeds, and was there informed that the Swiss was not within, that he had been three days absent, and that where he was the porter could not tell. The Lords immediately presented an address to the King, requesting him to give orders that the ports might be stopped and the fugitive arrested. But Robart was already in Holland on his way to his native mountains.

The flight of this man made it impossible for the Commons to proceed. They vehemently accused Leeds of having sent away the witness who alone could furnish legal proof of that which was already established by moral proof. Leeds, now at ease as to the event of the impeachment, gave himself the airs of an injured man. "My Lords," he said, "the conduct of the Commons is without precedent. They impeach me of a high crime : they promise to prove it : then they find that they have not the means of proving it ; and they revile me for not supplying them with the means. Surely they ought not to have brought a charge like this, without well considering whether they had or had not evidence sufficient to support it. If Robart's testimony be, as they now say, indispensable, why did they not send for him and hear his story before they made up their minds ? They may thank their own intemperance, their own precipitancy, for his disappearance. He is a foreigner : he is timid : he hears that a transaction in which he has been concerned has been pronounced by the House of Commons to be highly criminal, that his master is impeached, that his friend Bates is in prison, that his own turn is coming. He naturally takes fright : he escapes to his own country ; and, from what I know of him, I will venture to predict that it will be long before he trusts himself again within reach of the Speaker's warrant. But what is that to me ? Am I to lie all my life under the stigma of an accusation like this, merely because the violence of my accusers has scared their own witness out of England ? I demand an immediate trial. I move your Lordships to resolve that, unless the Commons shall proceed before the end of the session, the impeachment shall be dismissed." A few friendly voices cried out "Well moved." But the Peers were generally unwilling to take a step which would have been in the highest degree offensive to the Lower House, and to the great body of those whom that House represented. The Duke's motion fell to the ground ; and a few hours later the Parliament was prorogued.*

* Exact Collection ; Lords' Journals, May 3. 1695 ; Commons' Journals, May 2, 3. ; L'Hermitage, May $\frac{1}{3}\frac{3}{3}$.; London Gazette, May 13.

The impeachment was never revived. The evidence which would warrant a formal verdict of guilty was not forthcoming; and a formal verdict of guilty would hardly have answered Wharton's purpose better than the informal verdict of guilty which the whole nation had already pronounced. The work was done. The Whigs were dominant. Leeds was no longer chief minister, was indeed no longer a minister at all. William, from respect probably for the memory of the beloved wife whom he had lately lost, and to whom Leeds had shown peculiar attachment, avoided every thing that could look like harshness. The fallen statesman was suffered to retain during a considerable time the title of Lord President, and to walk on public occasions between the Great Seal and the Privy Seal. But he was told that he would do well not to show himself at Council: the business and the patronage even of the department of which he was the nominal head passed into other hands; and the place which he ostensibly filled was considered in political circles as really vacant.*

He hastened into the country, and hid himself there, during some months, from the public eye. When the Parliament met again, however, he emerged from his retreat. Though he was well stricken in years and cruelly tortured by disease, his ambition was still as ardent as ever. With indefatigable energy he began a third time to climb, as he flattered himself, towards that dizzy pinnacle which he had twice reached, and from which he had twice fallen. He took a prominent part in debate: but, though his eloquence and knowledge always secured to him the attention of his hearers, he was never again, even when the Tory party was in power, admitted to the smallest share in the direction of affairs.

There was one great humiliation which he could not be spared. William was about to take the command of the army in the Netherlands; and it was necessary that, before he sailed, he should determine by whom the government should be administered during his absence. Hitherto Mary had acted as his vicegerent when he was out of England: but she was gone. He therefore delegated his authority to seven Lords Justices, Tenison, Archbishop of Canterbury, Somers, Keeper of the Great Seal, Pembroke, Keeper of the Privy Seal, Devonshire, Lord Steward, Dorset, Lord Chamberlain, Shrewsbury, Secretary of State, and Godolphin, First Commissioner of the Treasury. It is easy to judge from this list of names which way the balance of power was now leaning. Godolphin alone of the

* L'Hermitage, May $\frac{10}{20}$. 1695; Vernon to Shrewsbury, June 22. 1697.

seven was a Tory. The Lord President, still second in rank, and a few days before first in power, of the great lay dignitaries of the realm, was passed over ; and the omission was universally regarded as an official announcement of his disgrace.*

There were some who wondered that the Princess of Denmark was not appointed Regent. The reconciliation, which had been begun while Mary was dying, had since her death been, in external show at least, completed. This was one of those occasions on which Sunderland was peculiarly qualified to be useful. He was admirably fitted to manage a personal negotiation, to soften resentment, to soothe wounded pride, to select, among all the objects of human desire, the very bait which was most likely to allure the mind with which he was dealing. On this occasion his task was not difficult. He had two excellent assistants, Marlborough in the household of Anne, and Somers in the cabinet of William.

Marlborough was now as desirous to support the government as he had once been to subvert it. The death of Mary had produced a complete change in all his schemes. There was one event to which he looked forward with the most intense longing, the accession of the Princess to the English throne. It was certain that, on the day on which she began to reign, he would be in her Court all that Buckingham had been in the Court of James the First. Marlborough too must have been conscious of powers of a very different order from those which Buckingham had possessed, of a genius for politics not inferior to that of Richelieu, of a genius for war not inferior to that of Turenne. Perhaps the disgraced General, in obscurity and inaction, anticipated the day when his power to help and hurt in Europe would be equal to that of her mightiest princes, when he would be servilely flattered and courted by Cæsar on one side and by Lewis the Great on the other, and when every year would add another hundred thousand pounds to the largest fortune that had ever been accumulated by any English subject. All this might be if Mrs. Morley were Queen. But that Mr. Freeman should ever see Mrs. Morley Queen had till lately been not very probable. Mary's life was a much better life than his, and quite as good a life as her sister's. That William would have issue seemed unlikely. But it was generally expected that he would soon die. His widow might marry again, and might leave children who would succeed her. In these circumstances Marlborough might well think that he had very little interest in maintaining that settlement of the Crown

* London Gazette, May 6. 1695.

which had been made by the Convention. Nothing was so likely to serve his purpose as confusion, civil war, another revolution, another abdication, another vacancy of the throne. Perhaps the nation, incensed against William, yet not reconciled to James, and distracted between hatred of foreigners and hatred of Jesuits, might prefer both to the Dutch King and to the Popish King one who was at once a native of our country and a member of our Church. That this was the real explanation of Marlborough's dark and complicated plots was, as we have seen, firmly believed by some of the most zealous Jacobites, and is in the highest degree probable. It is certain that during several years he had spared no efforts to inflame the army and the nation against the government. But all was now changed. Mary was gone. By the Bill of Rights the Crown was entailed on Anne after the death of William. The death of William could not be far distant. Indeed all the physicians who attended him wondered that he was still alive ; and, when the risks of war were added to the risks of disease, the probability seemed to be that in a few months he would be in his grave. Marlborough saw that it would now be madness to throw every thing into disorder and to put every thing to hazard. He had done his best to shake the throne while it seemed unlikely that Anne would ever mount it except by violent means. But he did his best to fix it firmly, as soon as it became highly probably that she would soon be called to fill it in the regular course of nature and of law.

The Princess was easily induced by the Churchills to write to the King a submissive and affectionate letter of condolence. The King, who was never much inclined to engage in a commerce of insincere compliments, and who was still in the first agonies of his grief, showed little disposition to meet her advances. But Somers, who felt that every thing was at stake, went to Kensington, and made his way into the royal closet. William was sitting there, so deeply sunk in melancholy that he did not seem to perceive that any person had entered the room. The Lord Keeper, after a respectful pause, broke silence, and, doubtless with all that cautious delicacy which was characteristic of him, and which eminently qualified him to touch the sore places of the mind without hurting them, implored His Majesty to be reconciled to the Princess. "Do what you will," said William ; "I can think of no business." Thus authorised, the mediators speedily concluded a treaty.* Anne came to

* Letter from Mrs. Burnet to the Duchess of Marlborough, 1704, quoted by Coxe ; Shrewsbury to Russell, January 24. 1695 ; Burnett, ii. 149.

Kensington, and was graciously received : she was lodged in Saint James's Palace : a guard of honour was again placed at her door ; and the Gazettes again, after a long interval, announced that foreign ministers had had the honour of being presented to her.* The Churchills were again permitted to dwell under the royal roof. But William did not at first include them in the peace which he had made with their mistress. Marlborough remained excluded from military and political employment ; and it was not without much difficulty that he was admitted into the circle at Kensington, and permitted to kiss the royal hand.† The feeling with which he was regarded by the King explains why Anne was not appointed Regent. The Regency of Anne would have been the Regency of Marlborough ; and it is not strange that a man whom it was not thought safe to entrust with any office in the State or the army should not have been entrusted with the whole government of the kingdom.

Had Marlborough been of a proud and vindictive nature he might have been provoked into raising another quarrel in the royal family, and into forming new cabals in the army. But all his passions, except ambition and avarice, were under strict regulation. He was destitute alike of the sentiment of gratitude and of the sentiment of revenge. He had conspired against the government while it was loading him with favours. He now supported it, though it requited his support with contumely. He perfectly understood his own interest : he had perfect command of his temper : he endured decorously the hardships of his present situation, and contented himself by looking forward to a reversion which would amply repay him for a few years of patience. He did not indeed cease to correspond with the Court of Saint Germains : but the correspondence gradually became more and more slack, and seems, on his part, to have been made up of vague professions and trifling excuses.

The event which had changed all Marlborough's views had filled the minds of fiercer and more pertinacious politicians with wild hopes and atrocious projects.

During the two years and a half which followed the execution of Grandval, no serious design had been formed against the life of William. Some hotheaded malecontents had indeed laid schemes for kidnapping or murdering him : but those schemes were not, while his wife lived, countenanced by her

* London Gazette, April 8. 15. 29. 1695.
† Shrewsbury to Russell, January 24. 1695 ; Narcissus Luttrell's Diary.

father. James did not feel, and, to do him justice, was not such a hypocrite as to pretend to feel, any scruple about removing his enemies by those means which he had justly thought base and wicked when employed by his enemies against himself. If any such scruple had arisen in his mind, there was no want, under his roof, of casuists willing and competent to soothe his conscience with sophisms such as had corrupted the far nobler natures of Anthony Babington and Everard Digby. To question the lawfulness of assassination, in cases where assassination might promote the interests of the Church, was to question the authority of the most illustrious Jesuits, of Bellarmine and Suarez, of Molina and Mariana : nay, it was to rebel against the Chair of Saint Peter. One Pope had walked in procession at the head of his cardinals, had proclaimed a jubilee, had ordered the guns of Saint Angelo to be fired, in honour of the perfidious butchery in which Coligni had perished. Another Pope had in a solemn allocution hymned the murder of Henry the Third of France in rapturous language borrowed from the ode of the prophet Habakkuk, and had extolled the murderer above Phinehas and Judith.* William was regarded at Saint Germains as a monster compared with whom Coligni and Henry the Third were saints. Nevertheless James, during some years, refused to sanction any attempt on his nephew's person. The reasons which he assigned for his refusal have come down to us, as he wrote them with his own hand. He did not affect to think that assassination was a sin which ought to be held in horror by a Christian, or a villany unworthy of a gentleman : he merely said that the difficulties were great, and that he would not push his friends on extreme danger when it would not be in his power to second them effectually.† In truth, while Mary lived, it might well be doubted whether the murder of her husband would really be a service to the Jacobite cause. By his death the government would lose indeed the strength derived from his eminent personal qualities, but would at the same time be relieved from the load of his personal unpopularity. His whole power would at once devolve on his widow ; and the nation would probably rally round her with enthusiasm. If her political abilities were not equal to his, she had not his repulsive manners, his foreign pronunciation, his partiality for every thing

* De Thou, liii. xcvi.

† Life of James, ii. 545., Orig. Mem. Of course James does not use the word assassination. He talks of the seizing and carrying away of the Prince of Orange.

Dutch and for every thing Calvinistic. Many, who had thought her culpably wanting in filial piety, would be of opinion that now at least she was absolved from all duty to a father stained with the blood of her husband. The whole machinery of the administration would continue to work without that interruption which ordinarily followed a demise of the Crown. There would be no dissolution of the Parliament, no suspension of the customs and excise : commissions would retain their force ; and all that James would have gained by the fall of his enemy would have been a barren revenge.

The death of the Queen changed every thing. If a dagger or a bullet should now reach the heart of William, it was probable that there would instantly be general anarchy. The Parliament and the Privy Council would cease to exist. The authority of ministers and judges would expire with him from whom it was derived. It might seem not improbable that at such a moment a restoration might be effected without a blow.

Scarcely therefore had Mary been laid in the grave when restless and unprincipled men began to plot in earnest against the life of William. Foremost among these men in parts, in courage and in energy was Robert Charnock. He had been liberally educated, and had, in the late reign, been a fellow of Magdalene College, Oxford. Alone in that great society he had betrayed the common cause, had consented to be the tool of the High Commission, had publicly apostatized from the Church of England, and, while his college was a Popish seminary, had held the office of Vice President. The Revolution came, and altered at once the whole course of his life. Driven from the quiet cloister and the old grove of oaks on the bank of the Cherwell, he sought haunts of a very different kind. During several years he led the perilous and agitated life of a conspirator, passed and repassed on secret errands between England and France, changed his lodgings in London often, and was known at different coffeehouses by different names. His services had been requited with a captain's commission signed by the banished King.

With Charnock was closely connected George Porter, an adventurer who called himself a Roman Catholic and a Royalist, but who was in truth destitute of all religious and of all political principle. Porter's friends could not deny that he was a rake and a coxcomb, that he drank, that he swore, that he told extravagant lies about his amours, and that he had been convicted of manslaughter for a stab given in a brawl at the playhouse. His enemies affirmed that he was addicted to

nauseous and horrible kinds of debauchery, and that he procured the means of indulging his infamous tastes by cheating
and marauding; that he was one of a gang of clippers; that
he sometimes got on horseback late in the evening and stole
out in disguise, and that, when he returned from these mysterious
excursions, his appearance justified the suspicion that he had
been doing business on Hounslow Heath or Finchley Common.*

Cardell Goodman, popularly called Scum Goodman, a knave
more abandoned, if possible, than Porter, was in the plot.
Goodman had been on the stage, had been kept, like some
much greater men, by the Duchess of Cleveland, had been
taken into her house, had been loaded by her with gifts, and had
requited her by bribing an Italian quack to poison two of her
children. As the poison had not been administered, Goodman
could be prosecuted only for a misdemeanour. He was tried,
convicted and sentenced to a ruinous fine. He had since
distinguished himself as one of the first forgers of bank notes.†

Sir William Parkyns, a wealthy knight bred to the law, who
had been conspicuous among the Tories in the days of the
Exclusion Bill, was one of the most important members of the
confederacy. He bore a much fairer character than most of
his accomplices: but in one respect he was more culpable than
any of them. For he had, in order to retain a lucrative office
which he held in the Court of Chancery, sworn allegiance to the
Prince against whose life he now conspired.

The design was imparted to Sir John Fenwick, celebrated on
account of the cowardly insult which he had offered to the
deceased Queen. Fenwick, if his own assertion is to be trusted,
was willing to join in an insurrection, but recoiled from the
thought of assassination, and showed so much of what was in
his mind as sufficed to make him an object of suspicion to his
less scrupulous associates. He kept their secret, however, as
strictly as if he had wished them success.

It should seem that, at first, a natural feeling restrained the
conspirators from calling their design by the proper name.
Even in their private consultations they did not as yet talk of
killing the Prince of Orange. They would try to seize him and
to carry him alive into France. If there were any resistance
they might be forced to use their swords and pistols, and

---

* Every thing bad that was known or rumoured about Porter came out
on the State Trials of 1696.

† As to Goodman see the evidence on the trial of Peter Cook; Clever-
skirke, $\frac{\text{Feb 28.}}{\text{March 9.}}$ 1696; L'Hermitage, April $\frac{19}{29}$. 1696; and a pasquinade
entitled the Duchess of Cleveland's Memorial.

nobody could be answerable for what a thrust or a shot might do. In the spring of 1695, the scheme of assassination, thus thinly veiled, was communicated to James, and his sanction was earnestly requested. But week followed week; and no answer arrived from him. He doubtless remained silent in the hope that his adherents would, after a short delay, venture to act on their own responsibility, and that he might thus have the advantage without the scandal of their crime. They seem indeed to have so understood him. He had not, they said, authorised the attempt: but he had not prohibited it; and, apprised as he was of their plan, the absence of prohibition was a sufficient warrant. They therefore determined to strike: but before they could make the necessary arrangements William set out for Flanders; and the plot against his life was necessarily suspended till his return.

It was on the twelfth of May that the King left Kensington for Gravesend, where he proposed to embark for the Continent. Three days before his departure the Parliament of Scotland had, after a recess of about two years, met again at Edinburgh. Hamilton, who had, in the preceding session, sate on the throne and held the sceptre, was dead; and it was necessary to find a new Lord High Commissioner. The person selected was John Hay, Marquess of Tweedale, Chancellor of the Realm, a man grown old in business, well informed, prudent, humane, blameless in private life, and, on the whole, as respectable as any Scottish lord who had been long and deeply concerned in the politics of those troubled times.

His task was not without difficulty. It was indeed well known that the Estates were generally inclined to support the government. But it was also well known that there was one subject which would require the most dexterous and delicate management. The cry of the blood shed more than three years before in Glencoe had at length made itself heard. Towards the close of the year 1693, the reports, which had at first been contemptuously derided as factious calumnies, began to be generally thought deserving of serious attention. Many people little disposed to place confidence in any thing that came forth from the secret presses of the Jacobites owned that, for the honour of the government, some inquiry ought to be instituted. The amiable Mary had been much shocked by what she heard. William had, at her request, empowered the Duke of Hamilton and several other Scotchmen of note to investigate the whole matter. But the Duke died: his colleagues were slack in the performance of their duty; and the

King, who knew little and cared little about Scotland, forgot to urge them.*

It now appeared that the government would have done wisely as well as rightly by anticipating the wishes of the country. The horrible story repeated by the nonjurors pertinaciously, confidently, and with so many circumstances as almost enforced belief, had at length roused all Scotland. The sensibility of a people eminently patriotic was galled by the taunts of southern pamphleteers, who asked whether there was on the north of the Tweed, no law, no justice, no humanity, no spirit to demand redress even for the foulest wrongs. Each of the two extreme parties, which were diametrically opposed to each other in general politics, was impelled by a peculiar feeling to call for inquiry. The Jacobites were delighted by the prospect of being able to make out a case which would bring discredit on the usurper, and which might be set off against the many offences imputed by the Whigs to Claverhouse and Mackenzie. The zealous Presbyterians were not less delighted at the prospect of being able to ruin the Master of Stair. They had never forgotten or forgiven the service which he had rendered to the House of Stuart in the time of the persecution. They knew that, though he had cordially concurred in the political revolution which had freed them from the hated dynasty, he had seen with displeasure that ecclesiastical revolution which was, in their view, even more important. They knew that church government was with him merely an affair of State, and that, looking at it as an affair of State, he preferred the episcopal to the synodical model. They could not without uneasiness see so adroit and eloquent an enemy of pure religion constantly attending the royal steps and constantly breathing counsel in the royal ear. They were therefore impatient for an investigation, which, if one half of what was rumoured were true, must produce revelations fatal to the power and fame of the minister whom they distrusted. Nor could that minister rely on the cordial support of all who held office under the Crown. His genius and influence had excited the jealousy of many less successful courtiers, and especially of his fellow secretary, Johnstone.

Thus, on the eve of the meeting of the Scottish Parliament, Glencoe was in the mouths of all Scotchmen of all factions and of all sects. William, who was just about to start for the Continent, learned that, on this subject, the Estates must have their way, and that the best thing that he could do would be to put

* See the preamble to the Commission of 1695.

himself at the head of a movement which it was impossible for him to resist. A Commission authorising Tweedale and several other privy councillors to examine fully into the matter about which the public mind was so strongly excited was signed by the King at Kensington, was sent down to Edinburgh, and was there sealed with the Great Seal of the realm. This was accomplished just in time.* The Parliament had scarcely entered on business when a member rose to move for an inquiry into the circumstances of the slaughter of Glencoe. Tweedale was able to inform the Estates that His Majesty's goodness had prevented their desires, that a Commission of Precognition had, a few hours before, passed in all the forms, and that the lords and gentlemen named in that instrument would hold their first meeting before night.† The Parliament unanimously voted thanks to the King for this instance of his paternal care : but some of those who joined in the vote of thanks expressed a very natural apprehension that the second investigation might end as unsatisfactorily as the first investigation had ended. The honour of the country, they said, was at stake ; and the Commissioners were bound to proceed with such diligence that the result of the inquest might be known before the end of the session. Tweedale gave assurances which, for a time, silenced the murmurers.‡ But, when three weeks had passed away, many members became mutinous and suspicious. On the fourteenth of June it was moved that the Commissioners should be ordered to report. The motion was not carried : but it was renewed day after day. In three successive sittings Tweedale was able to restrain the eagerness of the assembly. But, when he at length announced that the report had been completed, and added that it would not be laid before the Estates till it had been submitted to the King, there was a violent outcry. The public curiosity was intense : for the examination had been conducted with closed doors ; and both Commissioners and clerks had been sworn to secrecy. The King was in the Netherlands. Weeks must elapse before his pleasure could be taken ; and the session could not last much longer. In a fourth debate there were signs which convinced the Lord High Commissioner that it was expedient to yield ; and the report was produced.§

It is a paper highly creditable to those who framed it, an

* The Commission will be found in the Minutes of the Parliament.
† Act. Parl. Scot., May 21. 1695 ; London Gazette, May 30.
‡ Act. Parl. Scot., May 23. 1695.
§ Ibid. June 14. 18. 20. 1695 ; London Gazette, June 27.

excellent digest of evidence, clear, passionless, and austerely just. No source from which valuable information was likely to be derived had been neglected. Glengarry and Keppoch, though notoriously disaffected to the government, had been permitted to conduct the case on behalf of their unhappy kinsmen. Several of the Macdonalds who had escaped from the havoc of that night had been examined, and among them the reigning Mac Ian, the eldest son of the murdered Chief. The correspondence of the Master of Stair with the military men who commanded in the Highlands had been subjected to a strict but not unfair scrutiny. The conclusion to which the Commissioners came, and in which every intelligent and candid inquirer will concur, was that the slaughter of Glencoe was a barbarous murder, and that of this barbarous murder the letters of the Master of Stair were the sole warrant and cause.

That Breadalbane was an accomplice in the crime was not proved: but he did not come off quite clear. In the course of the investigation it was incidentally discovered that he had, while distributing the money of William among the Highland Chiefs, professed to them the warmest zeal for the interest of James, and advised them to take what they could get from the usurper, but to be constantly on the watch for a favourable opportunity of bringing back the rightful King. Breadalbane's defence was that he was a greater villain than his accusers imagined, and that he had pretended to be a Jacobite only in order to get at the bottom of the Jacobite plans. In truth the depths of this man's knavery were unfathomable. It was impossible to say which of his treasons were, to borrow the Italian classification, single treasons, and which double treasons. On this occasion the Parliament supposed him to have been guilty only of a single treason, and sent him to the Castle of Edinburgh. The government, on full consideration, gave credit to his assertion that he had been guilty of a double treason, and let him out again.*

The Report of the Commission was taken into immediate consideration by the Estates. They resolved, without one dissentient voice, that the order signed by William did not authorise the slaughter of Glencoe. They next resolved, but, it should seem, not unanimously, that the slaughter was a murder.† They proceeded to pass several votes, the sense of which was finally summed up in an address to the King. How that part of the address which related to the Master of Stair should be

* Burnet, ii. 157.; Act. Parl., June 10. 1695.
† Act. Parl., June 26. 1695; London Gazette, July 4.

framed was a question about which there was much debate. Several of his letters were called for and read; and several amendments were put to the vote. It should seem that the Jacobites and the extreme Presbyterians were, with but too good cause, on the side of severity. The majority, under the skilful management of the Lord High Commissioner, acquiesced in words which made it impossible for the guilty minister to retain his office, but which did not impute to him such criminality as would have affected his life or his estate. They censured him, but censured him in terms far too soft. They blamed his immoderate zeal against the unfortunate clan, and his warm directions about performing the execution by surprise. His excess in his letters they pronounced to have been the original cause of the massacre : but, instead of demanding that he should be brought to trial as a murderer, they declared that, in consideration of his absence and of his great place, they left it to the royal wisdom to deal with him in such a manner as might vindicate the honour of the government.

The indulgence which was shown to the principal offender was not extended to his subordinates. Hamilton, who had fled and had been vainly cited by proclamation at the City Cross to appear before the Estates, was pronounced not to be clear of the blood of the Glencoe men. Glenlyon, Captain Drummond, Lieutenant Lindsey, Ensign Lundie, and Serjeant Barbour, were still more distinctly designated as murderers; and the King was requested to command the Lord Advocate to prosecute them.

The Parliament of Scotland was undoubtedly, on this occasion, severe in the wrong place and lenient in the wrong place. The cruelty and baseness of Glenlyon and his comrades excite, even after the lapse of a hundred and sixty years, emotions which make it difficult to reason calmly. Yet whoever can bring himself to look at the conduct of these men with judicial impartiality will probably be of opinion that they could not, without great detriment to the commonwealth, have been treated as assassins. They had slain nobody whom they had not been positively directed by their commanding officer to slay. That subordination without which an army is the worst of all rabbles would be at an end, if every soldier were to be held answerable for the justice of every order in obedience to which he pulls his trigger. The case of Glencoe was, doubtless, an extreme case : but it cannot easily be distinguished in principle from cases which, in war, are of ordinary occurrence. Very terrible military executions are sometimes indispensable. Humanity itself may require them. Who then is to decide whether there be an emergency such as makes severity the truest mercy? Who is to determine whether it be or be not necessary to lay a thriving town in ashes, to decimate a large body of mutineers, to shoot a whole gang of banditti? Is the responsibility with the commanding officer, or with the rank and file whom he orders to make ready, present and fire? And if the general rule be that the responsibility is with the commanding officer, and not with those who obey him, is it possible to find any reason for pronouncing the case of Glencoe an exception to that rule? It is remarkable that no member of the Scottish Parliament proposed that any of the private men of Argyle's regiment should be prosecuted for murder. Absolute impunity was granted to every body below the rank of Serjeant. Yet on what principle? Surely, if military obedience was not a valid plea, every man who shot a Macdonald on that horrible night was a murderer. And, if military obedience was a valid plea for the musketeer who acted by order of Serjeant Barbour, why not for Barbour who acted by order of Glenlyon? And why not for Glenlyon who acted by order of Hamilton? It can scarcely be maintained that more deference is due from a private to a noncommissioned officer than from a noncommissioned officer to his captain, or from a captain to his colonel.

It may be said that the orders given to Glenlyon were of so peculiar a nature that, if he had been a man of virtue, he would have thrown up his commission, would have braved the displeasure of colonel, general, and Secretary of State, would have incurred the heaviest penalty which a Court Martial could inflict, rather than have performed the part assigned to him; and this is perfectly true: but the question is not whether he acted like a virtuous man, but whether he did that for which he could, without infringing a rule essential to the discipline of camps and to the security of nations, be hanged as a murderer. In this case, disobedience was assuredly a moral duty: but it does not follow that obedience was a legal crime.

It seems therefore that the guilt of Glenlyon and his fellows was not within the scope of the penal law. The only punishment which could properly be inflicted on them was that which made Cain cry out that it was greater than he could bear; to be vagabonds on the face of the earth, and to carry wherever they went a mark from which even bad men should turn away sick with horror.

It was not so with the Master of Stair. He had been

solemnly pronounced, both by the Commission of Precognition and by the Estates of the Realm in full Parliament, to be the original author of the massacre. That it was not advisable to make examples of his tools was the strongest reason for making an example of him. Every argument which can be urged against punishing the soldier who executes the unjust and inhuman orders of his superior is an argument for punishing with the utmost rigour of the law the superior who gives unjust and inhuman orders. Where there can be no responsibility below, there should be double responsibility above. What the Parliament of Scotland ought with one voice to have demanded was, not that a poor illiterate serjeant, who was hardly more accountable than his own halbert for the bloody work which he had done, should be hanged in the Grassmarket, but that the real murderer, the most politic, the most eloquent, the most powerful, of Scottish statesmen, should be brought to a public trial, and should, if found guilty, die the death of a felon. Nothing less than such a sacrifice could expiate such a crime. Unhappily the Estates, by extenuating the guilt of the chief offender, and, at the same time, demanding that his humble agents should be treated with a severity beyond the law, made the stain which the massacre had left on the honour of the nation broader and deeper than before.

Nor is it possible to acquit the King of a great breach of duty. It is, indeed, highly probable that, till he received the report of his Commissioners, he had been very imperfectly informed as to the circumstances of the slaughter. We can hardly suppose that he was much in the habit of reading Jacobite pamphlets ; and, if he did read them, he would have found in them such a quantity of absurd and rancorous invective against himself that he would have been very little inclined to credit any imputation which they might throw on his servants. He would have seen himself accused, in one tract, of being a concealed Papist, in another of having poisoned Jeffreys in the Tower, in a third of having contrived to have Talmash taken off at Brest. He would have seen it asserted that, in Ireland, he once ordered fifty of his wounded English soldiers to be burned alive. He would have seen that the unalterable affection which he felt from his boyhood to his death for three or four of the bravest and most trusty friends that ever prince had the happiness to possess was made a ground for imputing to him abominations as foul as those which are buried under the waters of the Dead Sea. He might therefore naturally be slow to believe frightful imputations thrown by writers whom he knew to be habitual liars on a statesman whose abilities he valued highly, and to whose exertions he had, on some great occasions, owed much. But he could not, after he had read the documents transmitted to him from Edinburgh by Tweedale, entertain the slightest doubt of the guilt of the Master of Stair. To visit that guilt with exemplary punishment was the sacred duty of a Sovereign who had sworn, with his hand lifted up towards heaven, that he would, in his kingdom of Scotland, repress, in all estates and degrees, all oppression, and would do justice, without acceptance of persons, as he hoped for mercy from the Father of all mercies. William contented himself with dismissing the Master from office. For this great fault, a fault amounting to a crime, Burnet tried to frame, not a defence, but an excuse. He would have us believe that the King, alarmed by finding how many persons had borne a part in the slaughter of Glencoe, thought it better to grant a general amnesty than to punish one massacre by another. But this representation is the very reverse of the truth. Numerous instruments had doubtless been employed in the work of death : but they had all received their impulse, directly or indirectly, from a single mind. High above the crowd of offenders towered one offender, preeminent in parts, knowledge, rank and power. In return for many victims immolated by treachery, only one victim was demanded by justice ; and it must ever be considered as a blemish on the fame of William that the demand was refused.

On the seventeenth of July the session of the Parliament of Scotland closed. The Estates had liberally voted such a supply as the poor country which they represented could afford. They had indeed been put into high good humour by the notion that they had found out a way of speedily making that poor country rich. Their attention had been divided between the inquiry into the slaughter of Glencoe and some specious commercial projects of which the nature will be explained and the fate related in a future chapter.

Meanwhile all Europe was looking anxiously towards the Low Countries. The great warrior who had been victorious at Fleurus, at Steinkirk and at Landen had not left his equal behind him. But France still possessed Marshals well qualified for high command. Already Catinat and Boufflers had given proofs of skill, of resolution, and of zeal for the interests of the state. Either of those distinguished officers would have been a successor worthy of Luxemburg and an antagonist worthy of William : but their master, unfortunately for himself, preferred to both the Duke of Villeroy. The new general had been Lewis's playmate when they were both children, had then become a favourite, and had never ceased to be so. In those superficial graces for which the French aristocracy was then renowned throughout Europe, Villeroy was preeminent among the French aristocracy. His stature was tall, his countenance handsome, his manners nobly and somewhat haughtily polite, his dress, his furniture, his equipages, his table, magnificent. No man told a story with more vivacity: no man sate his horse better in a hunting party: no man made love with more success: no man staked and lost heaps of gold with more agreeable unconcern: no man was more intimately acquainted with the adventures, the attachments, the enmities of the lords and ladies who daily filled the halls of Versailles. There were two characters especially which this fine gentleman had studied during many years, and of which he knew all the plaits and windings, the character of the King, and the character of her who was Queen in every thing but name. But there ended Villeroy's acquirements. He was profoundly ignorant both of books and of business. At the Council Board he never opened his mouth without exposing himself. For war he had not a single qualification except that personal courage which was common to him with the whole class of which he was a member. At every great crisis of his political and of his military life he was alternately drunk with arrogance and sunk in dejection. Just before he took a momentous step his self-confidence was boundless: he would listen to no suggestion: he would not admit into his mind the thought that failure was possible. On the first check he gave up every thing for lost became incapable of directing, and ran up and down in helpless despair. Lewis however loved him; and he, to do him justice, loved Lewis. The kindness of the master was proof against all the disasters which were brought on his kingdom by the rashness and weakness of the servant; and the gratitude of the servant was honourably, though not judiciously, manifested on more than one occasion after the death of the master.[*]

Such was the general to whom the direction of the campaign in the Netherlands was confided. The Duke of Maine was sent to learn the art of war under this preceptor. Maine, the natural son of Lewis by the Duchess of Montespan, had been brought up from childhood by Madame de Maintenon, and was loved by Lewis with the love of a father, by Madame de Maintenon with the not less tender love of a foster mother

[*] There is an excellent portrait of Villeroy in St. Simon's Memoirs.

Grave men were scandalized by the ostentatious manner in which the King, while making a high profession of piety, exhibited his partiality for this offspring of a double adultery. Kindness, they said, was doubtless due from a parent to a child : but decency was also due from a Sovereign to his people.    In spite of these murmurs the youth had been publicly acknowledged, loaded with wealth and dignities, created a Duke and Peer, placed, by an extraordinary act of royal power, above Dukes and Peers of older creation, married to a Princess of the blood royal, and appointed Grand Master of the Artillery of the Realm.    With abilities and courage he might have played a great part in the world.    But his intellect was small ; his nerves were weak ; and the women and priests who had educated him had effectually assisted nature.    He was orthodox in belief, correct in morals, insinuating in address, a hypocrite, a mischiefmaker and a coward.

It was expected at Versailles that Flanders would, during this year, be the chief theatre of war.    Here, therefore, a great army was collected.    Strong lines were formed from the Lys to the Scheld, and Villeroy fixed his headquarters near Tournay. Boufflers, with about twelve thousand men, guarded the banks of the Sambre.

On the other side the British and Dutch troops, who were under William's immediate command, mustered in the neighbourhood of Ghent.    The Elector of Bavaria, at the head of a great force, lay near Brussels.    A smaller army, consisting chiefly of Brandenburghers was encamped not far from Huy.

Early in June military operations commenced.    The first movements of William were mere feints intended to prevent the French generals from suspecting his real purpose.    He had set his heart on retaking Namur.    The loss of Namur had been the most mortifying of all the disasters of a disastrous war. The importance of Namur in a military point of view had always been great, and had become greater than ever during the three years which had elapsed since the last siege.    New works, the masterpieces of Vauban, had been added to the old defences which had been constructed with the utmost skill of Cohorn.    So ably had the two illustrious engineers vied with each other and cooperated with nature that the fortress was esteemed the strongest in Europe.    Over one gate had been placed a vaunting inscription which defied the allies to wrench the prize from the grasp of France.

William kept his own counsel so well that not a hint of his intention got abroad.    Some thought that Dunkirk, some that

Ypres was his object.   The marches and skirmishes by which he disguised his design were compared by Saint Simon to the moves of a skilful chess player.   Feuquieres, much more deeply versed in military science than Saint Simon, informs us that some of these moves were hazardous, and that such a game could not have been safely played against Luxemburg ; and this is probably true, but Luxemburg was gone ; and what Luxemburg had been to William, William now was to Villeroy.

While the King was thus employed, the Jacobites at home, being unable, in his absence, to prosecute their design against his person, contented themselves with plotting against his government.   They were somewhat less closely watched than during the preceding year : for the event of the trials at Manchester had discouraged Aaron Smith and his agents.   Trenchard, whose vigilance and severity had made him an object of terror and hatred, was no more, and had been succeeded, in what may be called the subordinate Secretaryship of State, by Sir William Trumball, a learned civilian and an experienced diplomatist, of moderate opinions, and of temper cautious to timidity.*   The malecontents were emboldened by the lenity of the administration.   William had scarcely sailed for the Continent when they held a great meeting at one of their favourite haunts, the Old King's Head in Leadenhall Street. Charnock, Porter, Goodman, Parkyns and Fenwick were present.   The Earl of Aylesbury was there, a man whose attachment to the exiled house was notorious, but who always denied that he had ever thought of effecting a restoration by immoral means.   His denial would be entitled to more credit if he had not, by taking the oaths to the government against which he was constantly intriguing, forfeited the right to be considered as a man of conscience and honour.   In the assembly was Sir John Friend, a nonjuror who had indeed a very slender wit, but who had made a very large fortune by brewing, and who spent it freely in sedition.   After dinner,—for the plans of the Jacobites were generally laid over wine, and generally bore some trace of the conviviality in which they had originated,—it was resolved that the time was come for an insurrection and a French invasion, and that a special messenger should carry the sense of the meeting to Saint Germains.   Charnock was selected. He undertook the commission, crossed the Channel, saw James, and had interviews with the ministers of Lewis, but could arrange nothing.   The English malecontents would not stir till

* Some curious traits of Trumball's character will be found in Pepys's Tangier Diary.

ten thousand French troops were in the island; and ten thousand French troops could not, without great risk, be withdrawn from the army which was contending against William in the Low Countries. When Charnock returned to report that his embassy had been unsuccessful, he found some of his confederates in gaol. They had during his absence amused themselves, after their fashion, by trying to raise a riot in London on the tenth of June, the birthday of the unfortunate Prince of Wales. They met at a tavern in Drury Lane, and, when hot with wine, sallied forth sword in hand, headed by Porter and Goodman, beat kettledrums, unfurled banners, and began to light bonfires. But the watch, supported by the populace, was too strong for the revellers. They were put to rout: the tavern where they had feasted was sacked by the mob: the ringleaders were apprehended, tried, fined and imprisoned, but regained their liberty in time to bear a part in a far more criminal design.*

By this time all was ready for the execution of the plan which William had formed. That plan had been communicated to the other chiefs of the allied forces, and had been warmly approved. Vaudemont was left in Flanders with a considerable force to watch Villeroy. The King, with the rest of his army, marched straight on Namur. At the same moment the Elector of Bavaria advanced towards the same point on one side, and the Brandenburghers on another. So well had these movements been concerted, and so rapidly were they performed, that the skilful and energetic Boufflers had but just time to throw himself into the fortress. He was accompanied by seven regiments of dragoons, by a strong body of gunners, sappers and miners, and by an officer named Megrigny, who was esteemed the best engineer in the French service with the exception of Vauban. A few hours after Boufflers had entered the place the besieging forces closed round it on every side; and the lines of circumvallation were rapidly formed.

The news excited no alarm at the French Court. There it was not doubted that William would soon be compelled to abandon his enterprise with grievous loss and ignominy. The town was strong: the castle was believed to be impregnable: the magazines were filled with provisions and ammunition sufficient to last till the time at which the armies of that age were expected to retire into winter quarters: the garrison consisted of sixteen thousand of the best troops in the world:

* Postboy, June 13., July 9. 11., 1695; Intelligence Domestic and Foreign, June 14. ; Pacquet Boat from Holland and Flanders, July 9.

they were commanded by an excellent general : he was assisted by an excellent engineer ; nor was it doubted that Villeroy would march with his great army to the assistance of Boufflers, and that the besiegers would then be in much more danger than the besieged.

These hopes were kept up by the despatches of Villeroy. He proposed, he said, first to annihilate the army of Vaudemont, and then to drive William from Namur. Vaudemont might try to avoid an action ; but he could not escape. The Marshal went so far as to promise his master news of a complete victory within twenty-four hours. Lewis passed a whole day in impatient expectation. At last, instead of an officer of high rank loaded with English and Dutch standards, arrived a courier bringing news that Vaudemont had effected a retreat with scarcely any loss, and was safe under the walls of Ghent. William extolled the generalship of his lieutenant in the warmest terms. " My cousin," he wrote, " you have shown yourself a greater master of your art than if you had won a pitched battle." * In the French camp, however, and at the French Court it was universally held that Vaudemont had been saved less by his own skill than by the misconduct of those to whom he was opposed. Some threw the whole blame on Villeroy ; and Villeroy made no attempt to vindicate himself. But it was generally believed that he might, at least to a great extent, have vindicated himself, had he not preferred royal favour to military renown. His plan, it was said, might have succeeded, had not the execution been entrusted to the Duke of Maine. At the first glimpse of danger the bastard's heart had died within him. He had not been able to conceal his poltroonery. He had stood trembling, stuttering, calling for his confessor, while the old officers round him, with tears in their eyes, urged him to advance. During a short time the disgrace of the son was concealed from the father. But the silence of Villeroy showed that there was a secret : the pleasantries of the Dutch gazettes soon elucidated the mystery ; and Lewis learned, if not the whole truth, yet enough to make him miserable. Never during his long reign had he been so moved. During some hours his gloomy irritability kept his servants, his courtiers, even his priests, in terror. He so far forgot the grace and dignity for which he was renowned throughout the world that, in the sight of all the splendid crowd of gentlemen and ladies who came to see him dine at Marli, he broke a cane on

* Vaudemont's Despatch and William's Answer are in the Monthly Mercury for July 1695.

the shoulders of a lacquey, and pursued the poor man with the handle.*

The siege of Namur meanwhile was vigorously pressed by the allies. The scientific part of their operations was under the direction of Cohorn, who was spurred by emulation to exert his utmost skill. He had suffered, three years before, the mortification of seeing the town, as he had fortified it, taken by his great master Vauban. To retake it, now that the fortifications had received Vauban's last improvements, would be a noble revenge.

On the second of July the trenches were opened. On the eighth a gallant sally of French dragoons was gallantly beaten back; and, late on the same evening, a strong body of infantry, the English footguards leading the way, stormed, after a bloody conflict, the outworks on the Brussels side. The King in person directed the attack; and his subjects were delighted to learn that, when the fight was hottest, he laid his hand on the shoulder of the Elector of Bavaria, and exclaimed, " Look, look at my brave English ! " Conspicuous in bravery even among those brave English was Cutts. In that bulldog courage which flinches from no danger, however terrible, he was un-rivalled. There was no difficulty in finding hardy volunteers, German, Dutch and British, to go on a forlorn hope: but Cutts was the only man who appeared to consider such an expedition as a party of pleasure. He was so much at his ease in the hottest fire of the French batteries that his soldiers gave him the honourable nickname of the Salamander.†

On the seventeenth the first counterscarp of the town was attacked. The English and Dutch were thrice repulsed with great slaughter, and returned thrice to the charge. At length, in spite of the exertions of the French officers, who fought valiantly sword in hand on the glacis, the assailants remained in possession of the disputed works. While the conflict was raging, William, who was giving his orders under a shower of bullets, saw with surprise and anger, among the officers of his staff, Michael Godfrey the Deputy Governor of the Bank of England. This gentleman had come to the King's head-quarters in order to make some arrangements for the speedy and safe remittance of money from England to the army in

---

* See Saint Simon's Memoirs, and his note upon Dangeau.

† London Gazette July 22. 1695 ; Monthly Mercury of August, 1695. Swift, ten years later, wrote a lampoon on Cutts, so dull and so nauseously scurrilous that Ward or Gildon would have been ashamed of it, entitled the Description of a Salamander.

the Netherlands, and was curious to see real war. Such curiosity William could not endure. "Mr. Godfrey," he said, "you ought not to run these hazards: you are not a soldier: you can be of no use to us here." "Sir," answered Godfrey, "I run no more hazard than Your Majesty." "Not so," said William; "I am where it is my duty to be; and I may without presumption commit my life to God's keeping: but you——" While they were talking a cannon ball from the ramparts laid Godfrey dead at the King's feet. It was not found however that the fear of being Godfreyed,—such was during some time the cant phrase,—sufficed to prevent idle gazers from coming to the trenches.* Though William forbade his coachmen, footmen and cooks to expose themselves, he repeatedly saw them skulking near the most dangerous spots and trying to get a peep at the fighting. He was sometimes, it is said, provoked into horsewhipping them out of the range of the French guns; and the story, whether true or false, is very characteristic.

On the twentieth of July the Bavarians and Brandenburghers, under the direction of Cohorn, made themselves masters, after a hard fight, of a line of works which Vauban had cut in the solid rock from the Sambre to the Meuse. Three days later, the English and Dutch, Cutts, as usual, in the front, lodged themselves on the second counterscarp. All was ready for a general assault, when a white flag was hung out from the ramparts. The effective strength of the garrison was now little more than one half of what it had been when the trenches were opened. Boufflers apprehended that it would be impossible for eight thousand men to defend the whole circuit of the walls much longer; but he felt confident that such a force would be sufficient to keep the stronghold on the summit of the rock. Terms of capitulation were speedily adjusted. A gate was delivered up to the allies. The French were allowed forty-eight hours to retire into the castle, and were assured that the wounded men whom they left below, about fifteen hundred in number, should be well treated. On the sixth the allies marched in. The contest for the possession of the town was over; and a second and more terrible contest began for the possession of the citadel.†

* London Gazette, July 29. 1695; Monthly Mercury for August 1695; Stepney to Lord Lexington, Aug. $\frac{1.6}{2.6}$.; Robert Fleming's Character of King William, 1702. It was in the attack of July $\frac{1.7}{2.7}$. that Captain Shandy received the memorable wound in his groin.

† London Gazette, Aug. 1. 5. 1695; Monthly Mercury of August 1695, containing the Letters of William and Dykvelt to the States General.

Villeroy had in the meantime made some petty conquests. Dixmuyde, which might have offered some resistance, had opened its gates to him, not without grave suspicion of treachery on the part of the governor. Deynse, which was less able to make any defence, had followed the example. The garrisons of both towns were, in violation of a convention which had been made for the exchange of prisoners, sent into France. The Marshal then advanced towards Brussels in the hope, as it should seem, that, by menacing that beautiful capital, he might induce the allies to raise the siege of the castle of Namur. During thirty-six hours he rained shells and redhot bullets on the city. The Electress of Bavaria, who was within the walls, miscarried from terror. Six convents perished. Fifteen hundred houses were at once in flames. The whole lower town would have been burned to the ground, had not the inhabitants stopped the conflagration by blowing up numerous buildings. Immense quantities of the finest lace and tapestry were destroyed: for the industry and trade which made Brussels famous throughout the world had hitherto been little affected by the war. Several of the stately piles which looked down on the market place were laid in ruins. The Town Hall itself, the noblest of the many noble senate houses reared by the burghers of the Netherlands, was in imminent peril. All this devastation, however, produced no effect except much private misery. William was not to be intimidated or provoked into relaxing the firm grasp with which he held Namur. The fire which his batteries kept up round the castle was such as had never been known in war. The French gunners were fairly driven from their pieces by the hail of balls, and forced to take refuge in vaulted galleries under the ground. Cohorn exultingly betted the Elector of Bavaria four hundred pistoles that the place would fall by the thirty-first of August, New Style. The great engineer lost his wager indeed, but lost it only by a few hours.*

Boufflers now began to feel that his only hope was in Villeroy. Villeroy had proceeded from Brussels to Enghien; he had there collected all the French troops that could be spared from the remotest fortresses of the Netherlands; and he now, at the head of more than eighty thousand men, marched towards Namur. Vaudemont meanwhile joined the besiegers. William therefore thought himself strong enough to offer battle to Villeroy, without intermitting for a moment

* Monthly Mercury for August 1695; Stepney to Lord Lexington, Aug. ¹⁹⁄₂₉.

the operations against Boufflers. The Elector of Bavaria was entrusted with the immediate direction of the siege. The King of England took up, on the west of the town, a strong position strongly intrenched, and there awaited the French, who were advancing from Enghien. Every thing seemed to indicate that a great day was at hand. Two of the most numerous and best ordered armies that Europe had ever seen were brought face to face. On the fifteenth of August the defenders of the castle saw from their watchtowers the mighty host of their countrymen. But between that host and the citadel was drawn up in battle order the not less mighty host of William. Villeroy, by a salute of ninety guns, conveyed to Boufflers the promise of a speedy rescue; and at night Boufflers, by fire signals which were seen far over the vast plain of the Meuse and Sambre, urged Villeroy to fulfil that promise without delay. In the capitals both of France and England the anxiety was intense. Lewis shut himself up in his oratory, confessed, received the Eucharist, and gave orders that the host should be exposed in his chapel. His wife ordered all her nuns to their knees.* London was kept in a state of distraction by a succession of rumours fabricated some by Jacobites and some by stockjobbers. Early one morning it was confidently averred that there had been a battle, that the allies had been beaten, that the King had been killed, that the siege had been raised. The Exchange, as soon as it was opened, was filled to overflowing by people who came to learn whether the bad news was true. The streets were stopped up all day by groups of talkers and listeners. In the afternoon the Gazette, which had been impatiently expected, and which was eagerly read by thousands, calmed the excitement, but not completely : for it was known that the Jacobites sometimes received, by the agency of privateers and smugglers who put to sea in all weathers, intelligence earlier than that which came through regular channels to the Secretary of State at Whitehall. Before night, however, the agitation had altogether subsided : but it was suddenly revived by a bold imposture. A horseman in the uniform of the Guards spurred through the City, announcing that the King had been killed. He would probably have raised a serious tumult, had not some apprentices, zealous for the Revolution and the Protestant religion, knocked him down and carried him to Newgate. The confidential corre-

---

* Monthly Mercury for August 1695 ; Letter from Paris, $\frac{\text{Aug. 26.}}{\text{Sept. 5.}}$ 1695, among the Lexington Papers.

spondent of the States General informed them that, in spite
of all the stories which the disaffected party invented and
circulated, the general persuasion was that the allies would
be successful. The touchstone of sincerity in England, he
said, was the betting. The Jacobites were ready enough to
prove that William must be defeated, or to assert that he had
been defeated : but they would not give the odds, and could
hardly be induced to take any moderate odds. The Whigs,
on the other hand, were ready to stake thousands of
guineas on the conduct and good fortune of the King.*

The event justified the confidence of the Whigs and the
backwardness of the Jacobites. On the sixteenth, the seventeenth, and the eighteenth of August the army of Villeroy
and the army of William confronted each other. It was fully
expected that the nineteenth would be the decisive day. The
allies were under arms before dawn. At four William mounted,
and continued till eight at night to ride from post to post,
disposing his own troops and watching the movements of the
enemy. The enemy approached his lines in several places,
near enough to see that it would not be easy to dislodge him :
but there was no fighting. He lay down to rest, expecting to
be attacked when the sun rose. But when the sun rose he
found that the French had fallen back some miles. He
immediately sent to request that the Elector would storm the
castle without delay. While the preparations were making,
Portland was sent to summon the garrison for the last time.
It was plain, he said to Boufflers, that Villeroy had given up
all hope of being able to raise the siege. It would therefore
be an useless waste of life to prolong the contest. Boufflers
however thought that another day of slaughter was necessary
to the honour of the French arms ; and Portland returned
unsuccessful.†

Early in the afternoon the assault was made in four places
at once by four divisions of the confederate army. One
point was assigned to the Brandenburghers, another to the
Dutch, a third to the Bavarians, and a fourth to the English.
The English were at first less fortunate than they had hitherto
been. The truth is that most of the regiments which had
seen service had marched with William to encounter Villeroy.
As soon as the signal was given by the blowing up of two
barrels of powder, Cutts, at the head of a small body of

* L'Hermitage, Aug. $\frac{13}{23}$. 1695.

† London Gazette, Aug. 26. 1695 ; Monthly Mercury ; Stepney to
Lexington, Aug. $\frac{20}{30}$.

grenadiers, marched first out of the trenches with drums beating and colours flying. This gallant band was to be supported by four battalions which had never been in action, and which, though full of spirit, wanted the steadiness which so terrible a service required. The officers fell fast. Every Colonel, every Lieutenant Colonel, was killed or severely wounded. Cutts received a shot in the head which for a time disabled him. The raw recruits, left almost without direction, rushed forward impetuously till they found themselves in disorder and out of breath, with a precipice before them, under a terrible fire, and under a shower, scarcely less terrible, of fragments of rock and wall. They lost heart, and rolled back in confusion, till Cutts, whose wound had by this time been dressed, succeeded in rallying them. He then led them, not to the place from which they had been driven back, but to another spot where a fearful battle was raging. The Bavarians had made their onset gallantly but unsuccessfully: their general had fallen; and they were beginning to waver when the arrival of the Salamander and his men changed the fate of the day. Two hundred English volunteers, bent on retrieving at all hazards the disgrace of the recent repulse, were the first to force a way, sword in hand, through the palisades, to storm a battery which had made great havoc among the Bavarians, and to turn the guns against the garrison. Meanwhile the Brandenburghers, excellently disciplined and excellently commanded, had performed, with no great loss, the duty assigned to them. The Dutch had been equally successful. When the evening closed in the allies had made a lodgment of a mile in extent on the outworks of the castle. The advantage had been purchased by the loss of two thousand men.*

And now Boufflers thought that he had done all that his duty required. On the morrow he asked for a truce of forty-eight hours in order that the hundreds of corpses which choked the ditches and which would soon have spread pestilence among both the besiegers and the besieged might be removed and interred. His request was granted; and, before the time expired, he intimated that he was disposed to capitulate. He would, he said, deliver up the castle in ten days, if he were not relieved sooner. He was informed that the allies would not treat with him on such terms, and that he must either consent

---

* Boyer's History of King William III., 1703; London Gazette, Aug. 29. 1695; Stepney to Lexington, Aug. $\frac{2\,0}{3\,0}$.; Blathwayt to Lexington Sept. 2.

to an immediate surrender, or prepare for an immediate assault. He yielded, and it was agreed that he and his men should be suffered to depart, leaving the citadel, the artillery, and the stores to the conquerors. Three peals from all the guns of the confederate army notified to Villeroy the fall of the stronghold which he had vainly attempted to succour. He instantly retreated towards Mons, leaving William to enjoy undisturbed a triumph which was made more delightful by the recollection of many misfortunes.

The twenty-sixth of August was fixed for an exhibition such as the oldest soldier in Europe had never seen, and such as, a few weeks before, the youngest had scarcely hoped to see. From the first battle of Condé to the last battle of Luxemburg, the tide of military success had run, without any serious interruption, in one direction. That tide had turned. For the first time, men said, since France had Marshals, a Marshal of France was to deliver up a fortress to a victorious enemy.

The allied forces, foot and horse, drawn up in two lines, formed a magnificent avenue from the breach which had lately been so desperately contested to the bank of the Meuse. The Elector of Bavaria, the Landgrave of Hesse, and many distinguished officers were on horseback in the vicinity of the castle. William was near them in his coach. The garrison, reduced to about five thousand men, came forth with drums beating and ensigns flying. Boufflers and his staff closed the procession. There had been some difficulty about the form of the greeting which was to be exchanged between him and the allied Sovereigns. An Elector of Bavaria was hardly entitled to be saluted by the Marshal with the sword. A King of England was undoubtedly entitled to such a mark of respect: but France did not recognise William as King of England. At last Boufflers consented to perform the salute without marking for which of the two princes it was intended. He lowered his sword. William alone acknowledged the compliment. A short conversation followed. The Marshal, in order to avoid the use of the words Sire and Majesty, addressed himself only to the Elector. The Elector, with every mark of deference, reported to William what had been said; and William gravely touched his hat. The officers of the garrison carried back to their country the news that the upstart who at Paris was designated only as Prince of Orange, was treated by the proudest potentates of the Germanic body with a respect as profound as that which Lewis exacted from the gentlemen of his bedchamber.*

The ceremonial was now over; and Boufflers passed on: but he had proceeded but a short way when he was stopped by Dykvelt who accompanied the allied army as deputy from the States General. "You must return to the town, Sir," said Dykvelt. "The King of England has ordered me to inform you that you are his prisoner." Boufflers was in transports of rage. His officers crowded round him and vowed to die in his defence. But resistance was out of the question: a strong body of Dutch cavalry came up; and the Brigadier who commanded them demanded the Marshal's sword. The Marshal uttered indignant exclamations: "This is an infamous breach of faith. Look at the terms of the capitulation. What have I done to deserve such an affront? Have I not behaved like a man of honour? Ought I not to be treated as such? But beware what you do, gentlemen. I serve a master who can and will avenge me." "I am a soldier, Sir," answered the Brigadier; "and my business is to obey orders without troubling myself about consequences." Dykvelt calmly and courteously replied to the Marshal's indignant exclamations. "The King of England has reluctantly followed the example set by your master. The soldiers who garrisoned Dixmuyde and Deynse have, in defiance of plighted faith, been sent prisoners into France. The Prince whom they serve would be wanting in his duty to them if he did not retaliate. His Majesty might with perfect justice have detained all the French who were in Namur. But he will not follow to such a length a precedent which he disapproves. He has determined to arrest you and you alone: and, Sir, you must not regard as an affront what is in truth a mark of his very particular esteem. How can he pay you a higher compliment than by showing that he considers you as fully equivalent to the five or six thousand men whom your sovereign wrongfully holds in captivity? Nay, you shall even now be permitted to proceed if you will give me your word of honour to return hither unless the garrisons of Dixmuyde and Deynse are released within a fortnight." "I do not at all know," answered Boufflers, "why the King my master detains those men; and therefore I cannot hold out any hope that he will liberate them. You have an army at your back: I am alone; and you must do

* Postscript to the Monthly Mercury for August 1695; London Gazette, Sept. 9.; Saint Simon Dangeau.

your pleasure." He gave up his sword, returned to Namur, and was sent thence to Huy, where he passed a few days in luxurious repose, was allowed to choose his own walks and rides, and was treated with marked respect by those who guarded him. In the shortest time in which it was possible to post from the place where he was confined to the French Court and back again, he received full powers to promise that the garrisons of Dixmuyde and Deynse should be sent back. He was instantly liberated; and he set off for Fontainebleau, where an honourable reception awaited him. He was created a Duke and a Peer. That he might be able to support his new dignities a considerable sum of money was bestowed on him; and, in the presence of the whole aristocracy of France, he was welcomed home by Lewis with an affectionate embrace.*

In all the countries which were united against France the news of the fall of Namur was received with joy: but here the exultation was greatest. During several generations our ancestors had achieved nothing considerable by land against foreign enemies. We had indeed occasionally furnished to our allies small bands of auxiliaries who had well maintained the honour of the nation. But from the day on which the two brave Talbots, father and son, had perished in the vain attempt to reconquer Guienne, till the Revolution, there had been on the Continent no campaign in which Englishmen had borne a principal part. At length our ancestors had again, after an interval of near two centuries and a half, begun to dispute with the warriors of France the palm of military prowess. The struggle had been hard. The genius of Luxemburg and the consummate discipline of the household troops of Lewis had pervailed in two great battles: but the event of those battles had been long doubtful; the victory had been dearly purchased, and the victor had gained little more than the honour of remaining master of the field of slaughter. Meanwhile he was himself training his adversaries. The recruits who survived his severe tuition speedily became veterans. Steinkirk and Landen had formed the volunteers who followed Cutts through the palisades of Namur. The judgment of all the great warriors whom all the nations of Western Europe had sent to the confluence of the Sambre and the Meuse was that the English subaltern was inferior to no subaltern and the English private

* Boyer, History of King William III., 1703; Postscript to the Monthly Mercury, Aug. 1695; London Gazette, Sept. 9. 12.; Blathwayt to Lexington, Sept. 6.; Saint Simon; Dangeau.

soldier to no private soldier in Christendom. The English officers of higher rank were thought hardly worthy to command such an army. Cutts, indeed, had distinguished himself by his intrepidity. But those who most admired him acknowledged that he had neither the capacity nor the science necessary to a general.

The joy of the conquerors was heightened by the recollection of the discomfiture which they had suffered, three years before, on the same spot, and of the insolence with which their enemy had then triumphed over them. They now triumphed in their turn. The Dutch struck medals. The Spaniards sang Te Deums. Many poems, serious and sportive, appeared, of which one only has lived. Prior burlesqued, with admirable spirit and pleasantry, the bombastic verses in which Boileau had celebrated the first taking of Namur. The two odes, printed side by side, were read with delight in London ; and the critics at Will's pronounced that, in wit as in arms, England had been victorious.

The fall of Namur was the great military event of this year. The Turkish war still kept a large part of the forces of the Emperor employed in indecisive operations on the Danube. Nothing deserving to be mentioned took place either in Piedmont or on the Rhine. In Catalonia the Spaniards obtained some slight advantages, advantages due to their English and Dutch allies, who seem to have done all that could be done to help a nation never much disposed to help itself. The maritime superiority of England and Holland was now fully established. During the whole year Russell was the undisputed master of the Mediterranean, passed and repassed between Spain and Italy, bombarded Palamos, spread terror along the whole shore of Provence, and kept the French fleet imprisoned in the harbour of Toulon. Meanwhile Berkeley was the undisputed master of the Channel, sailed to and fro in sight of the coasts of Artois, Picardy, Normandy and Brittany, threw shells into Saint Maloes, Calais and Dunkirk, and burned Granville to the ground. The navy of Lewis, which, five years before, had been the most formidable in Europe, which had ranged the British seas unopposed from the Downs to the Land's End, which had anchored in Torbay and had laid Teignmouth in ashes, now gave no sign of existence except by pillaging merchantmen which were unprovided with convoy. In this lucrative war the French privateers were, towards the close of the summer, very successful. Several vessels laden with sugar from Barbadoes were captured. The losses of the unfortunate East India

Company, already surrounded by difficulties and impoverished by boundless prodigality in corruption, were enormous. Five large ships returning from the Eastern seas, with cargoes of which the value was popularly estimated at a million, fell into the hands of the enemy. These misfortunes produced some murmuring on the Royal Exchange. But, on the whole, the temper of the capital and of the nation was better than it had been during some years.

Meanwhile events which no preceding historian has condescended to mention, but which were of far greater importance than the achievements of William's army or of Russell's fleet, were taking place in London. A great experiment was making. A great revolution was in progress. Newspapers had made their appearance.

While the Licensing Act was in force there was no newspaper in England except the London Gazette, which was edited by a clerk in the office of the Secretary of State, and which contained nothing but what the Secretary of State wished the nation to know. There were indeed many periodical papers: but none of those papers could be called a newspaper. Welwood, a zealous Whig, published a journal called the Observator: but his Observator, like the Observator which Lestrange had formerly edited, contained, not the news, but merely dissertations on politics. A crazy bookseller, named John Dunton, published the Athenian Mercury: but the Athenian Mercury merely discussed questions of natural philosophy, of casuistry and of gallantry. A fellow of the Royal Society, named John Houghton, published what he called a Collection for the Improvement of Industry and Trade. But his Collection contained little more than the prices of stocks, explanations of the modes of doing business in the City, puffs of new projects, and advertisements of books, quack medicines, chocolate, spa water, civet cats, surgeons wanting ships, valets wanting masters and ladies wanting husbands. If ever he printed any political news, he transcribed it from the Gazette. The Gazette was so partial and so meagre a chronicle of events that, though it had no competitors, it had but a small circulation. Only eight thousand copies were printed, much less than one to each parish in the kingdom. In truth a person who had studied the history of his own time only in the Gazette would have been ignorant of many events of the highest importance. He would, for example, have known nothing about the Court Martial on Torrington, the Lancashire Trials, the burning of the Bishop of Salisbury's Pastoral Letter or the impeachment of the Duke of Leeds. But the deficiencies of the Gazette were to a certain extent supplied in London by the coffeehouses, and in the country by the newsletters.

On the third of May 1695 the law which had subjected the press to a censorship expired. Within a fortnight, a stanch old Whig, named Harris, who had, in the days of the Exclusion Bill, attempted to set up a newspaper entitled Intelligence Domestic and Foreign, and who had been speedily forced to relinquish that design, announced that the Intelligence Domestic and Foreign, suppressed fourteen years before by tyranny, would again appear. Ten days after the first number of the Intelligence Domestic and Foreign was printed the first number of the English Courant. Then came the Packet Boat from Holland and Flanders, the Pegasus, the London Newsletter, the London Post, the Flying Post, the Old Postmaster, the Postboy and the Postman. The history of the newspapers of England from that time to the present day is a most interesting and instructive part of the history of the country. At first they were small and meanlooking. Even the Postboy and the Postman, which seem to have been the best conducted and the most prosperous, were wretchedly printed on scraps of dingy paper such as would not now be thought good enough for street ballads. Only two numbers came out in a week ; and a number contained little more matter than may be found in a single column of a daily paper of our time. What is now called a leading article seldom appeared, except when there was a scarcity of intelligence, when the Dutch mails were detained by the west wind, when the Rapparees were quiet in the Bog of Allen, when no stage coach had been stopped by highwaymen, when no nonjuring congregation had been dispersed by constables, when no ambassador had made his entry with a long train of coaches and six, when no lord or poet had been buried in the Abbey, and when consequently it was difficult to fill up four scanty pages. Yet the leading articles, though inserted, as it should seem, only in the absence of more attractive matter, are by no means contemptibly written.

It is a remarkable fact that the infant newspapers were all on the side of King William and the Revolution. This fact may be partly explained by the circumstance that the editors were, at first, on their good behaviour. It was by no means clear that their trade was not in itself illegal. The printing of newspapers was certainly not prohibited by any statute. But, towards the close of the reign of Charles the Second, the judges had pronounced that it was a misdemeanour at common

law to publish political intelligence without the King's license.
It is true that the judges who laid down this doctrine were
removable at the royal pleasure and were eager on all occasions
to exalt the royal prerogative. How the question, if it were
again raised, would be decided by Holt and Treby was doubtful; and the effect of the doubt was to make the ministers of
the Crown indulgent and to make the journalists cautious. On
neither side was there a wish to bring the question of right to
issue. The government therefore connived at the publication
of the newspapers; and the conductors of the newspapers
carefully abstained from publishing any thing that could
provoke or alarm the government. It is true that, in one of
the earliest numbers of one of the new journals, a paragraph
appeared which seemed intended to convey an insinuation that
the Princess Anne did not sincerely rejoice at the fall of
Namur. But the printer made haste to atone for his fault by
the most submissive apologies. During a considerable time
the unofficial gazettes, though much more garrulous and
amusing than the official gazette, were scarcely less courtly.
Whoever examines them will find that the King is always
mentioned with profound respect. About the debates and
divisions of the two Houses a reverential silence is preserved.
There is much invective: but it is almost all directed against
the Jacobites and the French. It seems certain that the
government of William gained not a little by the substitution
of these printed newspapers, composed under constant dread
of the Attorney General, for the old newsletters, which were
written with unbounded license.*

The pamphleteers were under less restraint than the journalists: yet no person who has studied with attention the
political controversies of that time can have failed to perceive
that the libels on William's person and government were

* There is a noble, and, I suppose, unique Collection of the newspapers
of William's reign in the British Museum. I have turned over every page
of that Collection. It is strange that neither Luttrell nor Evelyn should
have noticed the first appearance of the new journals. The earliest mention
of those journals which I have found, is in a despatch of L'Hermitage, dated
July $\frac{12}{22}$. 1695. I will transcribe his words:—"Depuis quelque tems on
imprime ici plusieurs feuilles volantes en forme de gazette, qui sont remplies
de toutes sortes de nouvelles. Cette licence est venue de ce que le parlement n'a pas achévé le bill ou projet d'acte qui avoit été porté dans la
Chambre des Communes pour régler l'imprimerie et empêcher que ces sortes
de choses n'arrivassent. Il n'y avoit ci-devant qu'un des commis des
Secrétaires d'Etat qui eût le pouvoir de faire des gazettes : mais aujourdhui
il s'en fait plusieurs sous d'autres noms." L'Hermitage mentions the
paragraph reflecting on the Princess, and the submission of the libeller.

decidedly less coarse and rancorous during the latter half of his reign than during the earlier half.   And the reason evidently is that the press, which had been fettered during the earlier half of his reign, was free during the latter half. While the censorship existed, no tract blaming, even in the most temperate and decorous language, the conduct of any public department, was likely to be printed with the approbation of the licenser.   To print such a tract without the approbation of the licenser was illegal.   In general, therefore, the respectable and moderate opponents of the Court, not being able to publish in the manner prescribed by law, and not thinking it right or safe to publish in a manner prohibited by law, held their peace, and left the business of criticizing the administration to two classes of men, fanatical nonjurors who sincerely thought that the Prince of Orange was entitled to as little charity or courtesy as the Prince of Darkness, and Grub Street hacks, coarseminded, badhearted and foulmouthed. Thus there was scarcely a single man of judgment, temper and integrity among the many who were in the habit of writing against the government.   Indeed the habit of writing against the government had, of itself, an unfavourable effect on the character.   For whoever was in the habit of writing against the government was in the habit of breaking the law; and the habit of breaking even an unreasonable law tends to make men altogether lawless.   However absurd a tariff may be, a smuggler is but too likely to be a knave and a ruffian.   However oppressive a game law may be, the transition is but too easy from a poacher to a murderer.   And so, though little indeed can be said in favour of the statutes which imposed restraints on literature, there was much risk that a man who was constantly violating those statutes would not be a man of high honour and rigid uprightness.   An author who was determined to print, and could not obtain the sanction of the licenser, must employ the services of needy and desperate outcasts, who, hunted by the peace officers, and forced to assume every week new aliases and new disguises, hid their paper and their types in those dens of vice which are the pest and the shame of great capitals.   Such wretches as these he must bribe to keep his secret and to run the chance of having their backs flayed and their ears clipped in his stead.   A man stooping to such companions and to such expedients could hardly retain unimpaired the delicacy of his sense of what was right and becoming.   The emancipation of the press produced a great and salutary change.   The best and wisest men in the ranks of the opposition now assumed an office which had hitherto been abandoned to the unprincipled or the hot-headed. Tracts against the government were written in a style not misbecoming statesmen and gentlemen; and even the compositions of the lower and fiercer class of malecontents became somewhat less brutal and less ribald than in the days of the licensers.

Some weak men had imagined that religion and morality stood in need of the protection of the licenser. The event signally proved that they were in error. In truth the censor-ship had scarcely put any restraint on licentiousness or profaneness. The Paradise Lost had narrowly escaped muti-lation : for the Paradise Lost was the work of a man whose politics were hateful to the ruling powers. But Etherege's She Would If She Could, Wycherley's Country Wife, Dryden's Translations from the Fourth Book of Lucretius, obtained the Imprimatur without difficulty : for Dryden, Etherege and Wycherley were courtiers. From the day on which the emancipation of our literature was accomplished, the purifica-tion of our literature began. That purification was effected, not by the intervention of senates or magistrates, but by the opinion of the great body of educated Englishmen, before whom good and evil were set, and who were left free to make their choice. During a hundred and sixty years the liberty of our press has been constantly becoming more and more entire; and during those hundred and sixty years the restraint imposed on writers by the general feeling of readers has been constantly becoming more and more strict. At length even that class of works in which it was formerly thought that a voluptuous imagination was privileged to disport itself, love songs, comedies, novels, have become more decorous than the sermons of the seventeenth century. At this day foreigners, who dare not print a word reflecting on the government under which they live, are at a loss to understand how it happens that the freest press in Europe is the most prudish.

On the tenth of October, the King, leaving his army in winter quarters, arrived in England, and was received with unwonted enthusiasm. During his passage through the capital to his palace, the bells of every church were ringing, and every street was lighted up. It was late before he made his way through the shouting crowds to Kensington. But, late as it was, a council was instantly held. An important point was to be decided. Should the House of Commons be permitted to sit again, or should there be an immediate dissolution ? The

King would probably have been willing to keep that House to the end of his reign. But this was not in his power. The Triennial Act had fixed the twenty-fifth of March as the latest day of the existence of the Parliament. If therefore there were not a general election in 1695, there must be a general election in 1696; and who could say what might be the state of the country in 1696? There might be an unfortunate campaign. There might be, indeed there was but too good reason to believe that there would be, a terrible commercial crisis. In either case, it was probable that there would be much ill humour. The campaign of 1695 had been brilliant: the nation was in an excellent temper; and William wisely determined to seize the fortunate moment. Two proclamations were immediately published. One of them announced, in the ordinary form, that His Majesty had determined to dissolve the old Parliament and had ordered writs to be issued for a new Parliament. The other proclamation was unprecedented. It signified the royal pleasure to be that every regiment quartered in a place where an election was to be held should march out of that place the day before the nomination, and should not return till the people had made their choice. From this order, which was generally considered as indicating a laudable respect for popular rights, the garrisons of fortified towns and castles were necessarily excepted.

But, though William carefully abstained from disgusting the constituent bodies by any thing that could look like coercion or intimidation, he did not disdain to influence their votes by milder means. He resolved to spend the six weeks of the general election in showing himself to the people of many districts which he had never yet visited. He hoped to acquire in this way a popularity which might have a considerable effect on the returns. He therefore forced himself to behave with a graciousness and affability in which he was too often deficient; and the consequence was that he received, at every stage of his progress, marks of the good will of his subjects. Before he set out he paid a visit in form to his sister in law, and was much pleased with his reception. The Duke of Gloucester, only six years old, with a little musket on his shoulder, came to meet his uncle, and presented arms. " I am learning my drill," the child said, " that I may help you to beat the French." The King laughed much, and, a few days later, rewarded the young soldier with the Garter.*

On the seventeenth of October William went to Newmarket,

* L'Hermitage, Oct. $\frac{15}{25}$., Nov. $\frac{15}{25}$. 1695.

now a place rather of business than of pleasure, but, in the autumns of the seventeenth century, the gayest and most luxurious spot in the island. It was not unusual for the whole Court and Cabinet to go down to the meetings. Jewellers and milliners, players and fiddlers, venal wits and venal beauties followed in crowds. The streets were made impassable by coaches and six. In the places of public resort peers flirted with maids of honour; and officers of the Life Guards, all plumes and gold lace, jostled professors in trencher caps and black gowns. For the neighbouring University of Cambridge always sent her highest functionaries with loyal addresses, and selected her ablest theologians to preach before the Sovereign and his splendid retinue. In the wild days of the Restoration, indeed, the most learned and eloquent divine might fail to draw a fashionable audience, particularly if Buckingham announced his intention of holding forth; for sometimes His Grace would enliven the dulness of a Sunday morning by addressing to the bevy of fine gentlemen and fine ladies a ribald exhortation which he called a sermon. But the Court of William was more decent; and the Academic dignitaries were treated with marked respect. With lords and ladies from Saint James's and Soho, and with doctors from Trinity College and King's College, were mingled the provincial aristocracy, foxhunting squires and their rosycheeked daughters, who had come in queerlooking family coaches drawn by carthorses from the remotest parishes of three or four counties to see their Sovereign. The heath was fringed by a wild gipsylike camp of vast extent. For the hope of being able to feed on the leavings of many sumptuous tables, and to pick up some of the guineas and crowns which the spendthrifts of London were throwing about, attracted thousands of peasants from a circle of many miles.*

William, after holding his court a few days at this joyous place, and receiving the homage of Cambridgeshire, Huntingdonshire and Suffolk, proceeded to Althorpe. It seems strange that he should, in the course of what was really a canvassing tour, have honoured with such a mark of favour a man so generally distrusted and hated as Sunderland. But the people were determined to be pleased. All Northamptonshire

* London Gazette, Oct. 24. 1695. See Evelyn's Account of Newmarket in 1671, and Pepys, July 18. 1668. From Tallard's despatches written after the Peace of Ryswick, it appears that the autumn meetings were not less numerous or splendid in the days of William than in those of his uncles.

crowded to kiss the royal hand in that fine gallery which had been embellished by the pencil of Vandyke and made classical by the muse of Waller; and the Earl tried to conciliate his neighbours by feasting them at eight tables, all blazing with plate. From Althorpe the King proceeded to Stamford. The Earl of Exeter, whose princely seat was, and still is, one of the great sights of England, had never taken the oaths, and had, in order to avoid an interview which must have been disagreeable, found some pretext for going up to London, but had left directions that the illustrious guest should be received with fitting hospitality. William was fond of architecture and of gardening; and his nobles could not flatter him more than by asking his opinion about the improvement of their country seats. At a time when he had many cares pressing on his mind he took a great interest in the building of Castle Howard; and a wooden model of that edifice, the finest specimen of a vicious style, was sent to Kensington for his inspection. We cannot therefore wonder that he should have seen Burleigh with delight. He was indeed not content with one view, but rose early on the following morning for the purpose of examining the building a second time. From Stamford he went on to Lincoln, where he was greeted by the clergy in full canonicals, by the magistrates in scarlet robes, and by a multitude of baronets, knights and esquires, from all parts of the immense plain which lies between the Trent and the German Ocean. After attending divine service in the magnificent cathedral, he took his departure, and journeyed eastward. On the frontier of Nottinghamshire the Lord Lieutenant of the county, John Holles, Duke of Newcastle, with a great following, met the royal carriages and escorted them to his seat at Welbeck, a mansion surrounded by gigantic oaks which scarcely seem older now than on the day when that splendid procession passed under their shade. The house in which William was then, during a few hours, a guest, passed long after his death, by female descents, from the Holleses to the Harleys, and from the Harleys to the Bentincks, and now contains the originals of those singularly interesting letters which passed between him and his trusty friend and servant Portland. At Welbeck the grandees of the north were assembled. The Lord Mayor of York came thither with a train of magistrates, and the Archbishop of York with a train of divines. William hunted several times in that forest, the finest in the kingdom, which in old times gave shelter to Robin Hood and Little John, and which is now portioned out into the princely domains of Welbeck, Thoresby, Clumber and Worksop. Four hundred gentlemen on horseback partook of his sport. The Nottinghamshire squires were delighted to hear him say at table, after a noble stag chase, that he hoped that this was not the last run which he should have with them, and that he must hire a hunting box among their delightful woods. He then turned southward. He was entertained during one day by the Earl of Stamford at Bradgate, the place where Lady Jane Grey sate alone reading the last words of Socrates while the deer was flying through the park followed by the whirlwind of hounds and hunters. On the morrow the Lord Brook welcomed his Sovereign to Warwick Castle, the finest of those fortresses of the middle ages which have been turned into peaceful dwellings. Guy's Tower was illuminated. A hundred and twenty gallons of punch were drunk to His Majesty's health ; and a mighty pile of faggots blazed in the middle of the spacious court overhung by ruins green with the ivy of centuries. The next morning the King, accompanied by a multitude of Warwickshire gentlemen on horseback, proceeded towards the borders of Gloucestershire. He deviated from his route to dine with Shrewsbury at a secluded mansion in the Wolds, and in the evening went on to Burford. The whole population of Burford met him, and entreated him to accept a small token of their love. Burford was then renowned for its saddles. One inhabitant of the town, in particular, was said by the English to be the best saddler in Europe. Two of his masterpieces were respectfully offered to William, who received them with much grace, and ordered them to be especially reserved for his own use.*

At Oxford he was received with great pomp, complimented in a Latin oration, presented with some of the most beautiful productions of the Academic press, entertained with music, and invited to a sumptuous feast in the Sheldonian theatre. He departed in a few hours, pleading as an excuse for the shortness of his stay that he had seen the colleges before, and that this was a visit, not of curiosity, but of kindness. As it was well known that he did not love the Oxonians and was not loved by them, his haste gave occasion to some idle rumours which found credit with the vulgar. It was said

* I have taken this account of William's progress chiefly from the London Gazettes, from the despatches of L'Hermitage, from Narcissus Luttrell's Diary, and from the letters of Vernon, Yard and Cartwright among the Lexington Papers.

that he hurried away without tasting the costly banquet which had been provided for him, because he had been warned by an anonymous letter, that, if he ate or drank in the theatre, he was a dead man. But it is difficult to believe that a Prince who could scarcely be induced, by the most earnest entreaties of his friends, to take the most common precautions against assassins of whose designs he had trustworthy evidence, would have been scared by so silly a hoax; and it is quite certain that the stages of his progress had been marked, and that he remained at Oxford as long as was compatible with arrangements previously made.*

He was welcomed back to his capital by a splendid show, which had been prepared at great cost during his absence. Sidney, now Earl of Romney and Master of the Ordnance, had determined to astonish London by an exhibition which had never been seen in England on so large a scale. The whole skill of the pyrotechnists of his department was employed to produce a display of fireworks which might vie with any that had been seen in the gardens of Versailles or on the great tank at the Hague. Saint James's Square was selected as the place for the spectacle. All the stately mansions on the northern, eastern and western sides were crowded with people of fashion. The King appeared at a window of Romney's drawing room. The Princess of Denmark, her husband and her court occupied a neighbouring house. The whole diplomatic body assembled at the dwelling of the minister of the United Provinces. A huge pyramid of flame in the centre of the area threw out brilliant cascades which were seen by hundreds of thousands who crowded the neighbouring streets and parks. The States General were informed by their correspondent that, great as the multitude was, the night had passed without the slightest disturbance.†

By this time the elections were almost completed. In every part of the country it had been manifest that the constituent bodies were generally zealous for the King and for the war. The City of London, which had returned four Tories in 1690, returned four Whigs in 1695. Of the proceedings at Westminster an account more than usually circumstantial has come down to us. In 1690 the electors, disgusted by the Sacheverell Clause, had returned two Tories. In 1695, as soon as it was known that a new Parliament was likely to be called, a meeting

---

* See the letter of Yard to Lexington, November 8. 1695, and the note by the editor of the Lexington Papers.

† L'Hermitage, Nov. $\frac{18}{28}$. 1695.

was held, at which it was resolved that a deputation should be sent with an invitation to two Commissioners of the Treasury, Charles Montague and Sir Stephen Fox. Sir Walter Clarges stood on the Tory interest. On the day of nomination near five thousand electors paraded the streets on horseback. They were divided into three bands; and at the head of each band rode one of the candidates. It was easy to estimate at a glance the comparative strength of the parties. For the cavalcade which followed Clarges was the least numerous of the three; and it was well known that the followers of Montague would vote for Fox, and the followers of Fox for Montague. The business of the day was interrupted by loud clamours. The Whigs cried shame on the Jacobite candidate who wished to make the English go to mass, eat frogs and wear wooden shoes. The Tories hooted the two placemen who were raising great estates out of the plunder of the poor overburdened nation. From words the incensed factions proceeded to blows; and there was a riot which was with some difficulty quelled. The High Bailiff then walked round the three companies of horsemen, and pronounced, on the view, that Montague and Fox were duly elected. A poll was demanded. The Tories exerted themselves strenuously. Neither money nor ink was spared. Clarges disbursed two thousand pounds in a few hours, a great outlay in times when the average income of a member of Parliament was not estimated at more than eight hundred a year. In the course of the night which followed the nomination, broadsides filled with invectives against the two courtly upstarts who had raised themselves by knavery from poverty and obscurity to opulence and power were scattered all over the capital. The Bishop of London canvassed openly against the government; for the interference of peers in elections had not yet been declared by the Commons to be a breach of privilege. But all was vain. Clarges was at the bottom of the poll without hope of rising. He withdrew; and Montague was carried on the shoulders of an immense multitude from Westminster Abbey to his office at Whitehall.*

The same feeling exhibited itself in many other places. The freeholders of Cumberland instructed their representatives to support the King, and to vote whatever supplies might be necessary for the purpose of carrying on the war with vigour; and this example was followed by several counties and towns.†
Russell did not arrive in England till after the writs had gone

* L'Hermitage, $\frac{Oct. 25.}{Nov. 4.}$ $\frac{Oct. 29}{Nov. 8}$ 1695.
† Ibid. Nov. $\frac{6}{16}$. 1695.

out.  But he had only to choose for what place he would sit. His popularity was immense : for his villanies were secret, and his public services were universally known.  He had won the battle of La Hogue.  He had commanded two years in the Mediterranean.  He had there shut up the French fleets in the harbour of Toulon, and had stopped and turned back the French armies in Catalonia.  He had taken many vessels, and among them two ships of the line ; and he had not, during his long absence in a remote sea, lost a single vessel either by war or by weather.  He had made the red cross of Saint George an object of terror to all the princes and commonwealths of Italy.  The effect of his successes was that embassies were on their way from Florence, Genoa and Venice, with tardy congratulations to William on his accession.  Russell's merits, artfully magnified by the Whigs, made such an impression that he was returned to Parliament not only by Portsmouth where his official situation gave him great influence, and by Cambridgeshire where his private property was considerable, but also by Middlesex.  This last distinction, indeed, he owed chiefly to the name which he bore.  Before his arrival in England it had been generally thought that two Tories would be returned for the metropolitan county.  Somers and Shrewsbury were of opinion that the only way to avert such a misfortune was to conjure with the name of the most virtuous of all the martyrs of English liberty.  They entreated Lady Russell to suffer her eldest son, a boy of fifteen, who was about to commence his studies at Cambridge, to be put in nomination.  He must, they said, drop, for one day, his new title of Marquess of Tavistock, and call himself Lord Russell. There will be no expense.  There will be no contest.  Thousands of gentlemen on horseback will escort him to the hustings ; nobody will dare to stand against him ; and he will not only come in himself, but bring in another Whig.  The widowed mother, in a letter written with all the excellent sense and feeling which distinguished her, refused to sacrifice her son to her party.  His education, she said, would be interrupted : his head would be turned : his triumph would be his undoing. Just at this conjuncture the Admiral arrived.  He made his appearance before the freeholders of Middlesex assembled on the top of Hampstead Hill, and was returned without opposition.*

* L'Hermitage, Nov. $\frac{5}{15}$. $\frac{18}{28}$. 1695 ; Sir James Forbes to Lady Russell, Oct. 3. 1695 ; Lady Russell to Lord Edward Russell ; The Postman, Nov. 16. 1695.

Meanwhile several noted malecontents received marks of public disapprobation. John Knight, the most factious and insolent of those Jacobites who had dishonestly sworn fealty to King William in order to qualify themselves to sit in Parliament, ceased to represent the great city of Bristol. Exeter, the capital of the west, was violently agitated. It had been long supposed that the ability, the eloquence, the experience, the ample fortune, the noble descent of Seymour would make it impossible to unseat him. But his moral character, which had never stood very high, had, during the last three or four years, been constantly sinking. He had been virulent in opposition till he had got a place. While he had a place he had defended the most unpopular acts of the government. As soon as he was out of place, he had again been virulent in opposition. His saltpetre contract had left a deep stain on his personal honour. Two candidates were therefore brought forward against him; and a contest, the longest and fiercest of that age, fixed the attention of the whole kingdom, and was watched with interest even by foreign governments. The poll was open five weeks. The expense on both sides was enormous. The freemen of Exeter, who, while the election lasted, fared sumptuously every day, were by no means impatient for the termination of their luxurious carnival. They ate and drank heartily; they turned out every evening with good cudgels to fight for Mother Church or for King William : but the votes came in very slowly. It was not till the eve of the meeting of Parliament that the return was made. Seymour was defeated, to his bitter mortification, and was forced to take refuge in the small borough of Totness.*

It is remarkable that, at this election as at the preceding election, John Hampden failed to obtain a seat. He had, since he ceased to be a member of Parliament, been brooding over his evil fate and his indelible shame, and occasionally venting his spleen in bitter pamphlets against the government. When the Whigs had become predominant at the Court and in the House of Commons, when Nottingham had retired, when Caermarthen had been impeached, Hampden, it should seem, again conceived the hope that he might play a great part in public life. But the leaders of his party, apparently, did not wish for an ally of so acrimonious and turbulent a spirit. He found himself still excluded from the House of Commons. He led, during a few months, a miser-

* There is a highly curious account of this contest in the despatches of L'Hermitage.

able life, sometimes trying to forget his cares among the well-
bred gamblers and frail beauties who filled the drawingroom
of the Duchess of Mazarine, and sometimes sunk in religious
melancholy. The thought of suicide often rose in his mind.
Soon there was a vacancy in the representation of Buckinghamshire, the county which had repeatedly sent himself and his
progenitors to Parliament ; and he expected that he should, by
the help of Wharton, whose dominion over the Buckinghamshire Whigs was absolute, be returned without difficulty.
Wharton, however, gave his interest to another candidate.
This was a final blow. The town was agitated by the news
that John Hampden had cut his throat, that he had survived
his wound a few hours, that he had professed deep penitence for
his sins, had requested the prayers of Burnet, and had sent a
solemn warning to the Duchess of Mazarine. A coroner's
jury found a verdict of insanity. The wretched man had
entered on life with the fairest prospects. He bore a name
which was more than noble. He was heir to an ample estate,
and to a patrimony much more precious, the confidence and
attachment of hundreds of thousands of his countrymen. His
own abilities were considerable, and had been carefully cultivated. Unhappily ambition and party spirit impelled him to
place himself in a situation full of danger. To that danger
his fortitude proved unequal. He stooped to supplications
which saved him and dishonoured him. From that moment,
he never knew peace of mind. His temper became perverse ;
and his understanding was perverted by his temper. He tried
to find relief in devotion and in revenge, in fashionable dissipation and in political turmoil. But the dark shade never passed
away from his mind, till, in the twelfth year of his humiliation,
his unhappy life was terminated by an unhappy death.*

The result of the general election proved that William had
chosen a fortunate moment for dissolving. The number of new
members was about a hundred and sixty ; and most of these
were known to be thoroughly well affected to the government.†

It was of the highest importance that the House of Commons
should, at that moment, be disposed to cooperate cordially
with the King. For it was absolutely necessary to apply a
remedy to an internal evil which had by slow degrees grown to
a fearful magnitude. The silver coin, which was then the

---

* Postman, Dec. 15. 17. 1696 ; Vernon to Shrewsbury, Dec. 13. 15. ;
Narcissus Luttrell's Diary ; Burnet, i. 647. ; Saint Evremond's Verses to
Hampden.
† L'Hermitage, Nov. $\frac{18}{28}$. 1695.

standard coin of the realm, was in a state at which the boldest and most enlightened statesmen stood aghast.*

Till the reign of Charles the Second our coin had been struck by a process as old as the thirteenth century. Edward the First had invited hither skilful artists from Florence, which, in his time, was to London what London, in the time of William the Third, was to Moscow. During many generations, the instruments which were then introduced into our mint continued to be employed with little alteration. The metal was divided with shears, and afterwards shaped and stamped by the hammer. In these operations much was left to the hand and eye of the workman. It necessarily happened that some pieces contained a little more and some a little less than the just quantity of silver : few pieces were exactly round ; and the rims were not marked. It was therefore in the course of years discovered that to clip the coin was one of the easiest and most profitable kinds of fraud. In the reign of Elizabeth it had been thought necessary to enact that the clipper should be, as the coiner had long been, liable to the penalties of high treason.† The practice of paring down money, however, was far too lucrative to be so checked ; and, about the time of the Restoration, people began to observe that a large proportion of the crowns, halfcrowns and shillings which were passing from hand to hand had undergone some slight mutilation.

That was a time fruitful of experiments and inventions in all the departments of science. A great improvement in the mode of shaping and striking the coin was suggested. A mill, which to a great extent superseded the human hand, was set up in the Tower of London. This mill was worked by horses, and would doubtless be considered by modern engineers as a rude and feeble machine. The pieces which it produced, however, were among the best in Europe. It was not easy to counterfeit them ; and, as their shape was exactly circular, and their edges were inscribed with a legend, clipping was not to be apprehended.‡ The hammered coins and the milled coins were current together. They were received without distinction in public, and consequently in private, payments. The financiers

---

* I have derived much valuable information on this subject from a MS. in the British Museum, Lansdowne Collection, No. 801. It is entitled Brief Memoires relating to the Silver and Gold Coins of England, with an Account of the Corruption of the Hammered Money, and of the Reform by the late Grand Coinage at the Tower and the Country Mints, by Hopton Haynes, Assay Master of the Mint.

† Stat. 5 Eliz. c. 11., and 18 Eliz. c. 1.

‡ Pepys's Diary, November 23. 1663.

of that age seem to have expected that the new money, which was excellent, would soon displace the old money which was much impaired. Yet any man of plain understanding might have known that, when the State treats perfect coin and light coin as of equal value, the perfect coin will not drive the light coin out of circulation, but will itself be driven out. A clipped crown, on English ground, went as far in the payment of a tax or a debt as a milled crown. But the milled crown, as soon as it had been flung into the crucible or carried across the Channel, became much more valuable than the clipped crown. It might therefore have been predicted, as confidently as any thing can be predicted which depends on the human will, that the inferior pieces would remain in the only market in which they could fetch the same price as the superior pieces, and that the superior pieces would take some form or fly to some place in which some advantage could be derived from their superiority.*

The politicians of that age, however, generally overlooked these very obvious considerations. They marvelled exceedingly that every body should be so perverse as to use light money in preference to good money. In other words, they marvelled that nobody chose to pay twelve ounces of silver when ten would serve the turn. The horse in the Tower still paced his rounds. Fresh waggon loads of choice money still came forth from the mill ; and still they vanished as fast as they appeared. Great masses were melted down ; great masses exported ; great

---

* The first writer who noticed the fact that, where good money and bad money are thown into circulation together, the bad money drives out the good money, was Aristophanes. He seems to have thought that the preference which his fellow citizens gave to light coins was to be attributed to a depraved taste, such as led them to entrust men like Cleon and Hyperbolus with the conduct of great affairs. But, though his political economy will not bear examination, his verses are excellent :—

> πολλάκις γ' ἡμῖν ἔδοξεν ἡ πόλις πεπονθέναι
> ταὐτὸν ἔς τε τῶν πολιτῶν τοὺς καλούς τε κἀγαθούς
> ἔς τε τἀρχαῖον νόμισμα καὶ τὸ καινὸν χρυσίον.
> οὔτε γὰρ τούτοισιν οὖσιν οὐ κεκιβδηλευμένοις
> ἀλλὰ καλλίστοις ἁπάντων, ὡς δοκεῖ, νομισμάτων,
> καὶ μόνοις ὀρθῶς κοπεῖσι, καὶ κεκωδωνισμένοις
> ἔν τε τοῖς Ἕλλησι καὶ τοῖς βαρβάροισι πανταχοῦ,
> χρώμεθ' οὐδέν, ἀλλὰ τούτοις τοῖς πονηροῖς χαλκίοις,
> χθές τε καὶ πρώην κοπεῖσι τῷ κακίστῳ κόμματι.
> τῶν πολιτῶν θ' οὓς μὲν ἴσμεν εὐγενεῖς καὶ σώφρονας
> ἄνδρας ὄντας, καὶ δικαίους, καὶ καλούς τε κἀγαθούς,
> καὶ τραφέντας ἐν παλαίστραις, καὶ χοροῖς καὶ μουσικῇ,
> προυσελοῦμεν· τοῖς δὲ χαλκοῖς, καὶ ξένοις, καὶ πυρρίαις,
> καὶ πονηροῖς, κἀκ πονηρῶν, εἰς ἅπαντα χρώμεθα.

masses hoarded : but scarcely one new piece was to be found in the till of a shop, or in the leathern bag which the farmer carried home from the cattle fair. In the receipts and payments of the Exchequer the milled money did not exceed ten shillings in a hundred pounds. A writer of that age mentions the case of a merchant who, in a sum of thirty-five pounds, received only a single halfcrown in milled silver. Meanwhile the shears of the clippers were constantly at work. The coiners too multiplied and prospered : for the worse the current money became the more easily it was imitated. During more than thirty years this evil had gone on increasing. At first it had been disregarded : but it had at length become an insupportable curse to the country. It was to no purpose that the rigorous laws against coining and clipping were rigorously executed. At every session that was held at the Old Bailey terrible examples were made. Hurdles, with four, five, six wretches convicted of counterfeiting or mutilating the money of the realm, were dragged month after month up Holborn Hill. On one morning seven men were hanged and a woman burned for clipping. But all was vain. The gains were such as to lawless spirits seemed more than proportioned to the risks. Some clippers were said to have made great fortunes. One in particular offered six thousand pounds for a pardon. His bribe was indeed rejected ; but the fame of his riches did much to counteract the effect which the spectacle of his death was designed to produce.* Nay the severity of the punishment gave encouragement to the crime. For the practice of clipping, pernicious as it was, did not excite in the common mind a detestation resembling that with which men regard murder, arson, robbery, nay, even theft. The injury done by the whole body of clippers to the whole society was indeed immense : but each particular act of clipping was a trifle. To pass a halfcrown, after paring a pennyworth of silver from it, seemed a minute, an almost imperceptible, fault. Even while the nation was crying out most loudly under the distress which the state of the currency had produced, every individual who was capitally punished for contributing to bring the currency into that state had the general sympathy on his side. Constables were unwilling to arrest the offenders. Justices were unwilling to commit. Witnesses were unwilling to tell the whole truth.

---

* Narcissus Luttrell's Diary is filled with accounts of these executions. " Le métier de rogneur de monnoye," says L'Hermitage, " est si lucratif et paroît si facile que, quelque chose qu'on fasse pour les détruire, il s'en trouve toujours d'autres pour prendre leur place. Oct. $\frac{1}{11}$. 1695."

Juries were unwilling to pronounce the word Guilty. It was vain to tell the common people that the mutilators of the coin were causing far more misery than all the highwaymen and housebreakers in the island. For, great as the aggregate of the evil was, only an infinitesimal part of that evil was brought home to the individual malefactor. There was, therefore, a general conspiracy to prevent the law from taking its course. The convictions, numerous as they might seem, were few indeed when compared with the offences; and the offenders who were convicted looked on themselves as murdered men, and were firm in the belief that their sin, if sin it were, was as venial as that of a schoolboy who goes nutting in the wood of a neighbour. All the eloquence of the ordinary could seldom induce them to conform to the wholesome usage of acknowledging in their dying speeches the enormity of their wickedness.*

The evil proceeded with constantly accelerating velocity. At length in the autumn of 1695 it could hardly be said that the country possessed, for practical purposes, any measure of the value of commodities. It was a mere chance whether what was called a shilling was really tenpence, sixpence or a groat. The results of some experiments which were tried at that time deserve to be mentioned. The officers of the Exchequer weighed fifty-seven thousand two hundred pounds of hammered money which had recently been paid in. The weight ought to have been above two hundred and twenty thousand ounces. It proved to be under one hundred and fourteen thousand ounces.† Three eminent London goldsmiths were

* As to the sympathy of the public with the clippers, see the very curious sermon which Fleetwood, afterwards Bishop of Ely, preached before the Lord Mayor in December 1694. Fleetwood says that "a soft pernicious tenderness slackened the care of magistrates, kept back the under officers, corrupted the juries, and withheld the evidence." He mentions the difficulty of convincing the criminals themselves that they had done wrong. See also a Sermon preached at York Castle by George Halley, a clergyman of the Cathedral, to some clippers who were to be hanged the next day. He mentions the impenitent ends which clippers generally made, and does his best to awaken the consciences of his hearers. He dwells on one aggravation of their crime which I should not have thought of. "If," says he, "the same question were to be put in this age, as of old, ' Whose is this image and superscription?' we could not answer the whole. We may guess at the image: but we cannot tell whose it is by the superscription: for that is all gone." The testimony of these two divines is confirmed by that of Tom Brown, who tells a facetious story, which I do not venture to quote, about a conversation between the ordinary of Newgate and a clipper.

† Lowndes's Essay for the Amendment of the Silver Coins, 1695.

G 37

invited to send a hundred pounds each in current silver to be tried by the balance. Three hundred pounds ought to have weighed about twelve hundred ounces. The actual weight proved to be six hundred and twenty-four ounces. The same test was applied in various parts of the kingdom. It was found that a hundred pounds, which should have weighed about four hundred ounces, did actually weigh at Bristol two hundred and forty ounces, at Cambridge two hundred and three, at Exeter one hundred and eighty, and at Oxford only one hundred and sixteen.* There were, indeed, some northern districts into which the clipped money had only begun to find its way. An honest Quaker, who lived in one of these districts, recorded, in some notes which are still extant, the amazement with which, when he travelled southward, shopkeepers and innkeepers stared at the broad and heavy halfcrowns with which he paid his way. They asked whence he came, and where such money was to be found. The guinea which he purchased for twenty-two shillings at Lancaster bore a different value at every stage of his journey. When he reached London it was worth thirty shillings, and would indeed have been worth more had not the government fixed that rate as the highest at which gold should be received in the payment of taxes.†

The evils produced by this state of the currency were not such as have generally been thought worthy to occupy a prominent place in history. Yet it may well be doubted whether all the misery which had been inflicted on the English nation in a quarter of a century by bad Kings, bad Ministers, bad Parliaments and bad Judges, was equal to the misery caused in a single year by bad crowns and bad shillings. Those events which furnish the best themes for pathetic or indignant eloquence are not always those which most affect the happiness of the great body of the people. The misgovernment of Charles and James, gross as it had been, had not prevented the common business of life from going steadily and prosperously on. While the honour and independence of the State were sold to a foreign power, while chartered rights were invaded, while fundamental laws were violated, hundreds of thousands of quiet, honest and industrious families laboured and traded, ate their meals and lay down to rest, in comfort and security. Whether Whigs or Tories, Protestants or Jesuits were uppermost, the grazier drove his beasts

* L'Hermitage, $\frac{\text{Nov. 29}}{\text{Dec. 9}}$ 1695.

† The Memoirs of this Lancashire Quaker were printed a few years ago in a most respectable newspaper, the Manchester Guardian.

to market : the grocer weighed out his currants : the draper measured out his broadcloth : the hum of buyers and sellers was as loud as ever in the towns : the harvest home was celebrated as joyously as ever in the hamlets : the cream over-flowed the pails of Cheshire : the apple juice foamed in the presses of Herefordshire : the piles of crockery glowed in the furnaces of the Trent ; and the barrows of coal rolled fast along the timber railways of the Tyne.   But when the great instru-ment of exchange became thoroughly deranged, all trade, all industry, were smitten as with a palsy.   The evil was felt daily and hourly in almost every place and by almost every class, in the dairy and on the threshing floor, by the anvil and by the loom, on the billows of the ocean and in the depths of the mine.   Nothing could be purchased without a dispute. Over every counter there was wrangling from morning to night. The workman and his employer had a quarrel as regularly as the Saturday came round.   On a fair day or a market day the clamours, the reproaches, the taunts, the curses, were inces-sant ; and it was well if no booth was overturned and no head broken.*   No merchant would contract to deliver goods without making some stipulation about the quality of the coin in which he was to be paid.   Even men of business were often bewil-dered by the confusion into which all pecuniary transactions were thrown.   The simple and the careless were pillaged without mercy by extortioners whose demands grew even more rapidly than the money shrank.   The price of the necessaries of life, of shoes, of ale, of oatmeal, rose fast.   The labourer found that the bit of metal which when he received it was called a shilling would hardly, when he wanted to purchase a pot of beer or a loaf of rye bread, go as far as sixpence.   Where artisans of more than usual intelligence were collected together in great numbers, as in the dockyard at Chatham, they were able to make their complaints heard and to obtain some redress.†   But the ignorant and helpless peasant was cruelly ground be-tween one class which would give money only by tale and another which would take it only by weight.   Yet his sufferings hardly exceeded those of the unfortunate race of authors.   Of the way in which obscure writers were treated we may easily form a judgment from the letters, still extant, of Dryden to his bookseller Tonson.   One day Tonson sends forty brass shillings, to say nothing of clipped money.   Another day he pays a debt with pieces so bad that none of them will go.   The great poet sends them all back, and demands in their place guineas at

* Lowndes's Essay.    † L'Hermitage, $\frac{\text{Dec. 24.}}{\text{Jan. 3.}}$ 1695.

twenty-nine shillings each. "I expect," he says in one letter, "good silver, not such as I have had formerly." "If you have any silver that will go," he says in another letter, "my wife will be glad of it. I lost thirty shillings or more by the last payment of fifty pounds." These complaints and demands, which have been preserved from destruction only by the eminence of the writer, are doubtless merely a fair sample of the correspondence which filled all the mail bags of England during several months.

In the midst of the public distress one class prospered greatly, the bankers; and among the bankers none could in skill or in luck bear a comparison with Charles Duncombe. He had been, not many years before, a goldsmith of very moderate wealth. He had probably, after the fashion of his craft, plied for customers under the arcades of the Royal Exchange, had saluted merchants with profound bows, and had begged to be allowed the honour of keeping their cash. But so dexterously did he now avail himself of the opportunities of profit which the general confusion of prices gave to a moneychanger, that, at the moment when the trade of the kingdom was depressed to the lowest point, he laid down near ninety thousand pounds for the estate of Helmsley in the North Riding of Yorkshire. That great property had, in a troubled time, been bestowed by the Commons of England on their victorious general Fairfax, and had been part of the dower which Fairfax's daughter had brought to the brilliant and dissolute Buckingham. Thither Buckingham, having wasted in mad intemperance, sensual and intellectual, all the choicest bounties of nature and of fortune, had carried the feeble ruins of his fine person and of his fine mind; and there he had closed his chequered life under that humble roof and on that coarse pallet which the great satirist of the succeeding generation described in immortal verse. The spacious domain passed to a new race; and in a few years a palace more splendid and costly than had ever been inhabited by the magnificent Villiers rose amidst the beautiful woods and waters which had been his, and was called by the once humble name of Duncombe.

Since the Revolution the state of the currency had been repeatedly discussed in Parliament. In 1689 a committee of the Commons had been appointed to investigate the subject, but had made no report. In 1690 another committee had reported that immense quantities of silver were carried out of the country by Jews, who, it was said, would do any thing for profit. Schemes were formed for encouraging the importation and discouraging the exportation of the precious metals.    One foolish bill after another was brought in and dropped.    At length, in the beginning of the year 1695, the question assumed so serious an aspect that the Houses applied themselves to it in earnest.    The only practical result of their deliberations, however, was a new penal law which, it was hoped, would prevent the clipping of the hammered coin and the melting and exporting of the milled coin.    It was enacted that every person who informed against a clipper should be entitled to a reward of forty pounds, that every clipper who informed against two clippers should be entitled to a pardon, and that whoever should be found in possession of silver filings or parings should be burned in the cheek with a redhot iron.    Certain officers were empowered to search for bullion.    If bullion were found in a house or on board of a ship, the burden of proving that it had never been part of the money of the realm was thrown on the owner.    If he failed in making out a satisfactory history of every ingot he was liable to severe penalties.    This Act was, as might have been expected, altogether ineffective. During the following summer and autumn, the coins went on dwindling, and the cry of distress from every county in the realm became louder and more piercing.

But happily for England there were among her rulers some who clearly perceived that it was not by halters and branding irons that her decaying industry and commerce could be restored to health.    The state of the currency had during some time occupied the serious attention of four eminent men closely connected by public and private ties.    Two of them were politicians who had never, in the midst of official and parliamentary business, ceased to love and honour philosophy ; and two were philosophers, in whom habits of abstruse meditation had not impaired the homely good sense without which even genius is mischievous in politics.    Never had there been an occasion which more urgently required both practical and speculative abilities ; and never had the world seen the highest practical and the highest speculative abilities united in an alliance so close, so harmonious, and so honourable as that which bound Somers and Montague to Locke and Newton.

It is much to be lamented that we have not a minute history of the conferences of the men to whom England owed the restoration of her currency and the long series of prosperous years which dates from that restoration.    It would be interesting to see how the pure gold of scientific truth found by the two philosophers was mingled by the two statesmen with just that quantity of alloy which was necessary for the working.   It would be curious to study the many plans which were propounded, discussed and rejected, some as inefficacious, some as unjust, some as too costly, some as too hazardous, till at length a plan was devised of which the wisdom was proved by the best evidence, complete success.

Newton has left to posterity no exposition of his opinions touching the currency.   But the tracts of Locke on this subject are happily still extant; and it may be doubted whether in any of his writings, even in those ingenious and deeply meditated chapters on language which form perhaps the most valuable part of the Essay on the Human Understanding, the force of his mind appears more conspicuously.   Whether he had ever been acquainted with Dudley North is not known.   In moral character the two men bore little resemblance to each other. They belonged to different parties.   Indeed, had not Locke taken shelter from tyranny in Holland, it is by no means impossible that he might have been sent to Tyburn by a jury which Dudley North had packed.   Intellectually, however, there was much in common between the Tory and the Whig. They had laboriously thought out, each for himself, a theory of political economy, substantially the same with that which Adam Smith afterwards expounded.   Nay, in some respects the theory of Locke and North was more complete and symmetrical than that of their illustrious successor.   Adam Smith has often been justly blamed for maintaining, in direct opposition to all his own principles, that the rate of interest ought to be regulated by the State ; and he is the more blamable because, long before he was born, both Locke and North had taught that it was as absurd to make laws fixing the price of money as to make laws fixing the price of cutlery or of broadcloth.*

Dudley North died in 1693.   A short time before his death he published, without his name, a small tract which contains a concise sketch of a plan for the restoration of the currency.   This plan appears to have been substantially the same with that which was afterwards fully developed and ably defended by Locke.

One question, which was doubtless the subject of many anxious deliberations, was whether any thing should be done while the war lasted.   In whatever way the restoration of the coin might be effected, great sacrifices must be made, either by

* It ought always to be remembered, to Adam Smith's honour, that he was entirely converted by Bentham's Defence of Usury, and acknowledged, with candour worthy of a true philosopher, that the doctrine laid down in the Wealth of Nations was erroneous.

the whole community or by a part of the community.    And to
call for such sacrifices at a time when the nation was already
paying taxes such as, ten years before, no financier would have
thought it possible to raise, was undoubtedly a course full of
danger.    Timorous politicians were for delay : but the deliberate
conviction of the great Whig leaders was that something must be
hazarded, or that every thing was lost.    Montague, in particular,
is said to have expressed in strong language his determination to
kill or cure.    If indeed there had been any hope that the evil
would merely continue to be what it was, it might have been
wise to defer till the return of peace an experiment which must
severely try the strength of the body politic.    But the evil was
one which daily made progress almost visible to the eye.    There
might have been a recoinage in 1694 with half the risk which
must be run in 1696 ; and, great as would be the risk in 1696,
that risk would be doubled if the coinage were postponed till
1698.

Those politicians whose voice was for delay gave less trouble
than another set of politicians, who were for a general and
immediate recoinage, but who insisted that the new shilling
should be worth only ninepence or ninepence halfpenny.    At
the head of this party was William Lowndes, Secretary of the
Treasury, and member of Parliament for the borough of Seaford,
a most respectable and industrious public servant, but much
more versed in the details of his office than in the higher parts
of political philosophy.    He was not in the least aware that a
piece of metal with the King's head on it was a commodity of
which the price was governed by the same laws which govern
the price of a piece of metal fashioned into a spoon or a buckle,
and that it was no more in the power of Parliament to make the
kingdom richer by calling a crown a pound than to make the
kingdom larger by calling a furlong a mile.    He seriously
believed, incredible as it may seem, that, if the ounce of silver
were divided into seven shillings instead of five, foreign nations
would sell us their wines and their silks for a smaller number of
ounces.    He had a considerable following, composed partly of dull
men who really believed what he told them, and partly of shrewd
men who were perfectly willing to be authorised by law to pay
a hundred pounds with eighty.    Had his arguments prevailed,
the evils of a vast confiscation would have been added to all the
other evils which afflicted the nation : public credit, still in its
tender and sickly infancy, would have been destroyed ; and
here would have been much risk of a general mutiny of the fleet
d army.    Happily Lowndes was completely refuted by Locke

in a paper drawn up for the use of Somers. Somers was delighted with this little treatise, and desired that it might be printed. It speedily became the text book of all the most enlightened politicians in the kingdom, and may still be read with pleasure and profit. The effect of Locke's forcible and perspicuous reasoning is greatly heightened by his evident anxiety to get at the truth, and by the singularly generous and graceful courtesy with which he treats an antagonist of powers far inferior to his own. Flamsteed, the Astronomer Royal, described the controversy well by saying that the point in dispute was whether five was six or only five.*

Thus far Somers and Montague entirely agreed with Locke: but as to the manner in which the restoration of the currency ought to be effected there was some difference of opinion. Locke recommended, as Dudley North had recommended, that the King should by proclamation fix a near day after which the hammered money should in all payments pass only by weight. The advantages of this plan were doubtless great and obvious. It was most simple, and, at the same time, most efficient. What searching, fining, branding, hanging, burning, had failed to do would be done in an instant. The clipping of the hammered pieces, the melting of the milled pieces would cease. Great quantities of good coin would come forth from secret drawers and from behind the panels of wainscots. The mutilated silver would gradually flow into the mint, and would come forth again in a form which would make mutilation impossible. In a short time the whole currency of the realm would be in a sound state, and, during the progress of this great change, there would never at any moment be any scarcity of money.

These were weighty considerations ; and to the joint authority of North and Locke on such a question great respect is due. Yet it must be owned that their plan was open to one serious objection, which did not indeed altogether escape their notice, but of which they seem to have thought too lightly. The restoration of the currency was a benefit to the whole community. On what principle then was the expense of restoring the currency to be borne by a part of the community ? It was most desirable doubtless that the words pound and shilling should again have a fixed signification, that every man should know what his contracts meant and what his property was worth.

* Lowndes's Essay for the Amendment of the Silver Coins ; Locke's Further Considerations concerning raising the Value of Money ; Locke to Molyneux, Nov. 20. 1695 ; Molyneux to Locke, Dec. 24. 1695.

But was it just to attain this excellent end by means of which the effect would be that every farmer who had put by a hundred pounds to pay his rent, every trader who had scraped together a hundred pounds to meet his acceptances, would find his hundred pounds reduced in a moment to fifty or sixty? It was not the fault of such a farmer or of such a trader that his crowns and halfcrowns were not of full weight. The government itself was to blame. The evil which the State had caused the State was bound to repair; and it would evidently have been wrong to throw the charge of the reparation on a particular class, merely because that class was so situated that it could conveniently be pillaged. It would have been as reasonable to require the timber merchants to bear the whole cost of fitting out the Channel fleet, or the gunsmiths to bear the whole cost of supplying arms to the regiments in Flanders, as to restore the currency of the kingdom at the expense of those individuals in whose hands the clipped silver happened at a particular moment to be.

Locke declared that he regretted the loss which, if his advice were taken, would fall on the holders of the short money. But it appeared to him that the nation must make a choice between evils. And in truth it was much easier to lay down the general proposition that the expenses of restoring the currency ought to be borne by the public than to devise any mode in which they could without extreme inconvenience and danger be so borne. Was it to be announced that every person who should within a term of a year or half a year carry to the mint a clipped crown should receive in exchange for it a milled crown, and that the difference between the value of the two pieces should be made good out of the public purse? That would be to offer a premium for clipping. The shears would be more busy than ever. The short money would every day become shorter. The difference which the taxpayers would have to make good would probably be greater by a million at the end of the term than at the beginning: and the whole of this million would go to reward malefactors. If the time allowed for the bringing in of the hammered coin were much shortened, the danger of further clipping would be proportionally diminished; but another danger would be incurred. The silver would flow into the mint so much faster than it could possibly flow out, that there must during some months be a grievous scarcity of money.

A singularly bold and ingenious expedient occurred to Somers and was approved by William. It was that a procla-

*G 37

mation should be prepared with great secresy, and published at once in all parts of the kingdom. This proclamation was to announce that hammered coins would thenceforth pass only by weight. But every possessor of such coins was to be invited to deliver them up within three days, in a sealed packet, to the public authorities. The coins were to be examined, numbered, weighed, and returned to the owner with a promissory note entitling him to receive from the Treasury at a future time the difference between the actual quantity of silver in his pieces and the quantity of silver which, according to the standard, those pieces ought to have contained.* Had this plan been adopted an immediate stop would have been put to the clipping, the melting and the exporting; and the expense of the restoration of the currency would have been borne, as was right, by the public. The inconvenience arising from a scarcity of money would have been of very short duration : for the mutilated pieces would have been detained only till they could be told and weighed : they would then have been sent back into circulation, and the recoinage would have taken place gradually and without any perceptible suspension or disturbance of trade. But against these great advantages were to be set off hazards, which Somers was prepared to brave, but from which it is not strange that politicians of less elevated character should have shrunk. The course which he recommended to his colleagues was indeed the safest for the country, but was by no means the safest for themselves. His plan could not be successful unless the execution were sudden : the execution could not be sudden if the previous sanction of Parliament were asked and obtained ; and to take a step of such fearful importance without the previous sanction of Parliament was to run the risk of censure, impeachment, imprisonment, ruin. The King and the Lord Keeper were alone in the Council. Even Montague quailed ; and it was determined to do nothing without the authority of the legislature. Montague undertook to submit to the Commons a scheme, which was not indeed without dangers and inconveniences, but which was probably the best which he could hope to carry.

On the twenty-second of November the Houses met. Foley was on that day again chosen Speaker. On the following day he was presented and approved. The King opened the session with a speech very skilfully framed. He congratulated his hearers on the success of the campaign on the Continent.

* Burnet, ii. 147.

That success he attributed, in language which must have gratified their feelings, to the bravery of the English army. He spoke of the evils which had arisen from the deplorable state of the coin, and of the necessity of applying a speedy remedy. He intimated very plainly his opinion that the expense of restoring the currency ought to be borne by the State : but he declared that he referred the whole matter to the wisdom of his Great Council. Before he concluded he addressed himself particularly to the newly elected House of Commons, and warmly expressed his approbation of the excellent choice which his people had made. The speech was received with a low but very significant hum of assent both from above and from below the bar, and was as favourably received by the public as by the Parliament.* In the Commons an address of thanks was moved by Wharton, faintly opposed by Musgrave, adopted without a division, and carried up by the whole House to Kensington. At the palace the loyalty of the crowd of gentlemen showed itself in a way which would now be thought hardly consistent with senatorial gravity. When refreshments were handed round in the ante-chamber, the Speaker filled his glass, and proposed two toasts, the health of King William, and confusion to King Lewis ; and both were drunk with loud acclamations. Yet near observers could perceive that, though the representatives of the nation were as a body zealous for civil liberty and for the Protestant religion, and though they were prepared to endure every thing rather than see their country again reduced to vassalage, they were anxious and dispirited. All were thinking of the state of the coin : all were saying that something must be done ; and all acknowledged that they did not know what could be done. " I am afraid," said a member who expressed what many felt, "that the nation can bear neither the disease nor the cure." †

There was indeed a minority by which the difficulties and dangers of that crisis were seen with malignant delight ; and of that minority the keenest, boldest and most factious leader was Howe, whom poverty had made more acrimonious than ever. He moved that the House should resolve itself into a Committee on the State of the Nation ; and the Ministry,— for that word may now with propriety be used,—readily consented. Indeed the great question touching the currency

* Commons' Journals, Nov. 22, 23. 26. 1695 ; L'Hermitage, $\frac{\text{Nov. 26.}}{\text{Dec. 6.}}$

† Commons' Journals, Nov. 26, 27, 28, 29. 1695 ; L'Hermitage, $\frac{\text{Nov. 26}}{\text{Dec. 6.}}$, $\frac{\text{Nov. 29}}{\text{Dec. 9.}}$, $\frac{\text{Dec. 3.}}{\text{13.}}$

could not be brought forward more conveniently than in such a Committee. When the Speaker had left the chair, Howe harangued against the war as vehemently as he had in former years harangued for it. He called for peace, peace on any terms. The nation, he said, resembled a wounded man, fighting desperately on, with blood flowing in torrents. During a short time the spirit might bear up the frame: but faintness must soon come on. No moral energy could long hold out against physical exhaustion. He found very little support. The great majority of his hearers were fully determined to put every thing to hazard rather than submit to France. It was sneeringly remarked that the state of his own finances had suggested to him the image of a man bleeding to death, and that, if a cordial were administered to him in the form of a salary, he would trouble himself little about the drained veins of the commonwealth. "We did not," said the Whig orators, "degrade ourselves by suing for peace when our flag was chased out of our own Channel, when Tourville's fleet lay at anchor in Torbay, when the Irish nation was in arms against us, when every post from the Netherlands brought news of some disaster, when we had to contend against the genius of Louvois in the Cabinet and of Luxemburg in the field. And are we to turn suppliants now, when no hostile squadron dares to show itself even in the Mediterranean, when our arms are victorious on the Continent, when God has removed the great statesman and the great soldier whose abilities long frustrated our efforts, and when the weakness of the French administration indicates, in a manner not to be mistaken, the ascendency of a female favourite?" Howe's suggestion was contemptuously rejected; and the Committee proceeded to take into consideration the state of the currency.*

Meanwhile the newly liberated presses of the capital never rested a moment. Innumerable pamphlets and broadsides about the coin lay on the counters of the booksellers, and were thrust into the hands of members of Parliament in the lobby. In one of the most curious and amusing of these pieces Lewis and his ministers are introduced, expressing the greatest alarm lest England should make herself the richest country in the world by the simple expedient of calling ninepence a shilling, and confidently predicting that, if the old standard were maintained, there would be another revolution. Some writers vehemently objected to the proposition that the public should bear the expense of restoring the

* Commons' Journals, Nov. 28, 29. 1695; L'Hermitage, Dec. $\frac{13}{23}$.

currency : some urged the government to take this opportunity of assimilating the money of England to the money of neighbouring nations : one projector was for coining guilders ; another for coining dollars.*

Within the walls of Parliament the debates continued during several anxious days.  At length Montague, after defeating, first those who were for letting things remain unaltered till the peace, and then those who were for the little shilling, carried eleven resolutions in which the outlines of his own plan were set forth.  It was resolved that the money of the kingdom should be recoined according to the old standard both of weight and of fineness ; that all the new pieces should be milled ; that the loss on the clipped pieces should be borne by the public ; that a time should be fixed after which no clipped money should pass, except in payments to the government ; and that a later time should be fixed, after which no clipped money should pass at all.  What divisions took place in the Committee cannot be ascertained.  When the resolutions were reported there was one division.  It was on the question whether the old standard of weight should be maintained.  The Noes were a hundred and fourteen ; the Ayes two hundred and twenty-five.†

It was ordered that a bill founded on the resolutions should be brought in.  A few days later the Chancellor of the Exchequer explained to the Commons, in a Committee of Ways and Means, the plan by which he proposed to meet the expense of the recoinage.  It was impossible to estimate with precision the charge of making good the deficiencies of the clipped money.  But it was certain that at least twelve hundred thousand pounds would be required.  Twelve hundred thousand pounds the Bank of England undertook to advance on good security.  It was a maxim received among financiers that no security which the government could offer

* L'Hermitage, $\frac{\text{Nov. 22.}}{\text{D}}$, Dec. $\frac{6}{13}$. 1695 ; An Abstract of the Consultations and Debates between the French King and his Council concerning the new Coin that is intended to be made in England, privately sent by a Friend of the Confederates from the French Court to his Brother at Brussels, Dec. 12. 1695 ; A Discourse of the General Notions of Money, Trade and Exchanges, by Mr. Clement of Bristol ; A Letter from an English Merchant at Amsterdam to his Friend in London ; A Fund for preserving and supplying our Coin ; An Essay for regulating the Coin, by A. V. ; A Proposal for supplying His Majesty with 1,200,000l., by mending the Coin, and yet preserving the ancient Standard of the Kingdom. These are a few of the tracts which were distributed among members of Parliament at this conjuncture.

† Commons' Journals, Dec. 10. 1695 ; L'Hermitage, Dec. $\frac{3}{13}$. $\frac{6}{16}$. $\frac{19}{29}$.

was so good as the old hearth money had been. That tax, odious as it was to the great majority of those who paid it, was remembered with regret at the Treasury and in the City. It occurred to the Chancellor of the Exchequer that it might be possible to devise an impost on houses, which might be not less productive nor less certain than the hearth money, but which might press less heavily on the poor, and might be collected by a less vexatious process. The number of hearths in a house could not be ascertained without domiciliary visits. The windows a collector might count without passing the threshold. Montague proposed that the inhabitants of cottages, who had been cruelly harassed by the chimney men, should be altogether exempted from the new duty. His plan was approved by the Committee of Ways and Means, and was sanctioned by the House without a division. Such was the origin of the window tax, a tax which, though doubtless a great evil, must be considered as a blessing when compared with the curse from which it rescued the nation.*

Thus far things had gone smoothly. But now came a crisis which required the most skilful steering. The news that the Parliament and the government were determined on a reform of the currency produced an ignorant panic among the common people. Every man wished to get rid of his clipped crowns and halfcrowns. No man liked to take them. There were brawls approaching to riots in half the streets of London. The Jacobites, always full of joy and hope in a day of adversity and public danger, ran about with eager looks and noisy tongues. The health of King James was publicly drunk in taverns and on ale benches. Many members of Parliament, who had hitherto supported the government, began to waver; and, that nothing might be wanting to the difficulties of the conjuncture, a dispute on a point of privilege arose between the Houses. The Recoinage Bill, framed in conformity with Montague's resolutions, had gone up to the Peers and had come back with amendments, some of which, in the opinion of the Commons, their Lordships had no right to make. The emergency was too serious to admit of delay. Montague brought in a new bill, which was in fact his former bill modified in some points to meet the wishes of the Lords: the Lords, though not perfectly contented with the new bill, passed it without any alteration; and the royal assent was immediately given. The fourth of May, a date long remembered over the whole kingdom and especially in the capital, was fixed as the day on which the

* Commons' Journals, Dec. 13. 1695.

government would cease to receive the clipped money in payment of taxes.*

The principles of the Recoinage Act are excellent. But some of the details, both of that Act and of a supplementary Act which was passed at a later period of the session, seem to prove that Montague had not fully considered what legislation can, and what it cannot, effect. For example, he persuaded the Parliament to enact that it should be penal to give or take more than twenty-two shillings for a guinea. It may be confidently affirmed that this enactment was not suggested or approved by Locke. He well knew that the high price of gold was not the evil which afflicted the State, but merely a symptom of that evil, and that a fall in the price of gold would inevitably follow, and could by no human power or ingenuity be made to precede, the recoinage of the silver. In fact, the penalty seems to have produced no effect whatever, good or bad. Till the milled silver was in circulation, the guinea continued, in spite of the law, to pass for thirty shillings. When the milled silver became plentiful, the guinea fell, not to twenty-two shillings, which was the highest price allowed by the law, but to twenty-one shillings and sixpence.†

Early in February the panic which had been caused by the first debates on the currency subsided; and, from that time till the fourth of May, the want of money was not very severely felt. The recoinage began. Ten furnaces were erected in the garden behind the Treasury; and every day huge heaps of pared and defaced crowns and shillings were turned into massy ingots which were instantly sent off to the mint in the Tower.‡

With the fate of the law which restored the currency was

* Stat. 7 Gul. 3. c. 1.; Lords' and Commons' Journals; L'Hermitage, $\frac{Dec. 31.}{Jan. 10.}$ Jan. $\frac{7}{17}$. $\frac{1}{2}\frac{0}{0}$. $\frac{1}{2}\frac{1}{4}$. 1696. L'Hermitage describes in strong language the extreme inconvenience caused by the dispute between the Houses :—" La longueur qu'il y a dans cette affaire est d'autant plus désagréable qu'il n'y a point de sujet sur lequel le peuple en général puisse souffrir plus d'incommodité, puisqu'il n'y a personne qui, à tous moments, n'aye occasion de l'esprouver."

† That Locke was not a party to the attempt to make gold cheaper by penal laws, I infer from a passage in which he notices Lowndes's complaints about the high price of guineas. "The only remedy," says Locke, "for that mischief, as well as a great many others, is the putting an end to the passing of clipp'd money by tale."—Locke's Further Considerations. That the penalty proved, as might have been expected, inefficacious, appears from several passages in the despatches of L'Hermitage, and even from Haynes's Brief Memoires, though Haynes was a devoted adherent of Montague.

‡ L'Hermitage, Jan. $\frac{1}{2}\frac{1}{4}$. 1696.

closely connected the fate of another law, which had been several years under the consideration of Parliament, and had caused several warm disputes between the hereditary and the elective branch of the legislature. The session had scarcely commenced when the Bill for regulating Trials in cases of High Treason was again laid on the table of the Commons. Of the debates to which it gave occasion nothing is known except one interesting circumstance which has been preserved by tradition. Among those who supported the bill appeared conspicuous a young Whig of high rank, of ample fortune, and of great abilities which had been assiduously improved by study. This was Anthony Ashley Cooper, Lord Ashley, eldest son of the second Earl of Shaftesbury, and grandson of that renowned politician who had, in the days of Charles the Second, been at one time the most unprincipled of ministers, and at another the most unprincipled of demagogues. Ashley had just been returned to Parliament for the borough of Poole, and was in his twenty-fifth year. In the course of his speech he faltered, stammered and seemed to lose the thread of his reasoning. The House, then, as now, indulgent to novices, and then, as now, well aware that, on a first appearance, the hesitation which is the effect of modesty and sensibility is quite as promising a sign as volubility of utterance and ease of manner, encouraged him to proceed. "How can I, Sir," said the young orator, recovering himself, "produce a stronger argument in favour of this bill than my own failure? My fortune, my character, my life, are not at stake. I am speaking to an audience whose kindness might well inspire me with courage. And yet, from mere nervousness, from mere want of practice in addressing large assemblies, I have lost my recollection: I am unable to go on with my argument. How helpless, then, must be a poor man who, never having opened his lips in public, is called upon to reply, without a moment's preparation, to the ablest and most experienced advocates in the kingdom, and whose faculties are paralysed by the thought that, if he fails to convince his hearers, he will in a few hours die on a gallows, and leave beggary and infamy to those who are dearest to him." It may reasonably be suspected that Ashley's confusion and the ingenious use which he made of it had been carefully premeditated. His speech, however, made a great impression, and probably raised expectations which were not fulfilled. His health was delicate: his taste was refined even to fastidiousness: he soon left politics to men whose bodies and minds were of coarser texture than his own, gave himself up to mer intellectual luxury, lost himself in the mazes of the old Academic philosophy, and aspired to the glory of reviving the old Academic eloquence.    His diction, affected and florid, but often singularly beautiful and melodious, fascinated many young enthusiasts.    He had not merely disciples, but worshippers.    His life was short: but he lived long enough to become the founder of a new sect of English freethinkers, diametrically opposed in opinions and feelings to that sect of freethinkers of which Hobbes was the oracle.    During many years the Characteristics continued to be the Gospel of romantic and sentimental unbelievers, while the Gospel of coldblooded and hardheaded unbelievers was the Leviathan.

The bill, so often brought in and so often lost, went through the Commons without a division, and was carried up to the Lords.    It soon came back with the long disputed clause altering the constitution of the Court of the Lord High Steward. A strong party among the representatives of the people was still unwilling to grant any new privilege to the nobility: but the moment was critical.    The misunderstanding which had arisen beween the Houses touching the Recoinage Bill had produced inconveniences which might well alarm even a bold politician.    It was necessary to purchase concession by concession.    The Commons, by a hundred and ninety-two votes to a hundred and fifty, agreed to the amendment on which the Lords had, during four years, so obstinately insisted; and the Lords in return immediately passed the Recoinage Bill without any amendment.

There had been much contention as to the time at which the new system of procedure in cases of high treason should come into operation; and the bill had once been lost in consequence of a dispute on this point.    Many persons were of opinion that the change ought not to take place till the close of the war. It was notorious, they said, that the foreign enemy was abetted by too many traitors at home; and, at such a time, the severity of the laws which protected the commonwealth against the machinations of bad citizens ought not to be relaxed.    It was at last determined that the new regulations should take effect on the twenty-fifth of March, the first day, according to the old Calendar, of the year 1696.

On the twenty-first of January the Recoinage Bill and the Bill for regulating Trials in cases of High Treason received the royal assent.    On the following day the Commons repaired to Kensington on an errand by no means agreeable either to themselves or to the King.    They were, as a body, fully resolved to support him, at whatever cost and at whatever hazard, against every foreign and domestic foe. But they were, as indeed every assembly of five hundred and thirteen English gentlemen that could by any process have been brought together must have been, jealous of the favour which he showed to the friends of his youth. He had set his heart on placing the house of Bentinck on a level in wealth and splendour with the houses of Howard and Seymour, of Russell and Cavendish. Some of the fairest hereditary domains of the Crown had been granted to Portland, not without murmuring on the part both of Whigs and Tories. Nothing had been done, it is true, which was not in conformity with the letter of the law and with a long series of precedents. Every English sovereign had from time immemorial considered the lands to which he had succeeded in virtue of his office as his private property. Every family that had been great in England, from the De Veres down to the Hydes, had been enriched by royal deeds of gift. Charles the Second had carved ducal estates for his bastards out of his hereditary domain. Nor did the Bill of Rights contain a word which could be construed to mean that the King was not at perfect liberty to alienate any part of the estates of the Crown. At first, therefore, William's liberality to his countrymen, though it caused much discontent, called forth no remonstrance from the Parliament. But he at length went too far. In 1695 he ordered the Lords of the Treasury to make out a warrant granting to Portland a magnificent estate in Denbighshire. This estate was said to be worth more than a hundred thousand pounds. The annual income, therefore, can hardly have been less than six thousand pounds ; and the annual rent which was reserved to the Crown was only six and eightpence. This, however, was not the worst. With the property were inseparably connected extensive royalties, which the people of North Wales could not patiently see in the hands of any subject. More than a century before Elizabeth had bestowed a part of the same territory on her favourite Leicester. On that occasion the population of Denbighshire had risen in arms ; and, after much tumult and several executions, Leicester had thought it advisable to resign his mistress's gift back to her. The opposition to Portland was less violent, but not less effective. Some of the chief gentlemen of the principality made strong representations to the ministers through whose offices the warrant had to pass, and at length brought the subject under the consideration of the Lower House. An address was unanimously voted requesting the King to stop the grant: Portland begged that he might not be the cause of a dispute between his master and the Parliament; and the King, though much mortified, yielded to the general wish of the nation.*

This unfortunate affair, though it terminated without an open quarrel, left much sore feeling. The King was angry with the Commons, and still more angry with the Whig ministers who had not ventured to defend his grant. The loyal affection which the Parliament had testified to him during the first days of the session had perceptibly cooled; and he was almost as unpopular as he had ever been, when an event took place which suddenly brought back to him the hearts of millions, and made him for a time as much the idol of the nation as he had been at the end of 1688.†

The plan of assassination which had been formed in the preceding spring had been given up in consequence of William's departure for the Continent. The plan of insurrection which had been formed in the summer had been given up for want of help from France. But before the end of the autumn both plans were resumed. William had returned to England; and the possibility of getting rid of him by a lucky shot or stab was again seriously discussed. The French troops had gone into winter quarters; and the force, which Charnock had in vain demanded while war was raging round Namur, might now be spared without inconvenience. Now, therefore, a plot was laid, more formidable than any that had yet threatened the throne and the life of William: or rather, as has more than once happened in our history, two plots were laid, one within the other. The object of the greater plot was an open insurrection, an insurrection which was to be supported by a foreign army. In this plot almost all the Jacobites of note were more or less concerned. Some laid in arms: some bought horses: some made lists of the servants and tenants in whom they could place firm reliance. The less warlike members of the party could at least take off bumpers to the

---

* Commons' Journals, Jan. 14. 17. 23. 1696; L'Hermitage, Jan. $\frac{14}{24}$; Gloria Cambriæ, or Speech of a Bold Briton against a Dutch Prince of Wales, 1702; Life of the late Honourable Robert Price, &c. 1734. Price was the bold Briton whose speech—never, I believe, spoken—was printed in 1702. He would have better deserved to be called bold, if he had published his impertinence while William was living. The Life of Price is a miserable performance, full of blunders and anachronisms.

† L'Hermitage mentions the unfavourable change in the temper of the Commons; and William alludes to it repeatedly in his letters to Heinsius, Jan. $\frac{24}{31}$. 1696, $\frac{Jan. 28.}{Feb. 7.}$

King over the water, and intimate by significant shrugs and whispers that he would not be over the water long. It was universally remarked that the malecontents looked wiser than usual when they were sober, and bragged more loudly than usual when they were drunk.* To the smaller plot, of which the object was the murder of William, only a few select traitors were privy.

Each of these plots was under the direction of a leader specially sent from Saint Germains. The more honourable mission was entrusted to Berwick. He was charged to communicate with the Jacobite nobility and gentry, to ascertain what force they could bring into the field, and to fix a time for the rising. He was authorised to assure them that the French government was collecting troops and transports at Calais, and that, as soon as it was known there that a rebellion had broken out in England, his father would embark with twelve thousand veteran soldiers, and would be among them in a few hours.

A more hazardous part was assigned to an emissary of lower rank, but of great address, activity and courage. This was Sir George Barclay, a Scotch gentleman who had served with credit under Dundee, and who, when the war in the Highlands had ended, had retired to Saint Germains. Barclay was called into the royal closet, and received his orders from the royal lips. He was directed to steal across the Channel and to repair to London. He was told that a few select officers and soldiers should speedily follow him by twos and threes. That they might have no difficulty in finding him, he was to walk, on Mondays and Thursdays, in the Piazza of Covent Garden after nightfall, with a white handkerchief hanging from his coat pocket. He was furnished with a considerable sum of money, and with a commission which was not only signed but written from beginning to end by James himself. This commission authorised the bearer to do from time to time such acts of hostility against the Prince of Orange and that Prince's adherents as should most conduce to the service of the King. What explanation of these very comprehensive words was orally given by James we are not informed.

Lest Barclay's absence from Saint Germains should cause any suspicion, it was given out that his loose way of life had made it necessary for him to put himself under the care of a

---

* The gaiety of the Jacobites is said by Van Cleverskirke to have been noticed during some time ; $\frac{\text{Feb. 25.}}{\text{March 6.}}$ 1696.

surgeon at Paris.* He set out with eight hundred pounds in his portmanteau, hastened to the coast, and embarked on board of a privateer which was employed by the Jacobites as a regular packet boat between France and England. This vessel conveyed him to a desolate spot in Romney Marsh. About half a mile from the landing place a smuggler named Hunt lived on a dreary and unwholesome fen where he had no neighbours but a few rude shepherds. His dwelling was singularly well situated for a contraband traffic in French wares. Cargoes of Lyons silk and Valenciennes lace sufficient to load thirty packhorses had repeatedly been landed in that dismal solitude without attracting notice. But, since the Revolution, Hunt had discovered that of all cargoes a cargo of traitors paid best. His lonely abode became the resort of men of high consideration, Earls and Barons, Knights and Doctors of Divinity. Some of them lodged many days under his roof while waiting for a passage. A clandestine post was established between his house and London. The couriers were constantly going and returning : they performed their journeys up and down on foot; but they appeared to be gentlemen, and it was whispered that one of them was the son of a titled man. The letters from Saint Germains were few and small. Those directed to Saint Germains were numerous and bulky : they were made up like parcels of millinery, and were buried in the morass till they were called for by the privateer.

Here Barclay landed in January 1696 ; and hence he took the road to London. He was followed, a few days later, by a tall youth, who concealed his name, but who produced credentials of the highest authority. This youth too proceeded to London. Hunt afterwards discovered that his humble roof had had the honour of sheltering the Duke of Berwick.†

The part which Barclay had to perform was difficult and hazardous ; and he omitted no precaution. He had been little in London ; and his face was consequently unknown to the agents of the government. Nevertheless he had several lodgings : he disguised himself so well that his oldest friends would not have known him by broad daylight; and yet he seldom ventured into the streets except in the dark. His chief agent was a monk who, under several names, heard confessions and said masses at the risk of his neck. This man intimated to some of the zealots with whom he consorted that

* Harris's deposition, March 28. 1696.
† Hunt's deposition.

a special agent of the royal family was to be spoken with in Covent Garden, on certain nights, at a certain hour, and might be known by certain signs.* In this way Barclay became acquainted with several men fit for his purpose. The first persons to whom he fully opened himself were Charnock and Parkyns. He talked with them about the plot which they and some of their friends had formed in the preceding spring against the life of William. Both Charnock and Parkyns declared that the scheme might easily be executed, that there was no want of resolute hearts among the Royalists, and that all that was wanting was some sign of His Majesty's approbation.

Then Barclay produced his commission. He showed his two accomplices that James had expressly commanded all good Englishmen, not only to rise in arms, not only to make war on the usurping government, not only to seize forts and towns, but also to do from time to time such other acts of hostility against the Prince of Orange as might be for the royal service. These words, Barclay said, plainly authorised an attack on the Prince's person. Charnock and Parkyns were satisfied. How in truth was it possible for them to doubt that James's confidential agent correctly construed James's expressions? Nay, how was it possible for them to understand the large words of the commission in any sense but one, even if Barclay had not been there to act as commentator? If indeed the subject had never been brought under James's consideration, it might well be thought that those words had dropped from his pen without any definite meaning. But he had been repeatedly apprised that some of his friends in England meditated a deed of blood, and that they were waiting only for his approbation. They had importuned him to speak one word, to give one sign. He had long kept silence; and, now that he had broken silence, he merely told them to do whatever might be beneficial to himself and prejudicial to the usurper. They had his authority as plainly given as they could reasonably expect to have it given in such a case.†

All that remained was to find a sufficient number of courageous and trustworthy assistants, to provide horses and weapons, and to fix the hour and the place of the slaughter. Forty or fifty men, it was thought, would be sufficient. Those troopers of James's guard who had already followed

* Fisher's and Harris's depositions.

† Barclay's narrative, in the Life of James, ii. 548.; Paper by Charnock among the MSS. in the Bodleian Library.

Barclay across the Channel made up nearly half that number.
James had himself seen some of these men before their
departure from Saint Germains, had given them money for
their journey, had told them by what name each of them
was to pass in England, had commanded them to act as
they should be directed by Barclay, and had informed them
where Barclay was to be found and by what tokens he was
to be known.* They were ordered to depart in small
parties, and to assign different reasons for going. Some
were ill: some were weary of the service: Cassels, one of
the most noisy and profane among them, announced that,
since he could not get military promotion, he should enter
at the Scotch college and study for a learned profession.
Under such pretexts about twenty picked men left the
palace of James, made their way by Romney Marsh to
London, and found their captain walking in the dim lamp-
light of the Piazza with the handkerchief hanging from his
pocket. One of these men was Ambrose Rookwood, who held
the rank of Brigadier, and who had a high reputation for
courage and honour: another was Major John Bernardi, an
adventurer of Genoese extraction, whose name has derived
a melancholy celebrity from a punishment so strangely prolonged that it at length shocked a generation which could not
remember his crime.†

It was in these adventurers from France that Barclay placed
his chief trust. In a moment of elation he once called them
his Janissaries, and expressed a hope that they would get him
the George and Garter. But twenty more assassins at least
were wanted. The conspirators probably expected valuable
help from Sir John Friend, who had received a Colonel's commission signed by James, and had been most active in en-
listing men and providing arms against the day when the
French should appear on the coast of Kent. The design was
imparted to him: but he thought it so rash, and so likely to bring
reproach and disaster on the good cause, that he would lend
no assistance to his friends, though he kept their secret
religiously.‡ Charnock undertook to find eight brave and
trusty fellows. He communicated the design to Porter, not
with Barclay's entire approbation; for Barclay appears to have
thought that a tavern brawler, who had recently been in prison
for swaggering drunk about the streets and huzzaing in honour

* Harris's deposition.
† Ibid.   Bernardi's autobiography is not at all to be trusted.
‡ See his trial.

of the Prince of Wales, was hardly to be trusted with a secret of such fearful import. Porter entered into the plot with enthusiasm, and promised to bring in others who would be useful. Among those whose help he engaged was his servant Thomas Keyes. Keyes was a far more formidable conspirator than might have been expected from his station in life. The household troops generally were devoted to William : but there was a taint of disaffection among the Blues. The chief conspirators had already been tampering with some Roman Catholics who were in that regiment ; and Keyes was excellently qualified to bear a part in this work : for he had formerly been trumpeter of the corps, and, though he had quitted the service, he still kept up an acquaintaince with some of the old soldiers in whose company he had lived at free quarter on the Somersetshire farmers after the battle of Sedgemoor.

Parkyns, who was old and gouty, could not himself take a share in the work of death. But he employed himself in providing horses, saddles and weapons for his younger and more active accomplices. In this department of business he was assisted by Charles Cranburne, a person who had long acted as a broker between Jacobite plotters and people who dealt in cutlery and firearms. Special orders were given by Barclay that the swords should be made rather for stabbing than for slashing. Barclay himself enlisted Edward Lowick, who had been a major in the Irish army, and who had, since the capitulation of Limerick, been living obscurely in London. The monk who had been Barclay's first confidant recommended two busy Papists, Richard Fisher and Christopher Knightley ; and this recommendation was thought sufficient. Knightley drew in Edward King, a Roman Catholic gentleman of hot and restless temper ; and King procured the assistance of a French gambler and bully named De la Rue.*

Meanwhile the heads of the conspiracy held frequent meetings at treason taverns, for the purpose of settling a plan of operations. Several schemes were proposed, applauded, and, on full consideration, abandoned. At one time it was thought that an attack on Kensington House at dead of night might probably be successful. The outer wall might easily be scaled. If once forty armed men were in the garden, the palace would soon be stormed or set on fire. Some were of opinion that it would be best to strike the blow on a Sunday as

* Fisher's deposition ; Knightley's deposition ; Cranburne's trial ; De la Rue's deposition.

William went from Kensington to attend divine service at the chapel of Saint James's Palace. The murderers might assemble near the spot where Apsley House and Hamilton Place now stand. Just as the royal coach passed out of Hyde Park, and was about to enter what has since been called the Green Park, thirty of the conspirators, well mounted, might fall on the guards. The guards were ordinarily only five and twenty. They would be taken completely by surprise; and probably half of them would be shot or cut down before they could strike a blow. Meanwhile ten or twelve resolute men on foot would stop the carriage by shooting the horses, and would then without difficulty despatch the King. At last the preference was given to a plan originally sketched by Fisher and put into shape by Porter. William was in the habit of going every Saturday from Kensington to hunt in Richmond Park. There was then no bridge over the Thames between London and Kingston. The King therefore went, in a coach escorted by some of his body guards, through Turnham Green to the river. There he took boat, crossed the water and found another coach and another set of guards ready to receive him on the Surrey side. The first coach and the first set of guards awaited his return on the northern bank. The conspirators ascertained with great precision the whole order of these journeys, and carefully examined the ground on both sides of the Thames. They thought that they should attack the King with more advantage on the Middlesex than on the Surrey bank, and when he was returning than when he was going. For, when he was going, he was often attended to the water side by a great retinue of lords and gentlemen; but on his return he had only his guards about him. The place and time were fixed. The place was to be a narrow and winding lane leading from the landingplace on the north of the river to Turnham Green. The spot may still be easily found. The ground has since been drained by trenches. But in the seventeenth century it was a quagmire, through which the royal coach was with difficulty tugged at a foot's pace. The time was to be the afternoon of Saturday the fifteenth of February. On that day the Forty were to assemble in small parties at public houses near the Green. When the signal was given that the coach was approaching they were to take horse and repair to their posts. As the cavalcade came up this lane Charnock was to attack the guards in the rear, Rookwood on one flank, Porter on the other. Meanwhile Barclay, with eight trusty men, was to stop the coach and to do the deed. That no movement of the King might escape notice, two orderlies were appointed to watch the palace.  One of these men, a bold and active Fleming, named Durant, was especially charged to keep Barclay well informed.  The other, whose business was to communicate with Charnock, was a ruffian named Chambers, who had served in the Irish army, had received a severe wound in the breast at the Boyne, and, on account of that wound, bore a savage personal hatred to William.*

While Barclay was making all his arrangements for the assassination, Berwick was endeavouring to persuade the Jacobite aristocracy to rise in arms.  But this was no easy task.  Several consultations were held; and there was one great muster of the party under the pretence of a masquerade, for which tickets were distributed among the initiated at one guinea each.†  All ended however in talking, singing and drinking.  Many men of rank and fortune indeed declared that they would draw their swords for their rightful Sovereign as soon as their rightful Sovereign was in the island with a French army; and Berwick had been empowered to assure them that a French army should be sent as soon as they had drawn the sword.  But between what they asked and what he was authorised to grant there was a difference which admitted of no compromise.  Lewis, situated as he was, would not risk ten or twelve thousand excellent soldiers on the mere faith of promises.  Similar promises had been made in 1690; and yet, when the fleet of Tourville had appeared on the coast of Devonshire, the western counties had risen as one man in defence of the government, and not a single malecontent had dared to utter a whisper in favour of the invaders.  Similar promises had been made in 1692; and to the confidence which had been placed in those promises was to be attributed the great disaster of La Hogue.  The French King would not be deceived a third time.  He would gladly help the English royalists: but he must first see them help themselves.  There was much reason in this; and there was reason also in what the Jacobites urged on the other side.  If, they said, they were to rise, without a single disciplined regiment to back them, against an usurper supported by a regular army, they should all be cut to pieces before the news that they were up could reach Versailles.  As Berwick could hold out no hope that there would be an invasion before there was an insurrection, and as his English friends were immovable in their determination

* See the trials and depositions.
† L'Hermitage, March $\frac{3}{13}$.

that there should be no insurrection till there was an invasion, he had nothing more to do here, and became impatient to depart.

He was the more impatient to depart because the fifteenth of February drew near. For he was in constant communication with Barclay, and was perfectly apprised of all the details of the crime which was to be perpetrated on that day. He was generally considered as a man of sturdy and even ungracious integrity. But to such a degree had his sense of right and wrong been perverted by his zeal for the interests of his family, and by his respect for the lessons of his priests, that he did not, as he has himself ingenuously confessed, think that he lay under any obligation to dissuade the assassins from the execution of their purpose. He had indeed only one objection to their design ; and that objection he kept to himself. It was simply this, that all who were concerned were very likely to be hanged. That, however, was their affair ; and, if they chose to run such a risk in the good cause, it was not his business to discourage them. His mission was quite distinct from theirs : he was not to act with them ; and he had no inclination to suffer with them. He therefore hastened down to Romney Marsh, and crossed to Calais.*

At Calais he found preparations making for a descent on Kent. Troops filled the town : transports filled the port. Boufflers had been ordered to repair thither from Flanders, and to take the command. James himself was daily expected. In fact he had already left Saint Germains. Berwick, however, would not wait. He took the road to Paris, met his father at Clermont, and made a full report of the state of things in England. His embassy had failed : the Royalist nobility and gentry seemed resolved not to rise till a French army was in the island : but there was still a hope : news would probably come within a few days that the usurper was no more ; and such news would change the whole aspect of affairs. James determined to go on to Calais, and there to await the event of Barclay's plot. Berwick hastened to Versailles for the purpose of giving explanations to Lewis. What the nature of the explanations was we know from Berwick's own narrative. He plainly told the French King that a small band of loyal men would in a short time make an attempt on the life of the great enemy of France. The next courier might bring tidings of an event which would probably subvert the English government and dissolve the European coalition. It might have been

* See Berwick's Memoirs.

thought that a prince who ostentatiously affected the character of a devout Christian and of a courteous knight would instantly have taken measures for conveying to his rival a caution which perhaps might still arrive in time, and would have severely reprimanded the guests who had so grossly abused his hospitality. Such, however, was not the conduct of Lewis. Had he been asked to give his sanction to a murder he would probably have refused with indignation. But he was not moved to indignation by learning that, without his sanction, a crime was likely to be committed which would be far more beneficial to his interests than ten such victories as that of Landen. He sent down orders to Calais that his fleet should be in such readiness as might enable him to take advantage of the great crisis which he anticipated. At Calais James waited with still more impatience for the signal that his nephew was no more. That signal was to be given by a fire, of which the fuel was already prepared on the cliffs of Kent, and which would be visible across the straits.*

But a peculiar fate has, in our country, always attended such conspiracies as that of Barclay and Charnock. The English regard assassination, and have during some ages regarded it, with a loathing peculiar to themselves. So English indeed is this sentiment that it cannot even now be called Irish, and till a recent period, it was not Scotch. In Ireland to this day the villain who shoots at his enemy from behind a hedge is too often protected from justice by public sympathy. In Scotland plans of assassination were often, during the sixteenth and seventeenth centuries, successfully executed, though known to great numbers of persons. The murders of Beaton, of Rizzio, of Darnley, of Murray, of Sharpe, are conspicuous instances. The royalists who murdered Lisle in Switzerland were Irishmen : the royalists who murdered Ascham at Madrid were Irishmen : the royalists who murdered Dorislaus at the Hague were Scotchmen. In England, as soon as such a design ceases to be a secret hidden in the recesses of one gloomy and ulcerated heart, the risk of detection and failure becomes extreme. Felton and Bellingham reposed trust in no human being ; and they were therefore able to accomplish their evil purposes. But Babington's conspiracy against Elizabeth,

---

* Van Cleverskirke, $\frac{\text{Feb 25.}}{\text{March 6}}$ 1696. I am confident that no sensible and impartial person, after attentively reading Berwick's narrative of these transactions and comparing it with the narrative in the Life of James (ii. 544.) which is taken, word for word, from the Original Memoirs, can doubt that James was accessory to the design of assassination.

Fawkes's conspiracy against James, Gerard's conspiracy against Cromwell, the Rye House conspiracy, the Cato Street conspiracy, were all discovered, frustrated and punished. In truth such a conspiracy is here exposed to equal danger from the good and from the bad qualities of the conspirators. Scarcely any Englishman, not utterly destitute of conscience and honour, will engage in a plot for slaying an unsuspecting fellow creature; and a wretch who has neither conscience nor honour is likely to think much on the danger which he incurs by being true to his associates, and on the rewards which he may obtain by betraying them. There are, it is true, persons in whom religious or political fanaticism has destroyed all moral sensibility on one particular point, and yet has left that sensibility generally unimpaired. Such a person was Digby. He had no scruple about blowing King, Lords and Commons into the air. Yet to his accomplices he was religiously and chivalrously faithful; nor could even the fear of the rack extort from him one word to their prejudice. But this union of depravity and heroism is very rare. The vast majority of men are either not vicious enough or not virtuous enough to be loyal and devoted members of treacherous and cruel confederacies; and, if a single member should want either the necessary vice or the necessary virtue, the whole confederacy is in danger. To bring together in one body forty Englishmen, all hardened cutthroats, and yet all so upright and generous that neither the hope of opulence nor the dread of the gallows can tempt any one of them to be false to the rest, has hitherto been found, and will, it is to be hoped, always be found impossible.

There were among Barclay's followers both men too bad and men too good to be trusted with such a secret as his. The first whose heart failed him was Fisher. Even before the time and place of the crime had been fixed, he obtained an audience of Portland, and told that lord that a design was forming against the King's life. Some days later Fisher came again with more precise intelligence. But his character was not such as entitled him to much credit; and the knavery of Fuller, of Young, of Whitney and of Taaffe, had made men of sense slow to believe stories of plots. Portland, therefore, though in general very easily alarmed where the safety of his master and friend was concerned, seems to have thought little about the matter. But, on the evening of the fourteenth of February, he received a visit from a person whose testimony he could not treat lightly. This was a Roman Catholic gentleman of known courage and honour, named Pendergrass.

He had, on the preceding day, come up to town from Hampshire, in consequence of a pressing summons from Porter, who, dissolute and unprincipled as he was, had to Pendergrass been a most kind friend, indeed almost a father. In a Jacobite insurrection Pendergrass would probably have been one of the foremost. But he learned with horror that he was expected to bear a part in a wicked and shameful deed. He found himself in one of those situations which most cruelly torture noble and sensitive natures. What was he to do? Was he to commit a murder? Was he to suffer a murder which he could prevent to be committed? Yet was he to betray one who, however culpable, had loaded him with benefits? Perhaps it might be possible to save William without harming Porter? Pendergrass determined to make the attempt. "My Lord," he said to Portland, "as you value King William's life, do not let him hunt tomorrow. He is the enemy of my religion: yet my religion constrains me to give him this caution. But the names of the conspirators I am resolved to conceal: some of them are my friends: one of them especially is my benefactor; and I will not betray them."

Portland went instantly to the King: but the King received the intelligence very coolly, and seemed determined not to be frightened out of a good day's sport by such an idle story. Portland argued and implored in vain. He was at last forced to threaten that he would immediately make the whole matter public, unless His Majesty would consent to remain within doors during the next day; and this threat was successful.*

Saturday the fifteenth came. The Forty were all ready to mount, when they received intelligence from the orderlies who watched Kensington House that the King did not mean to hunt that morning. "The fox," said Chambers, with vindictive bitterness, "keeps his earth." Then he opened his shirt, showed the great scar in his breast, and vowed revenge on William.

The first thought of the conspirators was that their design had been detected. But they were soon reassured. It was given out that the weather had kept the King at home; and indeed the day was cold and stormy. There was no sign of agitation at the palace. No extraordinary precaution was taken. No arrest was made. No ominous whisper was heard at the coffeehouses. The delay was vexatious: but Saturday the twenty-second would do as well.

* L'Hermitage, Feb. 25. / March 6.

But, before Saturday the twenty-second arrived, a third informer, De la Rue, had presented himself at the palace. His way of life did not entitle him to much respect; but his story agreed so exactly with what had been said by Fisher and Pendergrass that even William began to believe that there was real danger.

Very late in the evening of Friday the twenty-first, Pendergrass, who had as yet disclosed much less than either of the other informers, but whose single word was worth much more than their joint oath, was sent for to the royal closet. The faithful Portland and the gallant Cutts were the only persons who witnessed the singular interview between the King and his generous enemy. William, with courtesy and animation which he rarely showed, but which he never showed without making a deep impression, urged Pendergrass to speak out. "You are a man of true probity and honour: I am deeply obliged to you: but you must feel that the same considerations which have induced you to tell us so much ought to induce you to tell us something more. The cautions which you have as yet given can only make me suspect every body that comes near me. They are sufficient to embitter my life, but not sufficient to preserve it. You must let me know the names of these men." During more than half an hour the King continued to entreat and Pendergrass to refuse. At last Pendergrass said that he would give the information which was required, if he could be assured that it would be used only for the prevention of the crime, and not for the destruction of the criminals. "I give you my word of honour," said William, "that your evidence shall not be used against any person without your own free consent." It was long past midnight when Pendergrass wrote down the names of the chief conspirators.

While these things were passing at Kensington, a large party of the assassins were revelling at a Jacobite tavern in Maiden Lane. Here they received their final orders for the morrow. "Tomorrow or never," said King. "Tomorrow, boys," cried Cassels with a curse, "we shall have the plunder of the field." The morrow came. All was ready: the horses were saddled: the pistols were loaded: the swords were sharpened: the orderlies were on the alert: they early sent intelligence from the palace that the King was certainly going a hunting: all the usual preparations had been made: a party of guards had been sent round by Kingston Bridge to Richmond: the royal coaches, each with six horses, had gone from the stables at Charing Cross to Kensington. The chief murderers assembled in high glee at Porter's lodgings. Pendergrass, who, by the King's command, appeared among them, was greeted with ferocious mirth. "Pendergrass," said Porter, "you are named one of the eight who are to do his business. I have a musquetoon for you that will carry eight balls." "Mr. Pendergrass," said King, "pray do not be afraid of smashing the glass windows." From Porter's lodgings the party adjourned to the Blue Posts in Spring Gardens, where they meant to take some refreshment before they started for Turnham Green. They were at table when a message came from an orderly that the King had changed his mind and would not hunt; and scarcely had they recovered from their first surprise at this ominous news, when Keyes, who had been out scouting among his old comrades, arrived with news more ominous still. "The coaches have returned to Charing Cross. The guards that were sent round to Richmond have just come back to Kensington at full gallop, the flanks of the horses all white with foam. I have had a word with one of the Blues. He told me that strange things are muttered." Then the countenances of the assassins fell; and their hearts died within them. Porter made a feeble attempt to disguise his uneasiness. He took up an orange and squeezed it. "What cannot be done one day may be done another. Come, gentlemen, before we part let us have one glass to the squeezing of the rotten orange." The squeezing of the rotten orange was drunk; and the company dispersed.*

A few hours elapsed before all the conspirators abandoned all hope. Some of them derived comfort from a report that the King had taken physic, and that this was his only reason for not going to Richmond. If it were so, the blow might still be struck. Two Saturdays had been unpropitious. But Sunday was at hand. One of the plans which had formerly been discussed and abandoned might be resumed. The usurper might be set upon at Hyde Park Corner on his way to his chapel. Charnock was ready for any enterprise however desperate. If the hunt was up, it was better to die biting and scratching to the last than to be worried without resistance or revenge. He assembled some of his accomplices at one of the numerous houses at which he had lodgings, and plied them hard with healths to the King, to the Queen, to the Prince, and to

---

* My account of these events is taken chiefly from the trials and depositions. See also Burnet, ii. 165, 166, 167., and Blackmore's True and Impartial History, compiled under the direction of Shrewsbury and Somers, and Boyer's History of King William III., 1703.

the Grand Monarch, as they called Lewis.    But the terror and dejection of the gang were beyond the power of wine; and so many had stolen away that those who were left could effect nothing.    In the course of the afternoon it was known that the guards had been doubled at the palace; and soon after nightfall messengers from the Secretary of State's office were hurrying to and fro with torches through the streets, accompanied by files and musketeers.    Before the dawn of Sunday Charnock was in custody.    A little later, Rookwood and Bernardi were found in bed at a Jacobite alehouse on Tower Hill.    Seventeen more traitors were seized before noon; and three of the Blues were put under arrest.    That morning a Council was held; and, as soon as it rose, an express was sent off to call home some regiments from Flanders: Dorset set out for Sussex, of which he was Lord Lieutenant: Romney, who was Warden of the Cinque Ports, started for the coast of Kent; and Russell hastened down the Thames to take the command of the fleet.    In the evening the Council sate again.    Some of the prisoners were examined and committed.    The Lord Mayor was in attendance, was informed of what had been discovered, and was specially charged to look well to the peace of the capital.*

On Monday morning all the trainbands of the City were under arms.    The King went in state to the House of Lords, sent for the Commons, and from the throne told the Parliament that, but for the protection of a gracious Providence, he should at that moment have been a corpse, and the kingdom would have been invaded by a French army.    The danger of invasion, he added, was still great: but he had already given such orders as would, he hoped, suffice for the protection of the realm. Some traitors were in custody: warrants were out against others: he should do his part in this emergency; and he relied on the Houses to do theirs.†

The Houses instantly voted a joint address in which they thankfully acknowledged the divine goodness which had preserved him to his people, and implored him to take more than ordinary care of his person.    They concluded by exhorting him to seize and secure all persons whom he regarded as dangerous. On the same day two important bills were brought into the Commons.    By one the Habeas Corpus Act was suspended. The other provided that the Parliament should not be dissolved by the death of William.    Sir Rowland Gwyn, an honest

* Portland to Lexington, March $\frac{1}{15}$. 1696; Van Cleverskirke, Feb. 25. Mar. 6.; L'Hermitage, same date.

† Commons' Journals, Feb. 24. 1695.

country gentleman, made a motion of which he did not at all foresee the important consequences. He proposed that the members should enter into an association for the defence of their Sovereign and their country. Montague, who of all men was the quickest at taking and improving a hint, saw how much such an association would strengthen the government and the Whig party.* An instrument was immediately drawn up, by which the representatives of the people, each for himself, solemnly recognised William as rightful and lawful King, and bound themselves to stand by him and by each other against James and James's adherents. Lastly they vowed that, if His Majesty's life should be shortened by violence, they would avenge him signally on his murderers, and would, with one heart, strenuously support the order of succession settled by the Bill of Rights. It was ordered that the House should be called over the next morning.† The attendance was consequently great: the Association, engrossed on parchment, was on the table; and the members went up, county by county, to sign their names.‡

The King's speech, the joint address of both Houses, the Association framed by the Commons, and a proclamation, containing a list of the conspirators and offering a reward of a thousand pounds for the apprehension of any one of them, were soon cried in all the streets of the capital and carried out by all the postbags. Wherever the news came it raised the whole country. Those two hateful words, assassination and invasion, acted like a spell. No impressment was necessary. The seamen came forth from their hiding places by thousands to man the fleet. Only three days after the King had appealed to the nation, Russell sailed out of the Thames with one great squadron. Another was ready for action at Spithead. The militia of all the maritime counties from the Wash to the Land's End was under arms. For persons accused of offences merely political there was generally much sympathy. But Barclay's assassins were hunted like wolves by the whole population. The abhorrence which the English have, through many generations, felt for domiciliary visits, and for all those impediments which the police of continental states throws in the way of travellers, was for a time suspended. The gates of the City of London were kept many hours closed while a strict search was

* England's Enemies Exposed, 1701.
† Commons' Journals, Feb. 24. 169$\frac{5}{6}$.
‡ Ibid. Feb. 25. 169$\frac{5}{6}$; Van Cleverskirke, $\frac{\text{Feb 28.}}{\text{Mar. 9}}$; L'Hermitage, of the same date.

made within. The magistrates of almost every walled town in the kingdom followed the example of the capital. On every highway parties of armed men were posted with orders to stop passengers of suspicious appearance. During a few days it was hardly possible to perform a journey without a passport, or to procure posthorses without the authority of a justice of the peace. Nor was any voice raised against these precautions. The common people indeed were, if possible, more eager than the public functionaries to bring the traitors to justice. This eagerness may perhaps be in part ascribed to the great rewards promised by the royal proclamation. The hatred which every good Protestant felt for Popish cutthroats was not a little strengthened by the songs in which the street poets celebrated the lucky hackney coachman who had caught his traitor, had received his thousand pounds, and had set up as a gentleman.*
The zeal of the populace could in some places hardly be kept within the limits of the law. At the country seat of Parkyns in Warwickshire, arms and accoutrements sufficient to equip a troop of cavalry were found. As soon as this was known, a furious mob assembled, pulled down the house and laid the gardens utterly waste.† Parkyns himself was tracked to a garret in the Temple. Porter and Keyes, who had fled into Surrey, were pursued by the hue and cry, stopped by the country people near Leatherhead, and, after some show of resistance, secured and sent to prison. Friend was found hidden in the house of a Quaker. Knightley was caught in the dress of a fine lady, and recognised in spite of his patches and paint. In a few days all the chief conspirators were in custody except Barclay, who succeeded in making his escape to France.

At the same time some notorious malecontents were arrested, and were detained for a time on suspicion. Old Roger Lestrange, now in his eightieth year, was taken up. Ferguson was found hidden under a bed in Gray's Inn Lane, and was, to the general joy, locked up in Newgate.‡ Meanwhile a special commission was issued for the trial of the traitors. There was no want of evidence. For, of the conspirators who had been seized, ten or twelve were ready to save themselves by bearing witness against their associates. None had been deeper in guilt, and none

---

* According to L'Hermitage, $\frac{\text{Feb.}}{\text{Mar }9}$, there were two of these fortunate hackney coachmen. A shrewd and vigilant hackney coachman indeed was, from the nature of his calling, very likely to be successful in this sort of chase. The newspapers abound with proofs of the general enthusiasm.

† Postman, March 5. 169⅞.

‡ Ibid. Feb. 29., March 2., March 12., March 14. 169⅞.

shrank with more abject terror from death, than Porter. The government consented to spare him, and thus obtained, not only his evidence, but the much more respectable evidence of Pendergrass. Pendergrass was in no danger : he had committed no offence : his character was fair ; and his testimony would have far greater weight with a jury than the testimony of a crowd of approvers swearing for their necks. But he had the royal word of honour that he should not be a witness without his own consent ; and he was fully determined not to be a witness unless he were assured of Porter's safety. Porter was now safe ; and Pendergrass had no longer any scruple about relating the whole truth.

Charnock, King and Keyes were set first to the bar. The Chiefs of the three Courts of Common Law and several other Judges were on the bench ; and among the audience were many members of both Houses of Parliament.

It was the eleventh of March. The new Act which regulated the procedure in cases of high treason was not to come into force till the twenty-fifth. The culprits urged that, as the Legislature had, by passing that Act, recognised the justice of allowing them to see their indictment, and to avail themselves of the assistance of an advocate, the tribunal ought either to grant them what the highest authority had declared to be a reasonable indulgence, or to defer the trial for a fortnight. The Judges, however, would consent to no delay. They have therefore been accused by later writers of using the mere letter of the law in order to destroy men who, if that law had been construed according to its spirit, might have had some chance of escape. This accusation is unjust. The Judges undoubtedly carried the real intention of the Legislature into effect ; and, for whatever injustice was committed, the Legislature, and not the Judges, ought to be held accountable. The words, "twenty-fifth of March," had not slipped into the Act by mere inadvertence. All parties in Parliament had long been agreed as to the principle of the new regulations. The only matter about which there was any dispute was the time at which those regulations should take effect. After debates extending through several sessions, after repeated divisions with various results, a compromise had been made ; and it was surely not for the Courts to alter the terms of that compromise. It may indeed be confidently affirmed that, if the Houses had foreseen the Assassination Plot, they would have fixed, not an earlier, but a later day for the commencement of the new system. Undoubtedly the Parliament, and especially the Whig party, deserved serious blame.  For, if the old rules of procedure gave no unfair advantage to the Crown, there was no reason for altering them ; and if, as was generally admitted, they did give an unfair advantage to the Crown, and that against a defendant on trial for his life, they ought not to have been suffered to continue in force a single day.  But no blame is due to the tribunals for not acting in direct opposition both to the letter and to the spirit of the law.

The government might indeed have postponed the trials till the new Act came into force ; and it would have been wise, as well as right, to do so ; for the prisoners would have gained nothing by the delay.  The case against them was one on which all the ingenuity of the Inns of Court could have made no impression.  Porter, Pendergrass, De la Rue and others gave evidence which admitted of no answer.  Charnock said the very little that he had to say with readiness and presence of mind.  The jury found all the defendants guilty. It is not much to the honour of that age that the announcement of the verdict was received with loud huzzas by the crowd which surrounded the Courthouse.  Those huzzas were renewed when the three unhappy men, having heard their doom, were brought forth under a guard.*

Charnock had hitherto shown no sign of flinching : but when he was again in his cell his fortitude gave way.  He begged hard for mercy.  He would be content, he said, to pass the rest of his days in an easy confinement.  He asked only for his life.  In return for his life, he promised to discover all that he knew of the schemes of the Jacobites against the government.  If it should appear that he prevaricated or that he suppressed any thing, he was willing to undergo the utmost rigour of the law.  This offer produced much excitement, and some difference of opinion, among the councillors of William. But the King decided, as in such cases he seldom failed to decide, wisely and magnanimously.  He saw that the discovery of the Assassination Plot had changed the whole posture of affairs.  His throne, lately tottering, was fixed on an immovable basis.  His popularity had risen impetuously to as great a height as when he was on his march from Torbay to London. Many who had been out of humour with his administration, and who had, in their spleen, held some communication with Saint Germains, were shocked to find that they had been,

* Postman, March 12. 1696 ; Vernon to Lexington, March 13. ; Van Cleverskirke, March $\frac{1}{1}\frac{3}{3}$.  The proceedings are fully reported in the Collection of State Trials.

in some sense, leagued with murderers. He would not drive such persons to despair. He would not even put them to the blush. Not only should they not be punished: they should not undergo the humiliation of being pardoned. He would not know that they had offended. Charnock was left to his fate.* When he found that he had no chance of being received as a deserter, he assumed the dignity of a martyr, and played his part resolutely to the close. That he might bid farewell to the world with a better grace, he ordered a fine new coat to be hanged in, and was very particular on his last day about the powdering and curling of his wig.† Just before he was turned off, he delivered to the Sheriffs a paper in which he avowed that he had conspired against the life of the Prince of Orange, but solemnly denied that James had given any commission authorising assassination. The denial was doubtless literally correct: but Charnock did not deny, and assuredly could not with truth have denied, that he had seen a commission written and signed by James, and containing words which might without any violence be construed, and which were, by all to whom they were shown, actually construed, to authorise the murderous ambuscade of Turnham Green.

Indeed Charnock, in another paper, which is still in existence, but has never been printed, held very different language. He plainly said that, for reasons too obvious to be mentioned, he could not tell the whole truth in the paper which he had delivered to the Sheriffs. He acknowledged that the plot in which he had been engaged seemed, even to many loyal subjects, highly criminal. They called him assassin and murderer. Yet what had he done more than had been done by Mucius Scævola? Nay, what had he done more than had been done by every body who bore arms against the Prince of Orange? If an army of twenty thousand men had suddenly landed in England and surprised the usurper, this would have been called legitimate war. Did the difference between war and assassination depend merely on the number of persons engaged? What then was the smallest number which could lawfully surprise an enemy? Was it five thousand, or a

* Burnet, ii. 171.; The Present Disposition of England considered; The answer entitled England's Enemies Exposed, 1701; L'Hermitage, March $\frac{1}{2}\frac{7}{7}$. 1696. L'Hermitage says, "Charnock a fait des grandes instances pour avoir sa grace, et a offert de tout déclarer: mais elle lui a esté refusée."

† L'Hermitage, March $\frac{1}{2}\frac{7}{7}$.

thousand, or a hundred? Jonathan and his armourbearer were only two. Yet they made a great slaughter of the Philistines. Was that assassination? It cannot, said Charnock, be the mere act, it must be the cause, that makes killing assassination. It followed that it was not assassination to kill one,—and here the dying man gave a loose to all his hatred, —who had declared a war of extermination against loyal subjects, who hung, drew and quartered every man who stood up for the right, and who had laid waste England to enrich the Dutch. Charnock admitted that his enterprise would have been unjustifiable if it had not been authorised by James: but he maintained that it had been authorised, not indeed expressly, but by implication. His Majesty had indeed formerly prohibited similar attempts; but had prohibited them, not as in themselves criminal, but merely as inexpedient at this or that conjuncture of affairs. Circumstances had changed. The prohibition might therefore reasonably be considered as withdrawn. His Majesty's faithful subjects had then only to look to the words of his commission; and those words, beyond all doubt, fully warranted an attack on the person of the usurper.*

King and Keyes suffered with Charnock. King behaved with firmness and decency. He acknowledged his crime, and said that he repented of it. He thought it due to the Church of which he was a member, and on which his conduct had brought reproach, to declare that he had been misled, not by any casuistry about tyrannicide, but merely by the violence of his own evil passions. Poor Keyes was in an agony of terror. His tears and lamentations moved the pity of some of the spectators. It was said at the time, and it has often since been repeated, that a servant drawn into crime by a master was a proper object of royal clemency. But those who have blamed the severity with which Keyes was treated have alto-

---

* This most curious paper is among the Nairne MSS. in the Bodleian Library. A short, and not perfectly ingenuous, abstract of it will be found in the Life of James, ii. 555. Why Macpherson, who has printed many less interesting documents, did not choose to print this document, it is easy to guess. I will transcribe two or three important sentences. "It may reasonably be presumed that what, in one juncture, His Majesty had rejected he might in another accept, when his own and the public good necessarily required it. For I could not understand it in such a manner as if he had given a general prohibition that at no time the Prince of Orange should be touched. . . . . . Nobody that believes His Majesty to be lawful King of England can doubt but that in virtue of his commission to levy war against the Prince of Orange and his adherents, the setting upon his person is justifiable, as well by the laws of the land duly interpreted and explained as by the law of God."

gether omitted to notice the important circumstance which distinguished his case from that of every other conspirator. He had been one of the Blues. He had kept up to the last an intercourse with his old comrades. On the very day fixed for the murder he had contrived to mingle with them and to pick up intelligence from them. The regiment had been so deeply infected with disloyalty that it had been found necessary to confine some men and to dismiss many more. Surely, if any example was to be made, it was proper to make an example of the agent by whose instrumentality the men who meant to shoot the King communicated with the men whose business was to guard him.

Friend was tried next. His crime was not of so black a dye as that of the three conspirators who had just suffered. He had indeed invited foreign enemies to invade the realm, and had made preparations for joining them. But, though he had been privy to the design of assassination, he had not been a party to it. His large fortune however, and the use which he was well known to have made of it, marked him out as a fit object for punishment. He, like Charnock, asked for counsel, and, like Charnock, asked in vain. The Judges could not relax the law; and the Attorney General would not postpone the trial. The proceedings of that day furnish a strong argument in favour of the Act from the benefit of which Friend was excluded. It is impossible to read them over at this distance of time without feeling compassion for a silly ill educated man, unnerved by extreme danger, and opposed to cool, astute and experienced antagonists. Charnock had defended himself and those who were tried with him as well as any professional advocate could have done. But poor Friend was as helpless as a child. He could do little more than exclaim that he was a Protestant, and that the witnesses against him were Papists, who had dispensations from their priests for perjury, and who believed that to swear away the lives of heretics was a meritorious work. He was so grossly ignorant of law and history as to imagine that the statute of treasons, passed in the reign of Edward the Third, at a time when there was only one religion in Western Europe, contained a clause providing that no Papist should be a witness, and actually forced the Clerk of the Court to read the whole Act from beginning to end. About his guilt it was impossible that there could be a doubt in any rational mind. He was convicted; and he would have been convicted if he had been allowed the privileges for which he asked.

Parkyns came next. He had been deeply concerned in the worst part of the plot, and was, in one respect, less excusable than any of his accomplices: for they were all nonjurors; and he had taken the oaths to the existing government. He too insisted that he ought to be tried according to the provisions of the new Act. But the counsel for the Crown stood on their extreme right; and his request was denied. As he was a man of considerable abilities, and had been bred to the bar, he probably said for himself all that counsel could have said for him; and that all amounted to very little. He was found guilty, and received sentence of death on the evening of the twenty-fourth of March, within six hours of the time when the law of which he had vainly demanded the benefit was to come into force.*

The execution of the two knights was eagerly expected by the population of London. The States General were informed by their correspondent that, of all sights, that in which the English most delighted was a hanging, and that, of all hangings within the memory of the oldest man, that of Friend and Parkyns excited the greatest interest. The multitude had been incensed against Friend by reports touching the exceeding badness of the beer which he brewed. It was even rumoured that he had, in his zeal for the Jacobite cause, poisoned all the casks which he had furnished to the navy. An innumerable crowd accordingly assembled at Tyburn. Scaffolding had been put up which formed an immense amphitheatre round the gallows. On this scaffolding the wealthier spectators stood, row above row; and expectation was at the height when it was announced that the show was deferred. The mob broke up in bad humour, and not without many fights between those who had given money for their places and those who refused to return it.†

The cause of this severe disappointment was a resolution suddenly passed by the Commons. A member had proposed that a Committee should be sent to the Tower with authority to examine the prisoners, and to hold out to them the hope that they might, by a full and ingenuous confession, obtain the intercession of the House. The debate appears, from the scanty information which has come down to us, to have been a very curious one. Parties seemed to have changed characters. It might have been expected that the Whigs would

* The trials of Friend and Parkyns will be found, excellently reported, among the State Trials.

† L'Hermitage, April $\frac{3}{13}$. 1696.

*H 37

have been inexorably severe, and that, if there was any tenderness for the unhappy men, that tenderness would have been found among the Tories. But in truth many of the Whigs hoped that they might, by sparing two criminals who had no power to do mischief, be able to detect and destroy numerous criminals high in rank and office. On the other hand, every man who had ever had any dealings direct or indirect with Saint Germains, or who took an interest in any person likely to have had such dealings, looked forward with dread to the disclosures which the captives might, under the strong terrors of death, be induced to make. Seymour, simply because he had gone further in treason than almost any other member of the House, was louder than any other member of the House in exclaiming against all indulgence to his brother traitors. Would the Commons usurp the most sacred prerogative of the Crown? It was for His Majesty, and not for them, to judge whether lives justly forfeited could be without danger spared. The Whigs however carried their point. A Committee, consisting of all the Privy Councillors in the House, set off instantly for Newgate. Friend and Parkyns were interrogated, but to no purpose. They had, after sentence had been passed on them, shown at first some symptoms of weakness: but their courage had been fortified by the exhortations of nonjuring divines who had been admitted to the prison. The rumour was that Parkyns would have given way but for the entreaties of his daughter, who adjured him to suffer like a man for the good cause. The criminals acknowledged that they had done the acts of which they had been convicted, but, with a resolution which is the more respectable because it seems to have sprung, not from constitutional hardihood, but from sentiments of honour and religion, refused to say any thing which could compromise others.*

In a few hours the crowd again assembled at Tyburn; and this time the sightseers were not defrauded of their amusement. They saw indeed one sight which they had not expected, and which produced a greater sensation than the execution itself. Jeremy Collier and two other nonjuring divines of less celebrity, named Cook and Snatt, had attended the prisoners in Newgate, and were in the cart under the gallows. When the prayers were over, and just before the hangman did his office, the three schismatical priests stood up, and laid their hands on the heads of the dying men who

* Commons' Journals, April 1, 2. 1696; L'Hermitage, April $\frac{3}{13}$. 1696; Van Cleverskirke, of the same date.

continued to kneel.    Collier pronounced a form of absolution taken from the service for the Visitation of the Sick, and his brethren exclaimed " Amen ! "

This ceremony raised a great outcry; and the outcry became louder when, a few hours after the execution, the papers delivered by the two traitors to the Sheriffs were made public. It had been supposed that Parkyns at least would express some repentance for the crime which had brought him to the gallows.    Indeed he had, before the Committee of the Commons, owned that the Assassination Plot could not be justified.    But, in his last declaration, he avowed his share in that plot, not only without a word indicating remorse, but with something which resembled exultation.    Was this a man to be absolved by Christian divines, absolved before the eyes of tens of thousands, absolved with rites evidently intended to attract public attention, with rites of which there was no trace in the Book of Common Prayer or in the practice of the Church of England?

In journals, pamphlets and broadsides, the insolence of the three Levites, as they were called, was sharply reprehended. Warrants were soon out.    Cook and Snatt were taken and imprisoned : but Collier was able to conceal himself, and, by the help of one of the presses which were at the service of his party, sent forth from his hiding place a defence of his conduct.    He declared that he abhorred assassination as much as any of those who railed against him ; and his general character warrants us in believing that this declaration was perfectly sincere.    But the rash act into which he had been hurried by party spirit furnished his adversaries with very plausible reasons for questioning his sincerity.    A crowd of answers to his defence appeared.    Preeminent among them in importance was a solemn manifesto signed by the two Archbishops and by all the Bishops who were then in London, twelve in number.    Even Crewe of Durham and Sprat of Rochester set their names to this document.    They condemned the proceedings of the three nonjuring divines, as in form irregular and in substance impious.    To remit the sins of impenitent sinners was a profane abuse of the power which Christ had delegated to his ministers.    It was not denied that Parkyns had planned an assassination.    It was not pretended that he had professed any repentance for planning an assassination.    The plain inference was that the divines who absolved him did not think it sinful to assassinate King William. Collier rejoined : but, though a pugnacious controversialist, he on this occasion shrank from close conflict, and made his escape as well as he could under a cloud of quotations from Tertullian, Cyprian and Jerome, Albaspinæus and Hammond, the Council of Carthage and the Council of Toledo. The public feeling was strongly against the three absolvers. The government however wisely determined not to confer on them the honour of martyrdom. A bill was found against them by the grand jury of Middlesex : but they were not brought to trial. Cook and Snatt were set at liberty after a short detention ; and Collier would have been treated with equal lenity if he would have consented to put in bail. But he was determined to do no act which could be construed into a recognition of the usurping government. He was therefore outlawed ; and when he died, more than thirty years later, his outlawry had not been reversed.*

Parkyns was the last Englishman who was tried for high treason under the old system of procedure. The first who was tried under the new system was Rookwood. He was defended by Sir Bartholomew Shower, who in the preceding reign had made himself unenviably conspicuous as a servile and cruel sycophant, who had obtained from James the Recordership of London when Holt honourably resigned it, and who had, as Recorder, sent soldiers to the gibbet for breaches of military discipline. By his servile cruelty he had earned the nickname of the Manhunter. Shower deserved, if any offender deserved, to be excepted from the Act of Indemnity, and left to the utmost rigour of those laws which he had so shamelessly perverted. But he had been saved by the clemency of William, and had requited that clemency by pertinacious and malignant opposition.† It was doubtless on account of Shower's known leaning towards Jacobitism that he was employed on this occasion. He raised some technical objections which the Court overruled. On the merits of the case he could make no defence. The jury returned a verdict of guilty. Cranburne and Lowick were then tried and convicted. They suffered with Rookwood ; and there the executions stopped.‡

The temper of the nation was such that the government might have shed much more blood without incurring the reproach of cruelty. The feeling which had been called forth

---

* L'Hermitage, April $\frac{7}{17}$. 1696. The Declaration of the Bishops, Collier's Defence, and Further Defence, and a long legal argument for Cook and Snatt will be found in the Collection of State Trials.

† See the Manhunter, 1690.                    ‡ State Trials.

by the discovery of the plot continued during several weeks to increase day by day. Of that feeling the able men who were at the head of the Whig party made a singularly skilful use. They saw that the public enthusiasm, if left without guidance, would exhaust itself in huzzas, healths and bonfires, but might, if wisely guided, be the means of producing a great and lasting effect. The Association, into which the Commons had entered while the King's speech was still in their ears, furnished the means of combining four fifths of the nation in one vast club for the defence of the order of succession with which were inseparably combined the dearest liberties of the English people, and of establishing a test which would distinguish those who were zealous for that order of succession from those who sullenly and reluctantly acquiesced in it. Of the five hundred and thirty members of the Lower House about four hundred and twenty voluntarily subscribed the instrument which recognised William as rightful and lawful King of England. It was moved in the Upper House that the same form should be adopted : but objections were raised by the Tories. Nottingham, ever conscientious, honourable and narrow minded, declared that he could not assent to the words "rightful and lawful." He still held, as he had held from the first, that a prince who had taken the Crown, not by birthright, but by the gift of the Convention, could not properly be so described. William was doubtless King in fact, and, as King in fact, was entitled to the obedience of Christians. "No man," said Nottingham, "has served or will serve His Majesty more faithfully than I. But to this document I cannot set my hand." Rochester and Normanby held similar language. Monmouth, in a speech of two hours and a half, earnestly exhorted the Lords to agree with the Commons. Burnet was vehement on the same side. Wharton, whose father had lately died, and who was now Lord Wharton, appeared in the foremost rank of the Whig peers. But no man distinguished himself more in the debate than one whose life, both public and private, had been one long series of faults and disasters, the incestuous lover of Henrietta Berkeley, the unfortunate lieutenant of Monmouth. He had recently ceased to be called by the tarnished name of Grey of Wark, and was now Earl of Tankerville. He spoke on that day with great force and eloquence for the words, "rightful and lawful." Leeds, after expressing his regret that a question about a mere phrase should have produced dissension among noble persons who were all equally attached to the reigning Sovereign, undertook the office of mediator. He proposed that their Lordships, instead of recognising William as rightful and lawful King, should declare that William had the right by law to the English Crown, and that no other person had any right whatever to that Crown. Strange to say, almost all the Tory peers were perfectly satisfied with what Leeds had suggested. Among the Whigs there was some unwillingness to consent to a change which, slight as it was, might be thought to indicate a difference of opinion between the two Houses on a subject of grave importance. But Devonshire and Portland declared themselves content : their authority prevailed ; and the alteration was made. How a rightful and lawful possessor is to be distinguished from a possessor who has the exclusive right by law is a question which a Whig may, without any painful sense of shame, acknowledge to be beyond the reach of his faculties, and leave to be discussed by High Churchmen. Eighty-three peers immediately affixed their names to the amended form of association ; and Rochester was among them. Nottingham, not yet quite satisfied, asked time for consideration.*

Beyond the walls of Parliament there was none of this verbal quibbling. The language of the House of Commons was adopted by the whole country. The City of London led the way. Within thirty-six hours after the Association had been published under the direction of the Speaker it was subscribed by the Lord Mayor, by the Aldermen, and by almost all the members of the Common Council. The municipal corporations all over the kingdom followed the example. The spring assizes were just beginning ; and at every county town the grand jurors and the justices of the peace put down their names. Soon shopkeepers, artisans, yeomen, farmers, husbandmen, came by thousands to the tables where the parchments were laid out. In Westminster there were thirty-seven thousand associators, in the Tower Hamlets eight thousand, in Southwark eighteen thousand. The rural parts of Surrey furnished seventeen thousand. At Ipswich all the freemen signed except two. At Warwick all the male inhabitants who had attained the age of sixteen signed, except two Papists and two Quakers. At Taunton, where the memory of the Bloody Circuit was fresh, every man who could write gave in his adhesion to the government. All the churches and all the

* The best, indeed the only good, account of these debates is given by L'Hermitage, $\frac{Feb. 28}{Mar. 9.}$ 1696. He says, very truly : " La différence n'est qu'une dispute de mots, le droit qu'on a à une chose selon les loix estant aussy bon qu'il puisse estre."

meeting houses in the town were crowded, as they had never been crowded before, with people who came to thank God for having preserved him whom they fondly called William the Deliverer. Of all the counties of England Lancashire was the most Jacobitical. Yet Lancashire furnished fifty thousand signatures. Of all the great towns of England Norwich was the most Jacobitical. The magistrates of that city were supposed to be in the interest of the exiled dynasty. The nonjurors were numerous, and had, just before the discovery of the plot, seemed to be in unusual spirits and ventured to take unusual liberties. One of the chief divines of the schism had preached a sermon there which gave rise to strange suspicions. He had taken for his text the verse in which the Prophet Jeremiah announced that the day of vengeance was come, that the sword would be drunk with blood, that the Lord God of Hosts had a sacrifice in the north country by the river Euphrates. Very soon it was known that, at the time when this discourse was delivered, swords had actually been sharpening, under the direction of Barclay and Parkyns, for a bloody sacrifice on the north bank of the river Thames. The indignation of the common people of Norwich was not to be restrained. They came in multitudes, though discouraged by the municipal authorities, to plight faith to William, rightful and lawful King. In Norfolk the number of signatures amounted to forty-eight thousand, in Suffolk to seventy thousand. Upwards of five hundred rolls went up to London from every part of England. The number of names attached to twenty-seven of those rolls appears from the London Gazette to have been three hundred and fourteen thousand. After making the largest allowance for fraud, it seems certain that the Association included the great majority of the adult male inhabitants of England who were able to sign their names. The tide of popular feeling was so strong that a man who was known not to have signed ran considerable risk of being publicly affronted. In many places nobody appeared without wearing in his hat a red riband on which were embroidered the words, "General Association for King William." Once a party of Jacobites had the courage to parade a street in London with an emblematic device which seemed to indicate their contempt for the new Solemn League and Covenant. They were instantly put to rout by the mob, and their leader was well ducked. The enthusiasm spread to secluded isles, to factories in foreign countries, to remote colonies. The Association was signed by the rude fishermen of the Scilly Rocks, by the English merchants of Malaga, by the English merchants of Genoa, by the citizens of New York, by the tobacco planters of Virginia and by the sugar planters of Barbadoes.*

Emboldened by success, the Whig leaders ventured to proceed a step further. They brought into the Lower House a bill for the securing of the King's person and government. By this bill it was provided that whoever, while the war lasted, should come from France into England without the royal license should incur the penalties of treason, that the suspension of the Habeas Corpus Act should continue to the end of the year 1696, and that all functionaries appointed by William should retain their offices, notwithstanding his death, till his successor should be pleased to dismiss them. The form of Association which the House of Commons had adopted was solemnly ratified; and it was provided that no person should sit in that House or should hold any office, civil or military, without signing. The Lords were indulged in the use of their own form; and nothing was said about the clergy.

The Tories, headed by Finch and Seymour, complained bitterly of this new test, and ventured once to divide, but were defeated. Finch seems to have been heard patiently: but, notwithstanding all Seymour's eloquence, the contemptuous manner in which he spoke of the Association raised a storm against which he could not stand. Loud cries of "the Tower, the Tower," were heard. Haughty and imperious as he was, he was forced to explain away his words, and could scarcely, by apologizing in a manner to which he was little accustomed, save himself from the humiliation of being called to the bar and reprimanded on his knees. The bill went up to the Lords, and passed with great speed in spite of the opposition of Rochester and Nottingham.*

The nature and extent of the change which the discovery of the Assassination Plot had produced in the temper of the House of Commons and of the nation is strikingly illustrated by the history of a bill entitled a Bill for the further Regulation of Elections of Members of Parliament. The moneyed interest was almost entirely Whig, and was therefore an object of dislike to the Tories. The rapidly growing power of that interest was generally regarded with jealousy by landowners whether they were Whigs or Tories. It was something new

* See the London Gazettes during several weeks; L'Hermitage, March $\frac{17}{27}$., $\frac{\text{March 24.}}{\text{April 3.}}$, April $\frac{14}{24}$. 1696; Postman, April 9. 25. 30.

† Journals of the Commons and Lords; L'Hermitage, April $\frac{7}{17}$. $\frac{10}{20}$. 1696.

and monstrous to see a trader from Lombard Street, who had no tie to the soil of our island, and whose wealth was entirely personal and movable, post down to Devonshire or Sussex with a portmanteau full of guineas, offer himself as candidate for a borough in opposition to a neighbouring gentleman whose ancestors had been regularly returned ever since the Wars of the Roses, and come in at the head of the poll. Yet even this was not the worst. More than one seat in Parliament, it was said, had been bought and sold over a dish of coffee at Garraway's. The purchaser had not been required even to go through the form of showing himself to the electors. Without leaving his counting house in Cheapside, he had been chosen to represent a place which he had never seen. Such things were intolerable. No man, it was said, ought to sit in the English legislature who was not master of some hundreds of acres of English ground.* A bill was accordingly brought in which provided that every member of the House of Commons must have a certain estate in land. For a knight of a shire the qualification was fixed at five hundred a year; for a burgess at two hundred a year. Early in February this bill was read a second time and referred to a Select Committee. A motion was made that the Committee should be instructed to add a clause enacting that all elections should be by ballot. Whether this motion proceeded from a Whig or a Tory, by what arguments it was supported and on what grounds it was opposed, we have now no means of discovering. We know only that it was rejected without a division.

Before the bill came back from the Committee, some of the most respectable constituent bodies in the kingdom had raised their voices against the new restriction to which it was proposed to subject them. There had in general been little sympathy between the commercial towns and the Universities. For the commercial towns were the chief seats of Whiggism and Non-conformity; and the Universities were zealous for the Crown and the Church. Now, however, Oxford and Cambridge made common cause with London and Bristol. It was hard, said the Academics, that a grave and learned man, sent by a large body of grave and learned men to the Great Council of the nation, should be thought less fit to sit in that Council than a boozing clown who had scarcely literature enough to entitle

* See the Freeholder's Plea against Stockjobbing Elections of Parliament Men, and the Considerations upon Corrupt Elections of Members to serve in Parliament. Both these pamphlets were published in 1701.

him to the benefit of clergy. It was hard, said the traders, that a merchant prince, who had been the first magistrate of the first city in the world, whose name on the back of a bill commanded entire confidence at Smyrna and at Genoa, at Hamburg and at Amsterdam, who had at sea ships every one of which was worth a manor, and who had repeatedly, when the liberty and religion of the kingdom were in peril, advanced to the government, at an hour's notice, five or ten thousand pounds, should be supposed to have a less stake in the prosperity of the commonwealth than a squire who sold his own bullocks and hops over a pot of ale at the nearest market town. On the report, it was moved that the Universities should be excepted: but the motion was lost by a hundred and fifty-one votes to a hundred and forty-three. On the third reading it was moved that the City of London should be excepted: but it was not thought advisable to divide. The final question that the bill do pass, was carried by a hundred and seventy-three votes to a hundred and fifty on the day which preceded the discovery of the Assassination Plot. The Lords agreed to the bill without any amendment.

William had to consider whether he would give or withhold his assent. The commercial towns of the kingdom, and among them the City of London, which had always stood firmly by him, and which had extricated him many times from great embarrassments, implored his protection. It was represented to him that the Commons were far indeed from being unanimous on this subject; that, in the last stage, the majority had been only twenty-three in a full House; that the motion to except the Universities had been lost by a majority of only eight. On full consideration he resolved not to pass the bill. Nobody, he said, could accuse him of acting selfishly on this occasion: his prerogative was not concerned in the matter; and he could have no objection to the proposed law except that it would be mischievous to his people.

On the tenth of April 1696, therefore, the Clerk of the Parliament was commanded to inform the Houses that the King would consider of the Bill for the further Regulation of Elections. Some violent Tories in the House of Commons flattered themselves that they might be able to carry a resolution reflecting on the King. They moved that whoever had advised His Majesty to refuse his assent to their bill was an enemy to him and to the nation. Never was a greater blunder committed. The temper of the House was very different from what it had been on the day when the address against Portland's grant had been voted by acclamation. The detection of a murderous conspiracy, the apprehension of a French invasion, had changed every thing. The King was popular. Every day ten or twelve bales of parchment covered with the signatures of associators were laid at his feet. Nothing could be more imprudent than to propose, at such a time, a thinly disguised vote of censure on him. The moderate Tories accordingly separated themselves from their angry and unreasonable brethren. The motion was rejected by two hundred and nineteen votes to seventy ; and the House ordered the question and the numbers on both sides to be published, in order that the world might know how completely the attempt to produce a quarrel between the King and the Parliament had failed.*

The country gentlemen might perhaps have been more inclined to resent the loss of their bill, had they not been put into high goodhumour by another bill which they considered as even more important. The project of a Land Bank had been revived ; not in the form in which it had, two years before, been brought under the consideration of the House of Commons, but in a form much less shocking to common sense and less open to ridicule. Chamberlayne indeed protested loudly against all modifications of his plan, and proclaimed, with undiminished confidence, that he would make all his countrymen rich if they would only let him. He was not, he said, the first great discoverer whom princes and statesmen had regarded as a dreamer. Henry the Seventh had, in an evil hour, refused to listen to Christopher Columbus : the consequence had been that England had lost the mines of Mexico and Peru ; yet what were the mines of Mexico and Peru to the riches of a nation blessed with an unlimited paper currency ? But the united force of reason and ridicule had reduced the once numerous sect which followed Chamberlayne to a small and select company of incorrigible fools. Few even of the squires now believed in his two great doctrines ; the doctrine that the State can, by merely calling a bundle of old rags ten millions sterling, add ten millions sterling to the riches of the nation ; and the doctrine that a lease of land for a term of years may be worth many times the fee simple. But it was still the general opinion of the country gentlemen that a bank, of which it should be the special business to advance money on the security of land, might be a great blessing to the nation. Harley and the Speaker Foley now proposed that such a bank should be estab-

* The history of this bill will be found in the Journals of the Commons, and in a very interesting despatch of L'Hermitage, April $\frac{14}{24}$. 1696.

lished by Act of Parliament, and promised that, if their plan was adopted, the King should be amply supplied with money for the next campaign.

The Whig leaders, and especially Montague, saw that the scheme was a delusion, that it must speedily fail, and that, before it failed, it might not improbably ruin their own favourite institution, the Bank of England. But on this point they had against them, not only the whole Tory party, but also their master and many of their followers. The necessities of the State were pressing. The offers of the projectors were tempting. The Bank of England had, in return for its charter, advanced to the State only one million at eight per cent. The Land Bank would advance more than two millions and a half at seven per cent. William, whose chief object was to procure money for the service of the year, was little inclined to find fault with any source from which two millions and a half could be obtained. Sunderland, who generally exerted his influence in favour of the Whig leaders, failed them on this occasion. The Whig country gentlemen were delighted by the prospect of being able to repair their stables, replenish their cellars, and give portions to their daughters. It was impossible to contend against such a combination of force. A bill was passed which authorised the government to borrow two million five hundred and sixty-four thousand pounds at seven per cent. A fund, arising chiefly from a new tax on salt, was set apart for the payment of the interest. If, before the first of August, the subscription for one half of this loan should have been filled, and if one half of the sum subscribed should have been paid into the Exchequer, the subscribers were to become a corporate body, under the name of the National Land Bank. As this bank was expressly intended to accommodate country gentlemen, it was strictly interdicted from lending money on any private security other than a mortgage of land, and was bound to lend on mortgage at least half a million annually. The interest on this half million was not to exceed three and a half per cent., if the payments were quarterly, or four per cent., if the payments were half yearly. At that time the market rate of interest on the best mortgages was full six per cent. The shrewd observers at the Dutch Embassy therefore thought that capitalists would eschew all connection with what must necessarily be a losing concern, and that the subscription would never be half filled up ; and it seems strange that any sane person should have thought otherwise.*

* The Act is 7 & 8 Will. 3. c. 31. Its history may be traced in the Journals.

It was vain however to reason against the general infatuation. The Tories exultingly predicted that the Bank of Robert Harley would completely eclipse the Bank of Charles Montague. The bill passed both Houses. On the twenty-seventh of April it received the royal assent; and the Parliament was immediately afterwards prorogued.

## CHAPTER XXII

On the seventh of May 1696, William landed in Holland.* Thence he proceeded to Flanders, and took the command of the allied forces, which were collected in the neighbourhood of Ghent. Villeroy and Boufflers were already in the field. All Europe waited impatiently for great news from the Netherlands, but waited in vain. No aggressive movement was made. The object of the generals on both sides was to keep their troops from dying of hunger; and it was an object by no means easily attained. The treasuries both of France and England were empty. Lewis had, during the winter, created with great difficulty and expense a gigantic magazine at Givet on the frontier of his kingdom. The buildings were commodious and of vast extent. The quantity of provender laid up in them for horses was immense. The number of rations for men was commonly estimated at from three to four millions. But early in the spring Athlone and Cohorn had, by a bold and dexterous move, surprised Givet, and had utterly destroyed both storehouses and stores.† France, already fainting from exhaustion, was in no condition to repair such a loss. Sieges such as those of Mons and Namur were operations too costly for her means. The business of her army now was, not to conquer, but to subsist.

The army of William was reduced to straits not less painful. The material wealth of England, indeed, had not been very seriously impaired by the drain which the war had caused: but she was suffering severely from the defective state of that instrument by which her material wealth was distributed.

Saturday, the second of May, had been fixed by Parliament as the last day on which the clipped crowns, halfcrowns and

* London Gazette, May 4. 1696.
† Ibid. March 12. 16. 1696; Monthly Mercury for March, 1696.

shillings were to be received by tale in payment of taxes.*
The Exchequer was besieged from dawn till midnight by an
immense multitude. It was necessary to call in the guards for
the purpose of keeping order. On the following Monday
began a cruel agony of a few months, which was destined to
be succeeded by many years of almost unbroken prosperity.†

Most of the old silver had vanished. The new silver had
scarcely made its appearance. About four millions sterling, in
ingots and hammered coin, were lying in the vaults of the
Exchequer; and the milled money as yet came forth very
slowly from the Mint.‡ Alarmists predicted that the wealthiest
and most enlightened kingdom in Europe would be reduced
to the state of those barbarous societies in which a mat is
bought with a hatchet, and a pair of mocassins with a piece of
venison.

There were, indeed, some hammered pieces which had
escaped mutilation; and sixpences not clipped within the
innermost ring were still current. This old money and the
new money together made up a scanty stock of silver, which,
with the help of gold, was to carry the nation through the
summer.§ The manufacturers generally contrived, though with
extreme difficulty, to pay their workmen in coin.‖ The upper
classes seem to have lived to a great extent on credit. Even
an opulent man seldom had the means of discharging the
weekly bills of his baker and butcher.¶ A promissory note,
however, subscribed by such a man, was readily taken in the
district where his means and character were well known. The
notes of the wealthy moneychangers of Lombard Street circulated widely.** The paper of the Bank of England did much

* The Act provided that the clipped money must be brought in before
the fourth of May. As the third was a Sunday, the second was practically
the last day.

† L'Hermitage, May ₅⁄₁₅. 1696; London Newsletter, May 4., May 6.
In the Newsletter the fourth of May is mentioned as "the day so much
taken notice of for the universal concern people had in it."

‡ London Newsletter, May 21. 1696; Old Postmaster, June 25.;
L'Hermitage, May ₁₂⁄₂₈.

§ Haynes's Brief Memoirs, Lansdowne MSS. 801.

‖ See the petition from Birmingham in the Commons' Journals, Nov. 12.
1696; and the petition from Leicester, Nov. 21.

¶ "Money exceeding scarce, so that none was paid or received: but all
was on trust."—Evelyn, May 13. And again, on June 11.: "Want of
current money to carry on the smallest concerns, even for daily provisions
in the markets."

** L'Hermitage, May 22.⁄June 1. See a Letter of Dryden to Tonson, which
Malone, with great probability, supposes to have been written at this
time.

service, and would have done more, but for the unhappy error into which the Parliament had recently been led by Harley and Foley. The confidence which the public had felt in that powerful and opulent Company had been shaken by the Act which established the Land Bank. It might well be doubted whether there would be room for the two rival institutions; and of the two, the younger seemed to be the favourite of the government and of the legislature. The stock of the Bank of England had gone rapidly down from a hundred and ten to eighty-three. Meanwhile the goldsmiths, who had from the first been hostile to that great corporation, were plotting against it. They collected its paper from every quarter; and on the fourth of May, when the Exchequer had just swallowed up most of the old money, and when scarcely any of the new money had been issued, they flocked to Grocers' Hall, and insisted on immediate payment. A single goldsmith demanded thirty thousand pounds. The Directors, in this extremity, acted wisely and firmly. They refused to cash the notes which had been thus maliciously presented, and left the holders to seek a remedy in Westminster Hall. Other creditors, who came in good faith to ask for their due, were paid. The conspirators affected to triumph over the powerful body, which they hated and dreaded. The bank which had recently begun to exist under such splendid auspices, which had seemed destined to make a revolution in commerce and in finance, which had been the boast of London and the envy of Amsterdam, was already insolvent, ruined, dishonoured. Wretched pasquinades were published, the Trial of the Land Bank for murdering the Bank of England, the last Will and Testament of the Bank of England, the Epitaph of the Bank of England, the Inquest on the Bank of England. But, in spite of all this clamour and all this wit, the correspondents of the States General reported, that the Bank of England had not really suffered in the public esteem, and that the conduct of the goldsmiths was generally condemned.*

The Directors soon found it impossible to procure silver enough to meet every claim which was made on them in good faith. They then bethought them of a new expedient. They made a call of twenty per cent. on the proprietors, and thus raised a sum which enabled them to give every applicant fifteen

---

* L'Hermitage to the States General, May $\frac{8}{18}$.; Paris Gazette, June $\frac{2}{12}$.; Trial and Condemnation of the Land Bank at Exeter Change for murdering the Bank of England at Grocers' Hall, 1696. The Will and the Epitaph will be found in the Trial.

per cent. in milled money on what was due to him. They returned him his note, after making a minute upon it that part had been paid.* A few notes thus marked are still preserved among the archives of the Bank, as memorials of that terrible year. The paper of the Corporation continued to circulate : but the value fluctuated violently from day to day, and indeed from hour to hour ; for the public mind was in so excitable a state that the most absurd lie which a stockjobber could invent sufficed to send the price up or down. At one time the discount was only six per cent., at another time twenty-four per cent. A tenpound note, which had been taken in the morning as worth more than nine pounds, was often worth less than eight pounds before night.†

Another, and, at that conjuncture, a more effectual substitute for a metallic currency, owed its existence to the ingenuity of Charles Montague. He had succeeded in engrafting on Harley's Land Bank Bill a clause which empowered the government to issue negotiable paper bearing interest at the rate of threepence a day on a hundred pounds. In the midst of the general distress and confusion appeared the first Exchequer Bills, drawn for various amounts from a hundred pounds down to five pounds. These instruments were rapidly distributed over the kingdom by the post, and were every where welcome. The Jacobites talked violently against them in every coffee-house, and wrote much detestable verse against them, but to little purpose. The success of the plan was such, that the ministers at one time resolved to issue twentyshilling bills, and even fifteenshilling bills, for the payment of the troops. But it does not appear that this resolution was carried into effect.‡

* L'Hermitage, June $\frac{12}{22}$. 1696.

† On this subject see the Short History of the Last Parliament, 1699 ; Narcissus Luttrell's Diary ; the newspapers of 1696 passim, and the letters of L'Hermitage passim. See also the petition of the Clothiers of Gloucester in the Commons' Journal, Nov. 27. 1696. Oldmixon, who had been himself a sufferer, writes on this subject with even more than his usual acrimony.

‡ See L'Hermitage, June $\frac{12}{22}$., $\frac{June\ 23.}{July\ 3.}$, $\frac{June\ 30.}{July\ 10.}$, Aug. $\frac{1}{11}$., $\frac{Aug.\ 28.}{Sept.\ 7.}$ 1696. The Postman of August 15. mentions the great benefit derived from the Exchequer Bills. The Pegasus of Aug. 24. says : "The Exchequer Bills do more and more obtain with the public ; and 'tis no wonder." The Pegasus of Aug. 28. says : "They pass as money from hand to hand : 'tis observed that such as cry them down are ill affected to the government." "They are found by experience," says the Postman of the seventh of May following, "to be of extraordinary use to the merchants and traders of the City of London, and all other parts of the kingdom." I will give one specimen of

It is difficult to imagine how, without the Exchequer Bills, the government of the country could have been carried on during that year. Every source of revenue had been affected by the state of the currency; and one source, on which the Parliament had confidently reckoned for the means of defraying more than half the charge of the war, had yielded not a single farthing.

The sum expected from the Land Bank was near two million six hundred thousand pounds. Of this sum one half was to be subscribed, and one quarter paid up by the first of August. The King, just before his departure, had signed a warrant appointing certain commissioners, among whom Harley and Foley were the most eminent, to receive the names of the contributors.* A great meeting of persons interested in the scheme was held in the Hall of the Middle Temple. One office was opened at Exeter Change, another at Mercers' Hall. Forty agents went down into the country, and announced to the landed gentry of every shire the approach of the golden age of high rents and low interest. The Council of Regency, in order to set an example to the nation, put down the King's name for five thousand pounds; and the newspapers assured the world that the subscription would speedily be filled.† But when three weeks had passed away, it was found that only fifteen hundred pounds had been added to the five thousand contributed by the King. Many wondered at this: yet there was little cause for wonder. The sum which the friends of the project had undertaken to raise was a sum which only the enemies of the project could furnish. The country gentlemen wished well to Harley's scheme: but they wished well to it because they wanted to borrow money on easy terms; and, wanting to borrow money, they of course were not able to lend it. The moneyed class alone could supply what was necessary to the existence of the Land Bank; and the Land Bank was avowedly intended to diminish the profits, to destroy the political influence and to lower the social position of the moneyed class. As the usurers did

the unmetrical and almost unintelligible doggrel which the Jacobite poets published on this subject :—

> "Pray, Sir, did you hear of the late proclamation,
> Of sending paper for payment quite thro' the nation?
> Yes, Sir, I have : they're your Montague's notes,
> Tinctured and coloured by your Parliament votes.
> But 'tis plain on the people to be but a toast,
> They come by the carrier and go by the post."

* Commons' Journals, Nov. 25. 1696.

† L'Hermitage, June $\frac{2}{12}$. 1696; Commons' Journals, Nov. 25.; Postman, May 5., June 4., July 2.

not choose to take on themselves the expense of putting down usury, the whole plan failed in a manner which, if the aspect of public affairs had been less alarming, would have been exquisitely ludicrous. The day drew near. The neatly ruled pages of the subscription book at Mercers' Hall were still blank. The Commissioners stood aghast. In their distress they applied to the government for indulgence. Many great capitalists, they said, were desirous to subscribe, but stood aloof because the terms were too hard. There ought to be some relaxation. Would the Council of Regency consent to an abatement of three hundred thousand pounds? The finances were in such a state, and the letters in which the King represented his wants were so urgent, that the Council of Regency hesitated. The Commissioners were asked whether they would engage to raise the whole sum, with this abatement. Their answer was unsatisfactory. They did not venture to say that they could command more than eight hundred thousand pounds. The negotiation was, therefore, broken off. The first of August came; and the whole amount contributed by the whole nation to the magnificent undertaking from which so much had been expected was two thousand one hundred pounds.*

Just at this conjuncture Portland arrived from the Continent. He had been sent by William with charge to obtain money, at whatever cost and from whatever quarter. The King had strained his private credit in Holland to procure bread for his army. But all was insufficient. He wrote to his Ministers that, unless they could send him a speedy supply, his troops would either rise in mutiny or desert by thousands. He knew, he said, that it would be hazardous to call Parliament together during his absence. But, if no other resource could be devised, that hazard must be run.† The Council of Regency, in extreme embarrassment, began to wish that the terms, hard as they were, which had been offered by the Commissioners at Mercers' Hall had been accepted. The negotiation was renewed. Shrewsbury, Godolphin and Portland, as agents for the King, had several conferences with Harley and Foley, who had recently pretended that eight hundred thousand pounds were ready to be subscribed to the Land Bank. The Ministers gave assurances, that, if, at this conjuncture, even half that sum were advanced, those who had done this service to the State

* L'Hermitage, July $\frac{3}{13}$., $\frac{18}{28}$. 1696; Commons' Journals, Nov. 25.; Paris Gazette, June 30., Aug. 25.; Old Postmaster, July 9.
† William to Heinsius, July 30. 1696; William to Shrewsbury, July 23. 30. 31.

should, in the next session, be incorporated as a National Land Bank. Harley and Foley at first promised, with an air of confidence, to raise what was required. But they soon went back from their word : they showed a great inclination to be punctilious and quarrelsome about trifles : at length the eight hundred thousand pounds dwindled to forty thousand ; and even the forty thousand could be had only on hard conditions.* So ended the great delusion of the Land Bank. The commission expired ; and the offices were closed.

And now the Council of Regency, almost in despair, had recourse to the Bank of England. Two hundred thousand pounds was the very smallest sum which would suffice to meet the King's most pressing wants. Would the Bank of England advance that sum ? The capitalists who had the chief sway in that corporation were in bad humour, and not without reason. But fair words, earnest entreaties and large promises were not spared : all the influence of Montague, which was justly great, was exerted : the Directors promised to do their best : but they apprehended that it would be impossible for them to raise the money without making a second call of twenty per cent. on their constituents. It was necessary that the question should be submitted to a General Court : in such a court more than six hundred persons were entitled to vote ; and the result might well be doubted. The proprietors were summoned to meet on the fifteenth of August at Grocers' Hall. During the painful interval of suspense, Shrewsbury wrote to his master in language more tragic than is often found in official letters. " If this should not succeed, God knows what can be done. Any thing must be tried and ventured rather than lie down and die."† On the fifteenth of August, a great epoch in the history of the Bank, the General Court was held. In the chair sate Sir John Houblon, the Governor, who was also Lord Mayor of London, and, what would in our time be thought strange, a Commissioner of the Admiralty. Sir John, in a speech, every word of which had been written and had been carefully considered by the Directors, explained the case, and implored the assembly to stand by King William. There was at first a little murmuring. " If our notes would do," it was said, "we should be most willing to assist His Majesty : but two hundred thousand pounds in hard money

* Shrewsbury to William, July 28. 31., Aug. 4. 1696 ; L'Hermitage, Aug. 1⁄11.
† Shrewsbury to William, Aug. 7. 1696 ; L'Hermitage, ‡ ug. 11⁄4.; London Gazette, Aug. 13.

at a time like this——." The Governor announced explicitly that nothing but gold or silver would supply the necessities of the army in Flanders. At length the question was put to the vote ; and every hand in the Hall was held up for sending the money. The letters from the Dutch Embassy informed the States General that the events of that day had bound the Bank and the government together in close alliance, and that several of the ministers had, immediately after the meeting, purchased stock merely in order to give a pledge of their attachment to the body which had rendered so great a service to the State.*

Meanwhile strenuous exertions were making to hasten the recoinage. Since the Restoration the Mint had, like every other public establishment in the kingdom, been a nest of idlers and jobbers. The important office of Warden, worth between six and seven hundred a year, had become a mere sinecure, and had been filled by a succession of fine gentle-men, who were well known at the hazard table of Whitehall, but who never condescended to come near the Tower. This office had just become vacant, and Montague had obtained it for Newton.† The ability, the industry and the strict upright-ness of the great philosopher speedily produced a complete revolution throughout the department which was under his direction.‡ He devoted himself to his task with an activity

* L'Hermitage, Aug. $\frac{18}{28}$. 1696. Among the records of the Bank is a resolution of the Directors prescribing the very words which Sir John Houblon was to use. William's sense of the service done by the Bank on this occasion is expressed in his letter to Shrewsbury, of $\frac{\text{Aug. 24,}}{\text{Sept. 3.}}$ One of the Directors, in a letter concerning the Bank, printed in 1697, says : "The Directors could not have answered it to their members, had it been for any less occasion than the preservation of the kingdom."

† Haynes's Brief Memoires ; Lansdowne MSS. 801. Montague's friendly letter to Newton, announcing the appointment, has been repeat-edly printed. It bears date March 19. 169$\frac{5}{6}$.

‡ I have very great pleasure in quoting the words of Haynes, an able, experienced and practical man, who had been in the habit of transacting business with Newton. They have never, I believe, been printed. "Mr. Isaac Newton, public Professor of the Mathematicks in Cambridge, the greatest philosopher, and one of the best men of this age, was, by a great and wise statesman, recommended to the favour of the late King for Warden of the King's Mint and Exchanges, for which he was peculiarly qualified, because of his extraordinary skill in numbers, and his great integrity, by the first of which he could judge correctly of the Mint accounts and transactions as soon as he entered upon his office ; and by the latter— I mean his integrity—he sett a standard to the conduct and behaviour of every officer and clerk in the Mint. Well had it been for the publick, had he acted a few years sooner in that situation." It is interesting to compare this testimony, borne by a man who thoroughly understood the business of the Mint, with the childish talk of Pope. "Sir Isaac Newton," said Pope,

which left him no time to spare for those pursuits in which he had surpassed Archimedes and Galileo. Till the great work was completely done, he resisted firmly, and almost angrily, every attempt that was made by men of science, here or on the Continent, to draw him away from his official duties.* The old officers of the Mint had thought it a great feat to coin silver to the amount of fifteen thousand pounds in a week. When Montague talked of thirty or forty thousand, these men of form and precedent pronounced the thing impracticable. But the energy of the young Chancellor of the Exchequer and of his friend the Warden accomplished far greater wonders. Soon nineteen mills were going at once in the Tower. As fast as men could be trained to the work in London, bands of them were sent off to other parts of the kingdom. Mints were established at Bristol, York, Exeter, Norwich and Chester. This arrangement was in the highest degree popular. The machinery and the workmen were welcomed to the new stations with the ringing of bells and the firing of guns. The weekly issue increased to sixty thousand pounds, to eighty thousand, to a hundred thousand, and at length to a hundred and twenty thousand.† Yet even this issue, though great, not only beyond precedent, but beyond hope, was scanty when compared with the demands of the nation. Nor did all the newly stamped silver pass into circulation : for during the summer and autumn those politicians who were for raising the denomination of the coin were active and clamorous ; and it was generally expected that, as soon as the Parliament should reassemble, the standard would be lowered. Of course no person who thought it probable that he should, at a day not far distant, be able to pay a debt of a pound with three crown pieces instead of four, was willing to part with a crown piece till that day arrived. Most of the milled pieces were therefore

---

"though so deep in algebra and fluxions, could not readily make up a common account ; and, whilst he was Master of the Mint, used to get somebody to make up the accounts for him." Some of the statesmen with whom Pope lived might have told him that it is not always from ignorance of arithmetic that persons at the head of great departments leave to clerks the business of casting up pounds, shillings and pence.

* "I do not love," he wrote to Flamsteed, "to be printed on every occasion, much less to be dunned and teased by foreigners about mathematical things, or to be thought by our own people to be trifling away my time about them, when I am about the King's business."

† Hopton Haynes's Brief Memoires ; Lansdowne MSS. 801. ; the Old Postmaster, July 4. 1696 ; the Postman, May 30., July 4 , September 12. 19., October 8.; L'Hermitage's despatches of this summer and autumn, passim.

hoarded.* May, June and July passed away without any perceptible increase in the quantity of good money. It was not till August that the keenest observer could discern the first faint signs of returning prosperity.†

The distress of the common people was severe, and was aggravated by the follies of magistrates and by the arts of malecontents. A squire who was one of the quorum would sometimes think it his duty to administer to his neighbours, at this trying conjuncture, what seemed to him to be equity; and as no two of these rural prætors had exactly the same notion of what was equitable, their edicts added confusion to confusion. In one parish people were, in outrageous violation of the law, threatened with the stocks, if they refused to take clipped shillings by tale. In the next parish it was dangerous to pay such shillings except by weight.‡ The enemies of the government, at the same time, laboured indefatigably in their vocation. They harangued in every place of public resort, from the Chocolate House in Saint James's Street to the sanded kitchen of the alehouse on the village green. In verse and prose they incited the suffering multitude to rise up in arms. Of the tracts which they published at this time, the most remarkable was written by a deprived priest named Grascombe, of whose ferocity and scurrility the most respectable nonjurors had long been ashamed. He now did his best to persuade the rabble to tear in pieces those members of Parliament who had voted for the restoration of the currency.§ It would be too much to say that the malignant industry of this man and of men like him produced no effect on a population which was doubtless severely tried. There were riots in several parts of

* Paris Gazette, Aug. 11. 1696.

† On the 7th of August L'Hermitage remarked for the first time that money seemed to be more abundant.

‡ Compare Edmund Bohn's Letter to Carey of the 31st of July 1696 with the Paris Gazette of the same date. Bohn's description of the state of Norfolk is coloured, no doubt, by his constitutionally gloomy temper, and by the feeling with which he, not unnaturally, regarded the House of Commons. His statistics are not to be trusted; and his predictions were signally falsified. But he may be believed as to plain facts which happened in his immediate neighbourhood.

§ As to Grascombe's character, and the opinion entertained of him by the most estimable Jacobites, see the Life of Kettlewell, part iii., section 55. Lee, the compiler of the Life of Kettlewell, mentions with just censure some of Grascombe's writings, but makes no allusion to the worst of them, the Account of the Proceedings in the House of Commons in relation to the Recoining of the Clipped Money, and falling the price of Guineas. That Grascombe was the author, was proved before a Committee of the House of Commons. See the Journals, Nov. 30. 1696.

the country, but riots which were suppressed with little difficulty, and, as far as can be discovered, without the shedding of a drop of blood.* In one place a crowd of poor ignorant creatures, excited by some knavish agitator, besieged the house of a Whig member of Parliament, and clamorously insisted on having their short money changed. The gentleman consented, and desired to know how much they had brought. After some delay they were able to produce a single clipped halfcrown.† Such tumults as this were at a distance exaggerated into rebellions and massacres. At Paris it was gravely asserted in print that, in an English town which was not named, a soldier and a butcher had quarrelled about a piece of money, that the soldier had killed the butcher, that the butcher's man had snatched up a cleaver and killed the soldier, that a great fight had followed, and that fifty dead bodies had been left on the ground.‡ The truth was, that the behaviour of the great body of the people was beyond all praise. The Judges when, in September, they returned from their circuits, reported that the temper of the nation was excellent.§ There was a patience, a reasonableness, a good nature, a good faith, which nobody had anticipated. Every body felt that nothing but mutual help and mutual forbearance could prevent the dissolution of society. A hard creditor, who sternly demanded payment to the day in milled money, was pointed at in the streets, and was beset by his own creditors with demands which soon brought him to reason. Much uneasiness had been felt about the troops. It was scarcely possible to pay them regularly : if they were not paid regularly, it might well be apprehended that they would supply their wants by rapine ; and such rapine it was certain that the nation, altogether unaccustomed to military exaction and oppression, would not tamely endure. But, strange to say, there was, through this trying year, a better understanding than had ever been known between the soldiers and the rest of the community. The gentry, the farmers, the shopkeepers supplied the redcoats with necessaries in a manner so friendly and liberal that there was no brawling and no marauding. "Severely as these difficulties have been felt," L'Hermitage writes, "they have produced one happy effect : they have shown how good the spirit of the country is. No person, however favourable his opinion of the English may have been, could

* L'Hermitage, June ½²⁄², July ⁷⁄₁₇. 1696.
† See the Answer to Grascombe, entitled Reflections on a Scandalous Libel.
‡ Paris Gazette, Sept. 15. 1696.          § L'Hermitage, Oct. ²⁄₁₂. 1696.

have expected that a time of such suffering would have been a time of such tranquillity." *

Men who loved to trace, in the strangely complicated maze of human affairs, the marks of more than human wisdom, were of opinion that, but for the interference of a gracious Providence, the plan so elaborately devised by great statesmen and great philosophers would have failed completely and ignominiously. Often, since the Revolution, the English had been sullen and querulous, unreasonably jealous of the Dutch, and disposed to put the worst construction on every act of the King. Had the fourth of May found our ancestors in such a mood, it can scarcely be doubted that sharp distress, irritating minds already irritable, would have caused an outbreak which must have shaken and might have subverted the throne of William. Happily, at the moment at which the loyalty of the nation was put to the most severe test, the King was more popular than he had ever been since the day on which the Crown was tendered to him in the Banqueting House. The plot which had been laid against his life had excited general disgust and horror. His reserved manners, his foreign attachments were forgotten. He had become an object of personal interest and of personal affection to his people. They were every where coming in crowds to sign the instrument which bound them to defend and to avenge him. They were every where carrying about in their hats the badges of their loyalty to him. They could hardly be restrained from inflicting summary punishment on the few who still dared openly to question his title. Jacobite was now a synonyme for cutthroat. Noted Jacobite laymen had just planned a foul murder. Noted Jacobite priests had, in the face of day, and in the administration of a solemn ordinance of religion, indicated their approbation of that murder. Many honest and pious men, who thought that their allegiance was still due to James, had indignantly relinquished all connection with zealots who seemed to think that a righteous end justified the most unrighteous means. Such was the state of public feeling during the summer and autumn of 1696 ; and therefore it was that hardships which, in any of the seven preceding years, would certainly have produced a rebellion, and might perhaps have produced a counterrevolution, did not produce a single tumult too serious to be suppressed by the constable's staff.

Nevertheless, the effect of the commercial and financial crisis in England was felt through all the fleets and armies of

* L'Hermitage, July $\frac{2\,0}{3\,0}$., Oct. $\frac{2}{1\,3}$. $\frac{9}{1\,0}$. 1696.

the coalition. The great source of subsidies was dry. No important military operation could any where be attempted. Meanwhile overtures tending to peace had been made, and a negotiation had been opened. Callieres, one of the ablest of the many able envoys in the service of France, had been sent to the Netherlands, and had held many conferences with Dykvelt. Those conferences might perhaps have come to a speedy and satisfactory close, had not France, at this time, won a great diplomatic victory in another quarter. Lewis had, during seven years, been scheming and labouring in vain to break the great array of potentates whom the dread of his might and of his ambition had brought together and kept together. But, during seven years, all his arts had been baffled by the skill of William; and, when the eighth campaign opened, the confederacy had not been weakened by a single desertion. Soon however it began to be suspected that the Duke of Savoy was secretly treating with the enemy. He solemnly assured Galway, who represented England at the Court of Turin, that there was not the slightest ground for such suspicions, and sent to William letters filled with professions of zeal for the common cause, and with earnest entreaties for more money. This dissimulation continued till a French army, commanded by Catinat, appeared in Piedmont. Then the Duke threw off his disguise, concluded peace with France, joined his troops to those of Catinat, marched into the Milanese, and informed the allies whom he had just abandoned that, unless they wished to have him for an enemy, they must declare Italy neutral ground. The Courts of Vienna and Madrid, in great dismay, submitted to the terms which he dictated. William expostulated and protested in vain. His influence was no longer what it had been. The general opinion of Europe was, that the riches and the credit of England were completely exhausted; and both her confederates and her enemies imagined that they might safely treat her with indignity. Spain, true to her invariable maxim that every thing ought to be done for her and nothing by her, had the effrontery to reproach the Prince to whom she owed it that she had not lost the Netherlands and Catalonia, because he had not sent troops and ships to defend her possessions in Italy. The Imperial ministers formed and executed resolutions gravely affecting the interests of the coalition without consulting him who had been the author and the soul of the coalition.* Lewis had, after the failure of the

* The Monthly Mercuries; Correspondence between Shrewsbury and

I 37

Assassination Plot, made up his mind to the disagreeable necessity of recognising William, and had authorised Callieres to make a declaration to that effect. But the defection of Savoy, the neutrality of Italy, the disunion among the allies, and, above all, the distresses of England, exaggerated as they were in all the letters which the Jacobites of Saint Germains received from the Jacobites of London, produced a change. The tone of Callieres became high and arrogant: he went back from his word, and refused to give any pledge that his master would acknowledge the Prince of Orange as King of Great Britain. The joy was great among the nonjurors. They had always, they said, been certain that the Great Monarch would not be so unmindful of his own glory and of the common interest of Sovereigns as to abandon the cause of his unfortunate guests, and to call an usurper his brother. They knew from the best authority that His Most Christian Majesty had lately, at Fontainebleau, given satisfactory assurances on this subject to King James. Indeed, there is reason to believe that the project of an invasion of our island was again seriously discussed at Versailles.* Catinat's army was now at liberty. France, relieved from all apprehension on the side of Savoy, might spare twenty thousand men for a descent on England; and, if the misery and discontent here were such as was generally reported, the nation might be disposed to receive foreign deliverers with open arms.

So gloomy was the prospect which lay before William, when, in the autumn of 1696, he quitted his camp in the Netherlands for England. His servants here meanwhile were looking forward to his arrival with very strong and very various emotions. The whole political world had been thrown into confusion by a cause which did not at first appear commensurate to such an effect.

During his absence, the search for the Jacobites who had been concerned in the plots of the preceding winter had not been intermitted; and of these Jacobites none was in greater peril than Sir John Fenwick. His birth, his connections, the high situations which he had filled, the indefatigable activity with which he had, during several years, laboured to subvert the government, and the personal insolence with which he had treated the deceased Queen, marked him out as a man fit to

---

Galway; William to Heinsius, July 23. 30. 1696; Memoir of the Marquess of Leganes.

* William to Heinsius, $\frac{Aug. 27.}{Sept. 6.}$ Nov. $\frac{1}{2}\frac{6}{6}$., Nov. $\frac{1}{2}\frac{7}{7}$. 1696; Prior to Lexington, Nov. $\frac{1}{2}\frac{7}{7}$.; Villiers to Shrewsbury, Nov. $\frac{1}{2}\frac{3}{3}$.

be made an example. He succeeded, however, in concealing himself from the officers of justice till the first heat of pursuit was over. In his hiding place he thought of an ingenious device which might, as he conceived, save him from the fate of his friends Charnock and Parkyns. Two witnesses were necessary to convict him. It appeared from what had passed on the trials of his accomplices, that there were only two witnesses who could prove his guilt, Porter and Goodman. His life was safe if either of these men could be persuaded to abscond.

Fenwick was not the only person who had strong reason to wish that Porter or Goodman, or both, might be induced to leave England. Aylesbury had been arrested, and committed to the Tower; and he well knew that, if these men appeared against him, his head would be in serious danger. His friends and Fenwick's raised what was thought a sufficient sum; and two Irishmen, or, in the phrase of the newspapers of that day, bogtrotters, a barber named Clancy, and a disbanded captain named Donelagh, undertook the work of corruption.

The first attempt was made on Porter. Clancy contrived to fall in with him at a tavern, threw out significant hints, and, finding that those hints were favourably received, opened a regular negotiation. The terms offered were alluring; three hundred guineas down, three hundred more as soon as the witness should be beyond sea, a handsome annuity for life, a free pardon from King James, and a secure retreat in France. Porter seemed inclined, and perhaps was really inclined, to consent. He said that he still was what he had been, that he was at heart attached to the good cause, but that he had been tried beyond his strength. Life was sweet. It was easy for men who had never been in danger to say that none but a villain would save himself by hanging his associates: but a few hours in Newgate, with the near prospect of a journey on a sledge to Tyburn, would teach such boasters to be more charitable. After repeatedly conferring with Clancy, Porter was introduced to Fenwick's wife, Lady Mary, a sister of the Earl of Carlisle. Every thing was soon settled. Donelagh made the arrangements for the flight. A boat was in waiting. The letters which were to secure to the fugitive the protection of King James were prepared by Fenwick. The hour and place were fixed at which Porter was to receive the first instalment of the promised reward. But his heart misgave him. He had, in truth, gone such lengths that it would have been madness in him to turn back. He had sent Charnock, King,

Keyes, Friend, Parkyns, Rookwood, Cranburne, to the gallows. It was impossible that such a Judas could ever be really forgiven. In France, among the friends and comrades of those whom he had destroyed, his life would not be worth one day's purchase. No pardon under the Great Seal would avert the stroke of the avenger of blood. Nay, who could say that the bribe now offered was not a bait intended to lure the victim to the place where a terrible doom awaited him ? Porter resolved to be true to that government under which alone he could be safe : he carried to Whitehall information of the whole intrigue ; and he received full instructions from the ministers. On the eve of the day fixed for his departure he had a farewell meeting with Clancy at a tavern. Three hundred guineas were counted out on the table. Porter pocketed them, and gave a signal. Instantly several messengers from the office of the Secretary of State rushed into the room, and produced a warrant. The unlucky barber was carried off to prison, tried for his offence, convicted and pilloried.*

This mishap made Fenwick's situation more perilous than ever. At the next sessions for the City of London a bill of indictment against him, for high treason, was laid before the grand jury. Porter and Goodman appeared as witnesses for the Crown ; and the bill was found. Fenwick now thought that it was high time to steal away to the Continent. Arrangements were made for his passage. He quitted his hiding place, and repaired to Romney Marsh. There he hoped to find shelter till the vessel which was to convey him across the Channel should arrive. For, though Hunt's establishment had been broken up, there were still in that dreary region smugglers who carried on more than one lawless trade. It chanced that two of these men had just been arrested on a charge of harbouring traitors. The messenger who had taken them into custody was returning to London with them, when, on the high road, he met Fenwick face to face. Unfortunately for Fenwick, no face in England was better known than his. "It is Sir John," said the officer to the prisoners : "Stand by me, my good fellows, and, I warrant you, you will have your pardons, and a bag of guineas besides." The offer was too tempting to be refused : but Fenwick was better mounted than his

* My account of the attempt to corrupt Porter is taken from his examination before the House of Commons on Nov. 16. 1696, and from the following sources : Burnet, ii. 183.; L'Hermitage to the States General, May $\frac{8}{18}$. $\frac{12}{22}$. 1696 ; the Postboy, May 9. ; the Postman, May 9. ; Narcissus Luttrell's Diary ; London Gazette, Oct. 19. 1696.

assailants: he dashed through them, pistol in hand, and was soon out of sight. They pursued him: the hue and cry was raised: the bells of all the parish churches of the Marsh rang out the alarm: the whole country was up: every path was guarded: every thicket was beaten: every hut was searched; and at length the fugitive was found in bed. Just then a bark, of very suspicious appearance, came in sight: she soon approached the shore, and showed English colours: but to the practised eyes of the Kentish fishermen she looked much like a French privateer. It was not difficult to guess her errand. After waiting a short time in vain for her passenger, she stood out to sea.*

Fenwick, unluckily for himself, was able so far to elude the vigilance of those who had charge of him as to scrawl with a lead pencil a short letter to his wife. Every line contained evidence of his guilt. All, he wrote, was over: he was a dead man, unless, indeed, his friends could, by dint of solicitation, obtain a pardon for him. Perhaps the united entreaties of all the Howards might succeed. He would go abroad: he would solemnly promise never again to set foot on English ground, and never to draw sword against the government. Or would it be possible to bribe a juryman or two to starve out the rest? "That," he wrote, "or nothing can save me." This billet was intercepted in its way to the post, and sent up to Whitehall. Fenwick was soon carried to London and brought before the Lords Justices. At first he held high language and bade defiance to his accusers. He was told that he had not always been so confident; and his letter to his wife was laid before him. He had not till then been aware that it had fallen into hands for which it was not intended. His distress and confusion became great. He felt that, if he were instantly sent before a jury, a conviction was inevitable. One chance remained. If he could delay his trial for a short time, the judges would leave town for their circuits: a few weeks would be gained; and in the course of a few weeks something might be done.

He addressed himself particularly to the Lord Steward, Devonshire, with whom he had formerly had some connection of a friendly kind. The unhappy man declared that he threw himself entirely on the royal mercy, and offered to disclose all that he knew touching the plots of the Jacobites. That he knew much nobody could doubt. Devonshire advised his colleagues to postpone the trial till the pleasure of William could be known.

* London Gazette; Narcissus Luttrell; L'Hermitage, June $\frac{12}{22}$.; Postman, June 11.

This advice was taken. The King was informed of what had passed ; and he soon sent an answer directing Devonshire to receive the prisoner's confession in writing, and to send it over to the Netherlands with all speed.*

Fenwick had now to consider what he should confess. Had he, according to his promise, revealed all that he knew, there can be no doubt that his evidence would have seriously affected many Jacobite noblemen, gentlemen and clergymen. But, though he was very unwilling to die, attachment to his party was in his mind a stronger sentiment than the fear of death. The thought occurred to him that he might construct a story, which might possibly be considered as sufficient to earn his pardon, which would at least put off his trial some months, yet which would not injure a single sincere adherent of the banished dynasty, nay, which would cause distress and embarrassment to the enemies of that dynasty, and which would fill the Court, the Council, and the Parliament of William with fears and animosities. He would divulge nothing that could affect those true Jacobites who had repeatedly awaited, with pistols loaded and horses saddled, the landing of the rightful King accompanied by a French army. But if there were false Jacobites who had mocked their banished Sovereign year after year with professions of attachment and promises of service, and yet had, at every great crisis, found some excuse for disappointing him, and who were at that moment among the chief supports of the usurper's throne, why should they be spared? That there were such false Jacobites, high in political office and in military command, Fenwick had good reason to believe. He could indeed say nothing against them to which a Court of Justice would have listened : for none of them had ever entrusted him with any message or letter for France ; and all that he knew about their treachery he had learned at second hand and third hand. But of their guilt he had no doubt. One of them was Marlborough. He had, after betraying James to William, promised to make reparation by betraying William to James, and had, at last, after much shuffling, again betrayed James and made peace with William. Godolphin had practised similar deception. He had long been sending fair words to Saint Germains : in return for those fair words he had received a pardon ; and, with this pardon in his secret drawer, he had continued to administer the finances of the existing government. To ruin such a man would be a just punishment for his base-

* Life of William III., 1703 ; Vernon's evidence given in his place in the House of Commons, Nov. 16. 1696.

ness, and a great service to King James. Still more desirable was it to blast the fame and to destroy the influence of Russell and Shrewsbury. Both were distinguished members of that party which had, under different names, been, during three generations, implacably hostile to the Kings of the House of Stuart. Both had taken a great part in the Revolution. The names of both were subscribed to the instrument which had invited the Prince of Orange to England. One of them was now his Minister for Maritime Affairs; the other his Principal Secretary of State; but neither had been constantly faithful to him. Both had, soon after his accession, bitterly resented his wise and magnanimous impartiality, which, to their minds, disordered by party spirit, seemed to be unjust and ungrateful partiality for the Tory faction; and both had, in their spleen, listened to agents from Saint Germains. Russell had vowed by all that was most sacred that he would himself bring back his exiled Sovereign. But the vow was broken as soon as it had been uttered; and he to whom the royal family had looked as to a second Monk had crushed the hopes of that family at La Hogue. Shrewsbury had not gone such lengths. Yet he too, while out of humour with William, had tampered with the agents of James. With the power and reputation of these two great men was closely connected the power and reputation of the whole Whig party. That party, after some quarrels, which were in truth quarrels of lovers, was now cordially reconciled to William, and bound to him by the strongest ties. If those ties could be dissolved, if he could be induced to regard with distrust and aversion the only set of men which was on principle and with enthusiasm devoted to his interests, his enemies would indeed have reason to rejoice.

With such views as these Fenwick delivered to Devonshire a paper so cunningly composed that it would probably have brought some severe calamity on the Prince to whom it was addressed, had not that Prince been a man of singularly clear judgment and singularly lofty spirit. The paper contained scarcely any thing respecting those Jacobite plots in which the writer had been himself concerned, and of which he intimately knew all the details. It contained nothing which could be of the smallest prejudice to any person who was really hostile to the existing order of things. The whole narrative was made up of stories, too true for the most part, yet resting on no better authority than hearsay, about the intrigues of some eminent warriors and statesmen, who, whatever their former conduct might have been, were now at least hearty in support of William.

Godolphin, Fenwick averred, had accepted a seat at the Board of Treasury, with the sanction and for the benefit of King James. Marlborough had promised to carry over the army, Russell to carry over the fleet. Shrewsbury, while out of office, had plotted with Middleton against the government and King. Indeed the Whigs were now the favourites at Saint Germains. Many old friends of hereditary right were moved to jealousy by the preference which James gave to the new converts. Nay, he had been heard to express his confident hope that the monarchy would be set up again by the very hands which had pulled it down.

Such was Fenwick's confession. Devonshire received it and sent it by express to the Netherlands, without intimating to any of his fellow councillors what it contained. The accused ministers afterwards complained bitterly of this proceeding. Devonshire defended himself by saying that he had been specially deputed by the King to take the prisoner's information, and was bound, as a true servant of the Crown, to transmit that information to His Majesty and to His Majesty alone.

The messenger sent by Devonshire found William at Loo. The King read the confession, and saw at once with what objects it had been drawn up. It contained little more than what he had long known, and had long, with politic and generous dissimulation, affected not to know. If he spared, employed and promoted men who had been false to him, it was not because he was their dupe. His observation was quick and just : his intelligence was good ; and he had, during some years, had in his hands proofs of much that Fenwick had only gathered from wandering reports. It has seemed strange to many that a Prince of high spirit and acrimonious temper should have treated servants, who had so deeply wronged him, with a kindness hardly to be expected from the meekest of human beings. But William was emphatically a statesman. Ill humour, the natural and pardonable effect of much bodily and much mental suffering, might sometimes impel him to give a tart answer. But never did he on any important occasion indulge his angry passions at the expense of the great interests of which he was the guardian. For the sake of those interests, proud and imperious as he was by nature, he submitted patiently to galling restraints, bore cruel indignities and disappointments with the outward show of serenity, and not only forgave, but often pretended not to see, offences which might well have moved him to bitter resentment. He knew that he must work with such tools as he had.

If he was to govern England he must employ the public men of England; and in his age, the public men of England, with much of a peculiar kind of ability, were, as a class, lowminded and immoral. There were doubtless exceptions. Such was Nottingham among the Tories, and Somers among the Whigs. But the majority, both of the Tory and of the Whig ministers of William, were men whose characters had taken the ply in the days of the Antipuritan reaction. They had been formed in two evil schools, in the most unprincipled of courts, and the most unprincipled of oppositions, a court which took its character from Charles, an opposition headed by Shaftesbury. From men so trained it would have been unreasonable to expect disinterested and stedfast fidelity to any cause. But though they could not be trusted, they might be used and they might be useful. No reliance could be placed on their principles: but much reliance might be placed on their hopes and on their fears; and of the two Kings who laid claim to the English crown, the King from whom there was most to hope and most to fear was the King in possession. If therefore William had little reason to esteem these politicians his hearty friends, he had still less reason to number them among his hearty foes. Their conduct towards him, reprehensible as it was, might be called upright when compared with their conduct towards James. To the reigning Sovereign they had given valuable service; to the banished Sovereign little more than promises and professions. Shrewsbury might, in a moment of resentment or of weakness, have trafficked with Jacobite agents: but his general conduct had proved that he was as far as ever from being a Jacobite. Godolphin had been lavish of fair words to the dynasty which was out; but he had thriftily and skilfully managed the revenues of the dynasty which was in. Russell had sworn that he would desert with the English fleet; but he had burned the French fleet. Even Marlborough's known treasons,—for his share in the disaster of Brest and the death of Talmash was unsuspected,—had not done so much harm as his exertions at Walcourt, at Cork and at Kinsale had done good. William had therefore wisely resolved to shut his eyes to perfidy, which, however disgraceful it might be, had not injured him, and still to avail himself, with proper precautions, of the eminent talents which some of his unfaithful counsellors possessed. Having determined on this course, and having long followed it with happy effect, he could not but be annoyed and provoked by Fenwick's confession. Sir John, it was plain, thought himself a Machiavel. If his trick succeeded, the

*I 37

Princess, whom it was most important to keep in good humour, would be alienated from the government by the disgrace of Marlborough. The whole Whig party, the firmest support of the throne, would be alienated by the disgrace of Russell and Shrewsbury. In the meantime not one of those plotters whom Fenwick knew to have been deeply concerned in plans of insurrection, invasion, assassination, would be molested. This cunning schemer should find that he had not to do with a novice. William, instead of turning his accused servants out of their places, sent the confession to Shrewsbury, and desired that it might be laid before the Lords Justices. "I am astonished," the King wrote, "at the fellow's effrontery. You know me too well to think that such stories as his can make any impression on me. Observe this honest man's sincerity. He has nothing to say except against my friends. Not a word about the plans of his brother Jacobites." The King concluded by directing the Lords Justices to send Fenwick before a jury with all speed.*

The effect produced by William's letter was remarkable. Every one of the accused persons behaved himself in a manner singularly characteristic. Marlborough, the most culpable of all, preserved a serenity, mild, majestic and slightly contemptuous. Russell, scarcely less criminal than Marlborough, went into a towering passion, and breathed nothing but vengeance against the villanous informer. Godolphin, uneasy, but wary, reserved and selfpossessed, prepared himself to stand on the defensive. But Shrewsbury, who of all the four was the least to blame, was utterly overwhelmed. He wrote in extreme distress to William, acknowledged with warm expressions of gratitude the King's rare generosity, and protested that Fenwick had malignantly exaggerated and distorted mere trifles into enormous crimes. "My Lord Middleton,"—such was the substance of the letter,—"was certainly in communication with me about the time of the battle of La Hogue. We are relations: we frequently met: we supped together just before he returned to France: I promised to take care of his interests here: he in return offered to do me good offices there; but I told him that I had offended too deeply to be forgiven, and that I would not stoop to ask forgiveness." This, Shrewsbury averred, was the whole extent of his offence.† It is but too fully proved that this confession was by no means ingenuous; nor is it likely that William was

* William to Shrewsbury from Loo, Sept. 10. 1696.
† Shrewsbury to William, Sept. 18. 1696.

deceived. But he was determined to spare the repentant traitor the humiliation of owning a fault and accepting a pardon. "I can see," the King wrote, "no crime at all in what you have acknowledged. Be assured that these calumnies have made no unfavourable impression on me. Nay, you shall find that they have strengthened my confidence in you." * A man hardened in depravity would have been perfectly contented with an acquittal so complete, announced in language so gracious. But Shrewsbury was quite unnerved by a tenderness which he was conscious that he had not merited. He shrank from the thought of meeting the master whom he had wronged, and by whom he had been forgiven, and of sustaining the gaze of the peers, among whom his birth and his abilities had gained for him a station of which he felt that he was unworthy. The campaign in the Netherlands was over. The session of Parliament was approaching. The King was expected with the first fair wind. Shrewsbury left town and retired to the Wolds of Gloucestershire. In that district, then one of the wildest in the south of the island, he had a small country seat, surrounded by pleasant gardens and fish-ponds. William had, in his progress a year before, visited this dwelling, which lay far from the nearest high road and from the nearest market town, and had been much struck by the silence and loneliness of the retreat in which he found the most graceful and splendid of English courtiers.

At one in the morning of the sixth of October, the King landed at Margate. Late in the evening he reached Kensington. The following morning a brilliant crowd of ministers and nobles pressed to kiss his hand : but he missed one face which ought to have been there, and asked where the Duke of Shrewsbury was, and when he was expected in town. The next day came a letter from the Duke, averring that he had just had a bad fall in hunting. His side had been bruised : his lungs had suffered : he had spit blood, and could not venture to travel.†  That he had fallen and hurt himself was true : but even those who felt most kindly towards him suspected, and not without strong reason, that he made the most of his convenient misfortune, and, that if he had not shrunk from appearing in public, he would have performed the journey with little difficulty. His correspondents told him that, if he was really as ill as he thought himself, he would do well to consult the physicians

---

* William to Shrewsbury, Sept. 25. 1696.
† London Gazette, Oct. 8. 1696 ; Vernon to Shrewsbury, October 8. ; Shrewsbury to Portland, Oct. 11.

and surgeons of the capital.  Somers, especially, implored him in the most earnest manner to come up to London.  Every hour's delay was mischievous.  His Grace must conquer his sensibility.  He had only to face calumny courageously, and it would vanish.*  The King, in a few kind lines, expressed his sorrow for the accident.  "You are much wanted here," he wrote: "I am impatient to embrace you, and to assure you that my esteem for you is undiminished." †  Shrewsbury answered that he had resolved to resign the seals. ‡  Somers adjured him not to commit so fatal an error.  If at that moment His Grace should quit office, what could the world think, except that he was condemned by his own conscience?  He would, in fact, plead guilty : he would put a stain on his own honour, and on the honour of all who lay under the same accusation.  It would no longer be possible to treat Fenwick's story as a romance.  "Forgive me," Somers wrote, "for speaking after this free manner ; for I do own I can scarce be temperate in this matter."§  A few hours later William himself wrote to the same effect.  "I have so much regard for you, that, if I could, I would positively interdict you from doing what must bring such grave suspicions on you.  At any time, I should consider your resignation as a misfortune to myself : but I protest to you that, at this time, it is on your account more than on mine that I wish you to remain in my service." ‖  Sunderland, Portland, Russell and Wharton joined their entreaties to their master's ; and Shrewsbury consented to remain Secretary in name.  But nothing could induce him to face the Parliament which was about to meet.  A litter was sent down to him from London, but to no purpose.  He set out, but declared that he found it impossible to proceed, and took refuge again in his lonely mansion among the hills.¶

While these things were passing, the members of both Houses were from every part of the kingdom going up to Westminster.  To the opening of the session, not only England, but all Europe, looked forward with intense anxiety.  Public credit had been deeply injured by the failure of the Land Bank.  The restoration of the currency was not yet half accomplished.  The scarcity of money was still distressing.

* Vernon to Shrewsbury, Oct. 13. 1696 ; Somers to Shrewsbury, Oct. 15.
† William to Shrewsbury, Oct. 9. 1696.
‡ Shrewsbury to William, Oct. 11. 1696.
§ Somers to Shrewsbury, Oct. 19. 1696.
‖ William to Shrewsbury, Oct. 20. 1696.
¶ Vernon to Shrewsbury, Oct. 13. 15. ; Portland to Shrewsbury, Oct. 20.

Much of the milled silver was buried in private repositories as fast as it came forth from the Mint. Those politicians who were bent on raising the denomination of the coin had found too ready audience from a population suffering under severe pressure ; and, at one time, the general voice of the nation had seemed to be on their side.* Of course every person who thought it likely that the standard would be lowered, hoarded as much money as he could hoard ; and thus the cry for little shillings aggravated the pressure from which it had sprung.† Both the allies and the enemies of England imagined that her resources were spent, that her spirit was broken, that the Commons, so often querulous and parsimonious even in tranquil and prosperous times, would now positively refuse to bear any additional burden, and would, with an importunity not to be withstood, insist on having peace at any price.

But all these prognostications were confounded by the firmness and ability of the Whig leaders, and by the steadiness of the Whig majority. On the twentieth of October the Houses met. William addressed to them a speech remarkable even among all the remarkable speeches in which his own high thoughts and purposes were expressed in the dignified and judicious language of Somers. There was, the King said, great reason for congratulation. It was true that the funds voted in the preceding session for the support of the war had failed, and that the recoinage had produced great distress. Yet the enemy had obtained no advantage abroad : the State had been torn by no convulsion at home : the loyalty shown by the army and by the nation under severe trials had disappointed all the hopes of those who wished evil to England. Overtures tending to peace had been made. What might be the result of those overtures, was uncertain : but this was certain, that there could be no safe or honourable peace for a nation which was not prepared to wage vigorous war. "I am sure we shall all agree in opinion that the only way of treating with France is with our swords in our hands."

The Commons returned to their chamber ; and Foley read the speech from the chair. A debate followed which resounded through all Christendom. That was the proudest day of Montague's life, and one of the proudest days in the history of the English Parliament. In 1798, Burke held up the proceedings of that day as an example to the statesmen whose hearts had failed them in the conflict with the gigantic power of the French republic. In 1822, Huskisson held up the proceedings

* L'Hermitage, July ⅑⅒. 1696.　　　　† Lansdowne MS. 801.

of that day as an example to a legislature which, under the
pressure of severe distress, was tempted to alter the standard
of value and to break faith with the public creditor.    Before
the House rose the young Chancellor of the Exchequer, whose
ascendency, since the ludicrous failure of the Tory scheme of
finance, was undisputed, proposed and carried three memorable
resolutions.    The first, which passed with only one muttered
No, declared that the Commons would support the King
against all foreign and domestic enemies, and would enable him
to prosecute the war with vigour.    The second, which passed,
not without opposition, but without a division, declared that
the standard of money should not be altered in fineness,
weight or denomination.    The third, against which not a single
opponent of the government dared to raise his voice, pledged
the House to make good all the deficiencies of all parliamentary
funds established since the King's accession.    The task of
framing an answer to the royal speech was entrusted to a
Committee exclusively composed of Whigs.    Montague was
chairman ; and the eloquent and animated address which he
drew up may still be read in the Journals with interest and
pride.*

Within a fortnight two millions and a half were granted for
the military expenditure of the approaching year, and nearly
as much for the maritime expenditure.    Provision was made
without any dispute for forty thousand seamen.    About the
amount of the land force there was a division.    The King
asked for eighty-seven thousand soldiers ; and the Tories
thought that number too large.    The vote was carried by two
hundred and twenty-three to sixty-seven.

The malecontents flattered themselves, during a short time,
that the vigorous resolutions of the Commons would be nothing
more than resolutions, that it would be found impossible to
restore public credit, to obtain advances from capitalists, or to
wring taxes out of the distressed population, and that therefore
the forty thousand seamen and the eighty-seven thousand
soldiers would exist only on paper.    Howe, who had been
more cowed than was usual with him on the first day of the
session, attempted, a week later, to make a stand against the
Ministry.    "The King," he said, "must have been misinformed ;

---

* I take my account of these proceedings from the Commons' Journals,
from the despatches of Van Cleverskirke, and L'Hermitage to the States
General, and from Vernon's letter to Shrewsbury of the 27th of October
1696.    "I don't know," says Vernon, "that the House of Commons ever
acted with greater concert than they do at present."

or His Majesty never would have felicitated Parliament on the tranquil state of the country. I come from Gloucestershire. I know that part of the kingdom well. The people are all living on alms, or ruined by paying alms. The soldier helps himself, sword in hand, to what he wants. There have been serious riots already; and still more serious riots are to be apprehended." The disapprobation of the House was strongly expressed. Several members declared that in their counties every thing was quiet. If Gloucestershire were in a more disturbed state than the rest of England, might not the cause be that Gloucestershire was cursed with a more malignant and unprincipled agitator than all the rest of England could show? Some Gloucestershire gentlemen took issue with Howe on the facts. There was no such distress, they said, no such discontent, no such rioting as he had described. In that county, as in every other county, the great body of the population was fully determined to support the King in waging a vigorous war till he could make an honourable peace.*

In fact the tide had already turned. From the moment at which the Commons notified their fixed determination not to raise the denomination of the coin, the milled money began to come forth from a thousand strong boxes and private drawers. There was still pressure; but that pressure was less and less felt day by day. The nation, though still suffering, was joyful and grateful. Its feelings resembled those of a man who, having been long tortured by a malady which has embittered his life, has at last made up his mind to submit to the surgeon's knife, who has gone through a cruel operation with safety, and who, though still smarting from the steel, sees before him many years of health and enjoyment, and thanks God that the worst is over. Within four days after the meeting of Parliament there was a perceptible improvement in trade. The discount on bank notes had diminished by one third. The price of those wooden tallies, which, according to an usage handed to us from a rude age, were given as receipts for sums paid into the Exchequer, had risen. The exchanges, which had during many months been greatly against England, had begun to turn.† Soon the effect of the magnanimous firmness of the

---

* Vernon to Shrewsbury, Oct. 29. 1696; L'Hermitage, $\frac{Oct. 30.}{Nov. 9.}$ L'Hermitage calls Howe Jaques Haut. No doubt the Frenchman had always heard Howe spoken of as Jack.

† Postman, October 24. 1696; L'Hermitage, $\frac{Oct. 23.}{Nov. 2.}$ L'Hermitage says: "On commence déjà à ressentir des effets avantageux des promptes et favorables résolutions que la Chambre des Communes prit Mardy. Le

House of Commons was felt at every Court in Europe. So high indeed was the spirit of that assembly that the King had some difficulty in preventing the Whigs from moving and carrying a resolution that an address should be presented to him, requesting him to enter into no negotiation with France, till she should have acknowledged him as King of England.*
Such an address was unnecessary. The votes of the Parliament had already forced on Lewis the conviction that there was no chance of a counterrevolution. There was as little chance that he would be able to effect that compromise of which he had, in the course of the negotiations, thrown out hints. It was not to be hoped that either William or the English nation would ever consent to make the settlement of the English crown a matter of bargain with France. And even had William and the English nation been disposed to purchase peace by such a sacrifice of dignity, there would have been insuperable difficulties in another quarter. James could not endure to hear of the expedient which Lewis had suggested. " I can bear," the exile said to his benefactor, " I can bear with Christian patience to be robbed by the Prince of Orange ; but I never will consent to be robbed by my own son." Lewis never again mentioned the subject. Callieres received orders to make the concession on which the peace of the civilised world depended. He and Dykvelt came together at the Hague before Baron Lilienroth, the representative of the King of Sweden, whose mediation the belligerent powers had accepted. Dykvelt informed Lilienroth that the Most Christian King had engaged, whenever the Treaty of Peace should be signed, to recognise the Prince of Orange as King of Great Britain, and added, with a very intelligible allusion to the compromise proposed by France, that the recognition would be without restriction, condition or reserve. Callieres then declared that he confirmed, in the name of his master, what Dykvelt had said.† A letter from Prior, containing the good news, was delivered to James Vernon, the Under Secretary of State, in the House of Commons. The tidings ran along the benches—such is Vernon's expression—

---

discomte des billets de banque, qui estoit le jour auparavant à 18, est revenu à douze, et les actions ont aussy augmenté, aussy bien que les taillis."

* William to Heinsius, Nov. $\frac{13}{23}$. 1696.

† Actes et Mémoires des Négociations de la Paix de Ryswick, 1707 ; Villiers to Shrewsbury, Dec. $\frac{1}{11}$. $\frac{4}{14}$. 1696 ; Letter of Heinsius quoted by M. Sirtema de Grovestins. Of this letter I have not a copy.

like fire in a field of stubble. A load was taken away from every heart; and all was joy and triumph.* The Whig members might indeed well congratulate each other. For it was to the wisdom and resolution which they had shown, in a moment of extreme danger and distress, that their country was indebted for the near prospect of an honourable peace.

Meanwhile public credit, which had, in the autumn, sunk to the lowest point, was fast reviving. Ordinary financiers stood aghast when they learned that more than five millions were required to make good the deficiencies of past years. But Montague was not an ordinary financier. A bold and simple plan proposed by him, and popularly called the General Mortgage, restored confidence. New taxes were imposed; old taxes were augmented or continued; and thus a consolidated fund was formed sufficient to meet every just claim on the State. The Bank of England was at the same time enlarged by a new subscription; and the regulations for the payment of the subscription were framed in such a manner as to raise the value both of the notes of the corporation and of the public securities.

Meanwhile the mints were pouring forth the new silver faster than ever. The distress which began on the fourth of May 1696, which was almost insupportable during the five succeeding months, and which became lighter from the day on which the Commons declared their immutable resolution to maintain the old standard, ceased to be painfully felt in March 1697. Some months were still to elapse before credit completely recovered from the most tremendous shock that it has ever sustained. But already the deep and solid foundation had been laid on which was to rise the most gigantic fabric of commercial prosperity that the world had ever seen. The great body of the Whigs attributed the restoration of the health of the State to the genius and firmness of their leader Montague. His enemies were forced to confess, sulkily and sneeringly, that every one of his schemes had succeeded, the first Bank subscription, the second Bank subscription, the Recoinage, the General Mortgage, the Exchequer Bills. But some Tories muttered that he deserved no more praise than a prodigal who stakes his whole estate at hazard, and has a run of good luck. England had indeed passed safely through a terrible crisis, and was the stronger for having passed through it. But she had been in imminent danger of perishing; and the minister who had exposed her to that danger deserved, not to be praised, but

* Vernon to Shrewsbury, Dec. 8. 1696.

to be hanged. Others admitted that the plans which were popularly attributed to Montague were excellent, but denied that those plans were Montague's. The voice of detraction, however, was for a time drowned by the loud applauses of the Parliament and the City. The authority which the Chancellor of the Exchequer exercised in the House of Commons was unprecedented and unrivalled. In the Cabinet his influence was daily increasing. He had no longer a superior at the Board of Treasury. In consequence of Fenwick's confession, the last Tory who held a great and efficient office in the State had been removed, and there was at length a purely Whig Ministry.

It had been impossible to prevent reports about that confession from getting abroad. The prisoner, indeed, had found means of communicating with his friends, and had doubtless given them to understand that he had said nothing against them, and much against the creatures of the usurper. William wished the matter to be left to the ordinary tribunals, and was most unwilling that it should be debated elsewhere. But his counsellors, better acquainted than himself with the temper of large and divided assemblies, were of opinion that a parliamentary discussion, though perhaps undesirable, was inevitable. It was in the power of a single member of either House to force on such a discussion; and in both Houses there were members who, some from a sense of duty, some from mere love of mischief, were determined to know whether the prisoner had, as it was rumoured, brought grave charges against some of the most distinguished men in the kingdom. If there must be an inquiry, it was surely desirable that the accused statesmen should be the first to demand it. There was, however, one great difficulty. The Whigs, who formed the majority of the Lower House, were ready to vote, as one man, for the entire absolution of Russell and Shrewsbury, and had no wish to put a stigma on Marlborough, who was not in place, and therefore excited little jealousy. But a strong body of honest gentlemen, as Wharton called them, could not, by any management, be induced to join in a resolution acquitting Godolphin. To them Godolphin was an eyesore. All the other Tories who, in the earlier years of William's reign, had borne a chief part in the direction of affairs, had, one by one, been dismissed. Nottingham, Trevor, Leeds, were no longer in power. Pembroke could hardly be called a Tory, and had never been really in power. But Godolphin still retained his post at Whitehall; and to the men of the Revolution it seemed intolerable that one who had sate at the Council Board of Charles and James, and who had voted for a Regency, should be the principal minister of finance. Those who felt thus had learned with malicious delight that the First Lord of the Treasury was named in the confession about which all the world was talking; and they were determined not to let slip so good an opportunity of ejecting him from office. On the other hand, every body who had seen Fenwick's paper, and who had not, in the drunkenness of factious animosity, lost all sense of reason and justice, must have felt that it was impossible to make a distinction between two parts of that paper, and to treat all that related to Shrewsbury and Russell as false, and all that related to Godolphin as true. This was acknowledged even by Wharton, who of all public men was the least troubled by scruples or by shame.* If Godolphin had stedfastly refused to quit his place, the Whig leaders would have been in a most embarrassing position. But a politician of no common dexterity undertook to extricate them from their difficulties. In the art of reading and managing the minds of men Sunderland had no equal; and he was, as he had been during several years, desirous to see all the great posts in the kingdom filled by Whigs. By his skilful management Godolphin was induced to go into the royal closet, and to request permission to retire from office; and William granted that permission with a readiness by which Godolphin was much more surprised than pleased.†

One of the methods employed by the Whig junto, for the purpose of instituting and maintaining through all the ranks of the Whig party a discipline never before known, was the frequent holding of meetings of members of the House of Commons. Some of those meetings were numerous: others were select. The larger were held at the Rose, a tavern frequently mentioned in the political pasquinades of that time ‡; the smaller at Russell's in Covent Garden, or at Somers's in Lincoln's Inn Fields.

On the day on which Godolphin resigned his great office two select meetings were called. In the morning the place of assembly was Russell's house. In the afternoon there was a fuller muster at the Lord Keeper's. Fenwick's confession,

* Wharton to Shrewsbury, Oct. 27. 1696.

† Somers to Shrewsbury, Oct. 27. 31. 1696; Vernon to Shrewsbury, Oct. 31.; Wharton to Shrewsbury, Nov. 10. "I am apt to think," says Wharton, "there never was more management than in bringing that about."

‡ See for example a poem on the last Treasury day at Kensington, March 169⁷⁄₈.

which, till that time, had probably been known only by rumour to most of those who were present, was read. The indignation of the hearers was strongly excited, particularly by one passage, of which the sense seemed to be that not only Russell, not only Shrewsbury, but the great body of the Whig party was, and had long been, at heart Jacobite. "The fellow insinuates," it was said, "that the Assassination Plot itself was a Whig scheme." The general opinion was that such a charge could not be lightly passed over. There must be a solemn debate and decision in Parliament. The best course would be that the King should himself see and examine the prisoner, and that Russell should then request the royal permission to bring the subject before the House of Commons. As Fenwick did not pretend that he had any authority for the stories which he had told except mere hearsay, there could be no difficulty in carrying a resolution branding him as a slanderer, and an address to the throne requesting that he might be forthwith brought to trial for high treason.*

The opinion of the meeting was conveyed to William by his ministers; and he consented, though not without reluctance, to see the prisoner. Fenwick was brought into the royal closet at Kensington. A few of the great officers of state and the Crown lawyers were present. "Your papers, Sir John," said the King, "are altogether unsatisfactory. Instead of giving me an account of the plots formed by you and your accomplices, plots of which all the details must be exactly known to you, you tell me stories, without authority, without date, without place, about noblemen and gentlemen with whom you do not pretend to have had any intercourse. In short your confession appears to be a contrivance intended to screen those who are really engaged in designs against me, and to make me suspect and discard those in whom I have good reason to place confidence. If you look for any favour from me, give me, this moment and on this spot, a full and straightforward account of what you know of your own knowledge." Fenwick said that he was taken by surprise, and asked for time. "No, Sir," said the King. "For what purpose can you want time? You may indeed want time if you mean to draw up another paper like this. But what I require is a plain narrative of what you have yourself done and seen; and such a narrative you can give, if you will, without pen and ink." Then Fenwick positively refused to say any thing. "Be it so," said William. "I will neither hear you

* Somers to Shrewsbury, Oct. 31. 1696; Wharton to Shrewsbury, of the same date.

nor hear from you any more." *  Fenwick was carried back to
his prison.  He had at this audience shown a boldness and
determination which surprised those who had observed his
demeanour.  He had, ever since he had been in confinement,
appeared to be anxious and dejected : yet now, at the very
crisis of his fate, he had braved the displeasure of the Prince
whose clemency he had, a short time before, submissively
implored.  In a very few hours the mystery was explained.
Just before he had been summoned to Kensington, he had
received from his wife intelligence that his life was in no danger,
that there was only one witness against him, that she and her
friends had succeeded in corrupting Goodman.†

Goodman had been allowed a liberty which was afterwards,
with some reason, made matter of charge against the government.  For his testimony was most important : his character
was notoriously bad : the attempts which had been made to
seduce Porter proved that, if money could save Fenwick's life,
money would not be spared ; and Goodman had not, like
Porter, been instrumental in sending Jacobites to the gallows,
and therefore was not, like Porter, bound to the cause of
William by an indissoluble tie.  The families of the imprisoned
conspirators employed the agency of a cunning and daring
adventurer named O'Brien.  This man knew Goodman well.
Indeed they had belonged to the same gang of highwaymen.
They met at the Dog in Drury Lane, a tavern which was
frequented by lawless and desperate men.  O'Brien was accompanied by another Jacobite of determined character.  A simple
choice was offered to Goodman, to abscond and to be rewarded
with an annuity of five hundred a year, or to have his throat
cut on the spot.  He consented, half from cupidity, half from
fear.  O'Brien was not a man to be tricked as Clancy had been.
He never parted company with Goodman from the moment
when the bargain was struck till they were at Saint Germains.‡

On the afternoon of the day on which Fenwick was examined
by the King at Kensington it began to be noised abroad that
Goodman was missing.  He had been many hours absent from
his house.  He had not been seen at his usual haunts.  At
first a suspicion arose that he had been murdered by the Jacob-

---

* Somers to Shrewsbury, Nov. 3. 1696.  The King's unwillingness to
see Fenwick is mentioned in Somers's letter of the 15th of October.

† Vernon to Shrewsbury, Nov. 3. 1696.

‡ The circumstances of Goodman's flight were ascertained three years
later by the Earl of Manchester, when Ambassador at Paris, and by him
communicated to Jersey in a letter dated $\frac{\text{Sept. 25.}}{\text{Oct. 5.}}$ 1699.

ites ; and this suspicion was strengthened by a singular circumstance. Just after his disappearance, a human head was found
severed from the body to which it belonged, and so frightfully
mangled that no feature could be recognised. The multitude,
possessed by the notion that there was no crime which an Irish
Papist might not be found to commit, was inclined to believe
that the fate of Godfrey had befallen another victim. On
inquiry however it seemed certain that Goodman had designedly
withdrawn himself. A proclamation appeared promising a
reward of a thousand pounds to any person who should stop
the runaway : but it was too late.*

This event exasperated the Whigs beyond measure. No
jury could now find Fenwick guilty of high treason. Was he
then to escape ? Was a long series of offences against the State
to go unpunished merely because to those offences had now
been added the offence of bribing a witness to suppress his
evidence and to desert his bail ? Was there no extraordinary
method by which justice might strike a criminal who, solely
because he was worse than other criminals, was beyond the
reach of the ordinary law ? Such a method there was, a method
authorised by numerous precedents, a method used both by
Papists and by Protestants during the troubles of the sixteenth
century, a method used both by Roundheads and by Cavaliers
during the troubles of the seventeenth century, a method which
scarcely any leader of the Tory party could condemn without
condemning himself, a method of which Fenwick could not
decently complain, since he had, a few years before, been eager
to employ it against the unfortunate Monmouth. To that
method the party which was now supreme in the State determined to have recourse.

Soon after the Commons had met, on the morning of the
sixth of November, Russell rose in his place and requested to
be heard. The task which he had undertaken required courage
not of the most respectable kind : but to him no kind of courage
was wanting. Sir John Fenwick, he said, had sent to the King
a paper in which grave accusations were brought against some
of His Majesty's servants ; and His Majesty had, at the request
of his accused servants, graciously given orders that this paper
should be laid before the House. The confession was produced
and read. The Admiral then, with spirit and dignity worthy
of a better man, demanded justice for himself and Shrewsbury.
" If we are innocent, clear us. If we are guilty, punish us as

* London Gazette, Nov. 9. 1696 ; Vernon to Shrewsbury, Nov. 3. ; Van
Cleverskirke and L'Hermitage of the same date.

we deserve. I put myself on you as on my country, and am ready to stand or fall by your verdict."

It was immediately ordered that Fenwick should be brought to the bar with all speed. Cutts, who sate in the House as member for Cambridgeshire, was directed to provide a sufficient escort, and was especially enjoined to take care that the prisoner should have no opportunity of making or receiving any communication, oral or written, on the road from Newgate to Westminster. The House then adjourned till the afternoon.

At five o'clock, then a late hour, the mace was again put on the table : candles were lighted ; and the House and lobby were carefully cleared of strangers. Fenwick was in attendance under a strong guard. He was called in, and exhorted from the chair to make a full and ingenuous confession. He hesitated and evaded. "I cannot say any thing without the King's permission. His Majesty may be displeased if what ought to be known only to him should be divulged to others." He was told that his apprehensions were groundless. The King well knew that it was the right and the duty of his faithful Commons to inquire into whatever concerned the safety of his person and of his government. "I may be tried in a few days," said the prisoner. "I ought not to be asked to say any thing which may rise up in judgment against me." "You have nothing to fear," replied the Speaker, "if you will only make a full and free discovery. No man ever had reason to repent of having dealt candidly with the Commons of England." Then Fenwick begged for delay. He was not a ready orator : his memory was bad : he must have time to prepare himself. He was told, as he had been told a few days before in the royal closet, that, prepared or unprepared, he could not but remember the principal plots in which he had been engaged, and the names of his chief accomplices. If he would honestly relate what it was quite impossible that he could have forgotten, the House would make all fair allowances, and would grant him time to recollect subordinate details. Thrice he was removed from the bar ; and thrice he was brought back. He was solemnly informed that the opportunity then given him of earning the favour of the Commons would probably be the last. He persisted in his refusal, and was sent back to Newgate.

It was then moved that his confession was false and scandalous. Coningsby proposed to add that it was a contrivance to create jealousies between the King and good subjects for the purpose of screening real traitors. A few implacable and unmanageable Whigs, whose hatred of Godolphin had not been mitigated by his resignation, hinted their doubts whether the whole paper ought to be condemned. But after a debate in which Montague particularly distinguished himself the motion was carried. One or two voices cried " No : " but nobody ventured to demand a division.

Thus far all had gone smoothly : but in a few minutes the storm broke forth. The terrible words, Bill of Attainder, were pronounced ; and all the fiercest passions of both the great factions were instantly roused. The Tories had been taken by surprise, and many of them had left the house. Those who remained were loud in declaring that they never would consent to such a violation of the first principles of justice. The spirit of the Whigs was not less ardent, and their ranks were unbroken. The motion for leave to bring in a bill attainting Sir John Fenwick was carried very late at night by one hundred and seventy-nine votes to sixty-one : but it was plain that the struggle would be long and hard.*

In truth party spirit had seldom been more strongly excited. On both sides there was doubtless much honest zeal ; and on both sides an observant eye might have detected fear, hatred, and cupidity disguised under specious pretences of justice and public good. The baleful heat of faction rapidly warmed into life poisonous creeping things which had long been lying torpid, discarded spies and convicted false witnesses, the leavings of the scourge, the branding iron and the shears. Even Fuller hoped that he might again find dupes to listen to him. The world had forgotten him since his pillorying. He now had the effrontery to write to the Speaker, begging to be heard at the bar and promising much important information about Fenwick and others. On the ninth of November the Speaker informed the House that he had received this communication : but the House very properly refused even to suffer the letter of so notorious a villain to be read.

On the same day the Bill of Attainder, having been prepared by the Attorney and Solicitor General, was brought in and read a first time. The House was full and the debate sharp. John Manley, member for Bossiney, one of those

* The account of the events of this day I have taken from the Commons' Journals ; the valuable work entitled Proceedings in Parliament against Sir John Fenwick, Bart. upon a Bill of Attainder for High Treason, 1696 ; Vernon's Letter to Shrewsbury, November 6. 1696, and Somers's Letter to Shrewsbury, November 7. From both these letters it is plain that the Whig leaders had much difficulty in obtaining the absolution of Godolphin.

stanch Tories who, in the preceding session, had long refused to sign the Association, accused the majority, in no measured terms, of fawning on the Court and betraying the liberties of the people. His words were taken down; and, though he tried to explain them away, he was sent to the Tower. Seymour spoke strongly against the bill, and quoted the speech which Cæsar made in the Roman Senate against the motion that the accomplices of Catiline should be put to death in an irregular manner. A Whig orator keenly remarked that the worthy Baron had forgotten that Cæsar was grievously suspected of having been himself concerned in Catiline's plot.* In this stage a hundred and ninety-six members voted for the bill, a hundred and four against it. A copy was sent to Fenwick, in order that he might be prepared to defend himself. He begged to be heard by counsel: his request was granted; and the thirteenth was fixed for the hearing.

Never within the memory of the oldest member had there been such a stir round the House as on the morning of the thirteenth. The approaches were with some difficulty cleared; and no strangers, except peers, were suffered to come within the doors. Of peers the throng was so great that their presence had a perceptible influence on the debate. Even Seymour, who, having formerly been Speaker, ought to have been peculiarly mindful of the dignity of the Commons, so strangely forgot himself as once to say "My Lords." Fenwick, having been formally given up by the Sheriffs of London to the Serjeant at Arms, was put to the bar, attended by two barristers who were generally employed by Jacobite culprits, Sir Thomas Powis and Sir Bartholomew Shower. Counsel appointed by the House appeared in support of the bill.

The examination of the witnesses and the arguments of the advocates occupied three days. Porter was called in and interrogated. It was established, not indeed by legal proof, but by such moral proof as determines the conduct of men in the affairs of common life, that Goodman's absence was to be attributed to a scheme planned and executed by Fenwick's friends with Fenwick's privity. Secondary evidence of what Goodman, if he had been present, would have been able to prove, was, after a warm debate, admitted. His confession, made on oath and subscribed by his hand, was put in. Some of the grand jurymen who had found the bill against Sir John

---

* Commons' Journals, Nov. 9. 1696; Vernon to Shrewsbury, Nov. 10. The editor of the State Trials is mistaken in supposing that the quotation from Cæsar's speech was made in the debate of the 13th.

gave an account of what Goodman had sworn before them; and their testimony was confirmed by some of the petty jurymen who had convicted another conspirator. No evidence was produced in behalf of the prisoner. After counsel for him and against him had been heard, he was sent back to his cell.[*] Then the real struggle began. It was long and violent. The House repeatedly sate from daybreak till near midnight. Once the Speaker was in the chair fifteen hours without intermission. Strangers were freely admitted: for it was felt that, since the House chose to take on itself the functions of a court of justice, it ought, like a court of justice, to sit with open doors.[†] The substance of the debates has consequently been preserved in a report, meagre, indeed, when compared with the reports of our time, but for that age unusually full. Every man of note in the House took part in the discussion. The bill was opposed by Finch with that fluent and sonorous rhetoric which had gained him the name of Silvertongue, and by Howe with all the sharpness both of his wit and of his temper, by Seymour with characteristic energy, and by Harley with characteristic solemnity. On the other side Montague displayed the powers of a consummate debater, and was zealously supported by Littleton. Conspicuous in the front ranks of the hostile parties were two distinguished lawyers, Simon Harcourt and William Cowper. Both were gentlemen of honourable descent: both were distinguished by their fine persons and graceful manners: both were renowned for eloquence; and both loved learning and learned men. It may be added that both had early in life been noted for prodigality and love of pleasure. Dissipation had made them poor: poverty had made them industrious; and though they were still, as age is reckoned at the Inns of Court, very young men, Harcourt only thirty-six, Cowper only thirty-two, they already had the first practice at the bar. They were destined to rise still higher, to be the bearers of the great seal of the realm, and the founders of patrician houses. In politics they were diametrically opposed to each other. Harcourt had seen the Revolution with disgust, had not chosen to sit in the Convention, had with difficulty reconciled his conscience to the oaths, and had tardily and unwillingly signed the Association. Cowper had been in arms for the Prince of Orange and a free

[*] Commons' Journals, Nov. 13. 16, 17.; Proceedings against Sir John Fenwick.

[†] A Letter to a Friend in Vindication of the Proceedings against Sir John Fenwick, 1697.

Parliament, and had, in the short and tumultuary campaign which preceded the flight of James, distinguished himself by intelligence and courage. Since Somers had been removed to the Woolsack, the law officers of the Crown had not made a very distinguished figure in the Lower House, or indeed any where else; and their deficiencies had been more than once supplied by Cowper. His skill had, at the trial of Parkyns, recovered the verdict which the mismanagement of the Solicitor General had, for a moment, put in jeopardy. He had been chosen member for Hertford at the general election of 1695, and had scarcely taken his seat when he attained a high place among parliamentary speakers. Chesterfield many years later, in one of his letters to his son, described Cowper as an orator who never spoke without applause, but who reasoned feebly, and who owed the influence which he long exercised over great assemblies to the singular charm of his style, his voice and his action. Chesterfield was, beyond all doubt, intellectually qualified to form a correct judgment on such a subject. But it must be remembered that the object of his letters was to exalt good taste and politeness in opposition to much higher qualities. He therefore constantly and systematic-ally attributed the success of the most eminent persons of his age to their superiority, not in solid abilities and acquirements, but in superficial graces of diction and manner. He represented even Marlborough as a man of very ordinary capacity, who, solely because he was extremely well bred and well spoken, had risen from poverty and obscurity to the height of power and glory. It may confidently be pronounced that both to Marl-borough and to Cowper Chesterfield was unjust. The general who saved the Empire and conquered the Low Countries was assuredly something more than a fine gentleman; and the judge who presided during nine years in the Court of Chancery with the approbation of all parties must have been something more than a fine declaimer.

Whoever attentively and impartially studies the report of the debates will be of opinion that, on many points which were discussed at great length and with great animation, the Whigs had a decided superiority in argument, but that on the main question the Tories were in the right.

It was true that the crime of high treason was brought home to Fenwick by proofs which could leave no doubt on the mind of any man of common sense, and would have been brought home to him according to the strict rules of law, if he had not, by committing another crime, eluded the justice of the

ordinary tribunals.   It was true that he had, in the very act
of professing repentance and imploring mercy, added a new
offence to his former offences, that, while pretending to make
a perfectly ingenuous confession, he had, with cunning malice,
concealed every thing which it was for the interest of the
government that he should divulge, and proclaimed every
thing which it was for the interest of the government to bury
in silence.   It was a great evil that he should be beyond the
reach of punishment: it was plain that he could be reached
only by a bill of pains and penalties ; and it could not be
denied, either that many such bills had passed, or that no
such bill had ever passed in a clearer case of guilt or after a
fairer hearing.

All these propositions the Whigs seem to have fully
established.   They had also a decided advantage in the
dispute about the rule which requires two witnesses in cases of
high treason.   The truth is that the rule is absurd.   It is
impossible to understand why the evidence which would be
sufficient to prove that a man has fired at one of his fellow
subjects should not be sufficient to prove that he has fired at
his Sovereign.   It can by no means be laid down as a general
maxim that the assertion of two witnesses is more convincing
to the mind than the assertion of one witness.   The story told
by one witness may be in itself probable.   The story told by
two witnesses may be extravagant.   The story told by one
witness may be uncontradicted.   The story told by two
witnesses may be contradicted by four witnesses.   The story
told by one witness may be corroborated by a crowd of circumstances.   The story told by two witnesses may have no such
corroboration.   The one witness may be Tillotson or Ken.
The two witnesses may be Oates and Bedloe.

The chiefs of the Tory party, however, vehemently maintained that the law which required two witnesses was of universal
and eternal obligation, part of the law of nature, part of the
law of God.   Seymour quoted the book of Numbers and the
book of Deuteronomy to prove that no man ought to be
condemned to death by the mouth of a single witness.
" Caiaphas and his Sanhedrim," said Harley, " were ready
enough to set up the plea of expediency for a violation of
justice : they said,—and we have heard such things said,—
' We must slay this man, or the Romans will come and take
away our place and nation.'   Yet even Caiaphas and his
Sanhedrim, in that foulest act of judicial murder, did not
venture to set aside the sacred law which required two

witnesses." "Even Jezebel," said another orator, "did not dare to take Naboth's vineyard from him till she had suborned two men of Belial to swear falsely." "If the testimony of one grave elder had been sufficient," it was asked, "what would have become of the virtuous Susannah?" This last allusion called forth a cry of "Apocrypha, Apocrypha," from the ranks of the Low Churchmen.*

Over these arguments, which in truth can scarcely have imposed on those who condescended to use them, Montague obtained a complete and easy victory. "An eternal law! Where was this eternal law before the reign of Edward the Sixth? Where is it now, except in statutes which relate only to one very small class of offences. If these texts from the Pentateuch and these precedents from the practice of the Sanhedrim prove any thing, they prove the whole criminal jurisprudence of the realm to be a mass of injustice and impiety. One witness is sufficient to convict a murderer, a burglar, a highwayman, an incendiary, a ravisher. Nay, there are cases of high treason in which only one witness is required. One witness can send to Tyburn a gang of clippers and coiners. Are you, then, prepared to say that the whole law of evidence, according to which men have during ages been tried in this country for offences against life and property, is vicious and ought to be remodelled? If you shrink from saying this, you must admit that we are now proposing to dispense, not with a divine ordinance of universal and perpetual obligation, but simply with an English rule of procedure, which applies to not more than two or three crimes, which has not been in force a hundred and fifty years, which derives all its authority from an Act of Parliament, and which may therefore be by another Act abrogated or suspended without offence to God or men."

It was much less easy to answer the chiefs of the opposition when they set forth the danger of breaking down the partition which separates the functions of the legislator from those of the judge. "This man," it was said, "may be a bad Englishman; and yet his cause may be the cause of all good Englishmen. Only last year we passed an Act to regulate the procedure of the ordinary courts in cases of treason. We passed that Act because we thought that, in those courts, the life of a subject obnoxious to the government was not then sufficiently secured. Yet the life of a subject obnoxious to the government was then far more secure than it will be if this House takes on itself to

* This incident is mentioned by L'Hermitage.

be the supreme criminal judicature in political cases." Warm eulogies were pronounced on the ancient national mode of trial by twelve good men and true; and indeed the advantages of that mode of trial in political cases are obvious. The prisoner is allowed to challenge any number of jurors with cause, and a considerable number without cause. The twelve, from the moment at which they are invested with their short magistracy, till the moment when they lay it down, are kept separate from the rest of the community. Every precaution is taken to prevent any agent of power from soliciting or corrupting them. Every one of them must hear every word of the evidence and every argument used on either side. The case is then summed up by a judge who knows that, if he is guilty of partiality, he may be called to account by the great inquest of the nation. In the trial of Fenwick at the bar of the House of Commons all these securities were wanting. Some hundreds of gentlemen, every one of whom had much more than half made up his mind before the case was opened, performed the functions both of judge and jury. They were not restrained, as a judge is restrained, by the sense of responsibility; for who was to punish a Parliament? They were not selected, as a jury is selected, in a manner which enables the culprit to exclude his personal and political enemies. The arbiters of his fate came in and went out as they chose. They heard a fragment here and there of what was said against him, and a fragment here and there of what was said in his favour. During the progress of the bill they were exposed to every species of influence. One member was threatened by the electors of his borough with the loss of his seat: another might obtain a frigate for his brother from Russell: the vote of a third might be secured by the caresses and Burgundy of Wharton. In the debates arts were practised and passions excited which are unknown to well constituted tribunals, but from which no great popular assembly divided into parties ever was or ever will be free. The rhetoric of one orator called forth loud cries of "Hear him." Another was coughed and scraped down. A third spoke against time in order that his friends who were supping might come in to divide.* If the life of the most worthless man could be sported with thus, was the life of the most virtuous man secure?

The opponents of the bill did not, indeed, venture to say that there could be no public danger sufficient to justify an Act of Attainder. They admitted that there might be cases

* L'Hermitage tells us that such things took place in these debates.

in which the general rule must bend to an overpowering necessity. But was this such a case? Even if it were granted, for the sake of argument, that Strafford and Monmouth were justly attainted, was Fenwick, like Strafford, a great minister who had long ruled England north of Trent, and all Ireland, with absolute power, who was high in the royal favour, and whose capacity, eloquence and resolution made him an object of dread even in his fall? Or was Fenwick, like Monmouth, a pretender to the Crown and the idol of the common people? Were all the finest youths of three counties crowding to enlist under his banners? What was he but a subordinate plotter? He had indeed once had good employments: but he had long lost them. He had once had a good estate: but he had wasted it. Eminent abilities and weight of character he had never had. He was, no doubt, connected by marriage with a very noble family: but that family did not share his political prejudices. What importance, then, had he, except that importance which his persecutors were most unwisely giving him by breaking through all the fences which guard the lives of Englishmen in order to destroy him? Even if he were set at liberty, what could he do but haunt Jacobite coffeehouses, squeeze oranges, and drink the health of King James and the Prince of Wales? If, however, the government, supported by the Lords and the Commons, by the fleet and the army, by a militia one hundred and sixty thousand strong, and by the half million of men who had signed the Association, did really apprehend danger from this poor ruined baronet, the benefit of the Habeas Corpus Act might be withheld from him. He might be kept within four walls as long as there was the least chance of his doing mischief. It could hardly be contended that he was an enemy so terrible that the State could be safe only when he was in the grave.

It was acknowledged that precedents might be found for this bill, or even for a bill far more objectionable. But it was said that whoever reviewed our history would be disposed to regard such precedents rather as warnings than as examples. It had many times happened that an Act of Attainder, passed in a fit of servility or animosity, had, when fortune had changed, or when passion had cooled, been repealed and solemnly stigmatized as unjust. Thus, in old times, the Act which was passed against Roger Mortimer, in the paroxysm of a resentment not unprovoked, had been, at a calmer moment, rescinded on the ground that, however guilty he might have been, he had not had fair play for his life. Thus, within the memory of the existing generation, the law which attainted Strafford had been annulled, without one dissentient voice. Nor, it was added, ought it to be left unnoticed that, whether by virtue of the ordinary law of cause and effect, or by the extraordinary judgment of God, persons who had been eager to pass bills of pains and penalties, had repeatedly perished by such bills. No man had ever made a more unscrupulous use of the legislative power for the destruction of his enemies than Thomas Cromwell ; and it was by an unscrupulous use of the legislative power that he was himself destroyed. If it were true that the unhappy gentleman whose fate was now trembling in the balance had himself formerly borne a part in a proceeding similar to that which was now instituted against him, was not this a fact which ought to suggest very serious reflections ? Those who tauntingly reminded Fenwick that he had supported the bill which attainted Monmouth might perhaps themselves be tauntingly reminded, in some dark and terrible hour, that they had supported the bill which had attainted Fenwick. "Let us remember what vicissitudes we have seen. Let us, from so many signal examples of the inconstancy of fortune, learn moderation in prosperity. How little we thought, when we saw this man a favourite courtier at Whitehall, a general surrounded with military pomp at Hounslow, that we should live to see him standing at our bar, and awaiting his doom from our lips ! And how far is it from certain that we may not one day, in the bitterness of our souls, vainly invoke the protection of those mild laws which we now treat so lightly ! God forbid that we should ever again be subject to tyranny ! But God forbid, above all, that our tyrants should ever be able to plead, in justification of the worst that they can inflict upon us, precedents furnished by ourselves !"

These topics, skilfully handled, produced a great effect on many moderate Whigs. Montague did his best to rally his followers. We still possess the rude outline of what must have been a most effective peroration. "Gentlemen warn us"— this, or very nearly this, seems to have been what he said— "not to furnish King James with a precedent which, if ever he should be restored, he may use against ourselves. Do they really believe that, if that evil day shall ever come, this just and necessary law will be the pattern which he will imitate ? No, Sir, his model will be, not our bill of attainder, but his own ; not our bill, which, on full proof, and after a most fair hearing, inflicts deserved retribution on a single guilty head ; but his own bill, which, without a defence, without an investigation, without an accusation, doomed near three thousand people, whose only crimes were their English blood and their Protestant faith, the men to the gallows and the women to the stake. That is the precedent which he has set, and which he will follow. In order that he never may be able to follow it, in order that the fear of a righteous punishment may restrain those enemies of our country who wish to see him ruling in London as he ruled at Dublin, I give my vote for this bill."

In spite of all the eloquence and influence of the ministry, the minority grew stronger and stronger as the debates proceeded. The question that leave should be given to bring in the bill had been carried by nearly three to one. On the question that the bill should be committed, the Ayes were a hundred and eighty-six, the Noes a hundred and twenty-eight. On the question that the bill should pass, the Ayes were a hundred and eighty-nine, the Noes a hundred and fifty-six.

On the twenty-sixth of November the bill was carried up to the Lords. Before it arrived, the Lords had made preparations to receive it. Every peer who was absent from town had been summoned up : every peer who disobeyed the summons and was unable to give a satisfactory explanation of his disobedience was taken into custody by Black Rod. On the day fixed for the first reading, the crowd on the benches was unprecedented. The whole number of temporal Lords, exclusive of minors, Roman Catholics and nonjurors, was about a hundred and forty. Of these a hundred and five were in their places. Many thought that the Bishops ought to have been permitted, if not required, to withdraw : for, by an ancient canon, those who ministered at the altars of God were forbidden to take any part in the infliction of capital punishment. On the trial of a peer impeached of high treason, the prelates always retire, and leave the culprit to be absolved or condemned by laymen. And surely, if it be unseemly that a divine should doom his fellow creatures to death as a judge, it must be still more unseemly that he should doom them to death as a legislator. In the latter case, as in the former, he contracts that stain of blood which the Church regards with horror ; and it will scarcely be denied that there are some grave objections to the shedding of blood by Act of Attainder which do not apply to the shedding of blood in the ordinary course of justice. In fact, when the bill for taking away the life of Strafford was under consideration, all the spiritual peers withdrew. Now, however, the example of Cranmer, who had voted for some of the most infamous

K 37

acts of attainder that ever passed, was thought more worthy of imitation ; and there was a great muster of lawn sleeves. It was very properly resolved that, on this occasion, the privilege of voting by proxy should be suspended, that the House should be called over at the beginning and at the end of every sitting, and that every member who did not answer to his name should be taken into custody.*

Meanwhile the unquiet brain of Monmouth was teeming with strange designs. He had now reached a time of life at which youth could no longer be pleaded as an excuse for his faults : but he was more wayward and eccentric than ever. Both in his intellectual and in his moral character there was an abundance of those fine qualities which may be called luxuries, and a lamentable deficiency of those solid qualities which are of the first necessity. He had brilliant wit and ready invention without common sense, and chivalrous generosity and delicacy without common honesty. He was capable of rising to the part of the Black Prince ; and yet he was capable of sinking to the part of Fuller. His political life was blemished by some most dishonourable actions : yet he was not under the influence of those motives to which most of the dishonourable actions of politicians are to be ascribed. He valued power little and money less. Of fear he was utterly insensible. If he sometimes stooped to be a villain,—for no milder word will come up to the truth, —it was merely to amuse himself and to astonish other people. In civil as in military affairs, he loved ambuscades, surprises, night attacks. He now imagined that he had a glorious opportunity of making a sensation, of producing a great commotion ; and the temptation was irresistible to a spirit so restless as his.

He knew, or at least strongly suspected, that the stories which Fenwick had told on hearsay, and which King, Lords and Commons, Whigs and Tories, had agreed to treat as calumnies, were, in the main, true. Was it impossible to prove that they were true, to cross the wise policy of William, to bring disgrace at once on some of the most eminent men of both parties, to throw the whole political world into inextricable confusion ?

Nothing could be done without the help of the prisoner ; and with the prisoner it was impossible to communicate directly. It was necessary to employ the intervention of more than one female agent. The Duchess of Norfolk was a

* See the Lords' Journals, Nov. 14., Nov. 30., Dec. 1. 1696.

Mordaunt, and Monmouth's first cousin. Her gallantries were notorious; and her husband had, some years before, tried to induce his brother nobles to pass a bill for dissolving his marriage: but the attempt had been defeated, in consequence partly of the zeal with which Monmouth had fought the battle of his kinswoman. The lady, though separated from her lord, lived in a style suitable to her rank, and associated with many women of fashion, among others, with Lady Mary Fenwick, and with a relation of Lady Mary, named Elizabeth Lawson. By the instrumentality of the Duchess, Monmouth conveyed to the prisoner several papers containing suggestions framed with much art. Let Sir John,—such was the substance of these suggestions,—boldly affirm that his confession is true, that he has brought accusations, on hearsay indeed, but not on common hearsay, that he has derived his knowledge of the facts which he has asserted from the highest quarters; and let him point out a mode in which his veracity may be easily brought to the test. Let him pray that the Earls of Portland and Romney, who are well known to enjoy the royal confidence, may be called upon to declare whether they are not in possession of information agreeing with what he has related. Let him pray that the King may be requested to lay before Parliament the evidence which caused the sudden disgrace of Lord Marlborough, and any letters which may have been intercepted while passing between Saint Germains and Lord Godolphin. "Unless," said Monmouth to his female agents, "Sir John is under a fate, unless he is out of his mind, he will take my counsel. If he does, his life and honour are safe. If he does not, he is a dead man." Then this strange intriguer, with his usual license of speech, reviled William for what was in truth one of William's best titles to glory. "He is the worst of men. He has acted basely. He pretends not to believe these charges against Shrewsbury, Russell, Marlborough, Godolphin. And yet he knows,"—and Monmonth confirmed the assertion by a tremendous oath,—"he knows that every word of the charges is true."

The papers written by Monmouth were delivered by Lady Mary to her husband. If the advice which they contained had been followed, there can be little doubt that the object of the adviser would have been attained. The King would have been bitterly mortified: there would have been a general panic among public men of every party: even Marlborough's serene fortitude would have been severely tried; and Shrewsbury would probably have shot himself. But that Fenwick would have put himself in a better situation is by no means clear. Such was his own opinion. He saw that the step which he was urged to take was hazardous. He knew that he was urged to take that step, not because it was likely to save himself, but because it was certain to annoy others; and he was resolved not to be Monmouth's tool.

On the first of December the bill went through the earliest stage without a division. Then Fenwick's confession, which had, by the royal command, been laid on the table, was read; and then Marlborough stood up. "Nobody can wonder," he said, "that a man whose head is in danger should try to save himself by accusing others. I assure Your Lordships that, since the accession of his present Majesty, I have had no intercourse with Sir John on any subject whatever; and this I declare on my word of honour." * Marlborough's assertion may have been true: but it was perfectly compatible with the truth of all that Fenwick had said. Godolphin went further. "I certainly did," he said, "continue to the last in the service of King James and of his Queen. I was esteemed by them both. But I cannot think that a crime. It is possible that they and those who are about them may imagine that I am still attached to their interest. That I cannot help. But it is utterly false that I have had any such dealings with the Court of Saint Germains as are described in the paper which Your Lordships have heard read." †

Fenwick was then brought in, and asked whether he had any further confession to make. Several peers interrogated him, but to no purpose. Monmouth, who could not believe that the papers which he had sent to Newgate had produced no effect, put, in a friendly and encouraging manner, several questions intended to bring out answers which would have been by no means agreeable to the accused Lords. No such answer however was to be extracted from Fenwick. Monmouth saw that his ingenious machinations had failed. Enraged and disappointed, he suddenly turned round, and became more zealous for the bill than any other peer in the House. Every body noticed the rapid change in his temper and manner: but that change was at first imputed merely to his well known levity.

On the eighth of December the bill was again taken into consideration; and on that day Fenwick, accompanied by his counsel, was in attendance. But, before he was called in, a

---

* Wharton to Shrewsbury, Dec. 1. 1696; L'Hermitage, of same date.
† L'Hermitage, Dec. $\frac{4}{14}$. 1696; Wharton to Shrewsbury, Dec. 1.

previous question was raised. Several distinguished Tories, particularly Nottingham, Rochester, Normanby and Leeds, said that, in their opinion, it was idle to inquire whether the prisoner was guilty or not guilty, unless the House was of opinion that he was a person so formidable that, if guilty, he ought to be attainted by Act of Parliament. They did not wish, they said, to hear any evidence. For, even on the supposition that the evidence left no doubt of his criminality, they should still think it better to leave him unpunished than to make a law for punishing him. The general sense, however, was decidedly for proceeding.* The prisoner and his counsel were allowed another week to prepare themselves; and, at length, on the fifteenth of December, the struggle commenced in earnest.

The debates were the longest and the hottest, the divisions were the largest, the protests were the most numerously signed that had ever been known in the whole history of the House of Peers. Repeatedly the benches continued to be filled from ten in the morning till past midnight.† The health of many lords suffered severely: for the winter was bitterly cold; but the majority was not disposed to be indulgent. One evening Devonshire was unwell: he stole away and went to bed: but Black Rod was soon sent to bring him back. Leeds, whose constitution was extremely infirm, complained loudly. "It is very well," he said, "for young gentlemen to sit down to their suppers and their wine at two o'clock in the morning; but some of us old men are likely to be of as much use here as they; and we shall soon be in our graves if we are forced to keep such hours at such a season.‡ So strongly was party spirit excited that this appeal was disregarded, and the House continued to sit fourteen or fifteen hours a day. The chief opponents of the bill were Rochester, Nottingham, Normanby and Leeds. The chief orators on the other side were Tankerville, who, in spite of the deep stains which a life singularly unfortunate had left on his public and private character, always spoke with an eloquence which riveted the attention of his hearers; Burnet, who made a great display of historical learning; Wharton, whose lively and familiar style of speaking, acquired in the House of Commons, sometimes shocked the formality of the Lords; and Monmouth, who had always carried the liberty of debate to the verge of licentiousness, and who now never opened his lips without inflicting a wound on the feelings of some adversary. A very few nobles of great

* Lords' Journals, Dec. 8. 1696; L'Hermitage, of the same date.
† L'Hermitage, Dec. $\frac{4}{15}$. $\frac{4}{15}$. 1696.     ‡ Ibid. Dec. $\frac{4}{15}$. 1696.

weight, Devonshire, Dorset, Pembroke and Ormond, formed a third party. They were willing to use the Bill of Attainder as an instrument of torture for the purpose of wringing a full confession out of the prisoner. But they were determined not to give a final vote for sending him to the scaffold.

The first division was on the question whether secondary evidence of what Goodman could have proved should be admitted. On this occasion Burnet closed the debate by a powerful speech which none of the Tory orators could undertake to answer without premeditation. A hundred and twenty-six lords were present, a number unprecedented in our history. There were seventy-three Contents, and fifty-three Not Contents. Thirty-six of the minority protested against the decision of the House.*

The next great trial of strength was on the question whether the bill should be read a second time. The debate was diversified by a curious episode. Monmouth, in a vehement declamation, threw some severe and well merited reflections on the memory of the late Lord Jeffreys. The title and part of the ill gotten wealth of Jeffreys had descended to his son, a dissolute lad, who had lately come of age, and who was then sitting in the House. The young man fired at hearing his father reviled. The House was forced to interfere, and to make both the disputants promise that the matter should go no further. On this day a hundred and twenty-eight peers were present. The second reading was carried by seventy-three to fifty-five ; and forty-nine of the fifty-five protested.†

It was now thought by many that Fenwick's courage would give way. It was known that he was very unwilling to die. Hitherto he might have flattered himself with hopes that the bill would miscarry. But now that it had passed one House, and seemed certain to pass the other, it was probable that he would save himself by disclosing all that he knew. He was again put to the bar and interrogated. He refused to answer, on the ground that his answers might be used against him by the Crown at the Old Bailey. He was assured that the House would protect him : but he pretended that this assurance was not sufficient : the House was not always sitting : he might be brought to trial during a recess, and hanged before their Lord-

---

* Lords' Journals, Dec. 15. 1696 ; L'Hermitage, Dec. $\frac{15}{28}$. ; Vernon to Shrewsbury, Dec. 15. About the numbers there is a slight difference between Vernon and L'Hermitage. I have followed Vernon.

† Lords' Journals, Dec. 18. 1696 ; Vernon to Shrewsbury, Dec. 19. ; L'Hermitage, $\frac{\text{Dec. 22.}}{\text{Jan. 1.}}$ I take the numbers from Vernon.

ships met again. The royal word alone, he said, would be a complete guarantee. The Peers ordered him to be removed, and immediately resolved that Wharton should go to Kensington, and should entreat His Majesty to give the pledge which the prisoner required. Wharton hastened to Kensington, and hastened back with a gracious answer. Fenwick was again placed at the bar. The royal word, he was told, had been passed that nothing which he might say there should be used against him in any other place. Still he made difficulties. He might confess all that he knew, and yet might be told that he was still keeping something back. In short, he would say nothing till he had a pardon. He was then, for the last time, solemnly cautioned from the Woolsack. He was assured that, if he would deal ingenuously with the Lords, they would be intercessors for him at the foot of the throne, and that their intercession would not be unsuccessful. If he continued obstinate, they would proceed with the bill. A short interval was allowed him for consideration ; and he was then required to give his final answer. " I have given it," he said : " I have no security." If I had, I should be glad to satisfy the House." He was then carried back to his cell ; and the Peers separated, having sate far into the night.*

At noon they met again. The third reading was moved. Tenison spoke for the bill with more ability than was expected from him, and Monmouth with as much sharpness as in the previous debates. But Devonshire declared that he could go no further. He had hoped that fear would induce Fenwick to make a frank confession : that hope was at an end : the question now was simply whether this man should be put to death by an Act of Parliament ; and to that question Devonshire said that he must answer, " Not Content." It is not easy to understand on what principle he can have thought himself justified in threatening to do what he did not think himself justified in doing. He was, however, followed by Dorset, Ormond, Pembroke, and two or three others. Devon-

---

* Lords' Journals, Dec. 25. 1696 ; L'Hermitage, $\frac{\text{Dec. 26.}}{\text{Jan. 4.}}$ In the Vernon Correspondence there is a letter from Vernon to Shrewsbury giving an account of the transactions of this day ; but it is erroneously dated Dec. 2., and is placed according to that date. This is not the only blunder of the kind. A letter from Vernon to Shrewsbury, evidently written on the 7th of November 1696, is dated and placed as a letter of the 7th of January 1697. A letter of June 14. 1700 is dated and placed as a letter of June 14. 1698. The Vernon Correspondence is of great value : but it is so ill edited that it cannot be safely used without much caution, and constant reference to other authorities.

shire, in the name of his little party, and Rochester, in the name of the Tories, offered to waive all objections to the mode of proceeding, if the penalty were reduced from death to perpetual imprisonment. But the majority, though weakened by the defection of some considerable men, was still a majority, and would hear of no terms of compromise. The third reading was carried by only sixty-eight votes to sixty-one. Fifty-three Lords recorded their dissent; and forty-one subscribed a protest, in which the arguments against the bill were ably summed up.* The peers whom Fenwick had accused took different sides. Marlborough steadily voted with the majority, and induced Prince George to do the same. Godolphin as steadily voted with the minority, but, with characteristic wariness, abstained from giving any reasons for his votes. No part of his life warrants us in ascribing his conduct to any exalted motive. It is probable that, having been driven from office by the Whigs and forced to take refuge among the Tories, he thought it advisable to go with his party.†

As soon as the bill had been read a third time, the attention of the Peers was called to a matter which deeply concerned the honour of their order. Lady Mary Fenwick had been, not unnaturally, moved to the highest resentment by the conduct of Monmouth. He had, after professing a great desire to save her husband, suddenly turned round, and become the most merciless of her husband's persecutors; and all this solely because the unfortunate prisoner would not suffer himself to be used as an instrument for the accomplishing of a wild scheme of mischief. She might be excused for thinking that revenge would be sweet. In her rage she showed to her kinsman the Earl of Carlisle the papers which she had received from the Duchess of Norfolk. Carlisle brought the subject before the Lords. The papers were produced. Lady Mary declared that she had received them from the Duchess. The Duchess declared that she had received them from Monmouth. Elizabeth Lawson confirmed the evidence of her two friends. All the bitter things which the petulant Earl had said about William were repeated. The rage of both the great factions broke forth with ungovernable violence. The Whigs were exasperated by discovering that Monmouth had been secretly labouring to bring to shame and ruin two eminent men with whose reputation the reputation of the whole party was bound

* Lords' Journals, Dec. 23. 1696; Vernon to Shrewsbury, Dec. 24; L'Hermitage, $\frac{\text{Dec 25.}}{\text{Jan. 4.}}$

† Vernon to Shrewsbury, Dec. 24. 1696.

up. The Tories accused him of dealing treacherously and cruelly by the prisoner and the prisoner's wife. Both among the Whigs and among the Tories Monmouth had, by his sneers and invectives, made numerous personal enemies, whom fear of his wit and of his sword had hitherto kept in awe.* All these enemies were now openmouthed against him. There was great curiosity to know what he would be able to say in his defence. His eloquence, the correspondent of the States General wrote, had often annoyed others. He would now want it all to protect himself.† That eloquence indeed was of a kind much better suited to attack than to defence. Monmouth spoke near three hours in a confused and rambling manner, boasted extravagantly of his services and sacrifices, told the House that he had borne a great part in the Revolution, that he had made four voyages to Holland in the evil times, that he had since refused great places, that he had always held lucre in contempt. "I," he said, turning significantly to Nottingham, "have bought no great estate: I have built no palace: I am twenty thousand pounds poorer than when I entered public life. My old hereditary mansion is ready to fall about my ears. Who that remembers what I have done and suffered for His Majesty will believe that I would speak disrespectfully of him?" He solemnly declared,– and this was the most serious of the many serious faults of his long and unquiet life,—that he had nothing to do with the papers which had caused so much scandal. The Papists, he said, hated him: they had laid a scheme to ruin him: his ungrateful kinswoman had consented to be their implement, and had requited the strenuous efforts which he had made in defence of her honour by trying to blast his. When he concluded there was a long silence. He asked whether their Lordships wished him to withdraw. Then Leeds, to whom he had once professed a strong attachment, but whom he had deserted with characteristic inconstancy and assailed with characteristic petulance, seized the opportunity of revenging himself. "It is quite unnecessary," the shrewd old statesman said, "that the noble Earl should withdraw at present. The question which we have now to decide is merely whether these papers do or do not deserve our censure. Who wrote them is a

---

* Dohna, who knew Monmouth well, describes him thus : "Il avoit de l'esprit infiniment, et même du plus agréable ; mais il y avoit un peu trop de haut et de bas dans son fait. Il ne savoit ce que c'étoit que de ménager les gens ; et il turlupinoit à l'outrance ceux qui ne lui plaisoient pas."

† L'Hermitage, Jan. $\frac{12}{22}$. 1697.

question which may be considered hereafter." It was then moved and unanimously resolved that the papers were scandalous, and that the author had been guilty of a high crime and misdemeanour. Monmouth himself was, by these dexterous tactics, forced to join in condemning his own compositions.* Then the House proceeded to consider the charge against him. The character of his cousin the Duchess did not stand high; but her testimony was confirmed both by direct and by circumstantial evidence. Her husband said, with sour pleasantry, that he gave entire faith to what she had deposed. "My Lord Monmouth thought her good enough to be wife to me; and, if she is good enough to be wife to me, I am sure that she is good enough to be a witness against him." In a House of near eighty peers only eight or ten seemed inclined to show any favour to Monmouth. He was pronounced guilty of the act of which he had, in the most solemn manner, protested that he was innocent: he was sent to the Tower: he was turned out of all his places; and his name was struck out of the Council Book.† It might well have been thought that the ruin of his fame and of his fortunes was irreparable. But there was about his nature an elasticity which nothing could subdue. In his prison, indeed, he was as violent as a falcon just caged, and would, if he had been long detained, have died of mere impatience. His only solace was to contrive wild and romantic schemes for extricating himself from his difficulties and avenging himself on his enemies. When he regained his liberty, he stood alone in the world, a dishonoured man, more hated by the Whigs than any Tory, and by the Tories than any Whig, and reduced to such poverty that he talked of retiring to the country, living like a farmer, and putting his Countess into the dairy to churn and to make cheeses. Yet even after this fall, that mounting spirit rose again, and rose higher than ever. When he next appeared before the world, he had inherited the earldom of the head of his family: he had ceased to be called by the tarnished name of Monmouth; and he soon added new lustre to the name of Peterborough. He was still all air and fire. His ready wit and his dauntless courage made him formidable: some amiable qualities which contrasted strangely with his vices, and some great exploits of which the effect was heightened by the careless levity with which they were per-

* Lords' Journals, Jan. 9. 169$\frac{4}{5}$; Vernon to Shrewsbury, of the same date; L'Hermitage, Jan. $\frac{12}{22}$.

† Lords' Journals, Jan. 15. 169$\frac{4}{5}$; Vernon to Shrewsbury, of the same date; L'Hermitage, of the same date.

formed, made him popular; and his countrymen were willing to forget that a hero of whose achievements they were proud, and who was not more distinguished by parts and valour than by courtesy and generosity, had stooped to tricks worthy of the pillory.

It is interesting and instructive to compare the fate of Shrewsbury with the fate of Peterborough. The honour of Shrewsbury was safe. He had been triumphantly acquitted of the charges contained in Fenwick's confession. He was soon afterwards still more triumphantly acquitted of a still more odious charge. A wretched spy named Matthew Smith, who thought that he had not been sufficiently rewarded, and was bent on being revenged, affirmed that Shrewsbury had received early information of the Assassination Plot, but had suppressed that information, and had taken no measures to prevent the conspirators from accomplishing their design. That this was a foul calumny no person who has examined the evidence can doubt. The King declared that he could himself prove his minister's innocence; and the Peers, after examining Smith, pronounced the accusation unfounded. Shrewsbury was cleared as far as it was in the power of the Crown and of the Parliament to clear him. He had power and wealth, the favour of the King and the favour of the people. No man had a greater number of devoted friends. He was the idol of the Whigs: yet he was not personally disliked by the Tories. It should seem that his situation was one which Peterborough might well have envied. But happiness and misery are from within. Peterborough had one of those minds of which the deepest wounds heal and leave no scar. Shrewsbury had one of those minds in which the slightest scratch may fester to the death. He had been publicly accused of corresponding with Saint Germains; and, though King, Lords and Commons had pronounced him innocent, his conscience told him that he was guilty. The praises which he knew that he had not deserved sounded to him like reproaches. He never regained his lost peace of mind. He left office: but one cruel recollection accompanied him into retirement. He left England: but one cruel recollection pursued him over the Alps and the Apennines. On a memorable day, indeed, big with the fate of his country, he again, after many inactive and inglorious years, stood forth the Shrewsbury of 1688. Scarcely any thing in history is more melancholy than that late and solitary gleam, lighting up the close of a life which had dawned so splendidly, and which had so early become hopelessly troubled and gloomy.

On the day on which the Lords passed the Bill of Attainder, they adjourned over the Christmas holidays. The fate of Fenwick consequently remained during more than a fortnight in suspense. In the interval plans of escape were formed; and it was thought necessary to place a strong military guard round Newgate.* Some Jacobites knew William so little as to send him anonymous letters, threatening that he should be shot or stabbed if he dared to touch a hair of the prisoner's head.† On the morning of the eleventh of January he passed the bill. He at the same time passed a bill which authorised the government to detain Bernardi and some other conspirators in custody during twelve months. On the evening of that day a deeply mournful event was the talk of all London. The Countess of Aylesbury had watched with intense anxiety the proceedings against Sir John. Her lord had been as deep as Sir John in treason, was, like Sir John, in confinement, and had, like Sir John, been a party to Goodman's flight. She had learned with dismay that there was a method by which a criminal who was beyond the reach of the ordinary law might be punished. Her terror had increased at every stage in the progress of the Bill of Attainder. On the day on which the royal assent was to be given, her agitation became greater than her frame could support. When she heard the sound of the guns which announced that the King was on his way to Westminster, she fell into fits, and died in a few hours.‡

Even after the bill had become law, strenuous efforts were made to save Fenwick. His wife threw herself at William's feet, and offered him a petition. He took the petition, and said, very gently, that it should be considered, but that the matter was one of public concern, and that he must deliberate with his ministers before he decided.§ She then addressed herself to the Lords. She told them that her husband had not expected his doom, that he had not had time to prepare himself for death, that he had not, during his long imprisonment, seen a divine. They were easily induced to request that he might be respited for a week. A respite was granted: but, forty-eight hours before it expired, Lady Mary presented to the Lords another petition, imploring them to intercede with the King that her husband's punishment might be commuted to

* Postman, Dec. 29. 31. 1696.
† L'Hermitage, Jan. $\frac{1}{12}$. 1697.
‡ Van Cleverskirke, Jan. $\frac{12}{22}$. 1697; L'Hermitage, Jan. $\frac{14}{24}$.
§ L'Hermitage, Jan. $\frac{15}{25}$. 1697.

banishment. The House was taken by surprise ; and a motion to adjourn was with difficulty carried by two votes.* On the morrow, the last day of Fenwick's life, a similar petition was presented to the Commons. But the Whig leaders were on their guard : the attendance was full ; and a motion for reading the Orders of the Day was carried by a hundred and fifty-two to a hundred and seven.† In truth, neither branch of the legislature could, without condemning itself, request William to spare Fenwick's life. Jurymen, who have, in the discharge of a painful duty, pronounced a culprit guilty, may, with perfect consistency, recommend him to the favourable consideration of the Crown. But the Houses ought not to have passed the Bill of Attainder unless they were convinced, not merely that Sir John had committed high treason, but also that he could not, without serious danger to the Commonwealth, be suffered to live. He could not be at once a proper object of such a bill and a proper object of the royal mercy.

On the twenty-eighth of January the execution took place. In compliment to the noble families with which Fenwick was connected, orders were given that the ceremonial should be in all respects the same as when a peer of the realm suffers death. A scaffold was erected on Tower Hill and hung with black. The prisoner was brought from Newgate in the coach of his kinsman the Earl of Carlisle, which was surrounded by a troop of the Life Guards. Though the day was cold and stormy, the crowd of spectators was immense : but there was no disturbance, and no sign that the multitude sympathized with the criminal. He behaved with a firmness which had not been expected from him. He ascended the scaffold with steady steps, and bowed courteously to the persons who were assembled on it, but spoke to none, except White, the deprived Bishop of Peterborough. White prayed with him during about half an hour. In the prayer the King was commended to the Divine protection ; but no name which could give offence was pronounced. Fenwick then delivered a sealed paper to the Sheriffs, took leave of the Bishop, knelt down, laid his neck on the block, and exclaimed, "Lord Jesus, receive my soul." His head was severed from his body at a single blow. His remains were placed in a rich coffin, and buried that night, by torchlight, under the pave-

* Lords' Journals, Jan. 22. 26. 169⁹⁄₇ ; Vernon to Shrewsbury, Jan. 26.
† Commons' Journals, Jan. 27. 169⁹⁄₇. The entry in the Journals, which might easily escape notice, is explained by a letter of L'Hermitage, written $\frac{Jan. 29.}{Feb. 8}$

ment of Saint Martin's Church. No person has, since that day, suffered death in England by Act of Attainder.*

Meanwhile an important question, about which public feeling was much excited, had been under discussion. As soon as the Parliament met, a Bill for Regulating Elections, differing little in substance from the bill which the King had refused to pass in the preceding session, was brought into the House of Commons, was eagerly welcomed by the country gentlemen, and was pushed through every stage. On the report it was moved that five thousand pounds in personal estate should be a sufficient qualification for the representative of a city or borough. But this amendment was rejected. On the third reading a rider was added, which permitted a merchant possessed of five thousand pounds to represent the town in which he resided : but it was provided that no person should be considered as a merchant because he was a proprietor of Bank Stock or East India Stock. The fight was hard. Cowper distinguished himself among the opponents of the bill. His sarcastic remarks on the hunting, hawking boors, who wished to keep in their own hands the whole business of legislation, called forth some sharp rustic retorts. A plain squire, he was told, was as likely to serve the country well as the most fluent gownsman, who was ready, for a guinea, to prove that black was white. On the question whether the bill should pass, the Ayes were two hundred, the Noes a hundred and sixty.†

The Lords had, twelve months before, readily agreed to a similar bill ; but they had since reconsidered the subject and changed their opinion. The truth is that, if a law requiring every member of the House of Commons to possess an estate of some hundreds of pounds a year in land could have been strictly enforced, such a law would have been very advantageous to country gentlemen of moderate property, but would have been by no means advantageous to the grandees of the realm. A lord of a small manor would have stood for the town in the neighbourhood of which his family had resided during centuries, without any apprehension that he should be opposed by some alderman of London, whom the electors had never seen before the day of nomination, and whose chief title to their favour was a pocketbook full of bank notes. But a great nobleman, who had an estate of fifteen or twenty thousand

* L'Hermitage, $\frac{\text{Jan. 29}}{\text{Feb. 8}}$ 1697 ; London Gazette, Feb. 1. ; Paris Gazette ; Vernon to Shrewsbury, Jan. 28.; Burnet, ii. 193.

† Commons' Journals, December 19. 1696; Vernon to Shrewsbury, Nov. 28. 1696.

pounds a year, and who commanded two or three boroughs, would no longer be able to put his younger son, his younger brother, his man of business, into Parliament, or to earn a garter or a step in the peerage by finding a seat for a Lord of the Treasury or an Attorney General. On this occasion therefore the interest of the chiefs of the aristocracy, Norfolk and Somerset, Newcastle and Bedford, Pembroke and Dorset, coincided with that of the wealthy traders of the City and of the clever young aspirants of the Temple, and was diametrically opposed to the interest of a squire of a thousand or twelve hundred a year. On the day fixed for the second reading the attendance of lords was great. Several petitions from constituent bodies, which thought it hard that a new restriction should be imposed on the exercise of the elective franchise, were presented and read. After a debate of some hours the bill was rejected by sixty-two votes to thirty-seven.* Only three days later, a strong party in the Commons, burning with resentment, proposed to tack the bill which the Peers had just rejected to the Land Tax Bill. This motion would probably have been carried, had not Foley gone somewhat beyond the duties of his place, and, under pretence of speaking to order, shown that such a tack would be without a precedent in parliamentary history. When the question was put, the Ayes raised so loud a cry that it was believed that they were the majority : but on a division they proved to be only a hundred and thirty-five. The Noes were a hundred and sixty-three.†

Other parliamentary proceedings of this session deserve mention. While the Commons were busily engaged in the great work of restoring the finances, an incident took place which seemed, during a short time, likely to be fatal to the infant liberty of the press, but which eventually proved the means of confirming that liberty. Among the many newspapers which had been established since the expiration of the censorship, was one called the Flying Post. The editor, John Salisbury, was the tool of a band of stockjobbers in the City, whose interest it happened to be to cry down the public securities. He one day published a false and malicious paragraph, evidently intended to throw suspicion on the Ex-

---

* Lords' Journals, Jan. 23. 169⅞; Vernon to Shrewsbury, Jan. 23. ; L'Hermitage, $\frac{\text{Jan 26.}}{\text{Feb. 5.}}$

† Commons' Journals, Jan. 26. 169⅞ ; Vernon to Shrewsbury and Van Cleverskirke to the States General of the same date. It is curious that the King and the Lords should have made so strenuous a fight against the Commons in defence of one of the five points of the People's Charter.

chequer Bills. On the credit of the Exchequer Bills depended, at that moment, the political greatness and the commercial prosperity of the realm. The House of Commons was in a flame. The Speaker issued his warrant against Salisbury. It was resolved without a division that a bill should be brought in to prohibit the publishing of news without a license. Forty-eight hours later the bill was presented and read. But the members had now had time to cool. There was scarcely one of them whose residence in the country had not, during the preceding summer, been made more agreeable by the London journals. Meagre as those journals may seem to a person who has the Times daily on his breakfast table, they were to that generation a new and abundant source of pleasure. No Devonshire or Yorkshire gentleman, Whig or Tory, could bear the thought of being again dependent, during seven months of every year, for all information about what was doing in the world, on newsletters. If the bill passed, the sheets, which were now so impatiently expected twice a week at every country seat in the kingdom, would contain nothing but what it suited the Secretary of State to make public : they would be, in fact, so many London Gazettes ; and the most assiduous reader of the London Gazette might be utterly ignorant of the most important events of his time. A few voices, however, were raised in favour of a censorship. "These papers," it was said, "frequently contain mischievous matter." "Then why are they not prosecuted?" was the answer. "Has the Attorney-General filed an information against any one of them? And is it not absurd to ask us to give a new remedy by statute, when the old remedy afforded by the common law has never been tried?" On the question whether the bill should be read a second time, the Ayes were only sixteen, the Noes two hundred.*

Another bill, which fared better, ought to be noticed as an instance of the slow, but steady progress of civilisation. The ancient immunities enjoyed by some districts of the capital, of which the largest and the most infamous was Whitefriars, had

* Commons' Journals, April 1. 3. 1697 ; Narcissus Luttrell's Diary ; L'Hermitage, April $\frac{9}{19}$. $\frac{5}{16}$. L'Hermitage says, " La plupart des membres, lorsqu'ils sont à la campagne, estant bien aises d'estre informez par plus d'un endroit de ce qui se passe, et s'imaginant que la Gazette qui se fait sous la direction d'un des Sécrétaires d'Etat, ne contiendroit pas autant de choses que fait celle-cy, ne sont pas fâchez que d'autres les instruisent." The numbers on the division I take from L'Hermitage. They are not to be found in the Journals. But the Journals were not then so accurately kept as at present.

produced abuses which could no longer be endured. The Templars on one side of Alsatia, and the citizens on the other, had long been calling on the government and the legislature to put down so monstrous a nuisance. Yet still, bounded on the west by the great school of English jurisprudence, and on the east by the great mart of English trade, stood this labyrinth of squalid, tottering houses, close packed, every one, from cellar to cockloft, with outcasts whose life was one long war with society. The best part of the population consisted of debtors who were in fear of bailiffs. The rest were attorneys struck off the roll, witnesses who carried straw in their shoes as a sign to inform the public where a false oath might be procured for half a crown, sharpers, receivers of stolen goods, clippers of coin, forgers of bank notes, and tawdry women, blooming with paint and brandy, who, in their anger, made free use of their nails and their scissors, yet whose anger was less to be dreaded than their kindness. With these wretches the narrow alleys of the sanctuary swarmed. The rattling of dice, the call for more punch and more wine, and the noise of blasphemy and ribald song never ceased during the whole night. The benchers of the Inner Temple could bear the scandal and the annoyance no longer. They ordered the gate leading into Whitefriars to be bricked up. The Alsatians mustered in great force, attacked the workmen, killed one of them, pulled down the wall, knocked down the Sheriff who came to keep the peace, and carried off his gold chain, which, no doubt, was soon in the melting pot. The riot was not suppressed till a company of the Foot Guards arrived. This outrage excited general indignation. The City, indignant at the outrage offered to the Sheriff, cried loudly for justice. Yet, so difficult was it to execute any process in the dens of Whitefriars, that near two years elapsed before a single ringleader was apprehended.*

The Savoy was another place of the same kind, smaller indeed, and less renowned, but inhabited by a not less lawless population. An unfortunate tailor, who ventured to go thither for the purpose of demanding payment of a debt, was set upon by the whole mob of cheats, ruffians and courtesans. He offered to give a full discharge to his debtor and a treat to the rabble, but in vain. He had violated their franchises ; and this crime was not to be pardoned. He was knocked down, stripped, tarred, feathered. A rope was tied round his waist. He was dragged naked up and down the streets amidst yells of "A bailiff! A bailiff!" Finally he was compelled to kneel

* Narcissus Luttrell's Diary, June 1691, May 1693.

down and to curse his father and mother. Having performed this ceremony he was permitted,—and the permission was blamed by many of the Savoyards,—to limp home without a rag upon him.* The Bog of Allen, the passes of the Grampians, were not more unsafe than this small knot of lanes, surrounded by the mansions of the greatest nobles of a flourishing and enlightened kingdom.

At length, in 1697, a bill for abolishing the franchises of these places passed both Houses, and received the royal assent. The Alsatians and Savoyards were furious. Anonymous letters, containing menaces of assassination, were received by members of Parliament who had made themselves conspicuous by the zeal with which they had supported the bill : but such threats only strengthened the general conviction that it was high time to destroy these nests of knaves and ruffians. A fortnight's grace was allowed ; and it was made known that, when that time had expired, the vermin who had been the curse of London would be unearthed and hunted without mercy. There was a tumultuous flight to Ireland, to France, to the Colonies, to vaults and garrets in less notorious parts of the capital ; and when, on the prescribed day, the Sheriff's officers ventured to cross the boundary, they found those streets where, a few weeks before, the cry of " A writ ! " would have drawn together a thousand raging bullies and vixens, as quiet as the cloister of a cathedral.†

On the sixteenth of April, the King closed the session with a speech, in which he returned warm and well merited thanks to the Houses for the firmness and wisdom which had rescued the nation from commercial and financial difficulties unprecedented in our history. Before he set out for the Continent, he conferred some new honours, and made some new ministerial arrangements. Every member of the Whig junto was distinguished by some conspicuous mark of royal favour. Somers delivered up the seal, of which he was Keeper : he received it back again with the higher title of Chancellor, and was immediately commanded to affix it to a patent, by which he was created Baron Somers of Evesham.‡ Russell became Earl of Orford and Viscount Barfleur. No English title had ever before been taken from a place of battle lying within a foreign territory. But the precedent then set has been repeatedly followed ; and the names of Saint Vincent, Tra-

---

* Commons' Journals, Dec. 30. 1696 ; Postman, July 4. 1696
† Postman, April 22. 1696 ; Narcissus Luttrell's Diary.
‡ London Gazette, April 26. 29. 1697.

falgar, Camperdown, and Douro are now borne by the successors of great commanders. Russell seems to have accepted his earldom, after his fashion, not only without gratitude, but grumblingly, and as if some great wrong had been done him. What was a coronet to him? He had no child to inherit it. The only distinction which he should have prized was the garter; and the garter had been given to Portland. Of course, such things were for the Dutch; and it was strange presumption in an Englishman, though he might have won a victory which had saved the State, to expect that his pretensions would be considered till all the Mynheers about the palace had been served.*

Wharton, still retaining his place of Comptroller of the Household, obtained the lucrative office of Chief Justice in Eyre, South of Trent; and his brother, Godwin Wharton, was made a Lord of the Admiralty.†

Though the resignation of Godolphin had been accepted in October, no new commission of Treasury was issued till after the prorogation. Who should be First Commissioner was a question long and fiercely disputed. For Montague's faults had made him many enemies, and his merits many more. Dull formalists sneered at him as a wit and poet, who, no doubt, showed quick parts in debate, but who had already been raised far higher than his services merited or than his brain would bear. It would be absurd to place such a young coxcomb, merely because he could talk fluently and cleverly, in an office on which the well being of the kingdom depended. Surely Sir Stephen Fox was, of all the Lords of the Treasury, the fittest to be at the head of the Board. He was an elderly man, grave, experienced, exact, laborious; and he had never made a verse in his life. The King hesitated during a considerable time between the two candidates: but time was all in Montague's favour; for, from the first to the last day of the session, his fame was constantly rising. The voice of the House of Commons and of the City loudly designated him as preeminently qualified to be the chief minister of finance. At length Sir Stephen Fox withdrew from the competition, though not with a very good grace. He wished it to be notified in the London Gazette that the place of First Lord had been offered to him, and declined by him. Such a notification would have been an affront to Montague; and Montague, flushed with

* London Gazette, April 29. 1697; L'Hermitage, $\frac{\text{April 23.}}{\text{May 3.}}$
† London Gazette, April 26. 29. 1697; L'Hermitage, $\frac{\text{April 23.}}{\text{May 3.}}$

prosperity and glory, was not in a mood to put up with affronts. The dispute was compromised. Montague became First Lord of the Treasury ; and the vacant seat at the Board was filled by Sir Thomas Littleton, one of the ablest and most consistent Whigs in the House of Commons. But, from tenderness to Fox, these promotions were not announced in the Gazette.*

Dorset resigned the office of Chamberlain, but not in ill humour, and retired loaded with marks of royal favour. He was succeeded by Sunderland, who was also appointed one of the Lords Justices, not without much murmuring from various quarters.† To the Tories Sunderland was an object of unmixed detestation. Some of the Whig leaders had been unable to resist his insinuating address ; and others were grateful for the services which he had lately rendered to the party. But the leaders could not restrain their followers. Plain men, who were zealous for civil liberty and for the Protestant religion, who were beyond the range of Sunderland's irresistible fascination, and who knew that he had sate in the High Commission, concurred in the Declaration of Indulgence, borne witness against the Seven Bishops, and received the host from a Popish priest, could not, without indignation and shame, see him standing, with the staff in his hand, close to the throne. Still more monstrous was it that such a man should be entrusted with the administration of the government during the absence of the Sovereign. William did not understand these feelings. Sunderland was able : he was useful : he was unprincipled indeed : but so were all the English politicians of the generation which had learned, under the sullen tyranny of the Saints, to disbelieve in virtue, and which had, during the wild jubilee of the Restoration, been utterly dissolved in vice. He was a fair specimen of his class, a little worse, perhaps, than Leeds or Godolphin, and about as bad as Russell or Marlborough. Why he was to be hunted from the herd the King could not imagine.

Notwithstanding the discontent which was caused by Sunderland's elevation, England was, during this summer, perfectly quiet and in excellent temper. All but the fanatical Jacobites

* What the opinion of the public was we learn from a letter written by L'Hermitage immediately after Godolphin's resignation, Nov. $\frac{13}{25}$ 1696, " Le public tourne plus la veue sur le Sieur Montegu, qui a la seconde charge de la Trésorerie que sur aucun autre." The strange silence of the London Gazette is explained by a letter of Vernon to Shrewsbury, dated May 1. 1697.

† London Gazette, April 22. 26. 1697.

were elated by the rapid revival of trade and by the near prospect of peace. Nor were Ireland and Scotland less tranquil.

In Ireland nothing deserving to be minutely related had taken place since Sidney had ceased to be Lord Lieutenant. The government had suffered the colonists to domineer unchecked over the native population; and the colonists had in return been profoundly obsequious to the government. The proceedings of the local legislature which sate at Dublin had been in no respect more important or more interesting than the proceedings of the Assembly of Barbadoes. Perhaps the most momentous event in the parliamentary history of Ireland at this time was a dispute between the two Houses which was caused by a collision between the coach of the Speaker and the coach of the Chancellor. There were, indeed, factions, but factions which sprang merely from personal pretensions and animosities. The names of Whig and Tory had been carried across Saint George's Channel, but had in the passage lost all their meaning. A man who was called a Tory at Dublin would have passed at Westminster for as stanch a Whig as Wharton. The highest Churchmen in Ireland abhorred and dreaded Popery so much that they were disposed to consider every Protestant as a brother. They remembered the tyranny of James, the robberies, the burnings, the confiscations, the brass money, the Act of Attainder, with bitter resentment. They honoured William as their deliverer and preserver. Nay, they could not help feeling a certain respect even for the memory of Cromwell: for, whatever else he might have been, he had been the champion and the avenger of their race. Between the divisions of England, therefore, and the divisions of Ireland, there was scarcely any thing in common. In England there were two parties, of the same race and religion, contending with each other. In Ireland there were two castes, of different races and religions, one trampling on the other.

Scotland too was quiet. The harvest of the last year had indeed been scanty; and there was consequently much suffering. But the spirit of the nation was buoyed up by wild hopes, destined to end in cruel disappointment. A magnificent daydream of wealth and empire so completely occupied the minds of men that they hardly felt the present distress. How that dream originated, and by how terrible an awakening it was broken, will be related hereafter.

In the autumn of 1696 the Estates of Scotland met at Edinburgh. The attendance was thin; and the session lasted only five weeks. A supply amounting to little more than a hundred thousand pounds sterling was voted. Two Acts for the securing of the government were passed. One of those Acts required all persons in public trust to sign an Association similar to the Association which had been so generally subscribed in the south of the island. The other Act provided that the Parliament of Scotland should not be dissolved by the death of the King.

But by far the most important event of this short session was the passing of the Act for the settling of Schools. By this memorable law it was, in the Scotch phrase, statuted and ordained that every parish in the realm should provide a commodious schoolhouse and should pay a moderate stipend to a schoolmaster. The effect could not be immediately felt. But, before one generation had passed away, it began to be evident that the common people of Scotland were superior in intelligence to the common people of any other country in Europe. To whatever land the Scotchman might wander, to whatever calling he might betake himself, in America or in India, in trade or in war, the advantage which he derived from his early training raised him above his competitors. If he was taken into a warehouse as a porter, he soon became foreman. If he enlisted in the army, he soon became a serjeant. Scotland, meanwhile, in spite of the barrenness of her soil and the severity of her climate, made such progress in agriculture, in manufactures, in commerce, in letters, in science, in all that constitutes civilisation, as the Old World had never seen equalled, and as even the New World has scarcely seen surpassed.

This wonderful change is to be attributed, not indeed solely, but principally, to the national system of education. But to the men by whom that system was established posterity owes no gratitude. They knew not what they were doing. They were the unconscious instruments of enlightening the understandings and humanising the hearts of millions. But their own understandings were as dark and their own hearts as obdurate as those of the Familiars of the Inquisition at Lisbon. In the very month in which the Act for the settling of Schools was touched with the sceptre, the rulers of the Church and State in Scotland began to carry on with vigour two persecutions worthy of the tenth century, a persecution of witches and a persecution of infidels. A crowd of wretches, guilty only of being old and miserable, were accused of trafficking with the devil. The Privy Council was not ashamed to issue a Com-

mission for the trial of twenty-two of these poor creatures.*
The shops of the booksellers of Edinburgh were strictly
searched for heretical works. Impious books, among which
the sages of the Presbytery ranked Thomas Burnet's Sacred
Theory of the Earth, were strictly suppressed.† But the
destruction of mere paper and sheepskin would not satisfy the
bigots. Their hatred required victims who could feel, and
was not appeased till they had perpetrated a crime such as has
never since polluted the island.

A student of eighteen, named Thomas Aikenhead, whose
habits were studious and whose morals were irreproachable,
had, in the course of his reading, met with some of the
ordinary arguments against the Bible. He fancied that he
had lighted on a mine of wisdom which had been hidden from
the rest of mankind, and, with the conceit from which half
educated lads of quick parts are seldom free, proclaimed his
discoveries to four or five of his companions. Trinity in unity,
he said, was as much a contradiction as a square circle. Ezra
was the author of the Pentateuch. The Apocalypse was an
allegorical book about the philosopher's stone. Moses had
learned magic in Egypt. Christianity was a delusion which
would not last till the year 1800. For this wild talk, of which,
in all probability, he would himself have been ashamed long
before he was five and twenty, he was prosecuted by the Lord
Advocate. The Lord Advocate was that James Stewart who
had been so often a Whig and so often a Jacobite that it is
difficult to keep an account of his apostasies. He was now
a Whig for the third if not for the fourth time. Aikenhead
might undoubtedly have been, by the law of Scotland, punished
with imprisonment till he should retract his errors and do
penance before the congregation of his parish; and every man
of sense and humanity would have thought this a sufficient
punishment for the prate of a forward boy. But Stewart, as
cruel as he was base, called for blood. There was among the
Scottish statutes one which made it a capital crime to revile or
curse the Supreme Being or any person of the Trinity. Nothing
that Aikenhead had said could, without the most violent
straining, be brought within the scope of this statute. But the
Lord Advocate exerted all his subtlety. The poor youth at
the bar had no counsel. He was altogether unable to do
justice to his own cause. He was convicted, and sentenced to
be hanged and buried at the foot of the gallows. It was in

* Postman, Jan. 26., Mar. 7. 11. 169⅞., April 8. 1697.
† Ibid. Oct. 29. 1696.

vain that he with tears abjured his errors and begged piteously for mercy. Some of those who saw him in his dungeon believed that his recantation was sincere; and indeed it is by no means improbable that in him, as in many other pretenders to philosophy who imagine that they have completely emancipated themselves from the religion of their childhood, the near prospect of death may have produced an entire change of sentiment. He petitioned the Privy Council that, if his life could not be spared, he might be allowed a short respite to make his peace with the God whom he had offended. Some of the Councillors were for granting this small indulgence. Others thought that it ought not to be granted unless the ministers of Edinburgh would intercede. The two parties were evenly balanced; and the question was decided against the prisoner by the casting vote of the Chancellor. The Chancellor was a man who has been often mentioned in the course of this history, and never mentioned with honour. He was that Sir Patrick Hume whose disputatious and factious temper had brought ruin on the expedition of Argyle, and had caused not a little annoyance to the government of William. In the Club which had braved the King and domineered over the Parliament there had been no more noisy republican. But a title and a place had produced a wonderful conversion. Sir Patrick was now Lord Polwarth: he had the custody of the Great Seal of Scotland: he presided in the Privy Council; and thus he had it in his power to do the worst action of his bad life.

It remained to be seen how the clergy of Edinburgh would act. That divines should be deaf to the entreaties of a penitent who asks, not for pardon, but for a little more time to receive their instructions and to pray to Heaven for the mercy which cannot be extended to him on earth, seems almost incredible. Yet so it was. The ministers demanded, not only the poor boy's death, but his speedy death, though it should be his eternal death. Even from their pulpits they cried out for cutting him off. It is probable that their real reason for refusing him a respite of a few days was their apprehension that the circumstances of his case might be reported at Kensington, and that the King, who, while reciting the Coronation Oath, had declared from the throne that he would not be a persecutor, might send down positive orders that the sentence should not be executed. Aikenhead was hanged between Edinburgh and Leith. He professed deep repentance, and suffered with the Bible in his hand. The people of Edinburgh though assuredly not disposed to think lightly of his offence, were moved to compassion by his youth, by his penitence, and by the cruel haste with which he was hurried out of the world. It seems that there was some apprehension of a rescue: for a strong body of fusileers was under arms to support the civil power. The preachers who were the boy's murderers crowded round him at the gallows, and, while he was struggling in the last agony, insulted Heaven with prayers more blasphemous than any thing that he had ever uttered. Wodrow has told no blacker story of Dundee.*

On the whole, the British islands had not, during ten years, been so free from internal troubles as when William, at the close of April 1697, set out for the Continent. The war in the Netherlands was a little, and but a little, less languid than in the preceding year. The French generals opened the campaign by taking the small town of Aeth. They then meditated a far more important conquest. They made a sudden push for Brussels, and would probably have succeeded in their design but for the activity of William. He was encamped on ground which lies within sight of the Lion of Waterloo, when he received, late in the evening, intelligence that the capital of the Netherlands was in danger. He instantly put his forces in motion, marched all night, and, having traversed the field destined to acquire, a hundred and eighteen years later, a terrible renown, and threaded the long defiles of the Forest of Soignies, he was at ten in the morning on the spot from which Brussels had been bombarded two years before, and would, if he had been only three hours later, have been bombarded again. Here he surrounded himself with entrenchments which the enemy did not venture to attack. This was the most important military event which, during that summer, took place in the Low Countries In both camps there was an unwillingness to run any great risk on the eve of a general pacification.

Lewis had, early in the spring, for the first time during his long reign, spontaneously offered equitable and honourable conditions to his foes. He had declared himself willing to relinquish the conquests which he had made in the course of the war, to cede Lorraine to its own Duke, to give back Luxemburg to Spain, to give back Strasburg to the Empire and to acknowledge the existing government of England.†

---

* Howell's State Trials: Postman, Jan. $\frac{2}{5}$. 169$\frac{6}{7}$.

† See the Protocol of February 10. 1697 in the Actes et Mémoires des Négociations de la Paix de Ryswick, 1707.

Those who remembered the great woes which his faithless and merciless ambition had brought on Europe might well suspect that this unwonted moderation was not to be ascribed to sentiments of justice or humanity. But, whatever might be his motive for proposing such terms, it was plainly the interest and the duty of the Confederacy to accept them. For there was little hope indeed of wringing from him by war concessions larger than those which he now tendered as the price of peace. The most sanguine of his enemies could hardly expect a long series of campaigns as successful as the campaign of 1695. Yet in a long series of campaigns, as successful as that of 1695, the allies would hardly be able to retake all that he now professed himself ready to restore. William, who took, as usual, a clear and statesmanlike view of the whole situation, now gave his voice as decidedly for concluding peace as he had in former years given it for vigorously prosecuting the war; and he was backed by the public opinion both of England and of Holland. But, unhappily, just at the time when the two powers which alone, among the members of the coalition, had manfully done their duty in the long struggle, were beginning to rejoice in the near prospect of repose, some of those governments which had never furnished their full contingents, which had never been ready in time, which had been constantly sending excuses in return for subsidies, began to raise difficulties such as seemed likely to make the miseries of Europe eternal.

Spain had, as William, in the bitterness of his spirit, wrote to Heinsius, contributed nothing to the common cause but rodomontades. She had made no vigorous effort even to defend her own territories against invasion. She would have lost Flanders and Brabant but for the English and Dutch armies. She would have lost Catalonia but for the English and Dutch fleets. The Milanese she had saved, not by arms, but by concluding, in spite of the remonstrances of the English and Dutch governments, an ignominious treaty of neutrality. She had not a ship of war able to weather a gale. She had not a regiment that was not ill paid and ill disciplined, ragged and famished. Yet repeatedly, within the last two years, she had treated both William and the States General with an impertinence which showed that she was altogether ignorant of her place among states. She now became punctilious, demanded from Lewis concessions which the events of the war gave her no right to expect, and seemed to think it hard that allies, whom she was constantly treating with indignity, were not willing to lavish their blood and treasure for her during eight years more.

The conduct of Spain is to be attributed merely to arrogance and folly. But the unwillingness of the Emperor to consent even to the fairest terms of accommodation was the effect of selfish ambition. The Catholic King was childless : he was sickly : his life was not worth three years' purchase ; and when he died, his dominions would be left to be struggled for by a crowd of competitors. Both the House of Austria and the House of Bourbon had claims to that immense heritage. It was plainly for the interest of the House of Austria that the important day, come when it might, should find a great European coalition in arms against the House of Bourbon. The object of the Emperor therefore was that the war should continue to be carried on, as it had hitherto been carried on, at a light charge to him and a heavy charge to England and Holland, not till just conditions of peace could be obtained, but simply till the King of Spain should die. " The ministers of the Emperor," William wrote to Heinsius, "ought to be ashamed of their conduct. It is intolerable that a government which is doing every thing in its power to make the negotiations fail, should contribute nothing to the common defence."*

It is not strange that in such circumstances the work of pacification should have made little progress. International law, like other law, has its chicanery, its subtle pleadings, its technical forms, which may too easily be so employed as to make its substance inefficient. Those litigants therefore who did not wish the litigation to come to a speedy close had no difficulty in interposing delays. There was a long dispute about the place where the conferences should be held. The Emperor proposed Aix la Chapelle. The French objected, ard proposed the Hague. Then the Emperor objected in his turn. At last it was arranged that the ministers of the Allied Powers should meet at the Hague, and that the French plenipotentiaries should take up their abode five miles off at Delft.† To Delft accordingly repaired Harlay, a man of distinguished wit and good breeding, sprung from one of the

---

* William to Heinsius, Dec. $\frac{11}{21}$. 1696. There are similar expressions in other letters written by the King about the same time.

† See the papers drawn up at Vienna, and dated Sept. 16. 1696, and March 14. 1697. See also the protocol drawn up at the Hague, March $\frac{13}{23}$. 1697. These documents will be found in the Actes et Mémoires des Négociations de la Paix de Ryswick, 1707.

great families of the robe; Crecy, a shrewd, patient and
laborious diplomatist; and Cailleres, who, though he was
named only third in the credentials, was much better informed
than either of his colleagues touching all the points which
were likely to be debated.* At the Hague were the Earl of
Pembroke and Edward, Viscount Villiers, who represented
England. Prior accompanied them with the rank of Secretary.
At the head of the Imperial Legation was Count Kaunitz: at
the head of the Spanish Legation was Don Francisco Bernardo
de Quiros: the ministers of inferior rank it would be tedious
to enumerate.†

Half way between Delft and the Hague is a village named
Ryswick; and near it then stood, in a rectangular garden,
which was bounded by straight canals, and divided into
formal woods, flower beds and melon beds, a seat of the
Princes of Orange. The house seemed to have been built
expressly for the accommodation of such a set of diplomatists
as were to meet there. In the centre was a large hall painted
by Honthorst. On the right hand and on the left were wings
exactly corresponding to each other. Each wing was accessible
by its own bridge, its own gate and its own avenue. One wing
was assigned to the Allies, the other to the French, the hall in
the centre to the mediator.‡ Some preliminary questions of
etiquette were, not without difficulty, adjusted; and at length,
on the ninth of May, many coaches and six, attended by
harbingers, footmen and pages, approached the mansion by
different roads. The Swedish Minister alighted at the grand
entrance. The procession from the Hague came up the side
alley on the right. The procession from Delft came up the
side alley on the left. At the first meeting, the full powers of
the representatives of the belligerent governments were delivered
to the mediator. At the second meeting, forty-eight hours
later, the mediator performed the ceremony of exchanging
these full powers. Then several meetings were spent in
settling how many carriages, how many horses, how many
lacqueys, how many pages, each minister should be entitled to
bring to Ryswick; whether the serving men should carry
canes; whether they should wear swords; whether they
should have pistols in their holsters; who should take the

---

* Characters of all the three French ministers are given by Saint
Simon.

† Actes et Mémoires des Négociations de la Paix de Ryswick.

‡ An engraving and ground plan of the mansion will be found in the
Actes et Mémoires.

upper hand in the public walks, and whose carriage should break the way in the streets. It soon appeared that the mediator would have to mediate, not only between the coalition and the French, but also between the different members of the coalition. The Imperial Ambassadors claimed a right to sit at the head of the table. The Spanish Ambassador would not admit this pretension, and tried to thrust himself in between two of them. The Imperial Ambassadors refused to call the Ambassadors of Electors and Commonwealths by the title of Excellency. "If I am not called Excellency," said the Minister of the Elector of Brandenburg, "my master will withdraw his troops from Hungary." The Imperial Ambassadors insisted on having a room to themselves in the building, and on having a special place assigned to their carriages in the court. All the other Ministers of the Confederacy pronounced this a most unjustifiable demand, and a whole sitting was wasted in this childish dispute. It may easily be supposed that allies who were so punctilious in their dealings with each other were not likely to be very easy in their intercourse with the common enemy. The chief business of Harlay and Kaunitz was to watch each other's legs. Neither of them thought it consistent with the dignity of the Crown which he served to advance towards the other faster than the other advanced towards him. If therefore one of them perceived that he had inadvertently stepped forward too quick, he went back to the door, and the stately minuet began again. The ministers of Lewis drew up a paper in their own language. The German statesmen protested against this innovation, this insult to the dignity of the Holy Roman Empire, this encroachment on the rights of independent nations, and would not know any thing about the paper till it had been translated from good French into bad Latin. In the middle of April it was known to every body at the Hague that Charles the Eleventh, King of Sweden, was dead, and had been succeeded by his son: but it was contrary to etiquette that any of the assembled envoys should appear to be acquainted with this fact till Lilienroth had made a formal announcement: it was not less contrary to etiquette that Lilienroth should make such an announcement till his equipages and his household had been put into mourning; and some weeks elapsed before his coachmakers and tailors had completed their task. At length, on the twelfth of June, he came to Ryswick in a carriage lined with black and attended by servants in black liveries, and there, in full congress, proclaimed that it had pleased God to take to himself the most puissant King Charles the Eleventh. All the Ambassadors then condoled with him on the sad and unexpected news, and went home to put off their embroidery and to dress themselves in the garb of sorrow. In such solemn trifling week after week passed away. No real progress was made. Lilienroth had no wish to accelerate matters. While the congress lasted, his position was one of great dignity. He would willingly have gone on mediating for ever ; and he could not go on mediating, unless the parties on his right and on his left went on wrangling.*

In June the hope of peace began to grow faint. Men remembered that the last war had continued to rage, year after year, while a congress was sitting at Nimeguen. The mediators had made their entrance into that town in February 1676. The treaty had not been signed till February 1679. Yet the negotiation of Nimeguen had not proceeded more slowly than the negotiation of Ryswick. It seemed but too probable that the eighteenth century would find great armies still confronting each other on the Meuse and the Rhine, industrious populations still ground down by taxation, fertile provinces still lying waste, the ocean still made impassable by corsairs, and the plenipotentiaries still exchanging notes, drawing up protocols, and wrangling about the place where this minister should sit, and the title by which that minister should be called.

But William was fully determined to bring this mummery to a speedy close. He would have either peace or war. Either was, in his view, better than this intermediate state which united the disadvantages of both. While the negotiation was pending there could be no diminution of the burdens which pressed on his people ; and yet he could expect no energetic action from his allies. If France was really disposed to conclude a treaty on fair terms, that treaty should be concluded in spite of the imbecility of the Catholic King and in spite of the selfish cunning of the Emperor. If France was insecure, the sooner the truth was known, the sooner the farce which was acting at Ryswick was over, the sooner the people of England and Holland,—for on them every thing depended,—were told that they must make up their minds to great exertions and sacrifices, the better.

Pembroke and Villiers, though they had now the help of a

* Whoever wishes to be fully informed as to the idle controversies and mummeries in which the Congress wasted its time, may consult the Actes et Memoires.

veteran diplomatist, Sir Joseph Williamson, could do little or nothing to accelerate the proceedings of the Congress. For, though France had promised that, whenever peace should be made, she would recognise the Prince of Orange as King of Great Britain and Ireland, she had not yet recognised him. His ministers had therefore had no direct intercourse with Harlay, Crecy and Cailleres. William, with the judgment and decision of a true statesman, determined to open a communication with Lewis through one of the French Marshals who commanded in the Netherlands. Of those Marshals Villeroy was the highest in rank. But Villeroy was weak, rash, haughty, irritable. Such a negotiator was far more likely to embroil matters than to bring them to an amicable settlement. Boufflers was a man of sense and temper; and fortunately he had, during the few days which he had passed at Huy after the fall of Namur, been under the care of Portland, by whom he had been treated with the greatest courtesy and kindness. A friendship had sprung up between the prisoner and his keeper. They were both brave soldiers, honourable gentlemen, trusty servants. William justly thought that they were far more likely to come to an understanding than Harlay and Kaunitz even with the aid of Lilienroth. Portland indeed had all the essential qualities of an excellent diplomatist. In England, the people were prejudiced against him as a foreigner : his earldom, his garter, his lucrative places, his rapidly growing wealth, excited envy : his dialect was not understood : his manners were not those of the men of fashion who had been formed at Whitehall : his abilities were therefore greatly underrated ; and it was the fashion to call him a blockhead, fit only to carry messages. But, on the Continent, where he was judged without malevolence, he made a very different impression. It is a remarkable fact that this man, who in the drawingrooms and coffeehouses of London was described as an awkward, stupid, Hogan Mogan,—such was the phrase at that time,—was considered at Versailles as an eminently polished courtier and an eminently expert negotiator.* His chief

* Saint Simon was certainly as good a judge of men as any of those English grumblers who called Portland a dunce and a boor. Saint Simon too had every opportunity of forming a correct judgment ; for he saw Portland in a situation full of difficulties ; and Saint Simon says, in one place, "Benting, discret, secret, poli aux autres, fidèle à son maître, adroit en affaires, le servit très utilement ;" in another, "Portland parut avec un eclat personnel, une politesse, un air de monde et de cour, une galanterie et des grâces qui surprirent : avec cela, beaucoup de dignité, même de hauteur, mais avec discernement et un jugement prompt sans rien de hasardé." Boufflers too extols Portland's good breeding and tact. Boufflers to Lewis, July 9. 1697. This letter is in the archives of the French Foreign Office.

recommendation however was his incorruptible integrity. It was certain that the interests which were committed to his care would be as dear to him as his own life, and that every report which he made to his master would be literally exact.

Towards the close of June Portland sent to Boufflers a friendly message, begging for an interview of half an hour. Boufflers instantly sent off an express to Lewis, and received an answer in the shortest time in which it was possible for a courier to ride post to Versailles and back again. Lewis directed the Marshal to comply with Portland's request, to say as little as possible, and to learn as much as possible.*

On the twenty-eighth of June, according to the Old Style, the meeting took place in the neighbourhood of Hal, a town which lies about ten miles from Brussels, on the road to Mons. After the first civilities had been exchanged, Boufflers and Portland dismounted: their attendants retired; and the two negotiators were left alone in an orchard. Here they walked up and down during two hours, and, in that time, did much more business than the plenipotentiaries at Ryswick were able to despatch in as many months.†

Till this time the French government had entertained a suspicion, natural indeed, but altogether erroneous, that William was bent on protracting the war, that he had consented to treat merely because he could not venture to oppose himself to the public opinion both of England and of Holland, but that he wished the negotiation to be abortive, and that the perverse conduct of the House of Austria and the difficulties which had arisen at Ryswick were to be chiefly ascribed to his machinations. That suspicion was now removed. Compliments, cold, austere and full of dignity, yet respectful, were exchanged between the two great princes whose enmity had, during a quarter of a century, kept Europe in constant agitation. The negotiation between Boufflers and Portland proceeded as fast as the necessity of frequent reference to Versailles would permit. Their first five conferences were held in the open air; but, at their sixth meeting, they retired into a small house in which Portland had ordered tables, pens, ink and paper to be placed; and here the result of their labours was reduced to writing.

---

A translation will be found in the valuable collection published by M. Grimblot.

* Boufflers to Lewis, $\frac{June\ 21.}{July\ 1.}$ 1697 ; Lewis to Boufflers, $\frac{June\ 22.}{July\ 2.}$ ; Boufflers to Lewis, $\frac{June\ 25.}{July\ 5.}$

† Boufflers to Lewis, $\frac{June\ 28.}{July\ 8.?}$ $\frac{June\ 29.}{July\ 9.}$ 1697.

The really important points which had been in issue were four. William had at first demanded two concessions from Lewis; and Lewis had demanded two concessions from William.

William's first demand was that France should bind herself to give no help or countenance, directly or indirectly, to any attempt which might be made by James, or by James's adherents, to disturb the existing order of things in England.

William's second demand was that James should no longer be suffered to reside at a place so dangerously near to England as Saint Germains.

To the first of these demands Lewis replied that he was perfectly ready to bind himself by the most solemn engagements not to assist or countenance, in any manner, any attempt to disturb the existing order of things in England; but that it was inconsistent with his honour that the name of his kinsman and guest should appear in the treaty.

To the second demand Lewis replied that he could not refuse his hospitality to an unfortunate king who had taken refuge in his dominions, and that he could not promise even to indicate a wish that James would quit Saint Germains. But Boufflers, as if speaking his own thoughts, though doubtless saying nothing but what he knew to be in conformity to his master's wishes, hinted that the matter would probably be managed, and named Avignon as a place where the banished family might reside without giving any umbrage to the English government.

Lewis, on the other side, demanded, first, that a general amnesty should be granted to the Jacobites; and secondly, that Mary of Modena should receive her jointure of fifty thousand pounds a year.

With the first of these demands William peremptorily refused to comply. He should always be ready, of his own free will, to pardon the offences of men who showed a disposition to live quietly for the future under his government; but he could not consent to make the exercise of his prerogative of mercy a matter of stipulation with any foreign power. The annuity claimed by Mary of Modena he would willingly pay, if he could only be satisfied that it would not be expended in machinations against his throne and his person, in supporting, on the coast of Kent, another establishment like that of Hunt, or in buying horses and arms for another enterprise like that of Turnham Green. Boufflers had mentioned Avignon. If James and his Queen would take up their abode there, no difficulties would be made about the jointure.

At length all the questions in dispute were settled. After much discussion an article was framed by which Lewis pledged his word of honour that he would not favour, in any manner, any attempt to subvert or disturb the existing government of England. William, in return, gave his promise not to countenance any attempt against the government of France. This promise Lewis had not asked, and at first seemed inclined to consider as an affront. His throne, he said, was perfectly secure, his title undisputed. There were in his dominions no nonjurors, no conspirators ; and he did not think it consistent with his dignity to enter into a compact which seemed to imply that he was in fear of plots and insurrections such as a dynasty sprung from a revolution might naturally apprehend. On this point, however, he gave way ; and it was agreed that the covenants should be strictly reciprocal. William ceased to demand that James should be mentioned by name; and Lewis ceased to demand that an amnesty should be granted to James's adherents. It was determined that nothing should be said in the treaty, either about the place where the banished King of England should reside, or about the jointure of his Queen. But William authorised his plenipotentiaries at the Congress to declare that Mary of Modena should have whatever, on examination, it should appear that she was by law entitled to have. What she was by law entitled to have was a question which it would have puzzled all Westminster Hall to answer. But it was well understood that she would receive, without any contest, the utmost that she could have any pretence for asking as soon as she and her husband should retire to Provence or to Italy.*

* My account of this negotiation I have taken chiefly from the despatches in the French Foreign Office. Translations of those despatches have been published by M. Grimblot. See also Burnet, ii. 200, 201.

It has been frequently asserted that William promised to pay Mary of Modena fifty thousand pounds a year. Whoever takes the trouble to read the Protocol of Sept. $\frac{10}{20}$. 1697, among the Acts of the Peace of Ryswick, will see that my account is correct. Prior evidently understood the protocol as I understand it. For he says, in a letter to Lexington of Sept. 17. 1697, " No. 2. is the thing to which the King consents as to Queen Marie's settlements. It is fairly giving her what the law allows her. The mediator is to dictate this paper to the French, and enter it into his protocol ; and so I think we shall come off à bon marché upon that article."

It was rumoured at the time (see Boyer's History of King William III. 1703) that Portland and Boufflers had agreed on a secret article by which it was stipulated that, after the death of William, the Prince of Wales should succeed to the English throne. This fable has often been repeated, but was never believed by men of sense, and can hardly, since the publica-

Before the end of July every thing was settled, as far as France and England were concerned. Meanwhile it was known to the ministers assembled at Ryswick that Boufflers and Portland had repeatedly met in Brabant, and that they were negotiating in a most irregular and indecorous manner, without credentials, or mediation, or notes, or protocols, without counting each other's steps, and without calling each other Excellency. So barbarously ignorant were they of the rudiments of the noble science of diplomacy that they had very nearly accomplished the work of restoring peace to Christendom

---

tion of the letters which passed between Lewis and Boufflers, find credit even with the weakest. Dalrymple and other writers imagined that they had found in the Life of James (ii. 574, 575.) proof that the story of the secret article was true. The passage on which they relied was certainly not written by James, nor under his direction ; and the authority of those portions of the Life which were not written by him, or under his direction, is but small. Moreover, when we examine this passage, we shall find that it not only does not bear out the story of the secret article, but directly contradicts that story. The compiler of the Life tells us that, after James had declared that he never would consent to purchase the English throne for his posterity by surrendering his own rights, nothing more was said on the subject. Now it is quite certain that James, in his Memorial published in March 1697, a Memorial which will be found both in the Life (ii. 566.) and in the Acts of the Peace of Ryswick, declared to all Europe that he never would stoop so low and degenerate an action as to permit the Prince of Orange to reign on condition that the Prince of Wales should succeed. It follows, therefore, that nothing can have been said on this subject after March 1697. Nothing, therefore, can have been said on this subject in the conferences between Boufflers and Portland, which did not begin till late in June.

Was there then absolutely no foundation for the story ? I believe that there was a foundation ; and I have already related the facts on which this superstructure of fiction has been reared. It is quite certain that Lewis, in 1693, intimated to the allies, through the government of Sweden, his hope that some expedient might be devised which would reconcile the Princes who laid claim to the English crown. The expedient at which he hinted was, no doubt, that the Prince of Wales should succeed William and Mary. It is possible that, as the compiler of the Life of James says, William may have "show'd no great aversness" to this arrangement. He had no reason, public or private, for preferring his sister in law to his brother in law, if his brother in law were bred a Protestant. But William could do nothing without the concurrence of the Parliament ; and it is in the highest degree improbable that either he or the Parliament would ever have consented to make the settlement of the English crown a matter of stipulation with France. What he would or would not have done, however, we cannot with certainty pronounce. For James proved impracticable. Lewis consequently gave up all thoughts of effecting a compromise, and promised, as we have seen, to recognise William as King of England "without any difficulty, restriction, condition, or reserve." It seems certain that, after this promise, which was made in December 1696, the Prince of Wales was not again mentioned in the negotiations.

while walking up and down an alley under some apple trees. The English and Dutch loudly applauded William's prudence and decision. He had cut the knot which the Congress had only twisted and tangled. He had done in a month what all the formalists and pedants assembled at the Hague would not have done in ten years. Nor were the French plenipotentiaries ill pleased. "It is curious," said Harlay, a man of wit and sense, "that, while the Ambassadors are making war, the generals should be making peace." * But Spain preserved the same air of arrogant listlessness; and the ministers of the Emperor, forgetting apparently that their master had, a few months before, concluded a treaty of neutrality for Italy without consulting William, seemed to think it most extraordinary that William should presume to negotiate without consulting their master. It became daily more evident that the Court of Vienna was bent on prolonging the war. On the tenth of July the French ministers again proposed fair and honourable terms of peace, but added that, if those terms were not accepted by the twenty-first of August, the Most Christian King would not consider himself bound by his offer.† William in vain exhorted his allies to be reasonable. The senseless pride of one branch of the House of Austria and the selfish policy of the other were proof to all argument. The twenty-first of August came and passed; the treaty had not been signed: France was at liberty to raise her demands; and she did so. For just at this time news arrived of two great blows which had fallen on Spain, one in the Old and one in the New World. A French army, commanded by Vendome, had taken Barcelona. A French squadron had stolen out of Brest, had eluded the allied fleets, had crossed the Atlantic, had sacked Carthagena, and had returned to France laden with treasure.‡ The Spanish government passed at once from haughty apathy to abject terror, and was ready to accept any conditions which the conqueror might dictate. The French plenipotentiaries announced to the Congress that their master was determined to keep Strasburg, and that, unless the terms which he had offered, thus modified, were accepted by the tenth of September, he should hold himself at liberty to insist on further modifications. Never had the temper of William been more

* Prior MS.; Williamson to Lexington, July ²⁸/₃₈. 1697; Williamson to Shrewsbury, July 23./Aug. 2.

† The note of the French ministers, dated July ¹⁸/₂₈. 1697, will be found in the Actes et Mémoires.

‡ Monthly Mercuries for August and September, 1697.

severely tried. He was provoked by the perverseness of his allies : he was provoked by the imperious language of the enemy. It was not without a hard struggle and a sharp pang that he made up his mind to consent to what France now proposed. But he felt that it would be utterly impossible, even if it were desirable, to prevail on the House of Commons and on the States General to continue the war for the purpose of wresting from France a single fortress, a fortress in the fate of which neither England nor Holland had any immediate interest, a fortress, too, which had been lost to the Empire solely in consequence of the unreasonable obstinacy of the Imperial Court. He determined to accept the modified terms, and directed his Ambassadors at Ryswick to sign on the prescribed day. The Ambassadors of Spain and Holland received similar instructions. There was no doubt that the Emperor, though he murmured and protested, would soon follow the example of his confederates. That he might have time to make up his mind, it was stipulated that he should be included in the treaty if he notified his adhesion by the first of November.

Meanwhile James was moving the mirth and pity of all Europe by his lamentations and menaces. He had in vain insisted on his right to send, as the only true King of England, a minister to the Congress.* He had in vain addressed to all the Roman Catholic princes of the Confederacy a memorial in which he adjured them to join with France in a crusade against England for the purpose of restoring him to his inheritance, and of annulling that impious Bill of Rights which excluded members of the true Church from the throne.† When he found that this appeal was disregarded, he put forth a solemn protest against the validity of all treaties to which the existing government of England should be a party. He pronounced all the engagements into which his kingdom had entered since the Revolution null and void. He gave notice that he should not, if he should regain his power, think himself bound by any of those engagements. He admitted that he might, by breaking those engagements, bring great calamities both on his own dominions and on all Christendom. But for those calamities he declared that he should not think himself answerable either before God or before man. It seems almost incredible that even a Stuart, and the worst and dullest of the Stuarts, should

* Life of James, ii. 565.
† Actes et Mémoires des Négociations de la Paix de Ryswick ; Life of James, ii. 566.

have thought that the first duty, not merely of his own subjects, but of all mankind, was to support his rights; that Frenchmen, Germans, Italians, Spaniards, were guilty of a crime if they did not shed their blood and lavish their wealth, year after year, in his cause; that the interests of the sixty millions of human beings to whom peace would be a blessing were of absolutely no account when compared with the interests of one man.*

In spite of his protests the day of peace drew nigh. On the tenth of September the Ambassadors of France, England, Spain and the United Provinces, met at Ryswick. Three treaties were to be signed; and there was a long dispute on the momentous question which should be signed first. It was one in the morning before it was settled that the treaty between France and the States General should have precedence; and the day was breaking before all the instruments had been executed. Then the plenipotentiaries, with many bows, congratulated each other on having had the honour of contributing to so great a work.†

A sloop was in waiting for Prior. He hastened on board, and on the third day, after weathering an equinoctial gale, landed on the coast of Suffolk.‡

Very seldom had there been greater excitement in London than during the month which preceded his arrival. When the west wind kept back the Dutch packets, the anxiety of the people became intense. Every morning hundreds of thousands rose up hoping to hear that the treaty was signed; and every mail which came in without bringing the good news caused bitter disappointment. The malecontents, indeed, loudly asserted that there would be no peace, and that the negotiation would, even at this late hour, be broken off. One of them had seen a person just arrived from Saint Germains: another had had the privilege of reading a letter in the handwriting of Her Majesty; and all were confident that Lewis would never acknowledge the usurper. Many of those who held this language were under so strong a delusion that they backed their opinion by large wagers. When the intelligence of the fall of Barcelona arrived, all the treason taverns were in a ferment with nonjuring priests laughing, talking loud, and shaking each other by the hand.§

* James's Protest will be found in his Life, ii. 572.
† Actes et Mémoires des Négociations de la Paix de Ryswick; Williamson to Lexington, Sept. $\frac{14}{24}$. 1697; Prior MS.                    ‡ Prior MS.
§ L'Hermitage, July $\frac{20}{30}$., $\frac{\text{July 27.}}{\text{Aug. 6.}}$, $\frac{\text{Aug. 24.}}{\text{Sept. 3.}}$, $\frac{\text{Aug. 27.}}{\text{Sept. 6.}}$, $\frac{\text{Aug. 31.}}{\text{Sept. 10.}}$, 1697; Postman, Aug. 31.

At length, in the afternoon of the thirteenth of September, some speculators in the City received, by a private channel, certain intelligence that the treaty had been signed before dawn on the morning of the eleventh. They kept their own secret, and hastened to make a profitable use of it; but their eagerness to obtain Bank stock, and the high prices which they offered, excited suspicion; and there was a general belief that on the next day something important would be announced. On the next day Prior, with the treaty, presented himself before the Lords Justices at Whitehall. Instantly a flag was hoisted on the Abbey, another on Saint Martin's Church. The Tower guns proclaimed the glad tidings. All the spires and towers from Greenwich to Chelsea made answer. It was not one of the days on which the newspapers ordinarily appeared: but extraordinary numbers, with headings in large capitals, were, for the first time, cried about the streets. The price of Bank stock rose fast from eighty-four to ninety-seven. In a few hours triumphal arches began to rise in some places. Huge bonfires were blazing in others. The Dutch ambassador informed the States General that he should try to show his joy by a bonfire worthy of the commonwealth which he represented; and he kept his word; for no such pyre had ever been seen in London. A hundred and forty barrels of pitch roared and blazed before his house in Saint James's Square, and sent up a flame which made Pall Mall and Piccadilly as bright as at noonday.[*]

Among the Jacobites the dismay was great. Some of those who had betted deep on the constancy of Lewis took flight. One unfortunate zealot of divine right drowned himself. But soon the party again took heart. The treaty had been signed: but it surely would never be ratified. In a short time the ratification came: the peace was solemnly proclaimed by the heralds; and the most obstinate nonjurors began to despair. Some divines, who had during eight years continued true to James, now swore allegiance to William. They were probably men who held, with Sherlock, that a settled government, though illegitimate in its origin, is entitled to the obedience of Christians, but who had thought that the government of William could not properly be said to be settled while the greatest power in Europe not only refused to recognise him, but strenuously supported his competitor.[†] The fiercer and more

* Van Cleverskirke to the States General, Sept. $\frac{11}{21}$. 1697; L'Hermitage, Sept. $\frac{11}{21}$.; Postscript to the Postman, of the same date; Postman and Postboy of Sept. $\frac{13}{23}$., Postman of Sept. $\frac{18}{28}$.

† L'Hermitage, Sept. $\frac{17}{27}$., $\frac{Sept. 24}{Oct. 4}$ 1697, Oct. $\frac{19}{29}$.; Postman, Nov. 20.

determined adherents of the banished family were furious against Lewis. He had deceived, he had betrayed his suppliants. It was idle to talk about the misery of his people. It was idle to say that he had drained every source of revenue dry, and that, in all the provinces of his kingdom, the peasantry were clothed in rags, and were unable to eat their fill even of the coarsest and blackest bread. His first duty was that which he owed to the royal family of England. The Jacobites talked against him, and wrote against him, as absurdly, and almost as scurrilously, as they had long talked and written against William. One of their libels was so indecent that the Lords Justices ordered the author to be arrested and held to bail.*

But the rage and mortification were confined to a very small minority. Never, since the year of the Restoration, had there been such signs of public gladness. In every part of the kingdom where the peace was proclaimed, the general sentiment was manifested by banquets, pageants, loyal healths, salutes, beating of drums, blowing of trumpets, breaking up of hogsheads. At some places the whole population, of its own accord, repaired to the churches to give thanks. At others processions of girls, clad all in white, and crowned with laurels, carried banners inscribed with "God bless King William." At every county town a long cavalcade of the principal gentlemen, from a circle of many miles, escorted the mayor to the market cross. Nor was one holiday enough for the expression of so much joy. On the fourth of November, the anniversary of the King's birth, and on the fifth, the anniversary of his landing at Torbay, the bell-ringing, the shouting, and the illuminations were renewed both in London and all over the country.† On the day on which he

---

* L'Hermitage, $\frac{\text{Sept. 21.}}{\text{Oct. 1.}}$, Nov. $\frac{2}{13}$. 1697 ; Paris Gazette, Nov. $\frac{2}{6}\frac{0}{9}$.; Postboy, Nov. 2. At this time appeared a pasquinade entitled, A Satyr upon the French King, written after the Peace was concluded at Reswick, anno 1697, by a Non-Swearing Parson, and said to be drop'd out of his Pocket at Sam's Coffee House. I quote a few of the most decent couplets.

> " Lord ! with what monstrous lies and senseless shams
> Have we been cullied all along at Sam's !
> Who could have e'er believed, unless in spite
> Lewis le Grand would turn rank Williamite ?
> Thou that hast look'd so fierce and talk'd so big,
> In thine old age to dwindle to a Whig !
> Of Kings distress'd thou art a fine securer.
> Thou mak'st me swear, that am a known nonjuror.
> Were Job alive, and banter'd by such shufflers,
> He'd outrail Oates, and curse both thee and Boufflers.
> For thee I've lost, if I can rightly scan 'em,
> Two livings, worth full eightscore pounds *per annum*,
> *Bonæ et legalis Angliæ Monetæ.*
> But now I'm clearly routed by the treaty. '

† London Gazettes ; Postboy of Nov. 18. 1697 ; L'Hermitage, Nov. $\frac{5}{16}$.

returned to his capital no work was done, no shop was opened, in the two thousand streets of that immense mart. For that day the chiefs streets had, mile after mile, been covered with gravel : all the Companies had provided new banners ; all the magistrates new robes. Twelve thousand pounds had been expended in preparing fireworks. Great multitudes of people from all the neighbouring shires had come up to see the show. Never had the City been in a more loyal or more joyous mood. The evil days were past. The guinea had fallen to twenty-one shillings and sixpence. The bank note had risen to par. The new crowns and halfcrowns, broad, heavy and sharply milled, were ringing on all the counters. After some days of impatient expectation it was known, on the fourteenth of November, that His Majesty had landed at Margate. Late on the fifteenth he reached Greenwich, and rested in the stately building which, under his auspices, was turning from a palace into a hospital. On the next morning, a bright and soft morning, eighty coaches and six, filled with nobles, prelates, privy councillors and judges, came to swell his train. In Southwark he was met by the Lord Mayor and the Aldermen in all the pomp of office. The way through the Borough to the bridge was lined by the Surrey militia ; the way from the bridge to Walbrook by three regiments of the militia of the City. All along Cheapside, on the right hand and on the left, the livery were marshalled under the standards of their trades. At the east end of Saint Paul's churchyard stood the boys of the school of Edward the Sixth, wearing, as they still wear, the garb of the sixteenth century. Round the Cathedral, down Ludgate Hill and along Fleet Street, were drawn up three more regiments of Londoners. From Temple Bar to Whitehall gate the trainbands of Middlesex and the Foot Guards were under arms. The windows along the whole route were gay with tapestry, ribands and flags. But the finest part of the show was the innumerable crowd of spectators, all in their Sunday clothing, and such clothing as only the upper classes of other countries could afford to wear. "I never," William wrote that evening to Heinsius, "I never saw such a multitude of welldressed people." Nor was the King less struck by the indications of joy and affection with which he was greeted from the beginning to the end of his triumph. His coach, from the moment when he entered it at Greenwich till he alighted from it in the court of Whitehall, was accompanied by one long huzza. Scarcely had he reached his palace when addresses of congratulation, from all the great corporations of his kingdom, were presented to him.  It was remarked that the very foremost among those corporations was the University of Oxford.  The eloquent composition in which that learned body extolled the wisdom, the courage and the virtue of His Majesty, was read with cruel vexation by the nonjurors, and with exultation by the Whigs.*

The rejoicings were not yet over.  At a council which was held a few hours after the King's public entry, the second of December was appointed to be the day of thanksgiving for the peace.  The Chapter of Saint Paul's resolved that, on that day, their noble Cathedral, which had been long slowly rising on the ruins of a succession of pagan and Christian temples, should be opened for public worship.  William announced his intention of being one of the congregation.  But it was represented to him that, if he persisted in that intention, three hundred thousand people would assemble to see him pass, and all the parish churches of London would be left empty.  He therefore attended the service in his own chapel at Whitehall, and heard Burnet preach a sermon, somewhat too eulogistic for the place.†  At Saint Paul's the magistrates of the City appeared in all their state.  Compton ascended, for the first time, a throne rich with the sculpture of Gibbons, and thence exhorted a numerous and splendid assembly.  His discourse has not been preserved : but its purport may be easily guessed ; for he preached on that noble Psalm : " I was glad when they said unto me, Let us go into the house of the Lord."  He doubtless reminded his hearers that, in addition to the debt which was common to them with all Englishmen, they owed as Londoners a peculiar debt of gratitude to the divine goodness, which had permitted them to efface the last trace of the ravages of the great fire, and to assemble once more, for prayer and praise, after so many years, on that spot consecrated by the devotions of thirty generations.  Throughout London, and in every part of the realm, even to the remotest parishes of Cumberland and Cornwall, the churches were filled on the morning of that day ; and the evening was an evening of festivity.‡

These was indeed reason for joy and thankfulness.  England

* London Gazette, Nov. 18. 22. 1697 ; Van Cleverskirke, Nov. $\frac{18}{28}$. $\frac{19}{29}$. ; L'Hermitage, Nov. $\frac{18}{28}$. ; Postboy and Postman, Nov. 18. ; William to Heinsius, Nov. $\frac{18}{28}$.

† Evelyn's Diary, Dec. 2. 1697.  The sermon is extant ; and I must acknowledge that it deserves Evelyn's censure.

‡ London Gazette, Dec. 6. 1697 ; Postman, Dec. 4. ; Van Cleverskirke, Dec. $\frac{2}{12}$. ; L'Hermitage, Nov. $\frac{19}{28}$.

had passed through severe trials, and had come forth renewed in health and vigour. Ten years before, it had seemed that both her liberty and her independence were no more. Her liberty she had vindicated by a just and necessary revolution. Her independence she had reconquered by a not less just and necessary war. She had successfully defended the order of things established by the Bill of Rights against the mighty monarchy of France, against the aboriginal population of Ireland, against the avowed hostility of the nonjurors, against the more dangerous hostility of traitors who were ready to take any oath, and whom no oath could bind. Her open enemies had been victorious on many fields of battle. Her secret enemies had commanded her fleets and armies, had been in charge of her arsenals, had ministered at her altars, had taught at her Universities, had swarmed in her public offices, had sate in her Parliament, had bowed and fawned in the bedchamber of her King. More than once it had seemed impossible that any thing could avert a restoration which would inevitably have been followed, first by proscriptions and confiscations, by the violation of fundamental laws, and the persecution of the established religion, and then by a third rising up of the nation against that House which two depositions and two banishments had only made more obstinate in evil. To the dangers of war and the dangers of treason had recently been added the dangers of a terrible financial and commercial crisis. But all those dangers were over. There was peace abroad and at home. The kingdom, after many years of ignominious vassalage, had resumed its ancient place in the first rank of European powers. Many signs justified the hope that the Revolution of 1688 would be our last Revolution. The ancient constitution was adapting itself, by a natural, a gradual, a peaceful development, to the wants of a modern society. Already freedom of conscience and freedom of discussion existed to an extent unknown in any preceding age. The currency had been restored. Public credit had been reestablished. Trade had revived. The Exchequer was overflowing. There was a sense of relief every where, from the Royal Exchange to the most secluded hamlets among the mountains of Wales and the fens of Lincolnshire. The ploughmen, the shepherds, the miners of the Northumbrian coalpits, the artisans who toiled at the looms of Norwich and the anvils of Birmingham, felt the change, without understanding it; and the cheerful bustle in every seaport and every market town indicated, not obscurely, the commencement of a happier age.

## CHAPTER XXIII

THE rejoicings, by which London, on the second of December 1697, celebrated the return of peace and prosperity, continued till long after midnight. On the following morning the Parliament met; and one of the most laborious sessions of that age commenced.

Among the questions which it was necessary that the Houses should speedily decide, one stood forth preeminent in interest and importance. Even in the first transports of joy with which the bearer of the treaty of Ryswick had been welcomed to England, men had eagerly and anxiously asked one another what was to be done with that army which had been famed in Ireland and Belgium, which had learned, in many hard campaigns, to obey and to conquer, and which now consisted of eighty-seven thousand excellent soldiers Was any part of this great force to be retained in the service of the State? And, if any part, what part? The last two kings had, without the consent of the legislature, maintained military establishments in time of peace. But that they had done this in violation of the fundamental laws of England was acknowledged by all jurists, and had been expressly affirmed in the Bill of Rights. It was therefore impossible for William, now that the country was threatened by no foreign and no domestic enemy, to keep up even a single battalion without the sanction of the Estates of the Realm; and it might well be doubted whether such a sanction would be given.

It is not easy for us to see this question in the light in which it appeared to our ancestors.

No man of sense has, in our days, or in the days of our fathers, seriously maintained that our island could be safe without an army. And, even if our island were perfectly secure from attack, an army would still be indispensably necessary to us. The growth of the empire has left us no choice. The regions which we have colonized or conquered since the accession of the House of Hanover contain a population exceeding twenty-fold that which the House of Stuart governed. There are now more English soldiers on the other side of the tropic of Cancer in time of peace than Cromwell had under his command in time of war. All the troops of Charles II. would not have been sufficient to garrison the posts which we now occupy in the Mediterranean Sea alone. The regiments which defend the remote dependencies of the Crown cannot be duly recruited and relieved, unless a force far larger than that which James collected in the camp at Hounslow for the purpose of overawing his capital be constantly kept up within the kingdom. The old national antipathy to permanent military establishments, an antipathy which was once reasonable and salutary, but which lasted some time after it had become unreasonable and noxious, has gradually yielded to the irresistible force of circumstances. We have made the discovery, that an army may be so constituted as to be in the highest degree efficient against an enemy, and yet obsequious to the civil magistrate. We have long ceased to apprehend danger to law and to freedom from the license of troops, and from the ambition of victorious generals. An alarmist who should now talk such language as was common five generations ago, who should call for the entire disbanding of the land force of the realm, and who should gravely predict that the warriors of Inkerman and Delhi would depose the Queen, dissolve the Parliament, and plunder the Bank, would be regarded as fit only for a cell in Saint Luke's. But before the Revolution our ancestors had known a standing army only as an instrument of lawless power. Judging by their own experience, they thought it impossible that such an army should exist without danger to the rights both of the Crown and of the people. One class of politicians was never weary of repeating that an Apostolic Church, a loyal gentry, an ancient nobility, a sainted King, had been foully outraged by the Joyces and the Prides: another class recounted the atrocities committed by the Lambs of Kirke, and by the Beelzebubs and Lucifers of Dundee; and both classes, agreeing in scarcely any thing else, were disposed to agree in aversion to the red coats.

While such was the feeling of the nation, the King was, both as a statesman and as a general, most unwilling to see that superb body of troops which he had formed with infinite difficulty broken up and dispersed. But, as to this matter, he could not absolutely rely on the support of his ministers; nor could his ministers absolutely rely on the support of that parliamentary majority whose attachment had enabled them to confront enemies abroad and to crush traitors at home, to restore a debased currency, and to fix public credit on deep and solid foundations.

The difficulties of the King's situation are to be, in part at least, attributed to an error which he had committed in the preceding spring. The Gazette which announced that Sunderland had been appointed Chamberlain of the Royal Household, sworn of the Privy Council, and named one of the Lords Justices who were to administer the government during the summer, had caused great uneasiness among plain men who remembered all the windings and doublings of his long career. In truth, his countrymen were unjust to him. For they thought him, not only an unprincipled and faithless politician, which he was, but a deadly enemy of the liberties of the nation, which he was not. What he wanted was simply to be safe, rich and great. To these objects he had been constant through all the vicissitudes of his life. For these objects he had passed from Church to Church and from faction to faction, had joined the most turbulent of oppositions without any zeal for freedom, and had served the most arbitrary of monarchs without any zeal for monarchy ; had voted for the Exclusion Bill without being a Protestant, and had adored the Host without being a Papist ; had sold his country at once to both the great parties which divided the Continent, had taken money from France, and had sent intelligence to Holland. As far, however, as he could be said to have any opinions, his opinions were Whiggish. Since his return from exile, his influence had been generally exerted in favour of the Whig party. It was by his counsel that the Great Seal had been entrusted to Somers, that Nottingham had been sacrificed to Russell, and that Montague had been preferred to Fox. It was by his dexterous management that the Princess Anne had been detached from the opposition, and that Godolphin had been removed from the head of the Board of Treasury. The party which Sunderland had done so much to serve now held a new pledge for his fidelity. His only son, Charles Lord Spencer, was just entering on public life. The precocious maturity of the young man's intellectual and moral character had excited hopes which were not destined to be realized. His knowledge of ancient literature, and his skill in imitating the styles of the masters of Roman eloquence, were applauded by veteran scholars. The sedateness of his deportment and the apparent regularity of his life delighted austere moralists. He was known indeed to have one expensive taste ; but it was a taste of the most respectable kind. He loved books, and was bent on forming the most magnificent private library in England. While other heirs of noble houses were inspecting patterns of steinkirks and sword knots, dangling after actresses, or betting on fighting cocks, he was in pursuit of the Mentz editions of

Tully's Offices, of the Parmesan Statius, and of the inestimable Virgin of Zarottus.* It was natural that high expectations should be formed of the virtue and wisdom of a youth whose very luxury and prodigality had a grave and erudite air, and that even discerning men should be unable to detect the vices which were hidden under that show of premature sobriety.

Spencer was a Whig, unhappily for the Whig party, which, before the unhonoured and unlamented close of his life, was more than once brought to the verge of ruin by his violent temper and his crooked politics. His Whiggism differed widely from that of his father. It was not a languid, speculative, preference of one theory of government to another, but a fierce and dominant passion. Unfortunately, though an ardent, it was at the same time a corrupt and degenerate, Whiggism; a Whiggism so narrow and oligarchical as to be little, if at all, preferable to the worst forms of Toryism. The young lord's imagination had been fascinated by those swelling sentiments of liberty which abound in the Latin poets and orators; and he, like those poets and orators, meant by liberty something very different from the only liberty which is of importance to the happiness of mankind. Like them, he could see no danger to liberty except from kings. A commonwealth, oppressed and pillaged by such men as Opimius and Verres, was free, because it had no king. A member of the Grand Council of Venice, who passed his whole life under tutelage and in fear, who could not travel where he chose, or visit whom he chose, or invest his property as he chose, whose path was beset with spies, who saw at the corners of the streets the mouth of bronze gaping for anonymous accusations against him, and whom the Inquisitors of State could, at any moment, and for any or no reason, arrest, torture, fling into the Grand Canal, was free, because he had no king. To curtail, for the benefit of a small privileged class, prerogatives which the Sovereign possesses and ought to possess for the benefit of the whole nation, was the object on which Spencer's heart was set. During many years he was restrained by older and wiser men; and it was not till those whom he had early been accustomed to respect had passed away, and till he was

---

* Evelyn saw the Mentz edition of the Offices among Lord Spencer's books in April, 1699. Markland, in his preface to the Sylvæ of Statius, acknowledges his obligations to the very rare Parmesan edition in Lord Spencer's collection. As to the Virgil of Zarottus, which his Lordship bought for 46*l.*, see the extracts from Warley's Diary, in Nichols's Literary Anecdotes, i. 90.

himself at the head of affairs, that he openly attempted to obtain for the hereditary nobility a precarious and invidious ascendency in the State, at the expense both of the Commons and of the Throne.

In 1695, Spencer had taken his seat in the House of Commons as member for Tiverton, and had, during two sessions, conducted himself as a steady and zealous Whig. The party to which he had attached himself might perhaps have reasonably considered him as a hostage sufficient to ensure the good faith of his father ; for the Earl was approaching that time of life at which even the most ambitious and rapacious men generally toil rather for their children than for themselves. But the distrust which Sunderland inspired was such as no guarantee could quiet. Many fancied that he was,—with what object they never took the trouble to inquire, —employing the same arts which had ruined James for the purpose of ruining William. Each prince had had his weak side. One was too much a Papist, and the other too much a soldier, for such a nation as this. The same intriguing sycophant who had encouraged the Papist in one fatal error was now encouraging the soldier in another. It might well be apprehended that, under the influence of this evil counsellor, the nephew might alienate as many hearts by trying to make England a military country as the uncle had alienated by trying to make her a Roman Catholic country.

The parliamentary conflict on the great question of a standing army was preceded by a literary conflict. In the autumn of 1697 began a controversy of no common interest and importance. The press was now free. An exciting and momentous political question could be fairly discussed. Those who held uncourtly opinions could express those opinions without resorting to illegal expedients and employing the agency of desperate men. The consequence was that the dispute was carried on, though with sufficient keenness, yet, on the whole, with a decency which would have been thought extraordinary in the days of the censorship.

On this occasion the Tories, though they felt strongly, wrote but little. The paper war was almost entirely carried on between two sections of the Whig party. The combatants on both sides were generally anonymous. But it was well known that one of the foremost champions of the malecontent Whigs was John Trenchard, son of the late Secretary of State. Preeminent among the ministerial Whigs was one in whom admirable vigour and quickness of intellect were united to a not less admirable moderation and urbanity, one who looked on the history of past ages with the eye of a practical states- man, and on the events which were passing before him with the eye of a philosophical historian. It was not necessary for him to name himself. He could be none but Somers.

The pamphleteers who recommended the immediate and entire disbanding of the army had an easy task. If they were embarrassed, it was only by the abundance of the matter from which they had to make their selection. On their side were claptraps and historical commonplaces without number, the authority of a crowd of illustrious names, all the prejudices, all the traditions, of both the parties in the state. These writers laid it down as a fundamental principle of political science that a standing army and a free constitution could not exist together. What, they asked, had destroyed the noble commonwealths of Greece? What had enslaved the mighty Roman people? What had turned the Italian republics of the middle ages into lordships and duchies? How was it that so many of the kingdoms of modern Europe had been trans- formed from limited into absolute monarchies? The States General of France, the Cortes of Castile, the Grand Justiciary of Arragon, what had been fatal to them all? History was ransacked for instances of adventurers who, by the help of mercenary troops, had subjugated free nations or deposed legitimate princes; and such instances were easily found. Much was said about Pisistratus, Timophanes, Dionysius, Agathocles, Marius and Sylla, Julius Cæsar and Augustus Cæsar, Carthage besieged by her own mercenaries, Rome put up to auction by her own Prætorian cohorts, Sultan Osman butchered by his own Janissaries, Lewis Sforza sold into captivity by his own Switzers. But the favourite instance was taken from the recent history of our own land. Thousands still living had seen the great usurper, who, strong in the power of the sword, had triumphed over both royalty and freedom. The Tories were reminded that his soldiers had guarded the scaffold before the Banqueting House. The Whigs were reminded that those same soldiers had taken the mace from the table of the House of Commons. From such evils, it was said, no country could be secure which was cursed with a standing army. And what were the advantages which could be set off against such evils? Invasion was the bugbear with which the Court tried to frighten the nation. But we were not children to be scared by nursery tales. We were at peace; and, even in time of war, an enemy who should attempt to invade us would probably be intercepted by our fleet, and would assuredly, if he reached our shores, be repelled by our militia. Some people indeed talked as if a militia could achieve nothing great. But that base doctrine was refuted by all ancient and all modern history. What was the Lacedæmonian phalanx in the best days of Lacedæmon? What was the Roman legion in the best days of Rome? What were the armies which conquered at Cressy, at Poitiers, at Agincourt, at Halidon, or at Flodden? What was that mighty array which Elizabeth reviewed at Tilbury? In the fourteenth, fifteenth, and sixteenth centuries Englishmen who did not live by the trade of war had made war with success and glory. Were the English of the seventeenth century so degenerate that they could not be trusted to play the men for their own homesteads and parish churches?

For such reasons as these the disbanding of the forces was strongly recommended. Parliament, it was said, might perhaps, from respect and tenderness for the person of His Majesty, permit him to have guards enough to escort his coach and to pace the rounds before his palace. But this was the very utmost that it would be right to concede. The defence of the realm ought to be confided to the sailors and the militia. Even the Tower ought to have no garrison except the trainbands of the Tower Hamlets.

It must be evident to every intelligent and dispassionate man that these declaimers contradicted themselves. If an army composed of regular troops really was far more efficient than an army composed of husbandmen taken from the plough and burghers taken from the counter, how could the country be safe with no defenders but husbandmen and burghers, when a great prince, who was our nearest neighbour, who had a few months before been our enemy, and who might, in a few months, be our enemy again, kept up not less than a hundred and fifty thousand regular troops? If, on the other hand, the spirit of the English people was such that they would, with little or no training, encounter and defeat the most formidable array of veterans from the continent, was it not absurd to apprehend that such a people could be reduced to slavery by a few regiments of their own countrymen? But our ancestors were generally so much blinded by prejudice that this inconsistency passed unnoticed. They were secure where they ought to have been wary, and timorous where they might well have been secure. They were not shocked by hearing the same man maintain, in the same breath, that, if twenty thousand professional soldiers were kept up, the liberty and property of millions of Englishmen would be at the mercy of the Crown, and yet that those millions of Englishmen, fighting for liberty and property, would speedily annihilate an invading army composed of fifty or sixty thousand of the conquerors of Steinkirk and Landen. Whoever denied the former proposition was called a tool of the Court. Whoever denied the latter was accused of insulting and slandering the nation.

Somers was too wise to oppose himself directly to the strong current of popular feeling. With rare dexterity he took the tone, not of an advocate, but of a judge. The danger which seemed so terrible to many honest friends of liberty he did not venture to pronounce altogether visionary. But he reminded his countrymen that a choice between dangers was sometimes all that was left to the wisest of mankind. No lawgiver had ever been able to devise a perfect and immortal form of government. Perils lay thick on the right and on the left ; and to keep far from one evil was to draw near to another. That which, considered merely with reference to the internal polity of England, might be, to a certain extent, objectionable, might be absolutely essential to her rank among European Powers, and even to her independence. All that a statesman could do in such a case was to weigh inconveniences against each other, and carefully to observe which way the scale leaned. The evil of having regular soldiers, and the evil of not having them, Somers set forth and compared in a little treatise, which was once widely renowned as the Balancing Letter, and which was admitted, even by the malecontents, to be an able and plausible composition. He well knew that mere names exercise a mighty influence on the public mind ; that the most perfect tribunal which a legislator could construct would be unpopular if it were called the Star Chamber ; that the most judicious tax which a financier could devise would excite murmurs if it were called the Shipmoney ; and that the words Standing Army then had to English ears a sound as unpleasing as either Shipmoney or Star Chamber. He declared therefore that he abhorred the thought of a standing army. What he recommended was, not a standing, but a temporary army, an army of which Parliament would annually fix the number, an army for which Parliament would annually frame a military code, an army which would cease to exist as soon as either the Lords or the Commons should think that its services were not needed. From such an army surely the danger to public liberty could not by wise men be thought serious. On the other hand, the danger to which the kingdom would be exposed if all the troops were disbanded was such as might well disturb the firmest mind. Suppose a war with the greatest power in Christendom to break out suddenly, and to find us without one battalion of regular infantry, without one squadron of regular cavalry; what disasters might we not reasonably apprehend? It was idle to say that a descent could not take place without ample notice, and that we should have time to raise and discipline a great force. An absolute prince, whose orders, given in profound secresy, were promptly obeyed at once by his captains on the Rhine and on the Scheld, and by his admirals in the Bay of Biscay and in the Mediterranean, might be ready to strike a blow long before we were prepared to parry it. We might be appalled by learning that ships from widely remote parts, and troops from widely remote garrisons, had assembled at a single point within sight of our coast. To trust to our fleet was to trust to the winds and the waves. The breeze which was favourable to the invader might prevent our men of war from standing out to sea. Only nine years ago this had actually happened. The Protestant wind, before which the Dutch armament had run full sail down the Channel, had driven King James's navy back into the Thames. It must then be acknowledged to be not improbable that the enemy might land. And, if he landed, what would he find? An open country; a rich country; provisions everywhere; not a river but which could be forded; no natural fastnesses such as protect the fertile plains of Italy; no artificial fastnesses such as, at every step, impede the progress of a conqueror in the Netherlands. Every thing must then be staked on the steadiness of the militia; and it was pernicious flattery to represent the militia as equal to a conflict in the field with veterans whose whole life had been a preparation for the day of battle. The instances which it was the fashion to cite of the great achievements of soldiers taken from the threshing floor and the shopboard were fit only for a schoolboy's theme. Somers, who had studied ancient literature like a man,—a rare thing in his time,—said that those instances refuted the doctrine which they were meant to prove. He disposed of much idle declamation about the Lacedæmonians by saying, most concisely, correctly and happily, that the Lacedæmonian commonwealth really was a standing army which threatened all the rest of Greece. In fact, the Spartan had no calling except war. Of arts, sciences and letters he was ignorant. The labour of the spade and of the loom, and the petty gains of trade, he contemptuously abandoned to men of a lower caste.   His whole existence from childhood to old age was one long military training.   Meanwhile the Athenian, the Corinthian, the Argive, the Theban, gave his chief attention to his oliveyard or his vineyard, his warehouse or his workshop, and took up his shield and spear only for short terms and at long intervals.   The difference therefore between a Lacedæmonian phalanx and any other phalanx was long as great as the difference between a regiment of the French household troops and a regiment of the London trainbands.   Lacedæmon consequently continued to be dominant in Greece till other states began to employ regular troops.   Then her supremacy was at an end.   She was great while she was a standing army among militias.   She fell when she had to contend with other standing armies.   The lesson which is really to be learned from her ascendency and from her decline is this, that the occasional soldier is no match for the professional soldier.*

* The more minutely we examine the history of the decline and fall of Lacedæmon, the more reason we shall find to admire the sagacity of Somers.   The first great humiliation which befel the Lacedæmonians was the affair of Sphacteria.   It is remarkable that on this occasion they were vanquished by men who made a trade of war.   The force which Cleon carried out with him from Athens to the Bay of Pylos, and to which the event of the conflict is to be chiefly ascribed, consisted entirely of mercenaries,—archers from Scythia and light infantry from Thrace.   The victory gained by the Lacedæmonians over a great confederate army at Tegea retrieved that military reputation which the disaster of Sphacteria had impaired.   Yet even at Tegea it was signally proved that the Lacedæmonians, though far superior to occasional soldiers, were not equal to professional soldiers.   On every point but one the allies were put to rout; but on one point the Lacedæmonians gave way; and that was the point where they were opposed to a brigade of a thousand Argives, picked men, whom the state to which they belonged had during many years trained to war at the public charge, and who were, in fact, a standing army.   After the battle of Tegea, many years elapsed before the Lacedæmonians sustained a defeat.   At length a calamity befel them which astonished all their neighbours.   A division of the army of Agesilaus was cut off and destroyed almost to a man; and this exploit, which seemed almost portentous to the Greeks of that age, was achieved by Iphicrates, at the head of a body of mercenary light infantry.   But it was from the day of Leuctra that the fall of Sparta became rapid and violent.   Some time before that day the Thebans had resolved to follow the example set many years before by the Argives.   Some hundreds of athletic youths, carefully selected, were set apart, under the names of the City Band and the Sacred Band, to form a standing army.   Their business was war.   They encamped in the citadel; they were supported at the expense of the community; and they became, under assiduous training, the first soldiers in Greece.   They were constantly victorious till they were opposed to Philip's admirably disciplined phalanx at Chæronea; and even at Chæronea they were not defeated, but slain in their ranks, fighting to the last.   It was this band, directed by the skill of great

The same lesson Somers drew from the history of Rome ; and every scholar who really understands that history will admit that he was in the right. The finest militia that ever existed was probably that of Italy in the third century before Christ. It might have been thought that seven or eight hundred thousand fighting men, who assuredly wanted neither natural courage nor public spirit, would have been able to protect their own hearths and altars against an invader. An invader came, bringing with him an army small and exhausted by a march over the snows of the Alps, but familiar with battles and sieges. At the head of this army he traversed the peninsula to and fro, gained a succession of victories against immense numerical odds, slaughtered the hardy youth of Latium like sheep, by tens of thousands, encamped under the walls of Rome, continued during sixteen years to maintain himself in a hostile country, and was never dislodged till he had by a cruel discipline gradually taught his adversaries how to resist him.

It was idle to repeat the names of great battles won, in the middle ages, by men who did not make war their chief calling ; those battles proved only that one militia might beat another, and not that a militia could beat a regular army. As idle was it to declaim about the camp at Tilbury. We had indeed reason to be proud of the spirit which all classes of Englishmen, gentlemen and yeomen, peasants and burgesses, had so signally displayed in the great crisis of 1588. But we had also reason to be thankful that, with all their spirit, they were not brought face to face with the Spanish battalions. Somers related an anecdote, well worthy to be remembered, which had been preserved by tradition in the noble house of De Vere. One of the most illustrious men of that house, a captain who had acquired much experience and much fame in the Netherlands, had, in the crisis of peril, been summoned back to England by Elizabeth, and rode with her through the endless ranks of shouting pikemen. She asked him what he thought of the army. " It is," he said, " a brave army." There was something in his tone or manner which showed that he meant more than his words expressed. The Queen insisted on his speaking out. " Madam," he said, " Your Grace's army is

---

captains, which gave the decisive blow to the Lacedæmonian power. It is to be observed that there was no degeneracy among the Lacedæmonians. Even down to the time of Pyrrhus they seem to have been in all military qualities equal to their ancestors who conquered at Platæa. But their ancestors at Platæa had not such enemies to encounter.

brave indeed. I have not in the world the name of a coward; and yet I am the greatest coward here. All these fine fellows are praying that the enemy may land, and that there may be a battle; and I, who know that enemy well, cannot think of such a battle without dismay." De Vere was doubtless in the right. The Duke of Parma, indeed, would not have subjected our country; but it is by no means improbable that, if he had effected a landing, the island would have been the theatre of a war greatly resembling that which Hannibal waged in Italy, and that the invaders would not have been driven out till many cities had been sacked, till many counties had been wasted, and till multitudes of our stout-hearted rustics and artisans had perished in the carnage of days not less terrible than those of Thrasymene and Cannæ.

While the pamphlets of Trenchard and Somers were in every hand, the Parliament met.

The words with which the King opened the session brought the great question to a speedy issue. "The circumstances," he said, "of affairs abroad are such, that I think myself obliged to tell you my opinion, that, for the present, England cannot be safe without a land force; and I hope we shall not give those that mean us ill the opportunity of effecting that under the notion of a peace which they could not bring to pass by war."

The speech was well received; for that Parliament was thoroughly well affected to the Government. The members had, like the rest of the community, been put into high good humour by the return of peace and by the revival of trade. They were indeed still under the influence of the feelings of the preceding day; and they had still in their ears the thanksgiving sermons and thanksgiving anthems: all the bonfires had hardly burned out; and the rows of lamps and candles had hardly been taken down. Many, therefore, who did not assent to all that the King had said, joined in a loud hum of approbation when he concluded.* As soon as the Commons had retired to their own chamber, they resolved to present an address assuring His Majesty that they would stand by him in peace as firmly as they had stood by him in war. Seymour, who had, during the autumn, been going from shire to shire, for the purpose of inflaming the country gentlemen against the ministry, ventured to make some uncourtly remarks: but he gave so much offence that he was hissed down, and did not venture to demand a division.†

* L'Hermitage, Dec. $\frac{3}{13}$., $\frac{7}{17}$., 1697.
† Commons' Journals, Dec. 3. 1697. L'Hermitage, Dec. $\frac{7}{17}$.

The friends of the Government were greatly elated by the proceedings of this day. During the following week hopes were entertained that the Parliament might be induced to vote a peace establishment of thirty thousand men. But these hopes were delusive. The hum with which William's speech had been received, and the hiss which had drowned the voice of Seymour, had been misunderstood. The Commons were indeed warmly attached to the King's person and government, and quick to resent any disrespectful mention of his name. But the members who were disposed to let him have even half as many troops as he thought necessary were a minority. On the tenth of December his speech was considered in a Committee of the whole House; and Harley came forward as the chief of the opposition. He did not, like some hot headed men, among both the Whigs and the Tories, contend that there ought to be no regular soldiers. But he maintained that it was unnecessary to keep up, after the peace of Ryswick, a larger force than had been kept up after the peace of Nimeguen. He moved, therefore, that the military establishment should be reduced to what it had been in the year 1680. The Ministers found that, on this occasion, neither their honest nor their dishonest supporters could be trusted. For, in the minds of the most respectable men, the prejudice against standing armies was of too long growth and too deep root to be at once removed; and those means by which the Court might, at another time, have secured the help of venal politicians were, at that moment, of less avail than usual. The Triennial Act was beginning to produce its effects. A general election was at hand. Every member who had constituents was desirous to please them; and it was certain that no member would please his constituents by voting for a standing army: and the resolution moved by Harvey was strongly supported by Howe, was carried, was reported to the House on the following day, and, after a debate in which several orators made a great display of their knowledge of ancient and modern history, was confirmed by one hundred and eighty-five votes to one hundred and forty-eight.*

In this debate the fear and hatred with which many of the best friends of the Government regarded Sunderland were unequivocally manifested. "It is easy," such was the language of several members, "it is easy to guess by whom that unhappy sentence was inserted in the speech from the Throne. No person well acquainted with the disastrous and disgraceful

* L'Hermitage, Dec. $\frac{1}{8}\frac{0}{5}$., Dec. $\frac{1}{2}\frac{4}{4}$., Journals.

history of the last two reigns can doubt who the minister is, who is now whispering evil counsel in the ear of a third master.' The Chamberlain, thus fiercely attacked, was very feebly defended. There was indeed in the House of Commons a small knot of his creatures; and they were men not destitute of a certain kind of ability; but their moral character was as bad as his. One of them was the late Secretary of the Treasury, Guy, who had been turned out of his place for corruption. Another was the late Speaker, Trevor, who had, from the chair, put the question whether he was or was not a rogue, and had been forced to pronounce that the Ayes had it. A third was Charles Duncombe, long the greatest goldsmith of Lombard Street, and now one of the greatest landowners of the North Riding of Yorkshire. Possessed of a private fortune equal to that of any duke, he had not thought it beneath him to accept the place of Cashier of the Excise, and had perfectly understood how to make that place lucrative: but he had recently been ejected from office by Montague, who thought, with good reason, that he was not a man to be trusted. Such advocates as Trevor, Guy and Duncombe could do little for Sunderland in debate. The statesmen of the Junto would do nothing for him. They had undoubtedly owed much to him. His influence, cooperating with their own great abilities and with the force of circumstances, had induced the King to commit the direction of the internal administration of the realm to a Whig Cabinet. But the distrust which the old traitor and apostate inspired was not to be overcome. The ministers could not be sure that he was not, while smiling on them, whispering in confidential tones to them, pouring out, as it might seem, all his heart to them, really calumniating them in the closet or suggesting to the opposition some ingenious mode of attacking them. They had very recently been thwarted by him. They were bent on making Wharton a Secretary of State, and had therefore looked forward with impatience to the retirement of Trumball, who was indeed hardly equal to the duties of his great place. To their surprise and mortification they learned, on the eve of the meeting of Parliament, that Trumball had suddenly resigned, and Vernon, the Under Secretary, had been summoned to Kensington, and had returned thence with the seals. Vernon was a zealous Whig, and not personally unacceptable to the chiefs of his party. But the Lord Chancellor, the First Lord of the Treasury, and the First Lord of the Admiralty, might not unnaturally think it strange that a post of the highest importance should have been filled up in opposition to their known wishes, and with a haste and a secrecy which plainly showed that the King did not wish to be annoyed by their remonstrances. The Lord Chamberlain pretended that he had done all in his power to serve Wharton. But the Whig chiefs were not men to be duped by the professions of so notorious a liar. Montague bitterly described him as a fireship, dangerous at best, but on the whole most dangerous as a consort, and least dangerous when showing hostile colours. Smith, who was the most efficient of Montague's lieutenants, both in the Treasury and in the Parliament, cordially sympathised with his leader. Sunderland was therefore left undefended. His enemies became bolder and more vehement every day. Sir Thomas Dyke, member for Grinstead, and Lord Norris, son of the Earl of Abingdon, talked of moving an address requesting the King to banish for ever from the Court and the Council that evil adviser who had misled His Majesty's royal uncles, had betrayed the liberties of the people, and had abjured the Protestant religion.

Sunderland had been uneasy from the first moment at which his name had been mentioned in the House of Commons. He was now in an agony of terror. The whole enigma of his life, an enigma of which many unsatisfactory and some absurd explanations have been propounded, is at once solved if we consider him as a man insatiably greedy of wealth and power, and yet nervously apprehensive of danger. He rushed with ravenous eagerness at every bait which was offered to his cupidity. But any ominous shadow, any threatening murmur, sufficed to stop him in his full career, and to make him change his course or bury himself in a hiding place. He ought to have thought himself fortunate indeed, when, after all the crimes which he had committed, he found himself again enjoying his picture gallery and his woods at Althorpe, sitting in the House of Lords, admitted to the royal closet, pensioned from the Privy Purse, consulted about the most important affairs of state. But his ambition and avarice would not suffer him to rest till he held a high and lucrative office, till he was a regent of the kingdom. The consequence was, as might have been expected, a violent clamour ; and that clamour he had not the spirit to face.

His friends assured him that the threatened address would not be carried. Perhaps a hundred and sixty members might vote for it ; but hardly more. "A hundred and sixty !" he cried : "No minister can stand against a hundred and sixty. I am sure that I will not try." It must be remembered that a hundred and sixty votes in a House of five hundred and thirteen members would correspond to more than two hundred votes in the present House of Commons; a very formidable minority on the unfavourable side of a question deeply affecting the personal character of a public man.    William, unwilling to part with a servant whom he knew to be unprincipled, but whom he did not consider as more unprincipled than many other English politicians, and in whom he had found much of a very useful sort of knowledge, and of a very useful sort of ability, tried to induce the ministry to come to the rescue.    It was particularly important to soothe Wharton, who had been exasperated by his recent disappointment, and had probably exasperated the other members of the Junto.    He was sent for to the palace.    The King himself intreated him to be reconciled to the Lord Chamberlain, and to prevail on the Whig leaders in the Lower House to oppose any motion which Dyke or Norris might make.    Wharton answered in a manner which made it clear that from him no help was to be expected.    Sunderland's terrors now became insupportable.    He had requested some of his friends to come to his house that he might consult them; they came at the appointed hour, but found that he had gone to Kensington, and had left word that he should soon be back.    When he joined them, they observed that he had not the gold key which is the badge of the Lord Chamberlain, and asked where it was.    "At Kensington," answered Sunderland. They found that he had tendered his resignation, and that it had been, after a long struggle, accepted.    They blamed his haste, and told him that, since he had summoned them to advise him on that day, he might at least have waited till the morrow.    "To morrow," he exclaimed, "would have ruined me.    To night has saved me."

Meanwhile, both the disciples of Somers and the disciples of Trenchard were grumbling at Harley's resolution.    The disciples of Somers maintained that, if it was right to have an army at all, it must be right to have an efficient army.    The disciples of Trenchard complained that a great principle had been shamefully given up.    On the vital issue, Standing Army or no Standing Army, the Commons had pronounced an erroneous, a fatal decision.    Whether that army should consist of five regiments or of fifteen was hardly worth debating. The great dyke which kept out arbitrary power had been broken.    It was idle to say that the breach was narrow; for it would soon be widened by the flood which would rush in. The war of pamphlets raged more fiercely than ever.    At the same time alarming symptoms began to appear among the men

of the sword.    They saw themselves every day described in print
as the scum of society, as mortal enemies of the liberties of
their country.    Was it reasonable,—such was the language of
some scribblers,—that an honest gentleman should pay a
heavy land tax, in order to support in idleness and luxury a
set of fellows who requited him by seducing his dairy maids
and shooting his partridges?    Nor was it only in Grub Street
tracts that such reflections were to be found.    It was known
all over the town that uncivil things had been said of the
military profession in the House of Commons, and that Jack
Howe, in particular, had, on this subject, given the rein to his
wit and to his ill nature.    Some rough and daring veterans,
marked with the scars of Steinkirk and singed with the smoke
of Namur, threatened vengeance for these insults.    The
writers and speakers who had taken the greatest liberties went
in constant fear of being accosted by fierce-looking captains,
and required to make an immediate choice between fighting
and being caned.    One gentleman, who had made himself
conspicuous by the severity of his language, went about with
pistols in his pockets.    Howe, whose courage was not propor-
tionate to his malignity and petulance, was so much frightened,
that he retired into the country.    The King, well aware that
a single blow given, at that critical conjuncture, by a soldier
to a member of Parliament might produce disastrous consequences, ordered the officers of the army to their quarters,
and, by the vigorous exertion of his authority and influence,
succeeded in preventing all outrage.*

All this time the feeling in favour of a regular force seemed
to be growing in the House of Commons.    The resignation of
Sunderland had put many honest gentlemen in good humour.
The Whig leaders exerted themselves to rally their followers,
held meetings at the "Rose," and represented strongly the
dangers to which the country would be exposed, if defended
only by a militia.    The opposition asserted that neither bribes

* In the first act of Farquhar's Trip to the Jubilee, the passions which
about his time agitated society are exhibited with much spirit.    Alderman
Smuggler sees Colonel Standard, and exclaims, "There's another plague
of the nation, a red coat and feather."    "I'm disbanded," says the
Colonel.    "This very morning, in Hyde Park, my brave regiment, a
thousand men that looked like lions yesterday, were scattered and looked
as poor and simple as the herd of deer that grazed beside them."    "Fal
al deral!" cries the Alderman: "I'll have a bonfire this night, as high as
the monument."    "A bonfire!" answered the soldier; "thou dry,
withered, ill nature! had not those brave fellows' swords defended you,
your house had been a bonfire ere this about your ears."

nor promises were spared. The ministers at length flattered themselves that Harley's resolution might be rescinded. On the eighth of January they again tried their strength, and were again defeated, though by a smaller majority than before. A hundred and sixty-four members divided with them. A hundred and eighty-eight were for adhering to the vote of the eleventh of December. It was remarked that on this occasion the naval men, with Rooke at their head, voted against the Government.*

It was necessary to yield. All that remained was to put on the words of the resolution of the eleventh of December the most favourable sense that they could be made to bear. They did indeed admit of very different interpretations. The force which was actually in England in 1680 hardly amounted to five thousand men. But the garrison of Tangier and the regiments in the pay of the Batavian federation, which, as they were available for the defence of England against a foreign or domestic enemy, might be said to be in some sort part of the English army, amounted to at least five thousand more. The construction which the ministers put on the resolution of the eleventh of December was, that the army was to consist of ten thousand men; and in this construction the House acquiesced. It was not held to be necessary that the Parliament should, as in our time, fix the amount of the land force. The Commons thought that they sufficiently limited the number of soldiers by limiting the sum which was to be expended in maintaining soldiers. What that sum should be was a question which raised much debate. Harley was unwilling to give more than three hundred thousand pounds. Montague struggled for four hundred thousand. The general sense of the House was that Harley offered too little, and that Montague demanded too much. At last, on the fourteenth of January, a vote was taken for three hundred and fifty thousand pounds. Four days later the House resolved to grant half-pay to the disbanded officers till they should be otherwise provided for. The half-pay was meant to be a retainer as well as a reward. The effect of this important vote therefore was that, whenever a new war should break out, the nation would be able to command the services of many gentlemen of great military experience. The ministry afterwards succeeded in obtaining, much against the will of a portion of the opposition, a separate vote for three thousand marines.

A Mutiny Act, which had been passed in 1697, expired in the

* L'Hermitage, January ¹¹⁄₂₁.

spring of 1698. As yet no such Act had been passed except in time of war; and the temper of the Parliament and of the nation was such that the ministers did not venture to ask, in time of peace, for a renewal of powers unknown to the constitution. For the present, therefore, the soldier was again, as in the times which preceded the Revolution, subject to exactly the same law which governed the citizen.

It was only in matters relating to the army that the government found the Commons unmanageable. Liberal provision was made for the navy. The number of seamen was fixed at ten thousand, a great force, according to the notions of that age, for a time of peace. The funds assigned some years before for the support of the civil list had fallen short of the estimate. It was resolved that a new arrangement should be made, and that a certain income should be settled on the King. The amount was fixed, by an unanimous vote, at seven hundred thousand pounds; and the Commons declared that, by making this ample provision for his comfort and dignity, they meant to express their sense of the great things which he had done for the country. It is probable, however, that so large a sum would not have been given without debates and divisions, had it not been understood that he meant to take on himself the charge of the Duke of Gloucester's establishment, and that he would in all probability have to pay fifty thousand pounds a year to Mary of Modena. The Tories were unwilling to disoblige the Princess of Denmark; and the Jacobites abstained from offering any opposition to a grant in the benefit of which they hoped that the banished family would participate.

It was not merely by pecuniary liberality that the Parliament testified attachment to the Sovereign. A bill was rapidly passed which withheld the benefit of the Habeas Corpus Act, during twelve months more, from Bernardi and some other conspirators who had been concerned in the Assassination Plot, but whose guilt, though demonstrated to the conviction of every reasonable man, could not be proved by two witnesses. At the same time new securities were provided against a new danger which threatened the government. The peace had put an end to the apprehension that the throne of William might be subverted by foreign arms, but had, at the same time, facilitated domestic treason. It was no longer necessary for an agent from Saint Germains to cross the sea in a fishing boat, under the constant dread of being intercepted by a cruiser. It was no longer necessary for him to land on a desolate beach, to lodge in a thatched hovel, to dress himself like a carter, or to travel up to town on foot. He came openly by the Calais packet, walked into the best inn at Dover, and ordered post-horses for London. Meanwhile young Englishmen of quality and fortune were hastening in crowds to Paris. They would naturally wish to see him who had once been their king; and this curiosity, though in itself innocent, might have evil consequences. Artful tempters would doubtless be on the watch for every such traveller; and many such travellers might be well pleased to be courteously accosted, in a foreign land, by Englishmen of honourable name, distinguished appearance, and insinuating address. It was not to be expected that a lad fresh from the university would be able to refute all the sophisms and calumnies which might be breathed in his ear by dexterous and experienced seducers. Nor would it be strange if he should, in no long time, accept an invitation to a private audience at Saint Germains, should be charmed by the graces of Mary of Modena, should find something engaging in the childish innocence of the Prince of Wales, should kiss the hand of James, and should return home an ardent Jacobite. An Act was therefore passed forbidding English subjects to hold any intercourse orally, or by writing, or by message, with the exiled family. A day was fixed after which no English subject, who had, during the late war, gone into France without the royal permission or borne arms against his country was to be permitted to reside in this kingdom, except under a special license from the King. Whoever infringed these rules incurred the penalties of high treason.

The dismay was at first great among the malecontents. For English and Irish Jacobites, who had served under the standards of Lewis or hung about the Court of Saint Germains, had, since the peace, come over in multitudes to England. It was computed that thousands were within the scope of the new Act. But the severity of that Act was mitigated by a benefi-cent administration. Some fierce and stubborn non-jurors who would not debase themselves by asking for any indulgence, and some conspicuous enemies of the government who had asked for indulgence in vain, were under the necessity of taking refuge on the Continent. But the great majority of those offenders who promised to live peaceably under William's rule obtained his permission to remain in their native land.

In the case of one great offender there were some circum-stances which attracted general interest, and which might furnish a good subject to a novelist or a dramatist. Near fourteen years before this time, Sunderland, then Secretary of State to Charles the Second, had married his daughter Lady Elizabeth Spencer to Donough Macarthy, Earl of Clancarty, the lord of an immense domain in Munster. Both the bridegroom and the bride were mere children, the bridegroom only fifteen, the bride only eleven. After the ceremony they were separated; and many years full of strange vicissitudes elapsed before they again met. The boy soon visited his estates in Ireland. He had been bred a member of the Church of England; but his opinions and his practice were loose. He found himself among kinsmen who were zealous Roman Catholics. A Roman Catholic king was on the throne. To turn Roman Catholic was the best recommendation to favour both at Whitehall and at Dublin Castle. Clancarty speedily changed his religion, and from a dissolute Protestant became a dissolute Papist. After the Revolution he followed the fortunes of James; sate in the Celtic Parliament which met at the King's Inns; commanded a regiment in the Celtic army; was forced to surrender himself to Marlborough at Cork; was sent to England, and was imprisoned in the Tower. The Clancarty estates, which were supposed to yield a rent of not much less than ten thousand a year, were confiscated. They were charged with an annuity to the Earl's brother, and with another annuity to his wife: but the greater part was bestowed by the King on Lord Woodstock, the eldest son of Portland. During some time, the prisoner's life was not safe. For the popular voice accused him of outrages for which the utmost license of civil war would not furnish a plea. It is said that he was threatened with an appeal of murder by the widow of a Protestant clergyman who had been put to death during the troubles. After passing three years in confinement, Clancarty made his escape to the Continent, was graciously received at St. Germains, and was entrusted with the command of a corps of Irish refugees. When the treaty of Ryswick had put an end to the hope that the banished dynasty would be restored by foreign arms, he flattered himself that he might be able to make his peace with the English Government. But he was grievously disappointed. The interest of his wife's family was undoubtedly more than sufficient to obtain a pardon for him. But on that interest he could not reckon. The selfish, base, covetous, father-in-law was not at all desirous to have a highborn beggar and the posterity of a highborn beggar to maintain. The ruling passion of the brother-in-law was a stern and acrimonious party spirit. He could not bear to think that he was so nearly connected with an enemy of the Revolution and of the Bill of Rights, and would with pleasure have seen the odious tie severed even by the hand of the executioner. There was one, however, from whom the ruined, expatriated, proscribed young nobleman might hope to find a kind reception. He stole across the Channel in disguise, presented himself at Sunderland's door, and requested to see Lady Clancarty. He was charged, he said, with a message to her from her mother, who was then lying on a sick bed at Windsor. By this fiction he obtained admission, made himself known to his wife, whose thoughts had probably been constantly fixed on him during many years, and prevailed on her to give him the most tender proofs of an affection sanctioned by the laws both of God and of man. The secret was soon discovered and betrayed by a waiting woman. Spencer learned that very night that his sister had admitted her husband to her apartment. The fanatical young Whig, burning with animosity which he mistook for virtue, and eager to emulate the Corinthian who assassinated his brother, and the Roman who passed sentence of death on his son, flew to Vernon's office, gave information that the Irish rebel, who had once already escaped from custody, was in hiding hard by, and procured a warrant and a guard of soldiers. Clancarty was found in the arms of his wife, and dragged to the Tower. She followed him and implored permission to partake his cell. These events produced a great stir throughout the society of London. Sunderland professed everywhere that he heartily approved of his son's conduct : but the public had made up its mind about Sunderland's veracity, and paid very little attention to his professions on this or on any other subject. In general, honourable men of both parties, whatever might be their opinion of Clancarty, felt great compassion for his mother who was dying of a broken heart, and his poor young wife who was begging piteously to be admitted within the Traitor's Gate. Devonshire and Bedford joined with Ormond to ask for mercy. The aid of a still more powerful intercessor was called in. Lady Russell was esteemed by the King as a valuable friend : she was venerated by the nation generally as a saint, the widow of a martyr : and, when she deigned to solicit favours, it was scarcely possible that she should solicit in vain. She naturally felt a strong sympathy for the unhappy couple, who were parted by the walls of that gloomy old fortress in which she had herself exchanged the last sad endearments with one whose image was never absent from her. She took Lady Clancarty with her to the palace, obtained access to William, and put a petition into his hand. Clancarty was pardoned on condition that he should leave the kingdom and never return to it. A pension was granted to him, small when compared with the magnificent inheritance which he had forfeited, but quite sufficent to enable him to live like a gentleman on the Continent. He retired, accompanied by his Elizabeth, to Altona.

All this time the ways and means for the year were under consideration. The Parliament was able to grant some relief to the country. The land tax was reduced from four shillings in the pound to three. But nine expensive campaigns had left a heavy arrear behind them; and it was plain that the public burdens must, even in the time of peace, be such as, before the Revolution, would have been thought more than sufficient to support a vigorous war. A country gentleman was in no very good humour, when he compared the sums which were now exacted from him with those which he had been in the habit of paying under the last two kings; his discontent became stronger when he compared his own situation with that of courtiers, and above all of Dutch courtiers, who had been enriched by grants of Crown property; and both interest and envy made him willing to listen to politicians who assured him that, if those grants were resumed, he might be relieved from another shilling.

The arguments against such a resumption were not likely to be heard with favour by a popular assembly composed of taxpayers, but to statesmen and legislators will seem unanswerable.

There can be no doubt that the Sovereign was, by the old polity of the realm, competent to give or let the domains of the Crown in such manner as seemed good to him. No statute defined the length of the term which he might grant, or the amount of the rent which he must reserve. He might part with the fee simple of a forest extending over a hundred square miles in consideration of a tribute of a brace of hawks to be delivered annually to his falconer, or of a napkin of fine linen to be laid on the royal table at the coronation banquet. In fact, there had been hardly a reign since the Conquest, in which great estates had not been bestowed by our princes on favoured subjects. Anciently, indeed, what had been lavishly given was not seldom violently taken away. Several laws for the resumption of Crown lands were passed by the Parliaments of the fourteenth and fifteenth centuries. Of those laws the last was that which, in the year 1485, immediately after the battle of Bosworth, annulled the donations of the kings of the House of York. More than two hundred years had since elapsed without any Resumption Act. An estate derived from the royal liberality had long been universally thought as secure as an estate which had descended from father to son since the compilation of Domesday Book. No title was considered as more perfect than that of the Russells to Woburn, given by Henry the Eighth to the first Earl of Bedford, or than that of the Cecils to Hatfield, purchased from the Crown for less than a third of the real value by the first Earl of Salisbury. The Long Parliament did not, even in that celebrated instrument of nineteen articles, which was framed expressly for the purpose of making the King a mere Doge, propose to restrain him from dealing according to his pleasure with his parks and his castles, his fisheries and his mines. After the Restoration, under the government of an easy prince, who had indeed little disposition to give, but who could not bear to refuse, many noble private fortunes were carved out of the property of the Crown. Some of the persons who were thus enriched, Albemarle, for example, Sandwich and Clarendon, might be thought to have fairly earned their master's favour by their services. Others had merely amused his leisure or pandered to his vices. His mistresses were munificently rewarded. Estates sufficient to support the highest rank in the peerage were distributed among his illegitimate children. That these grants, however prodigal, were strictly legal, was tacitly admitted by the Estates of the Realm, when, in 1689, they recounted and condemned the unconstitutional acts of the kings of the House of Stuart. Neither in the Declaration of Right nor in the Bill of Rights is there a word on the subject. William, therefore, thought himself at liberty to give away his hereditary domains as freely as his predecessors had given away their's. There was much murmuring at the profusion with which he rewarded his Dutch favourites; and we have seen that, on one occasion in the year 1696, the House of Commons interfered for the purpose of restraining his liberality. An address was presented requesting him not to grant to Portland an extensive territory in North Wales. But it is to be observed that, though in this address a strong opinion was expressed that the grant would be mischievous, the Commons did not deny, and must therefore be considered as having admitted, that it would be perfectly legal. The King, however, yielded; and Portland was forced to content himself with ten or twelve manors scattered over various counties from Cumberland to Sussex.

It seems, therefore, clear that our princes were, by the law of the land, competent to do what they would with their hereditary estates. It is perfectly true that the law was defective, and that the profusion with which mansions, abbeys, chaces, warrens, beds of ore, whole streets, whole market towns, had been bestowed on courtiers was greatly to be lamented. Nothing could have been more proper than to pass a prospective statute tying up in strict entail the little which still remained of the Crown property. But to annul by a retrospective statute patents, which in Westminster Hall were held to be legally valid, would have been simply robbery. Such robbery must necessarily have made all property insecure ; and a statesman must be short-sighted indeed who imagines that what makes property insecure can really make society prosperous.

But it is vain to expect that men who are inflamed by anger, who are suffering distress, and who fancy that it is in their power to obtain immediate relief from their distresses at the expense of those who have excited their anger, will reason as calmly as the historian who, biassed neither by interest nor passion, reviews the events of a past age. The public burdens were heavy. To whatever extent the grants of royal domains were revoked, those burdens would be lightened. Some of the recent grants had undoubtedly been profuse. Some of the living grantees were unpopular. A cry was raised which soon became formidably loud. All the Tories, all the malecontent Whigs, and multitudes who, without being either Tories or malecontent Whigs, disliked taxes and disliked Dutchmen, called for a resumption of all the Crown property which King William had, as it was phrased, been deceived into giving away.

On the seventh of February 1698, this subject, destined to irritate the public mind at intervals during many years, was brought under the consideration of the House of Commons. The opposition asked leave to bring in a bill vacating all grants of Crown property which had been made since the Revolution. The ministers were in a great strait : the public feeling was strong ; a general election was approaching ; it was dangerous and it would probably be vain to encounter the prevailing sentiment directly. But the shock which could not be resisted might be eluded. The ministry accordingly professed to find no fault with the proposed bill, except that it did not go far enough, and moved for leave to bring in two more bills, one for annulling the grants of James the Second, the other for annulling the grants of Charles the Second. The Tories were caught in their own snare. For most of the grants of Charles and James had been made to Tories; and a resumption of those grants would have reduced some of the chiefs of the Tory party to poverty. Yet it was impossible to draw a distinction between the grants of William and those of his two predecessors. Nobody could pretend that the law had been altered since his accession. If, therefore, the grants of the Stuarts were legal, so were his: if his grants were illegal, so were the grants of his uncles. And, if both his grants and the grants of his uncles were illegal, it was absurd to say that the mere lapse of time made a difference. For not only was it part of the alphabet of the law that there was no prescription against the Crown, but the thirty-eight years which had elapsed since the Restoration would not have sufficed to bar a writ of right brought by a private demandant against a wrongful tenant. Nor could it be pretended that William had bestowed his favours less judiciously than Charles and James. Those who were least friendly to the Dutch would hardly venture to say that Portland, Zulestein and Ginkell was less deserving of the royal bounty than the Duchess of Cleveland and the Duchess of Portsmouth, than the progeny of Nell Gwynn, than the apostate Arlington or the butcher Jeffreys. The opposition, therefore, sullenly assented to what the ministry proposed. From that moment the scheme was doomed. Everybody affected to be for it; and everybody was really against it. The three bills were brought in together, read a second time together, ordered to be committed together, and were then, first mutilated, and at length quietly dropped.

In the history of the financial legislation of this session, there were some episodes which deserve to be related. Those members, a numerous body, who envied and dreaded Montague readily became the unconscious tools of the cunning malice of Sunderland, whom Montague had refused to defend in Parliament, and who, though detested by the opposition, contrived to exercise some influence over that party through the instrumentality of Charles Duncombe. Duncombe indeed had his own reasons for hating Montague, who had turned him out of the place of Cashier of the Excise. A serious charge was brought against the Board of Treasury, and especially against its chief. He was the inventor of Exchequer Bills; and they were popularly called Montague's notes. He had induced the Parliament to enact that those bills, even when at a discount in the market, should be received at par by the collectors of the revenue. This enactment, if honestly carried into effect, would have been unobjectionable. But it was strongly rumoured that there had been foul play, peculation, even forgery. Duncombe threw the most serious imputations on the Board of Treasury, and pretended that he had been put out of his office only because he was too shrewd to be deceived, and too honest to join in deceiving the public. Tories and malecontent Whigs, elated by the hope that Montague might be convicted of malversation, eagerly called for inquiry. An inquiry was instituted; but the result not only disappointed but utterly confounded the accusers. The persecuted minister obtained both a complete acquittal, and a signal revenge. Circumstances were discovered which seemed to indicate that Duncombe himself was not blameless. The clue was followed: he was severely cross-examined; he lost his head; made one unguarded admission after another, and was at length compelled to confess, on the floor of the House, that he had been guilty of an infamous fraud, which, but for his own confession, it would have been scarcely possible to bring home to him. He had been ordered by the Commissioners of the Excise to pay ten thousand pounds into the Exchequer for the public service. He had in his hands, as cashier, more than double that sum in good milled silver. With some of this money he bought Exchequer Bills which were then at a considerable discount: he paid those bills in; and he pocketed the discount, which amounted to about four hundred pounds. Nor was this all. In order to make it appear that the depreciated paper, which he had fraudulently substituted for silver, had been received by him in payment of taxes, he had employed a knavish Jew to forge endorsements of names, some real and some imaginary. This scandalous story, wrung out of his own lips, was heard by the opposition with consternation and shame, by the ministers and their friends with vindictive exultation. It was resolved, without any division, that he should be sent to the Tower, that he should be kept close prisoner there, that he should be expelled from the House. Whether any further punishment could be inflicted on him was a perplexing question. The English law touching forgery became, at a later period, barbarously severe; but, in 1698, it was absurdly lax. The prisoner's offence was certainly not a felony; and lawyers apprehended that there would be much difficulty in convicting him even of a misdemeanour. But a recent precedent was fresh in the minds of all men. The weapon which had reached Fenwick might reach Duncombe. A bill of pains and penalties was brought in, and carried through the earlier stages with less opposition than might have been expected. Some Noes might perhaps be uttered; but no members ventured to say that the Noes had it. The Tories were mad with shame and mortification, at finding that their rash attempt to ruin an enemy had produced no effect except the ruin of a friend. In their rage, they eagerly caught at a new hope of revenge, a hope destined to end, as their former hope had ended, in discomfiture and disgrace. They learned, from the agents of Sunderland, as many people suspected, but certainly from informants who were well acquainted with the offices about Whitehall, that some securities forfeited to the Crown in Ireland had been bestowed by the King ostensibly on one Thomas Railton, but really on the Chancellor of the Exchequer. The value of these securities was about ten thousand pounds. On the sixteenth of February this transaction was brought without any notice under the consideration of the House of Commons by Colonel Granville, a Tory member, nearly related to the Earl of Bath. Montague was taken completely by surprise, but manfully avowed the whole truth, and defended what he had done. The orators of the opposition declaimed against him with great animation and asperity. "This gentleman," they said, "has at once violated three distinct duties. He is a privy councillor, and, as such, is bound to advise the Crown with a view, not to his own selfish interests, but to the general good. He is the first minister of finance, and is, as such, bound to be a thrifty manager of the royal treasure. He is a member of this House, and is, as such, bound to see that the burdens borne by his constituents are not made heavier by rapacity and prodigality. To all these trusts he has been unfaithful. The advice of the privy councillor to his master is, 'Give me money.' The first Lord of the Treasury signs a warrrant for giving himself money out of the Treasury. The member for Westminster puts into his pocket money which his constituents must be taxed to replace." The surprise was complete; the onset was formidable: but the Whig majority, after a moment of dismay and wavering, rallied firmly round their leader. Several speakers declared that they highly approved of the prudent liberality with which His Majesty had requited the services of a most able, diligent and trusty counsellor. It was miserable economy indeed to grudge a reward of a few thousands to one who had made the State richer by millions. Would that all the largesses of former kings had been as well bestowed! How those largesses had been bestowed none knew better than some of the austere patriots who harangued so loudly against the avidity of Montague. If there is, it was said, a House in England which has been gorged with undeserved riches by the prodigality of weak sovereigns, it is the House of Bath. Does it lie in the mouth of a son of that house to blame the judicious munificence of a wise and good King? Before the Granvilles complain that distinguished merit has been rewarded with ten thousand pounds, let them refund some part of the hundreds of thousands which they have pocketed without any merit at all.

The rule was, and still is, that a member against whom a charge is made must be heard in his own defence, and must then leave the House. The Opposition insisted that Montague should retire. His friends maintained that this case did not fall within the rule. Distinctions were drawn; precedents were cited; and at length the question was put, that Mr. Montague do withdraw. The Ayes were only ninety-seven; the Noes two hundred and nine. This decisive result astonished both parties. The Tories lost heart and hope. The joy of the Whigs was boundless. It was instantly moved that the Honourable Charles Montague, Esquire, Chancellor of the Exchequer, for his good services to this Government does deserve His Majesty's favour. The Opposition, completely cowed, did not venture to demand another division. Montague scornfully thanked them for the inestimable service which they had done him. But for their malice he never should have had the honour and happiness of being solemnly pronounced by the Commons of England a benefactor of his country. As to the grant which had been the subject of debate, he was perfectly ready to give it up, if his accusers would engage to follow his example.

Even after this defeat the Tories returned to the charge. They pretended that the frauds which had been committed with respect to the Exchequer Bills had been facilitated by the mismanagement of the Board of Treasury, and moved a resolution which implied a censure on that Board, and especially on its chief. This resolution was rejected by a hundred and seventy votes to eighty-eight. It was remarked that Spencer, as if anxious to show that he had taken no part in the machinations of which his father was justly or unjustly suspected, spoke in this debate with great warmth against Duncombe and for Montague.

A few days later, the bill of pains and penalties against

Duncombe passed the Commons. It provided that two thirds of his enormous property, real and personal, should be confiscated and applied to the public service. Till the third reading there was no serious opposition. Then the Tories mustered their strength. They were defeated by a hundred and thirty-eight votes to a hundred and three; and the bill was carried up to the Lords by the Marquess of Hartington, a young nobleman whom the great body of Whigs respected as one of their hereditary chiefs, as the heir of Devonshire, and as the son in law of Russell.

That Duncombe had been guilty of shameful dishonesty was acknowledged by all men of sense and honour in the party to which he belonged. He had therefore little right to expect indulgence from the party which he had unfairly and malignantly assailed. Yet it is not creditable to the Whigs that they should have been so much disgusted by his frauds, or so much irritated by his attacks, as to have been bent on punishing him in a manner inconsistent with all the principles which governments ought to hold most sacred.

Those who concurred in the proceeding against Duncombe tried to vindicate their conduct by citing as an example the proceeding against Fenwick. So dangerous is it to violate, on any pretence, those principles which the experience of ages has proved to be the safeguards of all that is most precious to a community. Twelve months had hardly elapsed since the legislature had, in very peculiar circumstances, and for very plausible reasons, taken upon itself to try and to punish a great criminal whom it was impossible to reach in the ordinary course of justice; and already the breach then made in the fences which protect the dearest rights of Englishmen was widening fast. What had last year been defended only as a rare exception seemed now to be regarded as the ordinary rule. Nay, the bill of pains and penalties which now had an easy passage through the House of Commons was infinitely more objectionable than the bill which had been so obstinately resisted at every stage in the preceding session.

The writ of attainder against Fenwick was not, as the vulgar imagined and still imagine, objectionable because it was retrospective. It is always to be remembered that retrospective legislation is bad in principle only when it affects the substantive law. Statutes creating new crimes or increasing the punishment of old crimes ought in no case to be retrospective. But statutes which merely alter the procedure, if they are in themselves good statutes, ought to be retrospective. To take

*M 37

examples from the legislation of our own time, the Act passed in 1845, for punishing the malicious destruction of works of art with whipping, was most properly made prospective only. Whatever indignation the authors of that Act might feel against the ruffian who had broken the Barberini Vase, they knew that they could not, without the most serious detriment to the commonwealth, pass a law for scourging him. On the other hand the Act which allowed the affirmation of a Quaker to be received in criminal cases allowed, and most justly and reasonably, such affirmation to be received in the case of a past as well as of a future misdemeanour or felony. If we try the Act which attainted Fenwick by these rules we shall find that almost all the numerous writers who have condemned it have condemned it on wrong grounds. It made no retrospective change in the substantive law. The crime was not new. It was high treason as defined by the Statute of Edward the Third. The punishment was not new. It was the punishment which had been inflicted on traitors of ten generations. All that was new was the procedure; and, if the new procedure had been intrinsically better than the old procedure, the new procedure might with perfect propriety have been employed. But the procedure employed in Fenwick's case was the worst possible, and would have been the worst possible if it had been established from time immemorial. However clearly political crime may have been defined by ancient laws, a man accused of it ought not to be tried by a crowd of five hundred and thirteen eager politicians, of whom he can challenge none even with cause, who have no judge to guide them, who are allowed to come in and go out as they choose, who hear as much or as little as they choose of the accusation and of the defence, who are exposed, during the investigation, to every kind of corrupting influence, who are inflamed by all the passions which animated debates naturally excite, who cheer one orator and cough down another, who are roused from sleep to cry Aye or No, or who are hurried half drunk from their suppers to divide. For this reason, and for no other, the attainder of Fenwick is to be condemned. It was unjust and of evil example, not because it was a retrospective Act, but because it was an act essentially judicial, performed by a body destitute of all judicial qualities.

The bill for punishing Duncombe was open to all the objections which can be urged against the bill for punishing Fenwick, and to other objections of even greater weight. In both cases the judicial functions were usurped by a body unfit to exercise such functions.  But the bill against Duncombe really was, what the bill against Fenwick was not, objectionable as a retrospective bill.   It altered the substantive criminal law. It visited an offence with a penalty of which the offender, at the time when he offended, had no notice.

It may be thought a strange proposition that the bill against Duncombe was a worse bill than the bill against Fenwick, because the bill against Fenwick struck at life, and the bill against Duncombe struck only at property.   Yet this apparent paradox is a sober truth.  Life is indeed more precious than property.  But the power of arbitrarily taking away the lives of men is infinitely less likely to be abused than the power of arbitrarily taking away their property.  Even the lawless classes of society generally shrink from blood.  They commit thousands of offences against property to one murder; and most of the few murders which they do commit are committed for the purpose of facilitating or concealing some offence against property.  The unwillingness of juries to find a fellow creature guilty of a capital felony even on the clearest evidence is notorious; and it may well be suspected that they frequently violate their oaths in favour of life.   In civil suits, on the other hand, they too often forget that their duty is merely to give the plaintiff a compensation for evil suffered; and, if the conduct of the defendant has moved their indignation and his fortune is known to be large, they turn themselves into a criminal tribunal, and, under the name of damages, impose a large fine. As housebreakers are more likely to take plate and jewellery than to cut throats; as juries are far more likely to err on the side of pecuniary severity in assessing damages than to send to the gibbet any man who has not richly deserved it; so a legislature, which should be so unwise as to take on itself the functions properly belonging to the Courts of Law, would be far more likely to pass Acts of Confiscation than Acts of Attainder.  We naturally feel pity even for a bad man whose head is about to fall.  But, when a bad man is compelled to disgorge his ill-gotten gains, we naturally feel a vindictive pleasure, in which there is much danger that we may be tempted to indulge too largely.

The hearts of many stout Whigs doubtless bled at the thought of what Fenwick must have suffered, the agonizing struggle, in a mind not of the firmest temper, between the fear of shame and the fear of death, the parting from a tender wife, and all the gloomy solemnity of the last morning.  But whose heart was to bleed at the thought that Charles Duncombe, who was born to carry parcels and to sweep down a counting-house, was to be punished for his knavery by having his income reduced to eight thousand a year, more than most earls then possessed?

His judges were not likely to feel compassion for him ; and they all had strong selfish reasons to vote against him. They were all in fact bribed by the very bill by which he would be punished.

His property was supposed to amount to considerably more than four hundred thousand pounds. Two thirds of that property were equivalent to about sevenpence in the pound on the rental of the kingdom as assessed to the land tax. If, therefore, two thirds of that property could have been brought into the Exchequer, the land tax for 1699, a burden most painfully felt by the class which had the chief power in England, might have been reduced from three shillings to two and fivepence. Every squire of a thousand a year in the House of Commons would have had thirty pounds more to spend ; and that sum might well have made to him the whole difference between being at ease and being pinched during twelve months. If the bill had passed, if the gentry and yeomanry of the kingdom had found that it was possible for them to obtain a welcome remission of taxation by imposing on a Shylock or an Overreach, by a retrospective law, a fine not heavier than his misconduct might, in a moral view, seem to have deserved, it is impossible to believe that they would not soon have recurred to so simple and agreeable a resource. In every age it is easy to find rich men who have done bad things for which the law has provided no punishment or an inadequate punishment. The estates of such men would soon have been considered as a fund applicable to the public service. As often as it was necessary to vote an extraordinary supply to the Crown, the Committee of Ways and Means would have looked about for some unpopular capitalist to plunder. Appetite would have grown with indulgence. Accusations would have been eagerly welcomed. Rumours and suspicions would have been received as proofs. The wealth of the great goldsmiths of the Royal Exchange would have become as insecure as that of a Jew under the Plantagenets, as that of a Christian under a Turkish Pasha. Rich men would have tried to invest their acquisitions in some form in which they could lie closely hidden and could be speedily removed. In no long time it would have been found that of all financial resources the least productive is robbery, and that the public had really paid far more dearly for Duncombe's hundreds of thousands than if it had borrowed them at fifty per cent.

These considerations had more weight with the Lords than with the Commons. Indeed one of the principal uses of the Upper House is to defend the vested rights of property in cases in which those rights are unpopular, and are attacked on grounds which to shortsighted politicians seem valid. An assembly composed of men almost all of whom have inherited opulence, and who are not under the necessity of paying court to constituent bodies, will not easily be hurried by passion or seduced by sophistry into robbery. As soon as the bill for punishing Duncombe had been read at the table of the Peers, it became clear that there would be a sharp contest. Three great Tory noblemen, Rochester, Nottingham and Leeds, headed the opposition; and they were joined by some who did not ordinarily act with them. At an early stage of the proceedings a new and perplexing question was raised. How did it appear that the facts set forth in the preamble were true, that Duncombe had committed the frauds for which it was proposed to punish him in so extraordinary a manner? In the House of Commons, he had been taken by surprise: he had made admissions of which he had not foreseen the consequences; and he had then been so much disconcerted by the severe manner in which he had been interrogated that he had at length avowed everything. But he had now had time to prepare himself: he had been furnished with advice by counsel; and, when he was placed at the bar of the Peers, he refused to criminate himself and defied his persecutors to prove him guilty. He was sent back to the Tower. The Lords acquainted the Commons with the difficulty which had arisen. A conference was held in the Painted Chamber; and there Hartington, who appeared for the Commons, declared that he was authorized, by those who had sent him, to assure the Lords that Duncombe had, in his place in Parliament, owned the misdeeds which he now challenged his accusers to being home to him. The Lords, however, rightly thought that it would be a strange and a dangerous thing to receive a declaration of the House of Commons in its collective character as conclusive evidence of the fact that a man had committed a crime. The House of Commons was under none of those restraints which were thought necessary in ordinary cases to protect innocent defendants against false witnesses. The House of Commons could not be sworn, could not be cross-examined, could not be indicted, imprisoned, pilloried, mutilated, for perjury. Indeed the testimony of the House of Commons in its collective character was of less value than the uncontradicted testimony of a single member. For it was only the testimony of the majority of the House. There might be a large respectable minority whose recollections might materially differ from the recollections of the majority. This indeed was actually the case. For there had been a dispute among those who had heard Duncombe's confession as to the precise extent of what he had confessed ; and there had been a division ; and the statement which the Upper House was expected to receive as decisive on the point of fact had been at last carried only by ninety votes to sixty-eight. It should seem therefore that, whatever moral conviction the Lords might feel of Duncombe's guilt, they were bound, as righteous judges, to absolve him.

After much animated debate, they divided ; and the bill was lost by forty-eight votes to forty-seven. It was proposed by some of the minority that proxies should be called : but this scandalous proposition was strenuously resisted ; and the House, to its great honour, resolved that on questions which were substantially judicial, though they might be in form legislative, no peer who was absent should be allowed to have a voice.

Many of the Whig Lords protested. Among them were Orford and Wharton. It is to be lamented that Burnet, and the excellent Hough, who was now Bishop of Oxford, should have been impelled by party spirit to record their dissent from a decision which all sensible and candid men will now pronounce to have been just and salutary. Somers was present ; but his name is not attached to the protest which was subscribed by his brethren of the Junto. We may therefore not unreasonably infer that, on this as on many other occasions, that wise and virtuous statesman disapproved of the violence of his friends.

In rejecting the bill, the Lords had only exercised their indisputable right. But they immediately proceeded to take a step of which the legality was not equally clear. Rochester moved that Duncombe should be set at liberty. The motion was carried : a warrant for the discharge of the prisoner was sent to the Tower, and was obeyed without hesitation by Lord Lucas, who was Lieutenant of that fortress. As soon as this was known, the anger of the Commons broke forth with violence. It was by their order that the upstart Duncombe had been put in ward. He was their prisoner ; and it was monstrous insolence in the Peers to release him. The Peers defended what they had done by arguments which must be allowed to have been ingenious, if not satisfactory. It was quite true that Duncombe had originally been committed to the Tower by the Commons. But, it was said, the Commons, by sending a penal bill against him to the Lords, did, by necessary implication, send him also to the Lords. For it was plainly impossible for the Lords to pass the bill without hearing what he had to say against it. The Commons had felt this, and had not complained when he had, without their consent, been brought from his place of confinement, and set at the bar of the Peers. From that moment he was the prisoner of the Peers. He had been taken back from the bar to the Tower, not by virtue of the Speaker's warrant, of which the force was spent, but by virtue of their order which had remanded him. They, therefore, might with perfect propriety discharge him. Whatever a jurist might have thought of these arguments, they had no effect on the Commons. Indeed, violent as the spirit of party was in those times, it was less violent than the spirit of caste. Whenever a dispute arose between the two Houses, many members of both forgot that they were Whigs or Tories, and remembered only that they were Patricians or Plebeians. On this occasion nobody was louder in asserting the privileges of the representatives of the people in opposition to the encroachments of the nobility than Harley. Duncombe was again arrested by the Serjeant at Arms, and remained in confinement till the end of the session. Some eager men were for addressing the King to turn Lucas out of office. This was not done: but during several days the ill humour of the Lower House showed itself by a studied discourtesy. One of the members was wanted as a witness in a matter which the Lords were investigating. They sent two Judges with a message requesting the permission of the Commons to examine him. At any other time the Judges would have been called in immediately, and the permission would have been granted as of course. But on this occasion the Judges were kept waiting some hours at the door; and such difficulties were made about the permission that the Peers desisted from urging a request which seemed likely to be ungraciously refused.

The attention of the Parliament was, during the remainder of the session, chiefly occupied by commercial questions. Some of those questions required so much investigation, and gave occasion to so much dispute, that the prorogation did not take place till the fifth of July. There was consequently some illness and much discontent among both Lords and Commons. For, in that age, the London season usually ended soon after the first notes of the cuckoo had been heard, and before the poles had been decked for the dances and mummeries which welcomed the genial May day of the ancient calendar. Since the year of the Revolution, a year which was an exception to all ordinary rules, the members of the two Houses had never been detained from their woods and haycocks even so late as the beginning of June.

The Commons had, soon after they met, appointed a Committee to enquire into the state of trade, and had referred to this Committee several petitions from merchants and manufacturers who complained that they were in danger of being undersold, and who asked for additional protection.

A highly curious report on the importation of silks and the exportation of wool was soon presented to the House. It was in that age believed by all but a very few speculative men that the sound commercial policy was to keep out of the country the delicate and brilliantly tinted textures of southern looms, and to keep in the country the raw material on which most of our own looms were employed. It was now fully proved that, during eight years of war, the textures which it was thought desirable to keep out had been constantly coming in, and the material which it was thought desirable to keep in had been constantly going out. This interchange, an interchange, as it was imagined, pernicious to England, had been chiefly managed by an association of Huguenot refugees, residing in London. Whole fleets of boats with illicit cargoes had been passing and repassing between Kent and Picardy. The loading and unloading had taken place sometimes in Romney Marsh, sometimes on the beach under the cliffs between Dover and Folkstone. All the inhabitants of the south eastern coast were in the plot. It was a common saying among them that, if a gallows were set up every quarter of a mile along the coast, the trade would still go on briskly. It had been discovered, some years before, that the vessels and the hiding places which were necessary to the business of the smuggler had frequently afforded accommodation to the traitor. The report contained fresh evidence upon this point. It was proved that one of the contrabandists had provided the vessel in which the ruffian O'Brien had carried Scum Goodman over to France.

The inference which ought to have been drawn from these facts was that the prohibitory system was absurd. That system had not destroyed the trade which was so much dreaded, but had merely called into existence a desperate race of men who, accustomed to earn their daily bread by the breach of an unreasonable law, soon came to regard the most reasonable laws with contempt, and, having begun by eluding the custom house officers, ended by conspiring against the throne. And, if, in time of war, when the whole Channel was dotted with our cruisers, it had been found impossible to prevent the regular exchange of the fleeces of Cotswold for the alamodes of Lyons, what chance was there that any machinery which could be employed in time of peace would be more efficacious? The politicians of the seventeenth century, however, were of opinion that sharp laws sharply administered could not fail to save Englishmen from the intolerable grievance of selling dear what could be best produced by themselves, and of buying cheap what could be best produced by others. The penalty for importing French silks was made more severe. An Act was passed which gave to a joint stock company an absolute monopoly of lustrings for a term of fourteen years. The fruit of these wise counsels was such as might have been foreseen. French silks were still imported; and, long before the term of fourteen years had expired, the funds of the Lustring Company had been spent, its offices had been shut up, and its very name had been forgotten at Jonathan's and Garraway's.

Not content with prospective legislation, the Commons unanimously determined to treat the offences which the Committee had brought to light as high crimes against the State, and to employ against a few cunning mercers in Nicholas Lane and the Old Jewry all the gorgeous and cumbrous machinery which ought to be reserved for the delinquencies of great Ministers and Judges. It was resolved, without a division, that several Frenchmen and one Englishman who had been deeply concerned in the contraband trade should be impeached. Managers were appointed: articles were drawn up: preparations were made for fitting up Westminster Hall with benches and scarlet hangings: and at one time it was thought that the trials would last till the partridge shooting began. But the defendants, having little hope of acquittal, and not wishing that the Peers should come to the business of fixing the punishment in the temper which was likely to be the effect of an August passed in London, very wisely declined to give their lordships unnecessary trouble, and pleaded guilty. The sentences were consequently lenient. The French offenders were merely fined; and their fines probably did not amount to a fifth part of the sums which they had realised by unlawful traffic. The Englishman who had been active in managing the escape of Goodman was both fined and imprisoned.

The progress of the woollen manufactures of Ireland excited even more alarm and indignation than the contraband trade with France. The French question indeed had been simply commercial. The Irish question, originally commercial, became political. It was not merely the prosperity of the clothiers of Wiltshire and of the West Riding that was at stake; but the dignity of the Crown, the authority of the Parliament, and the unity of the empire. Already might be discerned among the Englishry, who were now, by the help and under the protection of the mother country, the lords of the conquered island, some signs of a spirit, feeble indeed, as yet, and such as might easily be put down by a few resolute words, but destined to revive at long intervals, and to be stronger and more formidable at every revival.

The person who on this occasion came forward as the champion of the colonists, the forerunner of Swift and of Grattan, was William Molyneux. He would have rejected the name of Irishman as indignantly as a citizen of Marseilles or Cyrene, proud of his pure Greek blood, and fully qualified to send a chariot to the Olympic race course, would have rejected the name of Gaul or Libyan. He was, in the phrase of that time, an English gentleman of family and fortune born in Ireland. He had studied at the Temple, had travelled on the Continent, had become well known to the most eminent scholars and philosophers of Oxford and Cambridge, had been elected a member of the Royal Society of London, and had been one of the founders of the Royal Society of Dublin. In the days of Popish ascendancy he had taken refuge among his friends here: he had returned to his home when the ascendancy of his own caste had been reestablished: and he had been chosen to represent the University of Dublin in the House of Commons. He had made great efforts to promote the manufactures of the kingdom in which he resided; and he had found those efforts impeded by an Act of the English Parliament which laid severe restrictions on the exportation of woollen goods from Ireland. In principle this Act was altogether indefensible. Practically it was altogether unimportant. Prohibitions were not needed to prevent the Ireland of the seventeenth century from being a great manufacturing country; nor could the most liberal bounties have made her so. The jealousy of commerce, however, is as fanciful and unreasonable as the jealousy of love. The clothiers of Wilts and Yorkshire were weak enough to imagine that they should be ruined by the competition of a half barbarous island, an island where there was far less capital than in England, where there was far less security for life and property than in England, and where there was far less industry and energy among the labouring classes than in England. Molyneux, on the other hand, had the sanguine temperament of a projector. He imagined that, but for the tyrannical interference of strangers, a Ghent would spring up in Connemara, and a Bruges in the Bog of Allen. And what right had strangers to interfere? Not content with showing that the law of which he complained was absurd and unjust, he undertook to prove that it was null and void. Early in the year 1698 he published and dedicated to the King a treatise in which it was asserted in plain terms that the English Parliament had no authority over Ireland.

Whoever considers without passion or prejudice the great constitutional question which was thus for the first time raised will probably be of opinion that Molyneux was in error. The right of the Parliament of England to legislate for Ireland rested on the broad general principle that the paramount authority of the mother country extends over all colonies planted by her sons in all parts of the world. This principle was the subject of much discussion at the time of the American troubles, and was then maintained, without any reservation, not only by the English Ministers, but by Burke and all the adherents of Rockingham, and was admitted, with one single reservation, even by the Americans themselves. Down to the moment of separation the Congress fully acknowledged the competency of the King, Lords and Commons to make laws, of any kind but one, for Massachusetts and Virginia. The only power which such men as Washington and Franklin denied to the Imperial legislature was the power of taxing. Within living memory, Acts which have made great political and social revolutions in our Colonies have been passed in this country; nor has the validity of those Acts ever been questioned: and conspicuous among them were the law of 1807 which abolished the slave trade, and the law of 1833 which abolished slavery.

The doctrine that the parent state has supreme power over the colonies is not only borne out by authority and by precedent, but will appear, when examined, to be in entire accordance with justice and with policy. During the feeble infancy of colonies independence would be pernicious, or rather fatal, to them. Undoubtedly, as they grow stronger and stronger, it will be wise in the home government to be more and more indulgent. No sensible parent deals with a son of twenty in the same way as with a son of ten. Nor will any government not infatuated treat such a province as Canada or Victoria in the way in which it might be proper to treat a little band of emigrants who have just begun to build their huts on a barbarous shore, and to whom the protection of the flag of a great nation is indispensably necessary. Nevertheless, there cannot really be more than one supreme power in a society. If, therefore, a time comes at which the mother country finds it expedient altogether to abdicate her paramount authority over a colony, one of two courses ought to be taken. There ought to be complete incorporation, if such incorporation be possible. If not, there ought to be complete separation. Very few propositions in politics can be so perfectly demonstrated as this, that parliamentary government cannot be carried on by two really equal and independent parliaments in one empire.

And, if we admit the general rule to be that the English parliament is competent to legislate for colonies planted by English subjects, what reason was there for considering the case of the colony in Ireland as an exception? For it is to be observed that the whole question was between the mother country and the colony. The aboriginal inhabitants, more than five sixths of the population, had no more interest in the matter than the swine or the poultry; or, if they had an interest, it was for their interest that the caste which domineered over them should not be emancipated from all external control. They were no more represented in the parliament which sate at Dublin than in the parliament which sate at Westminster. They had less to dread from legislation at Westminster than from legislation at Dublin. They were, indeed, likely to obtain but a very scanty measure of justice from the English Tories, a more scanty measure still from the English Whigs: but the most acrimonious English Whig did not feel towards them that intense antipathy, compounded of hatred, fear and scorn, with which they were regarded by the Cromwellian who dwelt among them.* For the Irishry

* That a portion at least of the native population of Ireland looked to the Parliament at Westminster for protection against the tyranny of the Parliament at Dublin appears from a paper entitled The Case of the Roman Catholic Nation of Ireland. This paper, written in 1711 by one of the oppressed race and religion, is in a MS. belonging to Lord Fingall.

Molyneux, though boasting that he was the champion of liberty, though professing to have learned his political principles from Locke's writings, and though confidently expecting Locke's applause, asked nothing but a more cruel and more hopeless slavery. What he claimed was that, as respected the colony to which he belonged, England should forego rights which she has exercised and is still exercising over every other colony that she has ever planted. And what reason could be given for making such a distinction? No colony had owed so much to England. No colony stood in such need of the support of England. Twice, within the memory of men then living, the natives had attempted to throw off the alien yoke; twice the intruders had been in imminent danger of extirpation; twice England had come to the rescue, and had put down the Celtic population under the feet of her own progeny. Millions of English money had been expended in the struggle. English blood had flowed at the Boyne and at Athlone, at Aghrim and at Limerick. The graves of thousands of English soldiers had been dug in the pestilential morass of Dundalk. It was owing to the exertions and sacrifices of the English people that, from the basaltic pillars of Ulster to the lakes of Kerry, the Saxon settlers were trampling on the children of the soil. The colony in Ireland was therefore emphatically a dependency; a dependency, not merely by the common law of the realm, but by the nature of things. It was absurd to claim independence for a community which could not cease to be dependent without ceasing to exist.

Molyneux soon found that he had ventured on a perilous undertaking. A member of the English House of Commons complained in his place that a book which attacked the most precious privileges of the supreme legislature was in circulation. The volume was produced: some passages were read; and a Committee was appointed to consider the whole subject. The Committee soon reported that the obnoxious pamphlet was only one of several symptoms which indicated a spirit such as

---

The Parliament of Ireland is accused of treating the Irish worse than the Turks treat the Christians, worse than the Egyptians treated the Israelites. " Therefore," says the writer, "they (the Irish) apply themselves to the present Parliament of Great Britain as a Parliament of nice honour and stanch justice. . . . Their request then is that this great Parliament may make good the Treaty of Limerick in all the Civil Articles." In order to propitiate those to whom he makes this appeal, he accuses the Irish Parliament of encroaching on the supreme authority of the English Parliament, and charges the colonists generally with ingratitude to the mother country to which they owe so much.

ought to be suppressed. The Crown of Ireland had been most improperly described in public instruments as an imperial Crown. The Irish Lords and Commons had presumed, not only to reenact an English Act passed expressly for the purpose of binding them, but to reenact it with alterations. The alterations were indeed small : but the alteration even of a letter was tantamount to a declaration of independence. Several addresses were voted without a division. The King was entreated to discourage all encroachments of subordinate powers on the supreme authority of the English legislature, to bring to justice the pamphleteer who had dared to question that authority, to enforce the Acts which had been passed for the protection of the woollen manufactures of England, and to direct the industry and capital of Ireland into the channel of the linen trade, a trade which might grow and flourish in Leinster and Ulster without exciting the smallest jealousy at Norwich or at Halifax.

The King promised to do what the Commons asked : but in truth there was little to be done. The Irish, conscious of their impotence, submitted without a murmur. The Irish woollen manufacture languished and disappeared, as it would, in all probability, have languished and disappeared if it had been left to itself. Had Molyneux lived a few months longer he would probably have been impeached. But the close of the session was approaching : and before the Houses met again a timely death had snatched him from their vengeance ; and the moment-ous question which had been first stirred by him slept a deep sleep till it was revived in a more formidable shape, after the lapse of twenty-six years, by the fourth letter of The Drapier.

Of the commercial questions which prolonged this session far into the summer the most important respected India. Four years had elapsed since the House of Commons had decided that all Englishmen had an equal right to traffic in the Asiatic Seas, unless prohibited by Parliament ; and in that decision the King had thought it prudent to acquiesce. Any merchant of London or Bristol might now fit out a ship for Bengal or for China, without the least apprehension of being molested by the Admiralty or sued in the Courts of Westminster. No wise man, however, was disposed to stake a large sum on such a venture. For the vote which protected him from annoyance here left him exposed to serious risks on the other side of the Cape of Good Hope. The Old Company, though its exclusive privileges were no more, and though its dividends had greatly diminished, was still in existence, and still retained its castles and warehouses, its fleet of fine merchantmen, and its able and zealous factors, thoroughly qualified by a long experience to transact business both in the palaces and in the bazaars of the East, and accustomed to look for direction to the India House alone. The private trader therefore still ran great risk of being treated as a smuggler, if not as a pirate. He might indeed, if he was wronged, apply for redress to the tribunals of his country. But years must elapse before his cause could be heard; his witnesses must be conveyed over fifteen thousand miles of sea; and in the meantime he was a ruined man. The experiment of free trade with India had therefore been tried under every disadvantage, or, to speak more correctly, had not been tried at all. The general opinion had always been that some restriction was necessary; and that opinion had been confirmed by all that had happened since the old restrictions had been removed. The doors of the House of Commons were again besieged by the two great contending factions of the City. The Old Company offered, in return for a monopoly secured by law, a loan of seven hundred thousand pounds; and the whole body of Tories was for accepting the offer. But those indefatigable agitators who had, ever since the Revolution, been striving to obtain a share in the trade of the Eastern seas exerted themselves at this conjuncture more strenuously than ever, and found a powerful patron in Montague.

That dexterous and eloquent statesman had two objects in view. One was to obtain for the State, as the price of the monopoly, a sum much larger than the Old Company was able to give. The other was to promote the interest of his own party. Nowhere was the conflict between Whigs and Tories sharper than in the City of London; and the influence of the City of London was felt to the remotest corner of the realm. To elevate the Whig section of that mighty commercial aristocracy which congregated under the arches of the Royal Exchange, and to depress the Tory section, had long been one of Montague's favourite schemes. He had already formed one citadel in the heart of that great emporium; and he now thought that it might be in his power to erect and garrison a second stronghold in a position scarcely less commanding. It had often been said, in times of civil war, that whoever was master of the Tower and of Tilbury Fort was master of London. The fastnesses by means of which Montague proposed to keep the capital obedient in times of peace and of constitutional government were of a different kind. The Bank was one of his fortresses; and he trusted that a new India House would be the other.

The task which he had undertaken was not an easy one. For, while his opponents were united, his adherents were divided. Most of those who were for a New Company thought that the New Company ought, like the Old Company, to trade on a joint stock. But there were some who held that our commerce with India would be best carried on by means of what is called a regulated Company. There was a Turkey Company, the members of which contributed to a general fund, and had in return the exclusive privilege of trafficking with the Levant: but those members trafficked, each on his own account: they forestalled each other; they undersold each other: one became rich; another became bankrupt. The Corporation meanwhile watched over the common interest of all the members, furnished the Crown with the means of maintaining an embassy at Constantinople, and placed at several important ports consuls and vice-consuls, whose business was to keep the Pacha and the Cadi in good humour, and to arbitrate in disputes among Englishmen. Why might not the same system be found to answer in regions lying still further to the east? Why should not every member of the New Company be at liberty to export European commodities to the countries beyond the Cape, and to bring back shawls, saltpetre and bohea to England, while the Company, in its collective capacity, might treat with Asiatic potentates, or exact reparation from them, and might be entrusted with powers for the administration of justice and for the government of forts and factories?

Montague tried to please all those whose support was necessary to him; and this he could effect only by bringing forward a plan so intricate that it cannot without some pains be understood. He wanted two millions to extricate the State from its financial embarrassments. That sum he proposed to raise by a loan at eight per cent. The lenders might be either individuals or corporations. But they were all, individuals and corporations, to be united in a new corporation, which was to be called the General Society. Every member of the General Society, whether individual or corporation, might trade separately with India to an extent not exceeding the amount which such member had advanced to the government. But all the members or any of them might, if they so thought fit, give up the privilege of trading separately, and unite themselves under a royal Charter for the purpose of trading in common. Thus the General Society was, by its original constitution, a regulated company ; but it was provided that either the whole Society or any part of it might become a joint stock company.

The opposition to the scheme was vehement and pertinacious. The Old Company presented petition after petition. The Tories, with Seymour at their head, appealed both to the good faith and to the compassion of Parliament. Much was said about the sanctity of the existing Charter, and much about the tenderness due to the numerous families which had, in reliance on that Charter, invested their substance in India stock. On the other side there was no want of plausible topics or of skill to use them. Was it not strange that those who talked so much about the Charter should have altogether overlooked the very clause of the Charter on which the whole question turned ? That clause expressly reserved to the government power of revocation, after three years' notice, if the Charter should not appear to be beneficial to the public. The Charter had not been found beneficial to the public ; the three years' notice should be given ; and in the year 1701 the revocation would take effect. What could be fairer ? If anybody was so weak as to imagine that the privileges of the Old Company were perpetual, when the very instrument which created those privileges expressly declared them to be terminable, what right had he to blame the Parliament, which was bound to do the best for the State, for not saving him, at the expense of the State, from the natural punishment of his own folly ? It was evident that nothing was proposed inconsistent with strict justice. And what right had the Old Company to more than strict justice ? These petitioners who implored the legislature to deal indulgently with them in their adversity, how had they used their boundless prosperity ? Had not the India House recently been the very den of corruption, the tainted spot from which the plague had spread to the Court and the Council, to the House of Commons and the House of Lords ? Were the disclosures of 1695 forgotten, the eighty thousand pounds of secret service money disbursed in one year, the enormous bribes direct and indirect, Seymour's saltpetre contracts, Leeds's bags of golds ? By the malpractices which the inquiry in the Exchequer Chamber then brought to light, the Charter had been forfeited ; and it would have been well if the forfeiture had been immediately enforced. " Had not time then pressed," said Montague, " had it not been necessary that the session should close, it is probable that the petitioners, who now cry out that they cannot get justice, would have got more justice than they desired. If they had been called to account for great and real wrong in 1695, we should not have had them here complaining of imaginary wrong in 1698."

The fight was protracted by the obstinacy and dexterity of the Old Company and its friends from the first week of May to the last week in June. It seems that many even of Montague's followers doubted whether the promised two millions would be forthcoming. His enemies confidently predicted that the General Society would be as complete a failure as the Land Bank had been in the year before the last, and that he would in the autumn find himself in charge of an empty exchequer. His activity and eloquence, however, prevailed. On the twenty-sixth of June, after many laborious sittings, the question was put that this Bill do pass, and was carried by one hundred and fifteen votes to seventy-eight. In the upper House, the conflict was short and sharp. Some peers declared that, in their opinion, the subscription to the proposed loan, far from amounting to the two millions which the Chancellor of the Exchequer expected, would fall far short of one million. Others, with much reason, complained that a law of such grave importance should have been sent up to them in such a shape that they must either take the whole or throw out the whole. The privilege of the Commons with respect to money bills had of late been grossly abused. The Bank had been created by one money bill; this General Society was to be created by another money bill. Such a bill the Lords could not amend: they might indeed reject it; but to reject it was to shake the foundations of public credit and to leave the kingdom defenceless. Thus one branch of the legislature was systematically put under duress by the other, and seemed likely to be reduced to utter insignificance. It was better that the government should be once pinched for money than that the House of Peers should cease to be part of the Constitution. So strong was this feeling that the Bill was carried only by sixty-five to forty-eight. It received the royal sanction on the fifth of July. The King then spoke from the throne. This was the first occasion on which a King of England had spoken to a Parliament of which the existence was about to be terminated, not by his own act, but by the act of the law. He could not, he said, take leave of the Lords and Gentlemen before him without publicly acknowledging the great things which they had done for his dignity and for the welfare of the nation. He recounted the chief services which they had, during three eventful sessions, rendered to the country.  "These things will," he said, "give a lasting reputation to this Parliament, and will be a subject of emulation to Parliaments which shall come after."  The Houses were then prorogued.

During the week which followed there was some anxiety as to the result of the subscription for the stock of the General Society.  If that subscription failed, there would be a deficit: public credit would be shaken; and Montague would be regarded as a pretender who had owed his reputation to a mere run of good luck, and who had tempted chance once too often.  But the event was such as even his sanguine spirit had scarcely ventured to anticipate.  At one in the afternoon of the 14th of July the books were opened at the Hall of the Company of Mercers in Cheapside.  An immense crowd was already collected in the street.  As soon as the doors were flung wide, wealthy citizens, with their money in their hands, pressed in, pushing and elbowing each other.  The guineas were paid down faster than the clerks could count them. Before night six hundred thousand pounds had been subscribed.  The next day the throng was as great.  More than one capitalist put down his name for thirty thousand pounds. To the astonishment of those ill boding politicians who were constantly repeating that the war, the debt, the taxes, the grants to Dutch courtiers, had ruined the kingdom, the sum, which it had been doubted whether England would be able to raise in many weeks, was subscribed by London in a few hours.  The applications from the provincial towns and rural districts came too late.  The merchants of Bristol had intended to take three hundred thousand pounds of the stock, but had waited to learn how the subscription went on before they gave their final orders; and, by the time that the mail had gone down to Bristol and returned, there was no more stock to be had.

This was the moment at which the fortunes of Montague reached the meridian.  The decline was close at hand.  His ability and his constant success were everywhere talked of with admiration and envy.  That man, it was commonly said, has never wanted, and never will want, an expedient.

During the long and busy session which had just closed, some interesting and important events had taken place which may properly be mentioned here.  One of those events was the destruction of the most celebrated palace in which the sovereigns of England have ever dwelt. On the evening of the 4th of January, a woman,—the patriotic journalists and pamphleteers of that time did not fail to note that she was a Dutchwoman,—who was employed as a laundress at Whitehall, lighted a charcoal fire in her room and placed some linen round it. The linen caught fire and burned furiously. The tapestry, the bedding, the wainscots were soon in a blaze. The unhappy woman who had done the mischief perished. Soon the flames burst out of the windows. All Westminster, all the Strand, all the river were in commotion. Before midnight the King's apartments, the Queen's apartments, the Wardrobe, the Treasury, the office of the Privy Council, the office of the Secretary of State, had been destroyed. The two chapels perished together: that ancient chapel where Wolsey had heard mass in the midst of gorgeous copes, golden candlesticks, and jewelled crosses, and that modern edifice which had been erected for the devotions of James and had been embellished by the pencil of Verrio and the chisel of Gibbons. Meanwhile a great extent of building had been blown up; and it was hoped that by this expedient a stop had been put to the conflagration. But early in the morning a new fire broke out of the heaps of combustible matter which the gunpowder had scattered to right and left. The guard room was consumed. No trace was left of that celebrated gallery which had witnessed so many balls and pageants, in which so many maids of honour had listened too easily to the vows and flatteries of gallants, and in which so many bags of gold had changed masters at the hazard table. During some time men despaired of the Banqueting House. The flames broke in on the south of that beautiful hall, and were with great difficulty extinguished by the exertions of the guards, to whom Cutts, mindful of his honourable nickname of the Salamander, set as good an example on this night of terror as he had set in the breach of Namur. Many lives were lost, and many grievous wounds were inflicted by the falling masses of stone and timber, before the fire was effectually subdued. When day broke, the heaps of smoking ruins spread from Scotland Yard to the Bowling Green, where the mansion of the Duke of Buccleuch now stands. The Banqueting House was safe; but the graceful columns and festoons designed by Inigo were so much defaced and blackened that their form could hardly be discerned. There had been time to move the most valuable effects which were moveable. Unfortunately some of Holbein's finest pictures were painted on the walls, and are consequently known to us only by copies and engravings. The books of the Treasury and of the Privy Council were rescued, and are still preserved. The Ministers whose offices had been burned down were provided with new offices in the neighbourhood. Henry the Eighth had built, close to St. James's Park, two appendages to the Palace of Whitehall, a cockpit and a tennis court. The Treasury now occupies the site of the cockpit, the Privy Council Office the site of the tennis court.

Notwithstanding the many associations which make the name of Whitehall still interesting to an Englishman, the old building was little regretted. It was spacious indeed and commodious, but mean and inelegant. The people of the capital had been annoyed by the scoffing way in which foreigners spoke of the principal residence of our sovereigns, and often said that it was a pity that the great fire had not spared the old portico of St. Paul's and the stately arcades of Gresham's Bourse, and taken in exchange that ugly old labyrinth of dingy brick and plastered timber. It might now be hoped that we should have a Louvre. Before the ashes of the old palace were cold, plans for a new palace were circulated and discussed. But William, who could not draw his breath in the air of Westminster, was little disposed to expend a million on a house which it would have been impossible for him to inhabit. Many blamed him for not restoring the dwelling of his predecessors; and a few Jacobites, whom evil temper and repeated disappointments had driven almost mad, accused him of having burned it down. It was not till long after his death that Tory writers ceased to call for the rebuilding of Whitehall, and to complain that the King of England had no better town house than St. James's, while the delightful spot where the Tudors and the Stuarts had held their councils and their revels was covered with the mansions of his jobbing courtiers.*

In the same week in which Whitehall perished, the Londoners were supplied with a new topic of conversation by a royal visit, which, of all royal visits, was the least pompous and ceremonious and yet the most interesting and important.

* London Gazette, Jan 6. 169⅞; Postman of the same date; Van Cleverskirke, Jan. 1̄7̄.; L'Hermitage, Jan. 1̄4̄. 1̄7̄.; Evelyn's Diary; Ward's London Spy; William to Heinsius, Jan. 1̄7̄.; "The loss," the King writes, "is less to me than it would be to another person, for I cannot live there. Yet it is serious." So late as 1758 Johnson described a furious Jacobite as firmly convinced that William burned down Whitehall in order to steal the furniture. Idler, No. 10. Pope, in Windsor Forest, a poem which has a stronger tinge of Toryism than anything else that he ever wrote, predicts the speedy restoration of the fallen palace.

"I see, I see, where two fair cities bend
    Their ample bow, a new Whitehall ascend."

See Ralph's bitter remarks on the fate of Whitehall.

On the 10th of January a vessel from Holland anchored off Greenwich and was welcomed with great respect. Peter the First, Czar of Muscovy, was on board. He took boat with a few attendants and was rowed up the Thames to Norfolk Street, where a house overlooking the river had been prepared for his reception.

His journey is an epoch in the history, not only of his own country, but of ours, and of the world. To the polished nations of Western Europe, the empire which he governed had till then been what Bokhara or Siam is to us. That empire indeed, though less extensive than at present, was the most extensive that had ever obeyed a single chief. The dominions of Alexander and of Trajan were small when compared with the immense area of the Scythian desert. But in the estimation of statesmen that boundless expanse of larch forest and morass, where the snow lay deep during eight months of every year, and where a wretched peasantry could with difficulty defend their hovels against troops of famished wolves, was of less account than the two or three square miles into which were crowded the counting houses, the warehouses, and the innumerable masts of Amsterdam. On the Baltic Russia had not then a single port. Her maritime trade with the other nations of Christendom was entirely carried on at Archangel, a place which had been created and was supported by adventurers from our island. In the days of the Tudors, a ship from England, seeking a north east passage to the land of silk and spice, had discovered the White Sea. The barbarians who dwelt on the shores of that dreary gulf had never before seen such a portent as a vessel of a hundred and sixty tons burden. They fled in terror; and, when they were pursued and overtaken, prostrated themselves before the chief of the strangers and kissed his feet. He succeeded in opening a friendly communication with them; and from that time there had been a regular commercial intercourse between our country and the subjects of the Czar. A Russia Company was incorporated in London. An English factory was built at Archangel. That factory was indeed, even in the latter part of the seventeenth century, a rude and mean building. The walls consisted of trees laid one upon another; and the roof was of birch bark. This shelter, however, was sufficient in the long summer day of the Arctic regions. Regularly at that season several English ships cast anchor in the bay. A fair was held on the beach. Traders came from a distance of many hundreds of miles to the only mart where they could exchange hemp and tar, hides and tallow, wax and honey, the fur of the sable and the wolverine, and the roe of the sturgeon of the Volga, for Manchester stuffs, Sheffield knives, Birmingham buttons, sugar from Jamaica and pepper from Malabar. The commerce in these articles was open. But there was a secret traffic which was not less active or less lucrative, though the Russian laws had made it punishable, and though the Russian divines pronounced it damnable. In general the mandates of princes and the lessons of priests were received by the Muscovite with profound reverence. But the authority of his princes and of his priests united could not keep him from tobacco. Pipes he could not obtain; but a cow's horn perforated served his turn. From every Archangel fair rolls of the best Virginia speedily found their way to Novgorod and Tobolsk.

The commercial intercourse between England and Russia made some diplomatic intercourse necessary. The diplomatic intercourse however was only occasional. The Czar had no permanent minister here. We had no permanent minister at Moscow; and even at Archangel we had no consul. Three or four times in a century extraordinary embassies were sent from Whitehall to the Kremlin and from the Kremlin to Whitehall.

The English embassies had historians whose narratives may still be read with interest. Those historians described vividly, and sometimes bitterly, the savage ignorance and the squalid poverty of the barbarous country in which they had sojourned. In that country, they said, there was neither literature nor science, neither school nor college. It was not till more than a hundred years after the invention of printing that a single printing press had been introduced into the Russian empire; and that printing press had speedily perished in a fire which was supposed to have been kindled by the priests. Even in the seventeenth century the library of a prelate of the first dignity consisted of a few manuscripts. Those manuscripts too were in long rolls: for the art of bookbinding was unknown. The best educated men could barely read and write. It was much if the secretary to whom was entrusted the direction of negotiations with foreign powers had a sufficient smattering of Dog Latin to make himself understood. The arithmetic was the arithmetic of the dark ages. The denary notation was unknown. Even in the Imperial Treasury the computations were made by the help of balls strung on wires. Round the person of the Sovereign there was a blaze of gold and jewels: but even in his most splendid palaces were to be found the filth and misery of an Irish cabin. So late as the year 1663 the gentlemen of the retinue of the Earl of Carlisle were, in the city of Moscow, thrust into a single bedroom, and were told that, if they did not remain together, they would be in danger of being devoured by rats.

Such was the report which the English legations made of what they had seen and suffered in Russia; and their evidence was confirmed by the appearance which the Russian legations made in England. The strangers spoke no civilised language. Their garb, their gestures, their salutations, had a wild and barbarous character. The ambassador and the grandees who accompanied him were so gorgeous that all London crowded to stare at them, and so filthy that nobody dared to touch them. They came to the court balls dropping pearls and vermin. It was said that one envoy cudgelled the lords of his train whenever they soiled or lost any part of their finery, and that another had with difficulty been prevented from putting his son to death for the crime of shaving and dressing after the French fashion.

Our ancestors therefore were not a little surprised to learn that a young barbarian, who had, at seventeen years of age, become the autocrat of the immense region stretching from the confines of Sweden to those of China, and whose education had been inferior to that of an English farmer or shopman, had planned gigantic improvements, had learned enough of some languages of Western Europe to enable him to communicate with civilised men, had begun to surround himself with able adventurers from various parts of the world, had sent many of his young subjects to study languages, arts and sciences in foreign cities, and finally had determined to travel as a private man, and to discover, by personal observation, the secret of the immense prosperity and power enjoyed by some communities whose whole territory was far less than the hundredth part of his dominions.

It might have been expected that France would have been the first object of his curiosity. For the grace and dignity of the French King, the splendour of the French Court, the discipline of the French armies, and the genius and learning of the French writers, were then renowned all over the world. But the Czar's mind had early taken a strange ply which it retained to the last. His empire was of all empires the least capable of being made a great naval power. The Swedish provinces lay between his States and the Baltic. The Bosporus and the Dardanelles lay between his States and the Mediterranean. He had access to the ocean only in a latitude in which navigation is, during a great part of every year, perilous and difficult. On the ocean he had only a single port, Archangel; and the whole shipping of Archangel was foreign. There did not exist a Russian vessel larger than a fishing-boat. Yet, from some cause which cannot now be traced, he had a taste for maritime pursuits which amounted to a passion, indeed almost to a monomania. His imagination was full of sails, yardarms, and rudders. That large mind, equal to the highest duties of the general and the statesman, contracted itself to the most minute details of naval architecture and naval discipline. The chief ambition of the great conqueror and legislator was to be a good boatswain and a good ship's carpenter. Holland and England therefore had for him an attraction which was wanting to the galleries and terraces of Versailles. He repaired to Amsterdam, took a lodging in the dockyard, assumed the garb of a pilot, put down his name on the list of workmen, wielded with his own hand the caulking iron and the mallet, fixed the pumps, and twisted the ropes. Ambassadors who came to pay their respects to him were forced, much against their will, to clamber up the rigging of a man of war, and found him enthroned on the cross trees.

Such was the prince whom the populace of London now crowded to behold. His stately form, his intellectual forehead, his piercing black eyes, his Tartar nose and mouth, his gracious smile, his frown black with all the stormy rage and hate of a barbarian tyrant, and above all a strange nervous convulsion which sometimes transformed his countenance during a few moments, into an object on which it was impossible to look without terror, the immense quantities of meat which he devoured, the pints of brandy which he swallowed, and which, it was said, he had carefully distilled with his own hands, the fool who jabbered at his feet, the monkey which grinned at the back of his chair, were, during some weeks, popular topics of conversation. He meanwhile shunned the public gaze with a haughty shyness which inflamed curiosity. He went to a play; but, as soon as he perceived that pit, boxes and galleries were staring, not at the stage, but at him, he retired to a back bench where he was screened from observation by his attendants. He was desirous to see a sitting of the House of Lords; but, as he was determined not to be seen, he was forced to climb up to the leads, and to peep through a small window. He heard with great interest the royal assent

N 37

given to a bill for raising fifteen hundred thousand pounds by land tax, and learned with amazement that this sum, though larger by one half than the whole revenue which he could wring from the population of the immense empire of which he was absolute master, was but a small part of what the Commons of England voluntarily granted every year to their constitutional King.

William judiciously humoured the whims of his illustrious guest, and stole to Norfolk Street so quietly that nobody in the neighbourhood recognised His Majesty in the thin gentleman who got out of the modest looking coach at the Czar's lodgings. The Czar returned the visit with the same precautions, and was admitted into Kensington House by a back door. It was afterwards known that he took no notice of the fine pictures with which the palace was adorned. But over the chimney of the royal sitting room was a plate which, by an ingenious machinery, indicated the direction of the wind; and with this plate he was in raptures.

He soon became weary of his residence. He found that he was too far from the objects of his curiosity, and too near to the crowds to which he was himself an object of curiosity. He accordingly removed to Deptford, and was there lodged in the house of John Evelyn, a house which had long been a favourite resort of men of letters, men of taste and men of science. Here Peter gave himself up to his favourite pursuits. He navigated a yacht every day up and down the river. His apartment was crowded with models of three deckers and two deckers, frigates, sloops and fireships. The only Englishman of rank in whose society he seemed to take much pleasure was the eccentric Caermarthen, whose passion for the sea bore some resemblance to his own, and who was very competent to give an opinion about every part of a ship from the stem to the stern. Caermarthen, indeed, became so great a favourite that he prevailed on the Czar to consent to the admission of a limited quantity of tobacco into Russia. There was reason to apprehend that the Russian clergy would cry out against any relaxation of the ancient rule, and would strenuously maintain that the practice of smoking was condemned by that text which declares that man is defiled, not by those things which enter in at the mouth, but by those which proceed out of it. This apprehension was expressed by a deputation of merchants who were admitted to an audience of the Czar: but they were reassured by the air with which he told them that he knew how to keep priests in order.

He was indeed so free from any bigoted attachment to the religion in which he had been brought up that both Papists and Protestants hoped at different times to make him a proselyte. Burnet, commissioned by his brethren, and impelled, no doubt, by his own restless curiosity and love of meddling, repaired to Deptford and was honoured with several audiences. The Czar could not be persuaded to exhibit himself at Saint Paul's; but he was induced to visit Lambeth palace. There he saw the ceremony of ordination performed, and expressed warm approbation of the Anglican ritual. Nothing in England astonished him so much as the Archiepiscopal library. It was the first good collection of books that he had seen; and he declared that he had never imagined that there were so many printed volumes in the world.

The impression which he made on Burnet was not favourable. The good bishop could not understand that a mind which seemed to be chiefly occupied with questions about the best place for a capstan and the best way of rigging a jury mast might be capable, not merely of ruling an empire, but of creating a nation. He complained that he had gone to see a great prince, and had found only an industrious shipwright. Nor does Evelyn seem to have formed a much more favourable opinion of his august tenant. It was, indeed, not in the character of tenant that the Czar was likely to gain the good word of civilised men. With all the high qualities which were peculiar to himself, he had all the filthy habits which were then common among his countrymen. To the end of his life, while disciplining armies, founding schools, framing codes, organising tribunals, building cities in deserts, joining distant seas by artificial rivers, he lived in his palace like a hog in a sty; and, when he was entertained by other sovereigns, never failed to leave on their tapestried walls and velvet state beds unequivocal proof that a savage had been there. Evelyn's house was left in such a state that the Treasury quieted his complaints with a considerable sum of money.

Towards the close of March the Czar visited Portsmouth, saw a sham sea-fight at Spithead, watched every movement of the contending fleets with intense interest, and expressed in warm terms his gratitude to the hospitable government which had provided so delightful a spectacle for his amusement and instruction. After passing more than three months in England, he departed in high good humour.*

* As to the Czar:—London Gazette; Van Citters, 1698; Jan. $\frac{11}{21}$. $\frac{14}{24}$.; Mar. $\frac{11}{21}$.; $\frac{\text{Mar. 2?}}{\text{April 1}}$; $\frac{\text{Mar. 29.}}{\text{April 8.}}$; L'Hermitage, Jan. $\frac{11}{21}$. $\frac{18}{28}$.; $\frac{\text{Jan. 25.}}{\text{Feb. 4.}}$; Feb. $\frac{1}{11}$.

His visit, his singular character, and what was rumoured of his great designs, excited much curiosity here, but nothing more than curiosity. England had as yet nothing to hope or to fear from his vast empire. All her serious apprehensions were directed towards a different quarter. None could say how soon France, so lately an enemy, might be an enemy again.

The new diplomatic relations between the two great western powers were widely different from those which had existed before the war. During the eighteen years which had elapsed between the signing of the Treaty of Dover and the Revolution, all the envoys who had been sent from Whitehall to Versailles had been mere sycophants of the great King. In England the French ambassador had been the object of a degrading worship. The chiefs of both the great parties had been his pensioners and his tools. The ministers of the Crown had paid him open homage. The leaders of the opposition had stolen into his house by the back door. Kings had stooped to implore his good offices, had persecuted him for money with the importunity of street beggars; and, when they had succeeded in obtaining from him a box of doubloons or a bill of exchange, had embraced him with tears of gratitude and joy. But those days were past. England would never again send a Preston or a Skelton to bow down before the majesty of France. France would never again send a Barillon to dictate to the cabinet of England. Henceforth the intercourse between the two states would be on terms of perfect equality.

William thought it necessary that the minister who was to represent him at the French Court should be a man of the first consideration, and one on whom entire reliance could be reposed. Portland was chosen for this important and delicate mission; and the choice was eminently judicious. He had, in the negotiations of the preceding year, shown more ability than was to be found in the whole crowd of formalists who had been exchanging notes and drawing up protocols at

$\frac{8}{18}$. $\frac{11}{21}$.; $\frac{\text{Feb 22}}{\text{Mar. 4.}}$; $\frac{\text{Feb. 25.}}{\text{Mar. 7.}}$; Mar. $\frac{4}{14}$., $\frac{\text{Mar 9.}}{\text{April 8.}}$; $\frac{\text{April 22.}}{\text{May 2.}}$. See also Evelyn's Diary; Burnet; Postman, Jan. 13. 15.; Feb. 10. 12. 24.; Mar. 24. 26. 31. As to Russia, see Hakluyt, Purchas, Voltaire, St. Simon. Estat de Russie par Margeret, Paris, 1607. State of Russia, London, 1671. La Relation des Trois Ambassades de M. Le Comte de Carlisle, Amsterdam, 1672. (There is an English translation from this French original.) North's Life of Dudley North. Seymour's History of London, ii. 426. Pepys and Evelyn on the Russian Embassies; Milton's account of Muscovy. On the personal habits of the Czar see the Memoirs of the Margravine of Bareuth.

Ryswick. Things which had been kept secret from the plenipotentiaries who had signed the treaty were well known to him. The clue of the whole foreign policy of England and Holland was in his possession. His fidelity and diligence were beyond all praise. These were strong recommendations. Yet it seemed strange to many that William should have been willing to part, for a considerable time, from a companion with whom he had during a quarter of a century lived on terms of entire confidence and affection. The truth was that the confidence was still what it had long been, but that the affection, though it was not yet extinct, though it had not even cooled, had become a cause of uneasiness to both parties. Till very recently, the little knot of personal friends who had followed William from his native land to his place of splendid banishment had been firmly united. The aversion which the English nation felt for them had given him much pain ; but he had not been annoyed by any quarrel among themselves. Zulestein and Auverquerque had, without a murmur, yielded to Portland the first place in the royal favour ; nor had Portland grudged to Zulestein and Auverquerque very solid and very signal proofs of their master's kindness. But a younger rival had lately obtained an influence which created much jealousy. Among the Dutch gentlemen who had sailed with the Prince of Orange from Helvoetsluys to Torbay was one named Arnold Van Keppel. Keppel had a sweet and obliging temper, winning manners, and a quick, though not a profound, understanding. Courage, loyalty and secresy were common between him and Portland. In other points they differed widely. Portland was naturally the very opposite of a flatterer, and, having been the intimate friend of the Prince of Orange at a time when the interval between the House of Orange and the House of Bentinck was not so wide as it afterwards became, had acquired a habit of plain speaking which he could not unlearn when the comrade of his youth had become the sovereign of three kingdoms. He was a most trusty, but not a very respectful, subject. There was nothing which he was not ready to do or suffer for William. But in his intercourse with William he was blunt and sometimes surly. Keppel, on the other hand, had a great desire to please, and looked up with unfeigned admiration to a master whom he had been accustomed, ever since he could remember, to consider as the first of living men. Arts, therefore, which were neglected by the elder courtier were assiduously practised by the younger. So early as the spring of 1691 shrewd observers were struck by the manner in which Keppel watched every turn of the King's eye, and anticipated the King's unuttered wishes. Gradually the new servant rose into favour. He was at length made Earl of Albemarle and Master of the Robes. But his elevation, though it furnished the Jacobites with a fresh topic for calumny and ribaldry, was not so offensive to the nation as the elevation of Portland had been. Portland's manners were thought dry and haughty; but envy was disarmed by the blandness of Albemarle's temper and by the affability of his deportment. Portland, though strictly honest, was covetous: Albemarle was generous. Portland had been naturalised here only in name and form: but Albemarle affected to have forgotten his own country, and to have become an Englishman in feelings and manners. The palace was soon disturbed by quarrels in which Portland seems to have been always the aggressor, and in which he found little support either among the English or among his own countrymen. William, indeed, was not the man to discard an old friend for a new one. He steadily gave, on all occasions, the preference to the companion of his youthful days. Portland had the first place in the bedchamber. He held high command in the army. On all great occasions he was trusted and consulted. He was far more powerful in Scotland than the Lord High Commissioner, and far deeper in the secret of foreign affairs than the Secretary of State. He wore the Garter, which sovereign princes coveted. Lands and money had been bestowed on him so liberally that he was one of the richest subjects in Europe. Albemarle had as yet not even a regiment; he had not been sworn of the Council: and the wealth which he owed to the royal bounty was a pittance when compared with the domains and the hoards of Portland. Yet Portland thought himself aggrieved. He could not bear to see any other person near him, though below him, in the royal favour. In his fits of resentful sullenness, he hinted an intention of retiring from the Court. William omitted nothing that a brother could have done to soothe and conciliate a brother. Letters are still extant in which he, with the utmost solemnity, calls God to witness that his affection for Bentinck still is what it was in their early days. At length a compromise was made. Portland, disgusted with Kensington, was not sorry to go to France as ambassador; and William with deep emotion consented to a separation longer than had ever taken place during an intimacy of twenty-five years. A day or two after the new plenipotentiary had set out on his mission, he received a touching letter from his master. "The loss of your society," the King wrote, " has affected me more than you can imagine. I should be very glad if I could believe that you felt as much pain at quitting me as I felt at seeing you depart: for then I might hope that you had ceased to doubt the truth of what I so solemnly declared to you on my oath. Assure yourself that I never was more sincere. My feeling towards you is one which nothing but death can alter." It should seem that the answer returned to these affectionate assurances was not perfectly gracious: for, when the King next wrote, he gently complained of an expression which had wounded him severely.

But, though Portland was an unreasonable and querulous friend, he was a most faithful and zealous minister. His despatches show how indefatigably he toiled for the interests, and how punctiliously he guarded the dignity, of the prince by whom he imagined that he had been unjustly and unkindly treated.

The embassy was the most magnificent that England had ever sent to any foreign court. Twelve men of honourable birth and ample fortune, some of whom afterwards filled high offices in the State, attended the mission at their own charge. Each of them had his own carriage, his own horses, and his own train of servants. Two less wealthy persons, who, in different ways, attained great note in literature, were of the company. Rapin, whose history of England might have been found, a century ago, in every library, was the preceptor of the ambassador's eldest son, Lord Woodstock. Prior was Secretary of Legation. His quick parts, his industry, his politeness, and his perfect knowledge of the French language, marked him out as eminently fitted for diplomatic employment. He had, however, found much difficulty in overcoming an odd prejudice which his chief had conceived against him. Portland, with good natural abilities and great expertness in business, was no scholar. He had probably never read an English book ; but he had a general notion, unhappily but too well founded, that the wits and poets who congregated at Will's were a most profane and licentious set ; and, being himself a man of orthodox opinions and regular life, he was not disposed to give his confidence to one whom he supposed to be a ribald scoffer. Prior, with much address, and perhaps with the help of a little hypocrisy, completely removed this unfavourable impression. He talked on serious subjects seriously, quoted the New Testament appositely, vindicated Hammond from the charge of popery, and, by way of a decisive blow, gave the

definition of a true Church from the nineteenth Article.
Portland stared at him. " I am glad, Mr. Prior, to find you
so good a Christian. I was afraid that you were an atheist."
"An atheist, my good lord ! " cried Prior. " What could lead
your Lordship to entertain such a suspicion ? " "Why," said
Portland, "I knew that you were a poet ; and I took it for
granted that you did not believe in God." "My lord," said
the wit, "you do us poets the greatest injustice. Of all people
we are the farthest from atheism. For the atheists do not even
worship the true God, whom the rest of mankind acknowledge;
and we are always invoking and hymning false gods whom
everybody else has renounced." This jest will be perfectly
intelligible to all who remember the eternally recurring allusions
to Venus and Minerva, Mars, Cupid and Apollo, which were
meant to be the ornaments, and are the blemishes, of Prior's
compositions. But Portland was much puzzled. However,
he declared himself satisfied ; and the young diplomatist
withdrew, laughing to think with how little learning a man
might shine in courts, lead armies, negotiate treaties, obtain a
coronet and a garter, and leave a fortune of half a million.

The citizens of Paris and the courtiers of Versailles, though
more accustomed than the Londoners to magnificent pageantry,
allowed that no minister from any foreign state had ever made
so superb an appearance as Portland. His horses, his liveries,
his plate, were unrivalled. His state carriage, drawn by eight
fine Neapolitan greys decorated with orange ribands, was
specially admired. On the day of his public entry the streets,
the balconies, and the windows were crowded with spectators
along a line of three miles. As he passed over the bridge on
which the statue of Henry IV. stands, he was much amused
by hearing one of the crowd exclaim : "Was it not this
gentleman's master that we burned on this very bridge eight
years ago ? " The Ambassador's hotel was constantly thronged
from morning to night by visitors in plumes and embroidery.
Several tables were sumptuously spread every day under his
roof ; and every English traveller of decent station and
character was welcome to dine there. The board at which the
master of the house presided in person, and at which he
entertained his most distinguished guests, was said to be more
luxurious than that of any prince of the House of Bourbon.
For there the most exquisite cookery of France was set off
by a certain neatness and comfort which then, as now,
peculiarly belonged to England. During the banquet the
room was filled with people of fashion, who went to see the

grandees eat and drink. The expense of all this splendour and hospitality was enormous, and was exaggerated by report. The cost to the English government really was fifty thousand pounds in five months. It is probable that the opulent gentlemen who accompanied the mission as volunteers laid out nearly as much more from their private resources.

The malecontents at the coffeehouses of London murmured at this profusion, and accused William of ostentation. But, as this fault was never, on any other occasion, imputed to him even by his detractors, we may not unreasonably attribute to policy what to superficial or malicious observers seemed to be vanity. He probably thought it important, at the commencement of a new era in the relations between the two great kingdoms of the West, to hold high the dignity of the Crown which he wore. He well knew, indeed, that the greatness of a prince does not depend on piles of silver bowls and chargers, trains of gilded coaches, and multitudes of running footmen in brocade, and led horses in velvet housings. But he knew also that the subjects of Lewis had, during the long reign of their magnificent sovereign, been accustomed to see power constantly associated with pomp, and would hardly believe that the substance existed unless they were dazzled by the trappings.

If the object of William was to strike the imagination of the French people, he completely succeeded. The stately and gorgeous appearance which the English embassy made on public occasions was, during some time, the general topic of conversation at Paris. Portland enjoyed a popularity which contrasts strangely with the extreme unpopularity which he had incurred in England. The contrast will perhaps seem less strange when we consider what immense sums he had accumulated at the expense of the English, and what immense sums he was laying out for the benefit of the French. It must also be remembered that he could not confer or correspond with Englishmen in their own language, and that the French tongue was at least as familiar to him as that of his native Holland. He, therefore, who here was called greedy, niggardly, dull, brutal, whom one English nobleman had described as a block of wood, and another as just capable of carrying a message right, was in the brilliant circles of France considered as a model of grace, of dignity and of munificence, as a dexterous negotiator and a finished gentleman. He was the better liked because he was a Dutchman. For, though fortune had favoured William, though considerations of policy had induced the Court of Versailles to acknowledge him, he was still, in the estimation of that Court, an usurper; and his English councillors and captains were perjured traitors who richly deserved axes and halters, and might, perhaps, get what they deserved. But Bentinck was not to be confounded with Leeds and Marlborough, Orford and Godolphin. He had broken no oath, had violated no law. He owed no allegiance to the House of Stuart; and the fidelity and zeal with which he had discharged his duties to his own country and his own master entitled him to respect. The noble and powerful vied with each other in paying honour to the stranger.

The Ambassador was splendidly entertained by the Duke of Orleans at St. Cloud, and by the Dauphin at Meudon. A Marshal of France was charged to do the honours of Marli; and Lewis graciously expressed his concern that the frosts of an ungenial spring prevented the fountains and flower beds from appearing to advantage. On one occasion Portland was distinguished, not only by being selected to hold the waxlight in the royal bedroom, but by being invited to go within the balustrade which surrounded the couch, a magic circle which the most illustrious foreigners had hitherto found impassable. The Secretary shared largely in the attentions which were paid to his chief. The Prince of Condé took pleasure in talking with him on literary subjects. The courtesy of the aged Bossuet, the glory of the Church of Rome, was long gratefully remembered by the young heretic. Boileau had the good sense and good feeling to exchange a friendly greeting with the aspiring novice who had administered to him a discipline as severe as he had administered to Quinault. The great King himself warmly praised Prior's manners and conversation, a circumstance which will be thought remarkable when it is remembered that His Majesty was an excellent model and an excellent judge of gentlemanlike deportment, and that Prior had passed his boyhood in drawing corks at a tavern, and his early manhood in the seclusion of a college. The Secretary did not however carry his politeness so far as to refrain from asserting, on proper occasions, the dignity of his country and of his master. He looked coldly on the twenty-one celebrated pictures in which Le Brun had represented on the ceiling of the gallery of Versailles the exploits of Lewis. When he was sneeringly asked whether Kensington Palace could boast of such decorations, he answered, with spirit and propriety: "No, Sir. The memorials of the great things which my master has done are to be seen in many places; but not in his own house."

Great as was the success of the embassy, there was one drawback. James was still at Saint Germains; and round the mock King were gathered a mock Court and Council, a Great Seal and a Privy Seal, a crowd of garters and collars, white staves and gold keys. Against the pleasure which the marked attentions of the French princes and grandees gave to Portland, was to be set off the vexation which he felt when Middleton crossed his path with the busy look of a real Secretary of State. But it was with emotions far deeper that the Ambassador saw on the terraces and in the antechambers of Versailles men who had been deeply implicated in plots against the life of his master. He expressed his indignation loudly and vehemently. "I hope," he said, "that there is no design in this; that these wretches are not purposely thrust in my way. When they come near me all my blood runs back in my veins." His words were reported to Lewis. Lewis employed Boufflers to smooth matters; and Boufflers took occasion to say something on the subject as if from himself. Portland easily divined that in talking with Boufflers he was really talking with Lewis, and eagerly seized the opportunity of representing the expediency, the absolute necessity, of removing James to a greater distance from England. "It was not contemplated, Marshal," he said, "when we arranged the terms of peace in Brabant, that a palace in the suburbs of Paris was to continue to be an asylum for outlaws and murderers." "Nay, my Lord," said Boufflers, uneasy doubtless on his own account, "you will not, I am sure, assert that I gave you any pledge that King James would be required to leave France. You are too honourable a man, you are too much my friend, to say any such thing." "It is true," answered Portland, "that I did not insist on a positive promise from you; but remember what passed. I proposed that King James should retire to Rome or Modena. Then you suggested Avignon; and I assented. Certainly my regard for you makes me very unwilling to do anything that would give you pain. But my master's interests are dearer to me than all the friends that I have in the world put together. I must tell His Most Christian Majesty all that passed between us; and I hope that, when I tell him, you will be present, and that you will be able to bear witness that I have not put a single word of mine into your mouth."

When Boufflers had argued and expostulated in vain, Villeroy was sent on the same errand, but had no better success. A few days later Portland had a long private audience of Lewis. Lewis declared that he was determined to keep his word, to preserve the peace of Europe, to abstain from everything which could give just cause of offence to England; but that, as a man of honour, as a man of humanity, he could not refuse shelter to an unfortunate King, his own first cousin. Portland replied that nobody questioned His Majesty's good faith; but that while Saint Germains was occupied by its present inmates it would be beyond even His Majesty's power to prevent eternal plotting between them and the malecontents on the other side of the Straits of Dover, and that, while such plotting went on, the peace must necessarily be insecure. The question was really not one of humanity. It was not asked, it was not wished, that James should be left destitute. Nay, the English government was willing to allow him an income larger than that which he derived from the munificence of France. Fifty thousand pounds a year, to which in strictness of law he had no right, awaited his acceptance, if he would only move to a greater distance from the country which, while he was near it, could never be at rest. If, in such circumstances, he refused to move, this was the strongest reason for believing that he could not safely be suffered to stay. The fact that he thought the difference between residing at Saint Germains and residing at Avignon worth more than fifty thousand a year sufficiently proved that he had not relinquished the hope of being restored to his throne by means of a rebellion or of something worse. Lewis answered that on that point his resolution was unalterable. He never would compel his guest and kinsman to depart. "There is another matter," said Portland, "about which I have felt it my duty to make representations. I mean the countenance given to the assassins." "I know nothing about assassins," said Lewis. "Of course," answered the Ambassador, "your Majesty knows nothing about such men. At least your Majesty does not know them for what they are. But I can point them out, and can furnish ample proofs of their guilt." He then named Berwick. For the English Government, which had been willing to make large allowances for Berwick's peculiar position as long as he confined himself to acts of open and manly hostility, conceived that he had forfeited all claim to indulgence by becoming privy to the Assassination Plot. This man, Portland said, constantly haunted Versailles. Barclay, whose guilt was of a still deeper dye,—Barclay, the chief contriver of the murderous ambuscade of Turnham Green,—had found in France, not only an asylum, but an honourable military position. The monk who was sometimes called Harrison and sometimes went by the alias of Johnson, but who, whether Harrison or Johnson, had been one of the earliest and one of the most bloodthirsty of Barclay's accomplices, was now comfortably settled as prior of a religious house in France. Lewis denied or evaded all these charges. "I never," he said, "heard of your Harrison. As to Barclay, he certainly once had a company : but it has been disbanded ; and what has become of him I do not know. It is true that Berwick was in London towards the close of 1695 ; but he was there only for the purpose of ascertaining whether a descent on England was practicable : and I am confident that he was no party to any cruel and dishonourable design." In truth Lewis had a strong personal motive for defending Berwick. The guilt of Berwick as respected the Assassination Plot does not appear to have extended beyond connivance ; and to the extent of connivance Lewis himself was guilty.

Thus the audience terminated. All that was left to Portland was to announce that the exiles must make their choice between Saint Germains and fifty thousand a year ; that the protocol of Ryswick bound the English government to pay to Mary of Modena only what the law gave her ; that the law gave her nothing ; that consequently the English government was bound to nothing ; and that, while she, her husband and her child remained where they were, she should have nothing. It was hoped that this announcement would produce a considerable effect even in James's household ; and indeed some of his hungry courtiers and priests seem to have thought the chance of a restoration so small that it would be absurd to refuse a splendid income, though coupled with a condition which might make that small chance somewhat smaller. But it is certain that, if there was murmuring among the Jacobites, it was disregarded by James. He was fully resolved not to move, and was only confirmed in his resolution by learning that he was regarded by the usurper as a dangerous neighbour. Lewis paid so much regard to Portland's complaints as to intimate to Middleton a request, equivalent to a command, that the Lords and gentlemen who formed the retinue of the banished King of England would not come to Versailles on days on which the representative of the actual King was expected there. But at other places there was constant risk of an encounter which might have produced several duels, if not an European war. James indeed, far from shunning such encounters, seems to have taken a perverse pleasure in thwarting his benefactor's wish to keep the peace, and in placing the Ambassador in embarrassing situations. One day his Excellency, while drawing on his boots for a run with the Dauphin's celebrated wolf pack, was informed that King James meant to be of the party, and was forced to stay at home.   Another day, when his Excellency had set his heart on having some sport with the royal staghounds, he was informed by the Grand Huntsman that King James might probably come to the rendezvous without any notice.   Melfort was particularly active in laying traps for the young noblemen and gentlemen of the Legation.   The Prince of Wales was more than once placed in such a situation that they could scarcely avoid passing close to him.   Were they to salute him?   Were they to stand erect and covered while every body else saluted him?   No Englishman zealous for the Bill of Rights and the Protestant religion would willingly do any thing which could be construed into an act of homage to a Popish pretender.   Yet no goodnatured and generous man, however firm in his Whig principles, would willingly offer any thing which could look like an affront to an innocent and a most unfortunate child.

Meanwhile other matters of grave importance claimed Portland's attention.   There was one matter in particular about which the French ministers anxiously expected him to say something, but about which he observed strict silence. How to interpret that silence they scarcely knew.   They were certain only that it could not be the effect of unconcern.   They were well assured that the subject which he so carefully avoided was never, during two waking hours together, out of his thoughts or out of the thoughts of his master.   Nay, there was not in all Christendom a single politician, from the greatest ministers of state down to the silliest newsmongers of coffeehouses, who really felt that indifference which the prudent Ambassador of England affected.   A momentous event, which had during many years been constantly becoming more and more probable, was now certain and near.   Charles the Second of Spain, the last descendant in the male line of the Emperor Charles the Fifth, would soon die without posterity.   Who would then be the heir to his many kingdoms, dukedoms, counties, lordships, acquired in different ways, held by different titles and subject to different laws?   That was a question about which jurists differed, and which it was not likely that jurists would, even if they were unanimous, be suffered to decide.   Among the claimants were the mightiest sovereigns of the continent: there was little chance that they would submit to any arbitration but that of the sword; and it could not be hoped that, if they appealed to the sword, other potentates who had no pretension to any part of the disputed inheritance would long remain neutral. For there was in Western Europe no government which did not feel that its own prosperity, dignity and security might depend on the event of the contest.

It is true that the empire, which had, in the preceding century, threatened both France and England with subjugation had of late been of hardly so much account as the Duchy of Savoy or the Electorate of Brandenburg. But it by no means followed that the fate of that empire was matter of indifference to the rest of the world. The paralytic helplessness and drowsiness of the body once so formidable could not be imputed to any deficiency of the natural elements of power. The dominions of the Catholic King were in extent and in population superior to those of Lewis and of William united. Spain alone, without a single dependency, ought to have been a kingdom of the first rank ; and Spain was but the nucleus of the Spanish monarchy. The outlying provinces of that monarchy in Europe would have sufficed to make three highly respectable states of the second order. One such state might have been formed in the Netherlands. It would have been a wide expanse of cornfield, orchard and meadow, intersected by navigable rivers and canals. At short intervals, in that thickly peopled and carefully tilled region, rose stately old towns, encircled by strong fortifications, embellished by fine cathedrals and senate-houses, and renowned either as seats of learning or as seats of mechanical industry. A second flourishing principality might have been created between the Alps and the Po, out of that well watered garden of olives and mulberry trees which spreads many miles on every side of the great white temple of Milan. Yet neither the Netherlands nor the Milanese could, in physical advantages, vie with the kingdom of the Two Sicilies, a land which nature had taken pleasure in enriching and adorning, a land which would have been paradise, if tyranny and superstition had not, during many ages, lavished all their noxious influences on the bay of Campania, the plain of Enna, and the sunny banks of Galesus.

In America the Spanish territories spread from the Equator northward and southward through all the signs of the Zodiac far into the temperate zone. Thence came gold and silver to be coined in all the mints, and curiously wrought in all the jewellers' shops, of Europe and Asia. Thence came the finest tobacco, the finest chocolate, the finest indigo, the finest cochineal, the hides of innumerable wild oxen, quinquina, coffee, sugar. Either the viceroyalty of Mexico or the viceroyalty of Peru would, as an independent state with ports open to all the world, have been an important member of the great community of nations.

And yet the aggregate, made up of so many parts, each of which separately might have been powerful and highly considered, was impotent to a degree which moved at once pity and laughter. Already one most remarkable experiment had been tried on this strange empire. A small fragment, hardly a three hundredth part of the whole in extent, hardly a thirtieth part of the whole in population, had been detached from the rest, had from that moment begun to display a new energy and to enjoy a new prosperity, and was now, after the lapse of a hundred and twenty years, far more feared and reverenced than the huge mass of which it had once been an obscure corner. What a contrast between the Holland which Alva had oppressed and plundered, and the Holland from which William had sailed to deliver England ! And who, with such an example before him, would venture to foretell what changes might be at hand, if the most languid and torpid of monarchies should be dissolved, and if every one of the members which had composed it should enter on an independent existence ?

To such a dissolution that monarchy was peculiarly liable. The King, and the King alone, held it together. The populations which acknowledged him as their chief either knew nothing of each other, or regarded each other with positive aversion. The Biscayan was in no sense the countryman of the Valencian, nor the Lombard of the Biscayan, nor the Fleming of the Lombard, nor the Sicilian of the Fleming. The Arragonese had never ceased to pine for their lost independence. Within the memory of many persons still living the Catalans had risen in rebellion, had entreated Lewis the Thirteenth of France to become their ruler with the old title of Count of Barcelona, and had actually sworn fealty to him. Before the Catalans had been quieted, the Neapolitans had taken arms, had abjured their foreign master, had proclaimed their city a republic, and had elected a Doge. In the New World the small caste of born Spaniards which had the exclusive enjoyment of power and dignity was hated by Creoles and Indians, Mestizos and Quadroons. The Mexicans especially had turned their eyes on a chief who bore the name and had inherited the blood of the unhappy Montezuma. Thus it seemed that the empire against which Elizabeth and Henry the Fourth had been scarcely able to contend would not improbably fall to pieces of itself, and that the first violent shock from without would scatter the ill-cemented parts of the huge frabric in all directions.

But, though such a dissolution had no terrors for the Catalonian or the Fleming, for the Lombard or the Calabrian, for the Mexican or the Peruvian, the thought of it was torture and madness to the Castilian. Castile enjoyed the supremacy in that great assemblage of races and languages. Castile sent out governors to Brussels, Milan, Naples, Mexico, Lima. To Castile came the annual galleons laden with the treasures of America. In Castile was ostentatiously displayed and lavishly spent great fortunes made in remote provinces by oppression and corruption. In Castile were the King and his Court. There stood the stately Escurial, once the centre of the politics of the world, the place to which distant potentates looked, some with hope and gratitude, some with dread and hatred, but none without anxiety and awe. The glory of the house had indeed departed. It was long since couriers bearing orders big with the fate of kings and commonwealths had ridden forth from those gloomy portals. Military renown, maritime ascendency, the policy once reputed so profound, the wealth once deemed inexhaustible, had passed away. An undisciplined army, a rotting fleet, an incapable council, an empty treasury, were all that remained of that which had been so great. Yet the proudest of nations could not bear to part even with the name and the shadow of a supremacy which was no more. All, from the grandee of the first class to the peasant, looked forward with dread to the day when God should be pleased to take their king to himself. Some of them might have a predilection for Germany : but such predilections were subordinate to a stronger feeling. The paramount object was the integrity of the empire of which Castile was the head ; and the prince who should appear to be most likely to preserve that integrity unviolated would have the best right to the allegiance of every true Castilian.

No man of sense, however, out of Castile, when he considered the nature of the inheritance and the situation of the claimants, could doubt that a partition was inevitable. Among those claimants three stood preeminent, the Dauphin, the Emperor Leopold, and the Electoral Prince of Bavaria.

If the question had been simply one of pedigree, the right of the Dauphin would have been incontestible. Lewis the Fourteeenth had married the Infanta Maria Theresa, eldest daughter of Philip the Fourth and sister of Charles the Second.

Her eldest son, the Dauphin, would therefore, in the regular course of things, have been her brother's successor. But she had, at the time of her marriage, renounced, for herself and her posterity, all pretensions to the Spanish crown.

To that renunciation her husband had assented. It had been made an article of the Treaty of the Pyrenees. The Pope had been requested to give his apostolical sanction to an arrangement so important to the peace of Europe; and Lewis had sworn, by every thing that could bind a gentleman, a king, and a Christian, by his honour, by his royal word, by the canon of the Mass, by the Holy Gospels, by the Cross of Christ, that he would hold the renunciation sacred.*

The claim of the Emperor was derived from his mother Mary Anne, daughter of Philip the Third, and aunt of Charles the Second, and could not therefore, if nearness of blood alone were to be regarded, come into competition with the claim of the Dauphin. But the claim of the Emperor was barred by no renunciation. The rival pretensions of the great Houses of Bourbon and Hapsburg furnished all Europe with an inexhaustible subject of discussion. Plausible topics were not wanting to the supporters of either cause. The partisans of the House of Austria dwelt on the sacredness of treaties; the partisans of France on the sacredness of birthright. How, it was asked on one side, can a Christian king have the effrontery, the impiety, to insist on a claim which he has with such solemnity renounced in the face of heaven and earth? How, it was asked on the other side, can the fundamental laws of a monarchy be annulled by any authority but that of the supreme legislature? The only body which was competent to take away from the children of Maria Theresa their hereditary rights was the Cortes. The Cortes had not ratified her renunciation. That renunciation was therefore a nullity; and no swearing, no signing, no sealing, could turn that nullity into a reality.

Which of these two mighty competitors had the better case may perhaps be doubted. What could not be doubted was that neither would obtain the prize without a struggle which

* It is worth while to transcribe the words of the engagement which Lewis, a chivalrous and a devout prince, violated without the smallest scruple. "Nous, Louis, par la grace de Dieu, Roi très Chrétien de France et de Navarre, promettons pour notre honneur, en foi et parole de Roi, jurons sur la croix, les saints Evangiles, et les canons de la Messe, que nous avons touchés, que nous observerons et accomplirons entièrement de bonne foi tous et chacun des points et articles contenus au traité de paix, renonciation, et amitié"

would shake the world. Nor can we justly blame either for refusing to give way to the other. For, on this occasion, the chief motive which actuated them was, not greediness, but the fear of degradation and ruin. Lewis, in resolving to put every thing to hazard rather than suffer the power of the House of Austria to be doubled; Leopold, in determining to put every thing to hazard rather than suffer the power of the House of Bourbon to be doubled; merely obeyed the law of self preservation. There was therefore one way, and one alone, by which the great woe which seemed to be coming on Europe could be averted. Was it possible that the dispute might be compromised? Might not the two great rivals be induced to make to a third party concessions such as neither could reasonably be expected to make to the other?

The third party, to whom all who were anxious for the peace of Christendom looked as their best hope, was a child of tender age, Joseph, son of the Elector of Bavaria. His mother, the Electress Mary Antoinette, was the only child of the Emperor Leopold by his first wife Margaret, a younger sister of the Queen of Lewis the Fourteenth. Prince Joseph was, therefore, nearer in blood to the Spanish throne than his grandfather the Emperor, or than the sons whom the Emperor had by his second wife. The Infanta Margaret had indeed, at the time of her marriage, renounced her rights to the kingdom of her forefathers. But the renunciation wanted many formalities which had been observed in her sister's case, and might be considered as cancelled by the will of Philip the Fourth, which had declared that, failing his issue male, Margaret and her posterity would be entitled to inherit his Crown. The partisans of France held that the Bavarian claim was better than the Austrian claim; the partisans of Austria held that the Bavarian claim was better than the French claim. But that which really constituted the strength of the Bavarian claim was the weakness of the Bavarian government. The Electoral Prince was the only candidate whose success would alarm nobody; would not make it necessary for any power to raise another regiment, to man another frigate, to have in store another barrel of gunpowder. He was therefore the favourite candidate of prudent and peaceable men in every country.

Thus all Europe was divided into the French, the Austrian, and the Bavarian factions. The contests of these factions were daily renewed in every place where men congregated, from Stockholm to Malta, and from Lisbon to Smyrna. But the fiercest and most obstinate conflict was that which raged in the palace of the Catholic King.  Much depended on him.  For, though it was not pretended that he was competent to alter by his sole authority the law which regulated the descent of the Crown, yet, in a case in which the law was doubtful, it was probable that his subjects might be disposed to accept the construction which he might put upon it, and to support the claimant whom he might, either by a solemn adoption or by will, designate as the rightful heir.  It was also in the power of the reigning sovereign to entrust all the most important offices in his kingdom, the government of all the provinces subject to him in the Old and in the New World, and the keys of all his fortresses and arsenals, to persons zealous for the family which he was inclined to favour.  It was difficult to say to what extent the fate of whole nations might be affected by the conduct of the officers who, at the time of his decease, might command the garrisons of Barcelona, of Mons, and of Namur.

The prince on whom so much depended was the most miserable of human beings.  In old times he would have been exposed as soon as he came into the world ; and to expose him would have been a kindness.  From his birth a blight was on his body and on his mind.  With difficulty his almost imperceptible spark of life had been screened and fanned into a dim and flickering flame.  His childhood, except when he could be rocked and sung into sickly sleep, was one long piteous wail. Till he was ten years old his days were passed on the laps of women ; and he was never once suffered to stand on his ricketty legs.  None of those tawny little urchins, clad in rags stolen from scarecrows, whom Murillo loved to paint begging or rolling in the sand, owed less to education than this despotic ruler of thirty millions of subjects.  The most important events in the history of his own kingdom, the very names of provinces and cities which were among his most valuable possessions, were unknown to him.  It may well be doubted whether he was aware that Sicily was an island, that Christopher Columbus had discovered America, or that the English were not Mahometans.  In his youth, however, though too imbecile for study or for business, he was not incapable of being amused.  He shot, hawked and hunted.  He enjoyed with the delight of a true Spaniard two delightful spectacles, a horse with its bowels gored out, and a Jew writhing in the fire.  The time came when the mightiest of instincts ordinarily wakens from its repose.  It was hoped that the young King would not prove invincible to female attractions, and that he would leave a Prince of Asturias to succeed him.  A consort was found for him in the royal family of France ; and her beauty and grace gave him a languid pleasure. He liked to adorn her with jewels, to see her dance, and to tell her what sport he had had with his dogs and his falcons. But it was soon whispered that she was a wife only in name. She died ; and her place was supplied by a German princess nearly allied to the Imperial House. But the second marriage, like the first, proved barren ; and, long before the King had passed the prime of life, all the politicians of Europe had begun to take it for granted in all their calculations that he would be the last descendant, in the male line, of Charles the Fifth. Meanwhile a sullen and abject melancholy took possession of his soul. The diversions which had been the serious employment of his youth became distasteful to him. He ceased to find pleasure in his nets and boar spears, in the fandango and the bullfight. Sometimes he shut himself up in an inner chamber from the eyes of his courtiers. Sometimes he loitered alone, from sunrise to sunset, in the dreary and rugged wilderness which surrounds the Escurial. The hours which he did not waste in listless indolence were divided between childish sports and childish devotions. He delighted in rare animals, and still more in dwarfs. When neither strange beasts nor little men could dispel the black thoughts which gathered in his mind, he repeated Aves and Credos : he walked in processions : sometimes he starved himself : sometimes he whipped himself. At length a complication of maladies completed the ruin of all his faculties. His stomach failed : nor was this strange ; for in him the malformation of the jaw, characteristic of his family, was so serious that he could not masticate his food ; and he was in the habit of swallowing ollas and sweetmeats in the state in which they were set before him. While suffering from indigestion he was attacked by ague. Every third day his convulsive tremblings, his dejection, his fits of wandering, seemed to indicate the approach of dissolution. His misery was increased by the knowledge that every body was calculating how long he had to live, and wondering what would become of his kingdoms when he should be dead. The stately dignitaries of his household, the physicians who ministered to his diseased body, the divines whose business was to soothe his not less diseased mind, the very wife who should have been intent on those gentle offices by which female tenderness can alleviate even the misery of hopeless decay, were all thinking of the new world which was to commence with his death, and would have been perfectly willing to see him in the hands of the embalmer if they could have been certain that his successor would be the prince whose interest they espoused. As yet the party of the Emperor seemed to predominate. Charles had a faint sort of preference for the House of Austria, which was his own house, and a faint sort of antipathy to the House of Bourbon, with which he had been quarrelling, he did not well know why, ever since he could remember. His Queen, whom he did not love, but of whom he stood greatly in awe, was devoted to the interests of her kinsman the Emperor; and with her was closely leagued the Count of Melgar, Hereditary Admiral of Castile and Prime Minister.

Such was the state of the question of the Spanish succession at the time when Portland had his first public audience at Versailles. The French ministers were certain that he must be constantly thinking about that question, and were therefore perplexed by his evident determination to say nothing about it. They watched his lips in the hope that he would at least let fall some unguarded word indicating the hopes or fears entertained by the English and Dutch Governments. But Portland was not a man out of whom much was to be got in that way. Nature and habit cooperating had made him the best keeper of secrets in Europe. Lewis therefore directed Pomponne and Torcy, two ministers of eminent ability, who had, under himself, the chief direction of foreign affairs, to introduce the subject which the discreet confidant of William seemed studiously to avoid. Pomponne and Torcy accordingly repaired to the English embassy, and there opened one of the most remarkable negotiations recorded in the annals of European diplomacy.

The two French statesmen professed in their master's name the most earnest desire, not only that the peace might remain unbroken, but that there might be a close union between the Courts of Versailles and Kensington. One event only seemed likely to raise new troubles. If the Catholic King should die before it had been settled who should succeed to his immense dominions, there was but too much reason to fear that the nations, which were just beginning to breathe after an exhausting and devastating struggle of nine years, would be again in arms. His Most Christian Majesty was therefore desirous to employ the short interval which might remain, in concerting with the King of England the means of preserving the tranquillity of the world.

Portland made a courteous but guarded answer. He could not, he said, presume to say exactly what William's sentiments were: but this he knew, that it was not solely or chiefly by the sentiments of the King of England that the policy of England on a great occasion would be regulated. The islanders must and would have their government administered according to certain maxims which they held sacred; and of those maxims they held none more sacred than this, that every increase of the power of France ought to be viewed with extreme jealousy.

Pomponne and Torcy answered that their master was most desirous to avoid every thing which could excite the jealousy of which Portland had spoken. But was it of France alone that a nation so enlightened as the English must be jealous? Was it forgotten that the House of Austria had once aspired to universal dominion? And would it be wise in the princes and commonwealths of Europe to lend their aid for the purpose of reconstructing the gigantic monarchy which, in the sixteenth century, had seemed likely to overwhelm them all?

Portland answered that, on this subject, he must be understood to express only the opinions of a private man. He had however now lived, during some years, among the English, and believed himself to be pretty well acquainted with their temper. They would not, he thought, be much alarmed by any augmentation of power which the Emperor might obtain. The sea was their element. Traffic by sea was the great source of their wealth; ascendency on the sea the great object of their ambition. Of the Emperor they had no fear. Extensive as was the area which he governed, he had not a frigate on the water; and they cared nothing for his Pandours and Croatians. But France had a great navy. The balance of maritime power was what would be anxiously watched in London; and the balance of maritime power would not be affected by an union between Spain and Austria, but would be most seriously deranged by an union between Spain and France.

Pomponne and Torcy declared that every thing should be done to quiet the apprehensions which Portland had described. It was not contemplated, it was not wished, that France and Spain should be united. The Dauphin and his eldest son the Duke of Burgundy would waive their rights. The younger brothers of the Duke of Burgundy, Philip Duke of Anjou and Charles Duke of Berry, were not named: but Portland perfectly understood what was meant. There would, he said, be scarcely less alarm in England if the Spanish dominions devolved on a grandson of His Most Christian Majesty than if they were annexed to the French crown. The laudable affection of the young princes for their country and their family, and their profound respect for the great monarch from whom they were descended, would inevitably determine their policy. The two kingdoms would be one; the two navies would be one; and all other states would be reduced to vassalage. England would rather see the Spanish monarchy added to the Emperor's dominions than governed by one of the younger French princes, who would, though nominally independent, be really a viceroy of France. But in truth there was no risk that the Spanish monarchy would be added to the Emperor's dominions. He and his eldest son the Archduke Joseph would, no doubt, be as ready to waive their rights as the Dauphin and the Duke of Burgundy could be; and thus the Austrian claim to the disputed heritage would pass to the younger Archduke Charles. A long discussion followed. At length Portland plainly avowed, always merely as his own private opinion, what was the opinion of every intelligent man who wished to preserve the peace of the world. "France is afraid," he said, "of every thing which can increase the power of the Emperor. All Europe is afraid of every thing which can increase the power of France. Why not put an end to all these uneasy feelings at once, by agreeing to place the Electoral Prince of Bavaria on the throne of Spain?" To this suggestion no decisive answer was returned. The conference ended; and a courier started for England with a despatch informing William of what had passed, and soliciting further instructions.

William, who was, as he had always been, his own Secretary for Foreign Affairs, did not think it necessary to discuss the contents of this despatch with any of his English ministers. The only person whom he consulted was Heinsius. Portland received a kind letter warmly approving all that he had said in the conference, and directing him to declare that the English government sincerely wished to avert the calamities which were but too likely to follow the death of the King of Spain, and would therefore be prepared to take into serious consideration any definite plan which His Most Christian Majesty might think fit to suggest. "I will own to you," William wrote to his friend, "that I am so unwilling to be again at war during the short time which I still have to live, that I will omit nothing that I can honestly and with a safe conscience do for the purpose of maintaining peace."

William's message was delivered by Portland to Lewis at a private audience. In a few days Pomponne and Torcy were authorised to propose a plan. They fully admitted that all neighbouring states were entitled to demand the strongest security against the union of the French and Spanish crowns. Such security should be given. The Spanish government might be requested to choose between the Duke of Anjou and the Duke of Berry. The youth who was selected would, at the utmost, be only fifteen years old, and could not be supposed to have any very deeply rooted national prejudices. He should be sent to Madrid without French attendants, should be educated by Spaniards, should become a Spaniard. It was absurd to imagine that such a prince would be a mere viceroy of France. Apprehensions had been sometimes hinted that a Bourbon, seated on the throne of Spain, might cede his dominions in the Netherlands to the head of his family. It was undoubtedly important to England, and all important to Holland, that those provinces should not become a part of the French monarchy. All danger might be averted by making them over to the Elector of Bavaria, who was now governing them as representative of the Catholic King. The Dauphin would be perfectly willing to renounce them for himself and for all his descendants. As to what concerned trade, England and Holland had only to say what they desired, and every thing in reason should be done to give them satisfaction.

As this plan was, in the main, the same which had been suggested by the French ministers in the former conference, Portland did little more than repeat what he had then said. As to the new scheme respecting the Netherlands, he shrewdly propounded a dilemma which silenced Pomponne and Torcy. If renunciations were of any value, the Dauphin and his posterity were excluded from the Spanish succession; and, if renunciations were of no value, it was idle to offer England and Holland a renunciation as a guarantee against a great danger.

The French Ministers withdrew to make their report to their master, and soon returned to say that their proposals had been merely first thoughts, that it was now the turn of King William to suggest something, and that whatever he might suggest should receive the fullest and fairest consideration.

And now the scene of the negotiation was shifted from Versailles to Kensington. The Count of Tallard had just set out for England as Ambassador. He was a fine gentleman: he was a brave soldier; and he was as yet reputed a skilful general. In all the arts and graces which were prized as qualifications for diplomatic missions of the highest class, he had, among the brilliant aristocracy to which he belonged, no superior and only one equal, the Marquess of Harcourt, who was entrusted with the care of the interests of the House of Bourbon at Madrid.

Tallard carried with him instructions carefully framed in the French Foreign Office. He was reminded that his situation would be widely different from that of his predecessors who had resided in England before the Revolution. Even his predecessors, however, had considered it as their duty to study the temper, not only of the Court, but of the nation. It would now be more than ever necessary to watch the movements of the public mind. A man of note was not to be slighted merely because he was out of place. Such a man, with a great name in the country and a strong following in Parliament, might exercise as much influence on the politics of England, and consequently of Europe, as any minister. The Ambassador must therefore try to be on good terms with those who were out as well as with those who were in. To this rule, however, there was one exception which he must constantly bear in mind. With nonjurors and persons suspected of plotting against the existing government he must not appear to have any connection. They must not be admitted into his house. The English people evidently wished to be at rest, and had given the best proof of their pacific disposition by insisting on the reduction of the army. The sure way to stir up jealousies and animosities which were just sinking to sleep would be to make the French embassy the head quarters of the Jacobite party. It would be wise in Tallard to say and to charge his agents to say, on all fit occasions, and particularly in societies where members of Parliament might be present, that the Most Christian King had never been an enemy of the liberties of England. His Majesty had indeed hoped that it might be in his power to restore his cousin, but not without the assent of the nation. In the original draft of the instructions was a curious paragraph which, on second thoughts, it was determined to omit. The Ambassador was directed to take proper opportunities of cautioning the English against a standing army, as the only thing which could really be fatal to their laws and liberties. This passage was suppressed, no doubt, because it occurred to Pomponne and Torcy that, with whatever approbation the English might listen to such language when uttered by a demagogue of their own race, they might be very differently affected by hearing it from a French diplomatist, and might think that there could not be a better reason for arming, than that Lewis and his emissaries earnestly wished them to disarm.

Tallard was instructed to gain, if possible, some members of the House of Commons. Every thing, he was told, was now subjected to the scrutiny of that assembly : accounts of the public income, of the public expenditure, of the army, of the navy, were regularly laid on the table ; and it would not be difficult to find persons who would supply the French legation with copious information on all these subjects.

The question of the Spanish succession was to be mentioned to William at a private audience. Tallard was fully informed of all that had passed in the conferences which the French ministers had held with Portland ; and was furnished with all the arguments that the ingenuity of publicists could devise in favour of the claim of the Dauphin.

The French embassy made as magnificent an appearance in England as the English embassy had made in France. The mansion of the Duke of Ormond, one of the finest houses in Saint James's Square, was taken for Tallard. On the day of the public entry, all the streets from Tower Hill to Pall Mall were crowded with gazers who admired the painting and gilding of his Excellency's carriages, the surpassing beauty of his horses, and the multitude of his running footmen, dressed in gorgeous liveries of scarlet and gold lace. The Ambassador was graciously received at Kensington, and was invited to accompany William to Newmarket, where the largest and most splendid Spring Meeting ever known was about to assemble. The attraction must be supposed to have been great : for the risks of the journey were not trifling. The peace had, all over Europe, and nowhere more than in England, turned crowds of old soldiers into marauders.* Several aristocratical equipages had been attacked even in Hyde Park. Every newspaper contained stories of travellers stripped, bound and flung into ditches. One day the Bristol mail was robbed ; another day the Dover coach ; then the Norwich waggon. On Hounslow Heath a company of horsemen, with masks on their faces, waited for the great people who had been to pay their court to the King at Windsor. Lord Ossulston escaped with the loss of two horses. The Duke of Saint Albans, with the help of his servants, beat off the assailants. His brother the Duke of

---

* George Psalmanazar's account of the state of the south of France at this time is curious. On the high road near Lyons he frequently passed corpses fastened to posts. "These," he says, "were the bodies of highwaymen, or rather of soldiers, sailors, mariners, and even galley slaves, disbanded after the peace of Reswick, who, having neither home nor occupation, used to infest the roads in troops, plunder towns and villages, and, when taken, were hanged at the county town by dozens, or even scores sometimes, after which their bodies were thus exposed along the highway *in terrorem.*"

Northumberland, less strongly guarded, fell into their hands. They succeeded in stopping thirty or forty coaches, and rode off with a great booty in guineas, watches and jewellery. No where, however, does the peril seem to have been so great as on the Newmarket road. There indeed robbery was organised on a scale unparalleled in the kingdom since the days of Robin Hood and Little John. A fraternity of plunderers, thirty in number according to the lowest estimate, squatted, near Waltham Cross, under the shades of Epping Forest, and built themselves huts, from which they sallied forth with sword and pistol to bid passengers stand. The King and Tallard were doubtless too well attended to be in jeopardy. But, soon after they had passed the dangerous spot, there was a fight on the highway attended with loss of life. A warrant of the Lord Chief Justice broke up the Maroon village for a short time : but the dispersed thieves soon mustered again, and had the impudence to bid defiance to the government in a cartel signed, it was said, with their real names. The civil power was unable to deal with this frightful evil. It was necessary that, during some time, cavalry should patrol every evening on the roads near the boundary between Middlesex and Essex.

The state of those roads, however, though contemporaries described it as dangerous beyond all example, did not deter men of rank and fashion from making the joyous pilgrimages to Newmarket. Half the Dukes in the kingdom were there. Most of the chief ministers of state swelled the crowd ; nor was the opposition unrepresented. Montague stole two or three days from the Treasury, and Orford from the Admiralty. Godolphin was there, looking after his horses and his bets, and probably went away a richer man than he came. But racing was only one of the many amusements of that festive season. On fine mornings there was hunting. For those who preferred hawking choice falcons had been brought from Holland. On rainy days the cockpit was encircled by stars and blue ribands. On Sundays William went to church in state, and the most eminent divines of the neighbouring University of Cambridge preached before him. He omitted no opportunity of showing marked civility to Tallard. The Ambassador informed his Court that his place at table was next to the royal arm chair, and that his health had been most graciously drunk by the King.

All this time, both at Kensington and Newmarket, the Spanish question was the subject of constant and earnest discussion. To trace all the windings of the negotiation would be tedious. The general course which it took may easily be described. The object of William was to place the Electoral Prince of Bavaria on the Spanish throne. To obtain the consent of Lewis to such an arrangement seemed all but impossible; but William manœuvred with rare skill. Though he frankly acknowledged that he preferred the Electoral Prince to any other candidate, he professed himself desirous to meet, as far as he honourably or safely could, the wishes of the French King. There were conditions on which England and Holland might perhaps consent, though not without reluctance, that a son of the Dauphin should reign at Madrid, and should be master of the treasures of the New World. Those conditions were that the Milanese and the Two Sicilies should belong to the Archduke Charles, that the Elector of Bavaria should have the Spanish Netherlands, that Lewis should give up some fortified towns in Artois for the purpose of strengthening the barrier which protected the United Provinces, and that some important places both in the Mediterranean sea and in the Gulf of Mexico should be made over to the English and Dutch for the security of trade. Minorca and Havanna were mentioned as what might satisfy England.

Against these terms Lewis exclaimed loudly. Nobody, he said, who knew with how sensitive a jealousy the Spaniards watched every encroachment on their colonial empire would believe that they would ever consent to give up any part of that empire either to England or to Holland. The demand which was made upon himself was altogether inadmissible. A barrier was not less necessary to France than to Holland; and he never would break the iron chain of frontier fastnesses which was the defence of his own kingdom, even in order to purchase another kingdom for his grandson. On that subject he begged that he might hear no more. The proposition was one which he would not discuss, one to which he would not listen.

As William, however, resolutely maintained that the terms which he had offered, hard as they might seem, were the only terms on which England and Holland could suffer a Bourbon to reign at Madrid, Lewis began seriously to consider whether it might not be on the whole for his interest and that of his family rather to sell the Spanish crown dear than to buy it dear. He therefore now offered to withdraw his opposition to the Bavarian claim, provided a portion of the disputed inheritance were assigned to him in consideration of his disinterestedness and moderation. William was perfectly willing and even eager to treat on this basis. The first demands of Lewis were,

as might have been expected, exorbitantly high.  He asked for
the kingdom of Navarre, which would have made him little
less than master of the whole Iberian peninsula, and for the
duchy of Luxemburg, which would have made him more
dangerous than ever to the United Provinces.  On both points
he encountered a steady resistance.  The impression which,
throughout these transactions, the firmness and good faith of
William made on Tallard is remarkable.  At first the dexterous
and keen witted Frenchman was all suspicion.  He imagined
that there was an evasion in every phrase, a hidden snare in
every offer.  But after a time he began to discover that he had
to do with a man far too wise to be false.  " The King of
England," he wrote, and it is impossible to doubt that he wrote
what he thought, "acts with good faith in every thing.  His
way of dealing is upright and sincere."* " The King of
England," he wrote a few days later, " has hitherto acted with
great sincerity; and I venture to say that, if he once enters
into a treaty, he will steadily adhere to it."  But in the same
letter the Ambassador thought it necessary to hint to his
master that the diplomatic chicanery which might be useful
in other negotiations would be all thrown away here.  " I must
venture to observe to Your Majesty that the King of England
is very sharpsighted, that his judgment is sound, and that, if
we try to spin the negotiation out, he will very soon perceive
that we are trifling with him." †

During some time projects and counterprojects continued to
pass and repass between Kensington and Versailles.  Something
was conceded on both sides; and when the session of Parliament
ended there seemed to be fair hopes of a settlement.  And
now the scene of the negotiation was again changed.  Having
been shifted from France to England, it was shifted from
England to Holland.  As soon as William had prorogued the
Houses, he was impatient to be again in his native land.  He
felt all the glee of a schoolboy who is leaving harsh masters
and quarrelsome comrades to pass the Christmas holidays at a
happy home.  That stern and composed face which had been
the same in the pursuit at the Boyne and in the rout at
Landen, and of which the keenest politicians had in vain tried

* " Il est de bonne foi dans tout ce qu'il fait.  Son procédé est droit et
sincère."  Tallard to Lewis, July 3. 1698.
† " Le Roi d'Angleterre, Sire, va très sincèrement jusqu'à présent ; et
j'ose dire que s'il entre une fois en traité avec Votre Majesté, il le tiendra
de bonne foi."—" Si je l'ose dire à V. M., il est très pénétrant, et a l'esprit
juste.  Il s'apercevra bientôt qu'on barguigne si les choses trainent trop de
long."  July 8.

to read the secrets, now wore an expression but too intelligible. The English were not a little provoked by seeing their King so happy. Hitherto his annual visits to the Continent had been not only pardoned but approved. It was necessary that he should be at the head of his army. If he had left his people, it had been in order to put his life in jeopardy for their independence, their liberty, and their religion. But they had hoped that, when peace had been restored, when no call of duty required him to cross the sea, he would generally, during the summer and autumn, reside in his fair palaces and parks on the banks of the Thames, or travel from country seat to country seat, and from cathedral town to cathedral town, making himself acquainted with every shire of his realm, and giving his hand to be kissed by multitudes of squires, clergymen and aldermen who were not likely ever to see him unless he came among them. It now appeared that he was sick of the noble residences which had descended to him from ancient princes; that he was sick even of those mansions which the liberality of Parliament had enabled him to build and embellish according to his own taste; that he was sick of Windsor, of Richmond, and of Hampton; that he promised himself no enjoyment from a progress through those flourishing and populous counties which he had never seen, Yorkshire and Norfolk, Cheshire, Shropshire and Worcestershire. While he was forced to be with us, he was weary of us, pining for his home, counting the hours to the prorogation. As soon as the passing of the last bill of supply had set him at liberty, he turned his back on his English subjects: he hastened to his seat in Guelders, where, during some months, he might be free from the annoyance of seeing English faces and hearing English words; and he would with difficulty tear himself away from his favourite spot when it became absolutely necessary that he should again ask for English money.

Thus his subjects murmured; but, in spite of their murmurs, he set off in high spirits. It had been arranged that Tallard should speedily follow him, and that the discussion in which they had been engaged at Kensington should be resumed at Loo.

Heinsius, whose cooperation was indispensable, would be there. Portland too would lend his assistance. He had just returned. He had always considered his mission as an extraordinary mission, of which the object was to put the relations between the two great Western powers on a proper footing after a long series of years during which England had been sometimes the enemy, but never the equal friend, of France. His task had been well performed: and he now came back, leaving behind him the reputation of an excellent minister, firm yet cautious as to substance, dignified yet conciliating in manner. His last audience at Versailles was unusually long; and no third person was present. Nothing could be more gracious than the language and demeanour of Lewis. He condescended to trace a route for the embassy, and insisted that Portland should make a circuit for the purpose of inspecting some of the superb fortresses of the French Netherlands. At every one of those fortresses the governors and engineers had orders to pay every attention to the distinguished stranger. Salutes were everywhere fired to welcome him. A guard of honour was everywhere in attendance on him. He stopped during three days at Chantilly, and was entertained there by the Prince of Condé with all that taste and magnificence for which Chantilly had long been renowned. There were boar hunts in the morning and concerts in the evening. Every gentleman of the legation had a gamekeeper specially assigned to him. The guests, who, in their own island were accustomed to give extravagant vails at every country house which they visited, learned, with admiration, that His Highness's servants were strictly forbidden to receive presents. At his luxurious table, by a refinement of politeness, choice cider from the orchards round the Malvern Hills made its appearance in company with the Champagne and the Burgundy.

Portland was welcomed by his master with all the kindness of old times. But that kindness availed nothing. For Albemarle was still in the royal household, and appeared to have been, during the last few months, making progress in the royal favour. Portland was angry, and the more angry because he could not but perceive that his enemies enjoyed his anger, and that even his friends generally thought it unreasonable; nor did he take any pains to conceal his vexation. But he was the very opposite of the vulgar crowd of courtiers who fawn on a master while they betray him. He neither disguised his ill humour, nor suffered it to interfere with the discharge of his duties. He gave his prince sullen looks, short answers, and faithful and strenuous services. His first wish, he said, was to retire altogether from public life. But he was sensible that, having borne a chief part in the negotiation on which the fate of Europe depended, he might be of use at Loo; and, with devoted loyalty, though with a sore heart and a gloomy brow, he prepared to attend William thither.

Before the King departed he delegated his power to nine Lords Justices. The public was well pleased to find that Sunderland was not among them. Two new names appeared in the list. That of Montague could excite no surprise. But that of Marlborough awakened many recollections and gave occasion to many speculations. He had once enjoyed a large measure of royal favour. He had then been dismissed, disgraced, imprisoned. The Princess Anne, for refusing to discard his wife, had been turned out of the palace, and deprived of the honours which had often been enjoyed by persons less near to the throne. Ministers who were supposed to have great influence in the closet had vainly tried to overcome the dislike with which their master regarded the Churchills. It was not till he had been some time reconciled to his sister in law that he ceased to regard her two favourite servants as his enemies. So late as the year 1696 he had been heard to say, " If I had been a private gentleman, my Lord Marlborough and I must have measured swords." All these things were now, it seemed, forgotten. The Duke of Gloucester's household had just been arranged. As he was not yet nine years old, and the civil list was burdened with a heavy debt, fifteen thousand pounds was thought for the present a sufficient provision. The child's literary education was directed by Burnet, with the title of Preceptor. Marlborough was appointed Governor ; and the London Gazette announced his appointment, not with official dryness, but in the fervid language of panegyric. He was at the same time again sworn a member of the Privy Council from which he had been expelled with ignominy ; and he was honoured a few days later with a still higher mark of the King's confidence, a seat at the board of Regency.

Some persons imagined that they saw in this strange reconciliation a sign that the influence of Portland was on the wane and that the influence of Albemarle was growing. For Marlborough had been many years at feud with Portland, and had even—a rare event indeed—been so much irritated as to speak of Portland in coarse and ungentlemanlike terms. With Albemarle, on the other hand, Marlborough had studiously ingratiated himself by all the arts which a mind singularly observant and sagacious could learn from a long experience in courts ; and it is possible that Albemarle may have removed some difficulties   It is hardly necessary, however, to resort to that supposition for the purpose of explaining why so wise a man as William forced himself, after some delay caused by very just and natural resentment, to act wisely. His opinion of Marlborough's character was probably unaltered. But he could not help perceiving that Marlborough's situation was widely different from what it had been a few years before. That very ambition, that very avarice, which had, in former times, impelled him to betray two masters, were now sufficient securities for his fidelity to the order of things which had been established by the Bill of Rights. If that order of things could be maintained inviolate, he could scarcely fail to be, in a few years, the greatest and wealthiest subject in Europe. His military and political talents might therefore now be used without any apprehension that they would be turned against the government which used them. It is to be remembered too that he derived his importance less from his military and political talents, great as they were, than from the dominion which, through the instrumentality of his wife, he exercised over the mind of the Princess. While he was on good terms with the Court it was certain that she would lend no countenance to any cabal which might attack either the title or the prerogatives of her brother in law. Confident that from this quarter, a quarter once the darkest and most stormy in the whole political horizon, nothing but sunshine and calm was now to be expected, William set out cheerfully on his expedition to his native country.

## CHAPTER XXIV

THE Gazette which informed the public that the King had set out for Holland announced also the names of the first members returned, in obedience to his writ, by the constituent bodies of the Realm. The history of those times has been so little studied that few persons are aware how remarkable an epoch the general election of 1698 is in the history of the English Constitution.

We have seen that the extreme inconvenience which had resulted from the capricious and headstrong conduct of the House of Commons during the years immediately following the Revolution had forced William to resort to a political machinery which had been unknown to his predecessors, and of which the nature and operation were but very imperfectly understood by himself or by his ablest advisers. For the first time the administration was confided to a small body of statesmen, who, on all grave and pressing questions, agreed with each other and with the majority of the representatives of the people. The direction of war and of diplomacy the King reserved to himself; and his servants, conscious that they were less versed than he in military affairs and in foreign affairs, were content to leave to him the command of the army, and to know only what he thought fit to communicate about the instructions which he gave to his own ambassadors and about the conferences which he held with the ambassadors of other princes. But, with these important exceptions, the government was entrusted to what then began to be called the Ministry.

The first English ministry was gradually formed; nor is it possible to say quite precisely when it began to exist. But, on the whole, the date from which the era of ministries may most properly be reckoned is the day of the meeting of the Parliament after the general election of 1695. That election had taken place at a time when peril and distress had called forth all the best qualities of the nation. The hearts of men were in the struggle against France for independence, for liberty, and for the Protestant religion. Everybody knew that such a struggle could not be carried on without large establishments and heavy taxes. The government therefore could hardly ask for more than the country was ready to give. A House of Commons was chosen in which the Whig party had a decided preponderance. The leaders of that party had recently been raised, one by one, to the highest executive offices. The majority, therefore, readily arranged itself in admirable order under the ministers, and during three sessions gave them on almost every occasion a cordial support. The consequence was that the country was rescued from its dangerous position, and, when that Parliament had lived out its three years, enjoyed prosperity after a terrible commercial crisis, peace after a long and sanguinary war, and liberty united with order after civil troubles which had lasted during two generations, and in which sometimes order and sometimes liberty had been in danger of perishing.

Such were the fruits of the general election of 1695. The ministers had flattered themselves that the general election of 1698 would be equally favourable to them, and that in the new Parliament the old Parliament would revive. Nor is it strange that they should have indulged such a hope. Since they had been called to the direction of affairs every thing had been changed, changed for the better, and changed chiefly by their wise and resolute policy, and by the firmness with which their party had stood by them. There was peace abroad and at home. The sentinels had ceased to watch by the beacons of Dorsetshire and Sussex. The merchant ships went forth without fear from the Thames and the Avon. Soldiers had been disbanded by tens of thousands. Taxes had been remitted. The value of all public and private securities had risen. Trade had never been so brisk. Credit had never been so solid. All over the kingdom the shopkeepers and the farmers, the artisans and the ploughmen, relieved, beyond all hope, from the daily and hourly misery of the clipped silver, were blessing the broad faces of the new shillings and half crowns. The statesmen whose administration had been so beneficent might be pardoned if they expected the gratitude and confidence which they had fairly earned. But it soon became clear that they had served their country only too well for their own interest. In 1695 adversity and danger had made men amenable to that control to which it is the glory of free nations to submit themselves, the control of superior minds. In 1698 prosperity and security had made men querulous, fastidious and unmanageable. The government was assailed with equal violence from widely different quarters. The opposition, made up of Tories many of whom carried Toryism to the length of Jacobitism, and of discontented Whigs some of whom carried Whiggism to the length of republicanism, called itself the Country party, a name which had been popular before the words Whig and Tory were known in England. The majority of the late House of Commons, a majority which had saved the State, was nicknamed the Court party. The Tory gentry, who were powerful in all the counties, had special grievances. The whole patronage of the government, they said, was in Whig hands. The old landed interest, the old Cavalier interest, had now no share in the favours of the Crown. Every public office, every bench of justice, every commission of Lieutenancy, was filled with Roundheads. The Tory rectors and vicars were not less exasperated. They accused the men in power of systematically protecting and preferring Presbyterians, Latitudinarians, Arians, Socinians, Deists, Atheists. An orthodox divine, a divine who held high the dignity of the priesthood and the mystical virtue of the sacraments, who thought schism as great a sin as theft and venerated the Icon as much as the Gospel, had no more chance of a bishopric or a deanery than a Papist recusant. Such complaints as these were not likely to call forth the sympathy of the Whig malecontents. But there were three war cries in which all the enemies of the government, from Trenchard to Seymour, could join: No standing army; No grants of Crown property; and No Dutchmen. Multitudes of honest freeholders and freemen were weak enough to believe that, unless the land force, which had already been reduced below what the public safety required, were altogether disbanded, the nation would be enslaved, and that, if the estates which the King had given away were resumed, all direct taxes might be abolished. The animosity to the Dutch mingled itself both with the animosity to standing armies and with the animosity to Crown grants. For a brigade of Dutch troops was part of the military establishment which was still kept up; and it was to Dutch favourites that William had been most liberal of the royal domains.

The elections, however, began auspiciously for the government. The first great contest was in Westminster. It must be remembered that Westminster was then by far the greatest city in the island, except only the neighbouring city of London, and contained more than three times as large a population as Bristol or Norwich, which came next in size. The right of voting at Westminster was in the householders paying scot and lot; and the householders paying scot and lot were many thousands. It is also to be observed that their political education was much further advanced than that of the great majority of the electors of the kingdom. A burgess in a country town, or a forty shilling freeholder in an agricultural district, then knew little about public affairs except what he could learn from reading the Postman at the alehouse, and from hearing, on the 30th of January, the 29th of May or the 5th of November, a sermon in which questions of state were discussed with more zeal than sense. But the citizen of Westminster passed his days in the vicinity of the palace, of the public offices, of the houses of parliament, of the courts of law. He was familiar with the faces and voices of ministers, senators and judges. In anxious times he walked in the great Hall to pick up news. When there was an important trial, he looked into the Court of King's Bench, and heard Cowper and Harcourt contending, and Holt moderating between them. When there was an interesting debate in the House of

Commons, he could at least squeeze himself into the lobby or the Court of Requests, and hear who had spoken, and how and what were the numbers on the division. He lived in a region of coffeehouses, of booksellers' shops, of clubs, of pamphlets, of newspapers, of theatres where poignant allusions to the most exciting questions of the day perpetually called forth applause and hisses, of pulpits where the doctrines of the High Churchman, of the Low Churchman, of the Nonjuror, of the Nonconformist, were explained and defended every Sunday by the most eloquent and learned divines of every persuasion. At that time, therefore, the metropolitan electors were, as a class, decidedly superior in intelligence and knowledge to the provincial electors.

Montague and Secretary Vernon were the ministerial candidates for Westminster. They were opposed by Sir Henry Colt, a dull, surly, stubborn professor of patriotism, who tired everybody to death with his endless railing at standing armies and placemen. The electors were summoned to meet on an open space just out of the streets. The first Lord of the Treasury and the Secretary of State appeared at the head of three thousand horsemen. Colt's followers were almost all on foot. He was a favourite with the keepers of pot-houses, and had enlisted a strong body of porters and chairmen. The two parties, after exchanging a good deal of abuse, came to blows. The adherents of the ministers were victorious, put the adverse mob to the rout, and cudgelled Colt himself into a muddy ditch. The poll was taken in Westminster Hall. From the first there was no doubt of the result. But Colt tried to prolong the contest by bringing up a voter an hour. When it became clear that this artifice was employed for the purpose of causing delay, the returning officer took on himself the responsibility of closing the books, and of declaring Montague and Vernon duly elected.

At Guildhall the Junto was less fortunate. Three ministerial Aldermen were returned. But the fourth member, Sir John Fleet, was not only a Tory, but was Governor of the old East India Company, and had distinguished himself by the pertinacity with which he had opposed the financial and commercial policy of the first Lord of the Treasury. While Montague suffered the mortification of finding that his empire over the city was less absolute than he had imagined, Wharton, notwithstanding his acknowledged preeminence in the art of electioneering, underwent a succession of defeats in boroughs and counties for which he had expected to name the members.

He failed at Brackley, at Malmesbury and at Cockermouth. He was unable to maintain possession even of his own strongholds, Wycombe and Aylesbury. He was beaten in Oxfordshire. The freeholders of Buckinghamshire, who had been true to him during many years, and who in 1685, when the Whig party was in the lowest state of depression, had, in spite of fraud and tyranny, not only placed him at the head of the poll but put their second votes at his disposal, now rejected one of his candidates, and could hardly be induced to return the other, his own brother, by a very small majority.

The elections for Exeter appear to have been in that age observed by the nation with peculiar interest. For Exeter was not only one of the largest and most thriving cities in the Kingdom, but was also the capital of the West of England, and was much frequented by the gentry of several counties. The franchise was popular. Party spirit ran high; and the contests were among the fiercest and the longest of which there is any record in our history. Seymour had represented Exeter in the Parliament of James, and in the two first Parliaments of William. In 1695, after a struggle of several weeks which had attracted much attention not only here but on the Continent, he had been defeated by two Whig candidates, and forced to take refuge in a small borough. But times had changed. He was now returned in his absence by a large majority; and with him was joined another Tory less able and, if possible, more unprincipled than himself, Sir Bartholomew Shower. Shower had been notorious as one of the hangmen of James. When that cruel King was bent on punishing with death soldiers who deserted from the army which he kept up in defiance of the constitution, he found that he could expect no assistance from Holt, who was the Recorder of London. Holt was accordingly removed. Shower was made Recorder, and showed his gratitude for his promotion by sending to Tyburn men who, as every barrister in the Inns of Court knew, were guilty of no offence at all. He richly deserved to have been excepted from the Act of Grace, and left to the vengeance of the laws which he had so foully perverted. The return which he made for the clemency which spared him was most characteristic. He missed no opportunity of thwarting and damaging the Government which had saved him from the gallows. Having shed innocent blood for the purpose of enabling James to keep up thirty thousand troops without the consent of Parliament, he now pretended to think it monstrous that William should keep up ten thousand with the consent of Parliament. That a great constituent body should be so forgetful of the past and so much out of humour with the present as to take this base and hardhearted pettifogger for a patriot was an omen which might well justify the most gloomy prognostications.

When the returns were complete, it appeared that the new House of Commons contained an unusual number of men about whom little was known, and on whose support neither the government nor the opposition could with any confidence reckon. The ranks of the staunch ministerial Whigs were certainly much thinned; but it did not appear that the Tory ranks were much fuller than before. That section of the representative body which was Whiggish without being ministerial had gained a great accession of strength, and seemed likely to have, during some time, the fate of the country in its hands. It was plain that the next session would be a trying one. Yet it was not impossible that the servants of the Crown might, by prudent management, succeed in obtaining a working majority. Towards the close of August the statesmen of the Junto, disappointed and anxious but not hopeless, dispersed in order to lay in a stock of health and vigour for the next parliamentary campaign. There were races at that season in the neighbourhood of Winchenden, Wharton's seat in Buckinghamshire; and a large party assembled there. Orford, Montague and Shrewsbury repaired to the muster. But Somers, whose chronic maladies, aggravated by sedulous application to judicial and political business, made it necessary for him to avoid crowds and luxurious banquets, retired to Tunbridge Wells, and tried to repair his exhausted frame with the water of the springs and the air of the heath. Just at this moment despatches of the gravest importance arrived from Guelders at Whitehall.

The long negotiation touching the Spanish succession had at length been brought to a conclusion. Tallard had joined William at Loo, and had there met Heinsius and Portland. After much discussion, the price in consideration of which the House of Bourbon would consent to waive all claim to Spain and the Indies, and to support the pretensions of the Electoral Prince of Bavaria, was definitively settled. The Dauphin was to have the Province of Guipuscoa, Naples, Sicily and some small Italian islands which were part of the Spanish monarchy. The Milanese was allotted to the Archduke Charles. As the Electoral Prince was still a child, it was agreed that his father, who was then governing the Spanish Netherlands as Viceroy, should be Regent of Spain during the minority. Such was the first Partition Treaty, a treaty which has been during five generations confidently and noisily condemned, and for which scarcely any writer has ventured to offer even a timid apology, but which it may perhaps not be impossible to defend by grave and temperate argument.

It was said, when first the terms of the Partition Treaty were made public, and has since been many times repeated, that the English and Dutch Governments, in making this covenant with France, were guilty of a violation of plighted faith. They had, it was affirmed, by a secret article of a Treaty of Alliance concluded in 1689, bound themselves to support the pretensions of the Emperor to the Spanish throne; and they now, in direct defiance of that article, agreed to an arrangement by which he was excluded from the Spanish throne. The truth is that the secret article will not, whether construed according to the letter or according to the spirit, bear the sense which has generally been put upon it. The stipulations of that article were introduced by a preamble, in which it was set forth that the Dauphin was preparing to assert by arms his claim to the great heritage which his mother had renounced, and that there was reason to believe that he also aspired to the dignity of King of the Romans. For these reasons, England and the States General, considering the evil consequences which must follow if he should succeed in attaining either of his objects, promised to support with all their power his Cæsarean Majesty against the French and their adherents. Surely we cannot reasonably interpret this engagement to mean that, when the dangers mentioned in the preamble had ceased to exist, when the eldest Archduke was King of the Romans, and when the Dauphin had, for the sake of peace, withdrawn his claim to the Spanish Crown, England and the United Provinces would be bound to go to war for the purpose of supporting the cause of the Emperor, not against the French but against his own grandson, against the only prince who could reign at Madrid without exciting fear and jealousy throughout all Christendom.

While some persons accused William of breaking faith with the House of Austria, others accused him of interfering unjustly in the internal affairs of Spain. In the most ingenious and humorous political satire extant in our language, Arbuthnot's History of John Bull, England and Holland are typified by a clothier and a linendraper, who take upon themselves to settle the estate of a bedridden old gentleman in their neighbourhood. They meet at the corner of his park with paper and pencils, a pole, a chain and a semicircle, measure his fields, calculate the value of his mines, and then proceed to his house in order to take an inventory of his plate and furniture. But this pleasantry, excellent as pleasantry, hardly deserves serious refutation. No person who has a right to give any opinion at all about politics can think that the question, whether two of the greatest empires in the world should be virtually united so as to form one irresistible mass, was a question with which other states had nothing to do, a question about which other states could not take counsel together without being guilty of impertinence as gross as that of a busybody in private life who should insist on being allowed to dictate the wills of other people. If the whole Spanish monarchy should pass to the House of Bourbon, it was highly probable that in a few years England would cease to be great and free, and that Holland would be a mere province of France. Such a danger England and Holland might lawfully have averted by war; and it would be absurd to say that a danger which may be lawfully averted by war cannot lawfully be averted by peaceable means. If nations are so deeply interested in a question that they would be justified in resorting to arms for the purpose of settling it, they must surely be sufficiently interested in it to be justified in resorting to amicable arrangements for the purpose of settling it. Yet, strange to say, a multitude of writers who have warmly praised the English and Dutch governments for waging a long and bloody war in order to prevent the question of the Spanish succession from being settled in a manner prejudicial to them, have severely blamed those governments for trying to attain the same end without the shedding of a drop of blood, without the addition of a crown to the taxation of any country in Christendom, and without a moment's interruption of the trade of the world by land or by sea.

It has been said to have been unjust that three states should have combined to divide a fourth state without its own consent; and, in recent times, the partition of the Spanish monarchy which was meditated in 1698 has been compared to the greatest political crime which stains the history of modern Europe, the partition of Poland. But those who hold such language cannot have well considered the nature of the Spanish monarchy in the seventeenth century. That monarchy was not a body pervaded by one principle of vitality and sensation. It was an assemblage of distinct bodies, none of which had any strong sympathy with the rest, and some of which had a positive antipathy for each other. The partition planned at Loo was therefore the very opposite of the partition of Poland.

The partition of Poland was the partition of a nation. It was such a partition as is effected by hacking a living man limb from limb. The partition planned at Loo was the partition of an ill governed empire which was not a nation. It was such a partition as is effected by setting loose a drove of slaves who have been fastened together with collars and handcuffs, and whose union has produced only pain, inconvenience and mutual disgust. There is not the slightest reason to believe that the Neapolitans would have preferred the Catholic King to the Dauphin, or that the Lombards would have preferred the Catholic King to the Archduke. How little the Guipuscoans would have disliked separation from Spain and annexation to France we may judge from the fact that, a few years later, the States of Guipuscoa actually offered to transfer their allegiance to France on condition that their peculiar franchises should be held sacred.

One wound the partition would undoubtedly have inflicted, a wound on the Castilian pride. But surely the pride which a nation takes in exercising over other nations a blighting and withering dominion, a dominion without prudence or energy, without justice or mercy, is not a feeling entitled to much respect. And even a Castilian who was not greatly deficient in sagacity must have seen that an inheritance claimed by two of the greatest potentates in Europe could hardly pass entire to one claimant; that a partition was therefore all but inevitable; and that the question was in truth merely between a partition effected by friendly compromise and a partition effected by means of a long and devastating war.

There seems, therefore, to be no ground at all for pronouncing the terms of the Treaty of Loo unjust to the Emperor, to the Spanish monarchy considered as a whole, or to any part of that monarchy. Whether those terms were or were not too favourable to France is quite another question. It has often been maintained that she would have gained more by permanently annexing to herself Guipuscoa, Naples and Sicily than by sending the Duke of Anjou or the Duke of Berry to reign at the Escurial. On this point, however, if on any point, respect is due to the opinion of William. That he thoroughly understood the politics of Europe is as certain as that jealousy of the greatness of France was with him a passion, a ruling passion, almost an infirmity. Before we blame him, therefore, for making large concessions to the power which it was the chief business of his life to keep within bounds, we shall do well to consider whether those concessions may not, on close examination, be found to be rather apparent than real. The truth is that they were so, and were well known to be so both by William and by Lewis.

Naples and Sicily formed indeed a noble kingdom, fertile, populous, blessed with a delicious climate, and excellently situated for trade. Such a kingdom, had it been contiguous to Provence, would indeed have been a most formidable addition to the French monarchy. But a glance at the map ought to have been sufficient to undeceive those who imagined that the great antagonist of the House of Bourbon could be so weak as to lay the liberties of Europe at the feet of that house. A King of France would, by acquiring territories in the South of Italy, have really bound himself over to keep the peace; for, as soon as he was at war with his neighbours, those territories were certain to be worse than useless to him. They were hostages at the mercy of his enemies. It would be easy to attack them. It would be hardly possible to defend them. A French army sent to them by land would have to force its way through the passes of the Alps, through Piedmont, through Tuscany, and through the Pontifical States, in opposition probably to great German armies. A French fleet would run great risk of being intercepted and destroyed by the squadrons of England and Holland. Of all this Lewis was perfectly aware. He repeatedly declared that he should consider the kingdom of the Two Sicilies as a source, not of strength, but of weakness. He accepted it at last with murmurs: he seems to have intended to make it over to one of his younger grandsons; and he would beyond all doubt have gladly given it in exchange for a thirtieth part of the same area in the Netherlands.* But in the Nether-

---

* I will quote from the despatches of Lewis to Tallard three or four passages which show that the value of the kingdom of the Two Sicilies was quite justly appreciated at Versailles. "À l'égard du royaume de Naples et de Sicile le roi d'Angleterre objectera que les places de ces états entre mes mains me rendront maître du commerce de la Méditeranée. Vous pourrez en ce cas laisser entendre, comme de vous même, qu'il serait si difficile de conserver ces royaumes unis à ma couronne, que les dépenses nécessaires pour y envoyer des secours seraient si grands, et qu'autrefois il a tant coûté à la France pour les maintenir dans son obéissance, que vraisemblablement j'établirois un roi pour les gouverner, et que peut-être ce serait le partage d'un de mes petits-fils qui voudroit régner independamment." April $\frac{7}{17}$. 1698. "Les royaumes de Naples et de Sicile ne peuvent se regarder comme un partage dont mon fils puisse se contenter pour lui tenir lieu de tous ses droits. Les exemples du passé n'ont que trop appris combien ces états coutent à la France, le peu d'utilité dont ils sont pour elle, et la difficulté de les conserver." May 16. 1698. "Je considère la cession de ces royaumes comme une source continuelle de dépenses et d'embarras. Il n'en a que trop coûté à la France pour les conserver; et

lands England and Holland were determined to allow him nothing. What he really obtained in Italy was little more than a splendid provision for a cadet of his house. Guipuscoa was then in truth the price in consideration of which France consented that the Electoral Prince of Bavaria should be King of Spain and the Indies. Guipuscoa, though a small, was doubtless a valuable province, and was in a military point of view highly important. But Guipuscoa was not in the Netherlands. Guipuscoa would not make Lewis a more formidable neighbour to England or to the United Provinces. And, if the Treaty should be broken off, if the vast Spanish empire should be struggled for and torn in pieces by the rival races of Bourbon and Hapsburg, was it not possible, was it not probable, that France might lay her iron grasp, not on Guipuscoa alone, but on Luxemburg and Namur, on Hainault, Brabant and Antwerp, on Flanders East and West? Was it certain that the united force of all her neighbours would be sufficient to compel her to relinquish her prey? Was it not certain that the contest would be long and terrible? And would not the English and Dutch think themselves most fortunate if, after many bloody and costly campaigns, the French King could be compelled to sign a treaty, the same, word for word, with that which he was ready uncompelled to sign now?

William, firmly relying on his own judgment, had not yet, in the whole course of this momentous negotiation, asked the advice or employed the agency of any English minister. But the treaty could not be formally concluded without the instrumentality of one of the Secretaries of State and of the Great Seal. Portland was directed to write to Vernon. The King himself wrote to the Chancellor. Somers was authorised to consult any of his colleagues whom he might think fit to be entrusted with so high a secret; and he was requested to give his own opinion of the proposed arrangement. If that opinion should be favourable, not a day must be lost. The King of Spain might die at any moment, and could hardly live till the winter. Full powers must be sent to Loo, sealed, but with blanks left for the names of the plenipotentiaries. Strict secresy must be observed; and care must be taken that the clerks whose duty it was to draw up the necessary documents

---

l'expérience a fait voir la necessité indispensable d'y entretenir toujours des troupes, et d'y envoyer incessamment des vaisseaux, et combien toutes ces peines ont été inutiles." May 29. 1698. It would be easy to cite other passages of the same kind. But these are sufficient to vindicate what I have said in the text.

should not entertain any suspicion of the importance of the work which they were performing.

The despatch from Loo found Somers at a distance from all his political friends, and almost incapacitated by infirmities and by remedies from attending to serious business, his delicate frame worn out by the labours and vigils of many months, his head aching and giddy with the first draughts from the chalybeate spring. He roused himself, however, and promptly communicated by writing with Shrewsbury and Orford. Montague and Vernon came down to Tunbridge Wells, and conferred fully with him. The opinion of the leading Whig statesmen was communicated to the King in a letter which was not many months later placed on the records of Parliament. These statesmen entirely agreed with William in wishing to see the question of the Spanish succession speedily and peaceably settled. They apprehended that, if Charles should die leaving that question unsettled, the immense power of the French King and the geographical situation of his dominions would enable him to take immediate possession of the most important parts of the great inheritance. Whether he was likely to venture on so bold a course, and whether, if he did venture on it, any continental government would have the means and the spirit to withstand him, were questions as to which the English ministers, with unfeigned deference, submitted their opinion to that of their master, whose knowledge of the interests and tempers of all the courts of Europe was unrivalled. But there was one important point which must not be left out of consideration, and about which his servants might perhaps be better informed than himself, the temper of their own country. It was, the Chancellor wrote, their duty to tell His Majesty that the recent elections had indicated the public feeling in a manner which had not been expected, but which could not be mistaken. The spirit which had borne the nation up through nine years of exertions and sacrifices seemed to be dead. The people were sick of taxes : they hated the thought of war. As it would, in such circumstances, be no easy matter to form a coalition capable of resisting the pretensions of France, it was most desirable that she should be induced to withdraw those pretensions ; and it was not to be expected that she would withdraw them without securing for herself a large compensation. The principle of the Treaty of Loo, therefore, the English Ministers cordially approved. But whether the articles of that treaty were or were not too favourable to the House of Bourbon, and whether the House of

Bourbon was likely faithfully to observe them, were questions about which Somers delicately hinted that he and his colleagues felt some misgivings. They had their fears that Lewis might be playing false. They had their fears also that, possessed of Sicily, he would be master of the trade of the Levant ; and that, possessed of Guipuscoa, he would be able at any moment to push an army into the heart of Castile. But they had been reassured by the thought that their Sovereign thoroughly understood this department of politics, that he had fully considered all these things, that he had neglected no precaution, and that the concessions which he had made to France were the smallest which could have averted the calamities impending over Christendom. It was added that the service which His Majesty had rendered to the House of Bavaria gave him a right to ask for some return. Would it be too much to expect, from the gratitude of the prince who was soon to be a great king, some relaxation of the rigorous system which excluded the English trade from the Spanish colonies ? Such a relaxation would greatly endear His Majesty to his subjects.

With these suggestions the Chancellor sent off the powers which the King wanted. They were drawn up by Vernon with his own hand, and sealed in such a manner that no subordinate officer was let into the secret. Blanks were left, as the King had directed, for the names of two Commissioners. But Somers gently hinted that it would be proper to fill those blanks with the names of persons who were English by naturalisation, if not by birth, and who would therefore be responsible to Parliament.

The King now had what he wanted from England. The peculiarity of the Batavian polity threw some difficulties in his way : but every difficulty yielded to his authority and to the dexterous management of Heinsius. And in truth the treaty could not but be favourably regarded by the States General ; for it had been carefully framed with the especial object of preventing France from obtaining any accession of territory or influence on the side of the Netherlands ; and Dutchmen, who remembered the terrible year when the camp of Lewis had been pitched between Utrecht and Amsterdam, were delighted to find that he was not to add to his dominions a single fortress in their neighbourhood, and were quite willing to buy him off with whole provinces under the Pyrenees and the Apennines. The sanction both of the federal and of the provincial governments was given with ease and expedition ; and in the evening of the fourth of September 1698, the treaty was signed.   As to the blanks in the English powers, William had attended to his Chancellor's suggestion, and had inserted the names of Sir Joseph Williamson, minister at the Hague, a born Englishman, and of Portland, a naturalised Englishman.   The Grand Pensionary and seven other Commissioners signed on behalf of the United Provinces.   Tallard alone signed for France. He seems to have been extravagantly elated by what seemed to be the happy issue of the negotiation in which he had borne so great a part, and in his next despatch to Lewis boasted of the new treaty as destined to be the most famous that had been made during many centuries.

William too was well pleased ; and he had reason to be so. Had the King of Spain died, as all men expected, before the end of that year, it is highly probable that France would have kept faith with England and the United Provinces ; and it is almost certain that, if France had kept faith, the treaty would have been carried into effect without any serious opposition in any quarter.   The Emperor might have complained and threatened ; but he must have submitted ; for what could he do ?   He had no fleet ; and it was therefore impossible for him even to attempt to possess himself of Castile, of Arragon, of Sicily, of the Indies, in opposition to the united navies of the three greatest maritime powers in the world.   In fact, the only part of the Spanish empire which he could hope to seize and hold by force against the will of the confederates of Loo was the Milanese ; and the Milanese the confederates of Loo had agreed to assign to his family.   He would scarcely have been so mad as to disturb the peace of the world when the only thing which he had any chance of gaining by war was offered him without war.   The Castilians would doubtless have resented the dismemberment of the unwieldy body of which they formed the head.   But they would have perceived that by resisting they were much more likely to lose the Indies than to preserve Guipuscoa.   As to Italy, they could no more make war there than in the moon.   Thus the crisis which had seemed likely to produce an European war of ten years would have produced nothing worse than a few angry notes and plaintive manifestoes.

Both the confederate Kings wished their compact to remain a secret while their brother Charles lived ; and it probably would have remained secret, had it been confided only to the English and French Ministers.   But the institutions of the United Provinces were not well fitted for the purpose of concealment. It had been necessary to trust so many deputies and magistrates that rumours of what had been passing at Loo got abroad. Quiros, the Spanish Ambassador at the Hague, followed the trail with such skill and perseverance that he discovered, if not the whole truth, yet enough to furnish materials for a despatch which produced much irritation and alarm at Madrid. A council was summoned, and sate long in deliberation. The grandees of the proudest of Courts could hardly fail to perceive that their next sovereign, be he who he might, would find it impossible to avoid sacrificing part of his defenceless and widely scattered empire in order to preserve the rest; they could not bear to think that a single fort, a single islet, in any of the four quarters of the world was about to escape from the sullen domination of Castile. To this sentiment all the passions and prejudices of the haughty race were subordinate. "We are ready," such was the phrase then in their mouths, "to go to any body, to go to the Dauphin, to go to the Devil, so that we all go together." In the hope of averting the threatened dismemberment, the Spanish ministers advised their master to adopt as his heir the candidate whose pretensions it was understood that France, England and Holland were inclined to support. The advice was taken; and it was soon every where known that His Catholic Majesty had solemnly designated as his successor his nephew Francis Joseph, Electoral Prince of Bavaria. France protested against this arrangement, not, as far as can now be judged, because she meant to violate the Treaty of Loo, but because it would have been difficult for her, if she did not protest, to insist on the full execution of that treaty. Had she silently acquiesced in the nomination of the Electoral Prince, she would have appeared to admit that the Dauphin's pretensions were unfounded; and, if she admitted the Dauphin's pretensions to be unfounded, she could not, without flagrant injustice, demand several provinces as the price in consideration of which she would consent to waive those pretensions. Meanwhile the confederates had secured the cooperation of a most important person, the Elector of Bavaria, who was actually Governor of the Netherlands, and was likely to be in a few months, at farthest, Regent of the whole Spanish monarchy. He was perfectly sensible that the consent of France, England and Holland to his son's elevation was worth purchasing at almost any cost, and, with much alacrity, promised that, when the time came, he would do all in his power to facilitate the execution of the Treaty of Partition. He was indeed bound by the strongest ties to the confederates of Loo. They had, by a secret article, added to the treaty, agreed that, if the Electoral Prince should become King of Spain, and then die without issue, his father should be his heir. The news that young Francis Joseph had been declared heir to the throne of Spain was welcome to all the potentates of Europe with the single exception of his grandfather the Emperor. The vexation and indignation of Leopold were extreme. But there could be no doubt that, graciously or ungraciously, he would submit. It would have been madness in him to contend against all Western Europe on land ; and it was physically impossible for him to wage war on the sea. William was therefore able to indulge, during some weeks, the pleasing belief that he had by skill and firmness averted from the civilised world a general war which had lately seemed to be imminent, and that he had secured the great community of nations against the undue predominance of one too powerful member.

But the pleasure and the pride with which he contemplated the success of his foreign policy gave place to very different feelings as soon as he again had to deal with our domestic factions. And, indeed, those who most revere his memory must acknowledge that, in dealing with these factions, he did not, at this time, show his wonted statesmanship. For a wise man, he seems never to have been sufficiently aware how much offence is given by discourtesy in small things. His ministers had apprised him that the result of the elections had been un-satisfactory, and that the temper of the new representatives of the people would require much management. Unfortunately he did not lay this intimation to heart. He had by proclamation fixed the opening of the Parliament for the 29th of November. This was then considered as a very late day. For the London season began together with Michaelmas Term ; and, even during the war, the King had scarcely ever failed to receive the compliments of his faithful Lords and Commons on the fifth of November, the anniversary both of his birth and of his memorable landing. The numerous members of the House of Commons who were in town, having their time on their hands, formed cabals, and heated themselves and each other by mur-muring at his partiality for the country of his birth. He had been off to Holland, they said, at the earliest possible moment. He was now lingering in Holland till the latest possible moment. This was not the worst. The twenty-ninth of November came : but the King was not come. It was neces-sary that the Lords Justices should prorogue the Parliament to the sixth of December. The delay was imputed, and justly, to adverse winds. But the malecontents asked, with some reason, whether His Majesty had not known that there were often gales from the West in the German Ocean, and whether, when he had made a solemn appointment with the Estates of his Realm for a particular day, he ought not to have arranged things in such a way that nothing short of a miracle could have prevented him from keeping that appointment.

Thus the ill humour which a large proportion of the new legislators had brought up from their country seats became more and more acrid every day, till they entered on their functions. One question was much agitated during this unpleasant interval. Who was to be Speaker? The Junto wished to place Sir Thomas Littleton in the chair. He was one of their ablest, most zealous and most steadfast friends; and had been, both in the House of Commons and at the Board of Treasury, an invaluable second to Montague. There was reason indeed to expect a strong opposition. That Littleton was a Whig was a grave objection to him in the opinion of the Tories. That he was a placeman, and that he was for a standing army, were grave objections to him in the opinion of many who were not Tories. But nobody else came forward. The health of the late Speaker Foley had failed. Musgrave was talked of in coffeehouses: but the rumour that he would be proposed soon died away. Seymour's name was in a few mouths: but Seymour's day had gone by. He still possessed, indeed, those advantages which had once made him the first of the country gentlemen of England, illustrious descent, ample fortune, ready and weighty eloquence, perfect familiarity with parliamentary business. But all these things could not do so much to raise him as his moral character did to drag him down. Haughtiness such as his, though it could never have been liked, might, if it had been united with elevated sentiments of virtue and honour, have been pardoned. But of all the forms of pride, even the pride of upstart wealth not excepted, the most offensive is the pride of ancestry when found in company with sordid and ignoble vices, greediness, mendacity, knavery and impudence; and such was the pride of Seymour. Many, even of those who were well pleased to see the ministers galled by his keen and skilful rhetoric, remembered that he had sold himself more than once, and suspected that he was impatient to sell himself again. On the very eve of the opening of Parliament, a little tract entitled "Considerations on the Choice of a Speaker" was widely circulated, and seems to have produced a great sensation. The writer cautioned the representatives of the people, at some length, against Littleton; and then, in even stronger language, though more concisely, against Seymour; but did not suggest any third person. The sixth of December came, and found the Country party, as it called itself, still unprovided with a candidate. The King, who had not been many hours in London, took his seat in the House of Lords. The Commons were summoned to the bar, and were directed to choose a Speaker. They returned to their Chamber. Hartington proposed Littleton; and the proposition was seconded by Spencer. No other person was put in nomination: but there was a warm debate of two hours. Seymour, exasperated by finding that no party was inclined to support his pretensions, spoke with extravagant violence. He who could well remember the military despotism of Cromwell, who had been an active politician in the days of the Cabal, and who had seen his own beautiful county turned into a Golgotha by the Bloody Circuit, declared that the liberties of the nation had never been in greater danger than at that moment, and that their doom would be fixed if a courtier should be called to the chair. The opposition insisted on dividing. Hartington's motion was carried by two hundred and forty-two votes to a hundred and thirty-five, Littleton himself, according to the childish old usage which has descended to our times, voting in the minority. Three days later, he was presented and approved.

The King then spoke from the throne. He declared his firm conviction that the Houses were disposed to do whatever was necessary for the safety, honour and happiness of the kingdom; and he asked them for nothing more. When they came to consider the military and naval establishments, they would remember that, unless England were secure from attack, she could not continue to hold the high place which she had won for herself among European powers: her trade would languish; her credit would fail; and even her internal tranquillity would be in danger. He also expressed a hope that some progress would be made in the discharge of the debts contracted during the War. "I think," he said, "an English Parliament can never make such a mistake as not to hold sacred all Parliamentary engagements."

The speech appeared to be well received; and during a short time William flattered himself that the great fault, as he considered it, of the preceding session would be repaired, that the army would be augmented, and that he should be able, at the important conjuncture which was approaching, to speak to foreign powers in tones of authority, and especially to keep France steady to her engagements. The Whigs of the Junto, better acquainted with the temper of the country and of the new House of Commons, pronounced it impossible to carry a vote for a land force of more than ten thousand men. Ten thousand men would probably be obtained if His Majesty would authorise his servants to ask in his name for that number, and to declare that with a smaller number he could not answer for the public safety. William, firmly convinced that twenty thousand would be too few, refused to make or empower others to make a proposition which seemed to him absurd and disgraceful. Thus, at a moment at which it was peculiarly desirable that all who bore a part in the executive administration should act cordially together, there was serious dissension between him and his ablest councillors. For that dissension neither he nor they can be severely blamed. They were differently situated, and necessarily saw the same objects from different points of view. He, as was natural, considered the question chiefly as an European question. They, as was natural, considered it chiefly as an English question. They had found the antipathy to a standing army insurmountably strong even in the late Parliament, a Parliament disposed to place large confidence in them and in their master. In the new Parliament that antipathy amounted almost to a mania. That liberty, law, property, could never be secured while the Sovereign had a large body of regular troops at his command in time of peace, and that of all regular troops foreign troops were the most to be dreaded, had, during the recent elections, been repeated in every town hall and market place, and scrawled upon every dead wall. The reductions of the preceding year, it was said, even if they had been honestly carried into effect, would not have been sufficient; and they had not been honestly carried into effect. On this subject the ministers pronounced the temper of the Commons to be such that, if any person high in office were to ask for what His Majesty thought necessary, there would assuredly be a violent explosion: the majority would probably be provoked into disbanding all that remained of the army; and the kingdom would be left without a single soldier. William, however, could not be brought to believe that the case was so hopeless. He listened too easily to some secret adviser,—Sunderland was probably the man,—who accused Montague and Somers of cowardice and insincerity. They had, it was whispered in the royal ear, a majority whenever they really wanted one.    They were bent upon placing their friend Littleton in the Speaker's chair; and they had carried their point triumphantly.    They would carry as triumphantly a vote for a respectable military establishment if the honour of their master and the safety of their country were as dear to them as the petty interests of their own faction. It was to no purpose that the King was told, what was nevertheless perfectly true, that not one half of the members who had voted for Littleton, could, by any art or eloquence, be induced to vote for an augmentation of the land force.    While he was urging his ministers to stand up manfully against the popular prejudice, and while they were respectfully representing to him that by so standing up they should only make that prejudice stronger and more noxious, the day came which the Commons had fixed for taking the royal speech into consideration.    The House resolved itself into a Committee.    The great question was instantly raised; What provision should be made for the defence of the realm?    It was naturally expected that the confidential advisers of the Crown would propose something. As they remained silent, Harley took the lead which properly belonged to them, and moved that the army should not exceed seven thousand men.    Sir Charles Sedley suggested ten thousand.    Vernon, who was present, was of opinion that this number would have been carried if it had been proposed by one who was known to speak on behalf of the King.    But few members cared to support an amendment which was certain to be less pleasing to their constituents, and did not appear to be more pleasing to the Court, than the original motion.    Harley's resolution passed the Committee.    On the morrow it was reported and approved.    The House also resolved that all the seven thousand men who were to be retained should be natural born English subjects.    Other votes were carried without a single division either in the Committee or when the mace was on the table.

The King's indignation and vexation were extreme.    He was angry with the opposition, with the ministers, with all England. The nation seemed to him to be under a judicial infatuation, blind to dangers which his sagacity perceived to be real, near and formidable, and morbidly apprehensive of dangers which his conscience told him were no dangers at all.    The perverse islanders were willing to trust every thing that was most precious to them, their independence, their property, their laws, their religion, to the moderation and good faith of France, to the winds and the waves, to the steadiness and expertness of bat-

talions of ploughmen commanded by squires; and yet they
were afraid to trust him with the means of protecting them lest
he should use those means for the destruction of the liberties
which he had saved from extreme peril, which he had fenced
with new securities, which he had defended with the hazard of
his life, and which from the day of his accession he had never
once violated.    He was attached, and not without reason, to
the Blue Dutch Foot Guards.    That brigade had served under
him for many years, and had been eminently distinguished by
courage, discipline and fidelity.    In December 1688 that
brigade had been the first in his army to enter the English
capital, and had been entrusted with the important duty of
occupying Whitehall and guarding the person of James.
Eighteen months later, that brigade had been the first to plunge
into the waters of the Boyne.    Nor had the conduct of these
veteran soldiers been less exemplary in their quarters than in
the field.    The vote which required the King to discard them
merely because they were what he himself was seemed to him
a personal affront.    All these vexations and scandals he
imagined that his ministers might have averted, if they had been
more solicitous for his honour and for the success of his great
schemes of policy, and less solicitous about their own popularity.    They, on the other hand, continued to assure him, and,
as far as can now be judged, to assure him with perfect truth,
that it was altogether out of their power to effect what he wished.
Something they might perhaps be able to do.    Many members
of the House of Commons had said in private that seven thousand men was too small a number.    If His Majesty would let
it be understood that he should consider those who should vote
for ten thousand as having done him good service, there might
be hopes.    But there could be no hope if gentlemen found that
by voting for ten thousand they should please nobody, that they
should be held up to the counties and towns which they represented as turncoats and slaves for going so far to meet his
wishes, and that they should be at the same time frowned upon
at Kensington for not going farther.    The King was not to be
moved.    He had been too great to sink into littleness without
a struggle.    He had been the soul of two great coalitions, the
dread of France, the hope of all oppressed nations.    And was
he to be degraded into a mere puppet of the Harleys and the
Howes, a petty prince who could neither help nor hurt, a less
formidable enemy and less valuable ally than the Elector of
Brandenburg or the Duke of Savoy?    His spirit, quite as arbitrary and as impatient of control as that of any of his prede-

cessors, Stuart, Tudor or Plantagenet, swelled high against this ignominious bondage. It was well known at Versailles that he was cruelly mortified and incensed ; and, during a short time, a strange hope was cherished there that, in the heat of his resentment, he might be induced to imitate his uncles, Charles and James, to conclude another treaty of Dover, and to sell himself into vassalage for a subsidy which might make him independent of his niggardly and mutinous Parliament. Such a subsidy, it was thought, might be disguised under the name of a compensation for the little principality of Orange, which Lewis had long been desirous to purchase even at a fancy price. A despatch was drawn up containing a paragraph by which Tallard was to be apprised of his master's views, and instructed not to hazard any distinct proposition, but to try the effect of cautious and delicate insinuations, and, if possible, to draw William on to speak first. This paragraph was, on second thoughts, cancelled ; but that it should ever have been written must be considered a most significant circumstance.

It may with confidence be affirmed that William would never have stooped to be the pensioner of France : but it was with difficulty that he was, at this conjuncture, dissuaded from throwing up the government of England. When first he threw out hints about retiring to the Continent, his ministers imagined that he was only trying to frighten them into making a desperate effort to obtain for him an efficient army. But they soon saw reason to believe that he was in earnest. That he was in earnest, indeed, can hardly be doubted. For, in a confidential letter to Heinsius, whom he could have no motive for deceiving, he intimated his intention very clearly. " I foresee," he writes, " that I shall be driven to take an extreme course, and that I shall see you again in Holland sooner than I had imagined." * In fact he had resolved to go down to the Lords, to send for the Commons, and to make his last speech from the throne. That speech he actually prepared and had it translated. He meant to tell his hearers that he had come to England to rescue their religion and their liberties ; that, for that end, he had been under the necessity of waging a long and cruel war ; that the war had, by the blessing of God, ended in an honourable and advantageous peace ; and that the nation might now be tranquil and happy, if only those precautions were adopted which he had on the first day of the session recommended as essential to the public security. Since, however, the Estates of the Realm thought fit to slight his advice, and to

* Dec. $\frac{29}{30}$. 1698

expose themselves to the imminent risk of ruin, he would not be the witness of calamities which he had not caused and which he could not avert. He must therefore request the Houses to present to him a bill providing for the government of the realm : he would pass that bill, and withdraw from a post in which he could no longer be useful ; but he should always take a deep interest in the welfare of England ; and, if what he foreboded should come to pass, if in some day of danger she should again need his services, his life should be hazarded as freely as ever in her defence.

When the King showed his speech to the Chancellor, that wise minister forgot for a moment his habitual self-command. "This is extravagance, Sir," he said : "this is madness. I implore your Majesty, for the sake of your own honour, not to say to anybody else what you have said to me." He argued the matter during two hours, and no doubt lucidly and forcibly. William listened patiently ; but his purpose remained unchanged.

The alarm of the ministers seems to have been increased by finding that the King's intention had been confided to Marlborough, the very last man to whom such a secret would have been imparted unless William had really made up his mind to abdicate in favour of the Princess of Denmark. Somers had another audience, and again began to expostulate. But William cut him short. "We shall not agree, my Lord ; my mind is made up." "Then, Sir," said Somers, "I have to request that I may be excused from assisting as Chancellor at the fatal act which Your Majesty meditates. It was from my King that I received this seal ; and I beg that he will take it from me while he is still my King."

In these circumstances the ministers, though with scarcely the faintest hope of success, determined to try what they could do to meet the King's wishes. A select Committee had been appointed by the House of Commons to frame a bill for the disbanding of all the troops above seven thousand. A motion was made by one of the Court party that this Committee should be instructed to reconsider the number of men. Vernon acquitted himself well in the debate. Montague spoke with even more than his wonted ability and energy, but in vain. So far was he from being able to rally round him such a majority as that which had supported him in the preceding Parliament, that he could not count on the support even of the placemen who sate at the same executive board with him. Thomas Pelham, who had, only a few months before, been made a Lord of the Treasury, tried to answer him. "I own," said Pelham, "that last year I thought a large land force necessary : this year I think such a force unnecessary ; but I deny that I have been guilty of any inconsistency. Last year the great question of the Spanish succession was unsettled, and there was serious danger of a general war. That question has now been settled in the best possible way ; and we may look forward to many years of peace." A Whig of still greater note and authority, the Marquess of Hartington, separated himself on this occasion from the Junto. The current was irresistible. At last the voices of those who tried to speak for the Instruction were drowned by clamour. When the question was put, there was a great shout of No, and the minority submitted. To divide would have been merely to have exposed their weakness.

By this time it became clear that the relations between the executive government and the Parliament were again what they had been before the year 1695. The history of our polity at this time is closely connected with the history of one man. Hitherto Montague's career had been more splendidly and uninterruptedly successful than that of any member of the House of Commons, since the House of Commons had begun to exist. And now fortune had turned. By the Tories he had long been hated as a Whig : and the rapidity of his rise, the brilliancy of his fame, and the unvarying good luck which seemed to attend him, had made many Whigs his enemies. He was absurdly compared to the upstart favourites of a former age, Carr and Villiers, men whom he resembled in nothing but in the speed with which he had mounted from a humble to a lofty position. They had, without rendering any service to the State, without showing any capacity for the conduct of great affairs, been elevated to the highest dignities, in spite of the murmurs of the whole nation, by the mere partiality of the Sovereign. Montague owed every thing to his own merit and to the public opinion of his merit. With his master he appears to have had very little intercourse, and none that was not official. He was in truth a living monument of what the Revolution had done for the Country. The Revolution had found him a young student in a cell by the Cam, poring on the diagrams which illustrated the newly discovered laws of centripetal and centrifugal force, writing little copies of verses, and indulging visions of parsonages with rich glebes, and of closes in old cathedral towns ; had developed in him new talents ; had held out to him the hope of prizes of a very different sort from a rectory or a prebend. His eloquence had gained for him the ear of the legislature.    His skill in fiscal and commercial affairs had won for him the confidence of the City.    During four years he had been the undisputed leader of the majority of the House of Commons ; and every one of those years he had made memorable by great parliamentary victories, and by great public services.    It should seem that his success ought to have been gratifying to the nation, and especially to that assembly of which he was the chief ornament, of which indeed he might be called the creature.    The representatives of the people ought to have been well pleased to find that their approbation could, in the new order of things, do for the man whom they delighted to honour all that the mightiest of the Tudors could do for Leicester, or the most arbitrary of the Stuarts for Strafford.    But, strange to say, the Commons soon began to regard with an evil eye that greatness which was their own work.    The fault indeed was partly Montague's.    With all his ability, he had not the wisdom to avert, by suavity and moderation, that curse, the inseparable concomitant of prosperity and glory, which the ancients personified under the name of Nemesis.    His head, strong for all the purposes of debate and arithmetical calculation, was weak  against the intoxicating influence of success and fame.    He became proud even to insolence.    Old companions, who, a very few years before, had punned and rhymed with him in garrets, had dined with him at cheap ordinaries, had sate with him in the pit, and had lent him some silver to pay his seamstress's bill, hardly knew their friend Charles in the great man who could not forget for one moment that he was First Lord of the Treasury, that he was Chancellor of the Exchequer, that he had been a Regent of the kingdom, that he had founded the Bank of England and the new East India Company, that he had restored the currency, that he had invented the Exchequer Bills, that he had planned the General Mortgage, and that he had been pronounced, by a solemn vote of the Commons, to have deserved all the favours which he had received from the Crown.    It was said that admiration of himself and contempt of others were indicated by all his gestures and written in all the lines of his face.    The very way in which the little jackanapes, as the hostile pamphleteers loved to call him, strutted through the lobby, making the most of his small figure, rising on his toe, and perking up his chin, made him enemies.    Rash and arrogant sayings were imputed to him, and perhaps invented for him.    He was accused of boasting that there was nothing that he could not carry through the House of Commons, that he could turn the majority round his finger.

A crowd of libellers assailed him with much more than political hatred. Boundless rapacity and corruption were laid to his charge. He was represented as selling all the places in the revenue department for three years' purchase. The opprobrious nickname of Filcher was fastened on him. His luxury, it was said, was not less inordinate than his avarice. There was indeed an attempt made at this time to raise against the leading Whig politicians and their allies, the great moneyed men of the City, a cry much resembling the cry which, seventy or eighty years later, was raised against the English Nabobs. Great wealth, suddenly acquired, is not often enjoyed with moderation, dignity and good taste. It is therefore not impossible that there may have been some small foundation for the extravagant stories with which malecontent pamphleteers amused the leisure of malecontent squires. In such stories Montague played a conspicuous part. He contrived, it was said, to be at once as rich as Crœsus and as riotous as Mark Antony. His stud and his cellar were beyond all price. His very lacqueys turned up their noses at claret. He and his confederates were described as spending the immense sums of which they had plundered the public in banquets of four courses, such as Lucullus might have eaten in the Hall of Apollo. A supper for twelve Whigs, enriched by jobs, grants, bribes, lucky purchases and lucky sales of stock, was cheap at eighty pounds. At the end of every course all the fine linen on the table was changed. Those who saw the pyramids of choice wild fowl imagined that the entertainment had been prepared for fifty epicures at the least. Only six birds' nests from the Nicobar islands were to be had in London : and all the six, bought at an enormous price, were smoking in soup on the board. These fables were destitute alike of probability and of evidence. But Grub Street could devise no fable injurious to Montague which was not certain to find credence in more than half the manor houses and vicarages of England.

It may seem strange that a man who loved literature passionately, and rewarded literary merit munificently, should have been more savagely reviled both in prose and verse than almost any other politician in our history. But there is really no cause for wonder. A powerful, liberal and discerning protector of genius is very likely to be mentioned with honour long after his death, but is very likely also to be most brutally libelled during his life. In every age there will be twenty bad writers for one good one ; and every bad writer will think himself a good one. A ruler who neglects all men of letters alike does not wound the self love of any man of letters.  But a ruler who shows favour to the few men of letters who deserve it inflicts on the many the miseries of disappointed hope, of affronted pride, of jealousy cruel as the grave.  All the rage of a multitude of authors, irritated at once by the sting of want and by the sting of vanity, is directed against the unfortunate patron.  It is true that the thanks and eulogies of those whom he has befriended will be remembered when the invectives of those whom he has neglected are forgotten.  But in his own time the obloquy will probably make as much noise and find as much credit as the panegyric.  The name of Mæcenas has been made immortal by Horace and Virgil, and is popularly used to designate an accomplished statesman, who lives in close intimacy with the greatest poets and wits of his time, and heaps benefits on them with the most delicate generosity.  But it may well be suspected that, if the verses of Alpinus and Fannius, of Bavius and Mævius, had come down to us, we might see Mæcenas represented as the most niggardly and tasteless of human beings, nay as a man who, on system, neglected and persecuted all intellectual superiority.  It is certain that Montague was thus represented by contemporary scribblers.  They told the world in essays, in letters, in dialogues, in ballads, that he would do nothing for anybody without being paid either in money or in some vile services ; that he not only never rewarded merit, but hated it whenever he saw it ; that he practised the meanest arts for the purpose of depressing it ; that those whom he protected and enriched were not men of ability and virtue, but wretches distinguished only by their sycophancy and their low debaucheries.  And this was said of the man who made the fortune of Joseph Addison, and of Isaac Newton.

Nothing had done more to diminish the influence of Montague in the House of Commons than a step which he had taken a few weeks before the meeting of the Parliament.  It would seem that the result of the general election had made him uneasy, and that he had looked anxiously round him for some harbour in which he might take refuge from the storms which seemed to be gathering.  While his thoughts were thus employed, he learned that the Auditorship of the Exchequer had suddenly become vacant.  The Auditorship was held for life.  The duties were formal and easy.  The gains were uncertain : for they rose and fell with the public expenditure : but they could hardly, in time of peace, and under the most economical administration, be less than four thousand pounds a year, and were likely, in time of war, to be more than double of that sum. Montague marked this great office for his own. He could not indeed take it, while he continued to be in charge of the public purse. For it would have been indecent, and perhaps illegal, that he should audit his own accounts. He therefore selected his brother Christopher, whom he had lately made a Commissioner of the Excise, to keep the place for him. There was, as may easily be supposed, no want of powerful and noble competitors for such a prize. Leeds had, more than twenty years before, obtained from Charles the Second a patent granting the reversion to Caermarthen. Godolphin, it was said, pleaded a promise made by William. But Montague maintained, and was, it seems, right in maintaining, that both the patent of Charles and the promise of William had been given under a mistake, and that the right of appointing the Auditor belonged, not to the Crown, but to the Board of Treasury. He carried his point with characteristic audacity and celerity. The news of the vacancy reached London on a Sunday. On the Tuesday the new Auditor was sworn in. The ministers were amazed. Even the Chancellor, with whom Montague was on terms of intimate friendship, had not been consulted. Godolphin devoured his ill temper. Caermarthen ordered out his wonderful yacht, and hastened to complain to the King, who was then at Loo. But what had been done could not be undone.

This bold stroke placed Montague's fortune, in the lower sense of the word, out of hazard, but increased the animosity of his enemies and cooled the zeal of his adherents. In a letter written by one of his colleagues, Secretary Vernon, on the day after the appointment, the Auditorship is described as at once a safe and lucrative place. " But I thought," Vernon proceeds, " Mr. Montague was too aspiring to stoop to any thing below the height he was in, and that he least considered profit." This feeling was no doubt shared by many of the friends of the ministry. It was plain that Montague was preparing a retreat for himself. This flinching of the captain, just on the eve of a perilous campaign, naturally disheartened the whole army. It deserves to be remarked that, more than eighty years later, another great parliamentary leader was placed in a very similar situation. The younger William Pitt held in 1784 the same offices which Montague had held in 1698. Pitt was pressed in 1784 by political difficulties not less than those with which Montague had contended in 1698. Pitt was also in 1784 a much poorer man than Montague in 1698. Pitt, in 1784, like Montague in 1698, had at his own absolute disposal a lucrative sinecure place in the Exchequer. Pitt gave away the office which would have made him an opulent man, and gave it away in such a manner as at once to reward unfortunate merit, and to relieve the country from a burden. For this disinterestedness he was repaid by the enthusiastic applause of his followers, by the enforced respect of his opponents, and by the confidence which, through all the vicissitudes of a chequered and at length disastrous career, the great body of Englishmen reposed in his public spirit and in his personal integrity. In the intellectual qualities of a statesman Montague was probably not inferior to Pitt. But the magnanimity, the dauntless courage, the contempt for riches and for baubles, to which, more than to any intellectual quality, Pitt owed his long ascendency, were wanting to Montague.

The faults of Montague were great ; but his punishment was cruel. It was indeed a punishment which must have been more bitter than the bitterness of death to a man whose vanity was exquisitely sensitive, and who had been spoiled by early and rapid success and by constant prosperity. Before the new Parliament had been a month sitting it was plain that his empire was at an end. He spoke with the old eloquence ; but his speeches no longer called forth the old response. Whatever he proposed was maliciously scrutinised. The success of his budget of the preceding year had surpassed all expectation. The two millions which he had undertaken to find had been raised with a rapidity which seemed magical. Yet for bringing the riches of the City, in an unprecedented flood, to overflow the Exchequer he was reviled as if his scheme had failed more ludicrously than the Tory Land Bank. Emboldened by his unpopularity, the Old East India Company presented a petition praying that the General Society Act, which his influence and eloquence had induced the late Parliament to pass, might be extensively modified. Howe took the matter up. It was moved that leave should be given to bring in a bill according to the prayer of the petition ; the motion was carried by a hundred and seventy-five votes to a hundred and forty-eight ; and the whole question of the trade with the Eastern seas was reopened. The bill was brought in, but was, with great difficulty and by a very small majority, thrown out on the second reading.* On other financial questions Montague, so lately

* Commons' Journals, February 24. 27. ; March 9. 169⅞. In the Vernon Correspondence a letter about the East India question which belongs to the year 1⁶⁹⁹⁄₁₇₀₀ is put under the date of Feb. 10. 169⅞. The truth is that this most valuable correspondence cannot be used to good purpose by any writer who does not do for himself all that the editor ought to have done.

the oracle of the Committee of Supply, was now heard with malevolent distrust. If his enemies were unable to detect any flaw in his reasonings and calculations, they could at least whisper that Mr. Montague was very cunning, that it was not easy to track him, but that it might be taken for granted that for whatever he did he had some sinister motive, and that the safest course was to negative whatever he proposed. Though that House of Commons was economical even to a vice, the majority preferred paying high interest to paying low interest, solely because the plan for raising money at low interest had been framed by him. In a despatch from the Dutch embassy the States General were informed that many of the votes of that session which had caused astonishment out of doors were to be ascribed to nothing but to the bitter envy which the ability and fame of Montague had excited. It was not without a hard struggle and a sharp pang that the first Englishman who has held that high position which has now been long called the Leadership of the House of Commons submitted to be deposed. But he was set upon with cowardly malignity by whole rows of small men none of whom singly would have dared to look him in the face. A contemporary pamphleteer compared him to an owl in the sunshine pursued and pecked to death by flights of tiny birds. On one occasion he was irritated into uttering an oath. Then there was a cry of Order; and he was threatened with the Serjeant and the Tower. On another occasion he was moved even to shedding tears of rage and vexation, tears which only moved the mockery of his low minded and bad hearted foes.

If a minister were now to find himself thus situated in a House of Commons which had just been elected, and from which it would therefore be idle to appeal to the electors, he would instantly resign his office, and his adversaries would take his place. The change would be most advantageous to the public, even if we suppose his successor to be both less virtuous and less able than himself. For it is much better for the country to have a bad ministry than to have no ministry at all; and there would be no ministry at all if the executive departments were filled by men whom the representatives of the people took every opportunity of thwarting and insulting. That an unprincipled man should be followed by a majority of the House of Commons is no doubt an evil. But, when this is the case, he will nowhere be so harmless as at the head of affairs. As he already possesses the power to do boundless mischief, it is desirable to give him a strong motive to abstain

from doing mischief; and such a motive he has from the moment
that he is entrusted with the administration. Office of itself does
much to equalise politicians. It by no means brings all characters
to a level; but it does bring high characters down and low
characters up towards a common standard. In power the
most patriotic and most enlightened statesman finds that he
must disappoint the expectations of his admirers; that, if he
effects any good, he must effect it by compromise; that he
must relinquish many favourite schemes; that he must bear
with many abuses. On the other hand, power turns the very
vices of the most worthless adventurer, his selfish ambition, his
sordid cupidity, his vanity, his cowardice, into a sort of public
spirit. The most greedy and cruel wrecker that ever put up
false lights to lure mariners to their destruction will do his best
to preserve a ship from going to pieces on the rocks, if he is
taken on board of her and made pilot: and so the most profligate Chancellor of the Exchequer must wish that trade may
flourish, that the revenue may come in well, and that he may
be able to take taxes off instead of putting them on. The
most profligate First Lord of the Admiralty must wish to
receive news of a victory like that of the Nile rather than of a
mutiny like that at the Nore. There is, therefore, a limit to
the evil which is to be apprehended from the worst ministry
that is likely ever to exist in England. But to the evil of
having no ministry, to the evil of having a House of Commons
permanently at war with the executive government, there is
absolutely no limit. This was signally proved in 1699 and
1700. Had the statesmen of the Junto, as soon as they had
ascertained the temper of the new Parliament, acted as statesmen similarly situated would now act, great calamities would
have been averted. The chiefs of the opposition must then
have been called upon to form a government. With the power
of the late ministry the responsibility of the late ministry would
have been transferred to them; and that responsibility would
at once have sobered them. The orator whose eloquence had
been the delight of the Country party would have had to exert
his ingenuity on a new set of topics. There would have been
an end of his invectives against courtiers and placemen, of
piteous moanings about the intolerable weight of the land tax,
of his boasts that the militia of Kent and Sussex, without the
help of a single regular soldier, would turn the conquerors of
Landen to the right about. He would himself have been a
courtier: he would himself have been a placeman: he would
have known that he should be held accountable for all

the misery which a national bankruptcy or a French invasion might produce : and, instead of labouring to get up a clamour for the reduction of imposts, and the disbanding of regiments, he would have employed all his talents and influence for the purpose of obtaining from Parliament the means of supporting public credit, and of putting the country in a good posture of defence.  Meanwhile the statesmen who were out might have watched the new men, might have checked them when they were wrong, might have come to their help when, by doing right, they had raised a mutiny in their own absurd and perverse faction.  In this way Montague and Somers might, in opposition, have been really far more powerful than they could be while they filled the highest posts in the executive government and were outvoted every day in the House of Commons.  Their retirement would have mitigated envy ; their abilities would have been missed and regretted ; their unpopularity would have passed to their successors, who would have grievously disappointed vulgar expectation, and would have been under the necessity of eating their own words in every debate.  The league between the Tories and the discontented Whigs would have been dissolved ; and it is probable that, in a session or two, the public voice would have loudly demanded the recall of the best Keeper of the Great Seal, and of the best First Lord of the Treasury, the oldest man living could remember.

But these lessons, the fruits of the experience of five generations, had never been taught to the politicians of the seventeenth century.  Notions imbibed before the Revolution still kept possession of the public mind.  Not even Somers, the foremost man of his age in civil wisdom, thought it strange that one party should be in possession of the executive administration while the other predominated in the legislature.  Thus, at the beginning of 1699, there ceased to be a ministry ; and years elapsed before the servants of the Crown and the representatives of the people were again joined in an union as harmonious as that which had existed from the general election of 1695 to the general election of 1698.  The anarchy lasted, with some short intervals of composedness, till the general election of 1705.  No portion of our parliamentary history is less pleasing or more instructive.  It will be seen that the House of Commons became altogether ungovernable, abused its gigantic power with unjust and insolent caprice, browbeat King and Lords, the Courts of Common Law and the Constituent bodies, violated rights guaranteed by the Great Charter, and at length made itself so odious that the people were glad to take shelter, under the protection of the throne and of the hereditary aristocracy, from the tyranny of the assembly which had been chosen by themselves.

The evil which had brought on so much discredit on representative institutions was of gradual though of rapid growth, and did not, in the first session of the Parliament of 1698, take the most alarming form. The lead of the House of Commons had, however, entirely passed away from Montague, who was still the first minister of finance, to the chiefs of the turbulent and discordant opposition. Among those chiefs the most powerful was Harley, who, while almost constantly acting with the Tories and High Churchmen, continued to use, on occasions cunningly selected, the political and religious phraseology which he had learned in his youth among the Roundheads. He thus, while high in the esteem of the country gentlemen and even of his hereditary enemies, the country parsons, retained a portion of the favour with which he and his ancestors had long been regarded by Whigs and Nonconformists. He was therefore peculiarly well qualified to act as mediator between the two sections of the majority.

The bill for the disbanding of the army passed with little opposition through the House till it reached the last stage. Then, at length, a stand was made, but in vain. Vernon wrote the next day to Shrewsbury that the ministers had had a division which they need not be ashamed of; for that they had mustered a hundred and fifty-four against two hundred and twenty-one. Such a division would not be considered as matter of boast by a Secretary of State in our time.

The bill went up to the House of Lords, where it was regarded with no great favour. But this was not one of those occasions on which the House of Lords can act effectually as a check on the popular branch of the legislature. No good would have been done by rejecting the bill for disbanding the troops, unless the King could have been furnished with the means of maintaining them; and with such means he could be furnished only by the House of Commons. Somers, in a speech of which both the eloquence and the wisdom were greatly admired, placed the question in the true light. He set forth strongly the dangers to which the jealousy and parsimony of the representatives of the people exposed the country. But any thing, he said, was better than that the King and the Peers should engage, without hope of success, in an acrimonious conflict with the Commons. Tankerville spoke with his usual ability on the same side. Nottingham and the other Tories remained silent; and the bill passed without a division.

By this time the King's strong understanding had mastered, as it seldom failed, after a struggle, to master, his rebellious temper. He had made up his mind to fulfil his great mission to the end. It was with no common pain that he admitted it to be necessary for him to give his assent to the disbanding bill. But in this case it would have been worse than useless to resort to his veto. For, if the bill had been rejected, the army would have been dissolved, and he would have been left without even the seven thousand men whom the Commons were willing to allow him. He determined, therefore, to comply with the wish of his people, and at the same time to give them a weighty and serious but friendly admonition. Never had he succeeded better in suppressing the outward signs of his emotions than on the day on which he carried this determination into effect. The public mind was much excited. The crowds in the parks and streets were immense. The Jacobites came in troops, hoping to enjoy the pleasure of reading shame and rage on the face of him whom they most hated and dreaded. The hope was disappointed. The Prussian Minister, a discerning observer, free from the passions which distracted English society, accompanied the royal procession from St. James's Palace to Westminster Hall. He well knew how bitterly William had been mortified, and was astonished to see him present himself to the public gaze with a serene and cheerful aspect.

The speech delivered from the throne was much admired; and the correspondent of the States General acknowledged that he despaired of exhibiting in a French translation the graces of style which distinguished the original. Indeed that weighty, simple and dignified eloquence which becomes the lips of a sovereign was seldom wanting in any composition of which the plan was furnished by William and the language by Somers. The King informed the Lords and Commons that he had come down to pass their bill as soon as it was ready for him. He could not indeed but think that they had carried the reduction of the army to a dangerous extent. He could not but feel that they had treated him unkindly in requiring him to part with those guards who had come over with him to deliver England, and who had since been near him on every field of battle. But it was his fixed opinion that nothing could be so pernicious to the State as that he should be regarded by his people with distrust, distrust of which he had not expected to be the object after what he had endeavoured, ventured, and acted, to restore and to secure their liberties. He had now, he said, told the Houses plainly the reason, the only reason, which had induced him to pass their bill; and it was his duty to tell them plainly, in discharge of his high trust, and in order that none might hold him accountable for the evils which he had vainly endeavoured to avert, that, in his judgment, the nation was left too much exposed.

When the Commons had returned to their chamber, and the King's speech had been read from the chair, Howe attempted to raise a storm. A gross insult had been offered to the House. The King ought to be asked who had put such words into his mouth. But the spiteful agitator found no support. The majority were so much pleased with the King for promptly passing the bill that they were not disposed to quarrel with him for frankly declaring that he disliked it. It was resolved without a division that an address should be presented, thanking him for his gracious speech and for his ready compliance with the wishes of his people, and assuring him that his grateful Commons would never forget the great things which he had done for the country, would never give him cause to think them unkind or undutiful, and would, on all occasions, stand by him against all enemies.

Just at this juncture tidings arrived which might well raise misgivings in the minds of those who had voted for reducing the national means of defence. The Electoral Prince of Bavaria was no more. The Gazette which announced that the Disbanding Bill had received the royal assent informed the public that he was dangerously ill at Brussels. The next Gazette contained the news of his death. Only a few weeks had elapsed since all who were anxious for the peace of the world had learned with joy that he had been named heir to the Spanish throne. That the boy just entering upon life with such hopes should die, while the wretched Charles, long ago half dead, continued to creep about between his bedroom and his chapel, was an event for which, notwithstanding the proverbial uncertainty of life, the minds of men were altogether unprepared. A peaceful solution of the great question now seemed impossible. France and Austria were left confronting each other. Within a month the whole Continent might be in arms. Pious men saw in this stroke, so sudden and so terrible, the plain signs of the divine displeasure. God had a controversy with the nations. Nine years of fire, of slaughter and of famine had not been sufficient to reclaim a guilty world; and a second and more severe chastisement was at hand. Others muttered that the event which all good men lamented was to be ascribed to unprincipled ambition. It would indeed have been strange if, in that age, so important a death, happening at so critical a moment, had not been imputed to poison. The father of the deceased Prince loudly accused the Court of Vienna; and the imputation, though not supported by the slightest evidence, was, during some time, believed by the vulgar.

The politicians at the Dutch embassy imagined that now at length the parliament would listen to reason. It seemed that even the country gentlemen must begin to contemplate the probability of an alarming crisis. The merchants of the Royal Exchange, much better acquainted than the country gentlemen with foreign lands, and much more accustomed than the country gentlemen to take large views, were in great agitation. Nobody could mistake the beat of that wonderful pulse which had recently begun, and has during five generations continued, to indicate the variations of the body politic. When Littleton was chosen speaker, the stocks rose. When it was resolved that the army should be reduced to seven thousand men, the stocks fell. When the death of the Electoral Prince was known, they fell still lower. The subscriptions to a new loan, which the Commons had, from mere spite to Montague, determined to raise on conditions of which he disapproved, came in very slowly. The signs of a reaction of feeling were discernible both in and out of Parliament. Many men are alarmists by constitution. Trenchard and Howe had frightened most men by writing and talking about the danger to which liberty and property would be exposed if the government were allowed to keep a large body of Janissaries in pay. The danger had ceased to exist; and those people who must always be afraid of something, as they could no longer be afraid of a standing army, began to be afraid of the French King. There was a turn in the tide of public opinion; and no part of statesmanship is more important than the art of taking the tide of public opinion at the turn. On more than one occasion William showed himself a master of that art. But, on the present occasion, a sentiment, in itself amiable and respectable, led him to commit the greatest mistake of his whole life. Had he at this conjuncture again earnestly pressed on the Houses the importance of providing for the defence of the kingdom, and asked of them an additional number of English troops, it is not improbable that he might have carried his point; it is certain that, if he had failed, there would have been nothing ignominious in his failure. Unhappily, instead of raising a great public question, on which he was in the right, on which he had a good chance of succeeding, and on which he might have been defeated without any loss of dignity, he chose to raise a personal question, on which he was in the wrong, on which, right or wrong, he was sure to be beaten, and on which he could not be beaten without being degraded. Instead of pressing for more English regiments, he exerted all his influence to obtain for the Dutch guards permission to remain in the island.

The first trial of strength was in the Upper House. A resolution was moved there to the effect that the Lords would gladly concur in any plan that could be suggested for retaining the services of the Dutch brigade. The motion was carried by fifty-four votes to thirty-eight. But a protest was entered, and was signed by all the minority. It is remarkable that Devonshire was, and that Marlborough was not, one of the Dissentients. Marlborough had formerly made himself conspicuous by the keenness and pertinacity with which he had attacked the Dutch. But he had now made his peace with the Court, and was in the receipt of a large salary from the civil list. He was in the House on that day ; and therefore, if he voted, must have voted with the majority. The Cavendishes had generally been strenuous supporters of the King and the Junto. But on the subject of the foreign troops Hartington in one House and his father in the other were intractable.

This vote of the Lords caused much murmuring among the Commons. It was said to be most unparliamentary to pass a bill one week, and the next week to pass a resolution condemning that bill. It was true that the bill had been passed before the death of the Electoral Prince was known in London. But that unhappy event, though it might be a good reason for increasing the English army, could be no reason for departing from the principle that the English army should consist of Englishmen. A gentleman who despised the vulgar clamour against professional soldiers, who held the doctrine of Somers's Balancing Letter, and who was prepared to vote for twenty or even thirty thousand men, might yet well ask why any of those men should be foreigners. Were our countrymen naturally inferior to men of other races in any of the qualities which, under proper training, make excellent soldiers ? That assuredly was not the opinion of the Prince who had, at the head of Ormond's Life Guards, driven the French household troops, till then invincible, back over the ruins of Neerwinden, and whose eagle eye and applauding voice had followed Cutts's grenadiers up the glacis of Namur. Bitter spirited malecontents muttered that, since there was no honourable service which could not be as well performed by the natives of the realm as by alien mercenaries, it might well be suspected that the King wanted his alien mercenaries for some service not honourable. If it were necessary to repel a French invasion or to put down an Irish insurrection, the Blues and the Buffs would stand by him to the death. But, if his object were to govern in defiance of the votes of his Parliament and of the cry of his people, he might well apprehend that English swords and muskets would, at the crisis, fail him, as they had failed his father in law, and might well wish to surround himself with men who were not of our blood, who had no reverence for our laws, and no sympathy with our feelings. Such imputations could find credit with no body superior in intelligence to those clownish squires who with difficulty managed to spell out Dyer's Letter over their ale. Men of sense and temper admitted that William had never shown any disposition to violate the solemn compact which he had made with the nation, and that, even if he were depraved enough to think of destroying the constitution by military violence, he was not imbecile enough to imagine that the Dutch brigade, or five such brigades, would suffice for his purpose. But such men, while they fully acquitted him of the design attributed to him by factious malignity, could not acquit him of a partiality which it was natural that he should feel, but which it would have been wise in him to hide, and with which it was impossible that his subjects should sympathise. He ought to have known that nothing is more offensive to free and proud nations than the sight of foreign uniforms and standards. Though not much conversant with books, he must have been acquainted with the chief events in the history of his own illustrious House ; and he could hardly have been ignorant that his great grandfather had commenced a long and glorious struggle against despotism by exciting the States General of Ghent to demand that all Spanish troops should be withdrawn from the Netherlands. The final parting between the tyrant and the future deliverer was not an event to be forgotten by any of the race of Nassau. " It was the States, Sir," said the Prince of Orange. Philip seized his wrist with a convulsive grasp, and exclaimed, " Not the States, but you, you, you."

William, however, determined to try whether a request made by himself in earnest and almost supplicating terms would induce his subjects to indulge his national partiality at the expense of their own. None of his ministers could flatter him with any hope of success. But on this subject he was too much excited to hear reason. He sent down to the Commons a message, not merely signed by himself according to the usual form, but written throughout with his own hand. He informed them that the necessary preparations had been made for sending away the guards who came with him to England, and that they would immediately embark, unless the House should, out of consideration for him, be disposed to retain them, which he should take very kindly. When the message had been read, a member proposed that a day might be fixed for the consideration of the subject. But the chiefs of the majority would not consent to any thing which might seem to indicate hesitation, and moved the previous question. The ministers were in a false position. It was out of their power to answer Harley when he sarcastically declared that he did not suspect them of having advised His Majesty on this occasion. If, he said, those gentlemen had thought it desirable that the Dutch brigade should remain in the kingdom, they would have done so before. There had been many opportunities of raising the question in a perfectly regular manner during the progress of the Disbanding Bill. Of those opportunities nobody had thought fit to avail himself ; and it was now too late to reopen the question. Most of the other members who spoke against taking the message into consideration took the same line, declined discussing points which might have been discussed when the Disbanding Bill was before the House, and declared merely that they could not consent to any thing so unparliamentary as the repealing of an Act which had just been passed. But this way of dealing with the message was far too mild and moderate to satisfy the implacable malice of Howe. In his courtly days he had vehemently called on the King to use the sword for the purpose of quelling the insubordination of the English regiments. "None but the Dutch troops," he said, "are to be trusted." He was now not ashamed to draw a parallel between those very Dutch troops and the Popish Kernes whom James had brought over from Munster and Connaught to enslave our island. The general feeling was such that the previous question was carried without a division. A Committee was immediately appointed to draw up an address explaining the reasons which made it impossible for the House to comply with His Majesty's wish. At the next sitting the Committee

*P 37

reported: and on the report there was an animated debate. The friends of the government thought the proposed address offensive. The most respectable members of the majority felt that it would be ungraceful to aggravate by harsh language the pain which must be caused by their conscientious opposition to the King's wishes. Some strong expressions were therefore softened down; some courtly phrases were inserted; but the House refused to omit one sentence which almost reproachfully reminded the King that in his memorable Declaration of 1688 he had promised to send back all the foreign forces as soon as he had effected the deliverance of this country. The division was, however, very close. There were one hundred and fifty-seven votes for omitting this passage, and one hundred and sixty-three for retaining it.*

The address was presented by the whole House. William's answer was as good as it was possible for him, in the unfortunate position in which he had placed himself, to return. It showed that he was deeply hurt; but it was temperate and dignified. Those who saw him in private knew that his feelings had been cruelly lacerated. His body sympathised with his mind. His sleep was broken. His headaches tormented him more than ever. From those whom he had been in the habit of considering as his friends, and who had failed him in the recent struggle, he did not attempt to conceal his displeasure. The lucrative see of Worcester was vacant; and some powerful Whigs of the cider country wished to obtain it for John Hall, Bishop of Bristol. One of the Foleys, a family zealous for the Revolution, but hostile to standing armies, spoke to the King on the subject. "I will pay as much respect to your wishes," said William, "as you and your's have paid to mine." Lloyd of St. Asaph was translated to Worcester.

The Dutch Guards immediately began to march to the coast. After all the clamour which had been raised against them, the populace witnessed their departure rather with sorrow than with triumph. They had been long domiciled here; they had

---

* I doubt whether there be extant a sentence of worse English than that on which the House divided. It is not merely inelegant and ungrammatical, but is evidently the work of a man of puzzled understanding, probably of Harley. "It is, Sir, to your loyal Commons an unspeakable grief, that any thing should be asked by Your Majesty's message to which they cannot consent, without doing violence to that constitution Your Majesty came over to restore and preserve; and did, at that time, in your gracious declaration, promise, that all those foreign forces which came over with you should be sent back."

been honest and inoffensive; and many of them were accompanied by English wives and by young children who talked no language but English. As they traversed the capital, not a single shout of exultation was raised; and they were almost everywhere greeted with kindness. One rude spectator, indeed, was heard to remark that Hans made a much better figure, now that he had been living ten years on the fat of the land, than when he first came. "A pretty figure you would have made," said a Dutch soldier, "if we had not come." And the retort was generally applauded. It would not, however, be reasonable to infer from the signs of public sympathy and good will with which the foreigners were dismissed that the nation wished them to remain. It was probably because they were going that they were regarded with favour by many who would never have seen them relieve guard at St. James's without black looks and muttered curses.

Side by side with the discussion about the land force had been proceeding a discussion, scarcely less animated, about the naval administration. The chief minister of marine was a man whom it had once been useless and even perilous to attack in the Commons. It was to no purpose that, in 1693, grave charges, resting on grave evidence, had been brought against the Russell who had conquered at La Hogue. The name of Russell acted as a spell on all who loved English freedom. The name of La Hogue acted as a spell on all who were proud of the glory of the English arms. The accusations, unexamined and unrefuted, were contemptuously flung aside; and the thanks of the House were voted to the accused commander without one dissentient voice. But times had changed. The Admiral still had zealous partisans: but the fame of his exploits had lost their gloss; people in general were quick to discern his faults; and his faults were but too discernible. That he had carried on a traitorous correspondence with Saint Germains had not been proved, and had been pronounced by the representatives of the people to be a foul calumny. Yet the imputation had left a stain on his name. His arrogant, insolent and quarrelsome temper made him an object of hatred. His vast and growing wealth made him an object of envy. What his official merits and demerits really were it is not easy to discover through the mist made up of factious abuse and factious panegyric. One set of writers described him as the most ravenous of all the plunderers of the poor overtaxed nation. Another set asserted that under him the ships were better built and rigged, the crews were better disciplined and better tempered, the biscuit was better, the beer was better, the slops were better, than under any of his predecessors; and yet that the charge to the public was less than it had been when the vessels were unseaworthy, when the sailors were riotous, when the food was alive with vermin, when the drink tasted like tanpickle, and when the clothes and hammocks were rotten. It may, however, be observed that these two representations are not inconsistent with each other; and there is strong reason to believe that both are, to a great extent, true. Orford was covetous and unprincipled; but he had great professional skill and knowledge, great industry, and a strong will. He was therefore an useful servant of the state when the interests of the state were not opposed to his own: and this was more than could be said of some who had preceded him. He was, for example, an incomparably better administrator than Torrington. For Torrington's weakness and negligence caused ten times as much mischief as his rapacity. But, when Orford had nothing to gain by doing what was wrong, he did what was right, and did it ably and diligently. Whatever Torrington did not embezzle he wasted. Orford may have embezzled as much as Torrington; but he wasted nothing.

Early in the session, the House of Commons resolved itself into a Committee on the state of the Navy. This Committee sate at intervals during more than three months. Orford's administration underwent a close scrutiny, and very narrowly escaped a severe censure. A resolution condemning the manner in which his accounts had been kept was lost by only one vote. There were a hundred and forty against him, and a hundred and forty-one for him. When the report was presented to the House, another attempt was made to put a stigma upon him. It was moved that the King should be requested to place the direction of maritime affairs in other hands. There were a hundred and sixty Ayes to a hundred and sixty-four Noes. With this victory, a victory hardly to be distinguished from a defeat, his friends were forced to be content. An address setting forth some of the abuses in the naval department, and beseeching King William to correct them, was voted without a division. In one of those abuses Orford was deeply interested. He was First Lord of the Admiralty; and he had held, ever since the Revolution, the lucrative place of Treasurer of the Navy. It was evidently improper that two offices, one of which was meant to be a check on the other, should be united in the same person; and this the Commons represented to the King.

Questions relating to the military and naval Establishments occupied the attention of the Commons so much during the session that, until the prorogation was at hand, little was said about the resumption of the Crown grants. But, just before the Land Tax Bill was sent up to the Lords, a clause was added to it by which seven Commissioners were empowered to take account of the property forfeited in Ireland during the late troubles. The selection of those Commissioners the House reserved to itself. Every member was directed to bring a list containing the names of seven persons who were not members ; and the seven names which appeared in the greatest number of lists were inserted in the bill. The result of the ballot was unfavourable to the government. Four of the seven on whom the choice fell were connected with the opposition ; and one of them, Trenchard, was the most conspicuous of the pamphleteers who had been during many months employed in raising a cry against the army.

The Land Tax Bill, with this clause tacked to it, was carried to the Upper House. The Peers complained, and not without reason, of this mode of proceeding. It may, they said, be very proper that Commissioners should be appointed by Act of Parliament to take account of the forfeited property in Ireland. But they should be appointed by a separate Act. Then we should be able to make amendments, to ask for conferences, to give and receive explanations. The Land Tax Bill we cannot amend. We may indeed reject it ; but we cannot reject it without shaking public credit, without leaving the kingdom defenceless, without raising a mutiny in the navy. The Lords yielded, but not without a protest which was signed by some strong Whigs and some strong Tories. The King was even more displeased than the Peers. " This Commission," he said, in one of his private letters, " will give plenty of trouble next winter." It did indeed give more trouble than he at all anticipated, and brought the nation nearer than it has ever since been to the verge of another revolution.

And now the supplies had been voted. The spring was brightening and blooming into summer. The lords and squires were sick of London ; and the King was sick of England. On the fourth day of May he prorogued the Houses with a speech very different from the speeches with which he had been in the habit of dismissing the preceding Parliament. He uttered not one word of thanks or praise. He expressed a hope that, when they should meet again, they would make effectual provision for the public safety. " I wish," these were his concluding words, "no mischief may happen in the mean time." The gentlemen who thronged the bar withdrew in wrath, and, as they could not take immediate vengeance, laid up his reproaches in their hearts against the beginning of the next session.

The Houses had broken up; but there was still much to be done before the King could set out for Loo. He did not yet perceive that the true way to escape from his difficulties was to form an entirely new ministry possessing the confidence of the majority which had, in the late session, been found so unmanageable. But some partial changes he could not help making. The recent votes of the Commons forced him seriously to consider the state of the Board of Admiralty. It was impossible that Orford could continue to preside at that Board and be at the same time Treasurer of the Navy. He was offered his option. His own wish was to keep the Treasurership, which was both the more lucrative and the more secure of his two places. But it was so strongly represented to him that he would disgrace himself by giving up great power for the sake of gains which, rich and childless as he was, ought to have been beneath his consideration, that he determined to remain at the Admiralty. He seems to have thought that the sacrifice which he had made entitled him to govern despotically the department at which he had been persuaded to remain. But he soon found that the King was determined to keep in his own hands the power of appointing and removing the Junior Lords. One of these Lords, especially, the First Commissioner hated, and was bent on ejecting, Sir George Rooke, who was Member of Parliament for Portsmouth. Rooke was a brave and skilful officer, and had, therefore, though a Tory in politics, been suffered to keep his place during the ascendency of the Whig Junto. Orford now complained to the King that Rooke had been in correspondence with the factious opposition which had given so much trouble, and had lent the weight of his professional and official authority to the accusations which had been brought against the naval administration. The King spoke to Rooke, who declared that Orford had been misinformed. "I have a great respect for my Lord; and on proper occasions I have not failed to express it in public. There have certainly been abuses at the Admiralty which I am unable to defend. When those abuses have been the subject of debate in the House of Commons, I have sate silent. But, whenever any personal attack has been made on my Lord, I have done him the best service that I could." William was satisfied, and thought that Orford should have been satisfied too. But that haughty and perverse nature could be content with nothing but absolute dominion. He tendered his resignation, and could not be induced to retract it. He said that he could be of no use. It would be easy to supply his place; and his successors should have his best wishes. He then retired to the country, where, as was reported and may easily be believed, he vented his ill humour in furious invectives against the King. The Treasurership of the Navy was given to the Speaker Littleton. The Earl of Bridgewater, a nobleman of very fair character and of some experience in business, became First Lord of the Admiralty.

Other changes were made at the same time. There had during some time been really no Lord President of the Council. Leeds, indeed, was still called Lord President, and, as such, took precedence of dukes of older creation; but he had not performed any of the duties of his office since the prosecution instituted against him by the Commons in 1695 had been suddenly stopped by an event which made the evidence of his guilt at once legally defective and morally complete. It seems strange that a statesman of eminent ability, who had been twice Prime Minister, should have wished to hold, by so ignominious a tenure, a place which can have had no attraction for him but the salary. To that salary, however, Leeds had clung, year after year; and he now relinquished it with a very bad grace. He was succeeded by Pembroke; and the Privy Seal which Pembroke laid down was put into the hands of a peer of recent creation, Viscount Lonsdale. Lonsdale had been distinguished in the House of Commons as Sir John Lowther, and had held high office, but had quitted public life in weariness and disgust, and had passed several years in retirement at his hereditary seat in Cumberland. He had planted forests round his house, and had employed Verrio to decorate the interior with gorgeous frescoes which represented the gods at their banquet of ambrosia. Very reluctantly, and only in compliance with the earnest and almost angry importunity of the King, Lonsdale consented to leave his magnificent retreat, and again to encounter the vexations of public life.

Trumball resigned the Secretaryship of State; and the Seals which he had held were given to Jersey, who was succeeded at Paris by the Earl of Manchester.

It is to be remarked that the new Privy Seal and the new Secretary of State were moderate Tories. The King had probably hoped that, by calling them to his councils, he should conciliate the opposition. But the device proved unsuccessful; and soon it appeared that the old practice of filling the chief offices of state with men taken from various parties, and hostile to one another, or, at least, unconnected with one another, was altogether unsuited to the new state of affairs ; and that, since the Commons had become possessed of supreme power, the only way to prevent them from abusing that power with boundless folly and violence was to intrust the government to a ministry which enjoyed their confidence.

While William was making these changes in the great offices of state, a change in which he took a still deeper interest was taking place in his own household. He had laboured in vain during many months to keep the peace between Portland and Albemarle. Albemarle, indeed, was all courtesy, good humour, and submission : but Portland would not be conciliated. Even to foreign ministers he railed at his rival and complained of his master. The whole Court was divided between the competitors, but divided very unequally. The majority took the side of Albemarle, whose manners were popular and whose power was evidently growing. Portland's few adherents were persons who, like him, had already made their fortunes, and who did not therefore think it worth their while to transfer their homage to a new patron. One of these persons tried to enlist Prior in Portland's faction, but with very little success. " Excuse me," said the poet, " if I follow your example and my Lord's. My Lord is a model to us all ; and you have imitated him to good purpose. He retires with half a million. You have large grants, a lucrative employment in Holland, a fine house. I have nothing of the kind. A court is like those fashionable churches into which we have looked at Paris. Those who have received the benediction are instantly away to the Opera House or the wood of Boulogne. Those who have not received the benediction are pressing and elbowing each other to get near the altar. You and my Lord have got your blessing, and are quite right to take yourselves off with it. I have not been blest, and must fight my way up as well as I can." Prior's wit was his own. But his worldly wisdom was common to him with multitudes ; and the crowd of those who wanted to be lords of the bedchamber, rangers of parks, and lieutenants of counties, neglected Portland and tried to ingratiate themselves with Albemarle.

By one person, however, Portland was still assiduously courted ; and that person was the King. Nothing was omitted which could soothe an irritated mind. Sometimes William argued, expostulated and implored during two hours together. But he found the comrade of his youth an altered man, unreasonable, obstinate and disrespectful even before the public eye.    The Prussian minister, an observant and impartial witness, declared that his hair had more than once stood on end to see the rude discourtesy with which the servant repelled the gracious advances of the master.    Over and over William invited his old friend to take the long accustomed seat in his royal coach, that seat which Prince George himself had never been permitted to invade ; and the invitation was over and over declined in a way which would have been thought uncivil even between equals. A sovereign could not, without a culpable sacrifice of his personal dignity, persist longer in such a contest.    Portland was permitted to withdraw from the palace.    To Heinsius, as to a common friend, William announced this separation in a letter which shows how deeply his feelings had been wounded.    "I cannot tell you what I have suffered.    I have done on my side every thing that I could do to satisfy him ; but it was decreed that a blind jealousy should make him regardless of every thing that ought to have been dear to him."    To Portland himself the King wrote in language still more touching.    "I hope that you will oblige me in one thing.    Keep your key of office.    I shall not consider you as bound to any attendance.    But I beg you to let me see you as often as possible.    That will be a great mitigation of the distress which you have caused me.    For, after all that has passed, I cannot help loving you tenderly."

Thus Portland retired to enjoy at his ease immense estates scattered over half the shires of England, and a hoard of ready money, such, it was said, as no other private man in Europe possessed.    His fortune still continued to grow.    For, though, after the fashion of his countrymen, he laid out large sums on the interior decoration of his houses, on his gardens, and on his aviaries, his other expenses were regulated with strict frugality.    His repose was, however, during some years not uninterrupted.    He had been trusted with such grave secrets, and employed in such high missions, that his assistance was still frequently necessary to the government ; and that assistance was given, not, as formerly, with the ardour of a devoted friend, but with the exactness of a conscientious servant.    He still continued to receive letters from William ; letters no longer indeed overflowing with kindness, but always indicative of perfect confidence and esteem.

The chief subject of those letters was the question which had been for a time settled in the previous autumn at Loo, and which had been reopened in the spring by the death of the Electoral Prince of Bavaria.

As soon as that event was known at Paris, Lewis directed

Tallard to sound William as to a new treaty. The first thought which occurred to William was that it might be possible to put the Elector of Bavaria in his son's place. But this suggestion was coldly received at Versailles, and not without reason. If, indeed, the young Francis Joseph had lived to succeed Charles, and had then died a minor without issue, the case would have been very different. Then the Elector would have been actually administering the government of the Spanish monarchy, and, supported by France, England and the United Provinces, might without much difficulty have continued to rule as King the empire which he had begun to rule as Regent. He would have had also, not indeed a right, but something which to the vulgar would have looked like a right, to be his son's heir. Now he was altogether unconnected with Spain. No more reason could be given for selecting him to be the Catholic King than for selecting the Margrave of Baden or the Grand Duke of Tuscany. Something was said about Victor Amadeus of Savoy, and something about the King of Portugal; but to both there were insurmountable objections. It seemed, therefore, that the only choice was between a French Prince and an Austrian Prince; and William learned, with agreeable surprise, that Lewis might possibly be induced to suffer the younger Archduke to be King of Spain and the Indies. It was intimated at the same time that the House of Bourbon would expect, in return for so great a concession to the rival House of Hapsburg, greater advantages than had been thought sufficient when the Dauphin consented to waive his claims in favour of a candidate whose elevation could cause no jealousies. What Lewis demanded, in addition to the portion formerly assigned to France, was the Milanese. With the Milanese he proposed to buy Lorraine from its Duke. To the Duke of Lorraine this arrangement would have been beneficial, and to the people of Lorraine more beneficial still. They were, and had long been, in a singularly unhappy situation. Lewis domineered over them as if they had been his subjects, and troubled himself as little about their happiness as if they had been his enemies. Since he exercised as absolute a power over them as over the Normans and Burgundians, it was desirable that he should have as great an interest in their welfare as in the welfare of the Normans and Burgundians.

On the basis proposed by France William was willing to negotiate; and, when, in June 1699, he left Kensington to pass the summer at Loo, the terms of the treaty known as the Second Treaty of Partition were very nearly adjusted. The great object now was to obtain the consent of the Emperor. That consent, it should seem, ought to have been readily and even eagerly given. Had it been given, it might perhaps have saved Christendom from a war of eleven years. But the policy of Austria was, at that time, strangely dilatory and irresolute. It was in vain that William and Heinsius represented the importance of every hour. " The Emperor's ministers go on dawdling," so the King wrote to Heinsius, " not because there is any difficulty about the matter, not because they mean to reject the terms, but solely because they are people who can make up their minds to nothing." While the negotiation at Vienna was thus drawn out into endless length, evil tidings came from Madrid.

Spain and her King had long been sunk so low that it seemed impossible for him to sink lower. Yet the political maladies of the monarchy and the physical maladies of the monarch went on growing, and exhibited every day some new and frightful symptom. Since the death of the Bavarian Prince, the Court had been divided between the Austrian faction, of which the Queen and the leading ministers Oropesa and Melgar were the chiefs, and the French faction, of which the most important member was Cardinal Portocarrero, Archbishop of Toledo. At length an event which, as far as can now be judged, was not the effect of a deeply meditated plan, and was altogether unconnected with the disputes about the succession, gave the advantage to the adherents of France. The government, having committed the great error of undertaking to supply Madrid with food, committed the still greater error of neglecting to perform what it had undertaken. The price of bread doubled. Complaints were made to the magistrates, and were heard with the indolent apathy characteristic of the Spanish administration from the highest to the lowest grade. Then the populace rose, attacked the house of Oropesa, poured by thousands into the great court of the palace, and insisted on seeing the King. The Queen appeared in a balcony, and told the rioters that His Majesty was asleep. Then the multitude set up a roar of fury. " It is false : we do not believe you. We will see him." " He has slept too long," said one threatening voice; " and it is high time that he should wake." The Queen retired weeping ; and the wretched being on whose dominions the sun never set tottered to the window, bowed as he had never bowed before, muttered some gracious promises, waved a handkerchief in the air, bowed again, and withdrew. Oropesa, afraid of being torn to pieces, retired to his country seat. Melgar made some show of resistance, garrisoned his house, and menaced the rabble with a shower of grenades, but was soon forced to go after Oropesa: and the supreme power passed to Portocarrero.

Portocarrero was one of a race of men of whom we, happily for us, have seen very little, but whose influence has been the curse of Roman Catholic countries. He was, like Sixtus the Fourth and Alexander the Sixth, a politician made out of an impious priest. Such politicians are generally worse than the worst of the laity, more merciless than any ruffian that can be found in camps, more dishonest than any pettifogger who haunts the tribunals. The sanctity of their profession has an unsanctifying influence on them. The lessons of the nursery, the habits of boyhood and of early youth, leave in the minds of the great majority of avowed infidels some traces of religion, which, in seasons of mourning and of sickness, become plainly discernible. But it is scarcely possible that any such trace should remain in the mind of the hypocrite who, during many years, is constantly going through what he considers as the mummery of preaching, saying mass, baptizing, shriving. When an ecclesiastic of this sort mixes in the contests of men of the world, he is indeed much to be dreaded as an enemy, but still more to be dreaded as an ally. From the pulpit where he daily employs his eloquence to embellish what he regards as fables, from the altar whence he daily looks down with secret scorn on the prostrate dupes who believe that he can turn a drop of wine into blood, from the confessional where he daily studies with cold and scientific attention the morbid anatomy of guilty consciences, he brings to courts some talents which may move the envy of the more cunning and unscrupulous of lay courtiers; a rare skill in reading characters and in managing tempers, a rare art of dissimulation, a rare dexterity in insinuating what it is not safe to affirm or to propose in explicit terms. There are two feelings which often prevent an unprincipled layman from becoming utterly depraved and despicable, domestic feeling, and chivalrous feeling. His heart may be softened by the endearments of a family. His pride may revolt from the thought of doing what does not become a gentleman. But neither with the domestic feeling nor with the chivalrous feeling has the wicked priest any sympathy. His gown excludes him from the closest and most tender of human relations, and at the same time dispenses him from the observation of the fashionable code of honour.

Such a priest was Portocarrero; and he seems to have been a consummate master of his craft. To the name of statesman he had no pretensions. The lofty part of his predecessor Ximenes was out of the range, not more of his intellectual, than his moral capacity. To reanimate a paralysed and torpid monarchy, to introduce order and economy into a bankrupt treasury, to restore the discipline of an army which had become a mob, to refit a navy which was perishing from mere rottenness, these were achievements beyond the power, beyond even the ambition, of that ignoble nature. But there was one task for which the new minister was admirably qualified, that of establishing, by means of superstitious terror, an absolute dominion over a feeble mind; and the feeblest of all minds was that of his unhappy sovereign. Even before the riot which had made the cardinal supreme in the state, he had succeeded in introducing into the palace a new confessor selected by himself. In a very short time the King's malady took a new form. That he was too weak to lift his food to his misshapen mouth, that, at thirty-seven, he had the bald head and wrinkled face of a man of seventy, that his complexion was turning from yellow to green, that he frequently fell down in fits and remained long insensible, these were no longer the worst symptoms of his malady. He had always been afraid of ghosts and demons; and it had long been necessary that three friars should watch every night by his restless bed as a guard against hobgoblins. But now he was firmly convinced that he was bewitched, that he was possessed, that there was a devil within him, that there were devils all around him. He was exorcised according to the forms of his Church: but this ceremony, instead of quieting him, scared him out of almost all the little reason that nature had given him. In his misery and despair he was induced to resort to irregular modes of relief. His confessor brought to court impostors who pretended that they could interrogate the powers of darkness. The Devil was called up, sworn and examined. This strange deponent made oath, as in the presence of God, that His Catholic Majesty was under a spell, which had been laid on him many years before, for the purpose of preventing the continuation of the royal line. A drug had been compounded out of the brains and kidneys of a human corpse, and had been administered in a cup of chocolate. This potion had dried up all the sources of life; and the best remedy to which the patient could now resort would be to swallow a bowl of consecrated oil every morning before breakfast. Unhappily, the authors of this story fell into contradictions which they could excuse only by throwing the blame on Satan, who, they said, was an unwilling witness, and a liar from the beginning. In the midst of their conjuring, the Inquisition came down upon them. It must be admitted that, if the Holy Office had reserved all its terrors for such cases, it would not now have been remembered as the most hateful judicature that was ever known among civilised men. The subaltern impostors were thrown into dungeons. But the chief criminal continued to be master of the King and of the kingdom. Meanwhile, in the distempered mind of Charles one mania succeeded another. A longing to pry into those mysteries of the grave from which human beings avert their thoughts had long been hereditary in his house. Juana, from whom the mental constitution of her posterity seems to have derived a morbid taint, had sate, year after year, by the bed on which lay the ghastly remains of her husband, apparelled in the rich embroidery and jewels which he had been wont to wear while living. Her son Charles found an eccentric pleasure in celebrating his own obsequies, in putting on his shroud, placing himself in the coffin, covering himself with the pall, and lying as one dead till the requiem had been sung, and the mourners had departed leaving him alone in the tomb. Philip the Second found a similar pleasure in gazing on the huge chest of bronze in which his remains were to be laid, and especially on the skull which, encircled with the crown of Spain, grinned at him from the cover. Philip the Fourth, too, hankered after burials and burial places, gratified his curiosity by gazing on the remains of his great grandfather, the Emperor, and sometimes stretched himself out at full length like a corpse in the niche which he had selected for himself in the royal cemetery. To that cemetery his son was now attracted by a strange fascination. Europe could show no more magnificent place of sepulture. A staircase encrusted with jasper led down from the stately church of the Escurial into an octagon situated just beneath the high altar. The vault, impervious to the sun, was rich with gold and precious marbles, which reflected the blaze from a huge chandelier of silver. On the right and on the left reposed, each in a massy sarcophagus, the departed kings and queens of Spain. Into this mausoleum the King descended with a long train of courtiers, and ordered the coffins to be unclosed. His mother had been embalmed with such consummate skill that she appeared as she had appeared on her death bed. The body of his grandfather too seemed entire, but crumbled into dust at the first touch. From

Charles neither the remains of his mother nor those of his grandfather could draw any sign of sensibility. But, when the gentle and graceful Louisa of Orleans, the miserable man's first wife, she who had lighted up his dark existence with one short and pale gleam of happiness, presented herself, after the lapse of ten years, to his eyes, his sullen apathy gave way. "She is in heaven," he cried; "and I shall soon be there with her:" and, with all the speed of which his limbs were capable, he tottered back to the upper air.

Such was the state of the Court of Spain when, in the autumn of 1699, it became known that, since the death of the Electoral Prince of Bavaria, the governments of France, of England and of the United Provinces, were busily engaged in framing a second Treaty of Partition. That Castilians would be indignant at learning that any foreign potentate meditated the dismemberment of that empire of which Castile was the head might have been foreseen. But it was less easy to foresee that William would be the chief and indeed almost the only object of their indignation. If the meditated partition really was unjustifiable, there could be no doubt that Lewis was far more to blame than William. For it was by Lewis, and not by William, that the partition had been originally suggested; and it was Lewis, and not William, who was to gain an accession of territory by the partition. Nobody could doubt that William would most gladly have acceded to any arrangement by which the Spanish monarchy, could be preserved entire without danger to the liberties of Europe, and that he had agreed to the division of that monarchy solely for the purpose of contenting Lewis. Nevertheless the Spanish ministers carefully avoided whatever could give offence to Lewis, and indemnified themselves by offering a gross indignity to William. The truth is that their pride had, as extravagant pride often has, a close affinity with meanness. They knew that it was unsafe to insult Lewis; and they believed that they might with perfect safety insult William. Lewis was absolute master of his large kingdom. He had at no great distance armies and fleets which one word from him would put in motion. If he were provoked, the white flag might in a few days be again flying on the walls of Barcelona. His immense power was contemplated by the Castilians with hope as well as with fear. He and he alone, they imagined, could avert that dismemberment of which they could not bear to think. Perhaps he might yet be induced to violate the engagements into which he had entered with England and Holland, if one of his grandsons were named successor to the Spanish throne. He, therefore, must be respected and courted. But William could at that moment do little to hurt or to help. He could hardly be said to have an army. He could take no step which would require an outlay of money without the sanction of the House of Commons; and it seemed to be the chief study of the House of Commons to cross him and to humble him. The history of the late session was known to the Spaniards principally by inaccurate reports brought by Irish friars. And, had those reports been accurate, the real nature of a Parliamentary struggle between the Court party and the Country party could have been but very imperfectly understood by the magnates of a realm in which there had not, during several generations, been any constitutional opposition to the royal pleasure. At one time it was generally believed at Madrid, not by the mere rabble, but by Grandees who had the envied privilege of going in coaches and four through the streets of the capital, that William had been deposed, that he had retired to Holland, that the Parliament had resolved that there should be no more kings, that a commonwealth had been proclaimed, and that a Doge was about to be appointed: and, though this rumour turned out to be false, it was but too true that the English government was, just at that conjuncture, in no condition to resent slights. Accordingly, the Marquess of Canales, who represented the Catholic King at Westminster, received instructions to remonstrate in strong language, and was not afraid to go beyond those instructions. He delivered to the Secretary of State a note abusive and impertinent beyond all example and all endurance. His master, he wrote, had learnt with amazement that King William, Holland and other powers,—for the ambassador, prudent even in his blustering, did not choose to name the King of France,—were engaged in framing a treaty, not only for settling the succession to the Spanish crown, but for the detestable purpose of dividing the Spanish monarchy. The whole scheme was vehemently condemned as contrary to the law of nature and to the law of God. The ambassador appealed from the King of England to the Parliament, to the nobility, and to the whole nation, and concluded by giving notice that he should lay the whole case before the two Houses when next they met.

The style of this paper shows how strong an impression had been made on foreign nations by the unfortunate events of the late session. The King, it was plain, was no longer considered as the head of the government. He was charged with having committed a wrong; but he was not asked to make reparation. He was treated as a subordinate officer who had been guilty of an offence against public law, and was threatened with the displeasure of the Commons, who, as the real rulers of the state, were bound to keep their servants in order. The Lords Justices read this outrageous note with indignation, and sent it with all speed to Loo. Thence they received, with equal speed, directions to send Canales out of the country. Our ambassador was at the same time recalled from Madrid; and all diplomatic intercourse between England and Spain was suspended.

It is probable that Canales would have expressed himself in a less unbecoming manner, had there not already existed a most unfortunate quarrel between Spain and William, a quarrel in which William was perfectly blameless, but in which the unanimous feeling of the English Parliament and of the English nation was on the side of Spain.

It is necessary to go back some years for the purpose of tracing the origin and progress of this quarrel. Few portions of our history are more interesting or instructive: but few have been more obscured and distorted by passion and prejudice. The story is an exciting one; and it has generally been told by writers whose judgment had been perverted by strong national partiality. Their invectives and lamentations have still to be temperately examined; and it may well be doubted whether, even now, after the lapse of more than a century and a half, feelings hardly compatible with temperate examination will not be stirred up in many minds by the name of Darien. In truth that name is associated with calamities so cruel that the recollection of them may not unnaturally disturb the equipoise even of a fair and sedate mind.

The man who brought these calamities on his country was not a mere visionary or a mere swindler. He was that William Paterson whose name is honourably associated with the auspicious commencement of a new era in English commerce and in English finance. His plan of a national bank, having been examined and approved by the most eminent statesmen who sate in the Parliament house at Westminster and by the most eminent merchants who walked the Exchange of London, had been carried into execution with signal success. He thought, and perhaps thought with reason, that his services had been ill requited. He was, indeed, one of the original Directors of the great corporation which owed its existence to him; but he was not reelected. It may easily be believed that his colleagues, citizens of ample fortune and of long experience in the practical part of trade, aldermen, wardens of companies, heads of firms well known in every Burse throughout the civilised world, were not well pleased to see among them in Grocers' Hall a foreign adventurer whose whole capital consisted in an inventive brain and a persuasive tongue. Some of them were probably weak enough to dislike him for being a Scot: some were probably mean enough to be jealous of his parts and knowledge: and even persons who were not unfavourably disposed to him might have discovered, before they had known him long, that, with all his cleverness, he was deficient in common sense; that his mind was full of schemes which, at the first glance, had a specious aspect, but which, on closer examination, appeared to be impracticable or pernicious; and that the benefit which the public had derived from one happy project formed by him would be very dearly purchased if it were taken for granted that all his other projects must be equally happy. Disgusted by what he considered as the ingratitude of the English, he repaired to the Continent, in the hope that he might be able to interest the traders of the Hanse Towns and the princes of the German Empire in his plans. From the Continent he returned unsuccessful to London; and then at length the thought that he might be more justly appreciated by his countrymen than by strangers seems to have risen in his mind. Just at this time he fell in with Fletcher of Saltoun, who happened to be in England. These eccentric men soon became intimate. Each of them had his monomania; and the two monomanias suited each other perfectly. Fletcher's whole soul was possessed by a sore, jealous, punctilious patriotism. His heart was ulcerated by the thought of the poverty, the feebleness, the political insignificance of Scotland, and of the indignities which she had suffered at the hand of her powerful and opulent neighbour. When he talked of her wrongs his dark meagre face took its sternest expression: his habitual frown grew blacker; and his eyes flashed more than their wonted fire. Paterson, on the other hand, firmly believed himself to have discovered the means of making any state which would follow his counsel great and prosperous in a time which, when compared with the life of an individual, could hardly be called long, and which, in the life of a nation, was but as a moment. There is not the least reason to believe that he was dishonest. Indeed he would have found more difficulty in deceiving others had he not begun by deceiving himself. His faith in his own schemes was strong even to martyrdom ; and the eloquence with which he illustrated and defended them had all the charm of sincerity and of enthusiasm. Very seldom has any blunder committed by fools, or any villany devised by impostors, brought on any society miseries so great as the dreams of these two friends, both of them men of integrity and both of them men of parts, were destined to bring on Scotland.

In 1695 the pair went down together to their native country The Parliament of that country was then about to meet under the presidency of Tweeddale, an old acquaintance and country neighbour of Fletcher. On Tweeddale the first attack was made. He was a shrewd, cautious, old politician. Yet it should seem that he was not able to hold out against the skill and energy of the assailants. Perhaps, however, he was not altogether a dupe. The public mind was at that moment violently agitated. Men of all parties were clamouring for an inquiry into the slaughter of Glencoe. There was reason to fear that the session which was about to commence would be stormy. In such circumstances the Lord High Commissioner might think that it would be prudent to appease the anger of the Estates by offering an almost irresistible bait to their cupidity. If such was the policy of Tweeddale, it was, for the moment, eminently successful. The Parliament, which met burning with indignation, was soothed into good humour. The blood of the murdered Macdonalds continued to cry for vengeance in vain. The schemes of Paterson, brought forward under the patronage of the ministers of the Crown, were sanctioned by the unanimous voice of the Legislature.

The great projector was the idol of the whole nation. Men spoke to him with more profound respect than to the Lord High Commissioner. His antechamber was crowded with solicitors desirous to catch some drops of that golden shower of which he was supposed to be the dispenser. To be seen walking with him in the High Street, to be honoured by him with a private interview of a quarter of an hour, were enviable distinctions. He, after the fashion of all the false prophets who have deluded themselves and others, drew new faith in his own lie from the credulity of his disciples. His countenance, his voice, his gestures, indicated boundless self-importance. When he appeared in public he looked,—such is the language of one who probably had often seen him,—like Atlas conscious that a world was on his shoulders. But the airs which he gave himself only heightened the respect and admiration which he inspired. His demeanour was regarded as a model. Scotchmen who wished to be thought wise looked as like Paterson as they could.

His plan, though as yet disclosed to the public only by glimpses, was applauded by all classes, factions and sects, lords, merchants, advocates, divines, Whigs and Jacobites, Cameronians and Episcopalians. In truth, of all the ten thousand bubbles of which history has preserved the memory, none was ever more skilfully puffed into existence; none ever soared higher, or glittered more brilliantly; and none ever burst with a more lamentable explosion. There was, however, a certain mixture of truth in the magnificent day dream which produced such fatal effects.

Scotland was, indeed, not blessed with a mild climate or a fertile soil. But the richest spots that had ever existed on the face of the earth had been spots quite as little favoured by nature. It was on a bare rock, surrounded by deep sea, that the streets of Tyre were piled up to a dizzy height. On that sterile crag were woven the robes of Persian satraps and Sicilian tyrants: there were fashioned silver bowls and chargers for the banquets of kings: and there Pomeranian amber was set in Lydian gold to adorn the necks of queens. In the warehouses were collected the fine linen of Egypt and the odorous gums of Arabia; the ivory of India, and the tin of Britain. In the port lay fleets of great ships which had weathered the storms of the Euxine and the Atlantic. Powerful and wealthy colonies in distant parts of the world looked up with filial reverence to the little island; and despots, who trampled on the laws and outraged the feelings of all the nations between the Hydaspes and the Ægean, condescended to court the population of that busy hive. At a later period, on a dreary bank formed by the soil which the Alpine streams swept down to the Adriatic, rose the palaces of Venice. Within a space which would not have been thought large enough for one of the parks of a rude northern baron were collected riches far exceeding those of a northern kingdom. In almost every one of the private dwellings which fringed the Great Canal were to be seen plate, mirrors, jewellery, tapestry, paintings, carving, such as might move the envy of the master of Holyrood. In the arsenal were munitions of war sufficient to maintain a contest against the whole power of the Ottoman Empire. And, before the grandeur of Venice had declined, another commonwealth, still less favoured, if possible, by nature, had rapidly risen to a power and opulence which the whole civilised world contemplated with envy and admiration. On a desolate marsh overhung by fogs and exhaling diseases, a marsh where there was neither wood nor stone, neither firm earth nor drinkable water, a marsh from which the ocean on one side and the Rhine on the other were with difficulty kept out by art, was to be found the most prosperous community in Europe. The wealth which was collected within five miles of the Stadthouse of Amsterdam would purchase the fee simple of Scotland. And why should this be? Was there any reason to believe that nature had bestowed on the Phœnician, on the Venetian, or on the Hollander, a larger measure of activity, of ingenuity, of forethought, of self command, than on the citizen of Edinburgh or Glasgow? The truth was that, in all those qualities which conduce to success in life, and especially in commercial life, the Scot had never been surpassed; perhaps he had never been equalled. All that was necessary was that his energy should take a proper direction; and a proper direction Paterson undertook to give.

His esoteric project was the original project of Christopher Columbus, extended and modified. Columbus had hoped to establish a communication between our quarter of the world and India across the great western ocean. But he was stopped by an unexpected obstacle. The American continent, stretching far north and far south into cold and inhospitable regions, presented what seemed an insurmountable barrier to his progress; and, in the same year in which he first set foot on that continent, Gama reached Malabar by doubling the Cape of Good Hope. The consequence was that during two hundred years the trade of Europe with the remoter parts of Asia had been carried on by rounding the immense peninsula of Africa. Paterson now revived the project of Columbus, and persuaded himself and others that it was possible to carry that project into effect in such a manner as to make his country the greatest emporium that had ever existed on our globe.

For this purpose it was necessary to occupy in America some spot which might be a resting place between Scotland and India. It was true that almost every habitable part of America had already been seized by some European power. Paterson, however, imagined that one province, the most important of all, had been overlooked by the short-sighted cupidity of vulgar politicians and vulgar traders. The isthmus which joined the two great continents of the New World remained, according to him, unappropriated. Great Spanish viceroyalties, he said, lay on the east and on the west; but the mountains and forests of Darien were abandoned to rude tribes which followed their own usages and obeyed their own princes. He had been in that part of the world, in what character was not quite clear. Some said that he had gone thither to convert the Indians, and some that he had gone thither to rob the Spaniards. But, missionary or pirate, he had visited Darien, and had brought away none but delightful recollections. The havens, he averred, were capacious and secure : the sea swarmed with turtle : the country was so mountainous that, within nine degrees of the equator, the climate was temperate ; and yet the inequalities of the ground offered no impediment to the conveyance of goods. Nothing would be easier than to construct roads along which a string of mules or a wheeled carriage might in the course of a single day pass from sea to sea. The soil was, to the depth of several feet, a rich black mould, on which a profusion of valuable herbs and fruits grew spontaneously, and on which all the choicest productions of tropical regions might easily be raised by human industry and art ; and yet the exuberant fertility of the earth had not tainted the purity of the air. Considered merely as a place of residence, the isthmus was a paradise. A colony placed there could not fail to prosper, even if it had no wealth except what was derived from agriculture. But agriculture was a secondary object in the colonization of Darien. Let but that precious neck of land be occupied by an intelligent, an enterprising, a thrifty race ; and, in a few years, the whole trade between India and Europe must be drawn to that point. The tedious and perilous passage round Africa would soon be abandoned. The merchant would no longer expose his cargoes to the mountainous billows and capricious gales of the Antarctic seas. The greater part of the voyage from Europe to Darien, and the whole voyage from Darien to the richest kingdoms of Asia, would be a rapid yet easy gliding before the trade winds over blue and sparkling waters. The voyage back across the Pacific would, in the latitude of Japan, be almost equally speedy and pleasant. Time, labour, money, would be saved. The returns would come in more quickly. Fewer hands would be required to navigate the ships. The loss of a vessel would be a rare event. The trade would increase fast. In a short time it would double ; and it would all pass through Darien. Whoever possessed that door of the sea, that key of the universe,—such were the bold figures which Paterson loved to employ,—would give law to both hemispheres ; and would, by peaceful arts, without shedding one drop of blood, establish an empire as splendid as that of Cyrus or Alexander. Of the kingdoms of Europe, Scotland was, as yet, the poorest and the least considered. If she would but occupy Darien, if she would but become one great free port, one great warehouse for the wealth which the soil of Darien might produce, and for the still greater wealth which would be poured into Darien from Canton and Siam, from Ceylon and the Moluccas, from the mouths of the Ganges and the Gulf of Cambay, she would at once take her place in the first rank among nations. No rival would be able to contend with her either in the West Indian or in the East Indian trade. The beggarly country, as it had been insolently called by the inhabitants of warmer and more fruitful regions, would be the great mart for the choicest luxuries, sugar, rum, coffee, chocolate, tobacco, the tea and porcelain of China, the muslin of Dacca, the shawls of Cashmere, the diamonds of Golconda, the pearls of Karrack, the delicious birds' nests of Nicobar, cinnamon and pepper, ivory and sandal wood. From Scotland would come all the finest jewels and brocade worn by duchesses at the balls of St. James's and Versailles. From Scotland would come all the saltpetre which would furnish the means of war to the fleets and armies of contending potentates. And on all the vast riches which would be constantly passing through the little kingdom a toll would be paid which would remain behind. There would be a prosperity such as might seem fabulous, a prosperity of which every Scotchman, from the peer to the cadie, would partake. Soon, all along the now desolate shores of the Forth and Clyde, villas and pleasure grounds would be as thick as along the edges of the Dutch canals. Edinburgh would vie with London and Paris; and the baillie of Glasgow or Dundee would have as stately and well furnished a mansion, and as fine a gallery of pictures, as any burgomaster of Amsterdam.

This magnificent plan was at first but partially disclosed to the public. A colony was to be planted: a vast trade was to be opened between both the Indies and Scotland: but the name of Darien was as yet pronounced only in whispers by Paterson and by his most confidential friends. He had however shown enough to excite boundless hopes and desires. How well he succeeded in inspiring others with his own feelings is sufficiently proved by the memorable Act to which the Lord High Commissioner gave the Royal sanction on the 26th of June 1695. By this Act some persons who were named, and such other persons as should join with them, were formed into a corporation, which was to be named the Company of Scotland trading to Africa and the Indies. The amount of the capital to be employed was not fixed by law; but it was provided that one half of the stock at least must be

held by Scotchmen resident in Scotland, and that no stock
which had been originally held by a Scotchman resident in
Scotland should ever be transferred to any but a Scotchman
resident in Scotland.  An entire monopoly of the trade with
Asia, Africa and America, for a term of thirty-one years, was
granted to the Company.  All goods imported by the Company
were during twenty-one years to be duty free, with the exception of foreign sugar and tobacco.  Sugar and tobacco grown
on the Company's own plantations were exempted from all
taxation.  Every member and every servant of the Company
was to be privileged against impressment and arrest.  If any of
these privileged persons was impressed or arrested, the Company was authorised to release him, and to demand the
assistance both of the civil and of the military power.  The
Company was authorised to take possession of unoccupied
territories in any part of Asia, Africa or America, and there to
plant colonies, to build towns and forts, to impose taxes, and
to provide magazines, arms and ammunition, to raise troops, to
wage war, to conclude treaties; and the King was made to
promise that, if any foreign state should injure the Company,
he would interpose, and would, at the public charge, obtain
reparation.  Lastly it was provided that, in order to give
greater security and solemnity to this most exorbitant grant,
the whole substance of the Act should be set forth in Letters
Patent to which the Chancellor was directed to put the Great
Seal without delay.

The letters were drawn : the Great Seal was affixed : the
subscription books were opened ; the shares were fixed at a
hundred pounds sterling each ; and from the Pentland Firth
to the Solway Firth every man who had a hundred pounds was
impatient to put down his name.  About two hundred and
twenty thousand pounds were actually paid up.  This may not,
at first sight, appear a large sum to those who remember the
bubbles of 1825 and of 1845, and would assuredly not have
sufficed to defray the charge of three months of war with
Spain.  Yet the effort was marvellous when it may be affirmed
with confidence that the Scotch people voluntarily contributed
for the colonisation of Darien a larger proportion of their
substance than any other people ever, in the same space of
time, voluntarily contributed to any commercial undertaking.
A great part of Scotland was then as poor and rude as
Iceland now is.  There were five or six shires which did not
altogether contain so many guineas and crowns as were tossed
about every day by the shovels of a single goldsmith in

Lombard Street. Even the nobles had very little ready money. They generally took a large part of their rents in kind, and were thus able, on their own domains, to live plentifully and hospitably. But there were many esquires in Kent and Somersetshire who received from their tenants a greater quantity of gold and silver than a Duke of Gordon or a Marquess of Atholl drew from extensive provinces. The pecuniary remuneration of the clergy was such as would have moved the pity of the most needy curate who thought it a privilege to drink his ale and smoke his pipe in the kitchen of an English manor house. Even in the fertile Merse there were parishes of which the minister received only from four to eight pounds sterling in cash. The official income of the Lord President of the Court of Session was only five hundred a year; that of the Lord Justice Clerk only four hundred a year. The land tax of the whole kingdom was fixed some years later by the Treaty of Union at little more than half the land tax of the single county of Norfolk. Four hundred thousand pounds probably bore as great a ratio to the wealth of Scotland then as forty millions would bear now.

The list of the members of the Darien Company deserves to be examined. The number of shareholders was about fourteen hundred. The largest quantity of stock registered in one name was three thousand pounds. The heads of three noble houses took three thousand pounds each, the Duke of Hamilton, the Duke of Queensbury and Lord Belhaven, a man of ability, spirit and patriotism, who had entered into the design with enthusiasm not inferior to that of Fletcher. Argyle held fifteen hundred pounds. John Dalrymple, but too well known as the Master of Stair, had just succeeded to his father's title and estate, and was now Viscount Stair. He put down his name for a thousand pounds. The number of Scotch peers who subscribed was between thirty and forty. The City of Edinburgh, in its corporate capacity, took three thousand pounds, the City of Glasgow three thousand, the City of Perth two thousand. But the great majority of the subscribers contributed only one hundred or two hundred pounds each. A very few divines who were settled in the capital or in other large towns were able to purchase shares. It is melancholy to see in the roll the name of more than one professional man whose paternal anxiety led him to lay out probably all his hardly earned savings in purchasing a hundred pound share for each of his children. If, indeed, Paterson's predictions had been verified, such a share would, according to the notions of that age and country, have been a handsome portion for the daughter of a writer or a surgeon.

That the Scotch are a people eminently intelligent, wary, resolute and self possessed, is obvious to the most superficial observation. That they are a people peculiarly liable to dangerous fits of passion and delusions of the imagination is less generally acknowledged, but is not less true. The whole kingdom seemed to have gone mad. Paterson had acquired an influence resembling rather that of the founder of a new religion, that of a Mahomet, that of a Joseph Smith, than that of a commercial projector. Blind faith in a religion, fanatical zeal for a religion, are too common to astonish us. But such faith and zeal seem strangely out of place in the transactions of the money market. It is true that we are judging after the event. But before the event materials sufficient for the forming of a sound judgment were within the reach of all who cared to use them. It seems incredible that men of sense, who had only a vague and general notion of Paterson's scheme, should have staked every thing on the success of that scheme. It seems more incredible still that men to whom the details of that scheme had been confided should not have looked into any of the common books of history or geography in which an account of Darien might have been found, and should not have asked themselves the simple question, whether Spain was likely to endure a Scotch colony in the midst of her Transatlantic dominions. It was notorious that she claimed the sovereignty of the isthmus on specious, nay, on solid, grounds. A Spaniard had been the first discoverer of the coast of Darien. A Spaniard had built a town and established a government on that coast. A Spaniard had, with great labour and peril, crossed the mountainous neck of land, had seen rolling beneath him the vast Pacific, never before revealed to European eyes, had descended, sword in hand, into the waves up to his girdle, and had there solemnly taken possession of sea and shore in the name of the Crown of Castile. It was true that the region which Paterson described as a paradise had been found by the first Castilian settlers to be a land of misery and death. The poisonous air, exhaled from rank jungle and stagnant water, had compelled them to remove to the neighbouring haven of Panama; and the Red Indians had been contemptuously permitted to live after their own fashion on the pestilential soil. But that soil was still considered, and might well be considered, by Spain as her own. In many countries there were tracts of morass, of mountain, of forest, in which governments did not think it worth while to be at the expense of maintaining order, and in which rude tribes enjoyed by connivance a kind of independence.   It was not necessary for the members of the Company of Scotland trading to Africa and the Indies to look very far for an example.   In some highland districts, not more than a hundred miles from Edinburgh, dwelt clans which had always regarded the authority of King, Parliament, Privy Council and Court of Session, quite as little as the aboriginal population of Darien regarded the authority of the Spanish Viceroys and Audiences.   Yet it would surely have been thought an outrageous violation of public law in the King of Spain to take possession of Appin and Lochaber.   And would it be a less outrageous violation of public law in the Scots to seize on a province in the very centre of his possessions, on the plea that this province was in the same state in which Appin and Lochaber had been during centuries?

So grossly unjust was Paterson's scheme; and yet it was less unjust than impolitic.   Torpid as Spain had become, there was still one point on which she was exquisitely sensitive.   The slightest encroachment of any other European power even on the outskirts of her American dominions sufficed to disturb her repose and to brace her paralysed nerves.   To imagine that she would tamely suffer adventurers from one of the most insignificant kingdoms of the Old World to form a settlement in the midst of her empire, within a day's sail of Portobello on one side and of Carthagena on the other, was ludicrously absurd.   She would have been just as likely to let them take possession of the Escurial.   It was, therefore, evident that, before the new Company could even begin its commercial operations, there must be a war with Spain and a complete triumph over Spain.   What means had the Company of waging such a war, and what chance of achieving such a triumph?   The ordinary revenue of Scotland in time of peace was between sixty and seventy thousand a year.   The extraordinary supplies granted to the Crown during the war with France had amounted perhaps to as much more.   Spain, it is true, was no longer the Spain of Pavia and Lepanto.   But, even in her decay, she possessed in Europe resources which exceeded thirty fold those of Scotland; and in America, where the struggle must take place, the disproportion was still greater. The Spanish fleets and arsenals were doubtless in wretched condition.   But there were Spanish fleets; there were Spanish arsenals.   The galleons, which sailed every year from Seville to the neighbourhood of Darien and from the neighbourhood

of Darien back to Seville, were in tolerable condition, and
formed, by themselves, a considerable armament. Scotland
had not a single ship of the line, nor a single dockyard
where such a ship could be built. A marine sufficient to
overpower that of Spain must be, not merely equipped and
manned, but created. An armed force sufficient to defend the
isthmus against the whole power of the viceroyalties of Mexico
and Peru must be sent over five thousand miles of ocean.
What was the charge of such an expedition likely to be?
Oliver had, in the preceding generation, wrested a West Indian
island from Spain: but, in order to do this, Oliver, a man who
thoroughly understood the administration of war, who wasted
nothing, and who so excellently served, had been forced to
spend, in a single year, on his navy alone, twenty times the
ordinary revenue of Scotland; and, since his days, war had
been constantly becoming more and more costly.

It was plain that Scotland could not alone support the charge
of a contest with the enemy whom Paterson was bent on pro-
voking. And what assistance was she likely to have from
abroad? Undoubtedly the vast colonial empire and the
narrow colonial policy of Spain were regarded with an evil eye
by more than one great maritime power. But there was no
great maritime power which would not far rather have seen the
isthmus between the Atlantic and the Pacific in the hands of
Spain than in the hands of the Darien Company. Lewis could
not but dread whatever tended to aggrandise a state governed
by William. To Holland the East India trade was as the
apple of her eye. She had been the chief gainer by the discoveries of Gama; and it might be expected that she would do
all that could be done by craft, and, if need were, by violence,
rather than suffer any rival to be to her what she had been to
Venice. England remained; and Paterson was sanguine
enough to flatter himself that England might be induced to lend
her powerful aid to the Company. He and Lord Belhaven
repaired to London, opened an office in Clement's Lane,
formed a Board of Directors auxiliary to the Central Board at
Edinburgh, and invited the capitalists of the Royal Exchange to
subscribe for the stock which had not been reserved for
Scotchmen resident in Scotland. A few moneyed men were
allured by the bait: but the clamour of the City was loud and
menacing; and from the City a feeling of indignation spread
fast through the country. In this feeling there was undoubtedly
a large mixture of evil. National antipathy operated on some
minds, religious antipathy on others. But it is impossible to

deny that the anger which Paterson's schemes excited throughout the south of the island was, in the main, just and reasonable. Though it was not yet generally known in what precise spot his colony was to be planted, there could be little doubt that he intended to occupy some part of America; and there could be as little doubt that such occupation would be resisted. There would be a maritime war; and such a war Scotland had no means of carrying on. The state of her finances was such that she must be quite unable to fit out even a single squadron of moderate size. Before the conflict had lasted three months, she would have neither money nor credit left. These things were obvious to every coffeehouse politician; and it was impossible to believe that they had escaped the notice of men so able and well informed as some who sate in the Privy Council and Parliament at Edinburgh. In one way only could the conduct of these schemers be explained. They meant to make a dupe and a tool of the Southron. The two British kingdoms were so closely connected, physically and politically, that it was scarcely possible for one of them to be at peace with a power with which the other was at war. If the Scotch drew King William into a quarrel, England must, from regard to her own dignity which was bound up with his, support him in it. She was to be tricked into a bloody and expensive contest in the event of which she had no interest; nay, into a contest in which victory would be a greater calamity to her than defeat. She was to lavish her wealth and the lives of her seamen, in order that a set of cunning foreigners might enjoy a monopoly by which she would be the chief sufferer. She was to conquer and defend provinces for this Scotch Corporation; and her reward was to be that her merchants were to be undersold, her customers decoyed away, her exchequer beggared. There would be an end to the disputes between the old East India Company and the new East India Company; for both Companies would be ruined alike. The two great springs of revenue would be dried up together. What would be the receipt of the Customs, what of the Excise, when vast magazines of sugar, rum, tobacco, coffee, chocolate, tea, spices, silks, muslins, all duty free, should be formed along the estuaries of the Forth and of the Clyde, and along the border from the mouth of the Esk to the mouth of the Tweed? What army, what fleet, would be sufficient to protect the interests of the government and of the fair trader when the whole kingdom of Scotland should be turned into one great smuggling establishment? Paterson's plan was simply this, that England should first spend millions in defence of the trade of his Company, and should then be plundered of twice as many millions by means of that very trade.

The cry of the city and of the nation was soon echoed by the legislature. When the Parliament met for the first time after the general election of 1695, Rochester called the attention of the Lords to the constitution and designs of the Company. Several witnesses were summoned to the bar, and gave evidence which produced a powerful effect on the House. " If these Scots are to have their way," said one peer, " I shall go and settle in Scotland, and not stay here to be made a beggar." The Lords resolved to represent strongly to the King the injustice of requiring England to exert her power in support of an enterprise which, if successful, must be fatal to her commerce and to her finances. A representation was drawn up and communicated to the Commons. The Commons eagerly concurred, and complimented the Peers on the promptitude with which their Lordships had, on this occasion, stood forth to protect the public interests. The two Houses went up together to Kensington with the address. William had been under the walls of Namur when the Act for incorporating the Company had been touched with his sceptre at Edinburgh, and had known nothing about that Act till his attention had been called to it by the clamour of his English subjects. He now said, in plain terms, that he had been ill served in Scotland, but that he would try to find a remedy for the evil which had been brought to his notice. The Lord High Commissioner Tweeddale and Secretary Johnstone were immediately dismissed. But the Act which had been passed by their management still continued to be law in Scotland ; nor was it in their master's power to undo what they had done.

The Commons were not content with addressing the throne. They instituted an inquiry into the proceedings of the Scotch Company in London. Belhaven made his escape to his own country, and was there beyond the reach of the Serjeant-at-Arms. But Paterson and some of his confederates were severely examined. It soon appeared that the Board which was sitting in Clement's Lane had done things which were certainly imprudent and perhaps illegal. The Act of Incorporation empowered the directors to take and to administer to their servants an oath of fidelity. But that Act was on the south of the Tweed a nullity. Nevertheless the directors had, in the heart of the City of London, taken and administered this oath, and had thus, by implication, asserted that the powers conferred on them by the legislature of Scotland accompanied them to England. It was resolved that they had been guilty of a high crime and misdemeanour, and that they should be impeached. A committee was appointed to frame articles of impeachment; but the task proved a difficult one; and the prosecution was suffered to drop, not however till the few English capitalists who had at first been friendly to Paterson's project had been terrified into renouncing all connection with him.

Now, surely, if not before, Paterson ought to have seen that his project could end in nothing but shame to himself and ruin to his worshippers. From the first it had been clear that England alone could protect his Company against the enmity of Spain; and it was now clear that Spain would be a less formidable enemy than England. It was impossible that his plan could excite greater indignation in the Council of the Indies at Madrid, or in the House of Trade at Seville, than it had excited in London. Unhappily he was given over to a strong delusion; and the blind multitude eagerly followed their blind leader. Indeed his dupes were maddened by that which should have sobered them. The proceedings of the Parliament which sate at Westminster, proceedings just and reasonable in substance, but in manner doubtless harsh and insolent, had roused the angry passions of a nation, feeble indeed in numbers and in material resources, but eminently high spirited. The proverbial pride of the Scotch was too much for their proverbial shrewdness. The votes of the English Lords and Commons were treated with marked contempt. The populace of Edinburgh burned Rochester in effigy. Money was poured faster than ever into the treasury of the Company. A stately house, in Milne Square, then the most modern and fashionable part of Edinburgh, was purchased and fitted up at once as an office and a warehouse. Ships adapted both for war and for trade were required: but the means of building such ships did not exist in Scotland; and no firm in the south of the island was disposed to enter into a contract which might not improbably be considered by the House of Commons as an impeachable offence. It was necessary to have recourse to the dockyards of Amsterdam and Hamburg. At an expense of fifty thousand pounds a few vessels were procured, the largest of which would hardly have ranked as sixtieth in the English navy; and with this force, a force not sufficient to keep the pirates of Sallee in check, the

Company threw down the gauntlet to all the maritime powers in the world.

It was not till the summer of 1698 that all was ready for the expedition which was to change the face of the globe. The number of seamen and colonists who embarked at Leith was twelve hundred. Of the colonists many were younger sons of honourable families, or officers who had been disbanded since the peace. It was impossible to find room for all who were desirous of emigrating. It is said that some persons who had vainly applied for a passage hid themselves in dark corners about the ships, and, when discovered, refused to depart, clung to the rigging, and were at last taken on shore by main force. This infatuation is the more extraordinary because few of the adventurers knew to what place they were going. All that was quite certain was that a colony was to be planted somewhere, and to be named Caledonia. The general opinion was that the fleet would steer for some part of the coast of America. But this opinion was not universal. At the Dutch Embassy in Saint James's Square there was an uneasy suspicion that the new Caledonia would be founded among those Eastern spice islands with which Amsterdam had long carried on a lucrative commerce.

The supreme direction of the expedition was entrusted to a Council of Seven. Two Presbyterian chaplains and a precentor were on board. A cargo had been laid in which was afterwards the subject of much mirth to the enemies of the Company, slippers innumerable, four thousand periwigs of all kinds from plain bobs to those magnificent structures which, in that age, towered high above the foreheads and descended to the elbows of men of fashion, bales of Scotch woollen stuffs which nobody within the tropics could wear, and many hundreds of English bibles which neither Spaniard nor Indian could read. Paterson, flushed with pride and hope, not only accompained the expedition, but took with him his wife, a comely dame, whose heart he had won in London, where she had presided over one of the great coffeehouses in the neighbourhood of the Royal Exchange. At length on the twenty-fifth of July the ships, followed by many tearful eyes, and commended to heaven in many vain prayers, sailed out of the estuary of the Forth.

The voyage was much longer than a voyage to the Antipodes now is; and the adventurers suffered much. The rations were scanty: there were bitter complaints both of the bread and of the meat; and, when the little fleet, after passing round the Orkneys and Ireland, touched at Madeira, those gentlemen who had fine clothes among their baggage were glad to exchange embroidered coats and laced waistcoats for provisions and wine. From Madeira the adventurers ran across the Atlantic, landed on an uninhabited islet lying between Porto Rico and St. Thomas, took possession of this desolate spot in the name of the Company, set up a tent, and hoisted the white cross of St. Andrew. Soon, however, they were warned off by an officer who was sent from St. Thomas to inform them that they were trespassing on the territory of the King of Denmark. They proceeded on their voyage, having obtained the services of an old buccaneer who knew the coast of Central America well. Under his pilotage they anchored on the first of November close to the Isthmus of Darien. One of the greatest princes of the country soon came on board. The courtiers who attended him, ten or twelve in number, were stark naked: but he was distinguished by a red coat, a pair of cotton drawers, and an old hat. He had a Spanish name, spoke Spanish, and affected the grave deportment of a Spanish don. The Scotch propitiated Andreas, as he was called, by a present of a new hat blazing with gold lace, and assured him that, if he would trade with them, they would treat him better than the Castilians had done.

A few hours later the chiefs of the expedition went on shore, took formal possession of the country, and named it Caledonia. They were pleased with the aspect of a small peninsula about three miles in length and a quarter of a mile in breadth, and determined to fix here the city of New Edinburgh, destined, as they hoped, to be the great emporium of both Indies. The peninsula terminated in a low promontory of about thirty acres, which might easily be turned into an island by digging a trench. The trench was dug; and on the ground thus separated from the main land a fort was constructed: fifty guns were placed on the ramparts; and within the enclosures houses were speedily built and thatched with palm leaves.

Negotiations were opened with the chieftains, as they were called, who governed the neighbouring tribes. Among these savage rulers were found as insatiable a cupidity, as watchful a jealousy, and as punctilious a pride, as among the potentates whose disputes had seemed likely to make the Congress of Ryswick eternal. One prince hated the Spaniards because a fine rifle had been taken away from him by the Governor of

Portobello on the plea that such a weapon was too good for a red man. Another loved the Spaniards because they had given him a stick tipped with silver. On the whole, the new comers succeeded in making friends of the aboriginal race. One mighty monarch, the Lewis the Great of the isthmus, who wore with pride a cap of white reeds lined with red silk and adorned with an ostrich feather, seemed well inclined to the strangers, received them hospitably in a palace built of canes and covered with palmetto royal, and regaled them with calabashes of a sort of ale brewed from Indian corn and potatoes. Another chief set his mark to a treaty of peace and alliance with the colony. A third consented to become a vassal of the Company, received with great delight a commission embellished with gold thread and flowered riband, and swallowed to the health of his new masters not a few bumpers of their own brandy.

Meanwhile the internal government of the colony was organised according to a plan devised by the directors at Edinburgh. The settlers were divided into bands of fifty or sixty : each band chose a representative ; and thus was formed an assembly which took the magnificent name of Parliament. This Parliament speedily framed a curious code. The first article provided that the precepts, instructions, examples, commands and prohibitions expressed and contained in the Holy Scriptures should have the full force and effect of laws in New Caledonia, an enactment which proves that those who drew it up either did not know what the Holy Scriptures contained or did not know what a law meant. There is another provision which shows not less clearly how far these legislators were from understanding the first principles of legislation. " Benefits received and good services done shall always be generously and thankfully compensated, whether a prior bargain hath been made or not ; and, if it shall happen to be otherwise, and the Benefactor obliged justly to complain of the ingratitude, the Ungrateful shall in such case be obliged to give threefold satisfaction at the least." An article much more creditable to the little Parliament, and much needed in a community which was likely to be constantly at war, prohibits, on pain of death, the violation of female captives.

By this time all the Antilles and all the shores of the Gulf of Mexico were in a ferment. The new colony was the object of universal hatred. The Spaniards began to fit out armaments. The chiefs of the French dependencies in the West Indies eagerly offered assistance to the Spaniards. The governors of the English settlements put forth proclamations interdicting all communication with this nest of buccaneers. Just at this time, the Dolphin, a vessel of fourteen guns, which was the property of the Scotch Company, was driven on shore by stress of weather under the walls of Carthagena. The ship and cargo were confiscated, the crew imprisoned and put in irons. Some of the sailors were treated as slaves, and compelled to sweep the streets and to work on the fortifications. Others, and among them the captain, were sent to Seville to be tried for piracy. Soon an envoy with a flag of truce arrived at Carthagena, and, in the name of the Council of Caledonia, demanded the release of the prisoners. He delivered to the authorities a letter threatening them with the vengeance of the King of Great Britain, and a copy of the Act of Parliament by which the Company had been created. The Castilian governor, who probably knew that William, as Sovereign of England, would not, and, as Sovereign of Scotland, could not, protect the squatters who had occupied Darien, flung away both letter and Act of Parliament with a gesture of contempt, called for a guard, and was with difficulty dissuaded from throwing the messenger into a dungeon. The Council of Caledonia, in great indignation, issued letters of mark and reprisal against Spanish vessels. What every man of common sense must have foreseen had taken place. The Scottish flag had been but a few months planted on the walls of New Edinburgh; and already a war, which Scotland, without the help of England, was utterly unable to sustain, had begun.

By this time it was known in Europe that the mysterious voyage of the adventurers from the Forth had ended at Darien. The ambassador of the Catholic King repaired to Kensington, and complained bitterly to William of this outrageous violation of the law of nations. Preparations were made in the Spanish ports for an expedition against the intruders ; and in no Spanish port were there more fervent wishes for the success of that expedition than in the cities of London and Bristol. In Scotland, on the other hand, the exultation was boundless. In the parish churches all over the kingdom the ministers gave public thanks to God for having vouchsafed thus far to protect and bless the infant colony. At some places a day was set apart for religious exercises on this account. In every borough bells were rung ; bonfires were lighted ; and candles were placed in the windows at night. During some months all the reports which arrived from the other side of the Atlantic were such as to excite hope and joy in the north of the island, and alarm and envy in the south. The colonists, it was asserted, had found rich gold mines, mines in which the precious metal was far more abundant and in a far purer state than on the coast of Guinea. Provisions were plentiful. The rainy season had not proved unhealthy. The settlement was well fortified. Sixty guns were mounted on the ramparts. An immense crop of Indian corn was expected. The aboriginal tribes were friendly. Emigrants from various quarters were coming in. The population of Caledonia had already increased from twelve hundred to ten thousand. The riches of the country,—these are the words of a newspaper of that time,—were great beyond imagination. The mania in Scotland rose to the highest point. Munitions of war and implements of agriculture were provided in large quantities. Multitudes were impatient to emigrate to the land of promise.

In August 1699 four ships, with thirteen hundred men on board, were despatched by the Company to Caledonia. The spiritual care of these emigrants was entrusted to divines of the Church of Scotland. One of these was that Alexander Shields whose Hind Let Loose proves that in his zeal for the Covenant he had forgotten the Gospel. To another, John Borland, we owe the best account of the voyage which is now extant. The General Assembly had charged the chaplains to divide the colonists into congregations, to appoint ruling elders, to constitute a presbytery, and to labour for the propagation of divine truth among the Pagan inhabitants of Darien. The second expedition sailed as the first had sailed, amidst the acclamations and blessings of all Scotland. During the earlier part of September the whole nation was dreaming a delightful dream of prosperity and glory; and triumphing, somewhat maliciously, in the vexation of the English. But, before the close of that month, it began to be rumoured about Lombard Street and Cheapside that letters had arrived from Jamaica with strange news. The colony from which so much had been hoped and dreaded was no more. It had disappeared from the face of the earth. The report spread to Edinburgh, but was received there with scornful incredulity. It was an impudent lie devised by some Englishmen who could not bear to see that, in spite of the votes of the English Parliament, in spite of the proclamations of the governors of the English colonies, Caledonia was waxing great and opulent. Nay, the inventor of the fable was named. It was declared to be quite certain that Secretary Vernon was the man. On the fourth of October was put forth a vehement contradiction of the story.

On the fifth the whole truth was known.  Letters were received from New York announcing that a few miserable men, the remains of the colony which was to have been the garden, the warehouse, the mart, of the whole world, their bones peeping through their skin, and hunger and fever written in their faces, had arrived in the Hudson.

The grief, the dismay and the rage of those who had a few hours before fancied themselves masters of all the wealth of both Indies may easily be imagined.  The Directors, in their fury, lost all self command, and, in their official letters, railed at the betrayers of Scotland, the white-livered deserters.  The truth is that those who used these hard words were far more deserving of blame than the wretches whom they had sent to destruction, and whom they now reviled for not staying to be utterly destroyed.  Nothing had happened but what might easily have been foreseen.  The Company had, in childish reliance on the word of an enthusiastic projector, and in defiance of facts known to every educated man in Europe, taken it for granted that emigrants born and bred within ten degrees of the Arctic Circle would enjoy excellent health within ten degrees of the Equator.  Nay, statesmen and scholars had been deluded into the belief that a country which, as they might have read in books so common as those of Hakluyt and Purchas, was noted even among tropical countries for its insalubrity, and had been abandoned by the Spaniards solely on account of its insalubrity, was a Montpelier.  Nor had any of Paterson's dupes considered how colonists from Fife or Lothian, who had never in their lives known what it was to feel the heat of a distressing midsummer day, could endure the labour of breaking clods and carrying burdens under the fierce blaze of a vertical sun.  It ought to have been remembered that such colonists would have to do for themselves what English, French, Dutch, and Spanish colonists employed Negroes or Indians to do for them.  It was seldom indeed that a white freeman in Barbadoes or Martinique, in Guiana or at Panama, was employed in severe bodily labour.  But the Scotch who settled at Darien must at first be without slaves, and must therefore dig the trench round their town, build their houses, cultivate their fields, hew wood, and draw water, with their own hands.  Such toil in such an atmosphere was too much for them.  The provisions which they had brought out had been of no good quality, and had not been improved by lapse of time or by change of climate.  The yams and plantains did not suit stomachs accustomed to good oatmeal. The flesh of wild animals and the green fat of the turtle, a luxury then unknown in Europe, went but a small way; and supplies were not to be expected from any foreign settlement. During the cool months, however, which immediately followed the occupation of the isthmus there were few deaths. But, before the equinox, disease began to make fearful havoc in the little community. The mortality gradually rose to ten or twelve a day. Both the clergymen who had accompanied the expedition died. Paterson buried his wife in that soil which, as he had assured his too credulous countrymen, exhaled health and vigour. He was himself stretched on his pallet by an intermittent fever. Still he would not admit that the climate of his promised land was bad. There could not be a purer air. This was merely the seasoning which people who passed from one country to another must expect. In November all would be well again. But the rate at which the emigrants died was such that none of them seemed likely to live till November. Those who were not laid on their beds were yellow, lean, feeble, hardly able to move the sick and to bury the dead, and quite unable to repel the expected attack of the Spaniards. The cry of the whole community was that death was all around them, and that they must, while they still had strength to weigh an anchor or spread a sail, fly to some less fatal region. The men and provisions were equally distributed among three ships, the Caledonia, the Unicorn, and the Saint Andrew. Paterson, though still too ill to sit in the Council, begged hard that he might be left behind with twenty or thirty companions to keep up a show of possession, and to await the next arrivals from Scotland. So small a number of people, he said, might easily subsist by catching fish and turtles. But his offer was disregarded: he was carried, utterly helpless, on board of the Saint Andrew; and the vessel stood out to sea.

The voyage was horrible. Scarcely any Guinea slave ship has ever had such a middle passage. Of two hundred and fifty persons who were on board of the Saint Andrew, one hundred and fifty fed the sharks of the Atlantic before Sandy Hook was in sight. The Unicorn lost almost all its officers, and about a hundred and forty men. The Caledonia, the healthiest ship of the three, threw overboard a hundred corpses. The squalid survivors, as if they were not sufficiently miserable, raged fiercely against one another. Charges of incapacity, cruelty, brutal insolence, were hurled backward and forward. The rigid Presbyterians attributed the calamities of the colony to the wickedness of Jacobites, Prelatists, Sabbath-breakers, Atheists, who hated in others that image of God which was wanting in themselves. The accused malignants, on the other hand, complained bitterly of the impertinence of meddling fanatics and hypocrites. Paterson was cruelly reviled, and was unable to defend himself. He had been completely prostrated by bodily and mental suffering. He looked like a skeleton. His heart was broken. His inventive faculties and his plausible eloquence were no more; and he seemed to have sunk into second childhood.

Meanwhile the second expedition had been on the seas. It reached Darien about four months after the first settlers had fled. The new comers had fully expected to find a flourishing young town, secure fortifications, cultivated fields, and a cordial welcome. They found a wilderness. The castle of New Edinburgh was in ruins. The huts had been burned. The site marked out for the proud capital which was to have been the Tyre, the Venice, the Amsterdam of the eighteenth century was overgrown with jungle, and inhabited only by the sloth and the baboon. The hearts of the adventurers sank within them. For their fleet had been fitted out, not to plant a colony, but to recruit a colony already planted and supposed to be prospering. They were therefore worse provided with every necessary of life than their predecessors had been. Some feeble attempts, however, were made to restore what had perished. A new fort was constructed on the old ground; and within the ramparts was built a hamlet, consisting of eighty or ninety cabins, generally of twelve feet by ten. But the work went on languidly. The alacrity which is the effect of hope, the strength which is the effect of union, were alike wanting to the little community. From the councillors down to the humblest settlers all was despondency and discontent. The stock of provisions was scanty. The stewards embezzled great part of it. The rations were small; and soon there was a cry that they were unfairly distributed. Factions were formed. Plots were laid. One ringleader of the malecontents was hanged. The Scotch were generally, as they still are, a religious people; and it might therefore have been expected that the influence of the divines to whom the spiritual charge of the colony had been confided would have been employed with advantage for the preserving of order and the calming of evil passions. Unfortunately those divines seem to have been at war with almost all the rest of the society. They described their companions as the most profligate of mankind, and declared that it was impossible to constitute a presbytery according to the directions of the General Assembly; for that persons fit to be ruling elders of a Christian Church were not to be found among the twelve or thirteen hundred emigrants. Where the blame lay it is now impossible to decide. All that can with confidence be said is that either the clergymen must have been most unreasonably and most uncharitably austere, or the laymen must have been most unfavourable specimens of the nation and class to which they belonged.

It may be added that the provision by the General Assembly for the spiritual wants of the colony was as defective as the provision made for temporal wants by the directors of the Company. Nearly one third of the emigrants who sailed with the second expedition were Highlanders, who did not understand a word of English; and not one of the four chaplains could speak a word of Gaelic. It was only through interpreters that a pastor could communicate with a large portion of the Christian flock of which he had charge. Even by the help of interpreters he could not impart religious instruction to those heathen tribes which the Church of Scotland had solemnly recommended to his care. In fact, the colonists left behind them no mark that baptized men had set foot on Darien, except a few Anglo-Saxon curses, which, having been uttered more frequently and with greater energy than any other words in our language, had caught the ear and been retained in the memory of the native population of the isthmus.

The months which immediately followed the arrival of the new comers were the coolest and most salubrious of the year. But, even in those months, the pestilential influence of a tropical sun, shining on swamps rank with impenetrable thickets of black mangroves, began to be felt. The mortality was great; and it was but too clear that, before the summer was far advanced, the second colony would, like the first, have to choose between death and flight. But the agony of the inevitable dissolution was shortened by violence. A fleet of eleven vessels under the flag of Castile anchored off New Edinburgh. At the same time an irregular army of Spaniards, creoles, negroes, mulattoes and Indians marched across the isthmus from Panama; and the fort was blockaded at once by sea and land.

A drummer soon came with a message from the besiegers, but a message which was utterly unintelligible to the besieged. Even after all that we have seen of the perverse imbecility of the directors of the Company, it must be thought strange that they should have sent a colony to a remote part of the world, where it was certain that there must be constant intercourse peaceable or hostile, with Spaniards, and yet should not have taken care that there should be in the whole colony a single person who knew a little Spanish.

With some difficulty a negotiation was carried on in such French and such Latin as the two parties could furnish. Before the end of March a treaty was signed by which the Scotch bound themselves to evacuate Darien in fourteen days ; and on the eleventh of April they departed, a much less numerous body than when they arrived. In little more than four months, although the healthiest months of the year, three hundred men out of thirteen hundred had been swept away by disease. Of the survivors very few lived to see their native country again. Two of the ships perished at sea. Many of the adventurers, who had left their homes flushed with hopes of speedy opulence, were glad to hire themselves out to the planters of Jamaica, and laid their bones in that land of exile. Shields died there, worn out and heart broken. Borland was the only minister who came back. In his curious and interesting narrative, he expresses his feelings, after the fashion of the school in which he had been bred, by grotesque allusions to the Old Testament, and by a profusion of Hebrew words. On his first arrival, he tells us, he found New Edinburgh a Ziklag. He had subsequently been compelled to dwell in the tents of Kedar. Once, indeed, during his sojourn, he had fallen in with a Beer-lahai-roi, and had set up his Ebenezer : but in general Darien was to him a Magor Missabib, a Kibroth-hattaavah. The sad story is introduced with the words in which a great man of old, delivered over to the malice of the Evil Power, was informed of the death of his children and of the ruin of his fortunes : " I alone am escaped to tell thee."

# CHAPTER XXV.

THE passions which had agitated the Parliament during the late session continued to ferment in the minds of men during the recess, and, having no longer a vent in the senate, broke forth in every part of the empire, destroyed the peace of towns, brought into peril the honour and the lives of innocent men, and impelled magistrates to leave the bench of justice and attack one another sword in hand. Private calamities, private brawls, which had nothing to do with the disputes between court and country, were turned by the political animosities of that unhappy summer into grave political events.

One mournful tale, which called forth the strongest feelings of the contending factions, is still remembered as a curious part of the history of our jurisprudence, and especially of the history of our medical jurisprudence. No Whig member of the Lower House, with the single exception of Montague, filled a larger space in the public eye than William Cowper. In the art of conciliating an audience, Cowper was preeminent. His graceful and engaging eloquence cast a spell on juries ; and the Commons, even in those stormy moments when no other defender of the administration could obtain a hearing, would always listen to him. He represented Hertford, a borough in which his family had considerable influence : but there was a strong Tory minority among the electors ; and he had not won his seat without a hard fight, which had left behind it many bitter recollections. His younger brother Spencer, a man of parts and learning, was fast rising into practice as a barrister on the Home Circuit.

At Hertford resided an opulent Quaker family named Stout. A pretty young woman of this family had lately sunk into a melancholy of a kind not very unusual in girls of strong sensibility and lively imagination who are subject to the restraints of austere religious societies. Her dress, her looks, her gestures, indicated the disturbance of her mind. She sometimes hinted her dislike of the sect to which she belonged. She complained that a canting waterman who was one of the brotherhood had held forth against her at a meeting. She threatened to go beyond sea, to throw herself out of window, to drown herself. To two or three of her associates she owned that she was in love ; and on one occasion she plainly said that the man whom she loved was one whom she never could marry. In fact, the object of her fondness was Spencer Cowper, who was already married. She at length wrote to him in language which she never would have used if her intellect had not been disordered. He, like an honest man, took no advantage of her unhappy state of mind, and did his best to avoid her. His prudence mortified her to such a degree that on one occasion she went into fits. It was necessary, however, that he should see her, when he came to Hertford at the spring assizes of 1699. For he had been entrusted with some money which was due to her on mortgage. He called on her for this purpose late one evening, and delivered a bag of gold to her. She pressed him to be the guest of her family; but he excused himself and retired. The next morning she was found dead among the stakes of a mill dam on the stream called the Priory River. That she had destroyed herself there could be no reasonable doubt. The coroner's inquest found that she had drowned herself while in a state of mental derangement. But her family was unwilling to admit that she had shortened her own life, and looked about for somebody who might be accused of murdering her. The last person who could be proved to have been in her company was Spencer Cowper. It chanced that two attorneys and a scrivener, who had come down from town to the Hertford assizes, had been overheard, on that unhappy night, talking over their wine about the charms and flirtations of the handsome Quaker girl, in the light way in which such subjects are sometimes discussed even at the circuit tables and mess tables of our more refined generation. Some wild words, susceptible of a double meaning, were used about the way in which she had jilted one lover, and the way in which another lover would punish her for her coquetry. On no better grounds than these her relations imagined that Spencer Cowper had, with the assistance of these three retainers of the law, strangled her, and thrown her corpse into the water. There was absolutely no evidence of the crime. There was no evidence that any one of the accused had any motive to commit such a crime; there was no evidence that Spencer Cowper had any connection with the persons who were said to be his accomplices. One of those persons, indeed, he had never seen. But no story is too absurd to be imposed on minds blinded by religious and political fanaticism. The Quakers and the Tories joined to raise a formidable clamour. The Quakers had, in those days, no scruples about capital punishments. They would, indeed, as Spencer Cowper said bitterly, but too truly, rather send four innocent men to the gallows than let it be believed that one who had their light within her had committed suicide. The Tories exulted in the prospect of winning two seats from the Whigs. The whole kingdom was divided between Stouts and Cowpers. At the summer assizes Hertford was crowded with anxious faces from London and from parts of England more distant than London. The prosecution was conducted with a malignity and unfairness which to us seem almost incredible; and, unfortunately, the dullest and most ignorant judge of the twelve was on the bench.

Cowper defended himself and those who were said to be his accomplices with admirable ability and self possession. His brother, much more distressed than himself, sate near him through the long agony of that day. The case against the prisoners rested chiefly on the vulgar error that a human body, found, as this poor girl's body had been found, floating in water, must have been thrown into the water while still alive. To prove this doctrine the counsel for the Crown called medical practitioners, of whom nothing is now known except that some of them had been active against the Whigs at Hertford elections. To confirm the evidence of these gentlemen two or three sailors were put into the witness box. On the other side appeared an array of men of science whose names are still remembered. Among them was William Cowper, not a kinsman of the defendant, but the most celebrated anatomist that England had then produced. He was, indeed, the founder of a dynasty illustrious in the history of science : for he was the teacher of William Cheselden, and William Cheselden was the teacher of John Hunter. On the same side appeared Samuel Garth, who, among the physicians of the capital, had no rival except Radcliffe, and Hans Sloane, the founder of the magnificent museum which is one of the glories of our country. The attempt of the prosecutors to make the superstitions of the forecastle evidence for the purpose of taking away the lives of men was treated by these philosophers with just disdain. The stupid judge asked Garth what he could say in answer to the testimony of the seamen. " My Lord," replied Garth, " I say that they are mistaken. I will find seamen in abundance to swear that they have known whistling raise the wind."

The jury found the prisoners Not guilty ; and the report carried back to London by persons who had been present at the trial was that everybody applauded the verdict, and that even the Stouts seemed to be convinced of their error. It it certain, however, that the malevolence of the defeated party soon revived in all its energy. The lives of the four men who had just been absolved were again attacked by means of the most absurd and odious proceeding known to our old law, the appeal of murder. This attack too failed. Every artifice of chicane was at length exhausted ; and nothing was left to the disappointed sect and the disappointed faction except to caluminate those whom it had been found impossible to murder. In a succession of libels Spencer Cowper was held up to the execration of the public. But the public did him justice. He rose to high eminence in his profession : he at length took his seat, with general applause, on the judicial bench, and there distinguished himself by the humanity which he never failed to show to unhappy men who stood, as he had once stood, at the bar.    Many who seldom trouble themselves about pedigrees may be interested by learning that he was the grandfather of that excellent man and excellent poet William Cowper, whose writings have long been peculiarly loved and prized by the members of the religious community which, under a strong delusion, sought to slay his innocent progenitor.*

Though Spencer Cowper had escaped with life and honour, the Tories had carried their point.    They had secured against the next election the support of the Quakers of Hertford ; and the consequence was that the borough was lost to the family and to the party which had lately predominated there.

In the very week in which the great trial took place at Hertford, a feud arising out of the late election for Buckinghamshire very nearly produced fatal effects.    Wharton, the chief of the Buckinghamshire Whigs, had with difficulty succeeded in bringing in his brother as one of the knights of the shire. Graham Viscount Cheyney, of the kingdom of Scotland, had been returned at the head of the poll by the Tories.    The two noblemen met at the quarter sessions.    In England Cheyney was before the Union merely an Esquire.    Wharton was undoubtedly entitled to take place of him, and had repeatedly taken place of him without any dispute.    But angry passions now ran so high that a decent pretext for indulging them was hardly thought necessary.    Cheyney fastened a quarrel on Wharton.    They drew.    Wharton, whose cool good humoured courage and skill in fence were the envy of all the swordsmen of that age, closed with his quarrelsome neighbour, disarmed him, and gave him his life.

A more tragical duel had just taken place at Westminster. Conway Seymour, the eldest son of Sir Edward Seymour, had lately come of age.    He was in possession of an independent fortune of seven thousand pounds a year, which he lavished in costly fopperies. The town had nicknamed him Beau Seymour. He was displaying his curls and his embroidery in Saint James's

* It is curious that all Cowper's biographers with whom I am acquainted, Hayley, Southey, Grimshawe, Chalmers, mention the Judge, the common ancestor of the poet, of his first love Theodora Cowper, and of Lady Hesketh ; but that none of those biographers makes the faintest allusion to the Hertford trial, the most remarkable event in the history of the family ; nor do I believe that any allusion to that trial can be found in any of the poet's numerous letters.

Park on a midsummer evening, after indulging too freely in wine, when a young officer of the Blues named Kirke, who was as tipsy as himself, passed near him. "There goes Beau Seymour," said Kirke. Seymour flew into a rage. Angry words were exchanged between the foolish boys. They immediately went beyond the precincts of the Court, drew, and exchanged some pushes. Seymour was wounded in the neck. The wound was not very serious; but, when his cure was only half completed, he revelled in fruit, ice and Burgundy till he threw himself into a violent fever. Though a coxcomb and a voluptuary, he seems to have had some fine qualities. On the last day of his life he saw Kirke. Kirke implored forgiveness; and the dying man declared that he forgave as he hoped to be forgiven. There can be no doubt that a person who kills another in a duel is, according to law, guilty of murder. But the law had never been strictly enforced against gentlemen in such cases; and in this case there was no peculiar atrocity, no deep seated malice, no suspicion of foul play. Sir Edward, however, vehemently declared that he would have life for life. Much indulgence is due to the resentment of an affectionate father maddened by the loss of a son. But there is but too much reason to believe that the implacability of Seymour was the implacability, not of an affectionate father, but of a factious and malignant agitator. He tried to make what is, in the jargon of our time, called political capital out of the desolation of his house and the blood of his first born. A brawl between two dissolute youths, a brawl distinguished by nothing but its unhappy result from the hundred brawls which took place every month in theatres and taverns, he magnified into an attack on the liberties of the nation, an attempt to introduce a military tyranny. The question was whether a soldier was to be permitted to insult English gentlemen, and, if they murmured, to cut their throats? It was moved in the Court of King's Bench that Kirke should either be brought to immediate trial or admitted to bail. Shower, as counsel for Seymour, opposed the motion. But Seymour was not content to leave the case in Shower's hands. In defiance of all decency, he went to Westminster Hall, demanded a hearing, and pronounced a harangue against standing armies. "Here," he said, "is a man who lives on money taken out of our pockets. The plea set up for taxing us in order to support him is that his sword protects us, and enables us to live in peace and security. And is he to be suffered to use that sword to destroy us?" Kirke was tried and found guilty of manslaughter. In his case, as in the case of Spencer Cowper, an attempt was made to obtain a writ of appeal. The attempt failed; and Seymour was disappointed of his revenge: but he was not left without consolation. If he had lost a son, he had found, what he seems to have prized quite as much, a fertile theme for invective.

The King, on his return from the Continent, found his subjects in no bland humour. All Scotland, exasperated by the fate of the first expedition to Darien, and anxiously waiting for news of the second, called loudly for a Parliament. Several of the Scottish peers carried to Kensington an address which was subscribed by thirty-six of their body, and which earnestly pressed William to convoke the Estates at Edinburgh, and to redress the wrongs which had been done to the colony of New Caledonia. A petition to the same effect was widely circulated among the commonalty of his Northern kingdom, and received, if report could be trusted, not less than thirty thousand signatures. Discontent was far from being as violent in England as in Scotland. Yet in England there was discontent enough to make even a resolute prince uneasy. The time drew near at which the Houses must reassemble; and how were the Commons to be managed? Montague, enraged, mortified, and intimidated by the baiting of the last session, was fully determined not again to appear in the character of chief minister of finance. The secure and luxurious retreat which he had, some months ago, prepared for himself was awaiting him. He took the Auditorship, and resigned his other places. Smith became Chancellor of the Exchequer. A new commission of Treasury issued; and the first name was that of Tankerville. He had entered on his career, more than twenty years before, with the fairest hopes, young, noble, nobly allied, of distinguished abilities, of graceful manners. There was no more brilliant man of fashion in the theatre and in the ring. There was no more popular tribune in Guildhall. Such was the commencement of a life so miserable that all the indignation excited by great faults is overpowered by pity. A guilty passion, amounting to a madness, left on the moral character of the unhappy man a stain at which even libertines looked grave. He tried to make the errors of his private life forgotten by splendid and perilous services to a public cause; and, having endured in that cause penury and exile, the gloom of a dungeon, the prospect of a scaffold, the ruin of a noble estate, he was so unfortunate as to be regarded by the party for which he had sacrificed every thing as a coward, if not a traitor. Yet, even against such accumulated disasters and disgraces, his vigorous and aspiring mind bore up. His parts and eloquence gained for him the ear of the House of Lords; and at length, though not till his constitution was so broken that he was fitter for flannel and cushions than for a laborious office at Whitehall, he was put at the head of one of the most important departments of the administration. It might have been expected that this appointment would call forth clamours from widely different quarters; that the Tories would be offended by the elevation of a rebel; that the Whigs would set up a cry against the captain to whose treachery or faintheartedness they had been in the habit of imputing the rout of Sedgemoor; and that the whole of that great body of Englishmen which cannot be said to be steadily Whig or Tory, but which is zealous for decency and the domestic virtues, would see with indignation a signal mark of royal favour bestowed on one who had been convicted of debauching a noble damsel, the sister of his own wife. But so capricious is public feeling that it will be difficult, if not impossible, to find, in any of the letters, essays, dialogues, and poems which bear the date of 1699 or of 1700, a single allusion to the vices or misfortunes of the new First Lord of the Treasury. It is probable that his infirm health and his isolated position were his protection. The chiefs of the opposition did not fear him enough to hate him. The Whig Junto was still their terror and their abhorrence. They continued to assail Montague and Orford, though with somewhat less ferocity than while Montague had the direction of the finances, and Orford of the marine. But the utmost spite of all the leading malecontents were concentrated on one object, the great magistrate who still held the highest civil post in the realm, and who was evidently determined to hold it in defiance of them. It was not so easy to get rid of him as it had been to drive his colleagues from office. His abilities the most intolerant Tories were forced grudgingly to acknowledge. His integrity might be questioned in nameless libels and in coffeehouse tattle, but was certain to come forth bright and pure from the most severe Parliamentary investigation. Nor was he guilty of those faults of temper and of manner to which, more than to any grave delinquency, the unpopularity of his associates is to be ascribed. He had as little of the insolence and perverseness of Orford as of the petulance and vain-gloriousness of Montague. One of the most severe trials to which the head and heart of man can be put is great and rapid elevation. To that trial both Montague and Somers were put. It was too much for Montague. But Somers was found equal to it. He was the son of a country attorney. At thirty-seven he had been sitting in a stuff gown on a back bench in the Court of King's Bench. At forty-two he was the first lay dignitary of the realm, and took precedence of the Archbishop of York, and of the Duke of Norfolk. He had risen from a lower point than Montague, had risen as fast as Montague, had risen as high as Montague, and yet had not excited envy such as dogged Montague through a long career. Garreteers, who were never weary of calling the cousin of the Earls of Manchester and Sandwich an upstart, could not, without an unwonted sense of shame, apply those words to the Chancellor, who, without one drop of patrician blood in his veins, had taken his place at the head of the patrician order with the quiet dignity of a man ennobled by nature. His serenity, his modesty, his selfcommand, proof even against the most sudden surprises of passion, his self-respect, which forced the proudest grandees of the kingdom to respect him, his urbanity, which won the hearts of the youngest lawyers of the Chancery Bar, gained for him many private friends and admirers among the most respectable members of the opposition. But such men as Howe and Seymour hated him implacably : they hated his commanding genius much : they hated the mild majesty of his virtue still more. They sought occasion against him everywhere ; and they at length flattered themselves that they had found it.

Some years before, while the war was still raging, there had been loud complaints in the city that even privateers of St. Malo's and Dunkirk caused less molestation to trade than another class of marauders. The English navy was fully employed in the Channel, in the Atlantic, and in the Mediterranean. The Indian Ocean, meanwhile, swarmed with pirates of whose rapacity and cruelty frightful stories were told. Many of these men, it was said, came from our North American colonies, and carried back to those colonies the spoils gained by crime. Adventurers who durst not show themselves in the Thames found a ready market for their ill-gotten spices and stuffs at New York. Even the Puritans of New England, who in sanctimonious austerity surpassed even their brethren of Scotland, were accused of conniving at the wickedness which enabled them to enjoy abundantly and cheaply the produce of Indian looms and Chinese tea plantations.

In 1695 Richard Coote, Earl of Bellamont, an Irish peer who sate in the English House of Commons, was appointed Governor of New York and Massachusets. He was a man of eminently fair character, upright, courageous and independent.

Though a decided Whig, he had distinguished himself by
bringing before the Parliament at Westminster some tyrannical
acts done by Whigs at Dublin, and particularly the execution,
if it is not rather to be called the murder, of Gafney. Before
Bellamont sailed for America, William spoke strongly to him
about the freebooting which was the disgrace of the colonies.
" I send you, my Lord, to New York," he said, " because an
honest and intrepid man is wanted to put these abuses down,
and because I believe you to be such a man." Bellamont
exerted himself to justify the high opinion which the King had
formed of him. It was soon known at New York that the
Governor who had just arrived from England was bent on the
suppression of piracy; and some colonists in whom he placed
great confidence suggested to him what they may perhaps have
thought the best mode of attaining that object. There was
then in the settlement a veteran mariner named William Kidd.
He had passed most of his life on the waves, had distinguished
himself by his seamanship, had had opportunities of showing
his valour in action with the French, and had retired on a
competence. No man knew the Eastern seas better. He was
perfectly acquainted with all the haunts of the pirates who
prowled between the Cape of Good Hope and the Straits of
Malacca; and he would undertake, if he were entrusted with a
single ship of thirty or forty guns, to clear the Indian Ocean of
the whole race. The brigantines of the rovers were numerous,
no doubt; but none of them was large: one man of war, which
in the royal navy would hardly rank as a fourth rate, would
easily deal with them all in succession; and the lawful spoils
of the enemies of mankind would much more than defray the
charges of the expedition. Bellamont was charmed with this
plan, and recommended it to the King. The King referred it
to the Admiralty. The Admiralty raised difficulties, such as
are perpetually raised by public boards when any deviation,
whether for the better or for the worse, from the established
course of proceeding is proposed. It then occurred to Bellamont that his favourite scheme might be carried into effect
without any cost to the state. A few public spirited men
might easily fit out a privateer which would soon make the
Arabian Gulph and the Bay of Bengal secure highways for trade.
He wrote to his friends in England imploring, remonstrating,
complaining of their lamentable want of public spirit. Six
thousand pounds would be enough. That sum would be
repaid, and repaid with large interest, from the sale of prizes;
and an inestimable benefit would be conferred on the kingdom

and on the world. His urgency succeeded. Shrewsbury and Romney contributed. Orford, though, as first Lord of the Admiralty, he had been unwilling to send Kidd to the Indian ocean with a king's ship, consented to subscribe a thousand pounds. Somers subscribed another thousand. A ship called the Adventure Galley was equipped in the port of London ; and Kidd took the command. He carried with him, besides the ordinary letters of marque, a commission under the Great Seal empowering him to seize pirates, and to take them to some place where they might be dealt with according to law. Whatever right the King might have to the goods found in the possession of these malefactors he granted, by letters patent, to the persons who had been at the expense of fitting out the expedition, reserving to himself only one tenth part of the gains of the adventure, which was to be paid into the treasury. With the claim of merchants to have back the property of which they had been robbed His Majesty of course did not interfere. He granted away, and could grant away, no rights but his own.

The press for sailors to man the royal navy was at that time so hot that Kidd could not obtain his full complement of hands in the Thames. He crossed the Atlantic, visited New York, and there found volunteers in abundance. At length, in February 1697, he sailed from the Hudson with a crew of more than a hundred and fifty men, and in July reached the coast of Madagascar.

It is possible that Kidd may at first have meant to act in accordance with his instructions. But, on the subject of piracy, he held the notions which were then common in the North American colonies ; and most of his crew were of the same mind. He found himself in a sea which was constantly traversed by rich and defenceless merchant ships ; and he had to determine whether he would plunder those ships or protect them. The gain which might be made by plundering them was immense, and might be snatched without the dangers of a battle or the delays of a trial. The rewards of protecting the lawful trade were likely to be comparatively small. Such as they were, they would be got only by first fighting with desperate ruffians who would rather be killed than taken, and by then instituting a proceeding and obtaining a judgment in a Court of Admiralty. The risk of being called to a severe reckoning might not unnaturally seem small to one who had seen many old buccaneers living in comfort and credit at New York and Boston. Kidd soon threw off the character of a privateer, and became a pirate. He established friendly communications, and exchanged arms and ammunition, with the most notorious of those rovers whom his commission authorised him to destroy, and made war on those peaceful traders whom he was sent to defend. He began by robbing Mussulmans, and speedily proceeded from Mussulmans to Armenians, and from Armenians to Portuguese. The Adventure Galley took such quantities of cotton and silk, sugar and coffee, cinnamon and pepper, that the very foremast men received from a hundred to two hundred pounds each, and that the captain's share of the spoil would have enabled him to live at home as an opulent gentleman. With the rapacity Kidd had the cruelty of his odious calling. He burned houses ; he massacred peasantry. His prisoners were tied up and beaten with naked cutlasses in order to extort information about their concealed hoards. One of his crew, whom he had called a dog, was provoked into exclaiming, in an agony of remorse, " Yes, I am a dog ; but it is you that have made me so." Kidd, in a fury, struck the man dead.

News then travelled very slowly from the eastern seas to England. But, in August 1698, it was known in London that the Adventure Galley from which so much had been hoped was the terror of the merchants of Surat, and of the villagers of the coast of Malabar. It was thought probable that Kidd would carry his booty to some colony. Orders were therefore sent from Whitehall to the governors of the transmarine possessions of the Crown, directing them to be on the watch for him. He meanwhile, having burned his ship and dismissed most of his men, who easily found berths in the sloops of other pirates, returned to New York with the means, as he flattered himself, of making his peace and of living in splendour. He had fabricated a long romance to which Bellamont, naturally unwilling to believe that he had been duped and had been the means of duping others, was at first disposed to listen with favour. But the truth soon came out. The governor did his duty firmly ; and Kidd was placed in close confinement till orders arrived from the Admiralty that he should be sent to England.

To an intelligent and candid judge of human actions it will not appear that any of the persons at whose expense the Adventure Galley was fitted out deserved serious blame. The worst that could be imputed even to Bellamont, who had drawn in all the rest, was that he had been led into a fault by his ardent zeal for the public service, and by the generosity of a nature as little prone to suspect as to devise villanies. His friends in England might surely be pardoned for giving credit to his recommendation. It is highly probable that the motive which induced some of them to aid his design was genuine public spirit. But, if we suppose them to have had a view to gain, it was to legitimate gain. Their conduct was the very opposite of corrupt. Not only had they taken no money. They had disbursed money largely, and had disbursed it with the certainty that they should never be reimbursed unless the outlay proved beneficial to the public. That they meant well they proved by staking thousands on the success of their plan ; and, if they erred in judgment, the loss of those thousands was surely a sufficient punishment for such an error. On this subject there would probably have been no difference of opinion had not Somers been one of the contributors. About the other patrons of Kidd the chiefs of the opposition cared little. Bellamont was far removed from the political scene. Romney could not, and Shrewsbury would not, play a first part. Orford had resigned his employments. But Somers still held the Great Seal, still presided in the House of Lords, still had constant access to the closet. The retreat of his friends had left him the sole and undisputed head of that party which had, in the late Parliament, been a majority, and which was, in the present Parliament, outnumbered indeed, disorganised and disheartened, but still numerous and respectable. His placid courage rose higher and higher to meet the dangers which threatened him. He provided for himself no refuge. He made no move towards flight ; and, without uttering one boastful word, gave his enemies to understand, by the mild firmness of his demeanour, that he dared them to do their worst.

In their eagerness to displace and destroy him they overreached themselves. Had they been content to accuse him of lending his countenance, with a rashness unbecoming his high place, to an ill-concerted scheme, that large part of mankind which judges of a plan simply by the event would probably have thought the accusation well founded. But the malice which they bore to him was not to be so satisfied. They affected to believe that he had from the first been aware of Kidd's character and designs. The Great Seal had been employed to sanction a piratical expedition. The head of the law had laid down a thousand pounds in the hope of receiving tens of thousands when his accomplices should return, laden with the spoils of ruined merchants. It was fortunate for the

Chancellor that the calumnies of which he was the object were too atrocious to be mischievous.

And now the time had come at which the hoarded illhumour of six months was at liberty to explode. On the sixteenth of November the Houses met. The King, in his speech, assured them in gracious and affectionate language that he was determined to do his best to merit their love by constant care to preserve their liberty and their religion, by a pure administration of justice, by countenancing virtue, by discouraging vice, by shrinking from no difficulty or danger when the welfare of the nation was at stake. "These," he said, "are my resolutions; and I am persuaded that you are come together with purposes on your part suitable to these on mine. Since then our aims are only for the general good, let us act with confidence in one another, which will not fail, by God's blessing, to make me a happy king, and you a great and flourishing people."

It might have been thought that no words less likely to give offence had ever been uttered from the English throne. But even in those words the malevolence of faction sought and found matter for a quarrel. The gentle exhortation, "Let us act with confidence in one another," must mean that such confidence did not now exist, that the King distrusted the Parliament, or that the Parliament had shown an unwarrantable distrust of the King. Such an exhortation was nothing less than a reproach; and such a reproach was a bad return for the gold and the blood which England had lavished in order to make and to keep him a great sovereign. There was a sharp debate, in which Seymour took part. With characteristic indelicacy and want of feeling he harangued the Commons as he had harangued the Court of King's Bench, about his son's death, and about the necessity of curbing the insolence of military men. There were loud complaints that the events of the preceding session had been misrepresented to the public, that emissaries of the Court, in every part of the kingdom, declaimed against the absurd jealousies or still more absurd parsimony which had refused to His Majesty the means of keeping up such an army as might secure the country against invasion. Even justices of the peace, it was said, even deputy-lieutenants, had used King James and King Lewis as bugbears, for the purpose of stirring up the people against honest and thrifty representatives. Angry resolutions were passed, declaring it to be the opinion of the House that the best way to establish entire confidence between the King and the Estates of the

Realm would be to put a brand on those evil advisers who had dared to breathe in the royal ear calumnies against a faithful Parliament. An address founded on these resolutions was voted ; many thought that a violent rupture was inevitable. But William returned an answer so prudent and gentle that malice itself could not prolong the dispute. By this time, indeed, a new dispute had begun. The address had scarcely been moved when the House called for copies of the papers relating to Kidd's expedition. Somers, conscious of innocence, knew that it was wise as well as right to be perfectly ingenuous, and resolved that there should be no concealment. His friends stood manfully by him, and his enemies struck at him with such blind fury that their blows injured only themselves. Howe raved like a maniac. "What is to become of the country, plundered by land, plundered by sea ? Our rulers have laid hold on our lands, our woods, our mines, our money. And all this is not enough. We cannot send a cargo to the farthest ends of the earth, but they must send a gang of thieves after it." Harley and Seymour tried to carry a vote of censure without giving the House time to read the papers. But the general feeling was strongly for a short delay. At length, on the sixth of December, the subject was considered in a committee of the whole House. Shower undertook to prove that the letters patent to which Somers had put the Great Seal were illegal. Cowper replied to him with immense applause, and seems to have completely refuted him. Some of the Tory orators had employed what was then a favourite claptrap. Very great men, no doubt, were concerned in this business. But were the Commons of England to stand in awe of great men ? Would not they have the spirit to censure corruption and oppression in the highest places ? Cowper answered finely that assuredly the House ought not to be deterred from the discharge of any duty by the fear of great men, but that fear was not the only base and evil passion of which great men were the objects, and that the flatterer who courted their favour was not a worse citizen than the envious calumniator who took pleasure in bringing whatever was eminent down to his own level. At length, after a debate which lasted from midday till nine at night, and in which all the leading members took part, the committee divided on the question that the letters patent was dishonourable to the King, inconsistent with the law of nations, contrary to the statutes of the realm, and destructive of property and trade. The Chancellor's enemies had felt confident of victory, and had made the resolution so strong

in order that it might be impossible for him to retain the Great
Seal. They soon found that it would have been wise to propose a gentler censure. Great numbers of their adherents,
convinced by Cowper's arguments, or unwilling to put a cruel
stigma on a man of whose genius and accomplishments the
nation was proud, stole away before the door was closed. To
the general astonishment there were only one hundred and thirty-
three Ayes to one hundred and eighty-nine Noes. That the
City of London did not consider Somers as the destroyer, and
his enemies as the protectors, of trade, was proved on the
following morning by the most unequivocal of signs. As soon
as the news of his triumph reached the Royal Exchange, the
price of stocks went up.

Some weeks elapsed before the Tories ventured again to
attack him. In the meantime they amused themselves by
trying to worry another person whom they hated even more
bitterly. When, in a financial debate, the arrangements of the
household of the Duke of Gloucester were incidentally
mentioned, one or two members took the opportunity of
throwing reflections on Burnet. Burnet's very name sufficed
to raise among the High Churchmen a storm of mingled
merriment and anger. The Speaker in vain reminded the
orators that they were wandering from the question. The
majority was determined to have some fun with the Right
Reverend Whig, and encouraged them to proceed. Nothing
appears to have been said on the other side. The chiefs of
the opposition inferred from the laughing and cheering of the
Bishop's enemies, and from the silence of his friends, that
there would be no difficulty in driving from Court, with contumely, the prelate whom of all prelates they most detested, as
the personification of the latitudinarian spirit, a Jack Presbyter
in lawn sleeves. They, therefore, after the lapse of a few hours,
moved quite unexpectedly an address requesting the King to
remove the Bishop of Salisbury from the place of preceptor to
the young heir apparent. But it soon appeared that many who
could not help smiling at Burnet's weaknesses did justice to
his abilities and virtues. The debate was hot. The unlucky
Pastoral Letter was of course not forgotten. It was asked
whether a man who had proclaimed that England was a
conquered country, a man whose servile pages the English
Commons had ordered to be burned by the hangman, could be
a fit instructor for an English Prince. Some reviled the
Bishop for being a Socinian, which he was not, and some for
being a Scotchman, which he was. His defenders fought his

battle gallantly. "Grant," they said, "that it is possible to find, amidst an immense mass of eloquent and learned matter published in defence of the Protestant religion and of the English Constitution, a paragraph which, though well intended, was not well considered, is that error of an unguarded minute to outweigh the services of more than twenty years? If one House of Commons, by a very small majority, censured a little tract of which his Lordship was the author, let it be remembered that another House of Commons unanimously voted thanks to him for a work of very different magnitude and importance, the History of the Reformation. And, as to what is said about his birthplace, is there not already ill humour enough in Scotland? Has not the failure of that unhappy expedition to Darien raised a sufficiently bitter feeling against us throughout that kingdom? Every wise and honest man is desirous to soothe the angry passions of our neighbours. And shall we, just at this moment, exasperate those passions by proclaiming that to be born on the north of the Tweed is a disqualification for all honourable trust?" The ministerial members would gladly have permitted the motion to be withdrawn. But the opposition, elated with hope, insisted on dividing, and were confounded by finding that, with all the advantage of a surprise, they were only one hundred and thirty-three to one hundred and seventy-three. Their defeat would probably have been less complete, had not all those members who were especially attached to the Princess of Denmark voted in the majority or absented themselves. Marlborough used all his influence against the motion; and he had strong reasons for doing so. He was by no means well pleased to see the Commons engaged in discussing the characters and past lives of the persons who were placed about the Duke of Gloucester. If the High Churchmen, by reviving old stories, succeeded in carrying a vote against the Preceptor, it was by no means unlikely that some malicious Whig might retaliate on the Governor. The Governor must have been conscious that he was not invulnerable; nor could he absolutely rely on the support of the whole body of Tories: for it was believed that their favourite leader, Rochester, thought himself the fittest person to superintend the education of his grand nephew.

From Burnet the opposition went back to Somers. Some Crown property near Reigate had been granted to Somers by the King. In this transaction there was nothing that deserved blame. The Great Seal ought always to be held by a lawyer of the highest distinction ; nor can such a lawyer discharge his duties in a perfectly efficient manner unless, with the Great Seal, he accepts a peerage. But he may not have accumulated a fortune such as will alone suffice to support a peerage : his peerage is permanent; and his tenure of the Great Seal is precarious. In a few weeks he may be dismissed from office, and may find that he has lost a lucrative profession, that he has got nothing but a costly dignity, that he has been transformed from a prosperous barrister into a mendicant lord. Such a risk no wise man will run. If, therefore, the state is to be well served in the highest civil post, it is absolutely necessary that a provision should be made for retired Chancellors. The Sovereign is now empowered by Act of Parliament to make such a provision out of the public revenue. In old times such a provision was ordinarily made out of the hereditary domain of the Crown. What had been bestowed on Somers appears to have amounted, after all deductions, to a net income of about sixteen hundred a year, a sum which will hardly shock us who have seen at one time five retired Chancellors enjoying pensions of five thousand a year each. For the crime, however, of accepting this grant the leaders of the opposition hoped that they should be able to punish Somers with disgrace and ruin. One difficulty stood in the way. All that he had received was but a pittance when compared with the wealth with which some of his persecutors had been loaded by the last two kings of the House of Stuart. It was not easy to pass any censure on him which should not imply a still more severe censure on two generations of Granvilles, on two generations of Hydes, and on two generations of Finches. At last some ingenious Tory thought of a device by which it might be possible to strike the enemy without wounding friends. The grants of Charles and James had been made in time of peace ; and William's grant to Somers had been made in time of war. Malice eagerly caught at this childish distinction. It was moved that any minister who had been concerned in passing a grant for his own benefit while the nation was under the heavy taxes of the late war had violated his trust ; as if the expenditure which is necessary to secure to the country a good administration of justice ought to be suspended by war ; or as if it were not criminal in a government to squander the resources of the state in time of peace. The motion was made by James Brydges, eldest son of the Lord Chandos, the James Brydges who afterwards became Duke of Chandos, who raised a gigantic fortune out of war taxes, to squander it in comfortless and tasteless ostentation, and who is still remembered as the Timon of Pope's keen and brilliant satire. It was remarked as extraordinary that Brydges brought forward and defended his motion merely as the assertion of an abstract truth, and avoided all mention of the Chancellor. It seemed still more extraordinary that Howe, whose whole eloquence consisted in cutting personalities, named nobody on this occasion, and contented himself with declaiming in general terms against corruption and profusion. It was plain that the enemies of Somers were at once urged forward by hatred and kept back by fear. They knew that they could not carry a resolution directly condemning him. They, therefore, cunningly brought forward a mere speculative proposition which many members might be willing to affirm without scrutinising it severely. But, as soon as the major premise had been admitted, the minor would be without difficulty established; and it would be impossible to avoid coming to the conclusion that Somers had violated his trust. Such tactics, however, have very seldom succeeded in English parliaments; for a little good sense and a little straightforwardness are quite sufficient to confound them. A sturdy Whig member, Sir Rowland Gwyn, disconcerted the whole scheme of operations. " Why this reserve ? " he said, " Everybody knows your meaning. Everybody sees that you have not the courage to name the great man whom you are trying to destroy." " That is false," cried Brydges : and a stormy altercation followed. It soon appeared that innocence would again triumph. The two parties seemed to have exchanged characters for one day. The friends of the government, who in the Parliament were generally humble and timorous, took a high tone, and spoke as it becomes men to speak who are defending persecuted genius and virtue. The malecontents, generally so insolent and turbulent, seemed to be completely cowed. They abased themselves so low as to protest, what no human being could believe, that they had no intention of attacking the Chancellor, and had framed their resolution without any view to him. Howe, from whose lips scarcely any thing ever dropped but gall and poison, went so far as to say : " My Lord Somers is a man of eminent merit, of merit so eminent that, if he had made a slip, we might well overlook it." At a late hour the question was put ; and the motion was rejected by a majority of fifty in a house of four hundred and nineteen members. It was long since there had been so large an attendance at a division.

The ignominious failure of the attacks on Somers and Burnet

seemed to prove that the assembly was coming round to a better temper. But the temper of a House of Commons left without the guidance of a ministry is never to be trusted. "Nobody can tell today," said an experienced politician of that time, "what the majority may take it into their heads to do tomorrow." Already a storm was gathering in which the Constitution itself was in danger of perishing, and from which none of the three branches of the legislature escaped without serious damage.

The question of the Irish forfeitures had been raised; and about that question the minds of men, both within and without the walls of Parliament, were in a strangely excitable state. Candid and intelligent men, whatever veneration they may feel for the memory of William, must find it impossible to deny that, in his eagerness to enrich and aggrandise his personal friends, he too often forgot what was due to his own reputation and to the public interest. It is true that in giving away the old domains of the Crown he did only what he had a right to do, and what all his predecessors had done; nor could the most factious opposition insist on resuming his grants of those domains without resuming at the same time the grants of his uncles. But between those domains and the estates recently forfeited in Ireland there was a distinction, which would not indeed have been recognised by the judges, but which to a popular assembly might well seem to be of grave importance. In the year 1690 a Bill had been brought in for applying the Irish forfeitures to the public service. That Bill passed the Commons, and would probably, with large amendments, have passed the Lords, had not the King, who was under the necessity of attending the Congress at the Hague, put an end to the session. In bidding the Houses farewell on that occasion, he assured them that he should not dispose of the property about which they had been deliberating, till they should have had another opportunity of settling that matter. He had, as he thought, strictly kept his word; for he had not disposed of this property till the Houses had repeatedly met and separated without presenting to him any bill on the subject. They had had the opportunity which he had assured them that they should have. They had had more than one such opportunity. The pledge which he had given had therefore been amply redeemed; and he did not conceive that he was bound to abstain longer from exercising his undoubted prerogative. But, though it could hardly be denied that he had literally fulfilled his promise, the general opinion was that such a promise ought to have been more than literally fulfilled. If his Parliament, overwhelmed with business which could not be postponed without danger to his throne and to his person, had been forced to defer, year after year, the consideration of so large and complex a question as that of the Irish forfeitures, it ill became him to take advantage of such a laches with the eagerness of a shrewd attorney. Many persons, therefore, who were sincerely attached to his government, and who on principle disapproved of resumptions, thought the case of these forfeitures an exception to the general rule.

The Commons had at the close of the last session tacked to the Land Tax Bill a clause impowering seven Commissioners, who were designated by name, to take account of the Irish forfeitures; and the Lords and the King, afraid of losing the Land Tax Bill, had reluctantly consented to this clause. During the recess, the commissioners had visited Ireland. They had since returned to England. Their report was soon laid before both Houses. By the Tories, and by their allies the republicans, it was eagerly hailed. It had, indeed, been framed for the express purpose of flattering and of inflaming them. Three of the commissioners had strongly objected to some passages as indecorous, and even calumnious : but the other four had overruled every objection. Of the four the chief was Trenchard. He was by calling a pamphleteer, and seems not to have been aware that the sharpness of style and of temper which may be tolerated in a pamphlet is inexcusable in a state paper. He was certain that he should be protected and rewarded by the party to which he owed his appointment, and was delighted to have it in his power to publish, with perfect security and with a semblance of official authority, bitter reflections on King and ministry, Dutch favourites, French refugees, and Irish Papists. The consequence was that only four names were subscribed to the report. The three dissentients presented a separate memorial. As to the main facts, however, there was little or no dispute. It appeared that more than a million of Irish acres, or about seventeen hundred thousand English acres, an area equal to that of Middlesex, Hertfordshire, Bedfordshire, Cambridgeshire, and Huntingdonshire together, had been forfeited during the late troubles. But of the value of this large territory very different estimates were formed. The commissioners acknowledged that they could obtain no certain information. In the absence of such information they conjectured the annual rent to be about two hundred thousand pounds, and the fee simple to be worth

thirteen years' purchase, that is to say, about two millions six
hundred thousand pounds. They seem not to have been aware
that much of the land had been let very low on perpetual
leases, and that much was burdened with mortgages. A contemporary writer, who was evidently well acquainted with
Ireland, asserted that the authors of the report had valued the
forfeited property in Carlow at six times the real market price,
and that the two million six hundred thousand pounds, of
which they talked, would be found to shrink to about half
a million, which, as the exchanges then stood between Dublin
and London, would have dwindled to four hundred thousand
pounds by the time that it reached the English Exchequer.
It was subsequently proved, beyond all dispute, that this
estimate was very much nearer the truth than that which had
been formed by Trenchard and Trenchard's colleagues.

Of the seventeen hundred thousand acres which had been
forfeited, above a fourth part had been restored to the ancient
proprietors in conformity with the civil articles of the treaty of
Limerick. About one seventh of the remaining three fourths
had been given back to unhappy families, which, though they
could not plead the letter of the treaty, had been thought fit
objects of clemency. The rest had been bestowed, partly on
persons whose services merited all and more than all that they
obtained, but chiefly on the King's personal friends. Romney
had obtained a considerable share of the royal bounty. But
of all the grants the largest was to Woodstock, the eldest son
of Portland; the next was to Albemarle. An admirer of
William cannot relate without pain that he divided between
these two foreigners an extent of country larger than Hertfordshire.

This fact, simply reported, would have sufficed to excite a
strong feeling of indignation in a House of Commons less irritable and querulous than that which then sate at Westminster.
But Trenchard and his confederates were not content with
simply reporting the fact. They employed all their skill to
inflame the passions of the majority. They at once applied
goads to its anger and held out baits to its cupidity.

They censured that part of William's conduct which deserved
high praise even more severely than that part of his conduct
for which it is impossible to set up any defence. They told
the Parliament that the old proprietors of the soil had been
treated with pernicious indulgence; that the capitulation of
Limerick had been construed in a manner far too favourable
to the conquered race; and that the King had suffered his

compassion to lead him into the error of showing indulgence to many who could not pretend that they were within the terms of the capitulation. Even now, after the lapse of eight years, it might be possible, by instituting a severe inquisition, and by giving proper encouragement to informers, to prove that many Papists, who were still permitted to enjoy their estates, had taken the side of James during the civil war. There would thus be a new and plentiful harvest of confiscations. The four bitterly complained that their task had been made more difficult by the hostility of persons who held office in Ireland, and by the secret influence of great men who were interested in concealing the truth. These grave charges were made in general terms. No name was mentioned : no fact was specified : no evidence was tendered.

Had the report stopped here, those who drew it up might justly have been blamed for the unfair and ill natured manner in which they had discharged their functions ; but they could not have been accused of usurping functions which did not belong to them for the purpose of insulting the Sovereign and exasperating the nation. But these men well knew in what way and for what purpose they might safely venture to exceed their commission. The Act of Parliament from which they derived their powers authorised them to report on estates forfeited during the late troubles. It contained not a word which could be construed into an authority to report on the old hereditary domain of the Crown. With that domain they had as little to do as with the seignorage levied on tin in the Duchy of Cornwall, or with the church patronage of the Duchy of Lancaster. But they had discovered that a part of that domain had been alienated by a grant which they could not deny themselves the pleasure of publishing to the world. It was indeed an unfortunate grant, a grant which could not be brought to light without much mischief and much scandal. It was long since William had ceased to be the lover of Elizabeth Villiers, long since he had asked her counsel or listened to her fascinating conversation except in the presence of other persons. She had been some years married to George Hamilton, a soldier who had distinguished himself by his courage in Ireland and Flanders, and who probably held the courtier like doctrine that a lady is not dishonoured by having been the paramour of a king. William was well pleased with the marriage, bestowed on the wife a portion of the old Crown property in Ireland, and created the husband a peer of Scotland by the title of Earl of Orkney. Assuredly William would not have raised his character by abandoning to poverty a woman whom he had loved, though with a criminal love. He was undoubtedly bound, as a man of humanity and honour, to provide liberally for her; but he should have provided for her rather by saving from his civil list than by alienating his hereditary revenue. The four male-content commissioners rejoiced with spiteful joy over this discovery. It was in vain that the other three represented that the grant to Lady Orkney was one with which they had nothing to do, and that, if they went out of their way to hold it up to obloquy, they might be justly said to fly in the King's face. "To fly in the King's face!" said one of the majority; "our business is to fly in the King's face. We were sent here to fly in the King's face." With this patriotic object a paragraph about Lady Orkney's grant was added to the report, a paragraph too in which the value of that grant was so monstrously exaggerated that William appeared to have surpassed the profligate extravagance of his uncle Charles. The estate bestowed on the countess was valued at twenty-four thousand pounds a year. The truth seems to be that the income which she derived from the royal bounty, after making allowance for incumbrances and for the rate of exchange, was about four thousand pounds.

The success of the report was complete. The nation and its representatives hated taxes, hated foreign favourites, and hated Irish Papists; and here was a document which held out the hope that England might, at the expense of foreign courtiers and of popish Celts, be relieved from a great load of taxes. Many, both within and without the walls of Parliament, gave entire faith to the estimate which the commissioners had formed by a wild guess, in the absence of trustworthy information. They gave entire faith also to the prediction that a strict inquiry would detect many traitors who had hitherto been permitted to escape with impunity, and that a large addition would thus be made to the extensive territory which had already been confiscated. It was popularly said that, if vigorous measures were taken, the gain to the kingdom would be not less than three hundred thousand pounds a year; and almost the whole of this sum, a sum more than sufficient to defray the whole charge of such an army as the Commons were disposed to keep up in time of peace, would be raised by simply taking away what had been unjustifiably given to Dutchmen, who would still retain immense wealth taken out of English pockets, or unjustifiably left to Irishmen, who thought it at once the most pleasant and the most pious of all employments to cut English throats. The

Lower House went to work with the double eagerness of
rapacity and of animosity. As soon as the report of the four
and the protest of the three had been laid on the table and
read by the clerk, it was resolved that a Resumption Bill should
be brought in. It was then resolved, in opposition to the
plainest principles of justice, that no petition from any person
who might think himself aggrieved by this bill should ever be
received. It was necessary to consider how the commissioners
should be remunerated for their services: and this question
was decided with impudent injustice. It was determined that
the commissioners who had signed the report should receive a
thousand pounds each. But a large party thought that the
dissentient three deserved no recompense; and two of them
were merely allowed what was thought sufficient to cover the
expense of their journey to Ireland. This was nothing less
than to give notice to every man who should ever be employed
in any similar inquiry that, if he wished to be paid, he must
report what would please the assembly which held the purse of
the state. In truth the House was despotic, and was fast
contracting the vices of a despot. It was proud of its antipathy
to courtiers; and it was calling into existence a new set of
courtiers who would study all its humours, who would flatter all
its weaknesses, who would prophesy to it smooth things, and
who would assuredly be, in no respect, less greedy, less faithless, or less abject than the sycophants who bow in the antechambers of kings.

Indeed the dissentient commissioners had worse evils to
apprehend than that of being left unremunerated. One of them,
Sir Richard Levinz, had mentioned in private to his friends
some disrespectful expressions which had been used by one of
his colleagues about the King. What he had mentioned in
private was, not perhaps very discreetly, repeated by Montague
in the House. The predominant party eagerly seized the
opportunity of worrying both Montague and Levinz. A resolution implying a severe censure on Montague was carried.
Levinz was brought to the bar and examined. The four were
also in attendance. They protested that he had misrepresented
them. Trenchard declared that he had always spoken of His
Majesty as a subject ought to speak of an excellent sovereign,
who had been deceived by evil counsellors, and who would be
grateful to those who should bring the truth to his knowledge.
He vehemently denied that he had called the grant to Lady
Orkney villainous. It was a word that he never used, a word
that never came out of the mouth of a gentleman. These

*R 37

assertions will be estimated at the proper value by those who are acquainted with Trenchard's pamphlets, pamphlets in which the shocking word villainous will without difficulty be found, and which are full of malignant reflections on William.* But the House was determined not to believe Levinz. He was voted a calumniator, and sent to the Tower, as an example to all who should be tempted to speak truth which the Commons might not like to hear.

Meanwhile the bill had been brought in, and was proceeding easily. It provided that all the property which had belonged to the Crown at the time of the accession of James the Second, or which had been forfeited to the Crown since that time, should be vested in trustees. These trustees were named in the bill; and among them were the four commissioners who had signed the report. All the Irish grants of William were annulled. The legal rights of persons other than the grantees were saved. But of those rights the trustees were to be judges, and judges without appeal. A claimant who gave them the trouble of attending to him, and could not make out his case, was to be heavily fined. Rewards were offered to informers who should discover any property which was liable to confiscation, and which had not yet been confiscated. Though eight years had elapsed since an arm had been lifted up in the conquered island against the domination of the Englishry, the unhappy children of the soil, who had been suffered to live, submissive and obscure, on their hereditary fields, were threatened with a new and severe inquisition into old offences.

Objectionable as many parts of the bill undoubtedly were, nobody who knew the House of Commons believed it to be possible to carry any amendment. The King flattered himself that a motion for leaving at his disposal a third part of the forfeitures would be favourably received. There can be little doubt that a compromise would have been willingly accepted twelve months earlier. But the report had made all compromise impossible. William, however, was bent on trying the experiment; and Vernon consented to go on what he considered as a forlorn hope. He made his speech and his motion: but the reception which he met with was such that he did not

* I give an example of Trenchard's mode of showing his profound respect for an excellent Sovereign. He speaks thus of the commencement of the reign of Henry the Third. " The kingdom was recently delivered from a bitter tyrant, King John, and had likewise got rid of their perfidious deliverer, the Dauphin of France, who after the English had accepted him for their King, had secretly vowed their extirpation."

venture to demand a division. This feeble attempt at obstruction only made the impetuous current chafe the more. Howe immediately moved two resolutions: one attributing the load of debts and taxes which lay on the nation to the Irish grants; the other censuring all who had been concerned in advising or passing those grants. Nobody was named; not because the majority was inclined to show any tenderness to the Whig ministers, but because some of the most objectionable grants had been sanctioned by the Board of Treasury when Godolphin and Seymour, who had great influence with the country party, sate at that board.

Howe's two resolutions were laid before the King by the Speaker, in whose train all the leaders of the opposition appeared at Kensington. Even Seymour, with characteristic effrontery, showed himself there as one of the chief authors of a vote which pronounced him guilty of a breach of duty. William's answer was that he had thought himself bound to reward out of the forfeited property those who had served him well, and especially those who had borne a principal part in the reduction of Ireland. The war, he said, had undoubtedly left behind it a heavy debt; and he should be glad to see that debt reduced by just and effectual means. This answer was but a bad one; and, in truth, it was hardly possible for him to return a good one. He had done what was indefensible; and, by attempting to defend himself, he made his case worse. It was not true that the Irish forfeitures, or one fifth part of them, had been granted to men who had distinguished themselves in the Irish war; and it was not judicious to hint that those forfeitures could not justly be applied to the discharge of the public debts. The Commons murmured, and not altogether without reason. "His Majesty tells us," they said, "that the debts fall to us and the forfeitures to him. We are to make good out of the purses of Englishmen what was spent upon the war; and he is to put into the purses of Dutchmen what was got by the war." When the House met again, Howe moved that whoever had advised the King to return such an answer was an enemy to His Majesty and the kingdom; and this resolution was carried with some slight modification.

To whatever criticism William's answer might be open, he had said one thing which well deserved the attention of the House. A small part of the forfeited property had been bestowed on men whose services to the state well deserved a much larger recompense; and that part could not be resumed without gross injustice and ingratitude. An estate of very moderate value had been given, with the title of Earl of Athlone, to Ginkell, whose skill and valour had brought the war in Ireland to a triumphant close. Another estate had been given, with the title of Earl of Galway, to Rouvigny, who, in the crisis of the decisive battle, at the very moment when Saint Ruth was waving his hat, and exclaiming that the English should be beaten back to Dublin, had, at the head of a gallant body of horse, struggled through the morass, turned the left wing of the Celtic army, and retrieved the day. But the predominant faction, drunk with insolence and animosity, made no distinction between courtiers who had been enriched by injudicious partiality and warriors who had been sparingly rewarded for great exploits achieved in defence of the liberties and the religion of our country. Athlone was a Dutchman : Galway was a Frenchman ; and it did not become a good Englishman to say a word in favour of either.

Yet this was not the most flagrant injustice of which the Commons were guilty. According to the plainest principles of common law and of common sense, no man can forfeit any rights except those which he has. All the donations which William had made he had made subject to this limitation. But by this limitation the Commons were too angry and too rapacious to be bound. They determined to vest in the trustees of the forfeited lands an estate greater than had ever belonged to the forfeiting landholders. Thus innocent persons were violently deprived of property which was theirs by descent or by purchase, of property which had been strictly respected by the King and by his grantees. No immunity was granted even to men who had fought on the English side, even to men who had lined the walls of Londonderry and rushed on the Irish guns at Newton Butler.

In some cases the Commons showed indulgence : but their indulgence was not less unjustifiable, nor of less pernicious example, than their severity. The ancient rule, a rule which is still strictly maintained, and which cannot be relaxed without danger of boundless profusion and shameless jobbery, is that whatever the Parliament grants shall be granted to the Sovereign, and that no public bounty shall be bestowed on any private person except by the Sovereign.

The Lower House now, contemptuously disregarding both principles and precedents, took on itself to carve estates out of the forfeitures for persons whom it was inclined to favour. To the Duke of Ormond especially, who ranked among the Tories and was distinguished by his dislike of the foreigners, marked partiality was shown. Some of his friends, indeed, hoped that they should be able to insert in the bill a clause bestowing on him all the confiscated estates in the county of Tipperary. But they found that it would be prudent in them to content themselves with conferring on him a boon smaller in amount, but equally objectionable in principle. He had owed very large debts to persons who had forfeited to the Crown all that belonged to them. Those debts were therefore now due from him to the Crown. The House determined to make him a present of the whole, that very House which would not consent to leave a single acre to the general who had stormed Athlone, who had gained the battle of Aghrim, who had entered Galway in triumph, and who had received the submission of Limerick.

That a bill so violent, so unjust, and so unconstitutional would pass the Lords without considerable alteration was hardly to be expected. The ruling demagogues, therefore, resolved to join it with the bill which granted to the Crown a land tax of two shillings in the pound for the service of the next year, and thus to place the Upper House under the necessity of either passing both bills together without the change of a word, or rejecting both together, and leaving the public creditor unpaid and the nation defenceless.

There was great indignation among the Peers. They were not indeed more disposed than the Commons to approve of the manner in which the Irish forfeitures had been granted away; for the antipathy to the foreigners, strong as it was in the nation generally, was strongest in the highest ranks. Old barons were angry at seeing themselves preceded by new earls from Holland and Guelders. Garters, gold keys, white staves, rangerships, which had been considered as peculiarly belonging to the hereditary grandees of the realm, were now intercepted by aliens. Every English nobleman felt that his chance of obtaining a share of the favours of the Crown was seriously diminished by the competition of Bentincks and Keppels, Auverquerques and Zulesteins. But, though the riches and dignities heaped on the little knot of Dutch courtiers might disgust him, the recent proceedings of the Commons could not but disgust him still more. The authority, the respectability, the existence of his order were threatened with destruction. Not only,—such were the just complaints of the Peers,—not only are we to be deprived of that coordinate legislative power to which we are, by the constitution of the realm, entitled. We are not to be allowed even a suspensive veto. We are not to dare to remonstrate, to suggest an amendment, to offer a reason, to ask for an explanation. Whenever the other House has passed a bill to which it is known that we have strong objections, that bill is to be tacked to a bill of supply. If we alter it, we are told that we are attacking the most sacred privilege of the representatives of the people, and that we must either take the whole or reject the whole. If we reject the whole, public credit is shaken; the Royal Exchange is in confusion; the Bank stops payment; the army is disbanded; the fleet is in mutiny; the island is left, without one regiment, without one frigate, at the mercy of every enemy. The danger of throwing out a bill of supply is doubtless great. Yet it may on the whole be better that we should face that danger, once for all, than that we should consent to be, what we are fast becoming, a body of no more importance than the Convocation.

Animated by such feelings as these, a party in the Upper House was eager to take the earliest opportunity of making a stand. On the fourth of April, the second reading was moved. Near a hundred lords were present. Somers, whose serene wisdom and persuasive eloquence had seldom been more needed, was confined to his room by illness; and his place on the woolsack was supplied by the Earl of Bridgewater. Several orators, both Whig and Tory, objected to proceeding farther. But the chiefs of both parties thought it better to try the almost hopeless experiment of committing the bill and sending it back amended to the Commons. The second reading was carried by seventy votes to twenty-three. It was remarked that both Portland and Albemarle voted in the majority.

In the Committee and on the third reading several amendments were proposed and carried. Wharton, the boldest and most active of the Whig peers, and the Lord Privy Seal Lonsdale, one of the most moderate and reasonable of the Tories, took the lead, and were strenuously supported by the Lord President Pembroke, and by the Archbishop of Canterbury, who seems on this occasion to have a little forgotten his habitual sobriety and caution. Two natural sons of Charles the Second, Richmond and Southampton, who had strong personal reasons for disliking resumption bills, were zealous on the same side. No peer, however, as far as can now be discovered, ventured to defend the way in which William had disposed of his Irish domains. The provisions which annulled the grants of those domains were left untouched. But the words of which the effect was to vest in the parliamentary trustees property which had never been forfeited to the King, and had never been given away by him, were altered; and the clauses by which estates and sums of money were, in defiance of constitutional principle and of immemorial practice, bestowed on persons who were favourites of the Commons, were so far modified as to be, in form, somewhat less exceptionable. The bill, improved by these changes, was sent down by two Judges to the Lower House.

The Lower House was all in a flame. There was now no difference of opinion there. Even those members who thought that the Resumption Bill and the Land Tax Bill ought not to have been tacked together, yet felt that, since those bills had been tacked together, it was impossible to agree to the amendments made by the Lords without surrendering one of the most precious privileges of the Commons. The amendments were rejected without one dissentient voice. It was resolved that a conference should be demanded; and the gentlemen who were to manage the conference were instructed to say merely that the Upper House had no right to alter a money bill; that the point had long been settled and was too clear for argument; that they should leave the bill with the Lords, and that they should leave with the Lords also the responsibility of stopping the supplies which were necessary for the public service. Several votes of menacing sound were passed at the same sitting. It was Monday the eighth of April. Tuesday the ninth was allowed to the other House for reflection and repentance. It was resolved that on the Wednesday morning the question of the Irish forfeitures should again be taken into consideration, and that every member who was in town should be then in his place on peril of the highest displeasure of the House. It was moved and carried that every Privy Councillor who had been concerned in procuring or passing any exorbitant grant for his own benefit had been guilty of a high crime and misdemeanour. Lest the courtiers should flatter themselves that this was meant to be a mere abstract proposition, it was ordered that a list of the members of the Privy Council should be laid on the table. As it was thought not improbable that the crisis might end in an appeal to the constituent bodies, nothing was omitted which could excite out of doors a feeling in favour of the bill. The Speaker was directed to print and publish the report signed by the four Commissioners, not accompanied, as in common justice it ought to have been, by the protest of the three dissentients, but accompanied by several extracts from the journals which were thought likely to produce an impression favourable to the House and unfavourable to the Court. All these resolutions passed without any division, and without, as far as appears, any debate. There was, indeed, much speaking, but all on one side. Seymour, Harley, Howe, Harcourt, Shower, Musgrave, declaimed, one after another, about the obstinacy of the other House, the alarming state of the country, the dangers which threatened the public peace and the public credit. If, it was said, none but Englishmen sate in the Parliament and in the Council, we might hope that they would relent at the thought of the calamities which impend over England. But we have to deal with men who are not Englishmen, with men who consider this country as their own only for evil, as their property, not as their home; who, when they have gorged themselves with our wealth, will, without one uneasy feeling, leave us sunk in bankruptcy, distracted by faction, exposed without defence to invasion. "A new war," said one of these orators, "a new war, as long, as bloody, and as costly as the last, would do less mischief than has been done by the introduction of that batch of Dutchmen among the barons of the realm." Another was so absurd as to call on the House to declare that whoever should advise a dissolution would be guilty of high treason. A third gave utterance to a sentiment which it is difficult to understand how any assembly of civilised and Christian men, even in a moment of strong excitement, should have heard without horror. "They object to tacking; do they? Let them take care that they do not provoke us to tack in earnest. How would they like to have bills of supply with bills of attainder tacked to them?" This atrocious threat, worthy of the tribune of the French Convention in the worst days of the Jacobin tyranny, seems to have passed unreprehended. It was meant—such at least was the impression at the Dutch embassy—to intimidate Somers. He was confined by illness. He had been unable to take any public part in the proceedings of the Lords; and he had privately blamed them for engaging in a conflict in which he justly thought that they could not be victorious. Nevertheless, the Tory leaders hoped that they might be able to direct against him the whole force of the storm which they had raised. Seymour, in particular, encouraged by the wild and almost savage temper of his hearers, harangued with rancorous violence against the wisdom and the virtue which presented the strongest contrast to his own turbulence, insolence, faithlessness, and rapacity. No doubt, he said, the Lord Chancellor was a man of parts. Anybody might be glad to have for counsel so acute and eloquent an advocate. But a very good advocate might be a very bad minister; and, of all the ministers who had brought the kingdom into difficulties, this plausible, fair-spoken person was the most dangerous. Nor was the old reprobate ashamed to add that he was afraid that his Lordship was no better than a Hobbist in religion.

After a long sitting the members separated; but they reassembled early on the morning of the following day, Tuesday the ninth of April. A conference was held; and Seymour, as chief manager for the Commons, returned the bill and the amendments to the Peers in the manner which had been prescribed to him. From the Painted Chamber he went back to the Lower House, and reported what had passed. "If," he said, "I may venture to judge by the looks and manner of their Lordships, all will go right." But within half an hour evil tidings came through the Court of Requests and the lobbies. The Lords had divided on the question whether they would adhere to their amendments. Forty-seven had voted for adhering, and thirty-four for giving way. The House of Commons broke up with gloomy looks, and in great agitation. All London looked forward to the next day with painful forebodings. The general feeling was in favour of the bill. It was rumoured that the majority which had determined to stand by the amendments had been swollen by several prelates, by several of the illegitimate sons of Charles the Second, and by several needy and greedy courtiers. The cry in all the public places of resort was that the nation would be ruined by the three B's, Bishops, Bastards, and Beggars. On Wednesday the tenth, at length, the contest came to a decisive issue. Both Houses were early crowded. The Lords demanded a conference. It was held; and Pembroke delivered back to Seymour the bill and the amendments, together with a paper containing a concise, but luminous and forcible, exposition of the grounds on which the Lords conceived themselves to be acting in a constitutional and strictly defensive manner. This paper was read at the bar: but, whatever effect it may now produce on a dispassionate student of history, it produced none on the thick ranks of country gentlemen. It was instantly resolved that the bill should again be sent back to the Lords with a peremptory announcement that the Commons' determination was unalterable.

The Lords again took the amendments into consideration. During the last forty-eight hours, great exertions had been made in various quarters to avert a complete rupture between the Houses. The statesmen of the Junto were far too wise not to see that it would be madness to continue the struggle longer. It was indeed necessary, unless the King and the Lords were to be of as little weight in the State as in 1648, unless the House of Commons was not merely to exercise a general control over the government, but to be, as in the days of the Rump, itself the whole government, the sole legislative chamber, the fountain from which were to flow all those favours which had hitherto been in the gift of the Crown, that a determined stand should be made. But, in order that such a stand might be successful, the ground must be carefully selected; for a defeat might be fatal. The Lords must wait for some occasion on which their privileges would be bound up with the privileges of all Englishmen, for some occasion on which the constituent bodies would, if an appeal were made to them, disavow the acts of the representative body; and this was not such an occasion. The enlightened and large minded few considered tacking as a practice so pernicious that it would be justified only by an emergency which would justify a resort to physical force. But, in the many, tacking, when employed for a popular end, excited little or no disapprobation. The public, which seldom troubles itself with nice distinctions, could not be made to understand that the question at issue was any other than this, whether a sum which was vulgarly estimated at millions, and which undoubtedly amounted to some hundreds of thousands, should be employed in paying the debts of the state and alleviating the load of taxation, or in making Dutchmen, who were already too rich, still richer. It was evident that on that question the Lords could not hope to have the country with them, and that, if a general election took place while that question was unsettled, the new House of Commons would be even more mutinous and impracticable than the present House. Somers, in his sick chamber, had given this opinion. Orford had voted for the bill in every stage. Montague, though no longer a minister, had obtained admission to the royal closet, and had strongly represented to the King the dangers which threatened the state. The King had at length consented to let it be understood that he considered the passing of the bill as on the whole the less of two great evils. It was soon clear that the temper of the Peers had undergone a considerable alteration since the preceding day. Scarcely any, indeed, changed sides. But not a few abstained from voting. Wharton, who had at first spoken powerfully for the amendments, left town for Newmarket. On the other hand, some Lords who had not yet taken their part came down to give a healing vote. Among them were the two persons to whom the education of the young heir apparent had been entrusted, Marlborough and Burnet. Marlborough showed his usual prudence. He had remained neutral while by taking a part he must have offended either the House of Commons or the King. He took a part as soon as he saw that it was possible to please both. Burnet, alarmed for the public peace, was in a state of great excitement, and, as was usual with him when in such a state, forgot dignity and decorum, called out "stuff" in a very audible voice while a noble Lord was haranguing in favour of the amendments, and was in great danger of being reprimanded at the bar or delivered over to Black Rod. The motion on which the division took place was that the House do adhere to the amendments. There were forty contents and thirty-seven not contents. Proxies were called; and the numbers were found to be exactly even. In the House of Lords there is no casting vote. When the numbers are even, the non contents have it. The motion to adhere had therefore been negatived. But this was not enough. It was necessary that an affirmative resolution should be moved to the effect that the House agreed to the bill without amendments; and, if the numbers should again be equal, this motion would also be lost. It was an anxious moment. Fortunately the Primate's heart failed him. He had obstinately fought the battle down to the last stage. But he probably felt that it was no light thing to take on himself, and to bring on his order, the responsibility of throwing the whole kingdom into confusion. He started up and hurried out of the House, beckoning to some of his brethren. His brethren followed him with a prompt obedience, which, serious as the crisis was, caused no small merriment. In consequence of this defection, the motion to agree was carried by a majority of five. Meanwhile the members of the other House had been impatiently waiting for news, and had been alternately elated and depressed by the reports which followed one another in rapid succession. At first it was confidently expected that the Peers would yield; and there was general good humour. Then came intelligence that the majority of the Lords present had voted for adhering to the amendments. "I believe," so Vernon wrote the next day, "I believe there was not one man in the House that did not think the nation ruined." The lobbies were cleared: the back doors were locked: the keys were laid on the table: the Serjeant at Arms was directed to take his post at the front door, and to suffer no member to withdraw. An awful interval followed, during which the angry passions of the assembly seemed to be subdued by terror. Some of the leaders of the opposition, men of grave character and of large property, stood aghast at finding that they were engaged,—they scarcely knew how,—in a conflict such as they had not at all expected, in a conflict in which they could be victorious only at the expense of the peace and order of society. Even Seymour was sobered by the greatness and nearness of the danger. Even Howe thought it advisable to hold conciliatory language. It was no time, he said, for wrangling. Court party and country party were Englishmen alike. Their duty was to forget all past grievances, and to cooperate heartily for the purpose of saving the country.

In a moment all was changed. A message from the Lords was announced. It was a message which lightened many heavy hearts. The bill had been passed without amendments. The leading malecontents, who, a few minutes before, scared by finding that their violence had brought on a crisis for which they were not prepared, had talked about the duty of mutual forgiveness and close union, instantly became again as rancorous as ever. One danger, they said, was over. So far well. But it was the duty of the representatives of the people to take such steps as might make it impossible that there should ever again be such danger. Every adviser of the Crown, who had been concerned in the procuring or passing of any exorbitant grant, ought to be excluded from all access to the royal ear. A list of the privy councillors, furnished in conformity with the order made two days before, was on the table. That list the clerk was ordered to read. Prince George of Denmark and the Archbishop of Canterbury passed without remark. But, as soon as the Chancellor's name had been pronounced, the rage of his enemies broke forth. Twice already, in the course of that stormy session, they had attempted to ruin his fame and his fortunes ; and twice his innocence and his calm fortitude had confounded all their politics. Perhaps, in the state of excitement to which the House had been wrought up, a third attack on him might be successful. Orator after orator declaimed against him. He was the great offender. He was responsible for all the grievances of which the nation complained. He had obtained exorbitant grants for himself. He had defended the exorbitant grants obtained by others. He had not, indeed, been able, in the late debates, to raise his own voice against the just demands of the nation. But it might well be suspected that he had in secret prompted the ungracious answer of the King and encouraged the pertinacious resistance of the Lords. Sir John Levison Gower, a noisy and acrimonious Tory, called for impeachment. But Musgrave, an abler and more experienced politician, saw that, if the imputations which the opposition had been in the habit of throwing on the Chancellor were exhibited with the precision of a legal charge, their futility would excite universal derision, and thought it more expedient to move that the House should, without assigning any reason, request the King to remove Lord Somers from His Majesty's counsels and presence for ever. Cowper defended his persecuted friend with great eloquence and effect; and he was warmly supported by many members who had been zealous for the resumption of the Irish grants. Only a hundred and six members went into the lobby with Musgrave; a hundred and sixty-seven voted against him. Such a division, in such a House of Commons, and on such a day, is sufficient evidence of the respect which the great qualities of Somers had extorted even from his political enemies.

The clerk then went on with the list. The Lord President and the Lord Privy Seal, who were well known to have stood up strongly for the privileges of the Lords, were reviled by some angry members; but no motion was made against either. And soon the Tories became uneasy in their turn: for the name of the Duke of Leeds was read. He was one of themselves. They were very unwilling to put a stigma on him. Yet how could they, just after declaiming against the Chancellor for accepting a very moderate and well earned provision, undertake the defence of a statesman who had, out of grants, pardons and bribes, accumulated a princely fortune? There was actually on the table evidence that His Grace was receiving from the bounty of the Crown more than thrice as much as had been bestowed on Somers; and nobody could doubt that His Grace's secret gains had very far exceeded those of which there was evidence on the table. It was accordingly moved that the House, which had indeed been sitting many hours, should adjourn. The motion was lost; but neither party was disposed to move that the consideration of the list should be resumed. It was however resolved, without a division, that an address should be presented to the King, requesting that no person not a native of his dominions, Prince George excepted, might be admitted to the Privy Council either of England or of Ireland. The evening was now far spent. The candles had been some time lighted; and the House rose. So ended one of the most anxious, turbulent, and variously eventful days in the long Parliamentary History of England.

What the morrow would have produced if time had been

allowed for a renewal of hostilities can only be guessed. The supplies had been voted. The King was determined not to receive the address which requested him to disgrace his dearest and most trusty friends. Indeed he would have prevented the passing of that address by proroguing Parliament on the preceding day, had not the Lords risen the moment after they had agreed to the Resumption Bill. He had actually come from Kensington to the Treasury for that purpose; and his robes and crown were in readiness. He now took care to be at Westminster in good time. The Commons had scarcely met when the knock of Black Rod was heard. They repaired to the other House. The bills were passed; and Bridgewater, by the royal command, prorogued the Parliament. For the first time since the Revolution the session closed without a speech from the throne. William was too angry to thank the Commons, and too prudent to reprimand them.

\*     \*     \*     \*     \*     \*

\*     \*     \*     \*     \*     \*

The health of James had been during some years declining: and he had at length, on Good Friday, 1701, suffered a shock from which he had never recovered. While he was listening in his chapel to the solemn service of the day, he fell down in a fit, and remained long insensible. Some people imagined that the words of the anthem which his choristers were chanting had produced in him emotions too violent to be borne by an enfeebled body and mind. For that anthem was taken from the plaintive elegy in which a servant of the true God, chastened by many sorrows and humiliations, banished, homesick, and living on the bounty of strangers, bewailed the fallen throne and the desolate Temple of Sion: " Remember, O Lord, what is come upon us; consider and behold our reproach. Our inheritance is turned to strangers, our houses to aliens; the crown is fallen from our head. Wherefore dost thou forget us for ever? "

The King's malady proved to be paralytic. Fagon, the first physician of the French Court, and, on medical questions, the oracle of all Europe, prescribed the waters of Bourbon. Lewis, with all his usual generosity, sent to Saint Germains ten thousand crowns in gold for the charges of the journey, and gave orders that every town along the road should receive his good brother with all the honours due to royalty.\*

James, after passing some time at Bourbon, returned to the

---

\* Life of James; St. Simon; Dangeau.

neighbourhood of Paris with health so far reestablished that he was able to take exercise on horseback, but with judgment and memory evidently impaired. On the thirteenth of September, he had a second fit in his chapel; and it soon became clear that this was a final stroke. He rallied the last energies of his failing body and mind to testify his firm belief in the religion for which he had sacrificed so much. He received the last sacraments with every mark of devotion, exhorted his son to hold fast to the true faith in spite of all temptations, and entreated Middleton, who, almost alone among the courtiers assembled in the bedchamber, professed himself a Protestant, to take refuge from doubt and error in the bosom of the one infallible Church. After the extreme unction had been administered, James declared that he pardoned all his enemies, and named particularly the Prince of Orange, the Princess of Denmark, and the Emperor. The Emperor's name he repeated with peculiar emphasis : " Take notice, father," he said to the confessor, " that I forgive the Emperor with all my heart." It may perhaps seem strange that he should have found this the hardest of all exercises of Christian charity. But it must be remembered that the Emperor was the only Roman Catholic Prince still living who had been accessory to the Revolution, and that James might not unnaturally consider Roman Catholics who had been accessory to the Revolution as more inexcusably guilty than heretics who might have deluded themselves into the belief that, in violating their duty to him, they were discharging their duty to God.

While James was still able to understand what was said to him, and make intelligible answers, Lewis visited him twice. The English exiles observed that the Most Christian King was to the last considerate and kind in the very slightest matters which concerned his unfortunate guest. He would not allow his coach to enter the court of Saint Germains, lest the noise of the wheels should be heard in the sick room. In both interviews he was gracious, friendly, and even tender. But he carefully abstained from saying anything about the future position of the family which was about to lose its head. Indeed he could say nothing : for he had not yet made up his own mind. Soon, however, it became necessary for him to form some resolution. On the sixteenth James sank into a stupor which indicated the near approach of death. While he lay in this helpless state, Madame de Maintenon visited his consort. To this visit many persons who were likely to be well informed attributed a long series of great events. We cannot wonder

that a woman should have been moved to pity by the misery
of a woman; that a devout Roman Catholic should have taken
a deep interest in the fate of a family persecuted, as she conceived, solely for being Roman Catholics; or that the pride
of the widow of Scarron should have been intensely gratified
by the supplications of a daughter of Este and a Queen of
England. From mixed motives, probably, the wife of Lewis
promised her powerful protection to the wife of James.

Madame de Maintenon was just leaving Saint Germains
when, on the brow of the hill which overlooks the valley of the
Seine, she met her husband, who had come to ask after his
guest. It was probable at this moment that he was persuaded
to form a resolution, of which neither he nor she by whom he
was governed foresaw the consequences. Before he announced
that resolution, however, he observed all the decent forms of
deliberation. A council was held that evening at Marli, and
was attended by the princes of the blood and by the ministers
of state. The question was propounded, whether, when God
should take James the Second of England to himself, France
should recognise the Pretender as King James the Third?

The ministers were, one and all, against the recognition.
Indeed, it seems difficult to understand how any person who
had any pretensions to the name of statesman should have been
of a different opinion. Torcy took his stand on the ground
that to recognise the Prince of Wales would be to violate the
Treaty of Ryswick. This was indeed an impregnable position.
By that treaty His Most Christian Majesty had bound himself
to do nothing which could, directly or indirectly, disturb the
existing order of things in England. And in what way, except
by an actual invasion, could he do more to disturb the existing
order of things in England than by solemnly declaring, in the
face of the whole world, that he did not consider that order of
things as legitimate, that he regarded the Bill of Rights and the
Act of Settlement as nullities, and the King in possession as an
usurper? The recognition would then be a breach of faith:
and, even if all considerations of morality were set aside, it was
plain that it would, at that moment, be wise in the French
government to avoid every thing which could with plausibility
be represented as a breach of faith. The crisis was a very
peculiar one. The great diplomatic victory won by France in
the preceding year had excited the fear and hatred of her
neighbours. Nevertheless there was, as yet, no great coalition
against her. The House of Austria, indeed, had appealed to
arms. But with the House of Austria alone the House of

Bourbon could easily deal. Other powers were still looking in doubt to England for the signal; and England, though her aspect was sullen and menacing, still preserved neutrality. That neutrality would not have lasted so long, if William could have relied on the support of his Parliament and of h's people. In his Parliament there were agents of France, who, though few, had obtained so much influence by clamouring against standing armies, profuse grants, and Dutch favourites, that they were often blindly followed by the majority; and his people, distracted by domestic factions, unaccustomed to busy themselves about continental politics, and remembering with bitterness the disasters and burdens of the last war, the carnage of Landen, the loss of the Smyrna fleet, the land tax at four shillings in the pound, hesitated about engaging in another contest, and would probably continue to hesitate while he continued to live. He could not live long. It had, indeed, often been prophesied that his death was at hand; and the prophets had hitherto been mistaken. But there was now no possibility of mistake. His cough was more violent than ever; his legs were swollen; his eyes, once bright and clear as those of a falcon, had grown dim; he who, on the day of the Boyne, had been sixteen hours on the backs of different horses, could now with great difficulty creep into his state coach.* The vigorous intellect, and the intrepid spirit, remained; but on the body fifty years had done the work of ninety. In a few months the vaults of Westminster would receive the emaciated and shattered frame which was animated by the most far-sighted, the most daring, the most commanding of souls. In a few months the British throne would be filled by a woman whose understanding was well known to be feeble, and who was believed to lean towards the party which was averse from war. To get over those few months without an open and violent rupture should have been the first object of the French government. Every engagement should have been punctually fulfilled: every occasion of quarrel should have been studiously avoided. Nothing should have been spared which could quiet the alarms and soothe the wounded pride of neighbouring nations.

The House of Bourbon was so situated that one year of moderation might not improbably be rewarded by thirty years of undisputed ascendency. Was it possible the politic and

* Poussin to Torcy, $\frac{\text{April 28.}}{\text{May 9}}$ 1701. "Le roi d'Angleterre tousse plus qu'il n'a jamais fait, et ses jambes sont fort enflés. Je le vis hier sortir du prêche de Saint James. Je le trouve fort cassé, les yeux éteints, et il eut beaucoup de peine à monter en carrosse."

experienced Lewis would at such a conjuncture offer a new and most galling provocation, not only to William, whose animosity was already as great as it could be, but to the people whom William had hitherto been vainly endeavouring to inspire with animosity resembling his own? How often, since the Revolution of 1688, had it seemed that the English were thoroughly weary of the new government. And how often had the detection of a Jacobite plot, or the approach of a French armament, changed the whole face of things. All at once the grumbling had ceased, the grumblers had crowded to sign loyal addresses to the usurper, had formed associations in support of his authority, had appeared in arms at the head of the militia, crying God save King William. So it would be now. Most of those who had taken a pleasure in crossing him on the question of his Dutch guards, on the question of his Irish grants, would be moved to vehement resentment when they learned that Lewis had, in direct violation of a treaty, determined to force on England a king of his own religion, a king bred in his own dominions, a king who would be at Westminster what Philip was at Madrid, a great feudatory of France.

These arguments were concisely but clearly and strongly urged by Torcy in a paper which is still extant, and which it is difficult to believe that his master can have read without great misgivings.* On one side were the faith of treaties, the peace of Europe, the welfare of France, nay the selfish interest of the House of Bourbon. On the other side were the influence of an artful woman, and the promptings of vanity which, we must in candour acknowledge, was ennobled by a mixture of compassion and chivalrous generosity. The King determined to act in direct opposition to the advice of all his ablest servants ; and the princes of the blood applauded his decision, as they would have applauded any decision which he had announced. Nowhere was he regarded with a more timorous, a more slavish, respect than in his own family.

On the following day he went again to Saint Germains, and, attended by a splendid retinue, entered James's bedchamber. The dying man scarcely opened his heavy eyes, and then closed them again. "I have something," said Lewis, "of great moment to communicate to Your Majesty." The courtiers who filled the room took this as a signal to retire, and were crowding towards the door, when they were stopped by that

* Mémoire sur la proposition de reconnoître au prince des Galles le titre du Roi de la Grande Bretagne, Sept. $\frac{9}{15}$. 1701.

commanding voice: "Let nobody withdraw. I come to tell Your Majesty that, whenever it shall please God to take you from us, I will be to your son what I have been to you, and will acknowledge him as King of England, Scotland and Ireland." The English exiles who were standing round the couch fell on their knees. Some burst into tears. Some poured forth praises and blessings with clamour such as was scarcely becoming in such a place and at such a time. Some indistinct murmurs which James uttered, and which were drowned by the noisy gratitude of his attendants, were interpreted to mean thanks. But from the most trustworthy accounts it appears that he was insensible to all that was passing around him.*

As soon as Lewis was again at Marli, he repeated to the Court assembled there the announcement which he had made at Saint Germains. The whole circle broke forth into exclamations of delight and admiration. What piety! What humanity! What magnanimity! Nor was this enthusiasm altogether feigned. For, in the estimation of the greater part of that brilliant crowd, nations were nothing and princes every thing. What could be more generous, more amiable, than to protect an innocent boy, who was kept out of his rightful inheritance by an ambitious kinsman? The fine gentlemen and fine ladies who talked thus forgot that, besides the innocent boy and that ambitious kinsman, five millions and a half of Englishmen were concerned, who were little disposed to consider themselves as the absolute property of any master, and who were still less disposed to accept a master chosen for them by the French King.

James lingered three days longer. He was occasionally sensible during a few minutes, and, during one of these lucid intervals, faintly expressed his gratitude to Lewis. On the sixteenth he died. His Queen retired that evening to the nunnery of Chaillot, where she could weep and pray undisturbed. She left Saint Germains in joyous agitation. A herald made his appearance before the palace gate, and, with sound of trumpet, proclaimed, in Latin, French and English, King James the Third of England and Eighth of Scotland. The streets, in consequence doubtless of orders from the government, were illuminated; and the townsmen with loud shouts wished a long reign to their illustrious neighbour. The poor lad received from his ministers, and delivered back to them,

* By the most trustworthy accounts I mean those of St. Simon and Dangeau. The reader may compare their narratives with the Life of James.

the seals of their offices, and held out his hand to be kissed. One of the first acts of his mock reign was to bestow some mock peerages in conformity with directions which he found in his father's will. Middleton, who had as yet no English title, was created Earl of Monmouth. Perth, who had stood high in the favour of his late master, both as an apostate from the Protestant religion, and as the author of the last improvements on the thumb screw, took the title of Duke.

Meanwhile the remains of James were escorted, in the dusk of the evening, by a slender retinue to the Chapel of the English Benedictines at Paris, and deposited there in the vain hope that, at some future time, they would be laid with kingly pomp at Westminster among the graves of the Plantagenets and Tudors.

Three days after these humble obsequies Lewis visited Saint Germains in form. On the morrow the visit was returned. The French Court was now at Versailles; and the Pretender was received there, in all points, as his father would have been, sate in his father's arm chair, took, as his father had always done, the right hand of the great monarch, and wore the long violet coloured mantle which was by ancient usage the mourning garb of the Kings of France. There was on that day a great concourse of ambassadors and envoys; but one well known figure was wanting. Manchester had sent off to Loo intelligence of the affront which had been offered to his country and his master, had solicited instructions, and had determined that, till these instructions should arrive, he would live in strict seclusion. He did not think that he should be justified in quitting his post without express orders; but his earnest hope was that he should be directed to turn his back in contemptuous defiance on the Court which had dared to treat England as a subject province.

As soon as the fault into which Lewis had been hurried by pity, by the desire of applause, and by female influence was complete and irreparable, he began to feel serious uneasiness. His ministers were directed to declare everywhere that their master had no intention of affronting the English government, that he had not violated the Treaty of Ryswick, that he had no intention of violating it, that he had merely meant to gratify an unfortunate family nearly related to himself by using names and observing forms which really meant nothing, and that he was resolved not to countenance any attempt to subvert the throne of William. Torcy, who had, a few days before, proved by irrefragable arguments that his master could not, without a gross breach of contract, recognise the Pretender, imagined that sophisms which had not imposed on himself might possibly impose on others. He visited the English embassy, obtained admittance, and, as was his duty, did his best to excuse the fatal act which he had done his best to prevent. Manchester's answer to this attempt at explanation was as strong and plain as it could be in the absence of precise instructions. The instructions speedily arrived. The courier who carried the news of the recognition to Loo arrived there when William was at table with some of his nobles and some princes of the German Empire who had visited him in his retreat. The King said not a word: but his pale cheek flushed: and he pulled his hat over his eyes to conceal the changes of his countenance. He hastened to send off several messengers. One carried a letter commanding Manchester to quit France without taking leave. Another started for London with a despatch which directed the Lords Justices to send Poussin instantly out of England.

England was already in a flame when it was first known there that James was dying. Some of his eager partisans formed plans and made preparations for a great public manifestation of feeling in different parts of the island. But the insolence of Lewis produced a burst of public indignation which scarcely any malecontent had the courage to face.

In the city of London, indeed, some zealots, who had probably swallowed too many bumpers to their new Sovereign, played one of those senseless pranks which were characteristic of their party. They dressed themselves in coats bearing some resemblance to the tabards of heralds, rode through the streets, halted at some places, and muttered something which nobody could understand. It was at first supposed that they were merely a company of prize fighters from Hockley in the Hole who had taken this way of advertising their performances with back sword, sword and buckler, and single falchion. But it was soon discovered that these gaudily dressed horsemen were proclaiming James the Third. In an instant the pageant was at an end. The mock kings at arms and pursuivants threw away their finery and fled for their lives in all directions, followed by yells and showers of stones.* Already the Common Council of London had met, and had voted, without one dissentient voice, an address expressing the highest resentment at the insult which France had offered to the King and the kingdom. A few hours after this address had been presented

* Lettres Historiques Mois de Novembre 1701.

to the Regents, the Livery assembled to choose a Lord Mayor. Duncombe, the Tory candidate, lately the popular favourite, was rejected, and a Whig alderman placed in the chair. All over the kingdom, corporations, grand juries, meetings of magistrates, meetings of freeholders, were passing resolutions breathing affection to William, and defiance to Lewis. It was necessary to enlarge the "London Gazette" from four columns to twelve; and even twelve were too few to hold the multitude of loyal and patriotic addresses. In some of those addresses severe reflections were thrown on the House of Commons. Our deliverer had been ungratefully requited, thwarted, mortified, denied the means of making the country respected and feared by neighbouring states. The factious wrangling, the penny wise economy, of three disgraceful years had produced the effect which might have been expected. His Majesty would never have been so grossly affronted abroad, if he had not first been affronted at home. But the eyes of his people were opened. He had only to appeal from the representatives to the constituents; and he would find that the nation was still sound at heart.

Poussin had been directed to offer to the Lords Justices explanations similar to those with which Torcy had attempted to appease Manchester. A memorial was accordingly drawn up and presented to Vernon: but Vernon refused to look at it. Soon a courier arrived from Loo with the letter in which William directed his vicegerents to send the French agent out of the kingdom. An officer of the royal household was charged with the execution of the order. He repaired to Poussin's lodgings: but Poussin was not at home: he was supping at the Blue Posts, a tavern much frequented by Jacobites, the very tavern indeed at which Charnock and his gang had breakfasted on the day fixed for the murderous ambuscade of Turnham Green. To this house the messenger went; and there he found Poussin at table with three of the most virulent Tory members of the House of Commons, Tredenham, who returned himself for Saint Mawes; Hammond, who had been sent to Parliament by the high churchmen of the University of Cambridge; and Davenant, who had recently, at Poussin's suggestion, been rewarded by Lewis for some savage invectives against the Whigs with a diamond ring worth three thousand pistoles. This supper party was, during some weeks, the chief topic of conversation. The exultation of the Whigs was boundless. These then were the true English patriots, the men who could not endure a foreigner, the men who would not suffer His

Majesty to bestow a moderate reward on the foreigners who had stormed Athlone, and turned the flank of the Celtic army at Aghrim. It now appeared they could be on excellent terms with a foreigner, provided only that he was the emissary of a tyrant hostile to the liberty, the independence, and the religion of their country. The Tories, vexed and abashed, heartily wished that, on that unlucky day, their friends had been supping somewhere else. Even the bronze of Davenant's forehead was not proof to the general reproach. He defended himself by pretending that Poussin, with whom he had passed whole days, who had corrected his scurrilous pamphlets, and who had paid him his shameful wages, was a stranger to him, and that the meeting at the Blue Posts was purely accidental. If his word was doubted, he was willing to repeat his assertion on oath. The public, however, which had formed a very correct notion of his character, thought that his word was worth as much as his oath, and that his oath was worth nothing.

Meanwhile the arrival of William was impatiently expected. From Loo he had gone to Breda, where he had passed some time in reviewing his troops, and in conferring with Marlborough and Heinsius. He had hoped to be in England early in October. But adverse winds detained him three weeks at the Hague. At length, in the afternoon of the fourth of November, it was known in London that he had landed early that morning at Margate. Great preparations were made for welcoming him to his capital on the following day, the thirteenth anniversary of his landing in Devonshire. But a journey across the bridge, and along Cornhill and Cheapside, Fleet Street, and the Strand, would have been too great an effort for his enfeebled frame. He accordingly slept at Greenwich, and thence proceeded to Hampton Court without entering London. His return was, however, celebrated by the populace with every sign of joy and attachment. The bonfires blazed, and the gunpowder roared, all night. In every parish from Mile End to Saint James's was to be seen enthroned on the shoulders of stout Protestant porters a pope, gorgeous in robes of tinsel and triple crown of pasteboard; and close to the ear of His Holiness stood a devil with horns, cloven hoof, and a snaky tail.

Even in his country house the King could find no refuge from the importunate loyalty of his people. Deputations from cities, counties, universities, besieged him all day. He was, he wrote to Heinsius, quite exhausted by the labour of hearing harangues and returning answers. The whole kingdom meanwhile was looking anxiously towards Hampton Court. Most of the ministers were assembled there. The most eminent men of the party which was out of power had repaired thither, to pay their duty to their sovereign, and to congratulate him on his safe return. It was remarked that Somers and Halifax, so malignantly persecuted a few months ago by the House of Commons, were received with such marks of esteem and kindness as William was little in the habit of vouchsafing to his English courtiers. The lower ranks of both the great factions were violently agitated. The Whigs, lately vanquished and dispirited, were full of hope and ardour. The Tories, lately triumphant and secure, were exasperated and alarmed. Both Whigs and Tories waited with intense anxiety for the decision of one momentous and pressing question. Would there be a dissolution? On the seventh of November the King propounded that question to his Privy Council. It was rumoured, and is highly probable, that Jersey, Wright and Hedges advised him to keep the existing Parliament. But they were not men whose opinion was likely to have much weight with him ; and Rochester, whose opinion might have had some weight, had set out to take possession of his Viceroyalty just before the death of James, and was still at Dublin. William, however, had, as he owned to Heinsius, some difficulty in making up his mind. He had no doubt that a general election would give him a better House of Commons : but a general election would cause delay ; and delay might cause much mischief. After balancing these considerations, during some hours, he determined to dissolve.

The writs were sent out with all expedition ; and in three days the whole kingdom was up. Never—such was the intelligence sent from the Dutch Embassy to the Hague—had there been more intriguing, more canvassing, more virulence of party feeling. It was in the capital that the first great contests took place. The decisions of the Metropolitan constituent bodies were impatiently expected as auguries of the general result. All the pens of Grub Street, all the presses of Little Britain, were hard at work. Handbills for and against every candidate were sent to every voter. The popular slogans on both sides were indefatigably repeated. Presbyterian, Papist, Tool of Holland, Pensioner of France, were the appellations interchanged between the contending factions. The Whig cry was that the Tory members of the last two Parliaments had, from a malignant desire to mortify the King, left the kingdom exposed to danger and insult, had unconstitutionally encroached both on the legislature and on the judicial functions of the House of Lords, had turned the House of Commons into a new Star

Chamber, had used as instruments of capricious tyranny those privileges which ought never to be employed but in defence of freedom, had persecuted, without regard to law, to natural justice, or to decorum, the great Commander who had saved the state at La Hogue, the great Financier who had restored the currency and reestablished public credit, the great Judge whom all persons not blinded by prejudice acknowledged to be, in virtue, in prudence, in learning and eloquence, the first of living English jurists and statesmen. The Tories answered that they had been only too moderate, only too merciful; that they had used the Speaker's warrant and the power of tacking only too sparingly; and that, if they ever again had a majority, the three Whig leaders who now imagined themselves secure should be impeached, not for high misdemeanours, but for high treason. It soon appeared that these threats were not likely to be very speedily executed. Four Whig and four Tory candidates contested the City of London. The show of hands was for the Whigs. A poll was demanded; and the Whigs polled nearly two votes to one. Sir John Levison Gower, who was supposed to have ingratiated himself with the whole body of shopkeepers by some parts of his parliamentary conduct, was put up for Westminster on the Tory interest; and the electors were reminded by puffs in the newspapers of the services which he had rendered to trade. But the dread of the French King, the Pope, and the Pretender, prevailed; and Sir John was at the bottom of the poll. Southwark not only returned Whigs, but gave them instructions of the most Whiggish character.

In the country, parties were more nearly balanced than in the capital. Yet the news from every quarter was that the Whigs had recovered part at least of the ground which they had lost. Wharton had regained his ascendency in Buckinghamshire. Musgrave was rejected by Westmoreland. Nothing did more harm to the Tory candidates than the story of Poussin's farewell supper. We learn from their own acrimonious invectives that the unlucky discovery of the three members of Parliament at the Blue Posts cost thirty honest gentlemen their seats. One of the criminals, Tredenham, escaped with impunity. For the dominion of his family over the borough of St. Mawes was absolute even to a proverb. The other two had the fate which they deserved. Davenant ceased to sit for Bedwin. Hammond, who had lately stood high in the favour of the University of Cambridge, was defeated by a great majority, and was succeeded by the glory of the Whig party, Isaac Newton.

There was one district to which the eyes of hundreds of thousands were turned with anxious interest, Gloucestershire. Would the patriotic and high spirited gentry and yeomanry of that great county again confide their dearest interests to the Impudent Scandal of parliaments, the renegade, the slanderer, the mountebank, who had been, during thirteen years, railing at his betters of every party with a spite restrained by nothing but the craven fear of corporal chastisement, and who had in the last Parliament made himself conspicuous by the abject court which he had paid to Lewis and by the impertinence with which he had spoken of William.

The Gloucestershire election became a national affair. Portmanteaus full of pamphlets and broadsides were sent down from London. Every freeholder in the county had several tracts left at his door. In every market place, on the market day, papers about the brazen forehead, the viperous tongue, and the white liver of Jack Howe, the French King's buffoon, flew about like flakes in a snow storm. Clowns from the Cotswold Hills and the forest of Dean, who had votes, but who did not know their letters, were invited to hear these satires read, and were asked whether they were prepared to endure the two great evils which were then considered by the common people of England as the inseparable concomitants of despotism, to wear wooden shoes, and to live on frogs. The dissenting preachers and the clothiers were peculiarly zealous. For Howe was considered as the enemy both of conventicles and of factories. Outvoters were brought up to Gloucester in extraordinary numbers. In the city of London the traders who frequented Blackwell Hall, then the great emporium for woollen goods, canvassed actively on the Whig side.

[*Here the revised part ends.*—EDITOR.]

Meanwhile reports about the state of the King's health were constantly becoming more and more alarming. His medical advisers, both English and Dutch, were at the end of their resources. He had consulted by letter all the most eminent physicians of Europe ; and, as he was apprehensive that they might return flattering answers if they knew who he was, he had written under feigned names. To Fagon he had described himself as a parish priest. Fagon replied, somewhat bluntly, that such symptoms could have only one meaning, and that the only advice which he had to give to the sick man was to prepare himself for death. Having obtained this plain answer, William consulted Fagon again without disguise, and obtained some prescriptions which were thought to have a little retarded the approach of the inevitable hour. But the great King's days were numbered. Headaches and shivering fits returned on him almost daily. He still rode and even hunted *; but he had no longer that firm seat or that perfect command of the bridle for which he had once been renowned. Still all his care was for the future. The filial respect and tenderness of Albemarle had been almost a necessary of life to him. But it was of importance that Heinsius should be fully informed both as to the whole plan of the next campaign and as to the state of the preparations. Albemarle was in full possession of the King's views on these subjects. He was therefore sent to the Hague. Heinsius was at that time suffering from indisposition, which was indeed a trifle when compared with the maladies under which William was sinking. But in the nature of William there was none of that selfishness which is the too common vice of invalids. On the twentieth of February he sent to Heinsius a letter in which he did not even allude to his own sufferings and infirmities. "I am," he said, "infinitely concerned to learn that your health is not yet quite re-established. May God be pleased to grant you a speedy recovery. I am unalterably your good friend, William." Those were the last lines of that long correspondence.

On the twentieth of February William was ambling on a favourite horse, named Sorrel, through the park of Hampton Court. He urged his horse to strike into a gallop just at the spot where a mole had been at work. Sorrel stumbled on the mole-hill, and went down on his knees. The King fell off, and broke his collar bone. The bone was set; and he returned to Kensington in his coach. The jolting of the rough roads of that time made it necessary to reduce the fracture again. To a young and vigorous man such an accident would have been a trifle. But the frame of William was not in a condition to bear even the slightest shock. He felt that his time was short, and grieved, with a grief such as only noble spirits feel, to think that he must leave his work but half finished. It was possible that he might still live until one of his plans should be carried into execution. He had long known that the relation in which England and Scotland stood to each other was at best precarious, and often unfriendly, and that it might

* Last letter to Heinsius.

be doubted whether, in an estimate of the British power, the resources of the smaller country ought not to be deducted from those of the larger. Recent events had proved that, without doubt, the two kingdoms could not possibly continue for another year to be on the terms on which they had been during the preceding century, and that there must be between them either absolute union or deadly enmity. Their enmity would bring frightful calamities, not on themselves alone, but on all the civilised world. Their union would be the best security for the prosperity of both, for the internal tranquillity of the island, for the just balance of power among European states, and for the immunities of all Protestant countries. On the twenty-eighth of February the Commons listened with uncovered heads to the last message that bore William's sign manual. An unhappy accident, he told them, had forced him to make to them in writing a communication which he would gladly have made from the throne. He had, in the first year of his reign, expressed his desire to see an union accomplished between England and Scotland. He was convinced that nothing could more conduce to the safety and happiness of both. He should think it his peculiar felicity if, before the close of his reign, some happy expedient could be devised for making the two kingdoms one; and he, in the most earnest manner, recommended the question to the consideration of the Houses. It was resolved that the message should be taken into consideration on Saturday, the seventh of March.

But on the first of March humours of menacing appearance showed themselves in the King's knee. On the fourth of March he was attacked by fever; on the fifth his strength failed greatly; and on the sixth he was scarcely kept alive by cordials. The Abjuration Bill and a money bill were awaiting his assent. That assent he felt that he should not be able to give in person. He therefore ordered a commission to be prepared for his signature. His hand was now too weak to form the letters of his name, and it was suggested that a stamp should be prepared. On the seventh of March the stamp was ready. The Lord Keeper and the clerks of the parliament came, according to usage, to witness the signing of the commission. But they were detained some hours in the antechamber while he was in one of the paroxysms of his malady. Meanwhile the Houses were sitting. It was Saturday, the seventh, the day on which the Commons had resolved to take into consideration the question of the union with Scotland. But that subject was not mentioned. It was known that the

King had but a few hours to live; and the members asked each other anxiously whether it was likely that the Abjuration and money bills would be passed before he died. After sitting long in the expectation of a message, the Commons adjourned till six in the afternoon. By that time William had recovered himself sufficiently to put the stamp on the parchment which authorised his commissioners to act for him. In the evening, when the Houses had assembled, Black Rod knocked. The Commons were summoned to the bar of the Lords; the commission was read, the Abjuration Bill and the Malt Bill became laws, and both Houses adjourned till nine o'clock in the morning of the following day. The following day was Sunday. But there was little chance that William would live through the night. It was of the highest importance that, within the shortest possible time after his decease, the successor designated by the Bill of Rights and the Act of Succession should receive the homage of the Estates of the Realm, and be publicly proclaimed in the Council: and the most rigid Pharisee in the Society for the Reformation of Manners could hardly deny that it was lawful to save the state, even on the Sabbath.

The King meanwhile was sinking fast. Albemarle had arrived at Kensington from the Hague, exhausted by rapid travelling. His master kindly bade him go to rest for some hours, and then summoned him to make his report. That report was in all respects satisfactory. The States General were in the best temper; the troops, the provisions and the magazines were in the best order. Every thing was in readiness for an early campaign. William received the intelligence with the calmness of a man whose work was done. He was under no illusion as to his danger. "I am fast drawing," he said, "to my end." His end was worthy of his life. His intellect was not for a moment clouded. His fortitude was the more admirable because he was not willing to die. He had very lately said to one of those whom he most loved: "You know that I never feared death; there have been times when I should have wished it; but, now that this great new prospect is opening before me, I do wish to stay here a little longer." Yet no weakness, no querulousness, disgraced the noble close of that noble career. To the physicians the King returned his thanks graciously and gently. "I know that you have done all that skill and learning could do for me: but the case is beyond your art; and I submit." From the words which escaped him he seemed to be frequently engaged in mental prayer. Burnet and Tenison remained many hours in the sick room. He professed to them his firm belief in the truth of the Christian religion, and received the sacrament from their hands with great seriousness. The antechambers were crowded all night with lords and privy councillors. He ordered several of them to be called in, and exerted himself to take leave of them with a few kind and cheerful words. Among the English who were admitted to his bedside were Devonshire and Ormond. But there were in the crowd those who felt as no Englishman could feel, friends of his youth who had been true to him, and to whom he had been true, through all vicissitudes of fortune ; who had served him with unalterable fidelity when his Secretaries of State, his Treasury and his Admiralty had betrayed him ; who had never on any field of battle, or in an atmosphere tainted with loathsome and deadly disease, shrunk from placing their own lives in jeopardy to save his, and whose truth he had at the cost of his own popularity rewarded with bounteous munificence. He strained his feeble voice to thank Auverquerque for the affectionate and loyal services of thirty years. To Albemarle he gave the keys of his closet, and of his private drawers. "You know," he said, "what to do with them." By this time he could scarcely respire. "Can this," he said to the physicians, "last long?" He was told that the end was approaching. He swallowed a cordial, and asked for Bentinck. Those were his last articulate words. Bentinck instantly came to the bedside, bent down, and placed his ear close to the King's mouth. The lips of the dying man moved ; but nothing could be heard. The King took the hand of his earliest friend, and pressed it tenderly to his heart. In that moment, no doubt, all that had cast a slight passing cloud over their long and pure friendship was forgotten. It was now between seven and eight in the morning. He closed his eyes, and gasped for breath. The bishops knelt down and read the commendatory prayer. When it ended William was no more.

When his remains were laid out, it was found that he wore next to his skin a small piece of black silk riband. The lords in waiting ordered it to be taken off. It contained a gold ring and a lock of the hair of Mary.

# INDEX

# INDEX

# EVERYMAN'S LIBRARY: A Selected List

This List covers a selection of volumes available in Everyman's Library. Tho volumes marked with a ★ indicate that a paperback edition of this title is also availabl Numbers only of hardback editions are given.

## BIOGRAPHY

**Brontë, Charlotte** (1816–55). LIFE, 1857. By *Mrs Gaskell.* 3
**Byron, Lord** (1788–1824). LETTERS. Edited by *R. G. Howarth,* B.LITT. 9
**Cellini, Benvenuto** (1500–71). ★THE LIFE OF BENVENUTO CELLINI, written by himself.
**Evelyn, John** (1620–1706). DIARY. Edited by *William Bray,* 1819. 2 vols. 220–
**Franklin, Benjamin** (1706–90). AUTOBIOGRAPHY, 1817. 2
**Goethe, Johann Wolfgang von** (1749–1832). LIFE, 1855. By *G. H. Lewes,* 1817–78. 2
**Hudson, William Henry** (1841–1922). FAR AWAY AND LONG AGO, 1918. 9
**Johnson, Dr Samuel** (1709–84). LIVES OF THE ENGLISH POETS, 1781. 2 vols. 770–
★BOSWELL'S LIFE OF JOHNSON, 1791. 2 vols. 1–2.
**Keats, John** (1795–1821). LIFE AND LETTERS, 1848. By *Lord Houghton* (1809–85). 8
**Nelson, Horatio, Viscount** (1758–1805). LIFE, 1813. By *Robert Southey* (1774–1843).
**Pepys, Samuel** (1633–1703). DIARY. Newly edited (1953), with modernized spellin
3 vols. 53–
**Plutarch** (46?–120). LIVES OF THE NOBLE GREEKS AND ROMANS. Dryden's editio 1683–6. Revised by *A. H. Clough,* 1859–61. 3 vols. 407–
**Rousseau, Jean Jacques** (1712–78). CONFESSIONS, 1782. Complete and unabridged.
2 vols. 859–
**Scott, Sir Walter** (1771–1832). LOCKHART'S LIFE OF SCOTT. An abridgment from th seven-volume work by *J. G. Lockhart* himself.
**Sévigné, Marie de Rabutin-Chantal, Marquise de** (1626–96). SELECTED LETTERS.
**Vasari, Giorgio** (1511–74). LIVES OF THE PAINTERS, SCULPTORS AND ARCHITECT Edited by *William Gaunt.* 4 vols. 784–
**Walpole, Horace** (1717–97). SELECTED LETTERS. Edited, with an Introduction, b *W. Hadley,* M.A. 7

## ESSAYS AND CRITICISM

**An Everyman Anthology.** Over a hundred authors from Everyman's Librar represented. 6
**Bacon, Francis, Lord Verulam** (1561–1626). ★ESSAYS. 1597–1626.
**Belloc, Hilaire** (1870–1953). ★STORIES, ESSAYS AND POEMS. 9
**Burke, Edmund** (1729–97). REFLECTIONS ON THE FRENCH REVOLUTION, 1790. 4
**Carlyle, Thomas** (1795–1881). ESSAYS. Introduction by *J. R. Lowell.* Essays on m and affairs. 2 vols. 703–4. PAST AND PRESENT, 1843. 608. SARTOR RESARTU 1838; and HEROES AND HERO-WORSHIP, 1841. 278
**Castiglioni, Baldassare** (1478–1529). THE BOOK OF THE COURTIER, 1528. *Sir Thom Hoby's* translation, 1561. 8
**Century.** ★A CENTURY OF ENGLISH ESSAYS FROM CAXTON TO BELLOC. 6
**Chesterfield, Earl of** (1694–1773). LETTERS TO HIS SON; AND OTHERS. 8
**Chesterton, Gilbert Keith** (1874–1936). ★STORIES, ESSAYS AND POEMS. 9
**Coleridge, Samuel Taylor** (1772–1834). BIOGRAPHIA LITERARIA, 1817. 11. SHAK SPEAREAN CRITICISM, 1849. Edited by *Prof. T. M. Raysor* (1960). 2 vols. 162, 18
**De Quincey, Thomas** (1785–1859). ★CONFESSIONS OF AN ENGLISH OPIUM-EATER, 182 223. THE ENGLISH MAIL-COACH AND OTHER WRITINGS. 609. REMINISCENC OF THE ENGLISH LAKE POETS. 163. All edited by *Prof. John E. Jordan.*
**Dryden, John** (1631–1700). OF DRAMATIC POESY AND OTHER CRITICAL ESSAYS. T whole of Dryden's critical writings. 2 vols. 568
**Elyot, Sir Thomas** (1490?–1546). THE GOVERNOR, 1531. Edited by *S. E. Lehmberg.* 2
**Emerson, Ralph Waldo** (1803–82). ESSAYS, 1841–4.
**Gray, Thomas** (1716–71). ESSAYS. (*See* Poetry and Drama Section.)
**Hamilton, Alexander** (1757–1804), and Others. THE FEDERALIST, 1787–8. 5
**Hazlitt, William** (1778–1830). LECTURES ON THE ENGLISH COMIC WRITERS, 1819; a FUGITIVE WRITINGS. 411. LECTURES ON THE ENGLISH POETS, 1818; and T SPIRIT OF THE AGE, 1825. 459. THE ROUND TABLE and CHARACTERS OF SHAK SPEAR'S PLAYS, 1817–18. 65. TABLE TALK, 1821–2, 1824. 321
**Holmes, Oliver Wendell** (1809–94). THE AUTOCRAT OF THE BREAKFAST-TABLE, 1858.

# FICTION

3

4

# REFERENCE

# RELIGION AND PHILOSOPHY

# SCIENCE

**Boyle, Robert** (1627–91). The Sceptical Chymist, 1661.
**Darwin, Charles** (1809–82). The Origin of Species, 1859. Embodies Darwin's additions.
**Eddington, Sir Arthur** (1882–1944). The Nature of the Physical World, 1928.
**Euclid** (fl. c. 330–c. 275 B.C.). The Elements of Euclid. Edited by *Isaac Todhun*

**Harvey, William** (1578–1657). The Circulation of the Blood.
**Locke, John** (1632–1704). Two Treatises of Civil Government, 1690.
**Malthus, Thomas Robert** (1766–1834). An Essay on the Principle of Populat 1798.
**Marx, Karl** (1818–83). Capital, 1867. Translated by *Eden* and *Cedar Paul.*
2 vols. 69
**Mill, John Stuart** (1806–73). Utilitarianism, 1863; Liberty, 1859; and Represen tive Government, 1861.
**Owen, Robert** (1771–1858). A New View of Society, 1813; and Other Writing

**Ricardo, David** (1772–1823). The Principles of Political Economy and Taxat 1817.
**Rousseau, Jean Jacques** (1712–78). The Social Contract, 1762; and Other Ess.

**Smith, Adam** (1723–90). The Wealth of Nations, 1766.        2 vols. 41?
**White, Gilbert** (1720–93). A Natural History of Selborne, 1789.
**Wollstonecraft, Mary** (1759–97). The Rights of Woman, 1792; and Mill, John St (1806–73), The Subjection of Women, 1869.

# TRAVEL AND TOPOGRAPHY

**Borrow, George** (1803–81). The Bible in Spain, 1843. 151.  Wild Wales, 1862
**Boswell, James** (1740–95). Journal of a Tour to the Hebrides with Sam Johnson, 1785.
**Cobbett, William** (1762–1835). Rural Rides, 1830.        2 vols. 63
**Cook, Captain James** (1728–79). Voyages of Discovery. Edited by *John Bar* F.R.S., F.S.A.
**Crèvecœur, St John de** (1735–1813). Letters from an American Farmer, 1782.
**Darwin, Charles** (1809–82). ★The Voyage of the 'Beagle', 1839.
**Defoe, Daniel** (1661?–1731). A Tour Through the Whole Island of Great Brit 1724–6.        2 vols. 82
**Hakluyt, Richard** (1552–1616). Voyages.      8 vols. 264–5; 313–14; 338–9; 38
**Kinglake, Alexander** (1809–91). Eothen, 1844.
**Lane, Edward William** (1801–76). Manners and Customs of the Modern Egypti 1836.
**Park, Mungo** (1771–1806). Travels.
**Polo, Marco** (1254–1324). Travels.
**Portuguese Voyages**, 1498–1663. Edited by *Charles David Ley.*
**Stevenson, Robert Louis** (1850–94). An Inland Voyage, 1878; Travels Wit Donkey, 1879; and The Silverado Squatters, 1883.
**Stow, John** (1525?–1605). ★The Survey of London. Elizabethan London.